Ubiquitous Developments in Knowledge Management:
Integrations and Trends

Murray E. Jennex
San Diego State University, USA

Information Science
REFERENCE

INFORMATION SCIENCE REFERENCE
Hershey · New York

Director of Editorial Content: Kristin Klinger
Director of Book Publications: Julia Mosemann
Development Editor: Julia Mosemann
Typesetter: Devvin Earnest, Sean Woznicki
Quality Control: Jamie Snavely
Cover Design: Lisa Tosheff
Printed at: Yurchak Printing Inc.

Published in the United States of America by
Information Science Reference (an imprint of IGI Global)
701 E. Chocolate Avenue
Hershey PA 17033
Tel: 717-533-8845
Fax: 717-533-8661
E-mail: cust@igi-global.com
Web site: http://www.igi-global.com/reference

Library of Congress Cataloging-in-Publication Data

Ubiquitous developments in knowledge management : integrations and trends / Murray Jennex, editor.
p. cm.

Includes bibliographical references and index.
Summary: "This book presents current research in Knowledge Management, highlighting new technologies, approaches, issues, solutions, or cases that can help an organization implement a knowledge management initiative or provide a knowledge base"--Provided by publisher.

ISBN 978-1-60566-954-0 (hbk.) -- ISBN 978-1-60566-955-7 (ebook) 1. Knowledge management. I. Jennex, Murray E., 1956-
HD30.2.U25 2010
658.4'038--dc22

2009052393

British Cataloguing in Publication Data
A Cataloguing in Publication record for this book is available from the British Library.

Advances in Knowledge Management Series (AKM)

ISBN: 1935-360X

Editor-in-Chief: Murray Jennex, San Diego State University, USA

Knowledge Management in Modern Organizations
IGI Publishing • copyright 2007 • 404 pp • H/C (ISBN: 1-59904-261-4) •
E-Book (ISBN: 1-59904-263-0)

Knowledge management has been growing in importance and popularity as a research topic and business initiative. Knowledge Management in Modern Organizations documents the latest key issues of knowledge management. The innovative chapters in this book discuss the philosophical foundations of knowledge management, serving as a viable resource for academicians, practitioners, researchers, and students. Knowledge Management in Modern Organizations depicts a global perspective as the contributors come from Asia, Europe, the Middle East, and the United States, and adds value to any course focused on KM in organizations.

Current Issues in Knowledge Management
Information Science Reference • copyright 2007 • 300pp • H/C (ISBN: 978-1-59904-916-8) •

As global enterprise grows increasingly reliant on electronic data, processes, and procedures, studies of the management of organizational knowledge are emergin at the forefront of critical research. Current Issues in Knowledge Management combines cutting-edge research on the cultural, technical, organizational, and human issues surrounding the creation, capture, transfer, and use of knowledge in today's organizations. Providing foremost information on topics such as organizational memory, knowledge management in enterprises, enablers and inhibitors of knowledge sharing and transfer, and emerging technologies of knowledge management, this estimable reference offers vital research information to practitioners and scholars in a variety of settings.

The Advances in Knowledge Management (AKM) Book Series covers all aspects of the knowledge management discipline, from organizational issues to technology support to knowledge representation. AKM provides a forum for global aspects of knowledge management and for differing cultural perspectives on the use of knowledge and knowledge management. The book series also focuses on cultural and organizational issues as well as technical issues associated with the creation and implementation of knowledge management systems. The Advances in Knowledge Management actively seeks out international depictions of knowledge management and how these applications are implemented into practical functions, as well as how these technologies create new developments for the advancement of information systems and the knowledge society. Because of the growing importance of knowledge management technologies, this series aims to bridge the gap in available literature, while furthering research principles.

IGI GLOBAL
DISSEMINATOR OF KNOWLEDGE

Hershey • New York

Order online at www.igi-global.com or call 717-533-8845 x 10 –
Mon-Fri 8:30 am - 5:00 pm (est) or fax 24 hours a day 717-533-8661

Editorial Advisory Board

Table of Contents

Detailed Table of Contents

The results reported in this chapter were obtained through the study of 43 work-units belonging to five business firms in a large group of Tunisian companies. Using the declarative, procedural and judgmental dimensions of organizational memory, interaction effects were detected between IT and organizational memory. Analyses of the data support the view that storage technologies interact with declarative memory contributing to reduce organizational information needs. But, contrary to expectations, storage technologies interact negatively with declarative memory on information provision. Furthermore, network technologies interact negatively with judgmental memory on information provision. These results raise issues that have been rarely encountered in the literature.

Organizational memories play a significant role in knowledge management, but several challenges confront their use. Artifacts of OM are many and varied. Access and use of the stored artifact are influenced by the user's understanding of these information objects as well as their context. Theories of distributed cognition and the notion of community of practice are used to develop a model of the knowledge management system. The present work looks at a model for managing organizational memory knowledge. Topic maps are used in the model to represent user cognition of contextualized information. A visual approach to topic maps proposed in the model also allows for access and analysis of stored memory artifacts. The design and implementation of a prototype to test the feasibility of the model is briefly examined.

This chapter investigates the phenomenon of virtual communities of practice, and proposes them to be efficient for individual's knowledge retrieval, when they work in a geographically dispersed organization, such as a multinational corporation. The virtual community of practice is likely to reduce the contextual gaps that typically exist between senders and receivers of knowledge, as it includes the possibility of feedback loops in the information exchange process. However, the organization must provide a knowledge-sharing friendly culture, and an institutional protectionism, in order to establish the required level of trust, being the foundation for knowledge exchanges within the virtual community.

Knowledge is increasingly being viewed as a critical component for organizations. It is largely people-based and the characteristics of groups of individuals, in the form of organizational cultures, may play a key role in the factors that lead to either the acceptance or rejection of knowledge management systems (KMS). The primary objective of this research is to explore how dimensions of organizational culture influence factors that lead to the acceptance of KMS. While researchers have agreed that culture plays an important role in KMS, the literature has only recently begun to examine organizational culture within this context. This chapter examined the effects of three dimensions of organizational culture through a research model that was tested and analyzed utilizing a field survey of corporate knowledge management users. Results indicate that both process-oriented and open communication system organizational cultures significantly influenced the factors that led to the acceptance of KMS.

Knowledge assets are an important organizational resource. Both research and practice literature has recognized that, if managed properly, knowledge resources have the potential to contribute to a firm's performance. Yet, the way in which organizations build knowledge management (KM) capability is relatively poorly understood. The diversity of knowledge assets existing within organizations makes it difficult to have a common understanding of how to utilize the knowledge resource most effectively. Drawing from both Resource Based View and Organizational Learning literature, the authors present a Knowledge Management (KM) framework that describes distinctly different types of knowledge assets within organizations. KM traditionally encompasses a range of activities associated with the knowledge lifecycle, including creation and capture of knowledge, transfer or sharing of this knowledge, and its

Knowledge is based on fact and is often obtained from experience or via association. Knowledge organization is the systematic management and organization of knowledge (Hodge, 2000). With the advent of Web 2.0, mashups have become a hot new thing on the Web. A mashup is a Web site or a Web application that combines content from more than one source and delivers it in an integrated way (Fichter, 2006). This chapter will first discuss knowledge and knowledge organization and review literature on these topics. Then the authors will explore the concept and look at the components of a typical mashup. In addition, they will provide an overview of various mashups on the Internet. From these facts, the chapter proceeds to draw some connections between knowledge organization and mashups, solidifying the authors' assertions with an elaboration on their real-world, a mashup experiment in an enterprise environment. The authors will describe how they mixed the content from two sets of data and created a new source of data: a novel way of organizing and displaying HP Labs Technical Reports. The findings from this project will be included and some best practices for creating enterprise mashups will be given. Finally, they will discuss the future of enterprise mashups.

In order to improve the level of decision making and competitive advantage, organizations are actively trying to develop and incorporate new knowledge management techniques that are suited for the evolving global economy; the notion of globally distributed team environments represents one area of heavy focus. In implementing a globally distributed work environment, decision makers are faced with an increasingly daunting task of reconciling disparate distributed and heterogeneous data sources. Further, these data sources are growing every day as corporations dedicate more of their resources to a multinational scenario, rather than to a domestic or geographically-specific focus. In order to address this growing problem of knowledge sharing, the authors propose a knowledge sharing model that incorporates the notion of the 24-Hour Knowledge Factory, in conjunction with grid computing and case-based reasoning (CBR). This chapter begins with a description of the 24-Hour Knowledge Factory, the Enterprise Common Knowledge Shared (ECKS) methodology, and the evolving time-shift sharing model. Next, a CBR-adapted approach, based on grid computing, is presented for use in a 24-Hour Knowledge Factory environment. Finally, several types of enterprise knowledge transfer mechanisms are presented in this paper.

Finding the right software is often hindered by different criteria as well as by technology changes. The authors performed an AHP (Analytic Hierarchy Process) analysis using Expert Choice to determine which data mining package was most suitable. Deliberating a dozen alternatives and objectives led them to a series of pair-wise comparisons. When further synthesizing the results, Expert Choice helped provide a clear rationale for the decision. The issue is, data mining technology is changing very rapidly. This chapter focused only on the major suppliers typically available in the market place. The method and the process that was used can be easily applied to analyze and compare other data mining software or knowledge management initiatives.

Knowledge sharing is a popular research topic; however, the construct has not been well defined theoretically or in terms of how to operationalize it, as there appears to be little consistency. This apparent lack of consistency is problematic for developing a cumulative understanding of the predictors and outcomes of this behavior. This study examines how other researchers have operationalized knowledge sharing, and conduct a qualitative study to further understand this construct. A knowledge sharing and hoarding classification system is developed, and six knowledge sharing behavioral categories are identified. Finally, recommendations are made for future research in knowledge management.

This study draws on literature in knowledge management and communities of practice to arrive at properties of a community that make it sustainable. These properties can then be viewed as a blueprint of what a community needs to have to achieve its function of fostering collaboration and hence, generating knowledge. In sum, this research is intended to help practitioners arrive at how best to design communities in knowledge management systems.

This chapter develops an argument for and provides case study evidence to demonstrate that knowledge management (KM) governance is a mechanism that strengthens the development and implementation of KM strategies. It achieves this through locating and formalizing risk management as a function of governance, establishing reporting structures and mechanisms to ensure feedback into the ongoing development of organizational KM. The author concludes that the operationalization of KM governance formalizes, locates and authorizes risk management as a structured response to the resolution of the cultural and structural risks and obstacles to KM strategy, and that it achieves this through developed capacity for analysis, articulation, strategic alignment and activity to address risks to effective, sustainable KM.

This chapter reports on types and roles of information and communication technologies (ICT) implemented in knowledge management (KM) solutions in local governments. A sample of nine local councils were rated on usage of various generic and KM specific ICT in supporting knowledge exploitation or exploration, and codification or personalization strategies. The results indicate a marked preference for generic types of ICT, and support for knowledge exploitation and codification approaches. These findings and their implications are further interpreted in terms of three stages of KM development in organizations.

This chapter reviews the plethora of user-generated video activity and the issues it creates for knowledge management activities. The ability for individuals to create and post videos online has become prolific and it has now become a source of potential liability for employees and the firm. Video can be used convey rich narratives that can facilitate sensemaking and knowledge sharing and transfer, but their needs to be standards and controls for content development and distribution. When video content is developed, structure and culture are important factors that must be considered in storytelling activities to increase the opportunity for effective sensemaking and message retention and to ensure the accuracy, relevance, and legitimacy of video content. Evidence and arguments are presented that should motivate organizations and academics to review video generation activities both internal and external to the organization. Issues concerning video content delivery, liability, spam, and search engine capabilities are discussed. Opportunities for new research inquiries are identified.

Preface: Why Knowledge Management?

INTRODUCTION

Welcome to Ubiquitous Developments in Knowledge Management: Integrations and Trends. This book presents current research in Knowledge Management. Each chapter presents new technologies, approaches, issues, solutions, or cases that can help an organization implement a knowledge management, KM, initiative or provide a knowledge base for the practitioner/academic researcher. This chapter provides a basic definition of KM and then explores why KM is important in today's world. Most readers are already convinced that KM is important; however, showing this quantitatively may be difficult. This chapter provides a discussion that shows KM is really, really important.

KM is the answer to why IS/IT Matters and even the Productivity Paradox. KM makes organizations more productive, but some would rather call it Business Intelligence, Competitive Intelligence, Social Capital, or some term other than KM; and actually go to great pains to avoid the use of the KM term. There is an identity crisis as to what KM is. Some consider KM to be a document management system, a data warehouse, a web portal, or a wiki or other collaboration tool; others consider it a process, a way of thinking, a strategy, or a social network. Jennex (2005) defines KM as the practice of selectively applying knowledge from previous experiences of decision-making to current and future decision making activities with the express purpose of improving the organization's effectiveness.

This is consistent with what Keen and Tan (2007) call a corporatist view of KM in that it is mission focused on using knowledge as an asset to improve processes. I see this as the necessary driver for KM and go a step further by stating that KM is really about two issues:

- Leveraging what the organization "knows" so that it can better utilize its knowledge assets, and
- Connecting knowledge generators, holders, and users to facilitate the flow of knowledge through the organization

These issues use the term "organization" very loosely. I view an organization as any group with a purpose. This means that an organization can be a formal business organization, a governmental organization, a multinational organization, or even an informal organization such as a community of practice. Also, an organization may have a formal command structure, an informal command structure, or be leaderless. This is a purposefully broad definition because were finding that KM can help all sorts of "organizations." I'm realizing that organizations are evolving into a variety of structures with various governance approaches and with various knowledge needs and tying ourselves to a set view of an organization will only limit the application of KM.

These issues also cause some of the KM identity crisis as many researchers and practitioners focus on one or the other of the issues and so view KM through their issue's particular lens. This is unfortunate and it is hoped that this chapter will encourage all KM practitioners and researchers to accept the dual nature of KM.

Finally, these issues drive the technologies, processes, methodologies, techniques, and practices used to implement KM. This book includes chapters on many of these and the reader is encouraged to remember that KM has a dual focus and to implement KM well and organization needs technologies, processes, methodologies, techniques, and practices for both issues. Additionally, the advent of web 2.0 technologies is driving resurgence in KMS development. Organizations are embracing the collaborative and semantic tools and processes Web 2.0 provide to create inexpensive but effective KMS. Wikis, blogs, social networks, YouTube, and web services are being used, mashed together, or incorporated into commercial products like SharePoint to create KMS that allow work groups up to full organizations to self organize knowledge and their knowledge sharing networks quickly and inexpensively. Concerns such as security and ontology are being overcome by the commercial products like SharePoint or by adjusting organizational processes while using shareware products. Issues such as organizational KM strategy and infrastructure are still being evolved to incorporate web 2.0 technologies and processes.

This book presents research which helps address these issues so they will not be explored further. What will be explored is why organizations need KM.

THE NEED FOR KNOWLEDGE MANAGEMENT

Organizations do KM because it makes sense, as KM, when done successfully has an impact on the organization and its members. This is illustrated by the Jennex Olfman Knowledge Management Success Model (Jennex and Olfman, 2006); see figure 1, as KM success is ultimately reflected in impacts to the organization. Jennex, Smolnik, and Croasdell (2008) refined this reflection of KM success into a definition of KM success:

KM success is a multidimensional concept. It is defined by capturing the right knowledge, getting the right knowledge to the right user, and using this knowledge to improve organizational and/or individual performance. KM success is measured by means of the dimensions: impact on business processes, impact on strategy, leadership, and knowledge content.

What is required for KM to be successful? Jennex and Olfman (2005) summarized and synthesized the literature on KM/KMS's critical success factors (CSF) into an ordered set of 12 KM CSFs identified from 17 studies of more than 200 KM projects. These CSFs were thereafter sequentially ordered according to the number of studies identifying them:

- A knowledge strategy that identifies users, sources, processes, storage strategy, knowledge, and links to knowledge for the KMS;
- Motivation and commitment of users, including incentives and training;
- Integrated technical infrastructure, including networks, databases/repositories, computers, software, and KMS experts;
- An organizational culture and structure that supports learning and the sharing and use of knowledge;

- A common enterprise-wide knowledge structure that is clearly articulated and easily understood;
- Senior management support, including allocation of resources, leadership, and training;
- Learning organization;
- The KMS has a clear goal and purpose;
- Measures are established to assess the impacts of the KMS and the use of knowledge, as well as verification that the right knowledge is being captured;
- The search, retrieval, and visualization functions of the KMS support facilitated use of knowledge;
- Work processes are designed that incorporate knowledge capture and use; and
- Knowledge is secured / protected.

The Jennex and Olfman (2006) KM Success Model (Figure 1) is derived using these CSFs and from analysis of case studies from several organizations and industries, and applying this analysis to the DeLone and McLean (1992, 2003) Information Success Model in order to generate a theoretically grounded KM Success model. The Jennex and Olfman KM Success Model has been tested in full and part by several studies and is considered to be reasonably validated.

While this may be enough to encourage organizations to pursue a KM initiative and show them what it takes to do it successfully, many organizations still need more basis to justify an investment in KM. Calculating Return on Investment, ROI, is a popular approach, but how is this done? There are some commonly accepted first steps:

- Find a need or an opportunity that KM satisfies, supports, or resolves.
- Identify the costs with the need or the benefits of the opportunity
- Identify the savings or potential earnings that implementing KM will provide
- Identify the costs of implementing KM

Easily stated but not easily done and the resulting financial numbers are often questionable. Do the numbers present the full story for KM? Many think they don't and that stories and anecdotes about KM need to be included to make KM real to management (Moore, 2008). This chapter is not about how to calculate the numbers; rather, this chapter is presenting some of the stories that are the other drivers that should be considered when determining if a KM initiative is appropriate. These stories are discussed below.

The Stories

Loss of Critical Knowledge

Organizations are facing severe stresses. 2008 and 2009 and probably 2010 are global recession years. Many organizations are being forced to cut back on expenditures as revenues and investment decline. The result in many organizations is a reduction in personnel. The more desperate the organization, the deeper the personnel cuts. Unfortunately personnel cuts do more than cut costs, they cut knowledge that the organization may need to compete later. Should organizations use KM to guide their cuts? Yes, they should but usually can't use KM to guide layoffs due to legal liabilities. Should organizations use KM to assess the risk of losing critical knowledge and try to capture that knowledge they need? Yes

Figure 1. Jennex Olfman Knowledge Management Success Model (Jennex and Olfman, 2006)

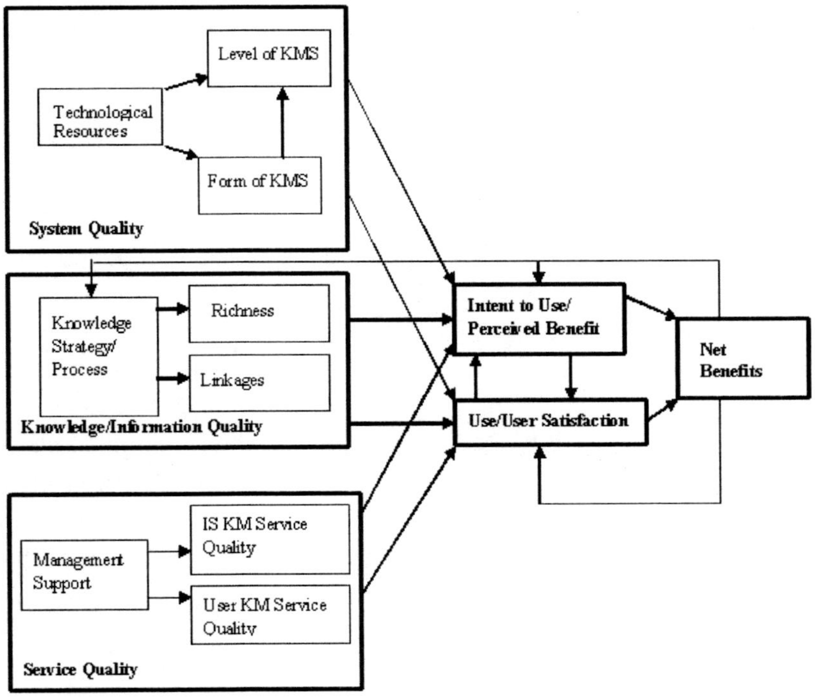

they should but most don't because of the energy and time needed to just stay in business takes away the time to assess, organize, and capture critical knowledge. How this loss of knowledge will affect future growth and competitiveness remains to be seen but it is anticipated that it will take more than the economy and financial sectors recovering before organizations will recover. Those organizations wanting to come out of the recession strong will have to recover lost knowledge and knowledge assets to give themselves a competitive edge.

Knowledge loss due to recession cutbacks is not the only cause of knowledge loss. Kosilov, Mazour, and Yanev (2006) report that the United States commercial nuclear industry faces the issue of a 'greying' workforce where literally half the current workers will be eligible to retire within the next five years (the aging of the Baby Boomer generation). The Federal Interagency Forum on Aging-Related Statistics (2006) reports that by 2010 more than 25% of the United States work force will have reached retirement age. The United States, Europe, Japan, and the rest of the developed countries are aging and will be losing knowledge as it retires and walks out the door. This is a rapidly approaching crisis; few organizations can withstand a 25% loss of personnel, all senior employees, without a loss in effectiveness. Parise, et al. (2006) recognized that while retirement is the most immediate contributor to knowledge loss, other factors, in particular job mobility, are major, continuing contributors requiring a process to capture critical knowledge. Additionally, Deloitte and Touche (2005) found that 69% of the 1396 human resources practitioners they surveyed said attracting new talent poses the greatest threat to competitiveness, followed by the inability to retain key talent (66%) and incoming workers with inadequate skills (34%). However, Parise, et al. (2006) report that only half of the above surveyed organizations had identified a list of critical skills needed for future growth and more than one-quarter viewed defining critical skills as unimportant. Additionally, Parise, et al. (2005) found that the key problem with many retention approaches is that they capture only a small fragment of what made an individual successful and knowledgeable. Ultimately, Massingham (2008) found that knowledge loss from losing an employee has three impacts:

- Loss of contribution to the organizational memory
- Loss of relational knowledge with the internal and external social network (fellow employees and customers).
- Loss of work performance resulting in decreased organizational productivity (there is a decrease in the organization's ability to perform the tasks it performed before the employee left).

Eucker (2007) summarizes this by saying a lost employee results in lost know-how, know-who, know-what.

Can KM mitigate this crisis? Yes, it can, but organizations need to start assessing what knowledge is critical, who has it, and what is the risk of these people leaving. Is KM preparing tools to assist organizations in doing this? The nuclear industry has been conducting research into knowledge loss due to its aging work force. There risk is made worse by a lack of new/replacement work force since few new nuclear plants have been built in the last 20 years, making this a less attractive career for engineers and other knowledge workers. The International Atomic Energy Agency, IAEA, has led research into methods to mitigate knowledge loss from retiring workers. This research culminated in the publication of their 2006 guide "Risk Management of Knowledge Loss in Nuclear Industry Organizations." (Kosilov, Mazour, and Yanev, 2006) The IAEA Knowledge Loss Risk Assessment is designed to identify positions/people where the potential knowledge loss is greatest and most imminent. It includes ratings based on two factors: time until retirement and position criticality; and provides focus - identifies "experts" where steps to mitigate knowledge loss may be needed. The Knowledge Loss Risk Assessment consists of three steps:

- Conduct a Knowledge Loss Risk Assessment
- Determine Approach to Capture Critical Knowledge
- Monitor and Evaluate

Additionally, Jennex (2009) has expanded the knowledge loss risk assessment to be worker, rather than position, specific. Jennex (2009) applied the standard risk formula: R=pxC to assess risk. Probability, p, was determined using factors that influence probability of knowledge loss including age, health, uniqueness of skills and knowledge, demand for skills and knowledge, and years of service. Consequence, C, was determined using factors that influence the importance of the employee to the organization and include criticality to competitive advantage, key skills possessed, key experience possessed, and if the employee is a key contributor. Consequence is mitigated by the ease of replacement of the employee and the uniqueness of the knowledge possessed by the employee. The determined risk was then adjusted based on the quality of the employee including time to loss of the employee, current health of the employee, time since employee acquired the critical knowledge, ability/willingness to share knowledge, and reason for leaving.

Other approaches include Kaplan (2008) who proposes using Communities of Practice, knowledge repositories, and mentoring and intern programs to assist the procurement industry in transferring knowledge from retiring workers to replacements. Parise, et al. (2006) propose using organizational network analysis to also assess the impact the loss of knowledge in a departing employee has on their work network and consider two network roles, Central Connector (those with technical expertise and organizational memory as well as a set of relationships that help many others get information or other resources to do their work) and Broker (broad knowledge of how the organization operates and ability to recognize and take advantage of opportunities that require integration of disparate expertise), as crucial roles requiring actions for capturing knowledge. Massingham (2008) supports the need for social network analysis as it was found that while loss of a critical employee may impact the social network by causing a loss of knowledge, it may also be mitigated because much of the knowledge possessed by the critical employee was distributed throughout their social network. Only by performing a social network analysis will the organization know which case (knowledge loss or loss mitigation) exists.

Ultimately, organizations need KM to help them understand and mitigate the potential loss of knowledge from employees leaving, retiring, being laid off, or lost for whatever reason.

Loss of Critical Knowledge: The United States Space Program

This example comes from a visit my eldest son and I made to the International Space Hall of Fame and Museum in Alamogordo, New Mexico. While there we talked to a retiree from the space program. During this conversation it came out that we were both engineers (he had served as a member of the capsule recovery team and a backup astronaut and my previous career before joining academia was as an engineer, manager, and project manager for a large nuclear utility). We got to talking engineering and he made the comment that it was too bad we couldn't get back to the moon. I of course agreed and expressed the desire for our government to allocate funds for it. He surprised me by saying it wasn't money that was the issue (although it would be if not for the following issue). What really prevents us from getting back to the moon is that we don't remember how to build Saturn V rockets, Apollo capsules, and Lunar Modules. It seems after the end of the Apollo program management ordered all the plans put on microfiche and all but two of the paper copies destroyed. This was done, however, when there was talk of going back to the moon and engineers went to retrieve the plans, the microfiche had decayed into unusable form, the saved two paper copies had been water damaged and were no longer readable and no other copies could be found, and everyone who knew how to build the rockets, capsules, and modules were either dead or retired. Additionally, when the younger engineers began to reverse engineer these components they were stymied because they didn't understand the technology from that time (the Apollo program used 1950s technology), technology had advanced so much that the engineers hadn't been taught some of the fundamental issues faced by engineers of that time. In other words, we had forgotten the knowledge from the experience of solving the problems that prevented moon flights. (Note: the above is the opinion of the interviewee, but it does reflect what I've observed in the commercial nuclear industry) (Jennex, 2006).

As previously stated, KM can be defined as the practice of selectively applying knowledge from previous experiences of decision making to current and future decision making activities with the express purpose of improving organizational effectiveness (Jennex, 2005). The above shows that the space program attempted to implement KM, but they are an example of failed KM. They attempted to store relevant knowledge but when it came time to retrieve it, it couldn't be retrieved and applied to the current decision making activity due to media volatility and a lack of capturing the relevant context that makes the critical knowledge usable. This is one of the issues organizations must prevent, the inability to retrieve and use knowledge once it is captured.

The retired astronaut and I discussed this for awhile and it occurred to me that we are facing similar issues in other industries. The Information Technology industry is an example of where we have forgotten fundamental issues and their solutions. I was trained to program using the IBM PC and XT. Those who remember these machines recall that we were restricted to approximately 1 Megahertz CPU speeds, 56 Kilobytes of usable memory, and hard drive storage of 10 Megabytes. The techniques used at that time for memory management and performance optimization were invalidated by newer generations of computers that ran faster with more memory making it unnecessary to train current students in these techniques. Additionally, with today's larger fixed drives (60 Gigabytes or more) there is no pressure on users to save only that which is necessary; the drives can hold it all; and if you need to move a lot of files there are Gigabyte sized flash drives. This is probably okay but what happens if we need to retrieve something critical? If we save everything it becomes difficult to find specific files, I know I'm guilty of this, I save all iterations of my papers and presentations and it is becoming difficult to organize my storage due to the thousands of files I am keeping (and often times gets me asking myself if I really need all these files). Several years ago I would have used risk management techniques to determine what file versions I truly could not afford to lose with the result that I would have had a fraction of the files to search through. (Jennex, 2006)

Additionally, what if we have to use an older machine or operating system or file management system to retrieve files? I recall my windows operating system corrupted a couple of years ago. I called the manufacturer's help desk to see if there was a way to recover and was told to reformat using the recovery CD. This would cause me to lose my files and I asked about copying them. The help desk didn't know how to do this but while I was talking to them I was fiddling with the computer and started it in DOS. I remembered how to move files using DOS commands and asked if that was an option. The help desk said they did not know DOS commands. To make a long story short I spent the next several minutes using basic DOS commands to backup my files on floppy disks while at the same time teaching the help desk how it could be done.

A final example is the commercial nuclear industry. The current generation of nuclear plants were designed and built by engineers who are now retiring or dead. This is a wealth of operational and design knowledge on using analog control and instrument systems, older material specifications, and older corrosion control systems that is no longer being taught to new engineers. Newer approaches rely on digital controls and displays, and newer materials with different corrosion control needs. Additionally, we have computerized processes that used to require manual calculations. As a young nuclear propulsion officer in the United States Navy I was taught to manually calculate estimated critical rod positions and reactor restart times (to name a few). These calculations are now done automatically and require little operator knowledge or input. This progress is good and is resulting in safer nuclear power plants, but I wonder what could happen if terrorists were able to successfully attack these new digital systems requiring operators to return to the old manual processes and analog systems. Would our operators know how it used to be done? Would we have the requisite knowledge and data to do it the old way? As a Year 2000 (Y2K) project manager for contingency planning for a large utility I learned that in many cases we no longer have the ability to backup our processes or systems using manual methods and that if we lost these components or systems we would not have the ability to maintain normal operations.

Storage Media

Is capturing knowledge enough? Hansen, et al. (1999) discusses the importance of a representation and storage strategy. The above space program situation is an example of having a strategy that identifies critical knowledge and stores it, but failed to identify a successful storage strategy. I don't believe this case is unique. Over the last 20 years I have seen a series of storage solutions, from microfiche to 8 inch floppies, 5 ¼ inch floppies, 3 ½ inch floppies, flash drives, storage networks, hard drive clusters, etc. Also, formats have changed from Wordstar in DOS to Word in Windows with a variety of software in-between (Word Perfect, various versions of Word, etc.). This also applies to database management systems (Dbase, Paradox, etc.) and spreadsheet systems (Visicalc, Lotus 123, etc.). What does this mean? Every time a standard changed I saw the most commonly used stored knowledge converted to the new standard, but the less used knowledge was left as is with the expectation that it would be converted later. Did later ever come? In many cases no, or at least not yet. So what is the issue? Potentially critical knowledge is now stored in a variety of formats and standards that organizations may not be able to read or retrieve from. Is there concern? I think there is but the concern is mild. Jennex (2008) found that use of knowledge had no correlation to its importance; in fact, it could almost be argued that knowledge that is seldom used is more valuable that that used frequently or even daily. Many don't understand what this means until they try to retrieve something from an old format and others possibly look at this as a good thing. After all, sales of music and videos tend to increase every time we change format and/or media. Video has gone from Beta to Laserdisc to VHS and now to DVD, where will it go next? Music has moved from 78s to 45s to 8 tracks to cassettes to CD to MP3, and is still changing. Books are moving from paper to audio to electronic books. Each of these changes ultimately causes owners to re-purchase their favorite titles when their old machines no longer work. I think content producers and distributors see this as a good thing. But is it? I don't think so; I think it only serves to keep us from facing the problem of lost data and knowledge.

Some Recommendations for Storage Issues

Bergeron (2002) has a fascinating book exploring the issue of media volatility and discussing how society will cope when the digital knowledge fails. He is not very optimistic. Can anything be done? Proposed actions include:

- Recognize consumer rights and require content producers and distributors when they change media and/or format to update products previously bought by consumers for the cost of the material. Consumers should not be forced to purchase new individual use copyrights when they already own them. This should force more organizations and individuals to consider the true costs of media and/or format changes and will raise awareness of how we are losing cultural treasures as after all, only those titles that are in consumer demand are re-mastered in the new media and/or format. As I get older I find this frustrating as it gets harder and harder to find playable versions of the music, videos, and books I grew up with and want to enjoy again (as an example, my favorite band, the Ozark Mountain Daredevils, had to buy back the rights to their music and re-issue their albums on CD themselves just to get it out to their fans).
- Organizations and individuals should use risk management techniques to select knowledge to be saved and continuously upgraded should media and/or formats change. As stated earlier, Jennex

(2008) found that there is no correlation between the importance of knowledge and its importance. Organizations should not use frequency of use as a guide to what knowledge should be converted. Organizations should apply risk management to determine the impact to the organization should that knowledge be lost. Organizations should establish an acceptable risk threshold and monitor how much risk they are assuming by not updating knowledge storage media/formats. Additionally, organizations should include aggregation assessments as much knowledge, when looked at alone, may seem to have minimal impact to the organization should it be lost. However, this same knowledge, when assessed as an aggregated whole with other related knowledge or all knowledge stored on the same media/format, may now have an unacceptable impact to the organization should it be lost.

- Finally, new technology and growing capacity is making it possible to capture everything. Is this a good thing? Again, I don't think so as we are overwhelming ourselves with data and knowledge of little value and making it harder for us to find those true golden nuggets of knowledge that provide innovative solutions to key problems. Shenk (1997) discusses this trend that he calls "Data Smog." His concern, and one I agree with, is that ultimately we will paralyze our decision making ability with an over abundance of information and knowledge. Managers and knowledge workers are afraid to make decisions on what to capture and what not to. The result is we capture so much because we can, not because there is a need. The problem is it makes retrieving critical knowledge harder as we have to search through these massive amounts of knowledge to find that which we need. Can we do anything about this? Again, yes we can. I am a strong proponent of the use of risk management techniques to identify critical knowledge for capture and retention. I strongly dislike the idea of capturing everything. Will we miss something at some point? Probably, but again, if we do our jobs right, it won't be impossible to recover from this.

Using Knowledge Correctly

Davenport and Prusak (1998) view knowledge as an evolving mix of framed experience, values, contextual information and expert insight that provides a framework for evaluating and incorporating new experiences and information. They found that in organizations, knowledge often becomes embedded in artifacts such as documents, video, audio or repositories and in organizational routines, processes, practices, and norms. They also say that for knowledge to have value it must include the human additions of context, culture, experience, and interpretation. Nonaka (1994) expands this view by stating that knowledge is about meaning in the sense that it is context-specific. This implies that users of knowledge must understand and have experience with the context, or surrounding conditions and influences, in which the knowledge is generated and used for it to have meaning to them. This also implies that for a knowledge repository to be useful it must also store the context in which the knowledge was generated. That knowledge is context specific argues against the idea that knowledge can be applied universally, however it does not argue against the concept of organizational knowledge. Organizational knowledge is considered to be an integral component of what organizational members remember and use meaning that knowledge is actionable.

What this means is that it is not enough to just capture knowledge and that taking action on knowledge without considering context and culture can lead to applying the wrong knowledge to the wrong situation, usually resulting in the wrong decisions being made. There are many examples of this being done but the one chosen for discussion is current and involves the stimulus package and budget that the United States government pushed through in early 2009.

Why this story? Consider that proponents of stimulus spending point to Roosevelt's public works spending as that government action that led to the end of the Great Depression. Opponents of stimulus spending point to Japan's public works spending in the 1990s that resulted in a huge public debt with little economic stimulus (Fackler, 2009) as the reason not to follow the stimulus spending plan. Which is right? The purpose of this chapter is not to make a political statement so the which is right question will not be answered. What will be answered is: are the examples being applied correctly?

The first story is the Roosevelt's public works program, the New Deal, used to spur the economy. Wikipedia (2009) describes the New Deal as the sequence of central economic planning and economic stimulus programs Roosevelt initiated between 1933 and 1938 with the goal of giving aid to the unemployed, reform of business and financial practices, and recovery of the economy during The Great Depression. The enactment of New Deal policies lasted from 1933 through 1939 and many consider them crucial to ending the Great Depression in the United States. Did these policies end the Great Depression? The opinions are mixed, it is agreed that the New Deal put people to work and created jobs, but most of these jobs were temporary and did not add to the economy. Many argue the Great Depression did not end until the onset of World War II with the resulting mobilization ending the Great Depression. The issue is that comparing the Great Depression and the remedies used to fight it may not be applicable to the current situation. Those using this story need to ensure that the context of the Great Depression matches that of today and I don't think it does. A KM approach would be to compare the political, economic, social, and legal environments in the 1930s to those in 2009. I expect they will be different but that doesn't make the story irrelevant to today, it just needs to be qualified and that context which matches identified and that context which doesn't analyzed for importance to applying this knowledge to the current situation. I don't seeing this being done by the various political pundits arguing the pros and cons of the stimulus package.

The second story is Japan's public works stimulus program from the 1990s. Fackler (2009) describes how this program created lots of infrastructure projects in Japan with the result that many projects were completed that weren't really needed driving Japan to having the largest public debt of any developed country. Many are using this result to say that the United States should not have a public works program. However, does the context match? Japan in the 1990s is probably much closer in context the United States of 2009 than the Great Depression is, with one major difference. Japan's infrastructure was fairly well destroyed during World War II requiring it to be rebuilt during the late 1940s, 1950s, and 1960s. This is important because the infrastructure projects of the 1990s were building on to this relatively new infrastructure. The United States in contrast did not suffer destruction of its infrastructure during World War II and instead is getting by in 2009 with infrastructure that was largely built in the early 1900s. This key difference in context needs to be considered when comparing Japan to the United States as it may very well be that the United States would benefit greatly from infrastructure projects that did Japan little to no good. Again, those political pundits using this story to argue for or against the current stimulus package need to analyze the context of each situation and use that to guide the discussion.

One final note, the above stories have not addressed culture. Both stories could be argued that cultural differences are significant between the story and the proposed application. However, due to chapter length considerations those differences are not addressed. This doesn't mean they aren't important, just too long to discuss here.

CONCLUSION

Why do we need Knowledge Management? We need KM because we need a formal process to help organizations identify, capture, store, and retrieve critical knowledge. We need KM processes to help organizations deal with changing storage strategies. We need KM to help us deal with the transience of knowledge workers. We need KM processes to help organizations manage a glut of knowledge. We need KM to ensure we apply knowledge correctly to differing situations. Ultimately, we need KM to help organizations make sense of what they know, to know what they know, and to effectively use what they know.

Murray E. Jennex
Editor

REFERENCES

Bergeron, B. (2002). *Dark Ages II: When the Digital Data Die*. Prentice Hall PTR.

Federal Interagency Forum on Aging-Related Statistics. (2006, May). Older Americans Update 2006: Key Indicators of Well-Being. Federal Interagency Forum on Aging-Related Statistics. Washington, DC: U.S. Government Printing Office.

Davenport, T.H. & Prusak, L. (1998). *Working Knowledge*. Harvard Business School Press.

Deloitte & Touche (2005, Feb. 15). *Retiring Workforce, Widening Skills Gap, Exodus of 'Critical Talent' Threatens Companies: Deloitte Consulting Survey*. Retrieved on November 28, 2008 from http://www.deloitte.com/dtt/press_release/0,1014,sid%253D5527%2526cid%253D102915,00.html

DeLone, W.H. & McLean, E.R., (1992). Information Systems Success: The Quest for the Dependent Variable. *Information Systems Research, 3*, 60-95.

DeLone, W.H. & McLean, E.R., (2003). The DeLone and McLean Model of Information Systems Success: A Ten-Year Update. *Journal of Management Information Systems, 19*(4), 9-30.

Eucker, T.R. (2007). Understanding the Impact of Tacit Knowledge Loss. *Knowledge Management Review, 10*(1), 10-13.

Fackler, M. (2009, February 6). Public Works Stimulus in Japan Offers Lessons. *The San Diego Union Tribune*, C1 & C3.

Hansen M.T., Nohria, N., & Tierney, T., (1999). What's your strategy for managing knowledge? *Harvard Business Review*, March-April, 106-116.

Jennex, M.E. (2005). What is Knowledge Management? *The International Journal of Knowledge Management, 1*(4), 1-4.

Jennex, M.E. (2006). Why We Can't Return to the Moon: The Need for Knowledge Management. *International Journal of Knowledge Management, 2*(1), 1-4.

Jennex, M.E., (2008). Exploring System Use as a Measure of Knowledge Management Success. *Journal of Organizational and End User Computing, 20*(1), 50-63.

Jennex, M.E., (2009). *Assessing Knowledge Loss Risk.* Paper presented at the 15th Americas Conference on Information Systems, AMCIS, Association for Information Systems, AIS.

Jennex, M.E. and Olfman, L., (2005). Assessing Knowledge Management Success. *International Journal of Knowledge Management, 1*(2), 33-49.

Jennex, M.E. and Olfman, L., (2006). A Model of Knowledge Management Success. *International Journal of Knowledge Management, 2*(3), 51-68.

Jennex, M.E., Smolnik, S., & Croasdell, D., (2008). Towards Measuring Knowledge Management Success. In *Proceedings of the 41st Hawaii International Conference on System Sciences, Hawaii, USA*. IEEE Computer Society Press.

Kaplan, B. (2008). *Managing the Risk of Knowledge Loss Due to Workforce Attrition: Retaining and Leveraging the Critical and Relevant Knowledge of the Procurement Workforce.* Professional Development Session National Association of State Procurement Officials, September 8, 2008. Retrieved November 15 from http://www.naspo.org/documents/Kaplan_Sep_08.pdf

Keen, P. & Tan, M., (2007). Knowledge Fusion: A Framework for Extending the Rigor and Relevance of Knowledge Management. *The International Journal of Knowledge Management, 3*(4), 1-17.

Kosilov, A., Mazour, T., & Yanev, Y., (2006). *Risk Management of Knowledge Loss in Nuclear Industry Organizations.* International Atomic Energy Agency.

Massingham, P., (2008). Measuring the Impact of Knowledge Loss: More than Ripples on a Pond? *Management Learning, 39*(5), 541-560

Moore, M., (2008). *Justifying Your Knowledge Management Programme* [White Paper]. Retrieved on March 30, 2009 from http://innotecture.files.wordpress.com/2008/11/justifying_your_km_prog3.pdf.

Nonaka, I., (1994). A Dynamic Theory of Organizational Knowledge Creation. *Organization Science, 5*(1), 14-37.

Parise, S., Cross, R., & Davenport, T.H., (2005). *It's Not What But Who You Know: How Organizational Network Analysis Can Help Address Knowledge Loss Crises.* Lost Knowledge Roundtable, The Network Roundtable at the University of Virginia.

Parise, S., Cross, R., & Davenport, T.H., (2006). Strategies for Preventing a Knowledge-Loss Crisis. *Sloan Management Review, 47*(4), 31-38.

Shenk, D. (1997). *Data Smog: Surviving the Information Glut.* HarperEdge Publishing.

Wikipedia (2009). *New Deal.* Retrieved on April 1, 2009 from http://en.wikipedia.org/wiki/New_Deal

Chapter 1
Do Organizational Memory and Information Technology Interact to Affect Organizational Information Needs and Provision?

Mohamed El Louadi
University of Tunis, Tunisia

Imen Tounsi
University of Sousse, Tunisia

ABSTRACT

The results reported in this chapter were obtained through the study of 43 work-units belonging to five business firms in a large group of Tunisian companies. Using the declarative, procedural and judgmental dimensions of organizational memory, interaction effects were detected between IT and organizational memory. Analyses of the data support the view that storage technologies interact with declarative memory contributing to reduce organizational information needs. But, contrary to expectations, storage technologies interact negatively with declarative memory on information provision. Furthermore, network technologies interact negatively with judgmental memory on information provision. These results raise issues that have been rarely encountered in the literature.

INTRODUCTION

Internal organization's information-processing capacity has almost always been related to struc-tural and technological mechanisms (Cummings & Cross, 2003; Girod, 1996; Huber, 1990; Walsham & Barrett, 2005). Quicker and easier access to external information and knowledge is becoming increasingly more important to organizations. Since the 1990s, the accumulation of data and information in organizations files and databases led researchers' interest to the study of organization memory too (Souren et al., 2004). Organization memory has become an additional mechanism allowing organizations to store, process, and disseminate information with the aim of speeding up organizational learning (Child & Rodrigues, 2001; Cohen, 1991).

Unfortunately, there has been very little empirical research on organizational memory and its relationship with the amounts of information needs and provision to date, despite the increasing realization that organizations are becoming more knowledge-based, relying not only on their computerized information systems but also on information and feedback from workers, customers, and partners. Even so, the knowledge-based company depends increasingly on knowledge, that is, patents, processes, management skills, old-fashioned experience, past failures and successes (Levitt & March, 1988; Walsh & Ungson, 1991). This is especially true in the case of organizations whose members are specialized in some particular task and where learning occurs essentially by doing. Such companies have managers who need to access more information about more aspects of the business, from more parts of the organization, and in shorter time spans (Huber, 1984).

While organizations develop uncertainty-reduction mechanisms by increasing their information-processing capacities favoring the acquisition, creation, and flow of new information (Galbraith, 1977), some other mechanisms are needed for the processing of information that the organization already possesses in order to foster learning. Some of the knowledge needed is accumulated in databases and archived documentation but the most important part lies in people's heads (Nonaka, 1995). An organization's knowledge capacity is therefore a function of the sum of everything everybody in the organization knows (Aschcraft, 1994; Walsh & Ungson, 1991).

Organizations do not need knowledge about past events only. They also need knowledge about past and present happenings and experiences. Learning cannot be dissociated from memory (Lehner et al., 1998, Walsh & Ungson, 1991); it is "...a process that involves the discovery, retention, and exploitation of stored knowledge" (Moorman & Miner 1998, p. 705). Mechanisms related to accumulated information about past and present events are collectively known as the organizational memory (Stein & Swass, 1995; Walsh & Ungson, 1991).

Past research has not always been consensual regarding the concepts of organizational learning, knowledge management, and organizational memory, probably due to the many disciplines in which they are studied. As a result, researchers and managers are often unclear as to what constitutes what.

Nickols (2001) attributes three meanings to the word "knowledge." The first refers to the "state of knowing" and is very close to what we commonly call the "know about." The second refers to the "the capacity for action" and is very close in meaning to what we call "know how." The former and the latter meanings thus point to the result of the cumulated knowledge. The third meaning refers to that which is codified and accumulated: facts, methods, principles, techniques, and so forth, in short, to that which was captured in the form of books, papers, formulae, formal procedures, computer code and so on (Nickols, 2001).

For Dodgson (1993, p. 377), organizational learning is building, supplementing, and organizing knowledge and routines around activities and within cultures by improving the use of the broad skills of the organization's workforces, leading to a change in behavior or, at least to a change in the range of potential behaviors (Huber, 1991). In order to be valid as organizational learning, this knowledge must be stored in the memory of the organization (Ortenblad, 2001). For Jennex and Croasdell (2004), organizational learning is the development of shared meanings and interpretations of those meanings to enhance future [organizational] activities

Huber (1991) considers that knowledge acquisition, information distribution, information interpretation, and organizational memory all contribute integrally to organizational learning (see Table 1). In his view, organizational memory cannot be separated from organizational learning: "[T]hat which has been learned must be stored in memory and then brought forth from memory" (Huber, 1996, p. 150). Whereas organizational learning need not be conscious, organizational memory needs to be continuously updated and refreshed, oftentimes consciously and while learning, in general, includes "unlearning" (forgetting) (Hedberg, 1981), memory is, by definition, the antonym of amnesia.

Finally, if organizational learning is primarily about changing the organizational knowledge base, it does not provide a clear indication as to what needs to be changed so that learning can take place. By contrast, because knowledge management addresses the process of acquiring, creating, distributing and using knowledge in organizations (Jennex & Croasdell, 2004), it provides a framework for managing the knowledge base in order for learning to be brought about (Büchel & Probst, 2000). Thus all of organizational learning, knowledge management, and organizational memory are as independent as, to borrow Spender's (1996) metaphor, the three elements in Ohm's Law, whereby voltage, current and resistance comprise a single system of concepts about electricity. Leaning is a process, knowledge management is a framework and organizational memory is about content.

This research endeavors to explore relationships between information technology (IT) and organizational memory, and their combined effect on the provision of information. It aims at answering the question as to whether organizational memory is associated with the degree of information availability and, if so, whether it is augmented by IT in providing needed information.

We have organized this paper as follows. First, we present a definition of organizational memory and three of its commonly used dimensions: declarative memory, procedural memory, and judgmental memory. Second, we present a conceptual overview of the concepts. Then, we introduce the method and data collection procedure. In the following section, we present the measures we used. Following this, we present the results of the tests of the relationships between the variables which we also discuss, and then we conclude the paper with the limitations of the study and propositions for future research.

Organizational Memory

Building on Walsh and Ungson (1991), Stein and Swass (1995) define organizational memory as

Table 1. The four elements of organizational learning (Huber, 1991); definitions adapted from Balasubramanian (1995).

Knowledge acquisition	Knowledge acquisition is about how knowledge is obtained. It is not limited to outside the organization but extends to the rearrangement of existing internal knowledge and to the updating of previous knowledge.
Information distribution	Information distribution is about how information is disseminated among organizational units and members thus promoting learning and producing new knowledge or understandings.
Information interpretation	Information interpretation is about how distributed information is viewed, interpreted, and given one or more commonly understood meanings.
Organizational memory	Organizational memory is about how knowledge is captured for future use.

"the means by which knowledge from the past is brought to bear on present activities" (p. 22).

Organizational memory has been conceptualized theoretically in several different ways. Ashcraft (1994), for example, classifies the different types of memories as episodic (knowledge of events personally experienced by people), semantic (factual knowledge), or procedural (skills learned, or as Markus (2001) calls it, "best practice"). Girod (1995) defines organizational memory as a set of competencies associated with beliefs and declarative and procedural knowledge borne out of inter and intra-organizational structural arrangements.

Synthesizing several literatures, Girod (1995, 1996) distinguishes between three memory categories. The first, called "declarative memory," is a mostly explicit memory containing knowledge accumulated in human memories about facts, things and events. The second, "procedural memory," is mostly tacit and contains knowledge about how to do things. And the third, "judgmental memory," contains memories related to the individual's experience.

Taken at the organizational, collective level, declarative and procedural memories are well known constructs in other management literatures (Anderson, 1983, Moorman & Miner, 1998) and to cognitive psychologists (Chase & Simon, 1973; Singley & Anderson, 1989). For that reason, organizational memory will be taken as composed of its three categories: declarative, procedural, and judgmental, which, according to Girod (1995) can also be conceptualized at the collective level as well.

Declarative Memory: The Know What

Declarative memory is the sum of technical, scientific, and administrative knowledge detained by organizational members which is related to their work and which, therefore, should be made available to the organization (Girod, 1996). It consists of explicit knowledge, that is, facts, propositions, events, situations, and so forth. (Moorman & Miner, 1998). Thus what individuals learn in school about the operation of machinery and which they bring into the organization upon their hiring is declarative knowledge. This knowledge can be stored in the individuals' memory or in archives, in the form of how-tos that other individuals can tap into. Girod considers that the memory containing declarative knowledge is not limited to individuals. It can be derived from the interaction of two or more people. In this case, it is considered collective declarative memory. It can be formalized and stored in databases for example (centralized collective declarative memory) or informal, implicit, unrecorded, and volatile (decentralized collective declarative memory).

At the collective level, declarative memory can be likened to what Walsh (1995) terms as "shared information." Moorman and Miner (1998) note that a key characteristic of declarative memory is the diversity of uses to which it can be put thus providing the basis for transfer of the same knowledge between different applications.

Procedural Memory: The Know How

Procedural memory is composed of the know-how that individuals apply in their day-to-day work-life (Cohen & Bacdayan, 1994). It is skill and action knowledge (Moorman & Miner, 1998). Unlike declarative knowledge, which is stored in declarative memories, procedural knowledge is the result of an individual's personal learning experience. A learning organization tries to transform this knowledge into organizational knowledge to make it available to everyone (Girod, 1996). Routine knowledge transformed into procedural knowledge is stored into rules and procedures (Cohen & Bacdayan, 1994) and is categorized as centralized collective procedural memory by Girod (1995). Moorman and Miner (1998) note that procedural memory generally becomes "automatic" or that it is accessible "unconsciously" (p. 708). Most often tacit, procedural memory can, however, be made explicit when it is documented and circulated in the shape of procedures, for example.

Judgmental Memory: The Know Why

Judgmental memory is the individuals' tendency to interpret information, events, and knowledge to derive proper action. It is memory about why things are done. Judgmental memory, also called "rationale memory" by Moran and Carroll (1996), relies forcibly on individuals' own experience and knowledge. It is what makes the opinion of an expert more valuable than a layperson's. It is also the type of memory that suffers the most from personnel turnover because it is very hard to extract and record. At the collective level, judgmental memory constitutes the sum of all organizational members' judgmental memories and the unique way that an organization senses and interprets events.

Organizational Memory and IT

Memory is increasingly being regarded as a resource, like labor and capital. In that, it is on the same path as information. In the information-processing view, an organization is viewed as an ensemble of information-processors (humans, machines, networks, etc.) matching information and knowledge acquired from the outside with information and knowledge accumulated in order to improve decision-making and effectiveness.

In an ethnographic study of a help line group, Ackerman and Halverson (2000) demonstrated the theoretical limitations of the metaphor of a single organizational memory. They contend that there is a supra-individual memory, maybe even several memories, complexly distributed among several people and technologies. Walsh and Ungson (1991) consider memory to include not only people but also archives, organizational procedures, organizational structures, and culture, but not information technology. In their model, Walsh and Ungson (1991) have categorized organ-izational memory as being spread over six organizational contexts: individuals (people's heads), culture, organizational transformations, structures, organizational ecology, and external archives. Ackerman (1996) argues that information repositories such as corporate manuals, databases, filing systems, and even anecdotal stories could also be included in the construct of organizational memory.

Yet, one of the objectives of IT is to make the required information easily accessible. IT plays an important role in disseminating information and in facilitating communication within organizations (Huber, 1990; Walsham, 2001). Like Huber (1990 p. 65), our hypothesis is that use of IT should lead to more information availability and greater information accessibility.

It can also be easily argued that IT represents a way for organizations to augment their organizational memory (Ackerman, 1996; Lehner et al., 1998; Moorman & Miner, 1998). As a consequence, IT would become embedded in a broader conceptualization of organizational memory as contended by Watson (1996) who considers organizational memory to be essentially technology driven, a comprehensive enterprise-wide database supported by multimedia, imaging, and electronic archiving and document management systems.

Conversely, a distinction can be made between memory that is based on IT, also called organizational memory systems (OMS) (Ackerman, 1996; Lehner et al., 1998), and organizational memory information systems (OMIS) (Wijnhoven, 1999). While Walsh and Ungson (1991) did not count computer files and databases among their components of organizational memory, Wijnhoven (1999), for example, includes in it individuals, culture, transformation, structure, ecology, external environment, computer-based information systems, and non-IT based records and files. Consequently, there would be two types of memories, one that is based on computer and communication technologies and another which is based on non IT-based mechanisms, both hypothesized to contribute positively to organizational information-processing capacity. As noted by Ackerman (1996):

"Organizational memory systems (OMS) offer the possibility that computer systems can better serve the information storage and retrieval needs of an organization's memory than can present technical and social methods" (Ackerman, 1996, p. 10).

Non IT-based memory, especially that which lies in people's heads has the advantage of being available and relatively more accessible within a known context, but it suffers from poor retention and is volatile because it is prone to leaving the organization once the individual holding it leaves (Stein & Zwass, 1995) causing what Borghoff and Pareschi (1997) and Kransdorff (1998) call "corporate amnesia." Thus, non-computer based memory can suffer corruption, decay in both detail and accuracy or even erasure with time. Knowledge in people's heads comes and goes as people come and go (Nonaka, 1995).

IT-based memory, on the other hand, is quasi-permanent; knowledge is logged, indexed, secured, and organized in such a way that it becomes accessible. However, IT-based memory suffers from limitations that have been pointed out by Ackerman (1996) such as the impossibility of having a unified organizational memory reflected in incomplete, fragmented and/or overlapping databases and files. Furthermore, IT often lacks the capability of providing necessary clues in light of the context in which memory is found most useful.

IT contributes to organizational memory in at least two ways: by making accumulated knowledge accessible to organization members or by making individuals with knowledge known (Ackerman, 1996; Jennex, 2006). However, there is still no agreement as to which technologies best support this memory and Lehner et al. (1998) suggest that organizational memory cannot be served by a single technology. Cross and Baird (2000) contend that it is not enough to accumulate information and knowledge in electronic repositories and that organizational members rely upon a network of relationships for information and advice. According to Cross and Baird (2000), people take advantage of databases only when more trained colleagues point them to a specific location in the database where they can find the information that they seek. For Cross and Baird, IT is only one form of memory that organizational members tap into when solving problems and its use is therefore limited.

In this chapter, we consider, like others (Huber, 1991; Jennex, 2006; Lehner et al., 1998; Stein & Zwass, 1995), that IT is also used to support organizational memory.

Setting

The study was conducted in Tunisia in 2002. Tunisia is a small, 10 million-populated North-African country. In 1995, it became the first Maghreb and Arab country to sign an association agreement with the European Union. Since then, Tunisia's economy has grown by over 4.5 percent annually. Three years later, it ratified the European Association Agreement which calls for the gradual removal of all tariffs on industrial goods by 2008. Today, Tunisia is seriously preparing its industrial sector, composed of more than 10,800 firms of more than 10 employees, to international competition through a $2.5 billion competitive restructuring program, launched in 1995 and dubbed "The Way to Competition." More than 2,360 Tunisian firms are totally exporting, and this number is increasing. These firms face the challenge to be as competitive as their European counterparts, maybe even as their other Asian and American partners.

Conscious of these implications, and encouraged by a set of governmental policies, the computer and telecommunication sectors have greatly contributed in making Tunisia an ideal regional telecommunications hub with access to Europe, the Middle East and Africa. More than

TD 1779 million were invested in IT as part of the 10th Plan (2002-2006) and TD 3107 million are planned in the 11th five-year Economic and Social Development Plan (2007-2011).

According to an International Herald Tribune article (Stratte-McClure, 2000), "Advances in telecommunications, the Internet and electronic commerce are appropriate symbols of Tunisia's industrial, social and economic strides." Having been the first African and Arab country to connect to the Internet in 1991, when there were only thirty-one countries connected (ITU, 2003), Tunisia now boasts more than 1,446,000 Internet users (roughly 14.5 percent of the population) .

In 2005, Tunisia was ranked 31st according to the Network Readiness Index developed by the World Economic Forum (WEF), up from the 40th position it was in the previous year (Forbes, 2005). It was ranked No.1 in Africa and in the Arab world for economic competitiveness in the 2007 WEF Global Competitiveness Report. Based on an assessment of the economies of 128 countries, the report ranks Tunisia the 29th most competitive country in the world. Tunisia was also ranked by the WEF as the first Arab and African country and 35th in the world in the field of global information technology. Tunisia is currently working out an overall IT strategy for the 2007-2011 period with the support of the World Bank, with an aim of reaching an IT infrastructure equivalent to that of the developed countries by 2011.

However, even though Tunisia has often been touted by the International Monetary Fund (IMF) and the World Bank as models for its emerging economies, IT, the main driver for its integration into world economy, seems to have been mostly adopted by the industry for clerical purposes. With a few exceptions, like the group of companies we studied.

Data Collection

The group of firms in which we conducted our study was created in 1967, 11 years after Tuni-sia's independence. In its beginnings, it was specialized in commercializing meat products such as chicken and turkey. In three decades, it expanded into a Holding composed of 30 firms organized in a matrix form and employing more than 6,000 people. Today, 95 percent of the Holding's products are either new in Tunisia (such as industrial ceramic) or manufactured using new technologies. It exports some of its products to more than 35 countries. Highly modernized, having complied with most ISO 9000 and restructuring programs, the group is reputed for its sense of organization, processes and procedures, overseen by a central audit structure in headquarters.

It was that central audit unit that selected the companies as well as the work-units within them which were to participate because the study was incorporated into a larger scale survey which was being made simultaneously. The only condition was that the questionnaire, written in French, that we used for data collection be handed to the same units across firms. The firms were geographically dispersed in four cities. The work-units in each firm were: (1) production, (2) commercial, (3) maintenance, (4) accounting, (5) finance, (6) quality assurance, (7) MIS, (8) purchasing, and (9) administrative and HR. The major focus of this study is on organizations work-units' memory and information needs and provision. We therefore concentrated on collecting data from various work-units in five firms all belonging to the same group of companies.

Because the use of multiple informants is ideal while measuring organization-level constructs (Van Bruggen et al., 2002), we polled several informants from each work-unit. While the use of multiple informants from each work-unit is preferable, the single informant approach allows for a larger number of work-units to be surveyed. In the face of resource constraints, we opted for the latter approach. Consequently, we took the precaution of wording our questionnaire so as to make clear that the entire organization is to be considered .

Our starting random sample of 45 (five firms x nine units) was reduced to 43 because two work-units did not respond in time or produced unusable answers. Forty three responses will consequently be used for analysis in the remainder of this paper (Table 2).

The Measures

Measures of organizational memory, IT penetration and information needs and provision were used for this study. These measures are explained below.

Organizational Memory

A measure composed of 15 items was specially designed for this study to measure organiza-tional memory. Factor analysis yielded a three factor solution explaining 64 percent of the variance. Coinciding with Girod's (1995) three dimensions, the factors were labeled: (1) procedural memory, (2) judgmental memory, and (3) declarative memory (see Table 3).

Amount of Information Needs and Provision

Information needs and provision of any organization can be classified as internal or external. Internal information is generated within the organization to satisfy its working members and decision-making functions. It pertains to the organization's internal operations. It supports decisions typically made by operations managers with short time horizons. External information is information that is of interest for the organization but which originates in its environment. It pertains to the organization's customers, competitors, and so forth. (Ewusi-Mensah, 1981).

Respondents were asked to rate, on a scale from 1 (not at all) to 5 (a lot), the extent of availability of 10 categories of external information and nine categories of internal external information. These measures were developed by El Louadi (1996) and their reliability and dimensionality were later further reassessed (El Louadi, 1998).

Degree of IT Adoption

Information technology refers to the technologies and applications which combine the information processing, storage and transmission powers of computers with the distance-transmission capabilities of telecommunication technologies (Bakopoulos, 1985). It also complements and supports knowledge processing (Tuomi, 2000). From our previous discussion, IT can also be conceptualized as a mechanism helping to augment organizational memory.

Some technologies, such as electronic filing cabinets, document archiving systems, relational databases, Intranet, groupware, data warehouses,

Table 2. Sample characteristics

	Main activity	No. of Work-units	#. employees (FTE)
1	Animal food industry	9	156
2	Animal food industry	9	48
3	Food industry	9	157
4	Food industry	9	324
5	Manufacturing	7	288
	Total	43	

navigators' information archiving with bookmarks, etc. have more of a memory focus than others. Unfortunately, there is still little evidence supporting the preeminence of some technologies over others with regards to organizational memory.

Shortly after its creation, the group in which we conducted our study was using a centrally controlled IT infrastructure with several systems and computer centers disseminated across the units. In the mean time, the group had diversified its activities to include eggs, ice cream, margarine, yogurt, wood, refrigerators, computer assembly, mufflers, tourism, and so forth. In 1991, it shifted towards clients-server computing progressively harmonizing its information systems until it adopted an ERP in 1998. In less than five years, it moved from unified transaction-processing to reporting to online analytical processing thus acquiring and fully exploiting a huge data warehouse fed by the many data marts scattered over the units. As a result, the group is probably one of the most, if not the most, developed IS shop in the Tunisian industry today. It uses electronic mail extensively (1,200 accounts at the time of the study) and hires its employees through its Web site.

For this reason, we included all technologies available in the work-units we surveyed.

In the questionnaire, we asked questions concerning the degree of adoption of IT using a 26-item list of information technologies. The respondents were asked to rate each technology on a scale from 1 (technology not operational) to 5 (operational on a widespread basis). Factor analysis with varimax (orthogonal) rotation and Kaiser normalization was then performed with the purpose of generating factors that are easily interpretable. A four-factor solution emerged

Table 3. Item-to-factor loadings for the organizational memory variable

	Procedural Memory	Judgmental Memory	Declarative Memory
Existence of documentation concerning past successful projects	.81		
Existence of documentation concerning past failed projects[a]	.79		
Existence of a procedure assuring the replacement of a leaving manager by another	.79		
Number of qualified or specialized members in the unit	.48		
The extent to which experimented unit members are solicited for help and advice		.79	
The extent to which help is available when an administrative problem occurs within the unit		.76	
The extent to which help is available when a technical problem occurs within the unit		.71	
The extent to which help is available when a social/relational problem occurs within the unit		.71	
Frequency of individual activity reports production			.95
Frequency of group activity reports production			.92
Frequency of meetings within the unit			.66

Extraction Method: Principal Component Analysis. Rotation Method: Varimax with Kaiser Normalization.

[a] *Reverse scored*

which explains 66 percent of the scale's variance. As shown in Table 4, the factors were labeled (1) software penetration, (2) storage penetration, (3) network penetration, and (4) communication penetration.

Analyses

Prior to analysis, the IT (software, storage, network, and communication) variables, the memory (procedural, judgmental, and declarative), and the information provision (external and internal) and information needs (external and internal) variables were examined through various SPSS programs for accuracy of data entry, missing values, and normality and multivariate analyses.

Because of the small size of our sample, we conducted tests of normality of variables following Tabachnick and Fidell (1989) recommendations by using descriptive programs for skewness. We found moderate negative skewness for the external information needs variable (skewness=-1.26). We corrected for skewness by computing the square root of the reflect of that variable. This reduced skewness considerably.

We calculated the Shapiro-Wilk statistic W (Shapiro & Wilk, 1965), which has become standard for small samples with 50 or fewer observations (Royston, 1982). The Shapiro-Wilk test revealed that the hypothesis of non-normality could not be rejected for 4 out of 7 independent variables and 2 out of four dependent variables (W varying between .84 and .94 significant at p=.024 or less).

We also looked for multivariate outliers. The tests revealed the existence of 11 multivariate outliers for which the Mahalanobis distance was greater than 3. Given the size of the data set, we were reluctant to eliminate them. However, we flagged the outliers with a dummy variable (see Tabachnick & Fidell 1989, p. 69) and applied the Shapiro-Wilk test on the remaining observations (the reduced sample). Thus, there were only three independent variables for which normality remained an issue ($W \geq .880$; $p \leq .015$).

Though the unit of analysis is the firm, not work-units or individuals, aggregating the data within work-units could present methodological issues for which there are yet no satisfactory solutions if members within a work-unit perceive the dimensions studied here differently. To test the assumption that participants from each work-unit responded similarly, a series of ANOVAs was performed (Dixon & Massey, 1969). Because we observed

Table 4. Item-to-factor loadings for the IT Variable

	Software Penetration	Storage Penetration	Network Penetration	Communication Penetration
Accounting Software	.79			
PC Software	.75			
Inventory Mgmt. Software	.69			
Personal Information Managers		.78		
Personal Computers		.77		
Databases (Access)		.59		
Data warehouse		.47		
Fax			.74	
Voice Mail			.74	
Wide Area Networks			.69	
External (Internet) e-mail				.85
Internal (Intranet) e-mail				.53

Extraction Method: Principal Component Analysis.
Rotation Method: Varimax with Kaiser Normalization.

large variances among individuals making up the groups and the way they are responding to the variables, the decision was not to pool individual responses to represent groups.

Table 5 summarizes the statistical properties of the variables used in this study.

T-tests revealed that though the need for internal information is not significantly greater than the need for external information, the provision of internal information is significantly greater than the provision of external information (t=5.59, 42 df, p<.0001) (see Table 5 and Figure 1). Furthermore, the need for information is significantly greater than provision whether it is internal (t=4.06, 42 df, p<.0001) or external (t=6.15, 42 df, p<.0001). The least we can infer from this result is that work-units in this sample do not suffer from information overload but rather from information poverty (Simon, 1982).

Interestingly, Table 5 shows that the judgmental memory variable has the greatest mean while one would have expected procedural memory to

Table 5. Statistical properties of the variables of the study

	Min	Max	Mean	Std-Dev	α
Organizational Memory					
Procedural Memory	1.00	4.75	3.32	.97	.75
Declarative Memory	1.00	5.00	2.97	1.04	.76
Judgmental Memory	2.00	5.00	**3.65**	.81	.83
IT					
Software Penetration	1.00	5.00	4.12	1.11	.67
Storage Penetration	1.40	5.00	3.97	.94	.70
Network Penetration	1.00	5.00	3.10	1.29	.63
Communication Penetration	1.00	5.00	**4.31**	.95	.65
Information Needs / Provision					
Internal Information Needs	2.00	5.00	**3.89**	.84	.88
Internal Information Provision	1.00	4.44	3.38	.81	.87
External Information Needs	1.00	5.00	3.63	.93	.89
External Information Provision	1.00	4.00	2.73	.73	.86

Figure 1. Statistically significant differences among the information variables:

- *information needs (mean=3.75) are significantly greater than overall information provision (mean=3.06) (t=6.048, p<.0001)*
- *internal information needs (3.89) are significantly greater than internal information provision (3.38) (t=4.06, p<.0001), and*
- *external information needs (3.63) are significantly greater than external information provision (2.73) (t=6.15, p<.0001).*

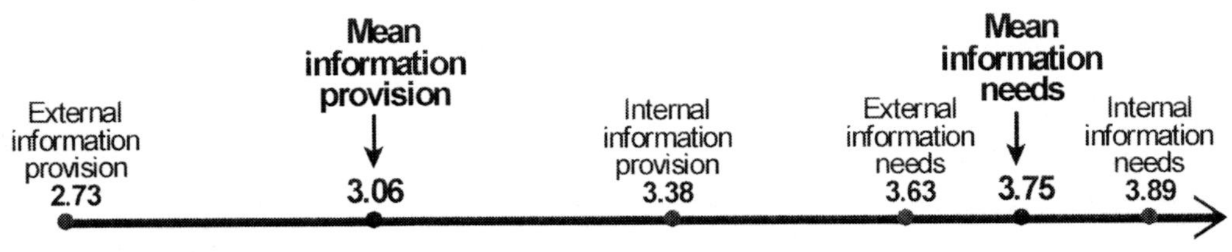

Table 6. Correlation matrix among the research variables

		1	2	3	4	5	6	7	8	9	10
1	Procedural Memory	-									
2	Declarative Memory	.23	-								
3	Judgmental Memory	**.35** *	.01	-							
4	Software Penetration	**.48** **	.02	**.29** *	-						
5	Storage Penetration	.16	.02	**.46** **	**.41** **	-					
6	Network Penetration	**.48** **	**-.28** *	.22	.24	.20	-				
7	Communication Penetration	.11	.17	.13	**.50** **	**.38** *	**.30** *	-			
8	Internal Information Needs	-.15	.06	.02	**-.26** *	-.21	.23	.11	-		
9	Internal Information Provision	-.01	-.13	.04	.14	-.08	**.29** *	**.37** *	**.52** ***	-	
10	External Information Provision	**.27** *	.06	.25	.18	.06	.14	**.26** *	.16	**.52** ***	-
11	External Information Needs[a]	.04	-.20	.16	.03	-.29	.14	-.08	**.47** **	.38 *	.34*

[a] Adjusted for sign due to correction for skewness by transformation.

* p <.05
** p<.005
*** p< .0001

be highest in this group of firms due to its over reliance on rules and procedures and where the employees are routinely evaluated on their compliance with these rules.

The correlations among the independent and the dependent variables are given in Table 6.

Interestingly, from among the three memory variables, only procedural memory and judgmental memory correlate positively with each other (.35, p=.011). There are also significant correlations between the memory variables and the technology variables ranging from .29 to .48. One can notice the .28 (p=.036) negative correlation between declarative memory and network penetration.

Only procedural memory correlates with the dependent information variable measuring external information provision. However, as one would expect, IT correlates with several information variables, either negatively with needs or positively with provision. For example, though not associated with information provision, software penetration is negatively associated with information needs (-.26, p=.046). Both network and communication penetrations are associated with internal information provision. The only variable other than procedural memory, correlating with external information provision is communication penetration (.26, p=.044). No independent variable correlates with external information needs.

The data of the correlation matrix raise two issues. First, most independent variables are significantly inter-correlated suggesting multicollinearity might be present. Second, the dependent variables demonstrate several significant intercorrelations. This is restrictive in the sense that running multivariate tests would inflate the possibility of Type I error. Coupled with the likely multicollinearity of the independent variables, the validity of the interpretation of the results could become questionable.

To address the first issue, we used the orthogonal factor scores extracted from the principal components analyses performed initially to extract an orthogonal set of component scores from all the independent variables (Tabachnick & Fidell, 1989). This procedure allowed us to form orthogonal variables which carry the same information as the original variables but which will not correlate, thus reducing multicollinearity.

To avoid the implications of the second issue, we used multiple analysis of variance (MANOVA) to analyze our data. It is inherent in the MANOVA procedure that tests on all univariate and multivariate effects are performed on the dependent variables taken together and separately. To perform these analyses, we split all the independent variables into two groups (low and high) based on their median.

Results

Given the exploratory nature of this study, a series of MANOVAs was conducted investigating main, multivariate and interaction effects between the independent variables and the information dependent variables. No significant results involved the procedural memory and software penetration variables. Furthermore, there were no main, multivariate, or interactive effects on the external information needs dependent variable.

There were, however, main effects and interactive effects involving the other variables. Main and interactive effects involved the storage, network, and communication variables as well as the declarative and judgmental memory variables.

The main effect of storage penetration was on the internal information provision (F=9.30, p=.004). Communication penetration had main effects on both the internal information needs (F=5.05, p=.031) and the external information provision (F=4.62, p=.039) variables.

Four interactive effects were detected. The first was between storage penetration and declarative memory on internal information needs (F=4.15, p=.050, see Figure 2). The second between storage penetration and declarative memory on internal information provision (F=14.70, p=.001, Figure 3). The third between storage penetration and declarative memory on external informa-tion provision (F=8.46, p=0.006, Figure 4). And the fourth between network penetration and judgmental memory on external information provision (F=5.20, p=.029, Figure 5).

The results thus clearly suggest that an interaction effect between memory and technological variables on information needs and provision exist.

We also note, from Figure 2, that, between low and high declarative memory, internal information needs are high when there is not enough storage. This result is to be expected since if technical, scientific, and administrative memories exist in the organization, but are not available in electronic form because there is not sufficient storage, the needs for technical, scientific, and administrative information will be augmented by the need to know where to find it. On the other hand, when both declarative memory and storage penetration are high, the need for internal information is low, probably because storage is used to also store this kind of information.

The next two results (Figures 3 and 4) show interaction effects of declarative memory and storage on both internal and external information provision. Both the nature and the form of these interaction effects are unexpected. In fact, one would assume the interaction to be in favor of increasing information provision when both storage and declarative memory are high. The opposite is observed.

Figure 2. Interaction effect between declarative memory and storage penetration on the amount of internal information needs

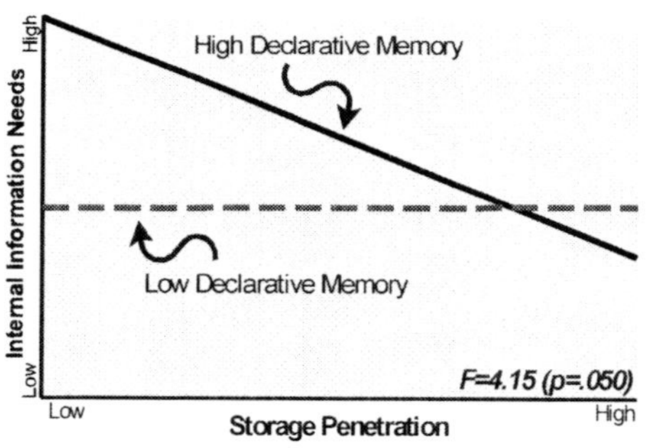

Figure 3. Interaction effect between declarative memory and storage penetration on the amount of internal information provision

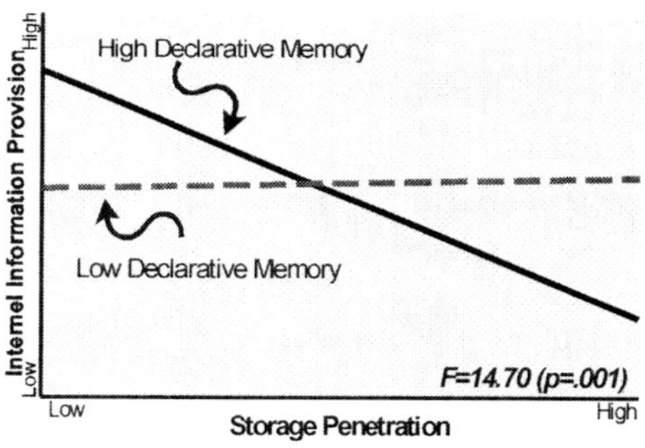

Figure 4. Interaction effect between declarative memory and storage penetration on the amount of external information provision

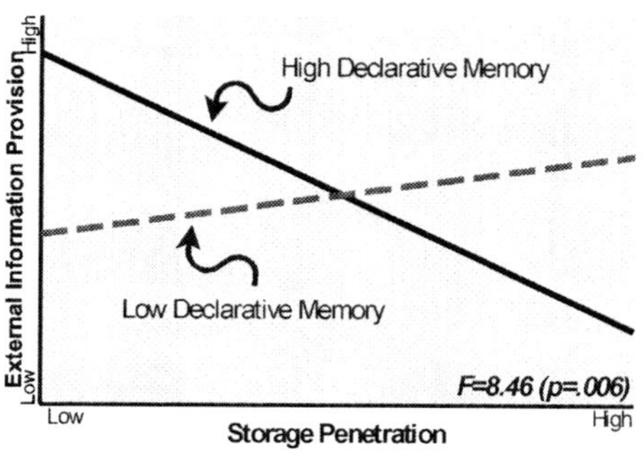

Figure 5. Interaction effect between judgmental memory and network penetration on the amount of external information provision

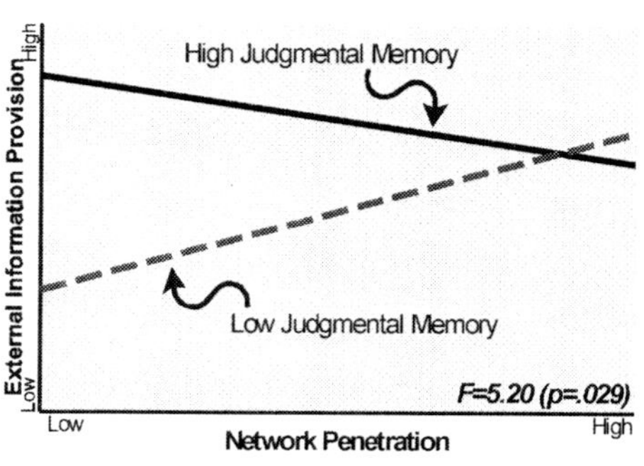

Figure 5 shows that judgmental memory and network penetration interact significantly on the amount of external information provision. Here, too, the same trend appears. In this case, it would seem that external information provision is better when judgmental memory is high and network penetration is low. This result goes counter to our expectations. Judgmental memory being more a matter of interpretation and experience, the fact that more technology is available does not make it perceived as more useful since it seems that provision gets lower when network penetration goes higher. But this would only explain one part of the results shown in Figure 5, that is, when both network penetration and judgmental memory are high. We could not find any explanation for the provision being higher when network penetration is low and judgmental memory is low than when they are both high.

CONCLUSION

The results of this study are somewhat unexpected. This is perhaps due to the lack of empirical studies having tackled the measurement of organizational memory and the inclusion of both IT and organizational memory in an integrated research model. This paper endeavored to overcome this shortcoming by incorporating both IT and memory concepts into the information-processing theory of the firm.

Unfortunately, most of our results do not support the view that IT and memory contribute simultaneously to increase the provision of information in organizations. While assertions found in the literature hypothesized that IT augments the benefits of organizational memory (Ackerman, 1996; Lehner et al., 1998), this study could not confirm all of them. In fact, it would seem as though IT and organizational memory have diverging effects on information provision.

These results are important because they highlight the effects that IT could have on learning in general and on memory in particular. Because organizations expect that IT would augment organizational memory, they would rely overly on it and expand less efforts in using other types of memories. Could this result in a net negative effect on information availability and has such a phenomenon been observed before?

We have already noted that IT-based and other memories differ in significant ways, one being the additional search effort needed to retrieve information and knowledge when they are stored electronically. Declarative memory, for example, has the characteristic of not being committed to a particular use which could become a drawback as was already noted by cognitive psychologists (Singley & Anderson, 1989) who note that "vast amounts of [declarative memory] are potentially relevant in any problem-solving situation, and this leads to serious problems of search" (p.220), a process by which stored information is recognized by its user as relevant to a particular problem or goal (Wijnhoven, 1999).

Search presumes knowledge about what to search (the information), where to search it (in computers or elsewhere) and, in the case of IT, how to search it. In effect, when information is stored in computer hard drives, servers and networks, there always needs to be programs or query routines to help access it. Organizational members need to know how to use these programs as well as tools to make sense out of the information found. With respect to computer-based memories, this is in conformity with Tuomi's (2000) notion of "reversed knowledge hierarchy" whereby meaningful information emerges only when we have knowledge about it.

If this was true, then the additional search effort entailed by computerized files and databases would increase the difficulty of having access to the information needed. This would increase the perception that information is less available since its access requires knowledge that may be lacking. Users may find it difficult even to select from the available sources those that are most appropriate given their needs (Lansdale, 1988). Or they may be unsure as to whether knowledge documented in repositories is current or out-of-date (Galunic & Weeks, 1999).

Another possible, and somewhat related, explanation could be found in both the psychological expectations of computer users (see Lansdale, 1988) and the computer credibility literature (Sheridan et al., 1983), which suggests that the trust that people put into computers may result in poorer performance. For example, when typing a text, people are less careful because they rely on the word-processor's spell checker; they lose their arithmetic skills because they rely on calculators, and their performance in using word-processor decreases when an intelligent agent, an Advisor, consisting of a context-sensitive function, is turned on (Galletta et al., 2005).

Limitations of the Study

No study is perfect and this empirical investigation is no exception. The first limitation is the small sample size which, coupled with the fact that all the work-units studied are affiliated to the same group of companies, precludes us from generalizing our results to other organizations.

The fact that the data was collected via questionnaires constitutes another limitation, especially that one of the advantages of questionnaires studies to tackle large samples has not been realized.

The third limitation is related to the operationalization of the memory variables. Because this was done for the first time and though the measures exhibited acceptable reliability, their content and construct validity are still not established.

Suggestions for Future Research

This study opens avenues for future research to test the hypothesis that IT and organizational memory have additive effects. This study failed to show this result. Other measures should perhaps be used, especially in the case of organizational memory.

In Randall et al.'s (2001) study, there was a general preference among workers to ask a local expert rather than interrogate manuals, computer screens, or other forms of knowledge support. If even knowledge workers such as Andersen Consulting consultants more often ask their colleagues for help to locate documents in the firm's repositories (Markus, 2001) and if engineers and scientists in search of assistance turn to colleagues five times more often than to a computerized data base (Cross et al., 2001), future research should probably explore what people would choose if they had the choice between IT and other means, and under what conditions.

Is national culture involved? Knowledge and memory have often been the subject of disagreements among researchers for whom knowledge is "a fundamentally cognitive concept" and researchers who consider it as a "socially and culturally" derived phenomenon (Ackermann and Halveson, 1998; Randall et al., 2001). More research is definitely needed studying knowledge management in Arab and/or North African countries perhaps through cross-comparisons with other cultures.

In this chapter, a distinction was made between IT-based memory and other types of memory. Aside from IT and human memory, there might still be a lot of knowledge stored mainly in the form of the organization and in the operation of the organization's socio-technical system (Lehner et al., 1998; Walsham & Barrett, 2005). Not all kinds of knowledge can be stored electronically; some knowledge could be supported by IT and knowledge could be found in control systems, such as standard procedures, rules and regulations, codes and codifications, descriptions of work processes (Feldman & March, 1981). Future studies might consider incorporating those aspects of organizational memory.

Clearly, the concepts related to organizational memory and their effects are yet to be discovered. Future studies should address the issue of homogeneity of needs or use larger samples if heterogeneity cannot be avoided. The issue of homogeneity has been addressed in several studies (Miner, 1990; Tushman & Anderson, 1986) and is suspected to reduce the value and effect of organizational memory. When organizational memory is heterogeneous, organizational members would find it easier to access the information they need than to have to search it.

It may be premature to conclude that no matter the IT advances in a firm, it still depends on its overall environment. The fact that this study is one of the first to be performed in Tunisia, a country that Henry (1998) describes as "information-shy" due to its seemingly peculiar approach to information management, may be an incentive to explore the concepts related to information and the way organizational memories are grasped in culturally different backgrounds and environments.

REFERENCES

Ackerman, M.S. (1996). Definitional and contextual issues in organizational and group memories. *Information Technology and People, 9*(1), 10-24.

Ackermann, M., & Halverson, C. (1998). Considering an organization's memory. In Proceedings of CSCW'98 (pp. 39-48). Seattle, Washington.

Ackerman, M.S., & Halverson, C. (2000). Reexamining organizational memory. *Communication of the ACM, 43*(1), 58-64.

Anderson, J.R. (1983). *The architecture of cognition*. Cambridge, MA: Harvard University Press.

Ashcraft, M.H. (1994). *Human memory and cognition (2nd ed.)*. New York, NY: HarperCollins College Publishers.

Bakopoulos, J.Y. (1985). Toward a more precise concept of information technology. *In Proceedings of the 6th International Conference on Information Systems (ICIS)*, (pp. 17-24).

Balasubramanian, V. (1995). Organizational Learning and Information Systems, E-Papyrus, Inc. Retrieved January 17, 2008 from http://www.e-papyrus.com/personal/orglrn.html

Borghoff, U.M., & Pareschi, R. (1997). Information technology for knowledge management. *Journal of Universal Computer Science, 3*(8), 835-842.

Büchel, B., & Probst, G. (2000). From organizational learning to knowledge management. Retrieved January 5, 2008 from http://www.hec.unige.ch/recherches_publications/cahiers/2000/2000.11.pdf

Chase, W.G., & Simon, H. (1973). Perceptions in chess. *Cognitive Psychology, 4*(1), 55-81.

Child, J., & Rodrigues, S. (2001). Social identity and organizational learning. In M. Easterby-Smith & M. A. Lyles (Eds.), *Handbook of organizational learning* (pp. 535-556). Oxford: Blackwell.

Cohen, M.D. (1991). Individual learning and organizational routine: Emerging connections. *Organization Science, 2*(1), 135-139.

Cohen, M.D., & Bacdayan, P. (1994). Organizational routines are stored as procedural memory: Evidence from a laboratory study. *Organizational Science, 5*(4), 554-568.

Cross, R., & Baird, L. (2000). Technology is not enough: Improving performance by building organizational memory. *Sloan Management Review, 41*(3), 69-78.

Cross, R., Parker, A., Prusak, L., & Borgatti, S.P. (2001). Knowing what we know: Supporting knowledge creation and sharing in social networks. *Organizational Dynamics, 30*(2), 100-120.

Cummings, J.N., & Cross, R. (2003). Structural properties of work groups and their consequences for performance. *Social Networks, 25*(3), 197-210.

Dixon, W.J., & Massey, F.J. Jr. (1969). *Introduction to statistical analysis*. New York, NY: McGraw-Hill.

Dodgson, M. (1993). Organizational learning: A review of some literatures. *Organization Studies, 14*(3), 375-394.

Duncan, R., & Weiss, A. (1979). *Organizational learning: Implications for organizational design. Research in organizational behavior*. Greenwich, CT: JAI Press Inc.

Ewusi-Mensah, K. (1981). The external organization environment and its impacts on management information systems. *Accounting, Organizations and Society, 6*(4), 301-316.

El Louadi, M. (1996, June 13-14). *Interaction between Organizational Structure and IT on Information Needs and Provision in Small Businesses.* Proceedings of the 41st International Conference on Small Business (ICSB) (pp. 195-216). Stockholm (Sweden).

El Louadi, M. (1998). The relationship among organizational structure. Information technology and information processing in small Canadian firms. *Canadian Journal of Administrative Sciences, 15*(2), 180-199.

Feldman, M.S., & March, J.G. (1981). Information in organizations as signal and symbols. *Administrative Science Quarterly, 26*(2), 171-186.

Forbes. (2005). IT Competitiveness Network Readiness Index 2005. Retrieved April 9, 2005 from http://www.forbes.com/technology/2005/03/09/cx_0309wefranking.html, see also http://www.weforum.org/pdf/Gcr/GITR_2003_2004/Rankings.pdf

Galbraith, J. (1977). *Organization design*. Reading, MA: Addison-Wesley.

Galletta, D.F., Durcikova, A., Everard, A., & Jones, B. (2005). Does spell-checking software need a warning label? *Communications of the ACM, 48*(7), 82-85.

Galunic, C., & Weeks, J. (1999). Managing knowledge at Booz-Allen & Hamilton: Knowledge On-line and Off, INSEAD, Fontainebleau, France. Retrieved August 23, 2007 from http://faculty.insead.edu/weeks/documents/Galunic-and-Weeks-Booz.pdf

Girod, M.S. (1995). La mémoire organisationnelle [Organizational Memory]. *Revue Française de Gestion, 105*, 30-42.

Girod, M.S. (1996). Pour une définition opérationnelle et une modélisation de la mémoire or-ganisationnelle [Towards an Operational and Modelization Definition of Organizational Memory]. *In Proceedings of the 5th Conference of the Association Internationale de Management Stratégique* (AIMS). Lille, May.

Hedberg, B. (1981). How organizations learn and unlearn. In P.C. Nystrom & W.H. Starbuck (Eds.), *Handbook of organizational design* (pp. 8-27). London.

Henry, C.M. (1998). Challenge of global capital markets to information-shy regimes: The case of Tunisia. Abu Dhabi. *The Emirates Center for Strategic Studies and Research, 53*(19).

Huber, G.P. (1984). The nature and design of post-industrial organizations. *Management Science, 30*(8), 928-951.

Huber, G.P. (1990). A theory of the effects of advanced information technologies on organizational design, intelligence, and decision making. *Academy of Management Review, 15*(1), 47-71.

Huber, G.P. (1991). Organizational Learning: The Contributing Processes and Literature. *Organization Science, 2*(1), 88-115.

Huber, G.P. (1996). Organizational learning: The contributing processes and the literature. In M.D.

Cohen & L.S. Sproull (Eds.), *Organizational learning* (pp. 124-162). Sage: Thousand Oaks.

ITU. (2003, December 9). World Telecommunication Development Report – Access Indicators for the Information Society. *International Telecommunication Union.*

Jennex, M. E. (2006, April 26-28). Technologies in support of knowledge management systems. *In the 6th International Forum on Knowledge Management,* Tunis. 21 pages.

Jennex, M., & Croasdell, D. (2004). Knowledge management, organizational memory & organizational learning cluster. In Proceedings of the 37th Hawaii International Conference on System Sciences, Hawaii, 1.

Kransdorff, A. (1998). *Corporate amnesia: Keeping know-how in the company.* New York, NY: Butterworth-Heinemann.

Lansdale, M. (1988). The psychology of personal information management. *Applied Ergonomics, 19*(1), 55-66.

Lehner, F., Maier, R., & Klosa, O. (1998). Organisational memory systems - application of advanced database & network technologies. Research Paper No. 19, University of Regensburg, Department of Business Informatics.

Levitt, B., & March, J.G. (1988). Organizational learning. *Annual Review of Sociology, 14*(3), 319-340.

Markus, M.L. (2001). Toward a theory of knowledge reuse: Types of knowledge reuse situations and factors in reuse success. *Journal of MIS, 18*(1), 57-93.

Miner, A.S. (1990). Structural evolution through idiosyncratic jobs: The potential for unplanned learning. *Organization Science, 1*(2), 195-210.

Moran, T.P., & Carroll, J.M. (1996). *Design rationale: Concepts, techniques, and use.* Mahwah, NJ: Lawrence Erlbaum.

Moorman, C., & Miner, A.S. (1998). Organization improvisation and organizational memory. *Academy of Management Review, 23*(4), 698-723.

Nickols, F. W. (2000). The Knowledge in Knowledge Management. In J.W. Cortada & J.A. Woods (Eds), *The knowledge management yearbook 2000-2001* (pp. 12-21). Boston, MA: Butterworth-Heinemann.

Nonaka, I. (1995). *The knowledge creating company.* New York, NY: Oxford University Press.

Ortenblad, A. (2001). On differences between organizational learning and learning organization. *The Learning Organization, 8*(3/4), 125-133.

Randall, D., Hughes, J., O'Brien, J., Rouncefield, M., & Tolmie, P. (2001). 'Memories are made of this:' Explicating organisational knowledge and memory. *European Journal of Information Systems, 10*(2), 113-121.

Royston, J.P. (1982). An extension of shapiro and wilk's W test for normality to large samples. *Applied Statistics, 31*(2), 115-124.

Shapiro, S.S., & Wilk, M.B. (1965). An analysis of variance test for normality (Complete Samples). *Biometrika, 52*(3, 4), 591-611.

Sheridan, T.B., Vamos, T., & Aida, S. (1983). Adapting automation to man, culture and society. *Automatica, 19*(6), 605-612.

Simon, H.A. (1982). *Designing organizations for an information-rich world, models for bounded rationality.* Cambridge, MA: MIT Press.

Singley, M.K., & Anderson, J.R. (1989). *The transfer of cognitive skill.* Cambridge, MA: Harvard University Press..

Souren, P., Haseman, W.D., & Ramamurthy, K. (2004). Collective memory support and cognitive-conflict group decision-making: An experimental investigation. *Decision Support Systems, 36*(3), 261-281.

Spender, J.-C. (1996). Organizational knowledge, learning and memory: Three concepts in search of a theory. *Journal of Organizational Change Management, 9*(1), 63-78.

Stein, E.W., & Zwass, V. (1995). Actualizing organizational memory with information systems. *Information Systems Research, 6*(2), 185-217.

Stratte-McClure, J. (2000). Taking the information highway to efficiency. International Herald Tribune, March 20.

Tabachnick, B.G., & Fidell, L.S. (1989). *Using multivariate statistics, (2nd ed.).* New York, NY: Harper Collins Publishers, Inc.

Tuomi, I. (2000). Data is more than knowledge: Implications of the reversed knowledge hierarchy for knowledge management and organizational memory. *Journal of MIS, 16*(3), 103-117.

Tushman, M.L., & Anderson, P. (1986). Technological discontinuities and organizational environments. *Administrative Science Quarterly, 31*(3), 439-465.

Van Bruggen, G.H., Lilien, G.L., & Kacker, M. (2002). Informants in organizational marketing research: Why use multiple informants and how to aggregate responses. *Journal of Marketing Research, 39*(4), 469-478.

Walsh, J.P. (1995). Managerial and organizational cognition: Notes from a trip down memory lane. *Organization Science, 6*(3), 280-321.

Walsh, J.P., & Ungson, G.R. (1991). Organizational memory. *Academy of Management Review, 16*(1), 57-91.

Walsham, G. (2001). Knowledge management: The benefits and limitations of computer systems. *European Management Journal, 19*(6), 599-608.

Walsham, G., & Barrett, M. (2005). *ICTs and changing processes of knowing in a global development agency. Judge Institute of Management Working Papers*, No.02/2005, University of Cambridge. Retrieved April 20, 2005 from www.jbs.cam.ac.uk/research/working_papers/2005/wp0502.pdf

Watson, R.T. (1996). *Data management: An organizational perspective.* New York, NY: Wiley.

Wijnhoven, F. (1999). Development scenarios for organizational memory information systems. *Journal of MIS, 16*(1), 121-146.

This work was previously published in the International Journal of Knowledge Management, Vol. 4, Issue 4, edited by M. Jennex, pp. 21-39, copyright 2008 by IGI Publishing (an imprint of IGI Global).

Chapter 2
Managing Knowledge in Organizational Memory Using Topic Maps[1]

Les Miller
Iowa State University, USA

Sree Nilakanta
Iowa State University, USA

Yunan Song
Iowa State University, USA

Lei Zhu
Iowa State University, USA

Ming Hua
Iowa State University, USA

ABSTRACT

Organizational memories play a significant role in knowledge management, but several challenges confront their use. Artifacts of OM are many and varied. Access and use of the stored artifact are influenced by the user's understanding of these information objects as well as their context. Theories of distributed cognition and the notion of community of practice are used to develop a model of the knowledge management system. In the present work we look at a model for managing organizational memory knowledge. Topic maps are used in the model to represent user cognition of contextualized information. A visual approach to topic maps proposed in the model also allows for access and analysis of stored memory artifacts. The design and implementation of a prototype to test the feasibility of the model is briefly examined.

INTRODUCTION

The late Dr. Peter Drucker had declared that we are in an era of knowledge economy. Understandably, any efficient functioning of the knowledge economy must rely on managing knowledge well. Individuals, organizations, countries, and economies must manage their knowledge through appropriate mechanisms and policies. Knowledge management requires the capture, storage, and use of several types of information and knowledge. Researchers have noted that organizational knowledge may be accumulated and retained using several organizational memory systems (Haseman et al., 2005; Nemati et al., 2002; Nevo & Wand, 2005). Advances in information technologies have helped in accumulating knowledge, but the paradigms applicable to collecting and storing the knowledge do little to motivate its use by managers and decision makers. Accessing and using organizational memories have been a challenge because of the multifaceted nature of memories and knowledge sources. Moreover, characteristics of the decision tasks where the knowledge and memory support are used pose interesting challenges in designing and developing knowledge management systems. In this article, we describe a model that makes use of topic maps to navigate the lattices of organizational memory and employ appropriate knowledge management and analysis tools.

ORGANIZATIONAL MEMORY AND KNOWLEDGE GENERATION

Organizational memory (OM) is a stored collection of organizational history reflected among the many parts (Walsh & Ungson, 1991). It includes both stored records and tacit knowledge and covers the various facets of organizational tasks, employees, and their task environments (Argote et al., 2003; Choy et al., 2005; Lee et al., 1999; Nonaka & Konno, 1998). Because it can be a large and valuable repository of information and knowledge, several researchers have recognized the import of organizational memory in effecting organizational performance (Akgun et al., 2006; Brockman & Morgan 2003; Jennex & Olfman 2002; Ji & Salvendy, 2004; Lesser & Storck, 2001).

Ackerman and Halverson (2004), however, take a critical view of prior research on OM and argue for a theoretical base to properly define and empirically validate future research. They state that as socio-technical systems, organizations and their memories conform to social structures and norms while employing technical models. They use the theory of distributed cognition to develop a theoretical foundation for organizational memory. The basic tenets of this theory are that knowledge evolves from a community of practice and that cognition and inferences result from the shared meaning among the participants (hence the distribution) (Hollan et al., 2000). Communities of practice fulfill a number of functions with respect to the creation, accumulation, and diffusion of knowledge in an organization through exchange and interpretation of information, by retaining knowledge, by stewarding competencies, and providing homes for identities (Wenger, 1998). Collective thinking creates knowledge that otherwise would not be evident. Additionally, changes in state of the memory, as in change from internal to external representation via artifact changes or through the movement of information among the participants (trajectory of information), are necessary to fully utilize an OM. A cycle of changes comprising contextualization to decontextualization and again to recontextualization of the information object takes place as organizational members relive their experience through the stored information object or artifact. An essential feature of knowledge management systems is this capability to change the state of the information object.

Using empirical data and qualitative methods, Ackerman and Halverson (2004) illustrate application of the theory of distributed cognition to validate the use of organizational memory in decision making. In order to build and test an organizational memory system to support knowledge management it is not sufficient to have a theory to test the effect of such systems on organizational performance. It is also necessary to have a design theory that would support the need for defining appropriate components upon which other theories can be tested. For example, a design component should be able to support the cycle of changes a stored information object might go through.

Markus et al. (2002) proposed the use of design theory (Walls, Widmeyer, & Sawy, 1992) to describe emergent knowledge processes, which are often found in situations similar to the use of OM and distributed cognition. Design theory brings together elements of user requirements, system features, and development guidelines into one package. Moreover, this set corresponds to an underlying theory (kernel theory), such as distributed cognition that may be tested empirically by examining the outcomes of the systems development for fit with the requirements. Design research proponents identify six nominal process steps, namely problem identification and motivation, objectives of a solution, design, and development, demonstration, evaluation, and communication (Peffers et al., 2006). The first four process steps are considered suitable for doing design research. In addition, when systems are built for testing and validating theory, the appropriate entry point for design research is indeed the design and development process. At this stage an artifact is built and theory is tested using the artifact. The main purpose is to yield a proof of concept of the theory and the system that supports it. The contribution of the present work is in the development of an organizational memory knowledge management model that supports the distributed cognition theory. The design and implementation are presented. We see the proposed model as providing an early step toward realizing the model proposed in Nilakanta et al. (2006).

As social and linguistic dimensions of knowledge become pertinent, users need appropriate tools to support the search and analysis of knowledge. Topic maps are one such tool.

Topic Maps

Smolnik and Erdman (2003) state that topic maps provide strong paradigms and concepts for the semantic structuring of link networks and therefore, they are a considerable solution for organizing and navigating large and, continuously growing organizational memories. The ISO standard ISO/IEC 13250 provides a standardized notation for interchangeably representing information about the structure of information resources used to define topics, and the relationships between topics. A set of one or more interrelated documents that employs the notation defined by this International Standard is called a *topic map*. The standard further states that a topic map defines a multidimensional topic space, a space in which the locations are topics, and in which the distances between topics are measurable in terms of the number of intervening topics which must be visited in order to get from one topic to another, and the kinds of relationships that define the path from one topic to another, if any, through the intervening topics, if any.

Topic maps provide a subject-based classification of resources where each resource represents a real world object. In topic maps, three constructs are provided for describing the subjects represented by the topics: names, occurrences, and associations. These describe the names, properties, and relationships of subjects, respectively. A name may be assigned to more than one topic and a topic may have more than one name. In addition by defining scope and types a name can become rich and complex. An occurrence links to one or more real knowledge sources. An occurrence, however, is not part of the topic map. Associations describe relationships among topics and are independent of the real knowledge objects. Associations add value through the relationships.

The Topic Map architecture is designed to facilitate merging topic maps without requiring the merged topic maps to be copied or modified. This feature makes it quite suitable for use in organizational memory systems. As Steiner, Essmayr, and Wagner (2001) state, the construction of large, complex organizational memories takes place over extended periods of time, growing incrementally both in size and structure. The ISO standard describes how topic maps may be used in situations such as that may be found in OM systems. For example, a topic map can be employed "to structure unstructured information objects, or to facilitate the creation of topic-oriented user interfaces that provide the effect of merging unstructured information bases with structured ones. The overlay mechanism of topic maps can be considered as a kind of *external markup mechanism*, in the sense that an arbitrary structure is imposed on the information without altering its original form." Knowledge management applications can also benefit from topic maps, especially when combined with ontologies. Korthaus, Henke, Aleksy, and Schader (2006) describe a topic grid architecture that enables a client application to view distributed topic maps of organizational knowledge as a combined virtual topic map. Each distributed topic map represents a different view of the underlying information.

MODEL

The goal of any organization is to make optimal use of the business knowledge that it has accumulated over the years. To do this, it is necessary to determine the sources of business knowledge and provide members of the organization access to it in a timely matter. Here we focus on the latter issue of providing access through retrieval, analysis, and learning tools. We assume that business knowledge sources are employee knowledge, transaction data, data warehouse data, memory artifacts (both internal and external), and the knowledge inferred from these sources.

The proposed model has been designed to provide support for accessing and analyzing the collective memory of the organization. We start by providing a simplistic overview of the model and then examining the important components in more detail.

Overview

We see the knowledge space of an organization's memory as consisting of data (transaction database data, warehouse data, and memory artifacts), knowledge (employee knowledge as well as knowledge inferred from the organization's memory), and tools (retrieval, analysis, and learning tools). Moreover, the knowledge space is distributed throughout the organization. Any model capable of managing the knowledge in such a space has to be flexible, scalable, and distributed. To meet the needs of such a space, we propose a model with the same characteristics. A block diagram of the proposed model is shown in Figure 1. It has been designed to provide support for accessing and analyzing the collective memory of an organization.

Topic maps that support access to an organization's knowledge via a combination of search terms and tools serve as the user's entry point. Note that the same knowledge space can take on different views based on the content of the topic map a user uses to navigate the space. To this end, we assume that the topic map framework in Figure 1 supports multiple topic maps. We see the choice of topic map as acting essentially like a view in that as the user logs on, the topic map framework presents the user with an initial topic map level that acts as a root to the topic maps that he or she is authorized to access. This approach was adopted rather than having a standard first level to simplify the user's access and restrict the topic map to the task at hand.

Figure 1. Block diagram of the primary model components

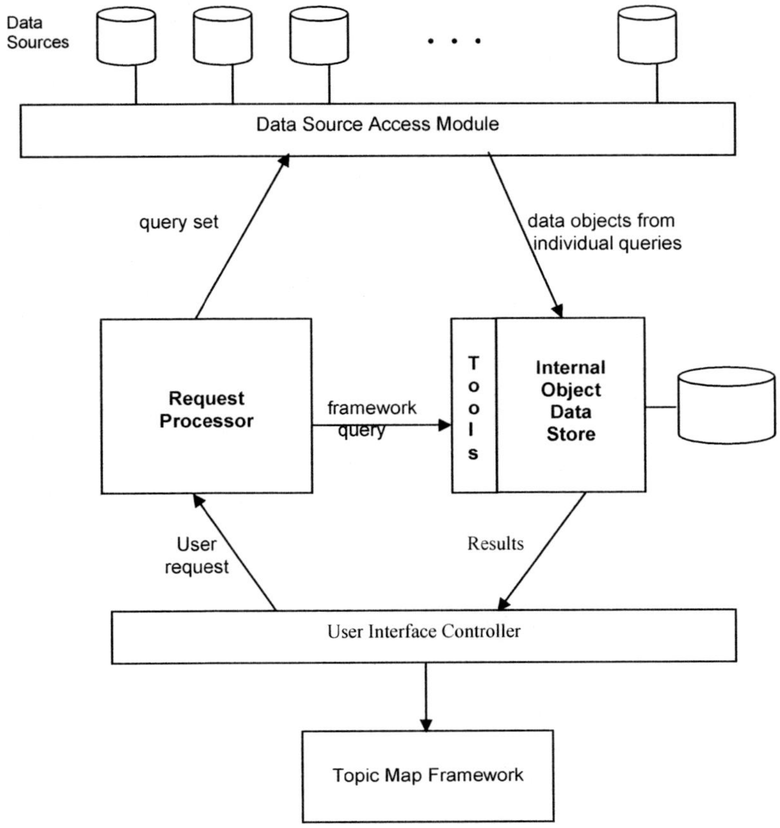

The framework that supports the topic map converts the user's request into a Request object and passes it to the User Interface Controller. The Request Processor converts the request into a set of queries (if required) and a framework query. If the requested information is not currently cached in the Internal Object Data Store, the set of queries are passed to the Data Source Access Module to be transmitted to the appropriate data source. Results from these queries are cached in the Internal Object Data Store as the queries are completed. When all the required data has been cached, the framework query is activated by calling the appropriate tools and data types. The results are returned to user.

Objects are used as the internal unit for storing and communicating artifacts due to the artifact's natural object structure. For example, the object structure of an e-mail is shown in Figure 2. The primary components make use of traditional wrappers and object views (Yen & Miller, 1995) that are used to support communication within the model.

Object Views

The object view type (Yen & Miller, 1995) is defined as being an extension of the object model. The views have a traditional object structure (attributes and methods) with the restriction that they support a derivation method. The derivation method is used to generate the public and private attributes of each object instance created through a local interface view.

Figure 2. E-mail object structure

```
public class E-mail{
private Person sender;
private Set<Person> receiverList;
private String subject;
private String body;
private Collection<Attachment> attachments;
...
}
```

Local Interface Views

The individual data sources are expected to have local control. The local interface view (Yen & Miller, 1995) is a view object type that is used by the local data administrator to provide a mechanism to make the local data accessible to the proposed model in object form. The local interface view allows distribution transparency and representation transparency, while hiding or converting (mapping) some of the data from the data source. The local interface view belongs to the data source. It interacts directly with the data source and passes the result to the wrapper which controls communication with other components of the proposed model. A given data source and its wrapper can support multiple local interface views in order to present its data in different ways to different applications or users.

Topic Map

A topic map is used in the model to provide users with visual access to both search and analysis. It is this interesting blend of semantic search and analysis that motivates its use in the model.

Here we define a topic map to be the directed acyclic graph T = (N,E), where N is the set of topic map terms, data types, or search/analysis tools. The directed edges in E are of the type (n1, n2), where n1 is a topic map term or a data type and n2 is a topic map term, a data type, or a search/analysis tool. An implicit node, called the root, points to the topic map terms, data types, or tools that make up the first level of the topic map. Nodes with out degree zero are said to be leaves of the topic map. Leaves point to the information in the organization's memory and carry any search terms or data types accumulated on the path from the root of the topic map to the leaf. Note that leaves that are either search terms or data types make use of an implicit search tool. In addition each nonleaf level of the topic map has a search tool that can be used to initiate a search based on the topic map terms that have been traversed to get to the topic level or arbitrary keywords entered by the user.

Data Types

The data types supported will depend to some extent on the nature of the organization. Typically, the data types will include the people that the organization relies on for expertise, transaction data, warehouse data, the artifacts that make up the organizations' memory, and knowledge inferred from these data. The typical artifacts are e-mails, meeting minutes, reports, tutorials, news releases, Web pages, and presentations. Extending the supported data types is simply a matter of ensuring that the appropriate object types and tools for search, analysis, and learning are available in the set of supported tools.

Data Sources

A block diagram of the layout of a data source is shown in Figure 3. The query string for a data source from the request processor is translated to the appropriate request string and passed to the local interface view (LIV) via the data source wrapper. The LIV interprets the request string and passes it to the data source and converts the response into the objects defined by the LIV view

Figure 3. Data source node layout and request/ data flow for retrieval

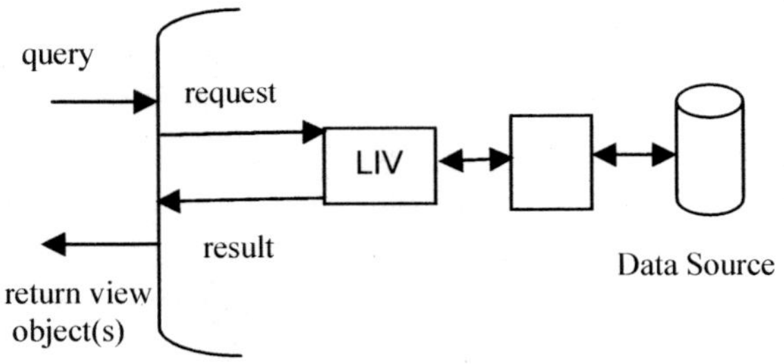

Figure 4. Polymorphic class hierarchy for two tools that extend the Request class

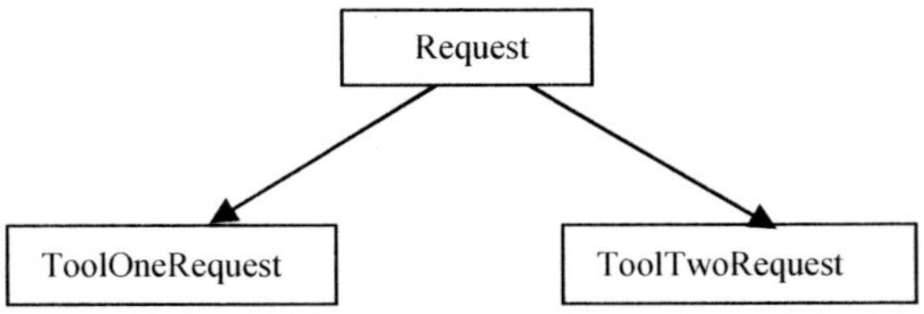

type. Note that the LIV may make use of local analysis and learning tools to process the data returned from the data source before returning it to the Internal Object Data Store. The set of result view objects are then passed back to the Data Source Access Module and cached in the Internal Object Data Store for analysis.

Internal Object Data Store

The Internal Object Data Store is based on our earlier work on object-oriented data warehouses (Miller, Honavar, Wong, & Nilakanta, 1998; Miller, Lu, Zhou, & Hurson, 2000). The Internal Object Data Store combines tools and cached data to allow in depth analysis of the data in the knowledge space. The tool set consists of a set of built in (kernel) tools for managing tools and data, as well as a set of user defined tools for analyzing or learning from data (Miller et al., 1998).

User Interface Controller and Topic Map Framework

The division between these two components in an implementation will depend on the nature of the tools used to set up the system. For example, in the case that the topic maps and results are delivered to the user via an Internet browser, the Topic Map Framework represents the HTML and JSP pages. The User Interface Controller would be implemented using a Web framework package such as Goodwill and Hightower (2003). For an implementation using a Java client as the user interface, the separate roles of the two components will be handled by different classes.

Request Processor

The request processor receives a Request object from the User Interface Controller that defines the required search criteria and the result format required to complete the request. The tool type and action is built into the class structure by employing the Polymorphic design pattern. The Request, shown in Figure 3.4 as the super class, provides the basic request attributes and behavior. Each tool that is added either implicitly or explicitly to the topic map requires the definition of a class that extends the Request class. These new classes add any additional information/actions required by the tool. Figure 4 shows the class hierarchy for two tools.

IMPLEMENTATION

To illustrate the functionality of the current implementation of the proposed model, we walk through a sample session and point out some details as the session unfolds. The current implementation has been implemented in Java with everything but the data sources being on a single machine. Our next version will expand this view to include the use of a Web browser as a user's client for accessing the organization's memory.

Figure 5 illustrates the initial view of the organizational memory topic map seen by a user as he or she accesses the system. The shape of a symbol on the screen provides an indication of how the topic or tool is used. Tools that provide more than basic information retrieval are represented by rectangles, while ovals indicate that the topic points to another level in the topic map or that the default information retrieval tool can be reached from the oval. The default information retrieval tool uses the path label to determine the domain (e.g., artifact type) or the search criteria (e.g., any nontool topics in the path label). In Figure 5, the *Find Expert* rectangle indicates the existence of a tool that maps areas of expertise to employees with the desired expertise. The user also has access to the default information retrieval tool by clicking on *Search By Arbitrary Terms*, *Committee Search,* or *Tutorial Search*. The difference between the three nodes is the domain that will be searched. Clicking on the *Search By Arbitrary Terms* oval will provide a keyword search of all artifacts stored in the organizational memory, while clicking on either of the other two ovals will provide a keyword based search on the domains indicated within the oval topic name, that is, committee information or tutorials, respectively. The *Search By Topics* oval represents the root of a subtopic map based on the general topic terms.

The *Search Memory Collections* oval points to the set of supported organizational memory data types. Figure 6 shows the result of clicking on it. Selecting one of the memory type ovals (e.g., e-mail, minutes, reports, etc.) provides access to the next level of the topic map that focuses on the options available for the artifact chosen. The *Search By Arbitrary Terms* oval at the bottom of the screen shown in Figure 6 gives access to the same search tool that was available on the first level. It gives the user the ability to select relevant artifacts on the basis of any terms from the artifact types identified on the screen. In our current implementation this tool makes use of a frequency based search as described in Hu, Miller, and Nilakanta (1998).

Figure 7 shows the next level in the organizational memory that the user moves to by clicking on the *E-mail* oval from Figure 6. Note that the path label at this point consists of the *Search Memory Collections* and *E-mail* topics and is used to restrict the domain of any of the tools to the e-mail domain. Because the only topics in the path label are designed to restrict the domain, the tools will have to provide their own search criteria.

Figure 5. Initial level of the topic map seen by users

Figure 6. Artifacts available by selecting the Search Memory Collections topic on the first level (Figure 5)

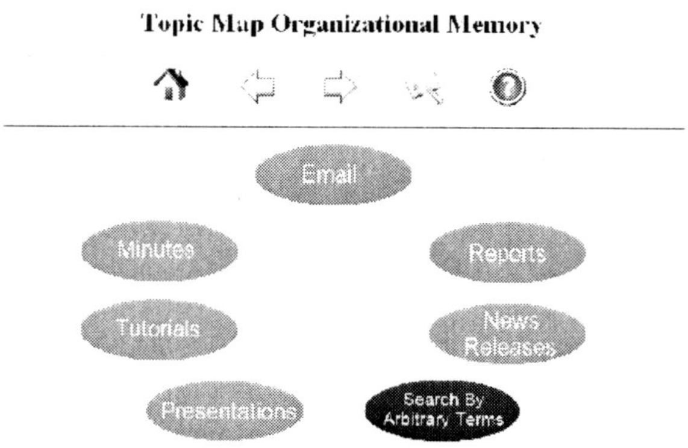

A user can always return to the top level of the topic map by clicking on the home icon at the top of the page. Navigation between pages that have already been traversed can be done by using the forward and backward arrows at the top of the page.

A key feature of any system designed to provide search and analysis of artifacts is that the tools have to be constructed so that the user can easily grasp the results of the search and analysis. To accomplish this it is useful for the tools to be interactive and make use of visual displays of results. We conclude this section by examining a simple e-mail tool that gives the user the ability to choose a set of search terms, a start and stop date, and the number of intervals. Figure 8 shows the screen segment for the results of this tool. The bar graph indicates the relative number of e-mails that matched the search condition for the intervals. The use of the tool is instructive in terms of what occurs within the prototype of the proposed model. The tool represented by Figure 8 is obtained by clicking on the *Frequency Analysis* rectangle at the bottom of the screen shown in Figure 7. Once the user clicked on the rectangle for the tool, the Topic Map Framework (Figure 1) would send the request to the Request Processor via the request class that extends the Request class for the e-mail tool. The system prompts (not shown) the user for the search terms, start and stop dates, and number of intervals. Submission of this request generates a search of the data sources that contain the relevant e-mails would take place and the results would be sent back to the Internal Object Data Store to be held there. The framework query for the tool's request creates the bar graph and presents it to the user. Our current implementation of the tool allows the user to click on any of the bars to see a list of e-mails that fall into the time interval represented by the bar. The user is then able to choose e-mails from the list to see the full text of the e-mail. Note that each time that the user operates on the data represented by the bar graph, the system only needs to go back to the Internal Object Data Store for the cached data.

Figure 7. Topic map level reached by clicking on the Email oval in Figure 6.

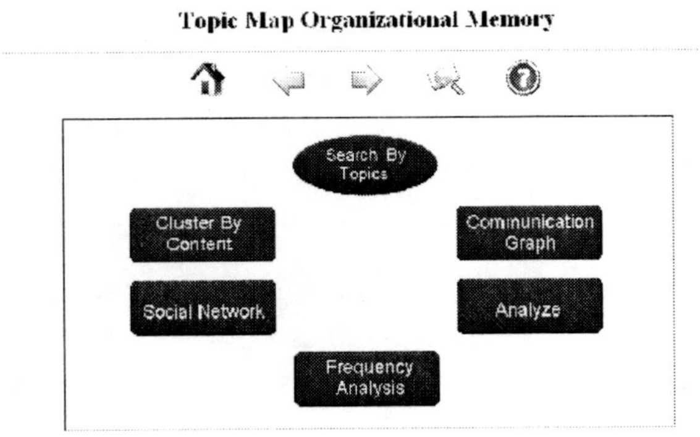

CONCLUSION AND FUTURE CONSIDERATIONS

A model of an environment for using topic maps to access knowledge from an organization's collective memory has been presented. The retrieved e-mail collection is representative of the collective thinking which creates knowledge that otherwise

Figure 8. Sample results for number of emails over fixed size intervals using days as the time unit

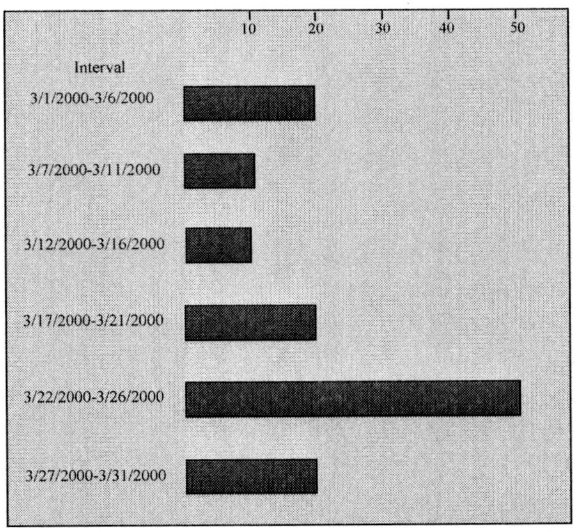

would not be evident. Additionally, changes in the state of the memory, as in change from local data source to the object store illustrated the trajectory of information and are necessary to fully utilize an OM. A cycle of changes comprising contextualization to decontextualization and again to recontextualization of the information object takes place as organizational members relive their experience through the stored information object or artifact. An essential feature of knowledge management systems is this capability to change the state of the information object. An initial version of the model has been implemented using Java as the programming language, Poet to store the objects, and Soap to communicate to data sources external to the system.

Future releases will make use of either Java Data Objects or a tool like Hibernate to replace the Poet database system. In the next version of the system, a Web interface will be developed based on the java versions of the tools supported in the current version.

REFERENCES

Ackerman, M., & Halverson, C. (2004). Organizational memory as objects, processes, and trajectories: An examination of organizational memory in use. *Computer Supported Cooperative Work (CSCW), 13*(2), 155-189.

Akgun, A. E., Byrne, J. C. et al. (2006). Transactive memory system in new product development teams. *IEEE Transactions on Engineering Management, 53(1)*, 95-111.

Argote, L., McEvily, B. et al. (2003). Managing knowledge in organizations: An integrative framework and review of emerging themes. *Management Science, 49*(4), 571-583.

Brockman, B. K., & Morgan, R. M. (2003). The role of existing knowledge in new product innovativeness and performance. *Decision Sciences, 34*(2), 385-419.

Choy, K. L., Lee, W. B. et al. (2005). A knowledge-based supplier intelligence retrieval system for outsource manufacturing. *Knowledge-Based Systems, 18*(1), 1-17.

Goodwill, J., & Hightower, R. (2004). *Professional Jakarta struts.* Hoboken, NJ: Wiley.

Haseman, W. D., Nazareth, D. L. et al. (2005). Implementation of a group decision support system utilizing collective memory. *Information and Management, 42*, 591-605.

Hollan, J., Hutchins, E. et al. (2000). Distributed cognition: Toward a new foundation for human-computer interaction research. *ACM Transactions on Computer-Human Interaction (TOCHI), 7(*2), 174-196.

Hu, W., Miller, W., & Nilakanta, S. (1998). PROMIS: A profiler of organizational memory and institutional systems. In *Proceedings of the International Conference of Information Resources Management Association,* Boston, MA, (pp. 399-405).

Jennex, M., & Olfman, L. (2002). Organizational memory/knowledge effects on productivity, a longitudinal study. In *Proceedings of the 35th Annual Hawaii International Conference on System Sciences.*

Ji, Y.G., & Salvendy, G. (2004). Interface methods for using intranet portal organizational memory information system. *Ergonomics, 47(*15), 1585-1597.

Korthaus, A., Henke, S., Aleksy, M., & Schader, M. (2006). A distributed topic map architecture for enterprise knowledge management. In *Proceedings of the 5th IEEE/ACIS International Conference on Computer and Information Science, ICIS-COMSAR 2006*, (pp. 96-102).

Lee, T., Chams, M. et al. (1999). Information integration with attribution support for corporate profiles. In *Proceedings of the Eighth International Conference on Information and Knowledge*

Management, Kansas City, MO, United States: ACM Press.

Lesser, E. L., & Storck, J. (2001). Communities of practice and organizational performance. *IBM Systems Journal, 40*(4), 831-841.

Markus, M. L., A. Majchrzak, et al. (2002). A Design Theory for Systems That Support Emergent Knowledge Processes. *MIS Quarterly 26*(3): 179-212.

Miller, L. L., Honavar, V., Wong, J., & Nilakanta, S. (1998). Object-oriented data warehouse for information fusion from heterogeneous distributed data and knowledge sources. In *Proceedings of the IEEE Information Technology Conference*, (pp. 27-31).

Miller, L. L., Lu, Y., Zhou, Y., & Hurson, A. R. (2000). A data warehouse based on materializing object-oriented views. In *Proceedings of the International Conference on Computers and Their Applications*. New Orleans, LA, (pp. 68-71).

Nemati, H. R., Steiger, D. M. et al. (2002). Knowledge warehouse: An architectural integration of knowledge management, decision support, artificial intelligence and data warehousing. *Decision Support Systems 33*(2), 143.

Nevo, D., & Wand, Y. (2005). Organizational memory information systems: A transactive memory approach. *Decision Support Systems, 39*, 549-562.

Nilakanta, S., Miller, L. L. et al. (2006). Organizational memory management technological and research issues. *Journal of Database Management, 17*(1), 85-94.

Nonaka, I., & Konno, N. (1998). The concept of "Ba": Building a foundation for knowledge creation. *California Management Review, 40*(3), 40-54.

Peffers, K., Tuunanen, T. et al. (2006). The design science research process: A model for producing and presenting information systems research. In *Proceedings of the International Conference on Design Science Research in Information Systems and Technology*, Claremont, CA.

Smolnik, S., & Erdmann, I. (2003). Visual navigation of distributed knowledge structures in groupware-based organizational memories. *Business Process Management Journal, 9*(3), 261.

Steiner, K., Essmayr, W., & Wagner, R. (2001). Topic maps - an enabling technology for knowledge management.In *Proceedings of the 12th International Workshop on Database and Expert Systems Applications*, (pp. 472-476).

Walsh, J. P., & Ungson, G. R. (1991). Organizational Memory. *The Academy of Management Review, 16*(1), 57.

Walls, J. G., Widmeyer, G. R., & Sawy, O. A. (1992). Building an information system design theory for vigilant EIS. *Information Systems Research, 3*(1), 36-59.

Wenger, E. (1998). Communities of practice: Learning as a social system. *The Systems Thinker, 9*(5).

Yen, C. H., & Miller, L. L. (1995). An extensible view system for multidatabase integration and interoperation. *Integrated Computer-Aided Engineering, 2*(2), 97-123.

ENDNOTE

[1] An earlier version of this article was presented at HICSS-40.

This work was previously published in the International Journal of Knowledge Management, Vol. 4, Issue 1, edited by M. Jennex, pp. 17-28, copyright 2008 by IGI Publishing (an imprint of IGI Global).

Chapter 3
Virtual Communities of Practice:
Knowledge Retrieval, Contextualization and Establishment of Weak Trust in Multinational Corporations

Jens Gammelgaard
Copenhagen Business School, Denmark

ABSTRACT

This chapter investigates the phenomenon of virtual communities of practice, and proposes them to be efficient for individual's knowledge retrieval, when they work in a geographically dispersed organization, such as a multinational corporation. The virtual community of practice is likely to reduce the contextual gaps that typically exist between senders and receivers of knowledge, as it includes the possibility of feedback loops in the information exchange process. However, the organization must provide a knowledge-sharing friendly culture, and an institutional protectionism, in order to establish the required level of trust, being the foundation for knowledge exchanges within the virtual community.

INTRODUCTION

This chapter focuses on virtual communities of practices, and whether participation in such forums improves knowledge retrieval processes by overcoming problems of contextual gaps between the sender and the receiver of knowledge. Most multinational corporations (MNCs) have invested heavily in computer systems that help employees to easily download documents, but problems still arise when the searched knowledge is removed from its context and thereby loses some or all of its meaning to the reader. This article, though, differentiates the conventional wisdom that employee socialization, resulting from physical proximity that facilitates contextualization and trust building processes allows transfer of complex and tacit knowledge, (Cohendet et al., 1999; Constant et al., 1994; Granovetter, 1972; Hansen, 1999; Nonaka & Takeuchi, 1995) as in the case of communities of practice (Brown & Duguid, 1991; Wenger, 1998). Here, it will be pointed out that proximity is seldom the case of the MNC – having operations spanning the globe – which makes most communication "global rather than local" (Li et al., 2007). In this chapter it will, therefore, be questioned whether knowledge retrieval can be

DOI: 10.4018/978-1-60566-954-0.ch003

efficient in a virtual setting, given the context of an MNC. The description of knowledge retrieval, and knowledge transfer processes in general, are well established, likewise the analyses and surveys of these processes in communities of practices. However, this chapter contributes by investigating these matters in the context of the *MNC* and the impact of knowledge retrieval processes when they take place in a *virtual* context.

The topic of knowledge retrieval is central to MNCs when they, to give one example, intend to implement best practices throughout the organization as it requires the application of knowledge from one context to another (Grant, 2005; Hornett & Stein, 2007). The question is which knowledge management strategy best fits knowledge retrieval. Typically, MNCs either practices socialization or codification strategies (Hansen et al., 1999). Hornett & Stein (2007) confirm this established fact since their survey company focused on the social or the technological part respectively, but seldom the combination of the two, i.e., the sociotechnical orientation. Hornett & Stein further vary the debate with the finding of the company's attention paid to the knowledge transfer *per se* more than the usefulness of the transferred knowledge. Adding to this finding, we believe that MNC managers can benefit from this chapter, as it theorizes on the underlying mechanism for efficient utilization of transferred knowledge, i.e. the establishment of a forum where knowledge is retrieved correctly. This issue has been investigated in geographically proxy environments, but in this chapter, the focus is the efficiency of a socio-technical knowledge management strategy - in this case virtual communities of practice.

The chapter proceeds in the following order: Section Two provides an overview of the knowledge retrieval process, followed by discussions of communities of practice and virtual communities of practice in the next two sections. Thereafter, knowledge retrieval is analyzed in the context of virtual communities and this discussion leads to the formulation of propositions. Conclusions are drawn in the finalizing section.

THE KNOWLEDGE RETRIEVAL PROCESS

Retrieval of knowledge takes place in a two step process: one employee acquires, encodes and stores knowledge in the corporate memory, after which another employee retrieves (finds, reads, and decode) the knowledge and then subsequently apply it in a certain setting (Alavi & Leidner, 2001; Holzner & Marx, 1979; Krippendorff 1975; Pentland, 1995; Stein & Zwass, 1995). Therefore, retrieval processes begin when an individual requires knowledge stored in the organizational memory in order to meet a specific goal (a consultant meeting a client's request, for example). Krippendorff (1975, p. 19) defines *retrieval* as "processes by which information is reconstituted or reconstructed and made available, by, for example, reading documents for what is encoded in them". Knowledge retrieval can be seen as a two-stage process that starts by identifying specific, relevant knowledge stored in the organizational memory and continues with its decodification. Though, these two stages are related, the focus will be on the second, with an emphasis on the interpretation of the knowledge (Paepcke, 1996). The research question being addressed is: How can the MNC employee decode knowledge stored in document, and written by a colleague working in a distant organizational unit when this distance often creates a contextual gap?

If we are to fully understand the retrieval process, we first require clarification of what "knowledge", "memory", "document", and "contextual gap" mean. Normally, distinctions are made between data, information and knowledge. Zack (1999, p. 46) provides the following definition: "data represent observations or facts out of context that are, therefore, not directly meaningful. Information results from placing data within some meaningful context, often in the form of a message. Knowledge is that which we come to believe and value on the basis of the meaningfully organized accumulation of information (messages) through experience, communication or inference." This indicates a hierarchy of complexity with knowledge at the top, making it hardest to retrieve. Here, Tiwana (2000) views knowledge as actionable information, which further puts an emphasis on efficient retrieval processes, as utilization of transferred knowledge depends on this condition.

Memory refers to all knowledge-storage media, encompassing a varied range of concepts beginning with the "individual brain", including "routines and learning practices" and ending with such media as documents and databases. The act of retrieval depends on the particular medium used for knowledge access. Our paper focuses on the retrieval of knowledge from the shared pool of available *written information* (possible actionable information) - the MNC organizational memory. In Krippendorff's (1975) words, this is a memory that involves a record, i.e. "a medium which thereby carries into the present some information about its past history" (p. 22). This paper chooses the written *document* as the media for investigation. A document contains information and knowledge and is the actual product of writing; it stores collection of data and refers to something physical like printed pages, or to a virtual document in an electronic format. An example of a document could be a written report, which contains the findings of an individual.

A context is a "set of premises used in interpreting an utterance" (Sperber & Wilson, 1995, p. 15). A context is, therefore, a psychological construct, based on the retriever's assumption about the world. These assumptions are not only based on information or "pure facts" but can be influenced by – as Sperber & Wilson write (p. 16) "expectations about the future, scientific hypotheses or religious beliefs, anecdotal memories, general cultural assumptions, beliefs about the mental state of the speaker". Secondly, assumptions relate to the situation in which knowledge was acquired or need to be applied; such as a customer relationship (Alavi & Leidner, 2001; Alvesson & Kärreman, 2000), a representation that will be included in the final document reporting these findings. Encoding, therefore, accounts for the way records come into being in a medium, whereas decoding refers to the act of retrieving (Krippendorf, 1975). Senders will typically design text (encode) to give meaning within their own context, and receivers will likewise retrieve knowledge in their context in order to apply it in a specific situation (Shotter, 1993; Wenger, 1998) – like a customer relationship relevant to the receiver. Therefore, a contextual gap exists between the sender and the receiver, keeping them apart (Nahapiet & Ghoshal, 1998). Contextual gaps in communication emanate from lack of mutual knowledge. If sender and retriever share mutual knowledge, every piece of contextual information in a message must be mutual known by the sender and retriever, and both actors must know that they *do* share mutual knowledge (Sperber & Wilson, 1995). However, this hypothetical state of symmetric information seldom exists, even in case of actors with very tight relationships.

Furthermore, when interpreting written utterances, imperfections in language (Alvesson & Kärreman, 2000) and problems when the receiver of knowledge needs to translate a written document into his or her native language (Welch et al., 2005) complicate retrieval processes. On top of that, specific acronyms and terms often relates to a specific practice. Further, written language is often imperfect in order to make accurate representations of perceived objects. One example is provided by Alvesson & Kärreman (2000) showing how an expression like "very little" can be measured and interpreted differently. Palmer (1993) provides another example showing how the use of different punctuations in the same sentence changes the meaning considerably. Using Barthes' words (1997, p. 272): "The text is plural. This does not mean just that it has several meanings, but rather that it achieves plurality of meaning, an *irreducible* plurality." Large amounts of situated verbal interaction, where the sender controls for correctly comprehended retrieval – is as pointed out by Reddy (1979) – needed to reduce plurality, since sender helps the receiver to remove limitations to her or his own understanding (Deetz, 1992) – and alignment of meaning is based on negotiation processes between the two actors (Shotter, 1993; Wenger, 1998). Face-to-face conversation and socialization is then often required to transfer knowledge (Nonaka & Takeuchi, 1995). However, meaningful communication, further, requires a shared context of codes and language (Boland & Tenaski, 1995). Codification, in itself, is not sufficient for minimizing contextual gaps. As Cowan et al., (2000, p. 225) write: "what is codified for one person or group may be tacit for another and an utterly impenetrable mystery for a third." Encoding might even impede retrieval, since the use of, for example, a metaphor creates ambiguity. *Shared* context and frequent communication diminishes, on the other hand, the distance between encoding and decoding. Shared contexts can be face-to-face or virtual, where past interpretations may, in fact, be documented (Kogut & Zander, 1992; Krippendorff, 1975). Lave & Wenger (1991) and Brown & Duguid (1991, 2000) observe that shared codes and language bring people together and further shape members perceptions. The importance of shared narratives has also been emphasized (Wenger, 1998). Context is, therefore, vital, as knowledge is not acquired and transferred in a mechanical way. Handley et al., (2006) elucidates this by referring to the failure of designing a computer program that can interpret (and not only "read") e.g., newspaper articles. Communities of practice has been viewed as an entity that encapsulate context, and where common sense is build through mutual engagement in a geographically proxy environment, which is helpful to knowledge retrieval.

COMMUNITIES OF PRACTICE

A community of practice is an informal group of people sharing common concerns or expertise, strengthening its bonds through ongoing interaction (McDermott, 1999; Wenger et al., 2002; Wenger & Snyder, 2000). The group aims to develop practices and domains of knowledge with a unique perspective, by which they can "undertake or engage fully in a task, job or profession" (Brown & Duguid, 2001, p. 203). Each community member has a distinctive identity and finds a unique place in the group (Wenger, 1998). Both the possession and contribution of knowledge are distributed asymmetrically, though knowledge is available to all members. This shared knowledge pool lets individuals work without having to know everything (Brown & Duguid, 2001; Wenger, 1998). On the other hand, individuals are aware of the others' membership, that is, they know who is who (Brown & Duguid, 1991; Lave & Wenger, 1991) and what different people know. The shared codes and language are most important, turning the community of practice into an effective means of communication. Brown & Duguid (1991) point to the sharing of practices as leading to common tacit knowledge, engendering knowledge transfers, communication and learning within the community. As such, information travels fast within real communities and is readily accessible to other members. Gertler (2003) views communities of practice as facilitators of tacit knowledge transfers through collaborative problem solving assisted by storytelling. Ibarra (1999) emphasizes the ability to develop a practice by imitating other community members. In general, communities of practice provide their members with the opportunity for conversation, experimentation and sharing expertise with colleagues (Pan & Leidner, 2003). The sharing of practice establishes one shared context that might overcome other contextual differences (Alvesson & Kärreman, 2000). However, a community is still needed to be viewed as a social group, and even though contextual distances is decreased in relation to knowledge transfer, conflicts might occur (Handley et al., 2006), and the distribution of power, e.g., a group containing of managers and blue color workers, will still be in place (Fowler et al., 2004). Well-known is the initial work by Lave & Wenger (1991) and their descriptions of the meat cutter community where full participation in the community was denied to novices by the more powerful practitioners.

The creation of meaning is of particular relevance discussing communities of practice. Wenger (1998, p. 47, italics added) explains:"Communities of practice are the prime context in which we can work out *common sense* through mutual engagement". Hereby, the interpretation of the term "common sense" goes beyond its meaning in colloquial English referring to "sound and prudent judgment", i.e. some fact or interpretation everybody can agree upon. Wenger refers explicitly to the shared understanding of participants in a community and the development of individual viewpoints. In Wenger's (1998, p.48) words: "We all have our own theories and ways of understanding the world, and our communities of practice are places where we develop, negotiate, and share them". Therefore, participation in a community of practice leads to a social production of meaning, since the community members negotiate meaning through reification processes, through which they produce shared understandings of e.g., symbols, stories, and metaphors. As such, common sense does not refer in this context to "minimal joint agreement" or "general fact of life" but to common sense-making, common sense-development and common sense-negotiation. The activities in communities of practice are, therefore, not centered around the identification and defense of one "common sense" (universal agreement) but are focused to offer members ample opportunity to develop their own thinking based on "common sense" (mutual understanding). According to Stein (2005), communities of practice, therefore, specify a knowledge domain of interest, within ongoing processes of sense-making, knowledge sharing and discovery take place among interested and interconnected participants.

Within communities a relationship become idiosyncratic and meaning is based in a detailed, complex, embedded shared understanding (Wenger, 1998). Consequently, personal and social relationships within the community are essential to sense-making processes. The concept of "social capital" is useful in this context as it helps to clarify the value of the resources that are embedded in the network of relationships extending from a particular individual or social unit (Burt, 1997; McElroy, 2002; Nahapiet & Ghoshal, 1998). Additionally, "social capital" expresses the sense of trust that develops from continued inter-personal connections – bridging cultural differences and creating a shared context of meaning (Daniel et al., 2003). In such embedded relationships, there will be exchanges of strategic and operational information that will not transferred in less embedded relationships, which reduces the uncertainty of the transaction (Fowler et al., 2004; Uzzi, 1997)

A community of practice has a flexible structure with no precise termination date. Numbers and intensity of participation fluctuate as people move in and out, but the group normally includes tens or even hundreds, although only a few take social and intellectual leadership (Lesser & Everest, 2001; Wenger, 1998; Wenger & Snyder, 2000). Participants seldom pursue an agreed, shared end goal. They are instead connected through a joint interest in a particular topic. Evolving without constraint of authority, the group is self-organized (Creplet et al., 2001; Lesser & Everest, 2001). Unlike informal networks of people who share information and build relationships, the community of practice focuses on something specific (Lave & Wenger, 1991; Nonaka et al., 2001). Furthermore, its informality and focus on knowledge-building and sharing distinguishes it from formal workgroups and project teams that concentrate instead on final products or services.

Early studies assume communities of practice form spontaneously. More recent work describes far more management-governed processes (Soo et al., 2002; Storck & Hill, 2000; Swan et al., 2002). This is exemplified by the fact of an increased used of consultancy firms to identify, establish, and manage communities within the firm (Roberts, 2006). In an "epistemic community", members accept the presence of a procedural authority that urges fulfillment of a specified goal (Cowan et al., 1998; Creplet et al., 2001). Management can on the one hand provide helpful support to a community by adding more systematic structures. On the other hand this attempt to control by adding structures might result in the demise of the community (Thompson, 2005). Self-governed communities are different to epistemic communities. When members of a community of practice pay attention to the increasing performance of a given practice, members of epistemic communities are cautious about peers' orders and rewards (Cohendet & Llerena, 2003). A reason is that communities of practice may have broadly intrinsic motivation while epistemic communities are more likely to be defined by extrinsic incentives.

This literature review clearly points out a range of factors that minimizes the contextual gap between senders and receivers of knowledge. In practice it also covers the situation where the reader of a written document either contact the original informant personally for additional information, or automatically are aware of the premises of decoding based on a prior process of negotiated meaning, and by the use of a shared set of resources such as methods, tools, theories and practices, as stated by Stein (2005). However, the same author opposes the electronic information exchange to the far much richer concept of proxy sense-making (p. 3). It is, therefore, reasonable do discuss the efficiency of virtual information retrieval, and whether communities of practice are replicable in a virtual context.

VIRTUAL COMMUNITIES OF PRACTICE

Virtual communities are, at first sight, very near to communities of practice – a group of frequently interactive individuals sharing a practice. What is different is that communication and coordination of work takes place in cyberspace through information technology. The community is, therefore, relational without reference to a specific location (Ahuja & Carley, 1999). Koh & Kim (2004) speak of *distributed community of practices,* and refer to a group of geographically distributed individuals who are informally bound together by shared expertise and shared interest of work. Like communities of practice, they operate with informal goals, common language, shared understanding and reasonable levels of trust.

Two factors stand out as being significantly different for communities established in a virtual context: (1) communication takes place in cyberspace, and (2) the lack of physical proximity between sender and receiver. With regard to the on-line communication, MNCs usually establish an "Intranet" as an essential part of their knowledge management system: a replication of Internet technology that uses a firewall to prevent external access (Boettcher, 1998; Bowman, 2002). An intranet allows establishment of discussion forums where the receiver taps into written database documents describing, for example, best practice and, subsequently, has the opportunity to discuss their reapplication with the original creators (Zack, 1999). In general, information technologies are cost-efficient instrument for information exchange over a geographical distance (Huber, 1991) by linking organizational units and individuals through standardized information flows (Bowman, 2002; Ensign, 1998) and established repositories of codified knowledge (Constant et al., 1997; Pickering & King, 1995; Purvis et al., 2001). In fact, by using databases, more people – or at least their written documents – serve the individual as information sources (Zhang & Watts, 2008). MNC computer networks present the opportunity to ask (a large number of) strangers for advice and people can respond without having to know their colleagues and without having to travel. Such networks connect those who do not enjoy physical proximity, shared histories or demographics. Communities are connected primarily by e-mail networks (Wenger & Snyder, 2000) and overcome spatial distance by using collaborative groupware technologies (McKnight & Bontis, 2002). Members of "on-line communities" feel part of a larger web of relationships in which there are ongoing exchanges of commonly-valued items together with long-lasting, maintained interactions and a developed shared history (Figallo, 1998). On-line communities not only offer the possibility for information exchange, but also enable people to socialize (Preece, 2000). The computer system thus supports and mediates social interaction, facilitating a sense of togetherness.

Both the communities of practice and the virtual communities of practice are characterized by strong and embedded ties among actors. However, Fowler et al. (2004) distinguish between what they call the socially embedded ties (communities) and virtual embedded ties (virtual communities). Social embedded networks create trust, whereas virtual embedded networks lead to transparency, as the information technology provide access to databases and more flows of information. Therefore, the information shared becomes widespread and reaches a larger audience (Granovetter, 1973).

To distinguish between intranet, newsgroups, and chat rooms on one side and virtual communities on the other, the former ones describe tools by which persons can be found and contacted but no long-term interest is needed, nor a strong common sense. The main purpose is provision of data and "ready made" knowledge, which can be retrieved without further interaction or any longer term interactions. By contrast, virtual communities of practice do have a common topic and a long-term working history, even though individual members may have joint recently. The common theme unites the members and they jointly are working to improve and develop the field of their interest. Thus, the demarcation between the two concepts is duration of membership (long for virtual communities), direction of communication (two-sided in virtual communities) and finally, the level of joint interests (high for virtual communities). However, despite the joint interest, the lack of physical proximity, through which people meet face-to-face and which provides the opportunity of warmth, attentiveness and other interpersonal affections, is expected to lead to a situation where trust may be unlikely to develop (Jarvenpaa & Leidner, 1999; Wenger et al., 2002). In decentralized and dispersed organizational structures, employees can – through the use of information technology - work anytime and anywhere, but the fraying of ties between people impedes trust-building, which again affects the extent of knowledge transfers and the kind of information the sender is willing to share (Wiesenfeld et al., 1999). The next section, therefore, the circumstances in which knowledge retrieval can be efficient in a virtual community.

VIRTUAL COMMUNITIES OF PRACTICE AND KNOWLEDGE RETRIEVAL

It has been debated whether virtual communities are an efficient knowledge management practice. Examples of this are Bartczak et al., (2007) survey of the knowledge management strategy of the US Air Force Material Command showed the difficulties of leveraging the otherwise efficient communities of practice in a virtual context, and Vizcaino et al., (2007) arguing that technological solutions seldom take into account the fundamental problems of transferring knowledge. Contrary, Cheuk (2007) reports how the British Council has established sense-making processes in a virtual context by initiating social networks. Wenger et al. (2002) also reports on the use of communities in the large MNCs including Shell Oil Company, Daimler Chrysler, Hewlett Packard Company, McKinsey etc., and that some of this communities are large and contains more than 1,500 members. Therefore, as Roberts (2003) argue, it makes sense to view the communities of MNCs as a collection of communities, which is also the more narrowly defined focus of this chapter.

Because of the doubts about trust mentioned earlier, the virtual community's efficacy, as a knowledge-retrieval medium is not clear. We must ask whether the lack of geographical proximity, the difficulty in building strong ties and the general rootlessness of social relationships severely hampers retrieval processes. Communities of practice normally rely on social capital rather than on technostructures (Alvesson & Kärreman, 2001) or the overall organizational knowledge management strategies emphasizing economic aspects (Davenport, 1998). The distance between scattered groups of employees means people do not meet by chance and face-to-face contact is rare. Participants, therefore, remain in separate national and company cultures representing organizational units that possess different capabilities. On the other hand, distance might down tone the conflicts among members that exist in proxy communities (Handley et al., 2004), and interaction will take place on a neutral ground.

The question is whether members of virtual communities do retrieve knowledge effectively. A literature review by Huysman et al. (2003) reveals that virtual teams generally solve such problems as lack of trust, lack of shared background knowledge, and coordination, behavior and interaction issues: however, these problems were in this case mostly solved using a combination of video conferencing and communication through e-mail. Cramton (2001) opposes this view and find in her survey that mutual knowledge is a problem of geographical dispersed groups due to failures in communicating, retaining and updating contextual information. Schenkel & Teigland (2008) also experienced in their survey that a physical break up of a proxy community broke an otherwise efficient learning curve. Lea & Spears (1991) provide one explanation, namely that computer-mediated communication reduces the number of cues available to the receiver relative to face-to-face communication. On the other hand, Zhang & Watts (2008) suggest that virtual communities are preferable to proximate communities, because of their "global" availability, the likelihood of approaching a large number of receivers, and that the use of boundary object such as a document puts an emphasis on the message, and these factors compensate for the filtering out of cues. Furthermore, feeling of solidarity and mutual interest in communities of practice should increase the will to retain and update contextual information and minimize polarization effects. As Amin (2002) suggests, it is rather the relational proximity than the geographical proximity that makes communities of practice efficient.

Strong ties among individuals are also seen as necessary for transferring complex knowledge, one reason being the awareness of contextual backgrounds (Granovetter, 1972; Hansen, 1999). Whether it is possible to establish strong ties between actors in a virtual setting (Preece, 2000) is questionable. Virtual strong ties are typically founded on initial face-to-face meetings that are then later maintained virtually (McDermott, 1999). Thus, computer-mediated communication supports *existing* ties, whether weak or strong (Pickering & King, 1995; Preece, 2000). The establishment of new on-line weak ties typically results from newsgroup and chat room participation, often organized around specific topics or demographics, and not necessarily involving proxy social relationships (Kraut, et al., 1998).

The virtual context addresses the question of whether or not the lack of face-to-face interaction in on-line relationships hinders or at least limits the retrieval processes that are otherwise characterized by frequent, long-lasting voluntary information transfer, where both partners are willing to develop companionship and accept mutual needs (Wellman & Gulia, 2000). However, different surveys suggest the possibility to build close on-line social relationships. With asynchronous and necessarily verbal information, this is more difficult and time-consuming to achieve (Walther, 1995). Other surveys indicate that group newcomers readily participate actively in on-line groups because the medium affords greater anonymity thus actually lower barriers to enter a group (Ahuja & Galvin, 2003). Gertler (2003) claims that even tacit knowledge will flow across regional and national boundaries if the virtual community is "strong enough." Nonaka & Takeuchi (1995) see the need of transferring knowledge through proxy socialization mechanisms. However, this claim should not be misread as a ply for face-to-face relationships because virtual socialization media do exist. In addition, through a combination of narratives or storytelling techniques and with the use of boundary objects such as documents (Boland & Tenkasi, 1995), the virtual community of practice is useful for retrieval processes. Studies by Yates et al., (1999) reveal that communities develop "genres", i.e. "socially recognized types of communicative actions … that are habitually enacted by members of a community to realize particular social purpose" (p. 84) and further particular forms (e.g., choice of media), structural features (like formatting) and linguistic features (specialized vocabulary) are developed in a communities, all in all helping receivers to retrieve knowledge correctly. A survey by Zucchermaglio & Talermo (2003) also showed how informality in communication was reached over time, even in the context of using electronic mail systems. This study also proves that sense-making processes can be established, but further, that the time aspect should be integrated into the analyses. Therefore, if the receiver is provided with the contextual background, and if codes and language can be aligned, the same degree of retrieval should be achievable even in a virtual context. As Wenger (1998, p. 74) writes: "Given the right context, talking on the phone, exchanging electronic mail, or being connected by radio can all be part of what makes mutual engagement possible." One has also to remember that physical proximity also triggers personality clashes and, as such, a community of practice might be less effective than a virtual community.

The remaining factor to stress is the issue of trust. Dirks & Ferrin (2001) emphasized its importance through a literature review, pointing out that trust within a group had a significant positive effect on openness in communication (Roberts, 2003; Zand, 1972), and in general trust, familiarity and mutual understanding is supportive to knowledge transfers (Roberts, 2000). Therefore, as Mayer et al. (1995, p. 712) write, information transfers depends on the sender's willingness "to be vulnerable to the action of another party based on the expectation that the other will perform a particular action important to the trustor, irrespective of the ability to monitor or control the other party". The question, here, is whether or not a sender will provide contextual information to a receiver whom he has never met and perhaps only has communicated with via e-mail. Regardless the media, it requires repeated interactions to build up a feeling of confidence in the other party's value and trustworthiness (Jones & George, 1998). This supports our argument that a virtual community of practice is a forum for repeated interaction and thus, enables the necessary feeling of confidence in a virtual environment. One example is Wasko & Faraj (2005) finding that employees to a high degree share knowledge when operating in networks characterized by dense relationships. Further, the degree of trust needed for transfer depends on the "criticalness" of the transferred information (Bhattacharya et al., 1998). One example is the case where an employee assesses his "market value" and bargaining power within the company, aiming for future career building – in respect of the uniqueness of the knowledge he possess. Such kind of knowledge is very critical and demands high levels of trust before it will be transferred (Constant et al., 1999; Husted & Michailova, 2002). However, communicating with the "unknown" do take place in the initial phase of a relationship that simultaneously is the most critical phase for trust building (as documented by Constant et al., 1999 see also McKnight et al., 1998). Trust in this stage is based on calculation, and, therefore, depends on the availability of relevant information (Lane, 1998). Trust can only proceed on the basis of institutionalized protection or the reputation of the receiver (Child et al., 2005). The question is when the corporation can provide the needed institutional protection in the beginning of the relationships between sender and receiver, where trust is to be characterized as fragile (Coleman, 1990). In organizations with a knowledge-friendly environment, knowledge will no be free flowing. For example, Kankanhalli et al. (2005) showed that the absence of trust negatively had an impact on codification processes within the firm. In addition, Bock et al. (2005) saw a link between an organizational climate where members affiliated with the organization, and where manager's assessments of staff members were viewed as fair, and the degree of knowledge sharing. Therefore, the organization can build up a knowledge-sharing friendly culture and, in general, align corporate norms and values through proper communication, which again increases the possibility of shared contextual backgrounds (Wiesenfeld et al., 1999).

A specific type of trust can be established in virtual communities. Meyerson et al. (1996) operate with the term *swift trust* in describing the creation of trust in temporary teams. When trust cannot be established through frequent face-to-face contact, group members instead *import* expectations of trust from other familiar settings. Likewise, the community's genre repertoire (i.e. the types of communicative actions and the forms it takes) typically reflects the organizational cultural context (Yates et al., 1999). Subsequent trust retaining then depends on the ongoing activity in the group. Virtual communities thereby establish swift trust *if* the organization in which the community is embedded has implemented a trust-based knowledge-sharing culture, and as Constant et al., (1999, p. 400) write: "a belief in organizational ownership of work encourages and mediates attitudes favoring sharing". In this respect, Jarvenpaa & Leidner (1999) test the swift trust framework and find that dispersed teams do experience "swift trust", though such trust is fragile and only temporal. Kasper-Fuehrer & Ashkanasy (2001) also find that a common business understanding and strong business ethics are needed to establish trust in virtual organizations. Though, Meyerson et al., (1996) provide three reasons for an initial high level of trust in interaction between individuals without any prior relationships (e.g., trusting a newcomer to a virtual community and vice versa): a) implicit threat within the organization that inefficient managed communities at the end of the day harm the organization; b) the prospects of future interaction between sender and receiver and c) role clarity where individuals rather act as role models. This effect is also described by Dawes (1994, p. 24): "we trust doctors because we trust modern medicine, and we have evidence that it works when antibiotics and operations cure people". If the trustworthiness and reputation of a particular group (e.g. engineers or business development team) in a particular organization is high, it will, following the line of thoughts from Meyerson et al., (1996), generate swift trust even in newly established virtual communities.

In fact, virtual communities, or at least geographically dispersed groups - like scientific communities - have existed for centuries and have been able to establish new paradigms despite the disadvantage of distance (Kuhn, 1962). Their use of conferences, sabbaticals and virtual communication as sense-making media (Pickering & King, 1995) leads us to question whether any opportunity to establish a common sense through mutual engagement can overcome problems such as the lack of geographical proximity (Wenger, 1998). CERN (The European Nuclear Research

Centre) and the establishment of the World Wide Web (WWW) are relevant examples. The Web was conceived by Tim Berners-Lee to solve problems of a dispersed group of scientist, all of whom were paying CERN short visits. They still needed to communicate with colleagues after their temporary assignments. Even though the coding problem among physicists seems manageable, there was no documentation of what happened during each individual's stay. In general, employees entering the organization were only given a few hints of whom to address (Naughton, 1999). The situation inspired Tim Berners-Lee to design the basic structure of the WWW, which primarily began as a search opportunity, not particularly helpful for decoding – even though the initial idea was that entered documents should be editable by the receiver (Naughton, 1999). On the other hand, the WWW is forceful as it makes it possible to create and share not only written text, but also multimedia by combining transfers of hypertext with transmissions of images and audio/video versions (Abbate, 1999). The story is similar to the invention of the telegraph and how it enabled industries like the railway (Chandler, 1990) or a company like Reuters (Witzel, 2003) to develop into geographical dispersed entities.

Today, IT is an integrated means to communicate among geographical dispersed actors. Pan & Leidner (2003) use a case study of Buckman Labs – a chemical company with operations in 21 different countries – to show how information technology supports knowledge sharing within and between communities of practice. Furthermore, Ryssen & Godar (2000) provide an example of students working in virtual teams communicating by e-mail and the web. Likewise, Zhang & Watts (2008) describe how virtual community members actively engage in their shared practice and identity development in a Chinese online community on traveling. Lee & Cole (2003) give an example, describing the development of the Linux operating system. In the improvement of this system, thousands of volunteers dispersed among both *organizational* and *geographical* boundaries collaborated via the Internet. Criticism impelled learning processes, review processes and error corrections, which enforced correct retrieval of written documents. Even though this type of problem solving approaches the dyadic cooperation that takes place in communities of practice, the contributions from virtual community members are more non-reciprocal in its character, and commitments are in general relatively minor or fleeting (Fowler et al., 2004). To conclude, Linux successfully uses culture as a social control mechanism to solve trust (and property rights) problems and as such illustrates that trust can be developed and maintained in virtual settings.

To conclude the above discussion; knowledge retrieval – between a sender and a receiver communicating in a far distant context within an MNC - can be more efficient in virtual communities of practice than compared to transfer activities outside such communities. By formulating propositions, the purpose of this chapter is to put an emphasis on those factors that *initially* in the communication process are going to (1) minimize contextual gaps between sender and receiver, and (2) increase the likelihood of communication among "stranger", i.e., a situation without trust building in a proxy environment, given the context of transfers and retrieval of written reports within a virtual community of an MNC. Over time, virtual communities of practices are anticipated to mirror the characteristics from proxy communities of practices, in cases where negotiation of meaning takes place among participants (such as asking for additional information via a phone call) and contextual gaps are minimized via experience. Huysman et al. (2003) have here demonstrated that a combination of using e-mail and video-conferencing solved retrieval problems. Therefore, if "negotiation of meaning" processes are established, virtual communities will contain the same characteristics as proxy communities, showing distinctive identities, full information availability, high level of "knowing who" information - including contextual background information, and in general that conversation, experimentation and shared expertise or passion overcome contextual differences.

However, the question is what makes an initial retrieval of a written document more efficient in a virtual community of practice compared to reading documents – accessed from the corporate intranet - in general. From our perspective, there are various points why the existence of virtual communities leads to more efficient retrieval processes: First, it is easier for the receiver to search a particular piece of information from the sender through a virtual community, since the amount of entries are less and more relevant as compared to a general database. As Zhang & Watts (2008, p. 58) writes: "In online communities the content of computer mediated communication – whether text-based or not – can easily be stored in various formats and made available for various manipulations, such as browsing, searching, retrieving, analyzing, and mining". Franco & Mariano (2007) also report that in general databases are typical split in several locations, useful knowledge is hidden behind cryptic filenames or folders, which in general produces lack of motivating of uploading new information

Second, swift trust is easier to establish if other group members act as role models: this does not help the receiver to retrieve *per se,* but it increases the acceptance and the acknowledgement of the relevance of the information. Third, sharing a practice means shared codes since members often possess the same theoretical and practical background (Håkanson, 2007). Writings in the concept of absorptive capacity also advocate for more fluently communication and retrieval when members share a professional and theoretical background (Cummings & Teng, 2003; Lane & Lubatkin, 1998; Reagans & McEvily, 2003; Schultz, 2003): to exemplify, shared theoretical and professional background will lead to shared vocabulary (Yates et al., 1999). This approaches the situation described by Sperber & Wilson (1995), where contextual information is mutual known, and actors are aware (because of the shared practice) of that contextual information is shared. Thus it is proposed:

P1: Individuals participating in virtual communities of practice more efficiently retrieve knowledge from written documents in this forum than from the corporate database, since senders and receivers of knowledge more often will share a theoretical and professional background.

Still, what really drive people apart in MNCs, even in cases of shared practice, are obviously national cultures. Hofstede (1980) is here famous for his assumptions of national culture characteristics. However, a recent survey by Li et al., (2007) showed that individual hostility rather than national cultural related factors impacted knowledge sharing through online communities of practice. One reason could be the anonymity that the virtual setting offers the individual, which brings all participants on the same ground, compared to a "face to face" meeting, where participants brings their national identity with them (Ahuja & Galvin, 2003). These assumptions are similar to the swift trust situation, where the "role the sender can play in relation to his practice" becomes more important than what he or she represents in relation to national background. Secondly, we argue that there will be less knowledge sharing hostility if members identify themselves with the community in which they participate. Even though that Fiol & O'Connor (2005) demonstrate ambiguous findings in the literature up to now, they still argue that members will be motivated to identify with the group because of the relatively high degree of uncertainty that participation in such a virtual group produced. Therefore, swift trust – importing trustworthiness from the organizational setting is a key factor to overcome problems of knowledge sharing hostility and uncertainty. Next, to provide institutional protection is essential. Here, Gupta et al., (1999) emphasized that in MNCs, characterized by geographical, linguistic and cultural distance, sincere information asymmetries between a parent company and its subsidiaries will exist. Though, knowledge will only flow back to headquarters, if the MNC establishes norms and values for such communication. Therefore it is proposed that lack of institutional protection will lead to failures in communicating, retaining and updating contextual information. The corporate culture is for that reason a crucial player for efficient knowledge retrieval. This produces our second proposition:

P2: Individuals' willingness to share knowledge through virtual communities of practice increases when the MNCs culture, and in relation hereto its norms and values, establish the needed institutional protection to establish swift trust.

CONCLUSION

This paper discusses conceptually the phenomenon of communities of practice when established in a virtual context by MNCs. Hereby the focus of this chapter is on the outcome for the individual employee to retrieve knowledge efficiently when participating in such a group. Communities of practice are recognized as being efficient for knowledge transfers in general. The aim of the paper was a discussion of whether this comes true in an intra-organizational virtual setting as well. Based on findings from the existing literature, we suggest that individual members will share knowledge more efficiently in a virtual context, if the organization provides institutional protection to establish swift trust situations. Furthermore, similarities in practice and theory initially minimize contextual gaps. Over time, negotiation of meaning processes needs to be established to copy the success of proxy communities of practice. In this case, the virtual community must be rich in its use of media, opening up the possibility of negotiation of meaning processes to supply members with other members' contextual background. Further, sharing practices, in the sense of a jointed professional and theoretical background, is further helpful for information retrieval, and it helps the receiver of information to acknowledge the sender as a relevant informant.

Referring to retrieval of written documents, the receiver often deals with text written by a "stranger" with whom the sender could not establish face-to-face contact. A weaker tie between the actors is foreseeable when compared to a local community of practice. The members are not "colleagues", in the sense that daily operations beyond the community area were to be fulfilled. To put the discussion in perspective, it is worthwhile to address whether a combination of the two community forms would be effective, such as a virtual community of practice including regular face-to-face meetings. We suggest that business (or virtual communities within MNCs) get inspired by the structure from scientific communities where members occasionally meet at conferences or pay each respective organization short visits and, subsequently, cooperate. As a part of that process they retrieve knowledge from written documents in a virtual context. A combination may encompass the positive sides but also carries costs and risks of inefficient resource allocation. We suggest that the evaluation of relative importance of these two mechanisms should form the basis for further research.

REFERENCES

Abbate, J. (1999). *Inventing the Internet*. Cambridge, MA: The MIT Press.

Ahuja, M. J., & Galvin, J. E. (2003). Socialization in virtual groups. *Journal of Management, 29*, 161–185. doi:10.1177/014920630302900203

Ahuja, M. K., & Carley, K. M. (1999). Network structure in virtual organizations. *Organization Science, 10*, 741–757. doi:10.1287/orsc.10.6.741

Alavi, M., & Leidner, D. (2001). Review: Knowledge management and knowledge management systems: conceptual foundations and research issues. *MIS Quarterly*, *25*, 107–136. doi:10.2307/3250961

Alvesson, M., & Kärreman, D. (2000). Taking the linguistic turn in organizational research: challenges, responses, consequences. *The Journal of Applied Behavioral Science*, *36*, 136–158. doi:10.1177/0021886300362002

Alvesson, M., & Kärreman, D. (2001). Odd couple: making sense of the curious concept of knowledge management. *Journal of Management Studies*, *38*, 995–1018. doi:10.1111/1467-6486.00269

Amin, A. (2002). Spatialities of globalisation. *Environment & Planning A*, *34*, 385–399. doi:10.1068/a3439

Bartczak, S. E., Turner, J. M., & England, E. C. (2007). Challenges in developing a knowledge management strategy: a case study of the Air Force Material Command. *International Journal of Knowledge Management*, *4*(1), 46–50.

Barthes, R. (1997). From work to text. In S. L. Feagin, & P. Maynard, P. (Eds.), *Aesthetics*. Oxford: Oxford University Press.

Bhattacharya, R., Devinney, T. M., & Pillutla, M. M. (1998). A formal model of trust based on outcomes. *Academy of Management Review*, *23*, 459–472. doi:10.2307/259289

Bock, G.-W., Zmud, R. W., & Kim, Y.-G. (2005). Behavioral intention formation in knowledge sharing: Examining the roles of extrinsic motivators, social-psychological forces, and organizational climate. *MIS Quarterly*, *29*(1), 87–111.

Boettcher, S. (1998). The Netscape Intranet Solution: Deploying the Full-service Intranet. New York: John Wiley & Sons.

Boland, R. J., & Tenkasi, R. V. (1995). Perspective making and perspective taking in communities of knowing. *Organization Science*, *6*, 350–372. doi:10.1287/orsc.6.4.350

Bowman, B. J. (2002). Building knowledge management systems. *Information Systems Management*, *19*, 32–40. doi:10.1201/1078/43201.19.3.20020601/37168.5

Brown, J. S., & Duguid, P. (1991). Organizational learning and communities-of-practice: toward a unified view of working, learning and innovation. *Organization Science*, *2*, 40–57. doi:10.1287/orsc.2.1.40

Brown, J. S., & Duguid, P. (2001). Knowledge and organization: a social-practice perspective. *Organization Science*, *12*, 198–213. doi:10.1287/orsc.12.2.198.10116

Burt, R. S. (1997). The contingent value of social capital. *Administrative Science Quarterly*, *42*, 339–365. doi:10.2307/2393923

Chandler, A. D. (1990). *Scale and Scope - the Dynamics of Industrial Capitalism*. Cambridge, MA: Belknap Press.

Cheuk, B. W. (2007). Using social networking analysis to facilitate knowledge sharing in the British Council. *International Journal of Knowledge Management*, *2*(4), 67–76.

Child, J. Faulkner, D. & Tallman, S. (2005). Cooperative Strategy: Managing Alliances, Networks, and Joint Ventures. Oxford: Oxford University Press.

Cohendet, P., Kern, F., Mehmanpazir, B., & Munier, F. (1999). Knowledge coordination, competence creation and integrated networks in globalised firms. *Cambridge Journal of Economics*, *23*, 225–241. doi:10.1093/cje/23.2.225

Cohendet, P., & Llerena, P. (2003). Routines and incentives: the role of communities in the firm. *Industrial and Corporate Change, 12*, 271–297. doi:10.1093/icc/12.2.271

Coleman, R. (1990). *Foundations of Social Theory.* Cambridge, MA: Belknap Press.

Constant, D., Kiesler, S., & Sproull, L. (1994). What's mine is ours, or is it? A study of attitudes about information sharing. *Information Systems Research, 5*(5), 400–421. doi:10.1287/isre.5.4.400

Constant, D., Sproull, L., & Kiesler, S. (1997). The kindness of strangers: on the usefulness of electronic weak ties for technical advice. In S. Kiesler (ed.), *Culture of the Internet.* Mahwah, NJ: Lawrence Erlbaum Associates.

Cowan, R., David, P. A., & Foray, D. (2000). The explicit economics of knowledge codification and tacitness. *Industrial and Corporate Change, 9*, 211–253. doi:10.1093/icc/9.2.211

Cramton, C. D. (2001). The mutual knowledge problem and its consequences for dispersed collaboration. *Organization Science, 12*, 347–371. doi:10.1287/orsc.12.3.346.10098

Creplet, F., Dupouet, O., Kern, F., Mehmanpazir, B., & Munier, F. (2001). Consultants and experts in management consulting firms. *Research Policy, 30*, 1517–1535. doi:10.1016/S0048-7333(01)00165-2

Cummings, J. L., & Teng, B. (2003). Transferring R&D knowledge: The key factors affecting knowledge transfer success. *Journal of Engineering and Technology Management, 20*, 39–68. doi:10.1016/S0923-4748(03)00004-3

Daniel, B., Schwier, R. A., & McCalla, G. (2003). Social capital in virtual learning communities and distributed communities of practice. *Canadian Journal of Learning and Technology, 29*, 113–139.

Davenport, T. H., & Prusak, L. (1998). *Working Knowledge: How Organizations Manage What They Know.* Boston: Harvard Business School Press.

Dawes, R. M. (1994). *House of Cards: Psychology and Psychotherapy Built on Myth.* New York: Free Press.

Deetz, S. A. (1992). *Democracy in an Age of Corporate Colonization: Developments in Communication and the Politics of Everyday Life.* Albany: State University of New York Press.

Dirks, K. T., & Ferrin, D. L. (2001). The role of trust in organizational settings. *Organization Science, 12*, 450–467. doi:10.1287/orsc.12.4.450.10640

Ensign, P. C. (1998). Interrelationships and horizontal strategy to achieve synergy and competitive advantage in the diversified firm. *Management Decision, 36*, 657–668. doi:10.1108/00251749810245318

Figallo, C. (1998). *Hosting Web Communities: Building Relationships, Increasing Customer Loyalty, and Maintaining a Competitive Edge.* New York: John Wiley & Sons.

Fiol, C. M., & O'Connor, E. J. (2005). Identification in face-to-face, hybrid, and pure virtual teams: untangling the contradictions. *Organization Science, 16*, 19–32. doi:10.1287/orsc.1040.0101

Fowler, S. W., Lawrence, T. B., & Morse, E. A. (2004). Virtual embedded ties. *Journal of Management, 30*(5), 647–666. doi:10.1016/j.jm.2004.02.005

Franco, M., & Mariano, S. (2007). Information technology repositories and knowledge management processes: a qualitative analysis. *The Journal of Information and Knowledge Management Systems, 37*(4), 440–451.

Gertler, M. S. (2003). Tacit knowledge and the economic geography of context or the undefinable tacitness of being (there). *Journal of Economic Geography*, *3*, 75–99. doi:10.1093/jeg/3.1.75

Granovetter, M. S. (1972). The strength of weak ties. *American Journal of Sociology*, *78*, 1360–1380. doi:10.1086/225469

Gupta, A. K., Govindarajan, V., & Malhorta, A. (1999). Feedback-seeking behavior within multinational corporations. *Strategic Management Journal*, *20*, 205–222. doi:10.1002/(SICI)1097-0266(199903)20:3<205::AID-SMJ17>3.0.CO;2-H

Håkanson, L. (2007). Creating knowledge – the power and logic of articulation. *Industrial and Corporate Change*, *16*(1), 51–88. doi:10.1093/icc/dtl033

Handley, K., Sturdy, A., Fincham, R., & Clark, T. (2006). Within and beyond communities of practice: making sense of learning through participation, identity, and practice. *Journal of Management Studies*, *43*(3), 641–653. doi:10.1111/j.1467-6486.2006.00605.x

Hansen, M. T. (1999). The search-transfer problem: the role of weak ties in sharing knowledge across organization subunits. *Administrative Science Quarterly*, *44*, 82–111. doi:10.2307/2667032

Hofstede, G. (1980). *Culture's Consequences: International Differences in Work-related Values*. Beverly Hills CA: Sage.

Holzner, B., & Marx, J. (1979). *The Knowledge Application: the Knowledge System in Society*. Boston: Allyn-Bacon.

Hornett, A., & Stein, E. W. (2007). Mapping the knowledge management domain of ideas: evidence from a practice group. *International Journal of Knowledge Management*, *3*(3), 1–25.

Huber, G. P. (1991). Organizational learning: the contributing process and the literatures. *Organization Science*, *2*, 88–115. doi:10.1287/orsc.2.1.88

Husted, K., & Michailova, S. (2002). Diagnosing and fighting knowledge sharing hostility. *Organizational Dynamics*, *31*, 60–73. doi:10.1016/S0090-2616(02)00072-4

Huysman, M., Steinfield, C., Jang, C., & David, K., Huis In 'T Veld, M., Poot, J. & Mulder, I. (2003). Virtual Teams and the appropriation of communication technology: exploring the concept of media stickiness. *Computer Supported Cooperative Work*, *12*, 411–436. doi:10.1023/A:1026145017609

Ibarra, H. (1999). Provisional selves: experimenting with image and identity in professional adaptation. *Administrative Science Quarterly*, *44*, 764–791. doi:10.2307/2667055

Jarvenpaa, S. L., & Leidner, D. E. (1999). Communication and trust in global virtual teams. *Organization Science*, *10*, 791–815. doi:10.1287/orsc.10.6.791

Jones, G. R., & George, J. M. (1998). The experience and evolution of trust: Implications for cooperation and teamwork. *Academy of Management Review*, *23*, 531–546. doi:10.2307/259293

Kankanhalli, A., Tan, B. C. Y., & Wei, K.-K. (2005). Contributing knowledge to electronic knowledge repositories: An empirical investigation. *MIS Quarterly*, *29*(1), 113–143.

Kasper-Fuehrer, E. C., & Ashkanasy, N. (2001). Communicating trustworthiness and building trust in interorganizational virtual organizations. *Journal of Management*, *27*, 235–254. doi:10.1016/S0149-2063(01)00090-3

Kogut, B., & Zander, U. (1992). Knowledge of the firm: combinative capabilities, and the replication of technology. *Organization Science*, *3*, 383–397. doi:10.1287/orsc.3.3.383

Koh, J., & Kim, Y.-G. (2004). Knowledge sharing in virtual communities: an e-business perspective. *Expert Systems with Applications*, *26*, 155–166. doi:10.1016/S0957-4174(03)00116-7

Kraut, R., Patterson, M., Lundmark, V., Kiesler, S., Mukopadhyay, T., & Scherlis, W. (1998). Internet paradox. *The American Psychologist*, *53*, 1017–1031. doi:10.1037/0003-066X.53.9.1017

Krippendorff, K. (1975). Some principles of information storage and retrieval in society. *General Systems*, *20*, 15–35.

Kuhn, T. S. (1962). *The Structure of Scientific Revolutions*. Chicago: The University of Chicago Press.

Lane, C. (1998). Introduction. In C. Lane, & R. Bachmann (eds.), *Trust Within and Between Organizations*. New York: Oxford University Press.

Lane, P. J., & Lubatkin, M. (1998). Relative absorptive capacity and interorganizational learning. *Strategic Management Journal*, *19*, 461–477. doi:10.1002/(SICI)1097-0266(199805)19:5<461::AID-SMJ953>3.0.CO;2-L

Lave, J., & Wenger, E. (1991). *Situated Learning: Legitimate Peripheral Participation*. New York: Cambridge University Press.

Lea, M., & Spears, R. (1991). Computer-mediated communication, deindividuation and group decision-making. *International Journal of Man-Machine Studies*, *34*, 283–301. doi:10.1016/0020-7373(91)90045-9

Lee, G. K., & Cole, R. E. (2003). From a firm-based to a community-based model of knowledge creation: the case of the Linux kernel development. *Organization Science*, *14*, 633–649. doi:10.1287/orsc.14.6.633.24866

Lesser, E., & Everest, K. (2001). Using communities of practice to managing intellectual capital. *Ivey Business Journal*, *65*, 37–41.

Li, W., Ardichivili, A., Maurer, M., Wentling, T., & Studemann, R. (2007). Impact of Chinese culture values of knowledge sharing through online communities of practice. *International Journal of Knowledge Management*, *3*, 46–59.

Mayer, R. C., Davis, J. H., & Schoorman, F. D. (1995). An integrative model of organizational trust. *Academy of Management Review*, *20*, 709–734. doi:10.2307/258792

McDermott, R. (1999). Why information technology inspired but cannot deliver knowledge management. *California Management Review*, *41*, 103–117.

McElroy, M. (2002). Social innovation capital. *Journal of Intellectual Capital*, *3*, 30–39. doi:10.1108/14691930210412827

McKnight, B., & Bontis, N. (2002). E-improvisation: collaborative groupware technology expands the reach and effectiveness of organizational improvisation. *Knowledge and Process Management*, *9*, 219–227. doi:10.1002/kpm.154

McKnight, D. H., Cummings, L. L., & Chervany, N. L. (1998). Initial trust formation in new organizational relationships. *Academy of Management Review*, *23*, 473–490. doi:10.2307/259290

Meyerson, D., Weick, K. E., & Kramer, R. M. (1996). Swift trust in temporary groups. In R. M. Kramer, & T. R. Tyler (eds.), *Trust in Organizations: Frontiers of Theory and Research*. Thousand Oaks: Sage Publications.

Nahapiet, J., & Ghoshal, S. (1998). Social capital, intellectual capital, and the organizational advantage. *Academy of Management Review*, *23*, 242–266. doi:10.2307/259373

Naughton, J. (1999). *A Brief History of the Future: The Origins of the Internet*. London: Weidenfield & Nicholson.

Nonaka, I., & Takeuchi, H. (1995). *The Knowledge-creating Company - How Japanese Companies Create the Dynamic of Innovation*. Oxford: Oxford University Press.

Nonaka, I., Toyama, R., & Konno, N. (2001). SECI, Ba and leadership: a unified model of dynamic knowledge creation. In I. Nonaka, & D. J. Teece (eds.), *Managing Industrial Knowledge: Creation, Transfer and Utilization*. London: Sage Publications.

Paepcke, A. (1996). Digital Libraries: Searching is not enough. *D-Lib Magazine*, (May): 1996.

Palmer, R. (1993). *Write in Style – A Guide to Good English*. London: E & FN Spon.

Pan, S. L., & Leidner, D. E. (2003). Bridging communities of practice with information technology in pursuit of global knowledge sharing. *The Journal of Strategic Information Systems*, *12*, 71–88. doi:10.1016/S0963-8687(02)00023-9

Pentland, B. T. (1995). Information systems and organizational learning: the social epistemology of organizational knowledge systems. *Accounting . Management and Information Technologies*, *5*, 1–21. doi:10.1016/0959-8022(95)90011-X

Pickering, J. M., & King, J. L. (1995). Hardwiring weak ties: interorganizational computer-mediated communication, occupational communities, and organizational change. *Organization Science*, *6*, 479–486. doi:10.1287/orsc.6.4.479

Preece, J. (2000). *Online Communities: Designing Usability, Supporting Sociability*. Chichester: John Viley & Sons.

Purvis, R. L., Sambamurthy, V., & Zmud, R. W. (2001). The assimilation of knowledge platforms in organizations: an empirical investigation. *Organization Science*, *12*, 117–135. doi:10.1287/orsc.12.2.117.10115

Reagans, R., & McEvily, B. (2003). Network structure and knowledge transfer: The effects of cohesion and range. *Administrative Science Quarterly*, *48*, 240–267. doi:10.2307/3556658

Reddy, M. L. (1979). The conduit metaphor: a case of frame conflict in our language about language. In A. Ortony (Ed.), *Metaphor and thought*. Cambridge: Cambridge University Press.

Roberts, J. (2000). From know-how to show-how: the role of information and communication technologies in the transfer of knowledge. *Technology Analysis and Strategic Management*, *12*(4), 429–443. doi:10.1080/713698499

Roberts, J. (2003). Limits to communities of practice. *Journal of Management Studies*, *43*(3), 623–639. doi:10.1111/j.1467-6486.2006.00618.x

Ryssen, S. V., & Godar, S. H. (2000). Going international without going international: multinational virtual teams. *Journal of International Management*, *6*, 49–60. doi:10.1016/S1075-4253(00)00019-3

Schenkel, A., & Teigland, R. (2008). Improved organizational performance through communities of practice. *Journal of Knowledge Management*, *12*(1), 106–118. doi:10.1108/13673270810852421

Schultz, M. (2003). Pathways of relevance: Exploring inflows of knowledge into subunits of multinational corporations. *Organization Science*, *14*, 440–459. doi:10.1287/orsc.14.4.440.17483

Shotter, J. (1993). *Conversational Realities: Constructing Life through Language*. London: Sage Publications.

Soo, C., Devinney, T., Midgley, D., & Deering, A. (2002). Knowledge management: philosophy, processes and pitfalls. *California Management Review, 44*, 129–150.

Sperber, D., & Wilson, D. (1995). *Relevance: Communication and Cognition*. Oxford UK: Blackwell.

Stein, E. W. (2005). A qualitative study of the characteristics of a community of practice for knowledge management and its success factors. *International Journal of Knowledge Management, 1*, 1–24.

Stein, E. W., & Zwass, V. (1995). Actualizing organizational memory with information systems. *Information Systems Research, 6*(2), 85–117. doi:10.1287/isre.6.2.85

Storck, J., & Hill, P. A. (2000). Knowledge diffusion through "strategic communities". *Sloan Management Review, 41*, 63–74.

Swan, J., Scarbrough, H., & Robertson, M. (2002). The construction of "communities of practice" in the management of innovation. *Management Learning, 33*, 477–496. doi:10.1177/1350507602334005

Szulanski, G. (2000). The process of knowledge transfer: A diachronic analysis of stickiness. *Organizational Behavior and Human Decision Processes, 82*, 9–27. doi:10.1006/obhd.2000.2884

Teece, D. J. (2001). Strategies for managing knowledge assets: the role of firm structure and industrial context. In I. Nonaka, I. & D. J. Teece (eds.), *Managing Industrial Knowledge: Creation, Transfer and Utilization*. London: Sage Publications.

Thompson, M. (2005). Structural and epistemic parameters in communities of practice. *Organization Science, 16*(2), 151–164. doi:10.1287/orsc.1050.0120

Tiwana, A. (2000). *The Knowledge Management Toolkit*. Prentice Hall: Upper Saddle River, NJ.

Uzzi, B. (1997). Social structure and competition in interfirm networks: the paradox of embeddedness. *Administrative Science Quarterly, 42*, 35–67. doi:10.2307/2393808

Vizcaino, A., Soto, J. P., Portillo-Rodríguez, J., & Piattini, M. (2007). Developing knowledge management systems form a knowledge-based and multi-agent approach. *International Journal of Knowledge Management, 3*(4), 67–83.

Walther, J. B. (1995). Relational aspects of computer-mediated communication: experimental observations over time. *Organization Science, 6*, 186–203. doi:10.1287/orsc.6.2.186

Wasko, M. M., & Faraj, S. (2005). Why should I share? Examining social capital and knowledge contribution in electronic networks of practice. *MIS Quarterly, 29*(1), 35–57.

Welch, D., Welch, L., & Piekkari, R. (2005). Speaking in tongues: The importance of language in international management processes. *International Studies of Management and Organization, 1*, 10–27.

Wellman, B., & Gulia, M. (1999). Virtual communities as communities: net surfers don't ride alone. In M. A. Smith, & P. Kollock, (eds.), *Communities in Cyberspace*. London: Routledge.

Wenger, E. (1998). *Communities of Practice: Learning, Meaning, and Identity*. Cambridge: Cambridge University Press.

Wenger, E., McDermott, R., & Snyder, W. M. (2002). *Cultivating Communities of Practice: A Guide to Managing Knowledge*. Boston, MA: Harvard Business School Press.

Wenger, E. C., & Snyder, W. M. (2000). Communities of Practice: The Organizational Frontier. *Harvard Business Review, 78*, 139–145.

Wiesenfeld, B. M., Raghuram, S., & Garud, R. (1999). Communication patterns as determinants of organizational identification in a virtual organization. *Organization Science*, *10*, 777–790. doi:10.1287/orsc.10.6.777

Witzel, M. (2003). The world's first virtual business organization. *European Business Forum,* Issue 13, 72-74.

Yates, J., Orlikowski, W., & Okamura, K. (1999). Explicit and Implicit Structuring of Genres in Electronic Communication: Reinforcement and Change of Social Interaction. *Organization Science*, *10*(1), 83–103. doi:10.1287/orsc.10.1.83

Zack, M. H. (1999). Managing codified knowledge. *Sloan Management Review*, *40*, 45–58.

Zand, D. E. (1972). Trust and managerial problem solving. *Administrative Science Quarterly*, *17*, 229–239. doi:10.2307/2393957

Zhang, W., & Watts, S. (2008). Online communities as communities of practice: a case study. *Journal of Knowledge Management*, *12*(4), 55–71. doi:10.1108/13673270810884255

Zucchermaglio, C., & Talamo, A. (2003). The development of a virtual community of practice using electronic mail and communicative genres. *Journal of Business and Technical Communication*, *17*, 259–284. doi:10.1177/1050651903017003001

Chapter 4
Organizational Culture for Knowledge Management Systems:
A Study of Corporate Users

Andrew P. Ciganek
Jacksonville State University, USA

En Mao
Nicholls State University, USA

Mark Srite
University of Wisconsin-Milwaukee, USA

ABSTRACT

Knowledge is increasingly being viewed as a critical component for organizations. It is largely people-based and the characteristics of groups of individuals, in the form of organizational cultures, may play a key role in the factors that lead to either the acceptance or rejection of knowledge management systems (KMS). The primary objective of this research is to explore how dimensions of organizational culture influence factors that lead to the acceptance of KMS. While researchers have agreed that culture plays an important role in KMS, the literature has only recently begun to examine organizational culture within this context. We examined the effects of three dimensions of organizational culture through a research model that was tested and analyzed utilizing a field survey of corporate knowledge management users. Our results indicated that both process-oriented and open communication system organizational cultures significantly influenced the factors that led to the acceptance of KMS.

INTRODUCTION

Organizational culture can either facilitate or be a major barrier to knowledge management system (KMS) acceptance (De Long & Fahey, 2000; Grover & Davenport, 2001; Ruppel & Harrington, 2001). On February 1, 2003, the space shuttle Columbia was lost during its return to Earth. The Columbia Accident Investigation Board (CAIB) concluded that NASA's organizational culture as well as the piece of Columbia's foam insulation that fell off during launch shared equal blame for the tragedy (CAIB, 2003). According to the CAIB, the prevailing culture at NASA was of a mindset that accidents were inevitable, which led to the unnecessary acceptance of known and preventable risks. Although a KMS to assist with hazard identification and risk assessment was available at NASA (the Lessons Learned Information System), personnel only used that system on an *ad hoc* basis which limited its usefulness (CAIB, 2003). NASA's organizational culture consequently interfered with open communication, impeded the sharing of lessons learned, caused duplication and unnecessary expenditure of resources, and prompted resistance to external advice (CAIB, 2003).

The Columbia incident is an illustration of knowledge management system use failure. The acceptance of KMS, however, is a pressing issue in organizations (Kwan & Balasubramanian, 2003; Money & Turner, 2005). As knowledge is increasingly viewed as a critical activity for decision making (Markus, Majchrzak, & Gasser, 2002; Miranda & Saunders, 2003), organizations are becoming more receptive to using technologies to facilitate knowledge management (Schultze & Leidner, 2002). KMS are often employed to enhance organizational performance (De Long & Fahey, 2000) and are a reason why the KMS market has become one of the fastest growing areas in software development. While it is widely recognized that information technologies have the potential to facilitate knowledge management, the management of knowledge-based systems is an intricate process that involves a complex interplay of technical and social factors.

Recent studies have begun to investigate a variety of social factors and phenomena related to knowledge creation, sharing, and transfer. For example, Wasko and Faraj (2005) studied how individual motivations and social capital influence knowledge sharing in KMS. Ko, Kirsch, and King (2005) found that individual communication capabilities, motivations, and interpersonal relationships affected the transfer of complex enterprise software knowledge. Bock, Zmud, Kim, and Lee (2005) found that subjective norms and organizational climate had a significant impact on people's intention to share knowledge. Kankanhalli, Tan, and Wei (2005) similarly discovered that several social factors, including prosharing norms, influenced knowledge contribution. These studies provided strong empirical evidence of the social influences in knowledge management. Some of the factors that have been examined are conceptually similar to organizational culture dimensions that have been identified in the management literature. A more systematic study of organizational culture on KMS acceptance would provide theoretical congruence to this recent literature.

The primary objective of this research is to explore how dimensions of organizational culture influence the factors that lead to the acceptance of KMS (e.g., perceived usefulness, perceived ease-of-use, perceived behavioral control, subjective norms). In our investigation, organizational culture is postulated as a distal determinant for an employee's intention to use a KMS. In the next section, we present a literature review to support our hypotheses, followed by a discussion of our research methodology. We then empirically test our hypotheses with a field survey of corporate KMS users, discuss the results, and finish with some concluding remarks.

LITERATURE REVIEW

Knowledge Management Systems

Knowledge is information that exists in the mind of individuals (Alavi & Leidner, 2001; Berman-Brown & Woodland, 1999; Grover & Davenport, 2001; Ruppel & Harrington, 2001). Given the nature of knowledge, which is created and applied in the minds of human beings, it is extremely difficult to manage and control (Alvesson & Karreman, 2001; Grover & Davenport, 2001). Indeed, an organization's efforts to facilitate knowledge sharing can be a "central competitive dimension" for a firm (Kogut & Zander, 1992, p. 384). Consequently, KMS are an organization's efforts to facilitate knowledge sharing through the use of information technology (IT) in order to obtain organizational benefits.

There are a variety of KMS that exist, such as knowledge repositories, corporate directories, and knowledge networks (Alavi & Leidner, 2001; Grover & Davenport, 2001). Knowledge repositories, the type of IT examined in this study, are the most common KMS in Western organizations (Grover & Davenport, 2001). These systems are typically used to capture knowledge from employees for subsequent and extensive use by others within the organization to assist in decision-making. Examples of knowledge that are contained in such systems may range from best practices and lessons learned to organizational strategies and recruitment efforts.

There have been a number of KMS reviews and meta-analyses done in the information systems (IS) domain. Alavi & Leidner (2001) provided a review of the knowledge management literature in different academic disciplines that identified some key areas of research, which included the concept of knowledge in organizations, knowledge management processes (i.e., knowledge creation, storage/retrieval, and transfer), and KMS. They indicated that while the design of a KMS is important, the extent of use by its intended users would also have a significant impact on KMS acceptance. Schultze & Leidner (2002) also examined knowledge management research in the IS area. They identified and classified knowledge management research into four theoretical streams, which are normative, interpretive, critical, and dialogic discourses. Subsequent case-based research (Alavi, Kayworth, & Leidner, 2005-2006; Leidner, Alavi, & Kayworth, 2006) has found that differences in organizational cultural values leads to different uses of KMS. These research efforts demonstrated the importance and saliency of KMS in the IS context.

Organizational Culture

NASA's organizational culture had as much to do with this accident as foam did. Columbia Accident Investigation Report (CAIB, 2003)

As suggested in the quotation above, organizational culture is important and inextricably linked to KMS within organizations (Alavi & Leidner, 2001; Alvesson & Karreman, 2001; Cronin, 2001; De Long & Fahey, 2000; Grover & Davenport, 2001; McDermott, 1999; Tanriverdi, 2005). Organizational culture has been extensively studied in management research, and therefore, it is surprising that the relationship between KMS and an organization's culture has not been more thoroughly explored in the IS literature. Culture has historically been a factor that has received insufficient attention in the IS acceptance literature (Cooper, 1994; Robey, Wishart, & Rodriguez-Diaz, 1995a; Ruppel & Harrington, 2001), but is increasingly being viewed as a key ingredient for an organization's ability to embrace KMS (Cronin, 2001).

Organizational culture is widely believed to be a major barrier to KMS acceptance (De Long & Fahey, 2000; Grover & Davenport, 2001; Ruppel & Harrington, 2001). Without a match between an organization's culture and the cultural assumptions embedded within an IT innovation, costly implementation failures are likely to happen (Ruppel & Harrington, 2001). For example, in organizational cultures that are not suited to share and utilize knowledge (e.g., an organization where miscommunication is common and mistrust is prevalent), acceptance of a KMS can be problematic (Ruppel & Harrington, 2001). Without acknowledging cultural mismatches or modifying the organizational culture to better fit the IT, the impact on the organization could be disastrous, as evidenced in the Colombia tragedy.

Hofstede (1991) views culture as being collective, but often intangible and is what distinguishes one group, organization, or nation from another. There are two main elements of culture: the internal values of culture (invisible) and external elements of culture (visible), which are known as practices (Hofstede, 1991). Practices are particularly important to investigate because they are the most direct means for changing behaviors needed to support knowledge creation, sharing, and use (De Long & Fahey, 2000). Hofstede, Neuijen, Ohayv, and Sanders (1990) measured the perceived practices in employees' work situations in 20 organizational units and discovered six dimensions underlying organizational culture. Contrary to his dimensions of national culture (Hofstede, 1991), these organizational dimensions deal with key sociological issues. In favor of depicting a more manageable research model, we examine three dimensions of organizational culture, process-oriented vs. results-oriented, employee-oriented vs. job-oriented, and open communication systems vs. closed communication systems.

Technology Acceptance

Previous findings from the technology acceptance literature, which has been widely popular in the IS field for the past few years, suggest that for an advantage to be attained, the technology in question must be accepted and used (Venkatesh, Morris, Davis, & Davis, 2003). Organizations typically employ KMS to leverage their collective knowledge for competitive advantage (Alavi & Leidner, 2001). There has been relatively little research, however, that explicitly examines the influence that dimensions of organizational culture have on technology acceptance.

In the technology acceptance literature, a variety of psychological constructs have been examined with the goal of understanding how and why individuals adopt new information technologies. This has generated several competing models of technology acceptance, each with different sets of determinants for acceptance (Venkatesh et al., 2003). The following is a concise review of attributes that have been consistently shown to account for a significant amount of variance in the prediction of intentions and behaviors (Rogers, 2003; Tornatzky & Klein, 1982; Venkatesh et al., 2003).

Attributes of the Acceptance and Use of Technology

Based upon conceptual and empirical similarities across eight prominent models in the user acceptance literature, Venkatesh et al. (2003) developed a unified theory of individual acceptance of technology (the unified theory of acceptance and use of technology or UTAUT). The UTAUT theorizes four constructs having a significant role as direct determinants of acceptance and usage behavior: performance expectancy, effort expectancy, social influence, and facilitating conditions. Although we did not test the full UTAUT because the model was not published at the time of our data collection, each of the constructs that we did examine was conceptually similar. The four constructs that we utilized and their relationships to the constructs of the UTAUT model are discussed next.

The first construct examined in our model is perceived usefulness. Originally proposed in Davis' (1989) technology acceptance model (TAM), this is contained within the UTAUT construct of performance expectancy and is defined as "the degree to which an individual believes that using the system will help him or her to attain gains in job performance" (Venkatesh et al., 2003, p. 447). The second construct examined in our model is perceived ease of use. This construct, originally in Davis' (1989) TAM, is incorporated into UTAUT as part of effort expectancy which is defined as "the degree of ease associated with the use of the system" (Venkatesh et al., 2003, p. 450). Perceived ease of use has a significant direct effect on perceived usefulness (Davis, 1989).

The third construct examined, perceived behavioral control, indicates that a person's motivation is influenced by how difficult the behaviors are perceived to be, as well as the perception of how successfully the individual can, or cannot, perform the activity. Perceived behavioral control, originally in the theory of planned behavior (TPB) (Ajzen, 1985; Ajzen & Madden, 1986), is part of UTAUT's facilitating conditions construct which is defined as "the degree to which an individual believes that an organizational and technical infrastructure exists to support the use of the system" (Venkatesh et al., 2003, p. 453). Subjective norms, the fourth construct examined in this model, deals with the influence of important others, such as coworkers, supervisors, and top management. Subjective norms, originally in Fishbein & Ajzen's (1975) theory of reasoned action (TRA), are incorporated into UTAUT's construct of social influence, which is defined as "the degree to which an individual perceives that important others believe he or she should use the system" (Venkatesh et al., 2003, p. 451).

RESEARCH HYPOTHESES

Organizational Culture's Impact on Perceived Usefulness

An organization's attitude toward change, often elicited and reflected by the introduction of technology innovations, impacts the adoption of these technologies (Damanpour, 1991). Some organizations are relatively *process-oriented* and may have conservative attitudes toward innovation and its associated risk, exerting minimal effort while preferring the use of existing or well-known methods (Hofstede et al., 1990). Such organizations innovate only when they are seriously challenged by their competition or by shifting consumer preferences (Miller & Friesen, 1982). In contrast, *results-oriented* organizations are risk-oriented and foster an environment that encourages and actively supports the use of innovative techniques for the survival and growth of the organization (Hofstede et al., 1990). As an organization's policies and practices are perceived by employees to encourage, cultivate, and reward their use of a technology (e.g., KMS) the stronger that culture will be for the implementation of that technology (Klein & Sorra, 1996). Organizations that promote innovativeness and a willingness to try new things among their employees have been found to have better success with a KMS implementation (Ruppel & Harrington, 2001). Such organizations and individuals usually try to obtain a competitive advantage by routinely making dramatic innovative changes and taking the inherent risks associated with those innovations. Consequently, employees in a results-oriented organization are likely to believe that using KMS would enhance their job performance. On the other hand, knowledge sharing is risky from an individual employees' perspective because their value depends largely on the knowledge they possess (Stenmark, 2000). A work environment that is more process-oriented, consequently, would view KMS as a threat and to be less useful for making decisions. This leads to the following hypothesis:

H1: *Employees who perceive their work environment to be more* ***results-oriented*** *will have higher levels of perceived usefulness than employees who perceive their work environment to be more* ***process-oriented****.*

Organizational Culture's Impact on Perceived Ease of Use

At one end of a continuum, job roles in an organizational environment are routine and similar from one day to the next (*process-oriented*) (Hofstede et al., 1990). Employees in this environment are resistant to change, new technology, and risk and will only exert minimal effort. At the opposite end of this continuum, job roles bring forth new challenges daily (*results-oriented*) (Hofstede et al., 1990). Employees in this results-oriented environment embrace risk, are comfortable in unknown situations, and are likely to more quickly exploit any opportunity that a technology may offer. These individuals are likely to have more experience using innovative or relatively complex technologies, and as a result, have a relatively high belief that using other complex technologies would not be difficult. In fact, complexity is the degree to which an innovation is perceived as being difficult to use and has the opposite meaning of ease of use (Davis, Bagozzi, & Warshaw, 1989; Moore & Benbasat, 1991; Thompson, Higgins, & Howell, 1991). Therefore, employees who work in an environment that is characterized as a results-oriented organization where using new or complex technologies in their daily tasks is common are more likely to believe that KMS are easy to use. Hence:

H2: *Employees who perceive their work environment to be more* ***results-oriented*** *will have higher levels of perceived ease of use than employees who perceive their work environment to be more* ***process-oriented****.*

Organizational Culture's Impact on Perceived Behavioral Control

When employees are asked to put what they know into a KMS, they tend to feel as if they have lost ownership of the knowledge that they alone had previously controlled (De Long & Fahey, 2000). Individuals tend to resist such systems because when giving up control of their knowledge they may perceive their worth as an employee to be marginal, which is only propagated by the understandable fear that their job position has become interchangeable. In such circumstances an organization's culture is critical for the acceptance of KMS. As stated earlier, *results-oriented* organizations are risk-oriented, fostering an environment of daily challenges where employees feel comfortable in unknown situations (Hofstede et al., 1990). Although employees in results-oriented organizations may encounter more risky events, their capacity to tolerate risks is much stronger. Employees in this type of risk inclined environment would likely have strong beliefs in their ability to control outcomes (Delfabbro & Winefield, 2000) and hence, will be less worried about the potential negative issues associated with sharing knowledge. The more control an employee thinks they possess, the greater should be that person's perceived control over their behavior (Ajzen & Madden, 1986). Therefore, employees that work in an environment that is characterized as a results-oriented organization would believe that they can control the technology they use, which would make them more likely to use KMS. Hence:

H3: *Employees who perceive their work environment to be more* ***results-oriented*** *will have higher levels of perceived behavioral control than employees who perceive their work environment to be more* ***process-oriented****.*

Environments that typically do not favor KMS emphasize unilateral control, have high stakes for winning and losing, and attempt to minimize negative emotions (Ruppel & Harrington, 2001). Competition thrives in such environments and mistrust in others is high as sharing information or helping fellow employees is frowned upon because it creates a disadvantage for the employee being generous. A *job-oriented* environment exemplifies this scenario as it is an atmosphere where employees feel pressured to complete work (Hofstede et al., 1990).

On the other hand, an *employee-oriented* environment is one where individual personal problems are addressed and the organization has a genuine concern for the employee's welfare (Hofstede et al., 1990). This is critical particularly in the acceptance of KMS where employees must be able divulge, support, and trust the knowledge provided by other employees via the technology. The human relations management and job enrichment literatures (Hackman & Oldham, 1980) suggest that intrinsic rewards (e.g., employee of the month recognition) are at times more important than extrinsic rewards (e.g., salary raises, promotion). Resource-based theory also acknowledges the vital role that human assets/resources play in the contemporary hypercompetitive external environments where progressive organizations strive to keep their employees satisfied and thus retain top talent. Indeed, Ruppel & Harrington (2001) found that early adoption of KMS was most likely to occur in organizations where the culture was characterized as having a high concern for its employees and a setting of mutual confidence and trust. Consequently, employees who work in an environment that is characterized as an employee-oriented organization would be more likely to believe that they have access to greater opportunities and resources to perform a behavior than in a pressure-filled, job-oriented environment. Hence:

H4: *Employees who perceive their work environment to be more* ***employee-oriented*** *will have higher levels of perceived behavioral control than employees who perceive their work environment to be more* ***job-oriented****.*

Organizational Culture's Impact on Subjective Norms

An organizational culture that discourages open communication engenders a context that undermines knowledge sharing (De Long & Fahey, 2000). This is similar to a *closed communication system*, an environment that is secretive and reserved and also one in which it takes a relatively long time for employees to "fit in" (Hofstede et al., 1990). For KMS to be widely accepted within an organization, it should have a culture that supports knowledge sharing from a wide spectrum of coworkers, supervisors, and managers. Without this support, employees may not be willing to share and disseminate their knowledge and experiences, thus making the KMS essentially useless. Indeed, instilling a culture of sharing and maintaining information is critical for KMS acceptance.

An *open communication system*, alternatively, is an environment that is characterized as being open to newcomers and outsiders where it takes a relatively short time for employees to feel comfortable in the organization (Hofstede et al., 1990). Employees in this type of environment are likely to more willingly share their experiences and to support one another when attempting to make decisions on complex and unknown topic areas (e.g., relevance and mastery of new technologies). It is reasonable to expect that users of KMS would be more willing and prepared to assume any challenges posed by the new technology environment in view of the support that they can expect from their colleagues. Employees who work in an environment characterized by an open communication system, therefore, are more likely to be influenced by the opinions of important others and be more likely to use KMS. Hence:

H5: *Employees who perceive their work environment to be more* ***open*** *will have higher levels of subjective norms than employees who perceive their work environment to be more* ***closed****.*

Consistent with the TAM, the TRA, the TPB, and the UTAUT, perceived usefulness, perceived ease of use, perceived behavioral control, and subjective norms are expected to influence behavioral intentions. Following the technology acceptance model, perceived ease of use is expected to influence perceived usefulness. These relationships as well as our research hypotheses are depicted in the proposed theoretical model (Figure 1).

METHODOLOGY

This research utilized a questionnaire borrowing scales from prior literature. We adopted measures of organizational culture from Hofstede et al. (1990), perceived usefulness, perceived ease of use, and behavioral intention to use from Davis (1989), and perceived behavioral control from Ajzen & Madden (1986). The subjective norms construct contains two dimensions: normative beliefs (similar to the construct developed by Fishbein & Ajzen (1975) and motivation to comply from Bandura (1977). The subjective norms construct was formed by multiplying pairs of items (normative beliefs * motivation to comply). The order of the statements in the questionnaire was scrambled randomly to control for order effects. The dependent variable, behavioral intention was selected as it has been validated in prior literature as a reliable proxy for actual use in behavioral research (Magnus & Niclas, 2003). The questionnaire employed a 7-point Likert-style scale, anchored from 1 (strongly disagree) to 7 (strongly agree).

Data Collection

The instrument was pilot tested using 24 MBA students who were familiar with KMS. The reliability and validity of all eight research constructs were found to be acceptable. A field survey was then administered via two procedures within a 1 week period. We first surveyed KMS users from a leading user group in a major Midwestern U.S. city. The KMS utilized by the users were repository-based and included applications for sharing corporate knowledge, best practices, and lessons learned, among others. We distributed paper-based surveys after briefly explaining our research agenda. There were 64 attendees that were solicited to participate with 41 completing the paper-based survey, yielding a response rate of 64%.

The initial participants in the study were subsequently asked to recruit additional KMS users within their firms via an online Web-based survey, which had the same questions in identical sequence as the paper-based version. The participants represented seven companies from a variety of industries, including manufacturing, finance, consulting, and education. The Web-based survey

Figure 1. Theoretical model

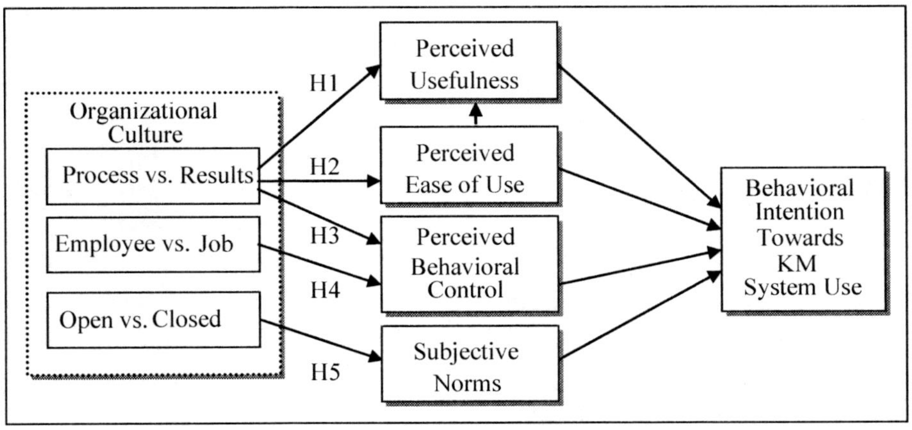

provided an additional 144 completed surveys from 7 companies, yielding an approximate response rate of 29% (144/500). This resulted in a total sample size of 185 (41 paper and 144 Web). With the exception of a single item, out of 31 total items, there were no significant differences between the paper-based and Web-based surveys after performing a series of t-tests at both the construct and item levels. The single item was not removed from the analysis because dropping it lowered the reliability of its construct. The mean age of the respondents was 38, and 60% of the participants were female and 40% were male. On average, the respondents had 15 years of work experience, 13 years of computing experience, and 2 years of KMS experience.

Consistent with the technology acceptance studies, gender (Venkatesh & Morris, 2000), age (Gist, Rosen, & Schwoerer, 1988; Igbaria, Parasuraman, & Baroudi, 1996), and experience (Venkatesh et al., 2003) were tested as control variables to see if they had a moderating effect on behavioral intention to use. Following Venkatesh et al. (2003), a hierarchical regression analysis was used to test the direct and moderating effects because sample size considerations prevented us from running the interaction terms in LISREL (our primary analysis tool). The moderating effects were modeled as interaction terms between the moderators and perceived usefulness (PU), perceived ease of use (PEOU), perceived behavioral control (PBC), and subjective norms (SN). With direct effects, PU, SN, and PBC were significant. With both direct and interaction effects, PU, PU x gender, PU x age, PU x gender x age, and PBC x experience were significant.

Psychometric Measures

The data were analyzed using the structural equation modeling (SEM) technique, which is suitable because our research model contains latent variables. The model was tested using the two-step approach where the measurement model fit was first assessed followed by the structural model testing in which the path coefficients were estimated (Bollen, 1989). The reliability and validity of the data were tested before model assessment and the results demonstrated acceptable psychometric properties. The reliability coefficients of all eight constructs, with two exceptions, were above .70, which is an acceptable value as stated by Nunnally (1967). The employee-oriented vs. job-oriented and open communication system vs. closed communication system constructs were at .69. They were retained because they were close to the cutoff levell.

Construct validity was assessed by comparing the correlation coefficients within and between constructs. The average within construct correlation was .40, which is higher than the between constructs correlation of .19. The within construct correlations were higher than between constructs correlations, indicating construct validity. In addition, we examined convergent and divergent validity and tested the data for normality. Even though the maximum likelihood estimator performs relatively well under various conditions (Hoyle & Panter, 1995), it assumes the normality of the data. The mean skewness and kurtosis values were -.47 and .33 respectively, indicating that the variables approximate a normal distribution and were acceptable for LISREL analysis (Bollen, 1989; Byrne, 1998; West, Finch, & Curran, 1995).

Chi-square goodness-of-fit statistic, comparative fit index, and the root mean square error of approximation were also assessed. Chi-square (χ^2) goodness-of-fit statistic assesses the degree of departure of the sample covariance matrix from the fitted covariance matrix (Hu & Bentler, 1999) . A nonsignificant and small chi-square is desirable. Because the chi-square statistic is a direct product of sample size, when the sample size is large and models contain a large number of indicators, the statistic can often be significant (Byrne, 1998). The comparative fit index (CFI) and root mean square error of approximation

(RMSEA), however, are not sensitive to sample size. The comparative fit index is an incremental fit index that measures the improvement in fit by comparing a target model with a restricted, nested base model (Hu & Bentler, 1999). In addition, it is suggested as the best approximation of the population value for a single model (Medsker, Williams, & Holahan, 1994). The general accepted value is above .90. The root mean square error of approximation, a type of absolute fit index, assesses how well sample data are reproduced from an *a priori* model (Hu & Bentler, 1999). The general accepted cutoff is .10.

Using LISREL 8.54, we first tested the measurement model. Its fit statistics were χ^2 (406 df, N = 185) = 685.63, p < .001, CFI = .95, and RMSEA = .061. Overall, the statistics demonstrated good fit and the measures were acceptable for structural model assessment. Good model statistics are indicative of unidimensionality and convergent validity (Gefen, Karahanna, & Straub, 2003). Divergent validity was assessed by comparing the original measurement model with an alterative model that includes all items as one construct (Segars, 1997). The χ^2 was significantly smaller in the original measurement model ($\chi^2_{\text{Alternative}}$ = 3234.07, χ^2 difference = 2548.44 with *df* change = 28, *p* = .00) establishing discriminant validity (Segars, 1997).

We assessed 10 paths in the structural model testing. The model fit statistics were χ^2 (421 df, N = 185) = 771.33, p < .001, CFI = .93, and RMSEA = .067. Overall, the statistics demonstrated a good fit of the model to the data. Figure 2 shows the estimated standardized path coefficients and their t-values in the structural model and the variance explained for each of the constructs. The asterisks on the path indicate the significance level and the variance explained are presented below the asterisks in parentheses. All links except those between an employee-oriented vs. job-oriented organizational culture and perceived behavioral control and between perceived ease of use and behavioral intention were significant. The model had adequate predictive power for several constructs, including perceived usefulness (R^2_{PU} = .43), subjective norms (R^2_{SN} = .22), and behavioral intention (R^2_{BI} = .61). However, the predictive power was somewhat less for perceived ease of use (R^2_{PEOU} = .03) and perceived behavioral control (R^2_{PBC} = .09). In regard to the variance extracted in behavioral intention, our model exhibited better predictive power (.61) than that shown in the hierarchical regression with direct effects (.48), as well as direct effects and interaction effects (e.g., age, gender, experience) combined (.58).

The theoretical model was modified to add direct paths of the cultural dimensions influencing behavioral intention. None of the direct paths from the cultural dimensions to behavioral intention were significant. The change between the theoretical model and the modified model in χ^2 was 5.49 with 3 degrees of freedom (p = .1392). This suggested that the effects of the cultural dimensions on behavioral intention were mediated and, consequently, the theoretical model was utilized.

DISCUSSION

There was support for four out of the five research hypotheses. These results suggest that the organizational culture dimensions play a key role in the factors that lead to the acceptance of KMS. Our research also examined several prominent technology acceptance relationships and had similar findings to other research that has investigated the applicability of such relationships with the user acceptance of a KMS (Money & Turner, 2005). The relationships between perceived usefulness and behavioral intention to use a KMS, subjective norms, and behavioral intention to use a KMS, perceived behavioral control, and behavioral intention to use a KMS, and perceived ease of use and perceived usefulness were all significant. The relationship between perceived ease of use and behavioral intention to use a KMS, however, was

Figure 2. Structural path coefficients

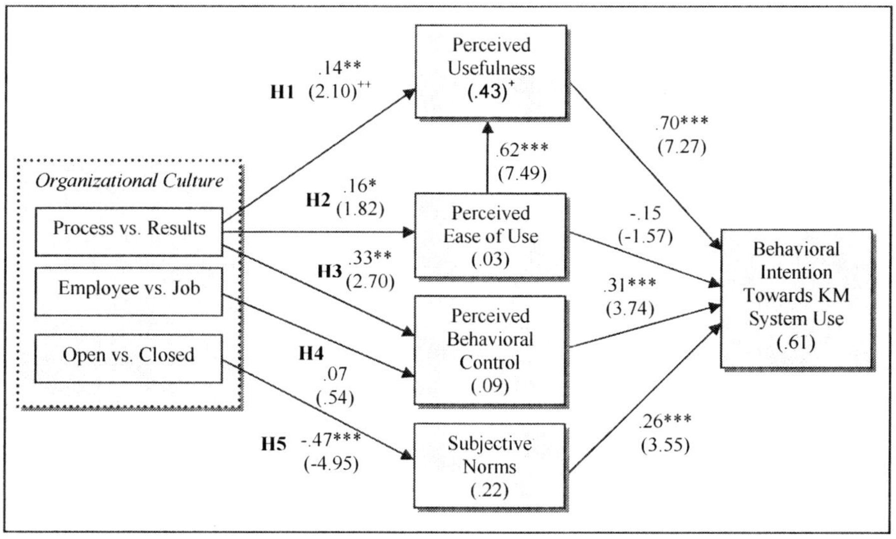

** P < .10, ** p < .05, *** p < .001*

not significant although there was still a significant path through the model incorporating perceived usefulness. These findings are consistent with other studies of extended technology acceptance models (e.g., Adams, Nelson, & Todd, 1992; Hu, Chau, Sheng, & Tam, 1999).

In general, our model explained a reasonable amount of variation of the key variables. The variation in process-oriented vs. results-oriented organizational cultures (as well as the variation in perceptions of ease of use) explained 43% of the variation in perceptions of usefulness. Furthermore, the variability in process-oriented vs. results-oriented cultures explained 3% of the variance of perceived ease of use. Similarly, open communication systems vs. closed communication systems organizational cultures explained 22% of the variance in subjective norms and 9% of the variance in perceived behavioral control. The model accounted for 61% of the variability in behavioral intention to use. Most of the R^2 values are acceptable for technology acceptance research. The large amount of variance in behavioral intention to use is an indication that organizational culture, subjective norms, perceived behavior control, and technology acceptance together are strong factors to study with respect to KMS acceptance.

IMPLICATIONS AND CONCLUSION

In conclusion, our research found that organizational culture does significantly influence the factors that lead to the acceptance of KMS. Our research model was developed using commonly accepted measures from the technology acceptance and organizational culture literatures, tested by surveying corporate KMS users, and analyzed utilizing structural equation modeling. Our results indicated that both process-oriented and open communication organizational cultures significantly influenced factors that lead to the acceptance of KMS.

This research has relevance for both practitioners and researchers. In this article, we examine the influence that three dimensions of organizational culture have on KMS acceptance. It is necessary to examine organizational culture when investigating KMS because such systems are different from traditional information systems. Knowledge, which is information that exists in the minds of individuals, is inextricably linked to knowledge management systems. The emphasis on this human component may not be as prominent in other information systems, and suggests that we incorporate constructs, such as organizational culture, to match the nature of this technology.

This research builds upon the growing IS literature that examines organizational culture, which had historically received insufficient attention (Cooper, 1994; Robey, Wishart, & Rodriguez-Diaz, 1995b; Ruppel & Harrington, 2001). In this study, we have demonstrated that organizational cultural elements are important and should be considered in studies of technology acceptance. For researchers in the culture field, our study extends the importance of examining organizational culture with respect to information systems.

This research also offers several implications for practitioners. We identify different dimensions of organizational culture that lead to greater KMS acceptance. These organizational culture practices are particularly valuable because they are the most direct tools for changing behaviors needed to support knowledge creation, sharing, and use (De Long & Fahey, 2000). Although organizational culture is likely to be inherent in IS practitioner's day-to-day interactions with employees and IT, knowledge of more formally defined dimensions as investigated in this study could lead to better understanding and management of organizational cultural issues, such as office politics. In addition, it has been found that organizations that share common goals, principles, values, and language help facilitate IT relatedness, which can enhance knowledge management capability and ultimately, firm performance (Tanriverdi, 2005). The findings in our research reveal specific dimensions of organizational culture that can influence the knowledge management capability of an organization. Consequently, managers should strive to foster a more results-oriented and open communication system environment in the workplace.

To develop a more results-oriented culture, managers need to encourage behaviors that are less risk averse, such as experimentation and exploration. Instead of a static technology with a limited adaptability, a KMS that has been experimented with by its users will generate new and novel uses of the system. Technologies are often not accepted due to a perceived misfit between the characteristics of the technology and the culture of the organization. Allowing employees the opportunity to adapt to the technology as an outcome of a results-oriented culture can generate a better fit. Consequently, managers should be required to focus more on the goals of job tasks instead of the processes of achieving the outcomes. The schemes for incentives and promotions of KMS users should be compatible with such strategies.

Allowing users time to experiment and explore the features of a new KMS could lead to increased perceptions of usefulness and ease of use, which were also found to influence KMS acceptance. As users experiment and find novel features of the system, they will find it to be more useful. Additionally, the increased time spent on the system would allow for greater perceptions of ease of use. Support for experimentation by management implies a tolerance for mistakes. With the understanding that a certain number of experiments will not have desirable outcomes, users would nevertheless still perceive a greater degree of control over the operation of the system.

Open communication plays a significant role in the acceptance of KMS. To develop a more open communication system culture, a number of strategies can be implemented. Users need to freely interact with their important others (such as coworkers, supervisors, and top management) as well as being included in the design, development, administration, and support of the system. Companies should encourage open communication through the use of forums and newsletters and can even design such features into a knowledge management system. Management can also reward users for openness, such as for voicing opinions regarding the system, and making suggestions for system improvements. These policies will cultivate the tendency to increase subjective norms among users and hence, increase KMS acceptance.

A limitation of our research is that it investigated only a few organizational culture dimensions. We believe that the dimensions most appropriate for KMS were captured in our study and that the germane features of other competing dimensions may be largely encapsulated in the dimensions that we investigated (Chatman & Jehn, 1994; Hofstede et al., 1990). Nonetheless, future research may wish to consider other cultural dimensions to examine the influence that they may have on KMS acceptance. Research can also pursue additional relationships among the cultural dimensions examined in this research, which may provide further insights into the influence that they have on the antecedents of KMS acceptance. The variance extracted for perceived ease of use and perceived behavioral control was less than 10%. It is important to recognize that due to limited variance extracted, the process/result-perceived ease of use and process/result-perceived behavioral control links need to be interpreted with caution and closely examined in future research (Falk & Miller, 1992). Another limitation is that the source of our data may be too limited to claim any universality for our research model. Certain industries, such as health and welfare, government, and retail were not represented in our sample. However, we believe that our research model is robust and will be suitable for testing in other environments and contexts.

REFERENCES

Adams, D. A., Nelson, R. R., & Todd, P. A. (1992). Perceived usefulness, ease of use, and usage of information technology: A replication. *MIS Quarterly, 16*(2), 227-247.

Ajzen, I. (1985). From intentions to actions: A theory of planned behavior. In J. K. A. J. Beckman (Ed.), *Action control: From cognition to behavior* (pp. 11-39). New York: Springer-Verlag.

Ajzen, I., & Madden, T. J. (1986). Prediction of goal-directed behavior: Attitudes, intentions, and perceived behavioral control. *Journal of experimental social psychology, 22*, 453-474.

Alavi, M., Kayworth, T., & Leidner, D. (2005-2006). An empirical examination of the influence of organizational culture on knowledge management practices. *Journal of Management Information Systems, 22*(3), 191-224.

Alavi, M., & Leidner, D. E. (2001). Review: Knowledge management and knowledge management systems: Conceptual foundations and research issues. *MIS Quarterly, 25*(1), 107-136.

Alvesson, M., & Karreman, D. (2001). Odd couple: Making sense of the curious concept of knowledge management. *Journal of Management Studies, 38*(7), 995-1018.

Bandura, A. (1977). Self-efficacy: Toward a unifying theory of behavioral change. *Psychological Review, 84*(2), 191-215.

Berman-Brown, R., & Woodland, M. J. (1999). Managing knowledge wisely: A case study in organisational behaviour. *Journal of Applied Management Studies, 8*(2), 175-198.

Bock, G.-W., Zmud, R. W., Kim, Y.-G., & Lee, J.-N. (2005). Behavioral intention formation in knowledge sharing: Examining the roles of extrinsic motivators, social-psychological forces, and organizational climate. *MIS Quarterly, 29*(1), 87-111.

Bollen, K. A. (1989). *Structural equations with latent variables*. New York: Wiley.

Byrne, B. M. (1998). *Structural equation modeling with LISREL, PRELIS, and SIMPLIS: Basic con-*

cepts, applications, and programming. Mahwah, NJ: Lawrence Erlbaum Associates.

CAIB. (2003). The Columbia accident investigation report. Retrieved August 12, 2007, from http://www.caib.us/news/report/pdf/vol1/full/caib_report_volume1.pdf

Chatman, J. A., & Jehn, K. A. (1994). Assessing the relationship between industry characteristics and organizational culture: How different can you be? *Academy of Management Journal, 37*(3), 522-553.

Cooper, R. (1994). The inertial impact of culture on IT implementation. *Information Management, 27*(1), 17-31.

Cronin, B. (2001). Knowledge management, organizational culture and Anglo-American higher education. *Journal of Information Science, 27*(3), 129-137.

Damanpour, F. (1991). Organizational innovation: A meta-analysis of effects of determinants and moderators. *Academy of Management Journal, 34*, 555-590.

Davenport, T., & Prusak, L. (1998). *Working knowledge*. Harvard Business School Press.

Davis, F. (1989). Perceived usefulness, perceived ease of use, and user acceptance of information technology. *MIS Quarterly, 13*(3), 319-339.

Davis, F., Bagozzi, R., & Warshaw, P. (1989). User acceptance of computer technology: A comparison of two theoretical models. *Management Science, 35*(8), 982-1003.

De Long, D. W., & Fahey, L. (2000). Diagnosing cultural barriers to knowledge management. *Academy of Management Executive, 14*(4), 113-127.

Delfabbro, P., & Winefield, A. (2000). Predictors of irrational thinking in regular slot machine gamblers. *The Journal of Psychology, 134*, 117-128.

Dembla, P., & Mao, E. (2002). A research framework for knowledge management. In D. White (Ed.), *Knowledge mapping and management* (pp. 297-310). Hershey, PA: Idea Group Publishing.

Falk, R., & Miller, N. B. (1992). *A primer for soft modeling*. Akron, OH: University of Akron Press.

Fishbein, M., & Ajzen, I. (1975). *Belief, attitude, intention and behavior: An introduction to theory and research*. Reading, MA: Addison-Wesley.

Gefen, D., Karahanna, E., & Straub, D. (2003). Inexperience and experience with online stores: The importance of TAM and trust. *IEEE Transactions on Engineering Management, 50*(3), 307-321.

Gist, M., Rosen, B., & Schwoerer, C. (1988). The influence of training method and trainee age on the acquisition of computer skills. *Personnel Psychology, 41*(2), 255-265.

Grover, V., & Davenport, T. (2001). General perspectives on knowledge management: Fostering a research agenda. *Journal of Management Information Systems, 18*(1), 5.

Hackman, J. R., & Oldham, G. R. (1980). *Work redesign*. Reading, MA: Addison-Wesley.

Hofstede, G. (1991). *Cultures and organizations: Software of the mind*. New York: McGraw-Hill.

Hofstede, G., Neuijen, B., Ohayv, D. D., & Sanders, G. (1990). Measuring organizational cultures: A qualilative and quantitative study across twenty cases. *Administrative Science Quarterly, 35*(2), 286-316.

Hoyle, R. H., & Panter, A. T. (1995). Writing about structural equation modeling. In R. H. Hoyle (Ed.), *Structural equation modeling: Concepts, issues, and applications* (pp. 158-176). Thousand Oaks, CA: Sage Publications.

Hu, L.-T., & Bentler, P. M. (1999). Cutoff criteria for fit indexes in covariance structure analysis: Conventional criteria versus new alternatives. *Structural Equation Modeling, 6*(1), 1-55.

Hu, P. J., Chau, P. Y. K., Sheng, O. R. L., & Tam, K. Y. (1999). Examining the technology acceptance model using physician acceptance of telemedicine technology. *Journal of Management Information Systems, 16(2)*, 91-112.

Igbaria, M., Parasuraman, S., & Baroudi, J. J. (1996). A motivational model of microcomputer usage. *Journal of Management Information Systems, 13*(1), 127-143.

Kankanhalli, A., Tan, B. C. Y., & Wei, K.-K. (2005). Contributing knowledge to electronic knowledge repositories: An empirical investigation. *MIS Quarterly, 29*(1), 113-143.

Klein, K. J., & Sorra, J. S. (1996). The challenge of innovation implementation. *Academy of Management Review, 21*(4), 1055-1080.

Ko, D.-G., Kirsch, L. J., & King, W. R. (2005). Antecedents of knowledge transfer from consultants to clients in enterprise system implementations. *MIS Quarterly, 29*(1), 59-85.

Kogut, B., & Zander, U. (1992). Knowledge of the firm, combinative capabilities, and the replication of technology. *Organization Science, 3*(3), 383-397.

Kwan, M. M., & Balasubramanian, P. (2003). KnowledgeScope: Managing knowledge in context. *Decision Support Systems, 35*(4), 467-486.

Leidner, D., Alavi, M., & Kayworth, T. (2006). The role of culture in knowledge management: A case study of two global firms. *The International Journal of Electronic Collaboration, 2(1)*, 17-40.

Magnus, S., & Niclas, O. (2003). Behavioral intentions in satisfaction research revisited. *Journal of Consumer Satisfaction, Dissatisfaction and Complaining Behavior, 16*, 53-66.

Markus, M. L., Majchrzak, A., & Gasser, L. (2002). A design theory for systems that support emergent knowledge processes. *MIS Quarterly, 26*(3), 179-212.

McDermott, R. (1999). Why information technology inspired but cannot deliver: Knowledge management. *California Management Review, 41*(4), 103-117.

Medsker, G. J., Williams, L. J., & Holahan, P. J. (1994). A review of current practices for evaluating causal models in organizational behavior and human resources management research. *Journal of Management Information Systems, 20*(2), 439-464.

Miller, D., & Friesen, P. H. (1982). Innovation in conservative and entrepreneurial firms: Two modes of strategic momentum. *Strategic Management Journal, 3*, 1-25.

Miranda, S. M., & Saunders, C. S. (2003). The social construction of meaning: An alternative perspective on information sharing. *Information Systems Research, 14*(1), 87-106.

Money, W., & Turner, A. (2005). Assessing knowledge management system user acceptance with the technology acceptance model. *International Journal of Knowledge Management, 1*(1), 8-26.

Moore, G. C., & Benbasat, I. (1991). Development of an instrument to measure the perceptions of adopting an information technology innovation. *Information Systems Research, 2*(3), 192-222.

Nunnally, J. C. (1967). *Psychometric theory*. New York: McGraw-Hill.

O'Reilly, C. A., Chatman, J. A., & Caldwell, D. F. (1991). People and organizational culture: A profile comparison approach to assessing person-organization fit. *Academy of Management Journal, 14*(1), 487-516.

Polanyi, M. (1958). *Personal knowledge*. Chicago, IL: University of Chicago Press.

Robey, D., Wishart, N. A., & Rodriguez-Diaz, A. G. (1995a). Merging the metaphors for organizational improvement: Business process reengineering as a component of organizational learning. *Accounting, Management and Information Technologies, 5*(1), 23-39.

Robey, D., Wishart, N. A., & Rodriguez-Diaz, A. G. (1995b). Merging the metaphors for organizational improvement: Business process reengineering as a component of organizational learning. *Accounting, Management and Information Technologies, 5*(1), 23-39.

Rogers, E. M. (2003). *Diffusion of innovations* (5th ed.). New York: Free Press.

Ruggles, R. (1998). The state of the notion: Knowledge management in practice. *California Management Review, 40*(3), 80-89.

Ruppel, C. P., & Harrington, S. J. (2001). Sharing knowledge through intranets: A study of organizational culture and intranet implementation. *IEEE Transactions on Professional Communication, 44*(1), 37-52.

Sarvary, M. (1999). Knowledge management and competition in the consulting industry. *California Management Review, 41*(2), 95-107.

Schultze, U., & Leidner, D. E. (2002). Studying knowledge management in information systems research: Discourses and theoretical assumptions. *MIS Quarterly, 26*(3), 213-242.

Segars, A. H. (1997). Assessing the unidimensionality of measurement: A paradigm and illustration within the context of information systems research. *Omega, 25*(1), 107-121.

Stenmark, D. (2000). Leveraging tacit organization knowledge. *Journal of Management Information Systems, 17*(3), 9-24.

Tanriverdi, H. (2005). Information technology relatedness, knowledge management capability, and performance of multibusiness firms. *MIS Quarterly, 29*(2), 311-334.

Thompson, R. L., Higgins, C. A., & Howell, J. (1991). Personal computing: Toward a conceptual model of utilization. *MIS Quarterly, 15*(1), 124-143.

Tornatzky, L. G., & Klein, K. J. (1982). Innovation characteristics and innovation adoption-implementation: A meta-analysis of findings. *IEEE Transactions on Engineering Management, 29*(1), 28-45.

Venkatesh, V., & Morris, M. (2000). Why don't men ever stop to ask for directions? Gender, social influence, and their role in technology acceptance and usage behavior. *MIS Quarterly, 24*(1), 115-139.

Venkatesh, V., Morris, M. G., Davis, G. B., & Davis, F. D. (2003). User acceptance of information t technology: Toward a unified view. *MIS Quarterly, 27*(3), 425-478.

Wasko, M. M., & Faraj, S. (2005). Why should I share? Examining social capital and knowledge contribution in electronic networks of practice. *MIS Quarterly, 29*(1), 35-57.

West, S. G., Finch, J. F., & Curran, P. J. (1995). Structural equation models with nonnormal variables. In R. H. Hoyle (Ed.), *Structural equation modeling: Concepts, issues, and applications* (pp. 56-75). Thousand Oaks, CA: Sage Publications.

ENDNOTE

1. An exploratory factor analysis was performed, but not included in this article due to space limitations. These results are available from the third author.

This work was previously published in the International Journal of Knowledge Management, Vol. 4, Issue 1, edited by M. Jennex, pp. 1-16, copyright 2008 by IGI Publishing (an imprint of IGI Global).

Chapter 5
Understanding the Composition of Knowledge Management Capability

Ronald D. Freeze
Arizona State University, USA

Uday Kulkarni
Arizona State University, USA

ABSTRACT

Knowledge assets are an important organizational resource. Both research and practice literature has recognized that, if managed properly, knowledge resources have the potential to contribute to a firm's performance. Yet, the way in which organizations build knowledge management (KM) capability is relatively poorly understood. The diversity of knowledge assets existing within organizations makes it difficult to have a common understanding of how to utilize the knowledge resource most effectively. Drawing from both Resource Based View and Organizational Learning literature, the authors present a Knowledge Management (KM) framework that describes distinctly different types of knowledge assets within organizations. KM traditionally encompasses a range of activities associated with the knowledge lifecycle, including creation and capture of knowledge, transfer or sharing of this knowledge, and its application and reuse in organizations. While explicating the characteristics of the different knowledge assets, our KM framework describes the unique activities required to manage these assets. Using this framework, organizations can evaluate their knowledge needs and selectively invest in knowledge resources, focusing on the activities required to manage them effectively. The authors believe that this framework will allow organizations to build optimal KM capabilities dictated by their business needs and goals, and in alignment with their overall business strategy.

INTRODUCTION

Knowledge Management (KM), as a discipline, is designed to provide strategy, process, and technology to increase organizational learning (Satyadas, 2001). The importance of Knowledge Management (KM) is succinctly provided in an article titled "If Only We Knew What We Know" (O'Dell, 1998). The predominant KM emphasis has been a system oriented view with a focus on technology applica-

DOI: 10.4018/978-1-60566-954-0.ch005

tions that range from traditional data-processing areas, such as knowledge enabled supply chain management (SCM) systems, to expert networks designed to facilitate expert-to-expert communication. The various system designs attempt to capture and capitalize on the existing explicit, implicit and, in some cases, tacit knowledge of organizations. This emphasis on technology masks the range of knowledge available in an organization and processes that facilitates the flow of knowledge. Organizations must develop an integrative approach to KM that covers all potential components of knowledge and leverages specific components strategically aligned to their business objectives. In addressing these issues of KM, the authors believe that an organization must move to a more knowledge oriented view and discover "what we know". This discovery should not be restrictive in the sense of targeting single organizational areas or single systems for improvement, but must encompass the entire organization and strategically map each area of strength and weakness. The authors develop an integrative framework by identifying knowledge assets that encompass all aspects of an organization's efforts to capture, store, retrieve, and use its knowledge assets.

Prior research has provided elucidation of knowledge assets and frameworks for their development. For example, (King et. al, 2002) identifies four KM application areas - knowledge repositories, lessons learned, expert networks and communities of practice. (Harigopal and Satyadas, 2001) introduced the Cognizant Enterprise Maturity Model - CEMM which identified 15 Key Maturity Areas within an organization to improve business value. Although an adequate start, King does not explicate the measurement necessary to sufficiently describe these application areas as knowledge assets. Conversely, the CEMM constructs and addresses capabilities beyond KM and into business process modeling, business innovation and business integration. Consequently, neither approach covers the diversity of assets or complete the descriptions of the composition of the knowledge assets. Nevertheless, these recent efforts to identify and study various knowledge areas highlight the need for extended organizational research within KM. Through the presentation of the KM framework and knowledge asset description, a more uniform level of abstraction is provided that will increase the level of understanding, and result in an improvement in the monitoring and management of these knowledge assets.

In this research we have proposed a description of a variety of separate sources of organizational knowledge, validated these sources as separate processes within the knowledge lifecycle, presented these sources as knowledge capabilities or KCs, and described their relationships to measures of organizational performance. Our description of these knowledge assets is sufficiently generic to capture the capabilities of an organization across a wide range of technologies, processes, and job responsibilities. The view of knowledge for this research incorporates the capability perspective as described by Alavi and Leidner (2001). This perspective incorporates both the potential for influencing future action (Carlsson et. al, 1996) and the capacity to use information (Watson, 1999) in the building of core competencies. Competencies were identified as dynamic capabilities in an approach to stress the exploitation of existing internal and external firm-specific competences to address changing environments (Teece et. al, 1997). This view of knowledge as a capability, as opposed to a resource, recognizes that capabilities are firm-specific and embedded in the organization and its processes. Capabilities are built internally and refer to a firm's capacity to deploy resources, while resources are selected and can be purchased external to the firm (Makadok, 2001). Five knowledge capabilities (expertise, knowledge documents, lessons learned, policies & procedures, and data) that a firm can build internally are identified for presentation and description as knowledge assets or KCs. Each KC is described and posited to be sufficiently diverse to merit separate analysis. The origins of each KC selection and the basis of their differences are presented through literature review.

In the following section, the authors identify various kinds of knowledge and introduce each of the proposed knowledge capabilities: Lessons Learned, Knowledge Documents, Expertise, Data and Policies & Procedures. This section will provide definitions of each Knowledge Capability (KC), highlight unique characteristics of that KC, and indicate the business importance of each KC. The next section provides coverage of prior research that provides the groundwork for proposing and creating the KCs as knowledge assets, establishes the unique characteristics of each KC and contrasts the significant differences between the KCs in terms of the Data/Information/Knowledge debate and an analysis of the Tacit/Implicit/Explicit components of each KC. The next two sections will review the validation of a subset of the proposed KCs and their relationships to organizationally important performance criteria through an extensive field study. Our concluding sections will discuss the implications for viewing each of these knowledge capabilities as separate knowledge assets, what conclusions can be drawn from this line of research and indicate the direction that our current research is pursuing in the measurement of knowledge assets.

KNOWLEDGE CAPABILITIES

A multitude of sources and experiences can be responsible for a firm's ability to initiate action from knowledge. A coworker's comment concerning a supplier's market standing may bring understanding to a negotiation process that enhances the final agreement for both companies. A mentor's question concerning why a particular process was used may facilitate improved efficiency that was previously unrecognized by both the mentor and apprentice. These seemingly disparate events highlight the need to create a framework of study to understand knowledge and all its diversity. To facilitate this study, five Knowledge Capabilities (KCs), Expertise, Knowledge Documents, Lessons Learned, Policies & Procedures and Data, are presented and discussed in order to further understand knowledge and its management.

In our conceptualization, knowledge can flow between KCs; it can transition from one KC to another in its representation. The implication is that singular knowledge can exist as differing depictions or interpretations across the KCs. The singular knowledge required to resolve a low product quality issue may be represented as "raw material X requires a purity level of Y% for quality level Z". The depictions of this knowledge, leading to the quality issue resolution, can manifest itself through three different capabilities, Expertise, Lessons Learned and Policies & Procedures, illustrated by the following example. An expert who tacitly possesses this singular knowledge may recognize the quality issue while checking the raw material manifest for the purity level of material X and initiate corrective action. On the other hand, the technician responsible for the outgoing product may consult with an explicit list of prior quality issue resolution lessons, match the conditions with probable causes, verify the cause of the low quality issue and initiate corrective action. Finally, this singular knowledge may also reside on an incoming procedural check list that rejects raw material X of an undesired purity and prevent the quality issue from arising. In each differing depiction of the singular knowledge, a high knowledge capability will either facilitate prompt resolution or prevent the issue from becoming a problem. The presentation of knowledge capabilities as separate and distinct are for analytic convenience only. This separation is designed to provide an understanding of differing methods to obtain the singular knowledge required for accelerated problem resolution and prevention.

It is beneficial to segregate how knowledge is viewed in order to effectively study its flows and identify its points of management. The authors

Figure 1. Knowledge Management Framework

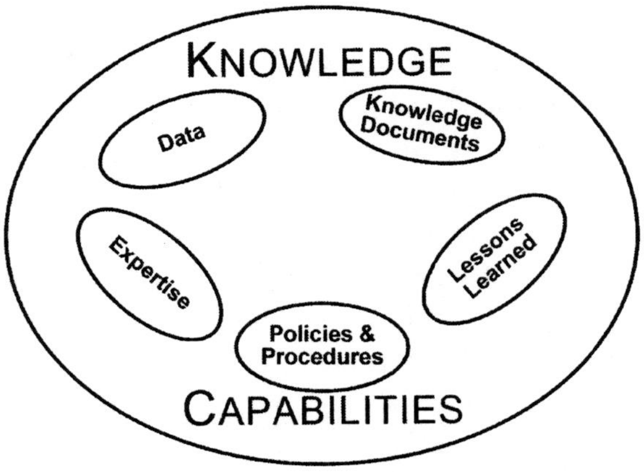

therefore view each of the KCs as a separate knowledge asset that is considered a part of an organizations overall collection of knowledge capabilities (Figure 1). Each KC is constructed to represent a combination of constructs comprising each knowledge asset. To identify the consistency of knowledge, the constructs are designed to measure the life cycle of each individual KC. However, the knowledge types within each KC also present unique characteristics that justify the separation into different knowledge assets. One of these differences may be the point in the lifecycle that the knowledge is emphasized. The definitions of each KC will provide the basis for which to contrast these separate knowledge assets. Additionally, the unique characteristics of each KC will be highlighted along with the business importance of that particular KC. To operationalize each KC and extract immediate business value, each KC is posited to be at different levels within an organization. To assess and report a firm's existing capability level, an aggregated indicator can be utilized for the set of latent constructs. In the business sense, KCs are posited to apply to organizational objects as a whole as well as the business units within an organization.

Expertise

Expertise knowledge is described as highly tacit/implicit, domain-specific, and originating through experience, formal education and collaboration. Corporate directories have been created to map internal Expertise (Alavi and Leidner, 2001) and many articles have been devoted to experts and expertise identification (Dooley et. al, 2002; Tiwana and Mcleen, 2005). Experts and their expertise have been studied extensively and are the source of a great deal of organizational knowledge. The Personalization Strategy (Hansen et. al, 1999) relied extensively on the identification of experts in various areas of their expertise. This strategy viewed knowledge transfer as occurring through human-human interaction such as mentoring.

The organizational strategy for utilizing the Expertise KC is one of connection between the expert and the knowledge needs of the organization. The strategy must target the retention of Expertise and promote its utilization, thereby maintaining and enhancing the core as well as related competencies of the organization. The processes necessary to reach this goal includes: identification of experts in core and related areas, registration of their expertise, facilitation of expert contacts, and the growth of expertise through one-on-one and group collaborations. The technologies that can facilitate these processes include well-developed expertise taxonomies and collaboration systems.

Expertise KC is generally characterized by volatility due to the challenges in maintaining and extending its prevalence within an organization. This volatility resides in several aspects of uncertainty (mobility, knowledge depth and reputation) that exists with a firm's identified experts. The mobility of experts provides an uncertainty with respect to the prevalence of this knowledge resource within a firm. Better job offers, changes in career path and personal circumstances (serious illness of expert or family members) all contribute to the potential that a valuable knowledge resource can be immediately unavailable. The depth of knowledge for any particular expert is always uncertain. Growth, enhancement and prevalence of an experts skills can all be improved through the opportunities available to upgrade their skills via education, research and continued on the job involvement. Reputation and accessibility (not just ability to contact) impact how well the expert is utilized. An expert that builds an aloof reputation degrades the value of their knowledge as a firm resource. Other knowledge workers will not make use of these types of experts when assistance is necessary. Each of these uncertainties can be mitigated by recognizing that experts also have a wealth of tacit/implicit knowledge. As part of the organization's human capital, a dual responsibility can be placed on these experts to participate in the transfer of their tacit knowledge to other community members and, where possible, explicating their implicit knowledge to ensure its retention within the organization.

Lessons Learned

Knowledge gained while completing tasks or projects usually comprises the Lessons Learned KC. Lessons Learned is also referred to as best known methods, best practices and internal benchmarking. Lessons Learned, as internal benchmarking or best practice transfer, has been identified as "one of the most common applications" (Alavi and Leidner, 2001). O'Dell and Grayson (1998) defined internal benchmarking as the process of identifying, sharing, and using the knowledge and practices inside its own organization. They cite anecdotal evidence of gains due to the transfer of best practices that include: $40 million from Dow Chemical, $20 million per year at Chevron and $1.5 billion in extra wafer fabrication capacity at Texas Instruments. While the lessons may be learned in a specific situation, a mature process and strategy can be developed to promote their use in varying alternative but similar circumstances.

Lessons Learned is singular to situations and processes, and predominantly represents implicit structured knowledge that has been recently codified or made explicit. The creation of this knowledge, and therefore its source, does not necessarily come from identified experts. The organizational strategy is to capture this implicit learning from all aspects of the organization's human capital. Once a lesson has been learned, it must be appropriately documented and stored before it can be applied and reused. Hence, enabling technologies must utilize a codification taxonomy.

Organizations must focus on matching current situations to similar, prior situations in order to transfer the knowledge successfully and extract value from this KC. With many organizations, the creation of a best practices repository is easy. However, as processes move forward, the best practices of yesterday may become either the standard practice of today or obsolete and therefore of questionable value. This KC's volatility highlights the life span of this type of structured knowledge and indicates its relatively brief currency. A knowledge base of lessons learned can assist in ramping up multiple facilities for the production of a particular product (i.e. 3.5" floppy disks or CDs). The usefulness of the same knowledge base will became devalued with the introduction and expansion of the products market replacement (i.e. USB thumb drive or DVD). Lessons Learned can be descriptively summarized as recently implicit knowledge that can be captured and documented in explicit form for wider use. This structured knowledge has a suspected short currency due to its high volatility, originating from any of an organization's human capital. The strategic hurdle is the correct transfer of knowledge to similar circumstances from prior learnings. This knowledge has potentially high immediate value when correctly applied.

Knowledge Documents

The Knowledge Documents KC represents a highly explicit form of codified knowledge that can originate either internally or externally and generally has extended currency. This "field of information (codified knowledge) can include statistics, maps, procedures, analyses…" (McDermott, 1999). While much of codified knowledge can originate internally, "knowledge sources may (also) lie outside the firm" (Zack, 1999a). Knowledge Documents can be traditional structured knowledge in text-based forms that include: project reports, technical reports, research reports and publications. Alternatively, it can be in unstructured forms which can include: pictures, drawings, diagrams, presentations, audio and video clips, on-line manuals, tutorials, etc. In this sense, knowledge documents may not be "documents" in the traditional sense, but must represent fully explicit knowledge with an extended currency of diverse types.

The codifications strategy presented by (Hansen, 1999) identified the creation of "knowledge objects" that allows the reuse of codified knowledge without the need to contact the individual who originally developed the objects. Thus the strategy for the Knowledge Documents KC is to achieve easy identification of relevant sources of knowledge that enhance learning. The source of knowledge for this KC goes beyond the organization's human capital and into its suppliers, customers and published reports (e.g. Gartner reports, industry trends, competitive intelligence analysis, etc.).

A critical enabling technology for this KC is the Search technology, preferably augmented by intuitive taxonomies, nimble indexing, and diverse search methods. The processes for using Knowledge Documents include cataloging, storage, and retrieval methods. These processes must be designed to access both structured and unstructured knowledge in its many diverse forms. Although unstructured knowledge may exist within other KCs (especially Lessons Learned), the Knowledge Document KC would focus significantly on incorporating this type of knowledge alongside more traditional structured forms of knowledge. Finally, knowledge documents should also be obtainable both in summary and their complete original form. Since knowledge documents represent highly explicit knowledge, the organization's human capital should understand, be educated about and recognize standard locations for obtaining this form of knowledge.

Data

A review of the very early literature suggests that the distinction between data and information is not clear, although it may be implicitly understood and considered natural and obvious by IS researchers. Information is the product of processing input data (raw material) to add or create utility and meaning (Gray, 2003). A commonly held view is that data consists of raw numbers and facts. A conventional hierarchical view is that data is aggregated to form information in order to provide knowledge. The iconoclastic view reverses the hierarchy and posits knowledge must first exist before information can be formulated and data is measured to form information (Bach and Belardo, 2003). "We recognize that raw data has been lavished with computerization during the past forty years" (Davenport et. al, 1998). These processing systems contain actionable information for making knowledgeable decisions that impact organizational direction and these databases are the most basic of knowledge management tools (Brown, 2000). Data, as a KC which is viewed as business intelligence, may therefore provide many complementary benefits to the leveraging of other KCs. Its inclusion as a KC is justified theoretically due to the face validity of its actionable information.

Data includes the summarized facts or figures (highly explicit knowledge) obtained from operations, experiments, surveys, etc. The strategic use of data is in the promotion of data-driven decision-making (a potentially implicit process). The organizational processes include identification, collection, maintenance, and analysis of this actionable data. New product introductions may be molded based on models constructed from prior successful (and maybe unsuccessful) introductions that correctly (or incorrectly) targeted a specific consumer segment. These models can drive marketing campaigns that include the use of mailings, TV/radio ads, or print advertising. The enabling technologies employed to facilitate this KC include transaction processing systems and data warehouses that can automate the capture of this knowledge. Data has a long currency with a tacit component that is recognized when a new view or vision is constructed that becomes actionable for the organization.

Policies & Procedures

It is argued that much of the organization's knowledge is embedded in its practices in the form of routines and operating procedures (Nelson, 1982). Huber (1991) cited that a great deal of organizational knowledge about how to do things is stored in the form of standard operating procedures, routines, and scripts. Policies & Procedures has been defined to represent institutional knowledge required for efficient and consistent operation of an organization. In exploring the tacit to explicit nature of Policies & Procedures, "we must recognize that there may be a large gap between what a task looks like in a procedure and what it looks like in reality" (Brown and Duguid, 2000). Procedures document the workflows for routine operations. The clarity and consistency of those procedures assist in the assimilation (learning) of new personnel as well as promote and enforce the smooth operation for existing personnel. The strategy in formulation is therefore to promote and provide clear and concise articulation of functional knowledge for the appropriate audience.

The knowledge transfer facilitated by the KC of Policies & Procedures is more a transfer of know-how rather than know-why. The documents referred to in the KC of Knowledge Documents must include knowledge that identifies the know-why since they are designed to be informative. The documents for the KC of Policies & Procedures are designed to provide the know-how of a process, are instructive and represent an endeavor to embed knowledge within the organization. A knowledge worker following a procedure can still discover the know-why of the process, but it is not a necessity to the continued smooth operation of the organization. An example can be identified from the Xerox technician's utilization of error codes to diagnose and solve problems with their copy machines (Brown and Duguid, 2000) in which the error codes facilitate problem resolution but do not provide the know-why of; 1) how the problem arose or 2) the problem resolution process. The source of these Policies & Procedures may originate from the tacit aspects of both the Lessons Learned KC and Expertise KC. This demarcation is recognized by (Argote et. al, 2003) when they stated that knowledge can be embedded in individual members (still tacit knowledge), in the organization's rules, routines (made explicit), cultures, structures and technologies. The organizational strategy is one of transfer from other learnings and KCs to insure an extended prevalence for retention of this

Table 1. KCs Contrasted: Knowledge Recognition

	Source of Knowledge	Origin of Knowledge	Nature of Knowledge	Currency of Knowledge	Lifecycle Initiation
Expertise	Expert	Internal High External Low	Broad	Long - Adaptable	Retrieval
Lessons Learned	Front Line	Internal High	Specific	Short - Limited adaptable	Creation
Knowledge Documents	Process Reports	Internal Low External High	General Procedural	Long – Modifiable	Retrieval
Data	Data Warehouses	Internal High External Med	Aggregated	Long – Static Models	Storage (Automated)
Policies & Procedures	Firm Leadership from top to bottom	Internal High	Specific Procedural	Short – Static	Retrieval

knowledge. Once made explicit, the organization's Policies & Procedures obtain the force of history and become embedded practice.

CHARACTERISTICS OF KNOWLEDGE CAPABILITIES

To further establish each KC's characteristics and unique contribution, as described previously, we highlight each KC's varying composition, identify interactions between KCs and provide additional historical and literature support for the KC selections as well as their composition. Each KC has been posited to contribute separately to organizational performance and yet each must interact with the others in the knowledge life cycle. Four tables are presented that contrast the varying composition of each KC. Table 1 begins with the knowledge life cycle and identifies distinct differences in the source, origin, nature and potential currency of the knowledge within each KC. Differences in the knowledge life cycle reinforce the need to manage and leverage these knowledge assets differently. These differences emphasize the need for varying strategies, technologies and processes that further differentiate the KCs. The Knowledge Life Cycle and Management differences represent an external recognition of the KCs. The final two sections approach differences in the knowledge that resides within the KCs. These differences are defined within the Data/Information/Knowledge debate and expounded upon by recognizing their Tacit/Implicit/Explicit composition.

The Knowledge Life Cycle

Knowledge assets are complex and, most importantly, not a static resource. In order to acknowledge the ownership of knowledge and how the organizational, technological, and physical factors interplay, companies that want to develop and use knowledge most profitably should start treating it differently according to the stages of its life (Birkinshaw and Sheehan, 2002). The KM research domain takes several views of these stages of knowledge: knowledge flows, steps to knowledge management (Satyadas et. al, 2001), architectures for explicit knowledge (Zack, 1999b), and knowledge life cycle (Birkinshaw, 2002). The differing views of the number of explicit stages or steps of knowledge transfer also varies from a three stage acquisition/storage/retrieval cycle (Birkinshaw and Sheehan, 2002) to a five step acquire/refine/store/distribute/present architecture (Zack, 1999b). In order to provide a parsimonious comparison, the different lifecycle stages are viewed as part of a four stage acquisition-creation/storage/retrieval/use cycle.

It is important to understand the knowledge lifecycle as a circular phenomenon without a specific "first" stage. An emphasis on a "beginning" and an "end" stage is neither prudent nor wise. In order to leverage each KC effectively, the overemphasis on the predominantly identified "first" stage of acquisition-creation ignores the contributions of and how the human capital must function within each KC. Each KC continually negotiates the cyclical pattern represented by the knowledge life cycle. The stage of emphasis is identified for each KC in order to provide the point of leverage necessary for management to make effective use of that particular KC. Table 1 – KCs Contrasted – Knowledge Recognition identifies the stage of the lifecycle that should be emphasized in order to leverage knowledge within that KC.

While the emphasized stage of the knowledge lifecycle identifies the point of leverage for each KC, the choice of that stage is determined by several factors relating to the type of knowledge and where the knowledge to be transferred resides. Table 1 identifies the source of the knowledge within each KC. The KC source must recognize both differing knowledge workers (social enablers) and differing repositories (technical enablers) that exist to facilitate a transfer of knowledge. While the origin of the knowledge will be viewed by the recipient as coming from the source, taking an organizational perspective of the knowledge as a composition of internal/external origin within each KC can identify complexities associated with capturing and transferring that knowledge as well as presentation of the knowledge. The nature of the knowledge within each KC identifies the extent of the context for which it may apply. The currency describes within each KC the long term usability and adaptability of that knowledge.

The KCs of Expertise, Knowledge Documents, and Policies & Procedures have been identified as "starting" with the retrieval stage of the knowledge lifecycle. For Expertise, the knowledge required is initiated by retrieving an expert. This transfer requires an expert contact whose knowledge is broad and adaptable to the context of the situation in which they have been called. Internal experts are considered highly valuable to firms due to the time required to create this resource. The cultivation of experts within a firm provides long term benefits when their expertise is utilized and disseminated throughout the firm. Knowledge contained within the KC of Knowledge Documents may also provide long term benefits but, due to the high external origin and technologically assisted retrieval, this knowledge will be more general and procedural in nature and potentially lack the context necessary for the situation in which retrieval was initiated. These knowledge documents are modifiable to improve the situational context. The Policies & Procedures KC contains embedded knowledge that has become a force of history within an organization. The origin of this knowledge is highly internal whose source is predominantly the firm's leadership. By its nature, this KC is procedural and specific to firm processes and is designed to bring efficiency to planned operations. A trade off within this KC occurs for the processes that are projected to be long term. This trade off is one of improved efficiency with a potential loss of flexibility. The knowledge within this KC is static due to its embedded nature and has prevalence only as long as the processes for which it was designed.

Knowledge transferred within the Lessons Learned KC occurs from the human capital responsible for the completion of tasks. This knowledge is highly specific in nature and is related directly to the processes and tasks associated with the firm's output. The origin of the knowledge is highly internal since those individuals directly involved with the production processes must recognize knowledge that has been created and needs to be captured for dissemination to other individuals within the organization. The highly specific nature of this knowledge makes the prevalence short with short renewal cycles and with only a limited degree of adaptability. Hence, the Lessons Learned KC

Table 2. KCs Contrasted: Management

	Strategy	Process	Enabling Technology
Expertise	ID Expert	Register & Construct	Expert Dir. & Expert Systems
Lessons Learned	ID Similar Situations	Special Interest Groups	Collaboration tools
Knowledge Documents	Relevant Classifications	Assemble Relevant Documents	Document Repository
Data	Assemble Relevant Information	Data Modeling	OLAP
Policies & Procedures	Embed Knowledge in Processes	Identify Standardized Knowledge	Departmental Process Repository

is unique in that the emphasis for the knowledge lifecycle must be at the creation phase.

The emphasis within the Data KC is on the storage stage of the lifecycle which should be automated for efficiency. This KC has its knowledge embedded in the form of aggregated information in data warehouses. The currency of the knowledge within this KC can be long, but is based on the various analytical models created to represent the stored knowledge. The data and information contained within this KC can be revealed in multiple ways based on the firm's ability to create new models.

The success of any attempt to leverage the knowledge assets of a firm is ultimately measured by whether knowledge transfer has occurred. The identification of which stage most effectively initiates this transfer is critical for the leveraging of these knowledge assets. When the differences between the KCs has been identified, strategic decisions can be made, enabling technologies identified and efficient process put in place to begin leveraging the knowledge within each KC.

Knowledge Assets as Organizational Resources

In spite of the call for research and practice for systematic leveraging of knowledge assets, a standardized and well-accepted description of knowledge assets has continued to be incomplete at best and non-existent at worst. In order to make effective use of knowledge assets, organizations must be able to identify and quantify these resources. Current literature has noted the lack of both how to effectively manage knowledge (Zack, 1999b) and the quantitative measures that need to be established for these intangible assets (Teece, 1998b). The authors have explicitly identified five knowledge assets through the conceptualization of the KCs. Recent groundwork has been laid from the area of strategic management and economic theory in the focus on the firm's resources and capabilities (Zack, 1999a). This perspective supports the view that knowledge assets are organizational resources as defined within the resource-based view of the firm. The management of these knowledge assets may be defined as the "discipline that provides the strategy, process, and technology to share and leverage information and expertise that will increase our level of understanding, to more effectively solve problems, and make decisions" (Harigopal and Satyadas, 2001). Therefore, in order to effectively differentiate the separate KCs, each KC should have a unique strategy, different technological enablers and distinctive processes that are utilized in order to extract value from the resident knowledge. Table 2 – KCs Contrasted – Management – has been constructed to identify how each KC differs with respect to their strategy, process and technology.

For any business unit within a firm, there exists a core capability within its community that relies on certain experts and the expertise they bring to the business processes in order to generate current value and facilitate future value for the firm. The strategic directive for the Expertise KC begins with identifying the core capabilities that exist and those individuals (experts) most conversant with the composition of those core capabilities. The technological enablers for utilizing these experts may include the creation of expert directories or the implementation of expert systems based on the firm's core capabilities. The processes implemented may include the registering of those experts as well as the distribution of contact information in order to leverage this knowledge asset.

Beyond the human capital's role of identified expert presented in the Expertise KC, the KC of Lessons Learned expands to include all individuals that may potentially contribute specific knowledge to other similar instances across the firm. An organizational strategy for knowledge contribution to other members of the organization begins with identifying similar situations that may contain efficiency or effectiveness lessons that can be transferred. A process implemented may be the construction of communities of practice or special interest groups revolving around the identified similar situations. Collaboration tools, as examples of enabling technologies, may mitigate the necessity of face to face meetings in order to leverage this knowledge asset.

Both Data and Knowledge Documents KCs encompass the assembly of relevant data and information into some form of repository or data warehouse. However, the strategies diverge in that the Knowledge Document KC must be concerned with relevant classification of objects and the Data KC must be concerned with the structuring of raw data. Both of these strategies reflect the differing processes for the two KCs of assembling relevant documents for retrieval (Knowledge Documents) or data modeling (Data).

Policies & Procedures KC attempts to embed organizational knowledge within the routine processes of the organization. Accomplishing this strategy includes the identification of standardized knowledge within the organization and is intended to solidify the processes of the organization. The goal is to minimize knowledge loss within the shifting human capital by embedding know-how into standard operating procedures.

The overall framework presented above describes knowledge assets in terms of their unique strategy, different technological enablers and distinctive processes. In order to evaluate the potential extensibility of this framework, an appraisal of whether differences ascribed to knowledge workers in different domains actually exist. Existing research notes domain differences that exist for knowledge workers. Unique terminology, tools, practices, or incentives that define each domain also establish knowledge boundaries across domains (Carlile and Rebentisch, 2003). Knowledge workers vary in important ways: by the work processes they follow, by status and influence, and by differentiation of work environment (Davenport et. al, 2002). However, these noted differences do not preclude that knowledge workers exist as part of a community, learn in similar fashions from community to community, or provide their unique skills to improve their organization's value. While each domain may vary in its use of technology tools, participate in different work flow processes, and supply different value to the organization, each domain; 1) utilizes a form of repository for their specific knowledge (Knowledge Documents), 2) incrementally improves their processes (Lessons Learned), 3) captures raw data representing their historical accomplishments (Data), 4) embs knowledge into their processes (Policies & Procedures), and 5) creates networks of experts and communities of participation to facilitate its learning (Expertise). These central concepts that occur from domain to domain indicate the extensibility of the KC framework.

Data/Information/Knowledge

A review of the hierarchical nature from which knowledge is created, via data and information, can further the understanding of each KC and the type of knowledge that resides within each KC. Taking

Table 3. KCs Contrasted: Data/Information/Knowledge

	Data	Information	Knowledge
Expertise	Minimal	Minimal	Maximum
Lessons Learned	Minimal	Medium	Minimal
Knowledge Documents	Medium	Maximum	Medium
Data	Maximum	Medium	Latent
Policies & Procedures	Minimal	Medium	Maximum

data as a concept, there is substantial agreement as to its nature and the potential lack of context from which it occurs when retrieved (Alavi and Leidner, 2001; Zack, 1999b). Data, as a KC, begins with the use of large quantities of raw aggregated data and must recognize this potential lack of context (see Table 3 – KCs Contrasted – Data/Information/Knowledge) in order to insure that context can be provided when designing processes that utilize this knowledge type. Information results from placing data within some meaningful context and can be viewed as processed data. The KCs of Knowledge Documents and Lessons Learned begin and depend on the context existing for which guidance is desired. When operating within these two KCs, knowledge workers are searching for answers in which the context of the situation is already known. An example can highlight this in which a knowledge worker is attempting to resolve an equipment problem that is resulting in a product deficiency (quality issue). The context of the situation is well known: equipment type, product specifications, production process, etc. The problem resides in pinpointing the exact step in the process that is creating the quality issue. The ease of search for similar past issues (Lessons Learned knowledge type) or vendor specifications review (Knowledge Document knowledge type) determines the speed of problem identification and the resolution of the issue.

If knowledge is not something different from data or information, then there is nothing new or interesting in knowledge management. The link between knowledge and information/data was solidified through the statement that knowledge is about imbuing data and information with decision- and action-relevant meaning (Fahey and Prusak, 1998). This view supports the three KCs already described as in that the data and information can be translated into decision- and action-relevant meaning. However, the knowledge contained with both the Expertise and Policies & Procedures KCs have a minimal amount of data and not much more information. For Expertise, the data would consist of contact information and possibly historical information concerning the expert. The knowledge contained within this KC resides tacitly within the experts and must be extracted essentially through a form of social interaction. For Policies & Procedures, knowledge has been embedded within the organizational processes. This knowledge of "why" to follow a process may not be immediately apparent. Greater effort may be required to extract this knowledge by inquiry of the initiators or writers of the procedures, following a construction thread of the procedure (if available) or utilizing another KC (such as Knowledge Documents) to provide the explanation of "why" the procedure was written.

Tacit/Implicit/Explicit Knowledge

Tacit knowledge has been described in a multitude of ways: practical know-how (Koskinen, 2003), difficult to articulate (Teece, 1998a), transferred only via observation and practice (Harigopal and Satyadas, 2001), subconsciously understood and applied (Zack, 1999b) and rooted in action, experience and involvement in a specific context (Nonaka, 1994). Similarly, explicit knowledge has a wealth of research to depict the essence of this knowledge type as being: embodied in a code or language (Koskinen, 2003), knowledge already documented (Harigopal and Satyadas, 2001), precisely or formally articulated (Zack, 1999b) and articulated, codified and communicated in symbolic form and/or natural language (Alavi and Leidner, 2001). A holistic view of organizational knowledge assets must encompass a view of both the tacit and explicit nature of knowledge. The connection between tacit and explicit knowledge has been recognized in which "tacit knowledge is the means by which explicit knowledge is captured, assimilated, created and disseminated" (Fahey, 1998) and where tacit knowledge forms the background necessary for assigning the structure to develop and interpret explicit knowledge (Alavi and Leidner, 2001; Polanyi, 1975). These connections imply a continuum that (Koskinen, 2003) provided as a scale of media richness vs. externalization that runs in order from: face-to-face (tacit knowledge), telephone, written personal, written formal, numeric formal (explicit knowledge).

Hence, if one were to view the range of tacit to explicit knowledge as a continuum, it hints at a phenomenon in which tacit knowledge is converted or transformed into explicit knowledge. This middle ground of knowledge between tacit and explicit is where the domain of implicit knowledge exists. The organizational learning literature has identified that implicit knowledge results from the induction of an abstract representation of the structure that the stimulus environment displays, and this knowledge is acquired in the absence of conscious, reflective strategies to learn (Reber, 1989). To place a knowledge management perspective on this definition, the tacit knowledge of experts has unconsciously been made implicit. This implicitness enables the possibility of transforming what was originally tacit knowledge into explicit knowledge. The OL literature has researched implicit learning such that "implicit knowledge can be retained for longer periods than explicit knowledge" (Tunney, 2003). This would indicate that, once tacit knowledge has been made implicit; there is an extended period of time in which the possibility of transferring that knowledge and making it explicit exists.

Implicit knowledge, however, does not have extended recognition within the KM and IS literature. That implicit knowledge resides on the continuum from tacit to explicit knowledge has been implied and recognized such that implicit knowledge is known to an expert and must be elicited from the expert and documented (Harigopal and Satyadas, 2001). More recently, it has been recognized that externalizing tacit knowledge into explicit knowledge means finding a way to express the "inexpressible". Herein resides the realm of implicit knowledge (Koskinen, 2003). Li and Gao (2003) went so far as to indicate that implicitness, another form of expressing knowing, does exist. It implies that one can articulate it, but is unwilling to do so because of specific reasons under certain settings. Identifying reasons for not transforming implicit knowledge to explicit knowledge indicate the need of organizational incentives to insure the transfer of knowledge assets.

While evaluating the KCs and their Tacit/Implicit/Explicit content, the KC of Expertise would be considered high in both tacit (uncodifiable) and implicit (potentially codifiable) knowledge (see Table 4 – KCs Contrasted – Tacit\Implicit\Explicit). Initiating processes in which an expert converts their implicit knowledge to explicit knowledge can insure a potential transfer of knowledge. This will allow the organization to retain its expert knowledge and potentially increase its store of Knowledge Documents. The predominant explicit knowledge within the KC of Expertise is the data and information on how to contact the expertise required for the problem at hand.

The KCs of Lessons Learned and Knowledge Documents are similar and therefore need their distinctiveness to be elaborated. The following

Table 4. KCs Contrasted: Tacit/Implicit/Explicit

	Tacit	Implicit	Explicit
Expertise	High	High	Low
Lessons Learned	Med	Med	Low
Knowledge Documents	Low	Low	High
Data	Low	Med	High
Policies & Proedures	Low	Med	Med

example can provide further understanding of the differences in these two KCs. An expert may create an incomplete document that assists in overcoming a current problem. This incomplete document would readily meet the criteria of a lesson learned that contains both tacit and implicit elements of knowledge (therefore the ranking of Med) that have not been fully explicated. In order for a document to be considered a knowledge document, it must be sufficiently complete to explain beyond the know-how and into the know-why of knowledge.

In its raw form, Data must be considered High in explicit knowledge. This composition is based on the immediate decision making capability that results from the review of operational or warehoused data. However, the indication that Data may contain implicit elements rises from the potential need to reformulate the data to a different granularity or different relational view to provide clarity. The reformulation can be achieved through a myriad of data manipulation and mining techniques, but the important aspect is that the firm's human capital can modify the implicit nature of the data into an explicit picture.

When assessing the composition of a firm's Policies & Procedures, each of the other KCs may contribute to an organizational process that becomes a typified embedded practice. These embedded practices contain both implicit and explicit elements of knowledge. The recognized knowledge residing in embedded practices is a significant force that enables any consistent practice to become an organizational policy or procedure. However, the know-why of a recently implemented process may be very explicit in its procedure and yet still contain implicit aspects not readily identifiable. As the organization matures and new human capital is applied to processes that contain embedded knowledge, the knowledge contained within that process may become highly implicit to those individuals participating in the procedures. This increase in implicit knowledge may result in the human capital not recognizing the full extent of the embedded knowledge in any policy or procedure.

VALIDATION OF KNOWLEDGE CAPABILITIES

Knowledge capabilities are inseparable from the organization's human capital. Developing an instrument to initially study and measure these various KCs was done in partnership with a large semiconductor manufacturing firm comprised of multiple business units in a global setting (Freeze and Kulkarni, 2008). The multi-year field study resulted in the development of a Knowledge Management Capability Assessment (KMCA) which was administered to four different groups within the organization. Consistent with the inseparability of each KC from the organization's human capital, the unit of analysis for the KMCA administration was the individual knowledge workers within each group studied.

Validation of the KCs was accomplished using two Structural Equation Modeling (SEM) tech-

Figure 2. Knowledge Capability Validation

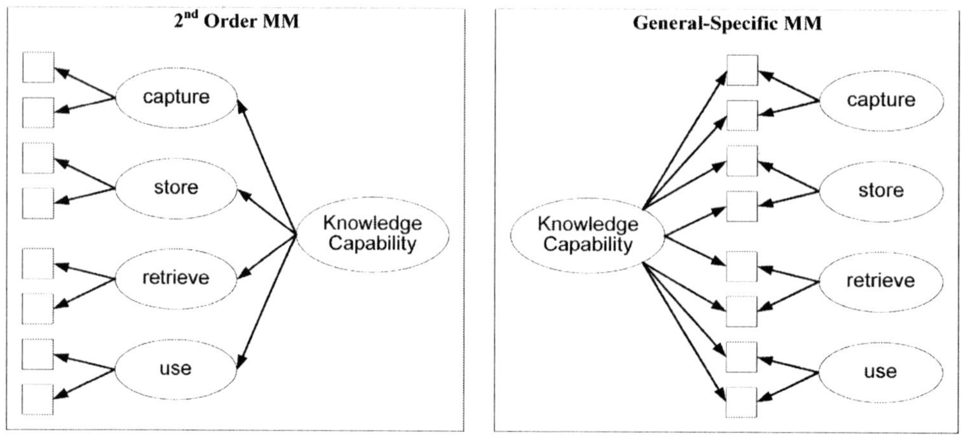

niques that confirmed the separately measureable knowledge processes of capture, store, retrieve, and use. The two SEM techniques are referred to as a Second Order Measurement Model (2nd Order MM) and a General-Specific Measurement Model (General-Specific MM) (Chen et. al, 2006). Together, these two SEM techniques were able to validate knowledge processes as part of the overall KC and that those knowledge processes had unique contributions to the overall KC (Figure 2 – Knowledge Capability Validation).

While this validation was consistent among the four organizational groups included in the field study, external validity becomes a question when studies are conducted within a single organization. Attention was therefore given to the differences between each of the study groups to provide a better determination of the external validity of the instrument. A high degree of autonomy was observed between each of the groups studied. In addition, substantial differences were noted in each group's job responsibilities, task performance, corporate directives and strategic goals. These observations are strong indicators that the KMCA development can be followed in multiple diverse organizational settings with similar results.

KNOWLEDGE CAPABILITIES AND PERFORMANCE

In the resource based view of the firm, capabilities can create a sustainable competitive advantage. Knowledge capabilities, as measured from an individual level, were investigated in several ways to begin to clarify their impact on organizational performance (Freeze R., 2006). This investigation was guided through the use of several research questions spanning the overall KM Capability, to the individual Knowledge Capabilities and finally to the individual knowledge processes for each KC.

- *What impact does KM Capability have on performance?*
- *What impact do knowledge capabilities have on performance?*
- *What impact does each knowledge process within a KC have on performance?*

Beginning with the most granular aspect of KM Capabilities, each knowledge process was shown to contribute to the overall knowledge capability. However, utilizing the knowledge workers satisfaction with each KC, the knowledge processes did not contribute consistently to increasing the

Figure 3. Knowledge Process Model

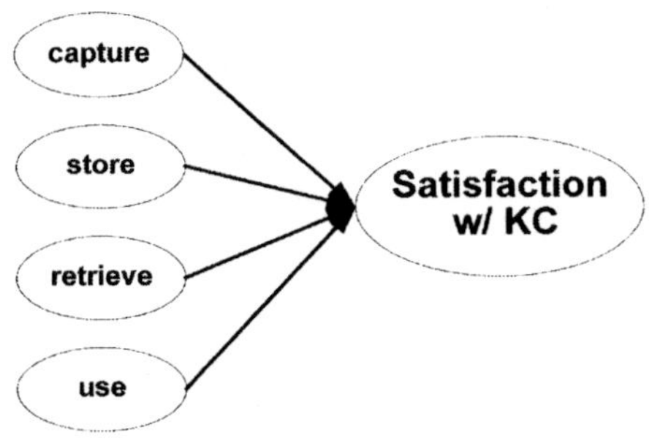

knowledge workers satisfaction with that KC. For example, the knowledge process for capturing expertise did not contribute to the knowledge workers satisfaction with the Expertise KC, but the knowledge process for using the Expertise KC contributed strongly. The distinct knowledge processes within each KC exhibited differences with their contributions to satisfaction with each KC (Figure 3 – Knowledge Process Model).

Given that the overall KM Capability of an organization is constructed by the individual knowledge capabilities, the overall satisfaction with the knowledge capabilities of the organization should be impacted by the levels of each KC. However, within organizations, the level of autonomy and strategic goals of each business unit may result in a specific KC having a greater impact on the satisfaction with all the KCs. This was discovered to be true for this field study. Each business unit valued either one KC much more highly than the others, or balanced their value between two KCs. This value was manifested in the stronger impact those KCs had on the business unit's satisfaction with the KCs as a whole (Figure 4 – Satisfaction with Knowledge Capability).

Figure 4. Satisfaction with Knowledge Capacity

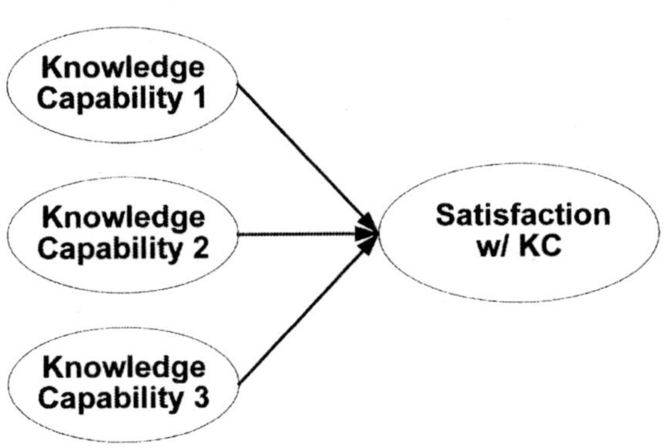

The KM Capability of an organization is constructed by the emphasis placed on the knowledge capabilities. However, the development of a knowledge sharing culture (KS Culture) has also been deemed as part of the KM Capability in the organization (Alavi & Leidner, 2001). Knowledge workers must perceive the usefulness of knowledge sharing (KS) within the organization. This perceived usefulness of KS can be impacted by both the KS Culture that has been developed as well as the KM Capability of the organization. These three aspects of knowledge within the organization should work together to impact the overall satisfaction that the knowledge workers have with KS. The field study results provided support for these relationships in that KS Culture contributed to the building of KM Capability, the improvement of the perceived usefulness of KS and had a positive impact on the overall KS satisfaction. Increased levels of KM Capability positively improved the perceived usefulness of KS. It did not have a direct impact on the overall KS satisfaction, but the perceived usefulness of KS did improve satisfaction (Figure 5 – Knowledge Sharing).

DISCUSSION

In today's knowledge-based economy, greater emphasis is being placed on managing organizational intangible knowledge assets. Continuing research is necessary in order to recognize and understand the potential use of corporate knowledge assets and how to effectively management them. The target audience for application and measurement of each proposed KC are the knowledge workers responsible for utilizing the processes and technologies provided by the organization. The

Figure 5. Knowledge Sharing

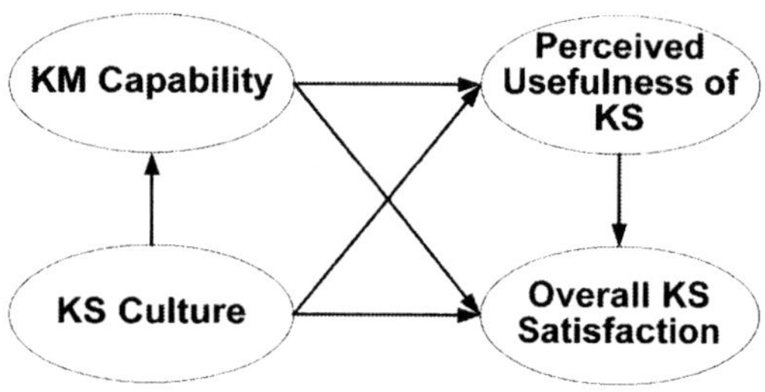

framework created a rich measurement instrument that was driven by the human capital responsible for utilizing knowledge within an organization. The KMCA allowed the observations that highlight the differing strategies, processes, and technologies necessary to effectively leverage different knowledge capabilities. The balanced assessment that incorporated each KC provided a more efficient view of how effectively corporate knowledge assets are managed.

Diverse organizational business units use each KC in a manner that supports the entire organization, but does not necessarily mirror the usage in other business units. The resulting contribution to management is that KC improvement can be targeted to specific KCs in order to maximize the return on any KM initiative investment. For example, a unit that is unable to identify the relevant experts and expertise when errant events occur will exhibit inefficiencies in problem resolution. These inefficiencies may be identified through the lack of a central repository for the storage of information about experts, who those experts are, what their expertise is, the difficulty of contacting experts or the lack of adequate training in the tools provided for this purpose. Another example of the emphasis on knowledge worker measurement rests with utilizing the resident human capital to capture lessons learned from the most highly relevant knowledge flows to create embedded practices that improve firm efficiencies. Recognizing that the knowledge flow of an organization must move through each of the identified KCs rests with the knowledge workers. Identifying that a shortcoming exists within one area can allow an organization to focus resources on addressing that shortcoming to improve its overall performance. Although recognition of relative capabilities can assist in targeting resources, firms must understand that the shifting nature of human capital, the inflow and outflow within a unit, can have an effect on the capability within each of the KCs. This effect can be positive, increased capability, when the inflow consists of human capital that know and understand the knowledge types and knowledge flows of each KC or negative when that understanding is limited.

CONCLUSION

The goal of this research was the identification and presentation of Knowledge Capabilities as identifiable components of the overall KM Capability. Each KC has an impact on separate business units within a single organization and those business unit differences indicate that the KCs could be studied across multiple industries and organizations. Each KC was presented as a sufficiently generic knowledge asset construct to represent and capture the knowledge activities across a wide range of knowledge worker domains.

The measurement and validation of these firm capabilities is a significant contribution that was augmented by the ability to parse both the KCs and KM Capability to investigate their differential impact on aspects of the knowledge workers' satisfaction. The parsing highlighted the difficulties in assessing KM Capability from only an organizational perspective. However, opportunities resulting from an improved understanding of the knowledge process impact can result in targeted improvements that will result in larger gains in knowledge sharing with smaller capital investments. The business impact ultimately desired from improving KM Capability is improving the firm's competitive standing.

CURRENT AND FUTURE RESEARCH

The current field study has provided additional measures of firm related performance currently being studied. These measures relate to the organizational benefits of reducing the time knowledge workers spend searching for the knowledge necessary to make decisions affecting their task responsibilities. The relationship of the knowledge processes to the organizational performance measures of time to access knowledge should vary from KC to KC as they did for the individual performance measures of satisfaction. However, the knowledge process of usage should consistently be the process that most effectively improves the efficiency of the knowledge workers and the business units in which they reside

The limitation of conducting a field study in a single organization is also currently being addressed through the application of the KMCA in an academic organization. That the KCs can be identified and measured in such a dissimilar organization from the original field study of a manufacturing organization will substantially strengthen the external validation of the KMCA. The opportunities present in the extension of the KMCA also allow an investigation into the formation of each KC and the accuracy with which these constructs can be transported to other research contexts.

REFERENCES

Alavi, M., & Leidner, D. (2001). Review: Knowledge Management and Knowledge Management Systems: Conceptual Foundations and Research Issues. *MIS Quarterly*, *25*(1), 107–136. doi:10.2307/3250961

Argote, L., McEvily, B., & Reagans, R. (2003). Managing knowledge in organizations: An integrative framework and review of emerging themes. *Management Science*, *49*(4), 571–582. doi:10.1287/mnsc.49.4.571.14424

Bach, C., & Belardo, S. (2003). Scientific and Philosophical Aspects of Information and the Relationships Among Data, Information, and Knowledge. *Ninth Americas Conference on Information Systems*, Tampa Bay, Fl (pp. 2629-2639).

Birkinshaw, J., & Sheehan, T. (2002). Managing the knowledge life cycle. *MIT Sloan Management Review*, *44*(1), 75–83.

Brown, J. S., & Duguid, P. (2000). Balancing act: How to capture knowledge without killing it. *Harvard Business Review*, *78*(3), 73.

Carlile, P. R., & Rebentisch, E. S. (2003). Into the black box: the knowledge transformation cycle. *Management Science*, *I*(9).

Carlsson, S. A., Sawy, O. E., Eriksson, I., & Raven, A. (1996). Gaining Competitive Advantage Through Shared Knowledge Creation: In Search of a New Design Theory for Strategic Information Systems. In *Proceedings of the Fourth European Conference on Information Systems*, Lisbon, Portugal (pp. 1067-1076).

Chen, F. F., West, S. G., & Sousa, K. H. (2006). A Comparison of Bifactor and Second-Order Models of Quality of Life. *Multivariate Behavioral Research*, *41*(2), 189–225. doi:10.1207/s15327906mbr4102_5

Davenport, T. H., De Long, D. W., & Beers, M. C. (1998). Successful knowledge management projects. *Sloan Management Review*, *39*(2), 43–57.

Davenport, T. H., Thomas, R. J., & Cantrell, S. (2002). The mysterious art and science of knowledge-worker performance. *Sloan Management Review*, *44*(1), 23–30.

Dooley, K. J., Corman, S. R., & McPhee, R. D. (2002). A Knowledge Directory for Identifying Experts and Areas of Expertise. *Human Systems Management*, *21*, 217–228.

Fahey, L., & Prusak, L. (1998). The eleven deadliest sins of knowledge management. *California Management Review*, *40*(3), 265.

Freeze, R. (2006). *Relating Knowledge Management Capability to Organizational Outcomes*. Dissertation, Completed August 10, 2006

Freeze, R., & Kulkarni, U. (2008). Validating Distinct Knowledge Assets: A Capability erspective. *International Journal of Knowledge Management*, *4*(4).

Gray, R. (2003). A Brief Historical Review of the Development of the Distinction Between Data and Information in the Information Systems Literature. *Ninth Americas Conference on Information Systems*, Tampa Bay, FL (pp. 2843-2849).

Hansen, M. T., Nohria, N., & Tierney, T. (1999). What's your strategy for managing knowledge? *Harvard Business Review*, *77*(2), 106–116.

Harigopal, U., & Satyadas, A. (2001). Cognizant enterprise maturity model (CEMM). *IEEE Transactions on Systems, Man and Cybernetics. Part C, Applications and Reviews*, *31*(4), 449–459. doi:10.1109/5326.983928

Huber, G. P. (1991). Organizational Learning: The Contributing Processes and the Literatures. *Organization Science*, *2*(1), 88–111. doi:10.1287/orsc.2.1.88

King, W. R., Marks, P. V., & McCoy, S. (2002). The most important issues in knowledge management. *Communications of the ACM*, *45*(9), 93–97. doi:10.1145/567498.567505

Koskinen, K. U. (2003). Evaluation of tacit knowledge utilization in work units. *Journal of Knowledge Management*, *7*(5), 67–81. doi:10.1108/13673270310505395

Li, M., & Gao, F. (2003). Why Nonaka highlights tacit knowledge: a critical review. *Journal of Knowledge Management*, *7*(4), 6–14. doi:10.1108/13673270310492903

Makadok, R. (2001). Toward a synthesis of the resource-based and dynamic-capability views of rent creation. *Strategic Management Journal*, *22*(5), 387–401. doi:10.1002/smj.158

McDermott, R. (1999). Why information technology inspired but cannot deliver knowledge management. *California Management Review*, *41*(4), 103.

Nelson, R. R., & Winter, S. G. (1982). *An evolutionary theory of economic change*. Cambridge, MA: Belknap Press of Harvard University Press.

Nonaka, I. (1994). A Dynamic Theory of Organizational Knowledge Creation. *Organization Science*, *5*(1), 14–37. doi:10.1287/orsc.5.1.14

O'Dell, C., & Grayson, C. J. (1998). If only we knew what we know: Identification and transfer of internal best practices. *California Management Review*, *40*(3), 154–174.

Polanyi, M. (1975). *Personal Knowledge*. Chicago: University of Chicago Press.

Reber, A. S. (1989). Implicit Learning and Tacit Knowledge. *Journal of Experimental Psychology. General*, *118*(3), 219–235. doi:10.1037/0096-3445.118.3.219

Satyadas, A., Harigopal, U., & Cassaigne, N. P. (2001). Knowledge management tutorial: An editorial overview. *IEEE Transactions on Systems, Man and Cybernetics. Part C, Applications and Reviews*, *31*(4), 429–437. doi:10.1109/5326.983926

Teece, D. J. (1998a). Capturing value from knowledge assets: The new economy, markets for know-how, and intangible assets. *California Management Review*, *40*(3), 55.

Teece, D. J. (1998b). Research directions for knowledge management. *California Management Review*, *40*(3), 289–292.

Teece, D. J., Pisano, G., & Shuen, A. (1997). Dynamic capabilities and strategic management. *Strategic Management Journal, 18*(7), 509–533. doi:10.1002/(SICI)1097-0266(199708)18:7<509::AID-SMJ882>3.0.CO;2-Z

Tiwana, A., & Mclean, E. R. (2005). Expertise integration and creativity in information systems development. *Journal of Management Information Systems, 22*(1), 13–43.

Tunney, R. J. (2003). Implicit and explicit knowledge decay at different rates: A dissociation between priming and recognition in artificial grammar learning. *Experimental Psychology, 50*(2), 124–130. doi:10.1026//1618-3169.50.2.124

Watson, R. T. (1999). *Data Management: Databases and Organizations* (2nd ed.). New York.

Zack, M. H. (1999a). Developing a knowledge strategy. *California Management Review, 41*(3), 125–145.

Zack, M. H. (1999b). Managing codified knowledge. *Sloan Management Review, 40*(4), 45.

Chapter 6
Work Unit's Knowledge Processing Style:
An Empirical Examination of its Determinants

Seokwoo Song
Weber State University, USA

ABSTRACT

Intraorganizational units play a critical role in KM processes of acquiring, creating, exchanging, and utilizing knowledge assets. While much attention has been directed to effective knowledge strategies for supporting organizational KM processes, there is a lack of insightful research on knowledge strategy and its implementation at the work-unit level. This study examines two types of work unit knowledge processing styles (i.e., codification and personalization) and explores the relationship between critical determinants (i.e., task, organizational culture, and technology) and knowledge processing styles. The results showed that task variety and task analyzability were strongly associated with both knowledge processing styles. Interestingly, task interdependence and autonomy were significantly related only to personalization, whereas IT support was strongly associated with codification. The findings from this study suggest that the unit's organizational variables should harmonize appropriately with its knowledge processing styles.

INTRODUCTION

In recent years, knowledge has been regarded as one of the most strategically important resources of the firm. A firm's ability to sustain its growth and competitive edge depends on how well it manages its stock of knowledge (Hansen & Oetinger, 2001; Teece, 2000). Much attention has been directed to understanding knowledge management (KM) practices at the organizational level, which includes how companies can leverage knowledge for value creation within organizations (Gold,

Malhotra, & Segars, 2001; Lee & Choi, 2003; Sabherwal & Becerra-Fernandez, 2003) as well as the choices of effective knowledge strategy and its implementation (Bierly & Chakrabarti, 1996; Choi & Lee, 2003; Earl, 2001; Hansen, Nohria, & Tierney, 1999; Scheepers, Venkitachalam, & Gibbs, 2004; Zack, 1999). While these research endeavors have been useful in explaining firm-level KM processes of creating, transferring, and utilizing knowledge, few studies have attempted to examine why the knowledge structure or configuration of some units within the organization differs from that of others.

Work units in an organization are not all alike in the nature of work they do and, therefore, in the type of knowledge they deal with. Thus, a unit may have its own way of processing knowledge. For example, if the knowledge a unit deals with is more structured or explicit, the unit is more likely to rely on "written tools," such as manuals, databases, repositories, and so forth, for the documentation and reuse of knowledge (Hansen et al., 1999; Zollo & Winter, 2002). In this study, different styles in processing knowledge will be referred to as knowledge processing (KP) styles. Particularly, considering that the choice of a unit's KP style depends upon the nature of knowledge the unit predominantly deals with, the article draws on two underlying types of a unit's KP style: *codification* and *personalization*[1].

Most KM activities, however, may not be managed effectively in a uniform manner throughout an organization due to differences in the organizational characteristics of various work units. Thus, researchers have given intensive attention to understanding the influence of the organizational factors on the successes of KM practices, including organizational culture and structures (Alavi, Kayworth, & Leidner, 2006; Gold et al., 2001; Holsapple & Joshi, 2000; Lee & Choi, 2003; Wasko & Faraj, 2005), as well as technology (Alavi & Leidner, 2001; Davenport & Klahr, 1998; Gupta & Govindarajan, 2000; Lee & Choi, 2003; Ryu, Kim, Chaudhury, & Rao, 2005). Further, a typical employee performs day-to-day tasks while interacting with other members within the same work unit, which involves KM activities such as knowledge creation, acquisition, transfer, and utilization. The specific task environments of a work unit may determine how effectively the unit processes knowledge, depending upon the nature of knowledge the unit deals with. However, there is a lack of insightful research which examines the influence of these work unit environments on the unit's knowledge strategy. This motivates the research questions for this study: *what are the critical determinants of a unit's knowledge processing style? How do these determinants affect the choice of appropriate knowledge processing style?*

The article is organized as follows. First, I will present my research model, corresponding to the research questions identified above, followed by the development of research hypotheses and a description of my research methodology. The article then presents the study results and a discussion of research findings, concluding with a discussion of the limitations and the implications of the study.

RESEARCH MODEL AND HYPOTHESES

This study will explore the effect of a work unit's organizational factors on its knowledge strategies (i.e., KP styles), which in turn ultimately affect the overall effectiveness of its KM practices (Choi & Lee, 2003; Scheepers et al., 2004). The research model, as depicted in Figure 1, consists of a number of research constructs related to work unit environments and its KP style.

KM practices are greatly influenced by specific types of cultural values such as collaboration and autonomy (Alavi et al., 2006). Further, researchers (e.g., Alavi et al., 2006; DeLong & Fahey, 2000; Gold et al., 2001; Janz & Prasarnphanich, 2003) have shown that organizational culture is significantly related to effective KM processes

Figure 1. Research model and hypotheses

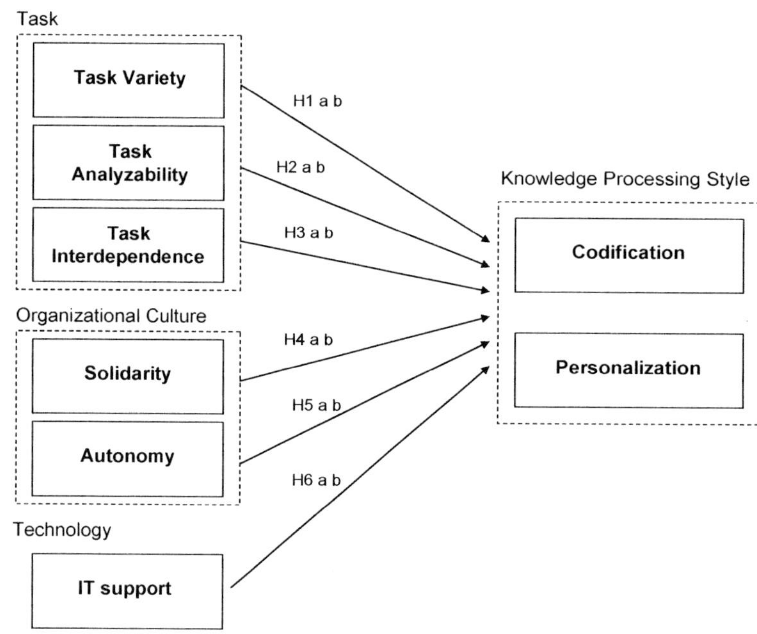

within an organization. On the other hand, an organization may enhance its ability to deal with environmental uncertainty by increasing its information processing capacity (Galbraith, 1973), which is greatly influenced by its task environments (Daft & Lengel, 1986; Perrow, 1967). Accordingly, this study has included a set of research constructs such as task, organizational culture, and technology. In what follows, I will first review the research literature on KP style as an outcome variable, and then discuss the development of my research hypotheses.

Knowledge Processing (KP) Style

Expertise, a scarce and valuable resource, is reflected in the knowledge that a work unit utilizes to perform tasks. The form and nature of this knowledge may vary across the units. Thus, in this study, a unit's KP style refers to the degree to which the unit predominantly relies on a certain type of knowledge (i.e., *explicit* or *tacit*) in the process of the KM cycle: creating, transferring, and utilizing knowledge within the unit. While some units prefer to deal with codified and explicitly represented forms of knowledge, others may rely on the tacit knowledge of personnel to solve problems.

Hansen et al. (1999) have classified an organization's primary approach to overall KM activities into two strategies: *codification* and *personalization*. Their classification was derived from the distinction between *explicit* and *tacit* knowledge (Alavi & Leidner, 2001; Nonaka & Takeuchi, 1995). This article draws on the former classification scheme to conceptualize a unit's KP style.

By evolving means for its effective storage and retrieval, *codification* promotes the documentation and reuse of knowledge and provides easy access to organizational knowledge across organizational boundaries (Gammelgaard & Ritter, 2005; Schulz & Jobe, 2001; Song & Teng, 2006). Further, *codification* greatly facilitates search and retrieval of relevant knowledge. The units may enjoy such benefits of codification by effectively executing the "operating routines" in written form (e.g., manuals, databases, repositories, etc.) (Zollo & Winter, 2002).

Personalization stimulates learning and knowledge creation through direct collaborative interaction with experts and colleagues (Janz & Prasarnphanich, 2003; Nonaka & Takeuchi, 1995). *Personalization* heavily depends on the ability of the people involved and their willingness to interact and share their knowledge with others. *Personalization* involves various learning mechanisms, such as face-to-face communication, informal dialogue, and accumulated experience (Prencipe & Tell, 2001; Song & Teng, 2006; Zollo & Winter, 2002). This is a desirable approach when the unit frequently deals with knowledge that does not lend itself to codification (Hansen et al., 1999). Such units commonly rely on extensive interactions between their members for the sharing and transfer of knowledge.

Research Hypotheses

Task

Organizations may implement structural or informal mechanisms to cope with uncertainty and information processing needs (Premkumar, Ramamurthy, & Saunders, 2005). Some units within the organization may engage in different KP styles than other units, depending upon the nature of knowledge (either *explicit* or *tacit*) required for achieving their tasks. A unit's tasks can be distinguished in terms of two underlying dimensions: task variety and task analyzability (Daft & Lengel, 1986; Daft & Macintosh, 1981; Perrow, 1967).

Task variety refers to the number and frequency of exceptional, unexpected, or novel events in the task over time (Daft & Macintosh, 1981). With high levels of task variety, people are expected to spend a larger amount of their time gathering or exchanging knowledge to deal with the unexpected events (Daft & Lengel, 1986; Daft & Macintosh, 1981), as well as to seek and request knowledge from others (Te'eni, 2001). In work units with higher level of task variety, therefore, more efforts would normally be devoted in seeking knowledge from formally recorded documents or computer files (*codification*) or by consulting colleagues through face-to-face contacts (*personalization*):

H1a: *In an organizational work unit, the level of task variety is positively associated with the extent of codification KM activities.*

H1b: *In an organizational work unit, the level of task variety is positively associated with the extent of personalization KM activities.*

Task analyzability refers to the extent to which a task can be "broken into small, well-defined components" (Ahuja & Carley, 1999; Perrow, 1967). Analyzable tasks involve more rules and procedures. Particularly in stable environments where tasks are comparatively routine, people are able to efficiently organize their activities (Olson, Slater, & Hult, 2005). Thus, when a unit's tasks are characterized as highly analyzable, people are more likely to process knowledge in a formalized and written form (*codification*). On the other hand, in the units with highly unanalyzable tasks, knowledge processing is more personal and ad hoc (Daft & Weick, 1984) than that in other units whose tasks are highly analyzable. Thus, in such units, people are expected to rely on extensive interaction (i.e., *personalization*), such as face-to-face communication and informal and formal meetings, for accomplishing their tasks (Rice, 1992; Van de Ven, Delbecq, & Koenig, 1976). Therefore,

H2a: *In an organization work unit, the level of task analyzability is positively associated with the extent of codification KM activities.*

H2b: *In an organization work unit, the level of task analyzability is negatively associated with the extent of personalization KM activities.*

Task interdependence is defined as the extent to which an individual needs information and support from others to accomplish his or her work (Campion, Medsker, & Higgs, 1993; Wageman, 1995; Van der Vegt, Van de Vliert, & Oosterhof, 2003). The degree of task interdependence typically increases as a task requires greater assistance from coworkers. The degree of task interdependence may vary among unit members (Van der Vegt et al., 2003) as well as across work units (Thompson, 1967). Further, task interdependence is closely related to levels of information exchange (Andres & Zmud, 2002; Sharma & Yetton, 2003). When the units exhibit a high degree of task interdependence, their members are able to accomplish their tasks or achieve the desired performance by sharing materials, information, or expertise with other colleagues (Campion et al., 1993; Cummings, 1978). Thus, in such units, members are expected to engage in extensive interaction and depend upon one another (*personalization*). On the other hand, a high degree of task interdependence may motivate the unit's members to use written tools (i.e., *codification*), such as manuals and decision support systems (Sharma & Yetton, 2003), for efficiently seeking and sharing knowledge. Thus,

H3a: *In an organizational work unit, the level of task interdependence is positively associated with the extent of codification KM activities.*

H3b: *In an organizational work unit, the level of task interdependence is positively associated with the extent of personalization KM activities.*

Organizational Culture

Cultural variables, which include solidarity and autonomy, play a critical role in the success of KM practices (Alavi et al., 2006; Bock, Zmud, Kim, & Lee, 2005; Gold et al., 2001; Janz & Prasarnphanich, 2003; Schulz, 2001). In this study, solidarity refers to a measure of a unit's ability "to pursue shared objectives quickly and effectively, regardless of social ties" (Goffee & Jones, 1996, p. 134). Solidarity is built upon shared experiences among members within the same unit who pursue common tasks or goals. A strong shared norm of behaviors (i.e., solidarity) may promote successful KM activities within work units by encouraging cooperation, reciprocity, and sharing (Ahuja, 2000). As one form of collaborative culture (Alavi et al., 2006; Lee & Choi, 2003), solidarity generates a strong sense of trust (Goffee & Jones, 1996), facilitating knowledge exchange through extensive interaction (i.e., *personalization*) such as formal or informal communication (von Krogh, 2002). Further, the value inherent in such collaborative culture can be expected to reduce the probability of individual opportunism and thus encourage knowledge exchange as well as knowledge creation (Gold et al., 2001; Hult, 2003; Janz & Prasarnphanich, 2003). In addition, a feeling of solidarity often motivates members to proactively engage in information processing activities (Kelly & Jones, 2001), which may be achieved through computer-mediated communication (e.g., *codification*). Thus,

H4a: *In an organizational work unit, the level of solidarity is positively associated with the extent of codification KM activities.*

H4b: *In an organizational work unit, the level of solidarity is positively associated with the extent of personalization KM activities.*

Autonomy refers to the degree to which an individual, or a group of individuals, has freedom, independence, and discretion in scheduling tasks as well as determining the procedures to be used in executing them (Hackman & Oldham, 1975; Henderson & Lee, 1992; Janz & Prasarnphanich, 2003). Previous studies have shown that autonomy is strongly associated with successful KM activities (Janz & Prasarnphanich, 2003; Schulz, 2001; Scott, 1998). High levels of autonomy facilitate the development of decentralized communication networks (Shaw, 1964), thus encouraging open communication among coworkers (Stewart & Barrick, 2000). Like typical knowledge workers, autonomous employees often try out new ideas and apply new skills to develop their own competency (Hackman & Oldham, 1975), and are willing to express their opinions, experiences, and beliefs (*personalization*). Further, Schulz (2001) found that autonomy is closely related to the combination and exploitation of knowledge, which requires knowledge available in written forms (*codification*). Therefore,

H5a: *The level of autonomy is positively associated with the extent of codification KM activities in a work unit.*

H5b: *The level of autonomy is positively associated with the extent of personalization KM activities in a work unit.*

Technology

IT plays a key role in facilitating the flow of knowledge in organizations (Becerra-Fernandez & Sabherwal, 2001; Dewett & Jones, 2001; Gold et. al., 2001; Kankanhalli, Tanudidjaja, Sutanto, & Tan, 2003) and contributes significantly to the knowledge creation process (Lee & Choi, 2003). Further, IT may improve organizational efficiency and effectiveness by promoting knowledge codification (Leidner & Elam, 1995), or by reducing the cost of communication (Pickering & King, 1995). Employee may enjoy the benefits of IT such as access to prior knowledge, searching for and absorbing new knowledge, and easily reaching experts in specialized areas (Dewett & Jones, 2001; Hansen, 1999). Thus, the units that heavily rely on documentation and reuse of knowledge entail extensive IT support to facilitate the acquisition, storage, retrieval, sharing, and transfer of knowledge assets (*codification*). In addition, IT promotes networks between people to exchange their skills, experiences, and expertise (Hansen et al., 1999; Majchrzak, Malhotra, & John, 2005; Scheepers et al., 2004). Further, IT support through collaborative tools, such as e-mail, video-conferencing, and online discussion networks, and so forth, enables people to easily reach other colleagues who are not physically proximate (Sarbaugh-Thompson & Feldman, 1998). Thus,

H6a: *The level of organizational IT support is positively associated with the extent of codification KM activities in a work unit.*

H6b: *The level of organizational IT support is positively associated with the extent of personalization KM activities in a work unit.*

RESEARCH METHODOLOGY

The survey method was used to empirically test the hypotheses. The items in the questionnaire were developed by adapting previously validated instruments. A pilot test was undertaken with 12 experienced knowledge workers, which resulted in the refinement of the questionnaire. The refined questionnaire was issued to MBA students enrolled in a major southern university's cohort-based program for working professionals, and a total of 149 useable responses have been collected.

Sample Characteristics

At the beginning of the questionnaire, a definition of knowledge was provided. A definition of "work unit" is also given, and the respondent is asked to indicate the name of the unit he/she belongs to, and also briefly describe its activities. In addition, the questionnaire also asks for basic demographic information from the respondents. The age of respondents ranged from 23 to 56 with an average of 39.58 (S.D. = 9.75). Consequently, knowledge workers of virtually all ages were represented in the sample. The presence of both genders in the sample also appears to be consistent with what one might expect in a population of knowledge workers: 64.2% male and 35.8% female. The mean number of years a respondent had spent with his/her present unit was 6.18 (S.D. = 6.17). Thus, we can be reasonably sure that they assessed the conditions in their units with a relatively high degree of accuracy. The average size of work units was 24.5 people (S.D. = 38.39). About one third (30.9 %) of the respondents classified themselves as managers, and the remainder consisted of engineers, analysts, specialists, and a variety of other knowledge workers. The types of industry include IT and consulting (27.7%), financial services (11.2%), manufacturing (19.6%), constructions and engineering (12.2%), health care (8.5%), and others (20.8%). These sample characteristics provide a strong indication that the respondents are reasonably representative of the population of experienced knowledge workers.

Measurement of Research Variables

A unit's KP style was classified into two underlying types: *codification* and *personalization*. The level of each KP style was assessed by using four questionnaire items. This study used the scales from the previous studies of Song and Teng (2006). The measures reflected the extent of relying on either formal documents or spontaneous face-to-face interaction throughout the process of the KM cycle, including knowledge creation, acquisition, sharing and transfer, and utilization.

For the work unit organizational variables, this study used the scales which were developed and validated by Daft and Macintosh (1981) for both *task variety* and *task analyzability*. In addition, three Likert-scale items adopted from Van der Vegt, Emans, and Van de Vliert (2001) were used to measure the degree of *task interdependence*. While three items adapted from the previous studies of Goffee and Jones (1996) and Jarvenpaa and Staples (2001) were used to measure the level of *solidarity*, the items for *autonomy* were adapted from Breaugh's (1985) multi-item scales, which have been widely used in prior studies. Finally, this study used the items of *IT support*, which were developed and validated by Song and Teng (2006).

All of the measurement items had seven-point Likert scales. The scale anchored by "to a very little extent" (1) and "to a very great extent" (7) was used for KP styles, task variety, and task analyzability measures, while the scale ranging from "strongly disagree" (1) to "strongly agree" (7) was used to measure the other variables, such as task interdependence, solidarity, autonomy, and IT support.

Reliability and Validity

Table 1 reports the descriptive statistics and correlations for independent and dependent variables. Given the size of the sample (N = 149), the research model was tested by using the partial least square (PLS) method with PLS Graph 3.0 (Chin, 2001). Before testing the various hypotheses, first the reliability and validity of the scales was examined. To assess inter-item reliability, I computed the internal composite reliability (ICR) values (see Table 1), which is interpreted as Cronbach's coefficients. Acceptable values of an ICR for perceptual measures should exceed 0.70 (Fornell & Larcker, 1981). If ICR values are less than 0.70, the items may be unrelated, or measuring more than one construct. As seen in the table, all ICR values are above 0.70 (range from 0.82 to 0.96), and thus deemed acceptable (Fornell & Larcker, 1981).

To ascertain the convergent validity of the constructs, the average variance extracted (AVE) is required to exceed 0.50, or the square root of AVE to be greater than the correlation between a construct and any other construct (Chin, 1998). The AVE refers to the amount of variance that a latent variable captures from its indicators relative to the amount due to measurement error

Table 1. Descriptive, ICRs, correlations, and AVE values of research variables (N = 149)

	Means	S.D.	ICR	Correlation							
				1	2	3	4	5	6	7	8
1. Codification	4.40	1.17	0.91	**0.85**							
2. Personalization	5.25	0.89	0.83	0.14*	**0.74**						
3. Task Variety	4.58	1.04	0.82	0.14*	.31**	**0.77**					
4. Task Analyzability	4.64	1.13	0.87	0.36**	-0.11	-0.12	**0.82**				
5. Task Interdependence	5.65	0.88	0.83	0.21**	0.38**	0.07	0.14*	**0.78**			
6. Solidarity	5.08	1.03	0.84	0.29**	0.32**	0.05	0.15*	0.37**	**0.80**		
7. Autonomy	4.21	1.13	0.89	0.21**	0.22**	0.16*	0.04	0.03	0.19*	**0.81**	
8. IT support	4.30	1.38	0.96	0.41**	0.15*	0.02	0.31**	0.12	0.25**	0.20**	**0.92**

ICR: Internal Composite Reliability; AVE: Average Variance Extracted
Note: Boldface numbers on the diagonal are the square roots of the AVE values.
** indicates p < 0.05 and ** indicates p < 0.01*

(Wasko & Faraj, 2005). All AVE values are above 0.50, ranging from 0.55 to 0.84, demonstrating convergent validity.

To assess discriminant validity, the AVE was compared with the shared variance among the constructs (Chin, 1998). As can be seen in Table 1, the square root of the AVEs (on the diagonal) is indeed greater than the corresponding correlations, which indicate adequate discriminant validity. In addition, I carried out an exploratory factor analysis with varimax rotation. The results, as indicated in Table 2, reveal that all the constructs were clearly delineated and that there was no cross loading above 0.40.

As in many other published IS studies, collecting all measures from a single respondent raises the concern of common method bias. Thus, I have examined the common method variance. Common method variance refers to variance resulting from the use of a common method rather than from the construct itself (Podsakoff, MacKenzie, Lee, & Podsakoff, 2003). Harman's single-factor test was performed (Podsakoff et al., 2003). In this study, all 29 items were analyzed by using a principal components factor analysis. The article found eight factors, in which the first factor accounted for 23.05% of the variance. Further, no general factor was apparent in the unrotated factor solution. The results indicated that common method variance was not a major problem in this study (Sabherwal & Becerra-Fernandez, 2003; Scott & Bruce, 1994).

Hypotheses Testing

Results of the PLS analysis, including all R^2 and path coefficients values, are reported in Table 3 and also indicated in Figure 2. R^2 values indicate the amount of variance explained by the model (Chin, 1998). The model explained 30% of the variance in the use of codification, and 32% of variance in the use of personalization.

The results showed that task variety was positively associated with the use of codification, providing support for H1a ($b = 0.16$, $t = 2.28$, $p < 0.05$). Also, there was a significant relationship with the work unit's personalization usage (H1b: $b = 0.22$ $t = 3.32$, $p < 0.001$). Task analyzability

Table 2. Exploratory factor loading for research variables (N = 149)

	Items	Factor1	Factor2	Factor3	Factor4	Factor5	Factor6	Factor7	Factor8
Codification	**CS1**	**0.79**	-0.07	0.06	0.17	0.07	-0.03	0.09	0.22
	CS2	**0.82**	0.09	0.03	0.12	0.02	0.09	0.20	0.13
	CS3	**0.86**	0.05	0.08	0.11	0.10	0.11	0.15	0.19
	CS4	**0.74**	0.02	0.06	0.12	0.02	0.25	-0.11	0.21
Personalization	**PS1**	0.11	**0.79**	0.09	-0.12	0.21	0.09	0.01	0.11
	PS2	-0.06	**0.83**	0.09	-0.03	0.14	0.18	0.10	0.09
	PS3	0.03	**0.82**	0.14	0.03	-0.05	0.03	0.09	0.06
	PS4	0.01	**0.57**	0.03	0.02	0.24	0.23	0.12	0.05
Task Variety	**TV1**	0.03	0.11	**0.79**	-0.10	0.02	-0.15	0.17	0.06
	TV2	-0.02	0.04	**0.81**	-0.01	-0.01	0.26	0.10	-0.08
	TV3	0.20	0.19	**0.65**	-0.04	0.10	-0.11	-0.09	0.00
Task	**TA1**	0.23	0.08	-0.15	**0.70**	0.20	0.11	-0.03	0.07
Analyzability	**TA2**	0.15	-0.09	-0.20	**0.78**	0.06	-0.02	0.01	0.22
	TA3	0.11	-0.09	0.16	**0.82**	-0.06	0.12	-0.01	0.17
Task	**Ti1**	0.08	0.09	-0.17	0.05	**0.52**	0.35	0.05	0.00
Interdependence	**Ti2**	0.02	0.13	0.14	0.02	**0.83**	0.07	-0.06	0.01
	Ti3	0.12	0.23	0.04	0.12	**0.80**	0.08	-0.02	0.08
Solidarity	**SOL1**	0.17	0.04	0.04	-0.01	-0.03	**0.75**	0.07	0.05
	SOL2	0.00	0.23	-0.05	0.05	0.21	**0.76**	0.07	0.13
	SOL3	0.13	0.20	0.01	0.19	0.11	**0.67**	0.04	0.13
Autonomy	**AT1**	0.06	0.07	-0.03	0.11	-0.09	0.10	**0.80**	0.21
	AT2	0.02	0.09	0.12	0.02	-0.06	0.11	**0.86**	0.10
	AT3	0.13	0.06	0.12	-0.13	-0.10	0.14	**0.75**	0.09
	AT4	0.08	0.08	-0.01	-0.02	0.20	-0.12	**0.76**	-0.07
IT Support	**IT1**	0.21	0.05	-0.03	0.04	-0.01	0.10	0.06	**0.86**
	IT2	0.21	0.03	0.03	0.13	-0.04	0.13	0.08	**0.90**
	IT3	0.18	0.06	0.01	0.10	0.01	0.02	0.04	**0.89**
	IT4	0.05	0.16	0.00	0.12	0.06	0.01	0.12	**0.89**
	IT5	0.13	0.07	-0.03	0.13	0.10	0.11	0.07	**0.89**

was positively associated with the codification approach (H2a: $b = 0.27$ t = 3.07, $p < 0.01$). The results revealed that task analyzability was negatively associated with the use of personalization (H2b: $b = -0.18$, t = 2.30, $p < 0.05$). As expected, task interdependence was significantly related to the use of personalization, supporting H3b ($b = 0.30$, t = 3.22, $p < 0.001$). However, there was no relationship between task interdependence and the codification approach, and thus no support for H3a ($b = 0.07$, t = 0.88). Solidarity was found to be significantly related to codification usage as well as the use of personalization, providing support for both H4a ($b = 0.13$, t = 1.70, $p < 0.05$) and H4b ($b = 0.21$, t = 2.21, $p < 0.05$). The results showed that autonomy was significantly related to the personalization approach (H5b: $b = 0.16$ t = 2.26, $p < 0.05$), but that there was no relationship

Table 3. Results of PLS analysis

		Codification	*Personalization*
	R^2	0.30	0.32
H1 a b	**Task Variety**		
	Path Coefficient	0.16*	0.22***
	t value	2.28	3.32
H2 a b	**Task Analyzability**		
	Path Coefficient	0.27**	-0.18*
	t value	3.07	2.30
H3 a b	**Task Interdependence**		
	Path Coefficient	0.07	0.30***
	t value	0.88	3.22
H4 a b	**Solidarity**		
	Path Coefficient	0.13*	0.21*
	t value	1.70	2.21
H5 a b	**Autonomy**		
	Path Coefficient	0.09	0.16*
	t value	1.40	2.26
H6 a b	**IT support**		
	Path Coefficient	0.27***	0.07
	t value	4.17	0.89

Note: * *indicates* $p < 0.05$, ** *indicates* $p < 0.01$, *and* *** *indicates* $p < 0.001$

Figure 2. Testing research model

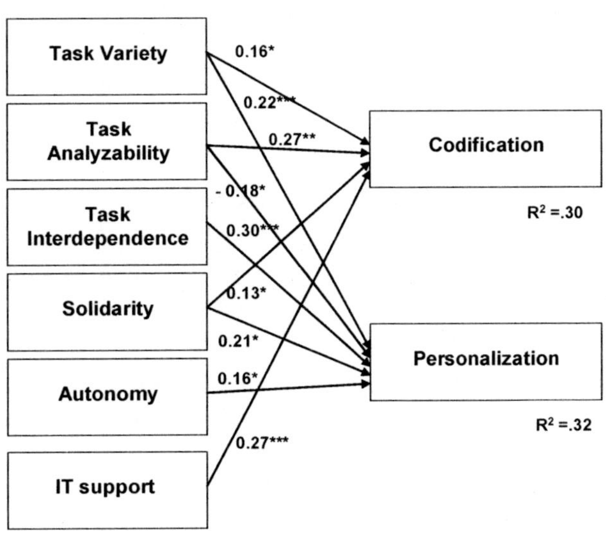

Note: * indicates $p < 0.05$, ** indicates $p < 0.01$, and *** indicates $p < 0.001$

between autonomy and the use of codification, thus not supporting H5a ($b = 0.09$, $t = 1.40$). As expected, IT support was positively associated with the codification approach, confirming H6a ($b = 0.27$, $t = 4.17$, $p < 0.001$). There, however, was no significant relationship between IT support and the personalization approach (H6b: $b = 0.07$, $t = 0.89$).

DISCUSSIONS

This study proposed a research model for investigating the influence of critical determinants on a unit's KP styles. The article identified two types of the unit's KP styles (i.e., *codification* and *personalization*), based upon the notions of knowledge strategy (Hansen et al., 1999). Further, the article discovered a set of constructs for representing the unit's crucial organizational variables in the process of its KM activities. In addition, this study empirically explored the relationship between such organizational variables and the unit's KP styles.

The results showed that task variety was significantly related to the use of both personalization and codification (H1a and H1b supported). This finding supports the view that the level of frequency and heterogeneity of tasks (i.e., task variety) is strongly associated with the extent of knowledge processing (Te'eni, 2001; Zollo & Winter, 2002). Task analyzability was found to be positively associated with the use of codification (H2a supported). This result is consistent with prior studies (Rice, 1992), indicating that people who deal with analyzable tasks are more likely to use formalized and written tools in processing information or knowledge. Interestingly, the results revealed strong support for the argument that task analyzability was negatively related to the use of personalization (H2b supported). This finding suggests that people engaged in unanalyzable tasks may rely on extensive interaction, such as face-to-face communication and informal dialogues, in the process of KM activities (Daft & Weick, 1984; Rice, 1992; Van de Ven et al., 1976).

As seen in Figure 2, task interdependence had a significant influence on the personalization approach (H3b supported), but not on the use of codification (H3a not supported). A possible explanation for the lack of support for H3a is that, as the degree of task interdependence increases, the *codification* mechanisms may become increasingly complex (Sharma & Yetton, 2003; Zollo & Winter, 2002). In order to develop and update complicated written tools (e.g., repositories, decision support systems, etc.), people are expected to make high level of cognitive and managerial effort, which includes time, resources, and managerial attention (Zollo & Winter, 2002). Thus, they may engage in open communication and cooperative interaction with other colleagues.

As hypothesized, the results showed that solidarity was positively associated with the use of both personalization and codification (H4a and H4b supported). The results support the prior studies (Kelly & Jones, 2001; von Krogh, 2002), demonstrating that feelings of solidarity may motivate people to engage in social interaction as well as computer-mediated communication for the overall KM activities. The article also found that autonomy was significantly related to the personalization approach (H5b supported), but not related to codification (H5a not supported). If the units hold a high level of autonomy, their typical members may be the professionals and experts who mostly rely on their *tacit* knowledge to accomplish their tasks (Lam, 2000; Stewart & Barrick, 2000). In such units, the members may be expected to engage in socialization, such as brainstorming and face-to-face contacts, to effectively exchange their *tacit* knowledge.

As indicated earlier, previous studies have suggested that IT support is crucial to facilitate KM process (Alavi & Leidner, 2001; Gold et al., 2001; Hansen et al., 1999; Lee & Choi, 2003). The results showed that organizational IT support was strongly associated with codification (H6a supported), but not with personalization (H6b not supported). The results support the prior studies (Dewett & Jones, 2001; Hansen, 1999), indicating that strong IT support in the process of KM activities encourages people to use formal documents, such as databases, decision support systems, and so forth, and thus, that people are able to enjoy benefits of access to prior knowledge, expertise, and resources, as well as efficiently searching for and absorbing new knowledge. Thus, it confirmed that codification strategies make greater use of IT in processing KM activities than personalization strategies. A possible explanation of the lack of support for H6b is that IT support for the overall KM activities might have minimally contributed to processing *tacit* knowledge (Hansen et al., 1999; Scheepers et al., 2004), which requires extensive interaction such as face-to-face contacts and informal dialogues.

Limitations

The article has uncovered a pattern in the influence of a work unit's organizational variables on the unit's knowledge processing styles that has not been previously examined. These results, however, should be interpreted with caution. First, the results are based on individual responses collected in the survey form. While the preliminary findings hold great promise, generalization of the results to work units universally requires further inquiries. Second, the standard limitations of self-reporting data such as self-selecting bias may apply to this research. Thus, I examined the common method variance, and found that common method bias has minimum impact on the validity of the results, as discussed earlier. Third, this study focused on the relationship between the unit's organizational variables and its KP styles. While the findings from this study provide insightful guidelines for an organization's KM practices, further investigation of how the unit's KP styles influence the overall effectiveness of its KM activities may be beneficial to the organization. Fourth, the article has examined a work unit's organizational factors (i.e., task, organizational culture, and technology) that influence its KP styles. Despite the fact that this study has revealed some interesting influence patterns of such organizational factors, further inquiries may be required to investigate the effect of other organizational characteristics, such as task complexity (Snowden, 2002), on KM practices and their relationships. Finally, in this exploratory study, the results depend upon the response of a single subject from each work unit. Although statistically legitimate, the results are limited by the extent that each respondent can accurately assess his or her work unit. Thus, future studies may incorporate measures drawn from multiple respondents of a unit.

CONCLUSION AND IMPLICATIONS

The current study attempted to enhance understanding of the influence of a work unit's task and structural environments on the unit's KP style. This study provides a significant contribution to the existing body of KM research. First, this study identifies two types of a unit's KP styles, which encompass the entire cycle of KM activities, including knowledge creation, sharing, and utilization. The concept of KP style may prove to be a key foundation of knowledge-based theory of the firm, and the findings from this study provide a valuable insight for future research. Second, this study examined the underlying factors that can potentially explain the complex phenomena in intraorganizational KM activities, which are the critical issues in current IS research. Thus, the results have shed more light on this emerging line of inquiry. Finally, the article suggests that a unit's critical organizational variables should harmonize appropriately with its knowledge processing styles. Recent studies (e.g., Kankanhalli et al., 2003) have illustrated how an organization can match various IT tools with different KM strategies. Further investigation may be required to explore the appropriate mixture of *personalization* and *codification* approaches under different work unit environments in order to achieve higher KM effectiveness.

The study has interesting and potentially substantive implications for KM practice. First, the article suggests that a work unit's task and structural environments should be a vital component in understanding the unit's KP style. Recognizing that a unit may ultimately improve its overall KM effectiveness by engaging in appropriate KP style (Hansel et al., 1999; Scheepers et al., 2004), the unit manager needs to give intensive attention to the unit's focal environments. Second, we see evidence that the unit's KP style is contingent upon the unit's task and structural environments. These findings suggest that there is potentially no universally appropriate KP style for a unit. Thus, the unit manager may improve the scope and effectiveness of the unit's KM practices by striking a balance between *personalization* and *codification*. Finally, the measurement items used in this study provides a detailed overview of essential KM activities in processing knowledge. For example, *personalization* involves face-to-face communication, informal dialogue, formal meetings, brainstorming, and accumulated experiences.

This study is among the first to focus attention on unit-level KM and specifically consider the influence of the unit's task and structural environments. This study is just one of the many steps necessary for understanding the unit's knowledge structure and its working mechanism. The results have provided a basis for future inquires which may, for example, examine the relationships between units' knowledge processing styles and firm-level knowledge strategy. In addition, future studies may provide richer understanding of the intraorganizational KM activities by systematically examining the mechanisms which explain why some units within the organization are more effective in their use of knowledge than others.

REFERENCES

Ahuja, G. (2000). Collaboration networks, structural holes, and innovation: A longitudinal study. *Administrative Science Quarterly, 45*(3), 425-455.

Ahuja, M.K., & Carley, K.M. (1999). Network structure in virtual organizations. *Organization Science, 10*(6), 741-757.

Alavi, M., Kayworth, T.R., & Leidner, D.E. (2006). An empirical examination of the influence of organizational culture on knowledge management practices. *Journal of Management Information Systems, 22*(3), 191-224.

Alavi, M., & Leidner, D.E. (2001). Review: Knowledge management and knowledge management systems: Conceptual foundations and research issues. *MIS Quarterly, 25(*1), 107-136.

Andres, H., & Zmud, R. (2002). A contingency approach to software project coordination. *Journal of Management Information Systems, 18*(3), 41-70.

Becerra-Fernandez, I., & Sabherwal, R. (2001). Organizational knowledge management: A contingency perspective. *Journal of Management Information Systems, 18*(1), 23-55.

Bierly, P., & Chakrabarti, A. (1996). Generic knowledge strategies in the U.S. pharmaceutical industry. *Strategic Management Journal, 17*, 123-135.

Bock, G.W., Zmud, R.W., Kim, Y.G., & Lee, J.N. (2005). Behavioral intention formation in knowledge sharing: Examining the roles of extrinsic motivators, social-psychological forces, and organizational climate. *MIS Quarterly, 29*(1), 87-111.

Breaugh, J.A. (1985). The work autonomy scales: Validity evidence. *Human Relations, 42*, 1033-1056.

Campion, M, Medsker, G., & Higgs, C. (1993). Relations between work group characteristics and effectiveness: Implications for designing effective work groups. *Personnel Psychology, 46*, 823-850.

Chin, W.W. (1998). The partial least squares approach to structural equation modeling. In G.A. Marcoulides (Ed.), *Modern methods for business research* (pp. 295-336). Mahway, NJ: Erlbaum.

Chin, W.W. (2001). PLS-graph user's guide version 3.0 (User's manual that accompanies PLS-GRAPH version 3.00 build 1126 provided by Wynn Chin). Calgary, Canada: University of Calgary.

Choi, B., & Lee, H. (2003). An empirical investigation of km styles and their effect on corporate performance. *Information & Management, 40*, 403-417.

Cummings, T.G. (1978). Self-regulating work groups: A socio-technical synthesis. *Academy of Management Review, 11*, 625-634.

Daft, R.L., & Lengel, R.H. (1986). Organizational information requirements, media richness and structural design. *Management Science, 32*(5), 554-571.

Daft, R.L., & MacIntosh, N.B. (1981). A tentative exploration into the amount and equivocality of information processing in organizational work units. *Administrative Science Quarterly, 26*, 207-224.

Daft, R.L., & Weick, K. (1984). Toward a model of organizations as interpretation systems. *Academy of Management Review, 9*, 284-295.

Davenport, T.H., & Klahr, P. (1998). Managing customer support knowledge. California *Management Review, 40*(3), 195-208.

DeLong, D.W., & Fahey, L. (2000). Diagnosing cultural barriers to knowledge management, *Academy of Management Executive, 14*(4), 113-128.

Dewett, T., & Jones, G. (2001). The role of information technology in the organization: A review, model, and assessment. *Journal of Management, 27*(3), 313-346.

Earl, M. J. (2001). Knowledge management strategies: Toward a taxonomy. *Journal of Management Information Systems, 18*(1), 215-233.

Fornell, C., & Larcker, D. (1981). Evaluating structural equation models with unobservable variables and measurement error. *Journal of Marketing, 18*(1), 39-50.

Galbraith, J. R. (1973). *Designing complex organizations.* Reading, MA: Addison-Wesley.

Gammelgaard, J., & Ritter, T. (2005). The knowledge retrieval matrix: Codification and personification as separate strategies, *Journal of Knowledge Management, 9*(4), 133-143.

Goffee, R., & Jones, G. (1996). What holds the modern company together? *Harvard Business Review, 74*(6), 133-148.

Gold, A.H., Malhotra, A., & Segars, A.H. (2001). Knowledge management: An organizational capabilities perspective. *Journal of Management Information Systems, 18*(1), 185-214.

Gupta, A.K., & Govindarajan, V. (2000). Knowledge flows within multinational corporations. *Strategic Management Journal, 21*(4), 473-496.

Hackman, J. R., & Oldham, G.R. (1975). Work redesign. Reading, MA: Addison-Wesley.

Hansen, M.T. (1999). The search-transfer problem: The role of weak ties in sharing knowledge across organization subunits. *Administrative Science Quarterly, 44*(1), 82-111.

Hansen, M.T., Nohria, N., & Tierney, T. (1999). What's your strategy for managing knowledge? *Harvard Business Review, 77*(2), 106-116.

Hansen, M.T., & von Oetinger, B. (2001). Introducing T-shaped managers: Knowledge management's next generation. *Harvard Business Review, 3*, 107-116.

Henderson, J.C., & Lee, S. (1992). Managing is design teams: A control theories perspective. *Management Science, 38*(6), 757-777.

Holsapple, C., & Joshi, K. (2000). An investigation of factors that influence the management of knowledge in organisations. *Journal of Strategic Information Systems, 9(*2-3), 235-261.

Hult, G.T.M. (2003). An integration of thoughts on knowledge management. *Decision Sciences, 34*(2), 189-195.

Janz, B.D., & Prasarnphanich, P. (2003). Understanding the antecedents of effective knowledge management: The importance of a knowledge-centered culture. *Decision Sciences, 34*(2), 351-384.

Jarvenpaa, S.L., & Staples, D.S. (2001). Exploring perceptions of organizational ownership of information and expertise. *Journal of Management Information Systems, 18(*1), 151-183.

Kankanhalli, A.M., Tanudidjaja, F., Sutanto, J., & Tan, B.C.Y. (2003). Role of information technology in successful knowledge management initiatives. Communications of the ACM, 46(9), 69-73.

Kelly, S., & Jones, M. (2001). Groupware and the social infrastructure of communication. *Communications of the ACM, 44*(12), 77-79.

Lam, A. (2000). Tacit knowledge, organizational learning and societal institutions: An integrated framework. *Organization Studies, 21*(3), 487-513.

Lee, H., & Choi, B. (2003). Knowledge management enablers, processes, and organizational performance: An integrative view and empirical examination. *Journal of Management Information Systems, 20*(1), 179-229.

Leidner, D.E., & Elam, J.J. (1995). The impact of executive information systems on organizational design, intelligence, and decision making. *Organization Science, 6*(6), 645-665.

Majchrzak, A., Malhotra, A., & John, R. (2005). Perceived individual collaboration know-how development through information technology-enabled contextualization: Evidence from distributed teams. *Information Systems Research, 16*(1), 9-27.

Nonaka, I., & Takeuchi, H. (1995). *The knowledge-creating company*. Oxford: Oxford University Press.

Olson, E.M., Slater, S.F., & Hult, G.T.M. (2005). The performance implications of fit among business strategy, marketing organization structure, and strategic behavior. *Journal of Marketing, 69*(3), 49-65.

Perrow, C. (1967). A framework for the comparative analysis of organizations. *American Sociological Review, 32,* 194-208.

Pickering, J.M., & King, J.L. (1995). Hardwiring weak ties: Interorganizational computer mediated communication, occupational communities and organizational change. *Organization Science, 6*, 479-504.

Podsakoff, S., MacKenzie, B., Lee, J.Y., & Podsakoff, N.P. (2003). Common method biases in behavioral research: A critical review of the literature and recommended remedies. *Journal of Applied Psychology, 88*(5), 879-903.

Premkumar, G., Ramamurthy, K., & Saunders, C.S. (2005). Information processing view of organizations: An exploratory examination of fit in the context of interorganizational relationships. *Journal of Management Information Systems, 22*(1), 257-298.

Prencipe, A., & Tell, F. (2001). Inter-project learning: Processes and outcomes of knowledge codification in project-based firms. *Research Policy, 30*(9), 597-621.

Rice, R.E. (1992). Task analyzability, use of new media, and effectiveness: A multi-site exploration of media richness. *Organization Science, 3*(4), 475-500.

Ryu, C., Kim, Y.J., Chaudhury, A., & Rao, H.R. (2005). Knowledge acquisition via three learning processes in enterprise information portals: Learning-by-investment, learning-by-doing, and learning-from-others. *MIS Quarterly, 29*(2), 245-278.

Sabherwal, R., & Becerra-Fernandez, I. (2003). An empirical study of the effect of knowledge management processes at individual, group, and organizational levels. *Decision Sciences, 34*(2), 225-260.

Sarbaugh-Thompson, M., & Feldman, M.S. (1998). Electronic mail and organizational communication: Does saying "hi" really matter? *Organizational Science, 9*(6), 685-698.

Scheepers R., Venkitachalam K., & Gibbs, M.R. (2004). Knowledge strategy in organizations: Refining the model of Hansen, Nohria and Tierney. *Journal of Strategic Information Systems, 13*(3), 201-222.

Schulz, M. (2001). The uncertain relevance of newness: Organizational learning and knowledge flows. *Academy of Management Journal, 44*(4), 661-681.

Schulz, M., & Jobe, L.A. (2001). Codification and tacitness as knowledge management strategies: An empirical exploration. *Journal of High Technology Management Research, 12,* 139-165.

Scott, J.E. (1998). Organizational knowledge and the Internet. *Decision Support Systems, 23,* 3-17.

Scott, S.G., & Bruce, R.A. (1994). Determinants of innovative behavior: A path model of individual innovation in the workplace. *Academy of Management Journal, 37*(3), 580-607.

Sharma, R., & Yetton, P. (2003). The contingent effects of management support and task interdependence on successful information systems implementation. *MIS Quarterly, 27*(4), 533-555.

Shaw, M.E. (1964). Communication networks. In L. Berkowitz (Ed.), *Advances in experimental social psychology* (Vol. 1, pp. 111-147). New York: Academic Press.

Snowden, D. (2002). Complex acts of knowing: Paradox and descriptive self-awareness. *Journal of Knowledge Management, 6*(2), 100-111.

Song, S., & Teng, J.T.C. (2006). Effective work unit knowledge management (KM): An exploratory investigation of the roles of network, task environment, and KM strategies. In *Proceedings of the 27th International Conference on Information Systems*, Milwaukee, WI.

Stewart, G.L., & Barrick, M.R. (2000). Team structure and performance: Assessing the mediating role of intra-team process and the moderating role of task type. *Academy of Management Journal, 43*(2), 135-148.

Teece, D.J. (2000). *Managing intellectual capital: Organizational, strategic, and policy dimensions.* Oxford University Press.

Te'eni, D. (2001). A cognitive-affective model of organizational communication for designing IT. *MIS Quarterly, 25*(2), 251-312.

Thompson, J.D. (1967). *Organizations in action.* New York: McGraw-Hill.

Van de Ven, A., Delbecq, A., & Koenig, R. (1976). Determinants of coordination modes within organizations. *American Sociological Review, 41*, 322-338.

Van der Vegt, G.S., Emans, B.J.M., & Van de Vliert, E. (2001). Patterns of interdependence in work teams: A two-level investigation of the relations with job and team satisfaction. *Personnel Psychology, 54*(1), 51-72.

Van der Vegt, G., Van de Vliert, E., & Oosterhof, A. (2003). Informational dissimilarity and organizational citizenship behavior: The role of intra-team interdependence and team identification. *Academy of Management Journal, 46*, 715-727.

von Krogh, G. (2002). The communal resource and information systems. *Journal of Strategic Information Systems, 11*, 85-107.

Wageman, R. (1995). Interdependence and group effectiveness. *Administrative Science Quarterly, 40*, 145-180.

Wasko, M.M., & Faraj, S. (2005). Why should I share? Examining social capital and knowledge contribution in electronic networks of practice. *MIS Quarterly, 29*(1), 35-57.

Zack, M.H. (1999). Developing a knowledge strategy. *California Management Review, 41*(3), 125-145.

Zollo, M., & Winter, S.G. (2002). Deliberate learning and the evolution of dynamic capabilities. *Organization Science, 13*(3), 339-351.

ENDNOTE

1 Hansen et al. (1999) proposed codification and personalization as two distinct KM strategies. This study makes use of their terminology to portray a unit's knowledge processing styles.

This work was previously published in the International Journal of Knowledge Management, Vol. 4, Issue 2, edited by M. Jennex, pp. 1-16, copyright 2008 by IGI Publishing (an imprint of IGI Global).

Chapter 7
Aligning a KM Strategy and Developing KM Capabilities:
Towards Taxonomies and Frameworks

Jean-Pierre Booto Ekionea
University of Moncton, Canada

Deborah E. Swain
North Carolina Central University, USA

ABSTRACT

Knowledge capitalization has become a major economic driver in business today and has created enormous requirements for organizations as they reconsider their goals and adapt their business strategies. However, the definition of knowledge management in an organizational context is a difficult task to realize (Spiegler, 2000). Although knowledge is a critical resource, it is generally poorly managed (Earl, 2001). Good knowledge management in an organization is likely to help achieve business goals, but require an alignment of knowledge management strategies (KMS) and business strategies (BS). Such alignment can be an effective approach to enhancing interactions and to applying knowledge. This chapter provides, first, a KMS and BS alignment framework and taxonomy in which concepts, links (contextual links among concepts), actors, actions and processes are defined and described to show how they provide the potential for effective knowledge management through alignment and interaction in an organization. Secondly, a KM capabilities framework and taxonomy in which three main dimensions and specific features is presented. The framework presented here is for managers in companies and organizations to use to align their KM strategies with business strategies to improve performance involving financial growth, cost reduction, and customer satisfaction.

INTRODUCTION

The resource-based view of a business firm includes the nature of resources possessed by organizations and details about the qualities that such resources must maintain in order to provide sustainable, competitive advantages over time (Barney, 1991; Wernerfelt, 1984). According to this view, "the organization must possess the ability to effectively and efficiently exploit the full potential of its resources, in order to develop and maintain any potential competitive advantages" (Adams and Lamont,

DOI: 10.4018/978-1-60566-954-0.ch007

2003). Furthermore, "knowledge is viewed by many as the most valuable resource, inimitable by others and sustainable if once acquired" Yu et al (2004, p.1). For this reason, large industrial groups are recognizing the strategic importance of knowledge and are improving their capability to exploit all inherited knowledge (Dieng et al, 2000) by means of good knowledge management (KM). Organizations know that knowledge could make a difference in performance, but they do not know where or how to begin management (Earl, 2003).

Because "knowledge is the critical resource rather than others and it is generally poorly managed" (Earl, 2001, p.215), KM research is needed. The literature in several disciplines and management practices indicate how important it is for knowledge to be managed. KM is a new science aiming at reorganizing business organizations around immaterial richness by a process of capturing, sharing and re-using knowledge (Davenport, 1998). As Jennex et al (2003, p.1) note: "Organizations are much more likely to capture knowledge benefits if they have an organizational KM strategy." The development, implementation and use of organizational knowledge require specific strategies suitable for setting up KM and the alignment of KM strategies with business strategies to ensure that KM is an integral part of a corporate strategy (Abou-Zeid, 2003 ; Asoh et al, 2003 ; Sharkie, 2003, Roth, 2003). As Asoh et al (2003) note, there has been little research into the alignment of KM with business strategies. Also, there seems to be a "lack of strategic models to link KM efforts and business strategy" (Maier, 2001, p.3). A lack of alignment can lead to poor strategic planning, which in turn can lead to the misuse of resources (Luftman, 2004) and poor performance.

Having the wrong strategy or no strategy causes organizations to fail to utilize their knowledge (Hansen et al, 1999). The authors of this article stress that it is not easy to undertake a study of the strategic alignment of KM and business. Such research requires clarification of terms, as Asoh et al (2003, pp.40-41) state: "First, the different perspectives of knowledge and KM may mean that researchers cannot come to terms concerning what exactly has to be aligned. Second, there is persistent confusion between the terms *information* and *knowledge*. Third, because of the confusion between information and knowledge, researchers may think they are working on KM when in fact they are researching information systems or information technologies (IS/IT). Fourth, there is a similar degree of confusion between knowledge strategies and KM strategies."

Although beneficial to international business, models for information strategy (Leidner and Galliers, 2003) can be limited in the help they provide organizations developing global ideas for knowledge management strategy and businesses strategy alignment (KMSABSA). Applying IS/IT strategy models can also lead to focusing on a scientific "fit" between knowledge management strategy (KMS) and business strategy (BS). As a result, KMS and BS global concepts and described behaviours can become derivatives vis-à-vis other concepts and sub-concepts. But KM as a conscious practice is so new that there are few successful models for executives to use as guides (Hansen et al, 1999). Nevertheless, "there is broad agreeing in the management literature that KM has to be solidly linked to business strategy and ultimately to the creation of economic value and competitive advantage in order to be a sustained effort" (Maier, 2001, p.3).

To support such an alignment, the design and implementation of a taxonomy and a conceptual framework for KMSABSA seem necessary to identify, define and connect the key concepts in managing knowledge. A taxonomy is needed (Earl, 1983; Hansen et al, 1999; Maier, 2001; Yu et al, 2004) to help answer questions such as: What concepts define accurately KMS and BS alignment? How do they interact? Who are the actors intervening on each level? During the last two decades, literature in knowledge management has tended to focus on KM strategies alignment to business strategies and how this alignment made it possible to attain business performance or business competitive advantages. Indeed, research advanced during the last two decades on the impact of knowledge management, as a strategic resource on businesses performance or business competitive advantages is still mainly limited to strategic alignment (Asoh et al, 2003). In consequence, actors need to develop organizational knowledge capabilities to make sure that they contribute to business performance or business competitive advantages (Peppart and Ward, 2004). Wha t are the KM capabilities that an organization can develop in order to attain business performance or to obtain sustained competitive advantage after aligning KMS to BS? Indeed, literature in KM (Abou-Zeid, 2003; Booto & Abou-Zeid, 2005; Chang & Ahn, 2005) presents the concept of KM capabilities in three dimensions: KM infrastructures, KM process and KM skills.

The interlinking among concepts, actors, actions, and processes in KMSABSA as defined and described in this article illustrates how businesses can implement these aspects of information systems while they interact based on the attributes associated with knowledge and business strategies. Following the cartographic – technocratic school of KM (Earl, 2001), a KMSABSA framework and taxonomy is presented. Information science research literature (Peppart & Ward, 2004) supports the concept that organizations need to develop organizational knowledge management capabilities to make sure that they contribute to the implementation of a knowledge management strategy that help to enrich business performance or sustained business competitive advantages (Peppart & Ward, 2004). Dierickx and Cool (1986) made the difference between resources, stocks and flow and defended the thesis according to which — the strategic factors necessary to obtain a durable competitive advantage — must be developed with the intern and cannot be in any case bought on the market. Therefore, in order to have a competitive advantage, the firm must develop resources and capabilities which would be difficult to imitate or to acquire by the competitors, i.e., intangible resource such as knowledge, reputation, etc. (Wernerfelt, 1984; Barney, 1991; Grant, 1991; Foss, 1996; Conner and Prahalad, 1996).

The second issue addressed in this article is to study the role of developing organizational capabilities in establishing sustained competitive advantage through the lens of RBV. Thus, the remainder of this article is organized as follows. In the next section, the link between KM strategy and business strategy is discussed. Il the second section, the Resource-Based View of Firm's Competitive Advantage is briefly discussed. In the third section a taxonomy and a framework of the alignment of business strategies with KM strategies are introduced. In the fourth section a conceptual hierarchy for actions by principal actors in the strategic alignment of KM and business. In the fifth section a framework for studying KM capabilities is introduced. The conclusion is a discussion of the possible significance and contribution of this framework, as well as possible areas for future research. The authors hope that this article will encourage further study of strategies and alignments for KM and KM capabilities.

ALIGNMENT IN THE CONTEXT OF PERFORMANCE: BUSINESS STRATEGY AND KM STRATEGY

To define clearly organizational business strategies, we call upon the classification diagram of strategy types adopted from Miles and Snow (1978). This diagram (see top of Figure 1) defines three possible types of business strategy that an organization can adopt (defender, prospector, and analyzer) in the context of business performance. The *defender* does not tend to seek new occasions apart from his field of competence and seldom carries out major adjustments in a business structure or technology. Defenders are the

Figure 1. Strategic Alignment of KM Strategies with Business Strategies (adapted from Miles and Snow, 1978)

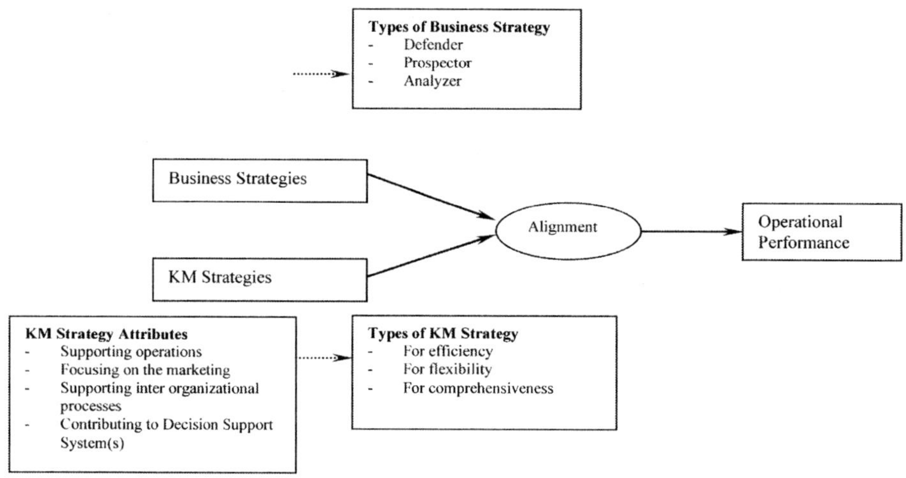

most stable among the three types of strategies. Someone who follows this type of strategy offers high quality products (but within the standard) or provides services at low price. Defender aims to control customers by the improvement of business processes. The *prospector* prefers to research without interruption and looks for new products or market opportunities. The prospector is the change-maker in a specific market. While basing the business on innovation, the prospector strongly invests in research and development. To function in a broad and dynamic field, this type of strategist seeks flexibility concerning technology. Lastly, the *analyzer* shares certain characteristics with each of the other two strategy types. However, he carries out a combination of strategies from the defender and the prospector. This type of strategist seeks to reduce risk to a minimum while simultaneously maximizing opportunities for growth and change. Each has the goal to improve business performance.

If an organization wants to launch a KM process, the strategists must determine which type(s) of operational performance (OP) it wants to improve by setting up a knowledge management system (that is aligned with business strategies). This step leads to the definition of objectives that have short, average and long terms and that also are defined according to the type of strategy that the organization has adopted: defender, prospector or analyzer. Figure 1 illustrates the alignment of business strategy attributes and types with knowledge management strategy attributes and types.

Adapting the Miles and Snow strategy model to KM, Figure 1 illustrates a proposed alignment of knowledge management strategies with business strategies. As suggested in the figure, KM strategy types can be defined in terms of the performance attributes with which they align (Sabherwal and Chan, 2001). Definitions for the alignment and application of business strategy types to KM and to OP are shown in Table 1, which documents the main constructs and the types of strategy for both business and KM, and the resulting overall performance.

The performance level that a company can reach by using KM can be summarized according to different factors. An organization that wishes to set up a KMS must clearly determine whether it wants to reach only one particular factor, a precise set of certain factors, or all of the value factors. In an operation that differentiates, the business

Table 1. Summary definitions of constructs and types of strategies

No.	Principal Constructs	Strategy Types	Definitions
1	Business Strategy	Defender	Its objective is to control its customers by the improvement of her business processes (Miles et Snow, 1978).
		Prospector	Seek without interruption new opportunities (Miles and Snow, 1978).
		Analyser	Carry out a combination of the forces of the two preceding types and seeks to reduce to the minimum simultaneously the risk while maximizing occasions for the growth (Miles and Snow, 1978).
2	KM Strategy	For Efficiency	For the Defenders, alignment between the KMS and the strategy type on KM for efficiency are perceived like a business performance (Sabherwal and Chan, 2001).
		For Flexibility	For the Prospectors, the KMS alignment and the type of strategy on KM for flexibility are perceived like a business performance (Sabherwal and Chan, 2001)
		For Comprehensiveness	For the Analyzers strategy, this performance is seen by the prism of the comprehensiveness of the strategy on KM (Sabherwal and Chan, 2001).
3	Operational Performance	Differentiation	OP is perceived as aiming to increase returns, to reduce costs and to increase customer satisfaction (Miles and Snow, 1978; Lawrence and Lorsh, 1967).
		Integration	The OP is perceived as aiming at the effectiveness or the output of the resources, at enrichment from processes and at the effectiveness of processes (Miles and Snow, 1978; Lawrence and Lorsh, 1967); plus, shared decision making (Earl, 2003).

value factors to choose from can be divided into three groups.

1. Factors related to a firm's increase on returns and financial growth: *knowledge capitalization* (the capture and dissemination of knowledge related to research and development experiments, or new ideas from within or outside the firm) and *knowledge management systems and technologies (*by which specific knowledge can constitute a commercial resource).
2. The cost reduction in providing a service or developing a product due to the installation of a knowledge management systems that supports innovation and facilitates knowledge-sharing and communication among all the stakeholders in the value chain (suppliers, customers, retailers, employees, industries, environment, etc.).
3. Improvement in customer satisfaction with knowledge capture and storage. Systems to treat information and to make knowledge available in an organization can lead to increased customer knowledge, improvement in customer services, and stronger customer loyalty (Cooper et al, 2000).

When the goal of operational performance is integration, there are three factors to consider that support organizational improvement:

- *Resource effectiveness*: capitalizing on tacit and explicit knowledge related to a product, a technology, or a service for the unspecified improvement of individual or collective competences (Nonaka, 1994).
- *Process enrichment*: knowledge capitalization using laws or regulations, industry rules, procedures or work specifications, standards, and methods.
- *Process effectiveness*: the capacity for coordination and innovation, which successful KM aims at within an organization by supporting or facilitating appropriate integration and differentiation: (The process or business entities that are integrated are individual, process or business entities that

have been differentiated according to specific organizational context.)

The research of Lawrence and Lorsh (1967) shows that an organization whose integration level and differentiation were high reached a high performance level. Therefore, concerning the definition of the OP level to be reached with a KMS, the principal question that should be posed by knowledge managers is which KM systems to recommend in order to reach a high level of both integration and differentiation at the same time? Because KM strategy types can be defined in terms of performance attributes (Sabherwal and Chan, 2001), to find the answer, a knowledge manager needs to determine the organization's strategy type based on the attributes for KM strategies that the organization has. The suggested attributes for KMS are supporting operations, focusing on the market, supporting inter-organisational processes, and providing assistance for decision-making systems. The strategy types for the attributes to be aligned with relate to how KMS impacts OP and refer to the performance concerns that a type emphasizes or is for: efficiency, flexibility or comprehensiveness. Thus, the alignment of KM strategies to the three types of business strategies (defenders, analyzers and prospectors) results in three concepts (efficiency, flexibility and comprehensiveness).

The theoretical and ideal values of the six attributes of business strategies can also be applied to the BS profiles or types: defenders, analyzers and/or prospectors (Miles and Snow, 1978). In comparison, there are three assumptions related to the alignment between business strategies and IS/IT strategies (Sabherwal and Chan, 2001) that can be applied to KMS (see Table 1). First, for the *defenders*, the strategic alignment of knowledge resources and the business strategy to improve efficiency is perceived in terms of business performance. Second, for the *prospectors*, the alignment of knowledge resource strategies and business strategies that support flexibility must be perceived in terms of business opportunities. Third, for the *analyzers*, business performance is seen through a comprehensive prism supporting both efficiency and flexibility for knowledge resources. (Note that Sabherwal and Chan also suggested a fourth concept, the perception of alignment, as a factor of performance.)

THE RESOURCE-BASED VIEW OF FIRM'S COMPETITIVE ADVANTAGE

Rooted in management strategy literature, the resource-based view of the firm posits that firms compete on the basis of "unique" corporate resources that are valuable, rare, difficult to imitate, and non-substitutable by other resources. It is based on two underlying assertions, as developed in strategic management theory (Barney, 1991; Barney, 1986; Conner, 1991; Rumelt, 1984; Wernerfelt, 1984): (1) that the resources and capabilities possessed by competing firms may differ (resource heterogeneity); and (2) that these differences may be long lasting (resource immobility).

The condition of resource heterogeneity is connected to sustained competitive advantage in the following way. If a firm possesses a resource that is not currently possessed by competing firms, the condition of resource heterogeneity is met, and a firm may obtain at least a temporary competitive advantage.

The second resource-based condition, the condition of resource immobility, becomes important in understanding when a firm's resources and capabilities will be sources of sustained competitive advantage. A resource is mobile if firms without a resource (or capability) face no cost disadvantage in developing, acquiring, and using that resource compared to firms that already possess and use it. In this case, that resource (i.e., mobile resource) can only be a source of temporary competitive advantage at best. On the other hand, if a firm without a resource or capability does face a cost disadvantage in obtaining, developing, and using it compared to a firm that already possesses that resource (i.e., resource immobility), then the firm that already possesses that resource can have a sustained competitive advantage (Barney, 1991).

TAXONOMY AND FRAMEWORK OF THE ALIGNMENT OF BUSINESSES STRATEGIES WITH KNOWLEDGE MANAGEMENT STRATEGIES

As Maier (2001, p.1) notes, "An organization should follow a KM strategy as part of comprehensive business strategy." For example, using the measurement results and indicators of businesses performance, one can measure critical success factors (Jennex and Olfman, 2005). Furthermore, critical success factors can contribute to measurements of business performance overall. Concerning KM, both the internal and external knowledge environments define the drivers for knowledge and a KMS. In this way, "key environment influences describe the external forces that drive the organization to exploit its knowledge to maintain its competitive position" (Jennex and Olfman, 2005, p.4).

Using definitions, influences and measures, (Henderson and Venkatraman, (1993) provide an entity-relationship analysis between the principal constructs (BS, KMS and OP) and the environment (internal and external) and drivers in business and knowledge management. As shown in Table 2, others (Abou-Zeid, 2003; Asoh et al, 2003; Sharkie, 2003; Miles and Snow, 1978) also suggest interactions and critical success factors among business constructs.

Maier (2001, p.1) suggests that "a KM strategy can be described using several dimensions." A procedural alignment of BS and KMS based on the definitions of principal constructs and strategy types provides dimensions for a KM framework. Figure 2 illustrates a schematic that can serve as a framework for the alignment of KM strategies with business strategies based on interactive attributes associated with knowledge. Specific steps are indicated by numbers in Figure 2 and show the dynamic nature of interactions involved in strategy building. These steps define the various business and KM concepts and how they are linked:

1. The external environment defines business drivers.
2. The internal environment defines business drivers.
3. Business drivers influence attributes for business strategies.
4. The attributes for business strategies determine the types of strategy.
5. The types of business strategy direct measurements of performance and use of key indicators.
6. The key indicators of business performance measure CSFs in business.
7. CSFs for business contribute to business performance.
8. The business strategies define attributes for KM strategies.
9. Both business and KM strategies influence overall performance.
10. The external environment defines KM drivers.
11. The internal environment defines KM drivers.
12. KM drivers influence attributes for KM strategies.
13. The attributes for KM strategies determine the types of strategy.
14. The types of business strategy interact with the types of KM strategy; the types of KM strategy interact with types of business strategy.
15. The types of KM strategy direct measurements of performance and use of key indicators.

Table 2. Description of the relationships between the principal constructs

No.	Relation	Constructs		Definitions
		Source	Target	
1	**Define**	External Environment	Business Drivers	The elements of the external environment define the conditions or the state of the businesses drivers (Henderson and Venkatraman, 1993).
2	**Define**	Internal Environment	Business Drivers	The elements of the internal environment define the conditions or the state of the businesses drivers (Henderson and Venkatraman, 1993).
3	**Influence**	Business Drivers	Business Strategies	The business drivers influences the definition of the business strategies (Henderson and Venkatraman, 1993).
4	**Determine**	Business Strategies	Types of Business Strategy	The business strategies determine which type of strategy an organization must adopt to achieve its business goals (Miles and Snow, 1978).
5	**Direct**	Types of Business Strategy	Measurements and indicators of businesses performance	The type of business strategy adopted directs the measurements choice and the indicators of businesses performance (Henderson and Venkatraman, 1993).
6	**Measure**	Measurements and indicators of performance	Critical Success Factors of businesses	Measurements and indicators of businesses performance measure the critical success factors of businesses (Henderson and Venkatraman, 1993).
7	**Contribute**	Critical Success Factors of businesses	Business Performance	The critical success factors of businesses contribute to the business performance (Henderson and Venkatraman, 1993).
8	**Define**	Business Strategies	KM Strategies	The business strategies define the KM strategies (Miles and Snow, 1978).
9	**Influence**	Business Strategies and KM Strategies	Performance	The businesses strategies and the KM strategies influence the business performance (Abou-Zeid, 2003; Asoh et al, 2003; Sharkie, 2003).
10	**Define**	KM External Environment	KM Drivers	The elements of the external environment define the conditions or the state of the KM drivers (Henderson and Venkatraman, 1993).
11	**Define**	KM Internal Environment	KM Drivers	The elements of the internal environment define the conditions or the state of the KM drivers (Abou-Zeid, 2003; Asoh et al, 2003; Sharkie, 2003).
12	**Influence**	KM Drivers	KM Strategies	The KM drivers influence the definition of the KM strategies (Abou-Zeid, 2003; Asoh et al, 2003; Sharkie, 2003).
13	**Determine**	KM Strategies	Types of KM Strategy	The KM strategies determine which type of KM strategy to achieve the businesses goals (Abou-Zeid, 2003; Asoh et al, 2003; Sharkie, 2003).
14a	**Interact with**	Types of Business Strategy	Types of KM Strategy	The types of businesses strategy interact with the types of KM strategy (Abou-Zeid, 2003)
14b	**Interact with**	Types of KM Strategy	Types of Business Strategy	The types of KM strategy interact with the types of business strategy (Abou-Zeid, 2003; Asoh et al, 2003 ; Sharkie, 2003).
15	**Direct**	Types of KM Strategy	Measurements and performance indicators of KM	The type of KM strategy adopted directs the choice of measurements and the indicators of business performance (Abou-Zeid, 2003 ; Asoh et al, 2003; Sharkie, 2003).
16	**Measure**	Measurements and performance indicators of KM	Critical Success Factors of KM	Measurements and the indicators of KM performance measure the critical success factors of KM (Abou-Zeid, 2003; Asoh et al, 2003; Sharkie, 2003).
17	**Contribute**	Success Criticize Factors of KM	Operational Performance	The critical success factors of KM contribute to the performance of businesses (Abou-Zeid, 2003; Asoh et al, 2003; Sharkie, 2003).

Figure 2. KM Alignment Framework

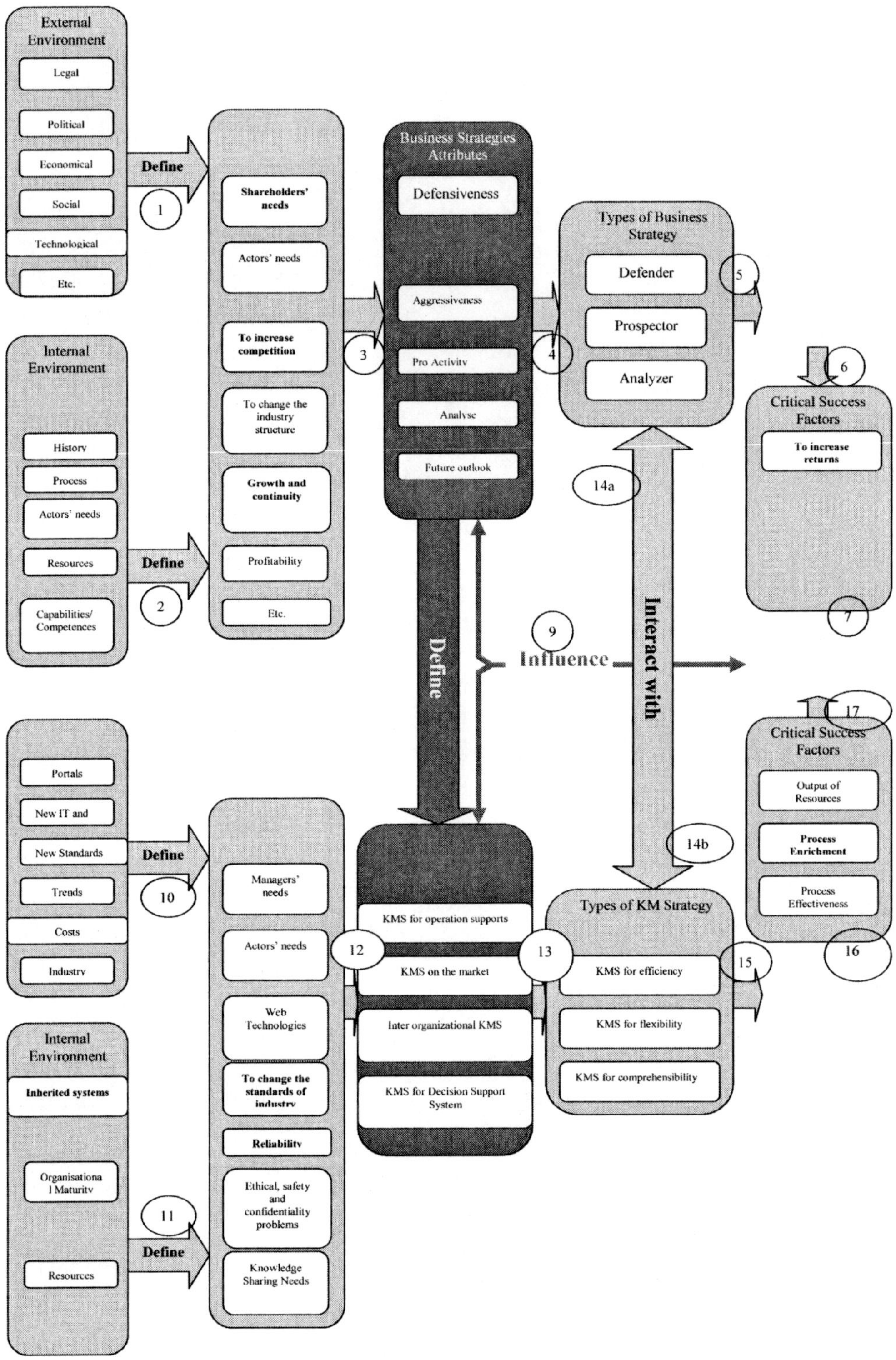

16. Key indicators of KM performance measure CSFs for KM.
17. CSFs for KM contribute to operational performance.

Differentiation in operations can promote growth in returns, reduction of costs, and increase of customer satisfactions, the three critical factors for successful business performance. With the management of knowledge, OP can be integrated in order to improve decision making for more output from resources, more enrichment from processes and increased effectiveness of processes, the critical factors for successful operations. Thus, through the alignment of KMS and BS, both business and operational performances are affected, and the overall performance by an organization can be strategically improved.

When evaluating models for strategic information planning, Earl (1990, 2003) found the organizational approach more effective among surveyed business managers than, for example, administrative or technological methods. The organizational method studied was based on requiring continued integration of decision making between IS and the rest of the organization. So concerning the overall performance level to be reached with a KMS, the principal question that should be posed by knowledge managers is which KM systems to recommend in order to reach a high level of both integration and differentiation at the same time?

Applying cartographic and technocratic techniques (Earl, 2001), Figure 3 illustrates topographically the taxonomy for aligning KM strategies with business strategies and provides a visualization of the interlinking of concepts and sub-concepts. As already defined and described, the interaction of attributes associated with strategies can lead to KM and business strategy alignment and can affect performance. Research in KM (Jennex et al, 2003; Davenport and Prusak, 1998) suggests that knowledge is an evolving mix of framed experience, values, contextual information and expert insight that can provide a way to evaluate and to incorporate new experiences and information. The KM alignment taxonomy supports a changing mix.

A CONCEPTUAL HIERARCHY FOR ACTIONS BY PRINCIPAL ACTORS IN THE STRATEGIC ALIGNMENT OF KM AND BUSINESS

To understand and apply the KMSABSA conceptual framework, internal and external actors can perform intervening actions that support the framework and taxonomy. The following definitions are provided to show the interactivity and links among organizations. The concepts of the KM strategic alignment are presented in a hierarchical order and the associated interactions by internal and external actors are defined to support the strategic management of knowledge in business.

A. Business Performance (Yu et al (2004, p.1) note that "organizations suffer from difficulties in evaluating performance of their KM initiatives." Indeed, the research of Lawrence and Lorsh (1967) showed that an organization whose integration level and differentiation was high reached a high performance level.)

AA. Differentiation

AA1. Financial Growth of a Company (Top management; - Managers; - KM Professionals): To define the KM activities or the KM practices that can be supported and the origins of any financial organizational performance criteria; to evaluate the contribution of the activities of KM to financial performance.

Figure 3. KM Alignment Taxonomy

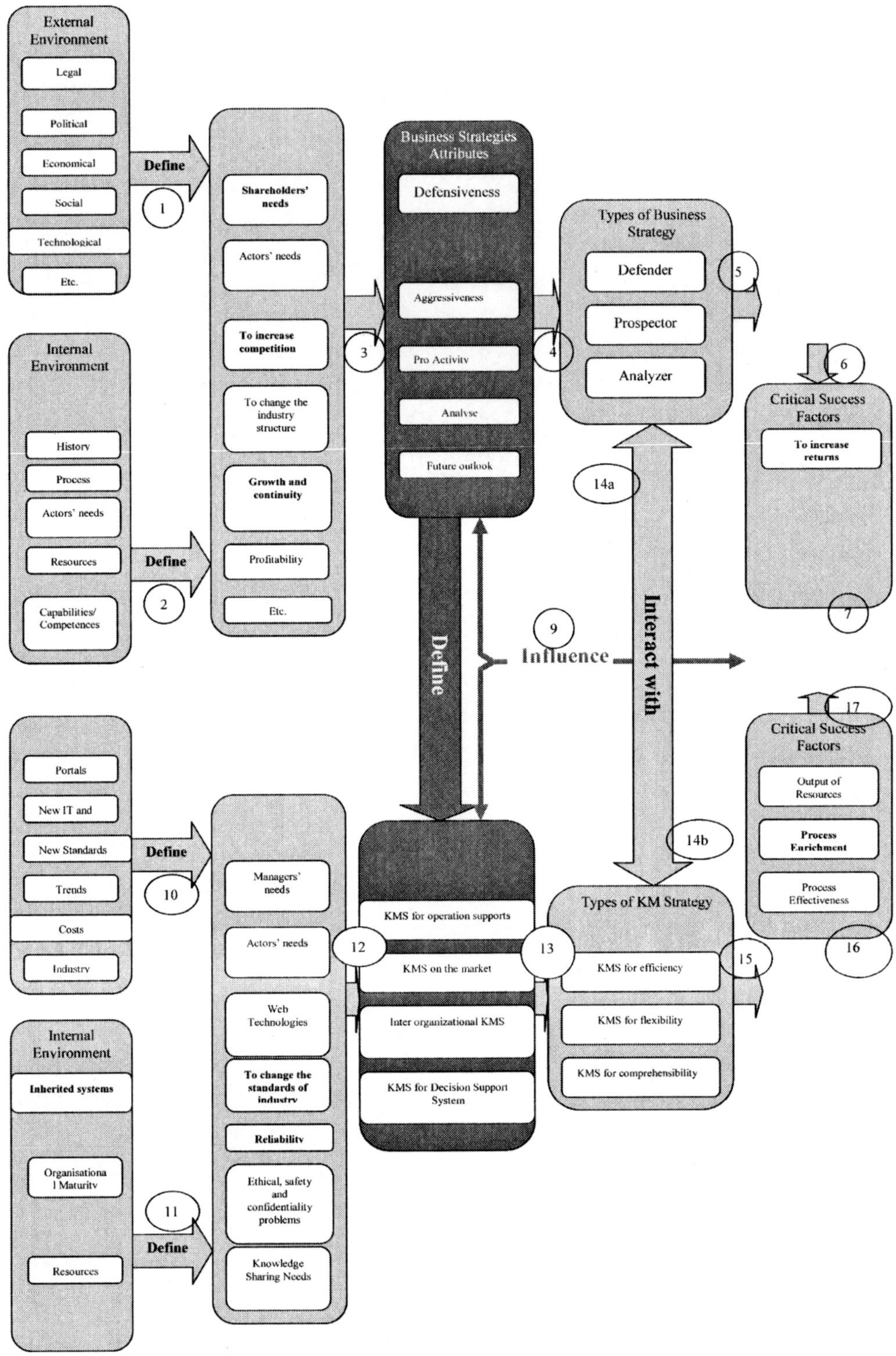

AA2. Reduction of Costs (Top management; Managers; KM Professionals): To identify and deploy the KMS or KM technologies which can help to reduce the operations costs and raise the level of knowledge in the value chain; to evaluate the contribution of KMS and KM technologies to the costs reduction.

AA3. Improvement of Customer Satisfaction (Top management; Managers; KM Professionals): To develop, exploit and use of a KMS, which makes it possible to improve customer knowledge; to evaluate the contribution of these KM systems to customer knowledge and to business practices and behaviours with respect to customer satisfaction with the whole of the system.

AB. Integration

AB1. Resource Effectiveness (Top management; Managers; KM Professionals): To identify the need for the capture and diffusion of knowledge resources; to evaluate the results and contribution of a KMS to the deployment of resources.

AB2. Process Enrichment (Top management; Managers; KM Professionals): To identify knowledge to be added or diffuse on each resource; to evaluate the contribution of the KMS on each resource to their enrichment.

AB3. Process Effectiveness (Top management; Managers; KM Professionals): To identify the requirements for knowledge by the processes, people, groups or whole organisational entity; to evaluate the contribution of a KMS to the effectiveness of the processes, people, groups or the whole organisational entity overall.

B. Business Strategy

BA. Business Drivers

BA1. Shareholders' Needs (Government; Top management; Board of directors; Managers): To define the customer's needs; - To define the requirements in information for the customers; to define needs of the governments and other partners; to define the requirements for consolidated information for the governments.

BA2. Actors' Needs (Concerned actors; IS/IT professionals; KM professionals): To identify needs of each actor concerned with the KMS; to define these needs; to represent these needs in comprehensible language about the information systems to the KM managers and professionals, and to the data processing professionals.

BA3. To Increase Competition (Top management; Managers): To develop the strategies likely to make the organization competitive; to define the priorities and the actions, using a well organized KM, in terms of costs reduction, business processes improvement, and productivity growth among employees to reach efficiency and effectiveness.

BA4. To Change Industry Structure (Top management; Professionals; Industries; Suppliers): To develop the strategies for research and development, which encourage the capture and dissemination of knowledge for knowledge sharing purposes, in order to improve the products and to influence industry rules; to ensure leadership based on product innovation and the business processes that can be generalized for the industry; to collaborate with other industry actors.

- **BA5. Growth and Continuity** (Top management; Managers): To define or adapt the rules and requirements for the growth needs of the customers; to anticipate the requirements in growth for the organization or the entity according to the industry and market data.
- **BA6. Profitability** (Top management; Managers): To restore or maintain an organization as competitive, effective and powerful; to define or redefine the rules of competitiveness, effectiveness and performance; to develop knowledge like an internal resource likely to bring value.

BB. Business Internal Environment

- **BB1. Organizational Culture** (Top management; Managers; Individuals): - To define the organisational vision directed towards the knowledge economy; - The definition, capture and diffusion of information to make it clear within the organization; - Integration of the company's culture and the individual culture, etc; - Development of a knowledge sharing culture between actors and entities in an organization.
- **BB2. History** (Top management; Managers; Individuals): To reconstitute the historical facts or to capitalize on the facts that provided a competitive advantage in the past; to develop and capture the culture from the organization's important historical facts.
- **BB3. Business Process** (Top management; Managers; People concerned): To redefine business process due to a new business orientation based on the knowledge economy; to adapt the processes and the ways of production along with the context for knowledge capture, storage, and exchange; to support the achievement of individual tasks by means of practice or through virtual communities.
- **BB4. Internal Actors' Needs** (Concerned individuals; IS Professionals; KM Professionals): To identify the requirements for information and knowledge of each internal actor concerned with a KMS; to define these needs; to translate these needs into comprehensible language for managers, IS and KM professionals, and computer professionals at the same time.
- **BB5. Resources** (Top management; Managers; Professionals or KM Experts): To allow substantial budgets for KM; to create KM structures and important KM stations; to ensure the training of leaders, managers and employees to understand the reality of KM; to grant the infrastructures and resources necessary for the correct operation of a KM structure.
- **BB6. Capabilities/Competencies** (Managers): To develop specific competencies in management in order to help control business processes; to develop specific competencies in KM; to express and describe requirements for information and knowledge about entities; to develop specific competencies in the management of KM technology and new technologies; to anticipate and ensure the management of consequential organisational changes due to the introduction of KM and policies required for the successful implementation, adoption and diffusion of KM technologies.
- **BB7. Leadership** (Top Management): To develop an organisational leadership and a businesses vision based on the knowledge economy and business intelligence; to develop leadership in

a KM organisation by identifying and developing critical knowledge likely to lead to innovation, to constitute a strategic resource, or to support the strategy and business process; to invest in the infrastructures supporting the capture, preservation, and exchange of knowledge in the places where the actors are; to anticipate the needs and uncertainties of the market and economic environment using policies based on businesses intelligence and KM organisation; to make KM the *leitmotiv* of change in order to improve organisational performance; to frame objectives and policies that motivate managers and employees to distinguish themselves during the installation of KM technologies.

BC. Business External Environment

- **BC1. Legal Environment** (Governmental and legislative authorities; Professional courses and courts; industry, orders; private partners): To define the laws and operations rules for an organization in general; to define the specific laws and rules related to KM.
- **BC2. Political Environment** (Governmental Authorities, Elected officials, International Organizations): To define the orientation of management and operations; to grant a favourable political space to the operation of an organization; to define a specific orientation to KM.
- **BC3. Economical Environment** (Governmental and Legislative Authorities; Industry and professional groups; Private partners): To define the organizational budget; definition of the overall and KM-specific economic situation; to fix prices and tariffs; to define of the laws and rules that recognize knowledge as an economic resource like other organizational resources.
- **BC4. Social Environment** (Trade unions, Socio-professional groups, Consumers rights and human right organizations): To take care of the benefits and working conditions of trade unionists in an industry; to request rights to protect conditions at work and respect for deontological codes; to take care of customer rights concerning information and data; to take care of the rights to confidentiality and the access to personal information; to take care of the rights of intellectual property, etc.
- **BC5. Technological Environment** (Managers and professionals, ITC Managers and professionals): To define adequate technological architecture; to include special, suitable technologies; to include information technologies and telecommunication (ITC) adapted for KM; to ensure the implementation, adoption and diffusion of technologies related to KM.

C. KM Strategy

CA. KM Drivers

- **CA1. Manager needs** (IS Professional; KM Professionals): To answer KM needs of the various entities in an organization; to identify, answer and frame the KM requirements for the entities or the organization.
- **CA2. Technologies** (IT Managers; IS Professionals; KM Professionals): To unearth recent KM technologies (gates, development tools, etc.) and to insert them into the organization's KMS; to develop specific KM technologies for an organization and particular entities within the organization.
- **CA3. To Change Industrial Standards** (IS Professional; KM Professionals): To

develop KM systems and technologies that allow wide use and to be able to influence industry practices.

CA4. KM Reliability (IT Managers; IS Professionals; KM Professionals): To develop or acquire a reliable KMS in terms of robustness, flexibility and ability to meet present and future organizational needs and the needs of specific entities.

CA5. Safety (Top management; Managers; IT Managers; IS Professionals; -KM Professionals): To establish a sedentary KMS in terms of confidentiality, software safety, and physics; to define the rules of clear and rigorous ethics for the use of IT and any KMS.

CA6 Knowledge in Real Time (Top management; Managers; IT Managers; IS Professionals; KM Professionals): To identify and define the requirements for knowledge in real time; to develop and deploy technologies likely to support the capture and sharing of knowledge in real time.

CB. KM Internal Environment

CB1. Inherited systems (Managers; IT Managers; IS Professionals; KM Professionals): To identify data and document management systems as data bases, knowledge bases, data warehouses, documentation data bases, ontology, the Web files, Tables, images, videos, etc; to define the possible integration of various existing systems into a new KMS.

CB2. Users (Concerned individuals; IT Managers; IS Professionals; KM Professionals): To define an organization's present and futures KM needs; to define the user interfaces that users want; to collaborate with IT professionals and KM professionals in the development process during a KM project; to frame the change process and KMS adoption as organisational technologies.

CB3. Organizational Maturity (Managers; IT Managers; IS Professionals; KM Professionals): To identify the KM organizational maturity level; to define a strategic plan aimed at moving from a lower level of maturity in an organization to a higher level of maturity in terms of KM.

CB4. KM Actors Requests (Managers; IT Managers; IS Professionals; KM Professionals): To adapt the KMS to new requests by various actors in a system; to establish a permanent dialogue with users of a system in order to obtain their loyalty and to be accountable for their knowledge requirements.

CB5. KM Resources (Top management; Managers; IT Managers; IS Professionals; KM Professionals): To recruit and educate human resources in order to develop KM expertise; to equip an organization with IT resources dedicated to KM; to equip an organization with a precise budget for the development and implementation of a KMS.

CB6. KM Capabilities/Competencies (Managers): To develop KM capabilities and competency.

CB7. KM Processes (Top management; Managers; IT Managers; IS Professionals; KM Professionals): To manage KM projects; to ensure the development of a KMS; to ensure the management of work partitioning or subcontracting for a KMS; to manage the processes of implementation, adoption and diffusion of a KMS within an organization; to manage the changes related to the introduction of a KMS.

CB8. KM Infrastructures (Top management; Managers; IT Managers; IS Professionals; KM Professionals): To equip an organization with the dedicated technological infrastructure required for KM; to develop the technological and KM infrastructures required for the types of business strategy retained by the organization.

CC. KM External Environment

CC1. News Technological Interfaces for KM (Managers; IT Managers; IS Professionals; KM Professionals): To define the requirements of IT for new technological interfaces for KM according to the needs for each system's actor.

CC2. News Technologies (Managers; IT Managers; IS Professionals; KM Professionals): To define the technological infrastructure likely to support a KMS.

CC3. KM Development/Acquisition Costs (Managers; IT Managers; IS Professionals; KM Professionals): To estimate acquisition or development costs for a KMS.

CC4. KM Market Trends (Managers; IT Managers; IS Professionals; KM Professionals): To study the market trends as regards the development and use of KM and a KMS standard.

CC5. KM Industry (Managers; IT Managers; IS Professionals; KM Professionals): To adapt a KMS to requirements or industry standards.

In order to answer the question "which are the KM capabilities that an organization can develop in order to attain business performance or to obtain sustained competitive advantage?", the next section helps.

KNOWLEDGE-BASED VIEW OF FIRM'S RESOURCES AND CAPABILITIES

Organizational Knowledge as Strategic Assets

While having unique access to valuable resources is one way to create competitive advantage, in some cases either this may not be possible, or competitors may imitate or develop substitutes for those resources. Firms having superior knowledge, however, are able to coordinate and combine their traditional resources in new and distinctive ways, providing more value for their customers than can their competitors (Penrose, 1959; Teece, Pisano, & Shuen, 1997) . That is, by having superior *intellectual* resources, a firm can understand how to exploit and develop their traditional resources better than competitors. Therefore, *knowledge* can be considered the most important strategic resource, and the ability to generate, mobilize and utilize it the most important capability for building and sustaining competitive advantage (Grant, 1996; Kogut & Zander, 1992; Spender, 1994; Winter, 1987) . The broadest value proposition, then, for engaging in knowledge management is that it can enhance the organization's fundamental ability to compete.

However, which is the knowledge that makes the advantage sustainable? It is the context-specific and tacit knowledge embedded in complex organizational routines and developed from experience. Such type of organizational knowledge possesses four characteristics namely: being valuable; being rare; being inimitable; and being non-substitutable (Michalisin, Smith, & Kline, 1997). First, it is valuable as it usually results in improved products, processes, technologies, or services. Second, it is rare as it is dependent on the knowledge and experiences of current and past employees, and is built on specific organizational prior knowledge. Third, it is inimitable as it builds on the unique past history of the organization's own experiences

Figure 4. KM Capabilities Taxonomy

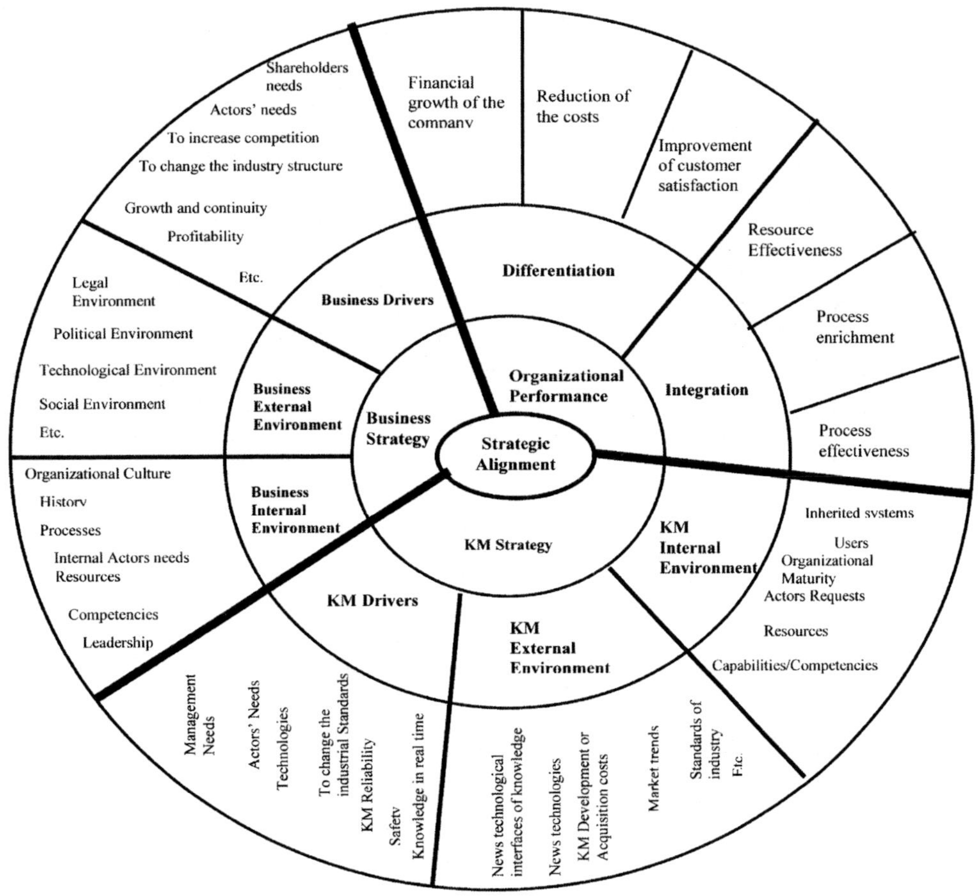

and accumulated expertise (Reed & DeFillippi, 1990). Finally, it is non-substitutable, as the context in which it has been created and used cannot be replicated.

Knowledge (K-) Capability of the Firm (Abou-Zeid, 2003).

Although proponents of the resource-based view generally tend to define resources broadly, to include tangible, intangible, and personnel-based resources, (Grant, 1991) distinguishes between *resources* and *capabilities*. While resources serve as the basic units of analyses, firms create competitive advantage by assembling resources that work together to create *organizational capabilities*. Capabilities, thus, refer to an *organization's ability to assemble, integrate, and deploy valued resources, usually, in combination or co-presence* (Amit & H, 1993; Russo & Fouts, 1997; Schendel, 1994). Extending the traditional notion of organizational capabilities to a firm's KM function, a firm's *KM capability* is defined here as its *ability to generate, mobilize and utilize organizational explicit and tacit knowledge in combination or co-presence with other resources and capabilities*. Thus, as shown in Figure 4, KM-capability in context of Km strategic alignment can be analyzed along three dimensions, namely: *knowledge (K)-infrastructures*, *knowledge (K)- processes*, and *knowledge (K)-skills*.

The *K-technical infrastructure* includes IT-enabled technologies that support KM activities such as business intelligence, collaboration and distributed learning, K-discovery, K-mapping, opportunity generation and security. The *K-structural infrastructure* refers to the presence of enabling formal organization structures and the organization's system of rewards and incentives.

The second dimension of the KM-capability, Knowledge (K)-processes, deals with the processes that change the states of organizational knowledge. Based on the literature review (e.g., (Firestone, 1999; Nissen, Kamel, & Sengupta, 2000; Nonaka, 1994; Probst, Raub, & Romhardt, 2000; Zack, 1999) and on analysis of several KM initiatives (e.g., (Davenport, 1998; Elliott, 1997, 1998) K-manipulation processes can be classified into three main categories, i.e., K-generation, K-mobilization and K-application. The knowledge generation process includes all activities by which new knowledge is generated within the organization. Knowledge mobilization means increasing the visibility of knowledge by sharing it or transferring it from one bearer (the knowledge provider, owner or source) to another (the knowledge seeker or target) through space or time. The knowledge bearer could be an artifact, such as technical documents or best practice databases, or human, such as experts in a certain domain. Based on the nature of the provider/source and seeker/target, four K-mobilization types can be distinguished, i.e., human-human, human-artifact, artifact-human and artifact-artifact (Abou-Zeid, 2002). Finally, during K-application processes knowledge is embodied in various forms. Knowledge can be used to develop new product/service/business processes or to improve existing ones. Associated with the processes of K-application are the processes of K-evaluation which includes all the activities that aim at justifying and measuring the business value of the knowledge.

However, knowledge processes are characterized by their dual nature. On the one hand there are K-manipulating processes, i.e., processes such as acquiring knowledge, converting it into a useful form, applying it, and protecting it. On the other hand, it has been identified that cultural and organizational issues are crucial in the successful deployment of KMS (Alavi & Leidner, 1999; von Krogh, Ichijo, & Nonaka, 2000). Therefore, each K-manipulating process should be associated with one or more K-enabling process such as managing conversation, mobilizing knowledge activists, creating the right context (von Krogh et al., 2000).

The last dimension of the K-capability is K-skills. KM processes are by their very nature multifaceted. They involve many dimensions such as cultural, technical, organizational and human. This characteristic of KM processes reflects on the nature of skills required to perform them. For example, Malhotra (Malhotra, 1997) defines a Senior Knowledge Executive, such as a Chief Knowledge Officer (CKO) or an Organizational Knowledge Architect, as the person who should have the combined capabilities of a business strategist, technology analyst, and a human resource professional. The ability to facilitate the ongoing process of knowledge sharing and knowledge renewal, the ability to develop the human and cultural infrastructure that facilitates information sharing, and the ability to utilize the available technologies for serving the creation, sharing and documentation of knowledge are some examples of the required skills.

In addition, there needs to be a procedure for implementation that would involve concepts, actors, actions and processes. The first step for businesses and organizations would be to identify their strategic character.as Defenders, Prospectors, or Analyzers (Swain & Ekionea, 2008). Finally, the *K-culture* and its involvement of elements such as corporate vision and the organization's system of values should be considsered (Gold et al., 2001).

CONCLUSION

The paradigm of the resources explains that it is from exploitation of rare, inimitable and non-substitutable resources valorized by the customer that the organization gets its competitive advantages; which enables it to maintain or to precede competition (Barney, 1991). Thus, developing KM strategic alignment and KM capabilities frameworks and taxonomies is very valuable for researchers and practitioners for understanding and using adequately concepts and terms in KM field. It seems that the "lack of a proper framework for assessing the current status of KM has cast doubt over the basic concept itself" (Yu et al, 2004, p.1). The principal contribution intended by this article is to encourage the classification of key words associated with KM strategy and KM capabilities in the context of alignment with business strategy. Therefore, the framework and taxonomies presented here aim to answer one of the concerns in the KM literature (Earl, 2001; Maier, 2001; Asoh et al., 2003; Yu et al, 2004) that there be a comprehensive, dynamic list of the concepts and definitions used in this research field. The approach to development is based on tables, figures and concept classification and is intended to focus on various aspects of KM and avoid the distraction of unnecessary details. Specific actions are offered for the strategic activities of intervening actors. Lastly, it is important to also note that the purpose of this work was not to undertake an exhaustive study on the subject of KM and business strategies, but to approach the issue in the field of KM that there is a need for taxonomies and frameworks to support better use of KM concepts in industry and in academic research.

REFERENCES

Abou-Zeid, E. (2002). A Knowledge Management Reference Model. *Journal of Knowledge Management*, *6*(5), 486–499. doi:10.1108/13673270210450432

Abou-Zeid, E. (2003). Developing Business Aligned Knowledge Management Strategy. In E. Coakes (Ed.), *Knowledge Management: Current Issues and Challenges* (pp. 156-172). IRM Press.

Adams, G. L., & Lamont, B. T. (2003). Knowledge Management systems and developing sustainable competitive advantage. *Journal of Knowledge Management*, *7*(2), 142–154. doi:10.1108/13673270310477342

Alavi, M., & Leidner, D. (1999). Knowledge Management Systems: Issues, Challenges, and Benefits. *Communication of the AIS, 1*(7). Retrieved from http://cais.isworld.org/articles/1-7/

Amit, R., & Shoemaker, P. J. H. (1993). Strategic Assets and Organizational Rents. *Strategic Management Journal*, *14*(1), 33–46. doi:10.1002/smj.4250140105

Asoh, D., Belardo, S., & Duchessi, P. (2003). Alignment: The missing link in knowledge management research. *Fourth European Conference on Knowledge Management* (pp. 39-47). Fergal McGrath University of Limerick.

Barney, J. (1991). Firm Resources and Sustained Competitive Advantage. *Journal of Management*, *17*(1), 99–120. doi:10.1177/014920639101700108

Barney, J. B. (1986). Organizational Culture: Can It Be a Source of Sustained Competitive Advantage. *Academy of Management Review*, *11*(3), 656–665. doi:10.2307/258317

Booto Ekionea, J.-P., & Abou-Zeid, E.-S. (2005). Knowledge Management and Sustained Competitive Advantage: A Resource-Based Analysis. *IRMA (Information Resources Management Association International Conference), Proceedings*. San Diego (USA). May, 15-18.

Chang, S.-G., & Ahn, J.-H. (2005). Product and Process Knowledge in the Performance-oriented Knowledge Management Approach. *Journal of Knowledge Management, 9*(4), 8–18. doi:10.1108/13673270510610378

Conner, K. R. (1991). A Historical Comparison of Resource-Based Theory and Five Schools of Thought within IIndustrial Organization Economics: Do We Have a New Theory of the Firm? *Journal of Management, 17*(1), 121–154. doi:10.1177/014920639101700109

Conner, K. R., & Prahalad, C. K. (1996). A Resource-Based Theory of the Firm: Knowledge Versus Opportunism. *Organization Science, 7*(5), 477–501. doi:10.1287/orsc.7.5.477

Cooper, B. L., Watson, H. J., Wixon, B. H., & Goodhue, D. L. (2000). Data Warehousing Supports Corporate Strategy at First American Corporation. *MIS Quarterly, 24*(4), 547–567. doi:10.2307/3250947

Davenport, T. H. (1998). Teltech: The Business of Knowledge Management Case Study. Retrieved from http://www.bus.utexas.edu/kman/telcase.htm.

Davenport, T. H., & Prusak, L. (1998). *Working knowledge*. Boston: Harvard Business School Press.

Dieng, R., et al. (2000). *Méthodes et outils pour la gestion des connaissances*. Paris: Dunod.

Dierickx, I., & Cool, K. (1989). Asset Stock Accumulation and Sustainablity of Competitive Advantage. *Management Science, 35*(12), 1504–1510. doi:10.1287/mnsc.35.12.1504

Earl, M. (2001). Knowledge Management Strategies: Toward a Taxonomy. *Journal of Management Information Systems, 18*(1), 215–233.

Earl, M. J. (1983). Emerging trends in managing new information technologies. Oxford Centre for Management Studies Research Paper 83/4. In Boland, R. J. & Hirschheim, R. A. (Eds.) (1987), *Critical Issues in Information Systems Research*. Chichester: Wiley.

Earl, M. J. (1990). *Proceedings of the International Conference on Information Systems*. Copenhagen, Denmark.

Earl, M. J. (2003). Approaches to Information Systems Planning: Experiences in strategic information systems planning. In D. Leidner & R. Galliers (Eds.), *Strategic Information Management*. Oxford: Butterworth-Heinemann/Elsevier.

Elliott, S. (1997). Case Corporation's Pilot Effort Proves Value of Knowledge Management. *Knowledge Management in Practice*, 10.

Elliott, S. (1998). Broderbund Builds Stong 'Case' for Internal, External Knowledge Sharing. Knowledge Management in Practice(14).

Firestone, J. (1999). Enterprise Knowledge Management Modeling and Distributed Knowledge Management Systems. Retrieved from http://www.dkms.com/EKMDKMS.html.

Foss, N. J., Knudsen, C., & Montgomery, C. A. (1997).An Exploration of Common Ground: Integrating Evolutionary and Strategic Theories of the Firm. In C.A. Montgomery (Ed.), *Resources-Based and Evolutionary of the firm*. Boston: Kluwer Academic Publishers.

Galliers, R. D. (1987). Information systems planning in the United Kingdom and Australia: a comparison of current practice. In P. I. Zorkorczy (Ed.), *Oxford Surveys in Information Technology, Vol. 4* (pp. 223-255). Oxford: Oxford University Press.

Gold, A., Malhotra, A., & Segars, A. (2001). Knowledge Management: An Organizational Capabilities Perspective. *Journal of Management Information Systems*, *18*(1), 185–214.

Grant, R. M. (1991). The Resource-Based Theory of Competitive Advantage: Implications for Strategy Formulation. *California Management Review*, *33*(3), 114–135.

Grant, R. M. (1996). Prospering in Dynamically-Competitive Environments: Organizational Capability as Knowledge Integration. *Organization Science*, *4*(July-August), 375–387. doi:10.1287/orsc.7.4.375

Hansen, M. T., Nohria, N., & Tierney, T. (1999). What's your strategy for managing knowledge? *Harvard Business Review*, (March-April): 106–116.

Henderson, J. C., & Venkatraman, N. (1993). Strategic Alignment: Leveraging Information Technology for Transforming Organizations. *IBM Systems Journal*, *32*(1).

Jennex, M. E., & Olfman, L. (2005). Assessing Knowledge Management Success. *International Journal of Knowledge Management*, *1*(2), 33–49.

Jennex, M. E., Olfman, L., & Addo, T. B. A. (2003). *The Need for an Organizational Knowledge Management Strategy*. Paper presented at the 36th Hawaii International Conference on System Sciences. HICSS36. IEEE Computer Society. January.

Kogut, B., & Zander, U. (1992). Knowledge of the Firm, Combinative Capabilities, and the Replication of Technology. *Organization Science*, *3*(3), 383–397. doi:10.1287/orsc.3.3.383

Lawrence, P. R., & Lorsch, J. W. (1967). *Organization and Environment*. Boston, MA: Harvard University Press.

Leidner, D., & Galliers, R. (Eds.). (2003). *Strategic Information Management*. Oxford: Butterworth-Heinemann/Elsevier.

Luftman, J. N., et al. (2004). *Managing the IT Resource: Leadership in the Information Age*. Pearson, Prentice Hall.

Maier, R. (2001). Towards a Framework for Knowledge Management Strategies: Process Orientation as Strategic Starting Point. In *Proceedings of the 34th Hawaii International Conference on System Sciences*. IEEE Computer Society.

Malhotra, Y. (1997). Profile of the Ideal Knowledge Manager/Architect. http://www.brint.com/wwwboard/messages/273.html.

Michalisin, M. D., Smith, R. D., & Kline, D. M. (1997). In Search of Strategic Assets. *The International Journal of Organizational Analysis*, (4): 360–387. doi:10.1108/eb028874

Miles, R. E., & Snow, C. C. (1978). *Organizational Strategy, Structure and Process*. New York: McGraw-Hill.

Nissen, M., Kamel, M., & Sengupta, K. (2000). Integrated Analysis and Design of Knowledge Systems and Processes. In Y. Malhotra (Ed.), *Knowledge Management and Virtual Organizations* (pp. 214-244). Idea Group Publishing.

Nolan, R. (1979). Managing the crises in data processing. *Harvard Business Review*, *57*(2).

Nonaka, I. (1994). A Dynamic Theory of Organizational Knowledge Creation. *Organization Science*, *5*(1), 14–37. doi:10.1287/orsc.5.1.14

Penrose, E. (1959). *The Theory of the Growth of the Firm*. New York: Wiley.

Peppart, J., & Ward, J. (2004). Beyond Strategic Information Systems: towards an IS capability. *The Journal of Strategic Information Systems*, *13*, 167–194. doi:10.1016/j.jsis.2004.02.002

Probst, G., Raub, S., & Romhardt, K. (2000). *Managing Knowledge: Building Block for Success*. John Wiley.

Reed, A., & DeFillippi, R. J. (1990). Causal Ambiguity, Barriers to Imitation, and Sustainable Competitive Advantage. *Academy of Management Review*, *15*(1), 88–102. doi:10.2307/258107

Roth, J. (2003). Enabling knowledge creation: learning from an R&D organization. *Journal of Knowledge Management*, *7*(1), 32–48. doi:10.1108/13673270310463608

Rumelt, R. P. (1984). Towards a Strategic Theory of the Firm. In A. B. Lamb (Ed.), *Competitive Strategic Management* (pp. 566-570). Englewood Cliffs, NJ: Prentice Hall.

Russo, M. V., & Fouts, P. A. (1997). A Resource-based Perspective on Corporate Environmental Performance and Profitability. *Academy of Management Journal*, *40*(3), 534–559. doi:10.2307/257052

Sabharwal, R., & Chan, Y. (2001). Alignment between business and IS strategies: A configurational approach. *Information Systems Research*, *12*(1), 11–33. doi:10.1287/isre.12.1.11.9714

Schendel, D. (1994). Introduction to Competitive Organizational Behavior: Toward an Organizationally Based Theory of Competitive Advantage. *Strategic Management Journal*, *15*, 1–4. doi:10.1002/smj.4250150901

Sharkie, R. (2003). Knowledge creation and its place in the development of sustainable competitive advantage. *Journal of Knowledge Management*, *7*(1), 20–31. doi:10.1108/13673270310463590

Spender, J.-C. (1994). Organizational Knowledge, Collective Practice and Penrose Rents. *International Business Review*, *3*(4), 353–367. doi:10.1016/0969-5931(94)90028-0

Spiegler, I. (2000). Knowledge Management: A New Idea or a Recycled Concept? *Communications of AIS (June)*, *3*(14).

Swain, D. & Ekionea, J.-P. B. (2008). A Framework for Developing and Aligning a Knowledge Management Strategy. *Journal of Information and Knowledge Management (June)*, *7*(2).

Teece, D. J., Pisano, G., & Shuen, A. (1997). Dynamic Capabilities and Strategic Management. *Strategic Management Journal*, *18*(7), 509–533. doi:10.1002/(SICI)1097-0266(199708)18:7<509::AID-SMJ882>3.0.CO;2-Z

von Krogh, G., Ichijo, K., & Nonaka, I. (2000). Enabling Knowledge Creation: How to Unlock the Mystery of Tacit Knowledge and Release the Power of Innovation: Oxford University Press.

Wernerfelt, B. (1984). A resource-based view of the firm. *Strategic Management Journal*, *5*(2), 171–180. doi:10.1002/smj.4250050207

Winter, S. G. (1987). Knowledge and Competence as Strategic Assets. In D. J. Teece (Ed.), *The Competitive Challenge: Strategies for Industrial Innovation and Renewal* (pp. 159-184). Cambridge, MA: Ballinger Publishing Company.

Yu, S.-H., Kim, Y.-G., & Kim, M.-Y. (2004). *Linking Organizational Knowledge Management Drivers to Knowledge Management Performance: An Exploratory Study*. Paper presented at the 37th Hawaii International Conference on System Sciences. HICSS36, IEEE Computer Society.

Zack, M. H. (1999). Managing Codified Knowledge. *Sloan Management Review*, *40*(4), 45–58.

Chapter 8
Knowledge Organization with Mashups:
A Mashup Experiment in an Enterprise Environment

Qin Zhu
HP Laboratories, USA

Justin Meza
HP Laboratories, USA

ABSTRACT

Knowledge is based on fact and is often obtained from experience or via association. Knowledge organization is the systematic management and organization of knowledge (Hodge, 2000). With the advent of Web 2.0, mashups have become a hot new thing on the Web. A mashup is a Web site or a Web application that combines content from more than one source and delivers it in an integrated way (Fichter, 2006). This chapter will first discuss knowledge and knowledge organization and review literature on these topics. Then the authors will explore the concept and look at the components of a typical mashup. In addition, they will provide an overview of various mashups on the Internet. From these facts, the chapter proceeds to draw some connections between knowledge organization and mashups, solidifying the authors' assertions with an elaboration on their real-world, a mashup experiment in an enterprise environment. The authors will describe how they mixed the content from two sets of data and created a new source of data: a novel way of organizing and displaying HP Labs Technical Reports. The findings from this project will be included and some best practices for creating enterprise mashups will be given. Finally, they will discuss the future of enterprise mashups.

INTRODUCTION

Knowledge is the understanding of facts or, information or knowing how to do something from experience or via association. Knowledge organization is the systematic management and organization of knowledge (Hodge, 2000). The new mashup technology can be used to organize, harvest, share, and leverage knowledge.

With the endless development of new technologies, more and more information—in a wide variety

DOI: 10.4018/978-1-60566-954-0.ch008

of formats—continues to become increasingly available on the Web, making it one of the most information-rich infrastructures ever built. With the advent of Web 2.0, mashups, which are combinations of content from different sources, have become a hot topic on the Web, gaining increasing popularity. According to Programmableweb.com (http://www.programmableweb.com/), there are currently 3.09 unique mashups being created each day, as programmers, Web developers, and hobbyists continue to blend data and services from different sources to produce entirely unique sets of content.

KNOWLEDGE AND KNOWLEDGE ORGANIZATION

What is knowledge? The Random House Dictionary of the English Language defines knowledge as "acquaintance with facts, truths, or principles, as from study or investigation." Webster's New Collegiate Dictionary defines knowledge as "the fact or condition of knowing something with familiarity gained through experience or association." According to Davenport and Prusak (1998), knowledge can be defined as a mix of framed experience, values, contextual information, and expert insight that provides a framework for evaluating and incorporating new experiences and information. Wilson (2002) more simply states that knowledge is what we know. Knowledge involves the mental processes of comprehension, understanding and learning that go on in the mind and only in the mind, however much they involve interaction with the world outside the mind, and interaction with others. These various definitions of knowledge can be boiled down to knowledge basically meaning knowing facts and information, and knowing how to do something. Knowledge is gained through past experience such as study or investigation.

Knowledge is often created in the mind of the individual. Knowledge would be of little value if it remained locked in the mind of the individual without knowledge representation, without knowledge sharing, and without knowledge accessing. Instead, however knowledge often is embedded in documents or repositories and in organizational routines, processes, practices and norms. Knowledge is also about meaning in the sense that it is context-specific (Huber, Davenport and King, 1998). For knowledge to be valuable and useful, it needs to be accessed and used. How can knowledge be accessible and usable? Knowledge organization addresses this question to some extent.

What is knowledge organization? One view from a Library and Information Science and information organization standpoint, is that knowledge organization is the management and organization of knowledge in a systematic way in order to support easier access to and retrieval of knowledge (Hodge, 2000). It also encompasses creating, sharing, and leveraging knowledge. Knowledge organization enables the management of a collection of materials, information, and documents, which represent recorded knowledge. It forms a bridge between the user's information need and the material in the collection. As the user browses, searches, and navigates, knowledge organization guides the user towards discovery. Knowledge organization also helps to answer questions about the scope of a collection (Hodge).

Knowledge organization has become a wide interdisciplinary field, with a broader focus than Library and Information Science. According to Hjerland (2003), there are also social and intellectual forms of knowledge organization. Social forms of knowledge organization are related to professional training, disciplines and social groups. The social perspective includes the social systems of genres and documents and the social system of knowledge producers, knowledge intermediaries and knowledge users. The social system of documents, genres and agents makes available a very complicated structure of potential subject access points, which may be used in information retrieval. This reflects what Huber, Davenport and King (1998) describe about knowledge: it becomes embedded in organizational norms and is context-sensitive.

Both Hodge (2000) and Hjerland (2003) mention semantic approaches to knowledge organization. Hodge proposes semantic networks and ontologies as schemes for knowledge organization. Hjerland describes how the basic unit in knowledge organization is the semantic relation between two concepts. But how to decide which things should be grouped together is not an easy task.

This leads to the points brought up by Wilde (2006): in any complex environment, it is unlikely that it is possible to design and build one unified knowledge organization system that will meet all requirements and be used by all people. Instead, systems often evolve out of practical needs. He points out that the constant changes make it challenging to formalize and organize knowledge. It becomes harder to re-design the system to better reflect the changes once the knowledge organization system and the underlying formalization get bigger and more complex. He proposes a mashup model, loosely coupled distributed system architecture, for knowledge organization. He also introduces Semantic Web technologies for shared understanding of the different domains covered by different components for knowledge organization. The Semantic Web was first thought up by Tim Berners-Lee. According to Berners-Lee (2001), for the Semantic Web, computers can access structured collections of information and sets of rules to be used for automated reasoning. By this means, people can create programs to collect Web content from diverse sources, process the information and exchange the results with other programs. Thus, it will be a universal linked Web for knowledge exchange. Semantic Web as a structure for programmatic access and process will open up the knowledge and workings of human kind to the next level. Potentially it can assist the evolution of human knowledge.

From the review of knowledge organization, we can see that, knowledge organization helps users harvest and share knowledge. Additionally knowledge organization assists in the reuse and leveraging of knowledge to, in turn, create new knowledge and stimulate innovations. By exploring and getting familiar with existing knowledge, people will have more chances to create new knowledge and innovation. Just as Koestler (1964) describes: when one "uncovers, selects, re-shuffles, combines, synthesizes already existing facts, ideas, faculties, skills. The more familiar the parts, the more striking the new whole."

WHAT IS A MASHUP?

A mashup is a Web site or a Web application that combines content from more than one source to produce something entirely new (Fichter, 2006). Sometimes the sources of the content may not be directly related. The newly created content on a Web site resulting from a mashup may provide something new or meaningful compared with the content from each individual source.

The word mashup originated in the music industry, where it referred to the mixing and blending of two or more tracks of recorded music or instruments in order to create an entirely new sound track. The underlying concept of mashups on the Web is not new. Since the start of the Web, people have been gathering information from various sources and mashing it together with HTML code to present it in a newer, more useful form: Web pages. In information services and the field of knowledge organization, the concept of mashups is not new either. In these fields there has historically been a tradition of information service providers and knowledge organization vendors working with various sources, such as publishers, to collect publication and citation information, combine the collected data, and provide abstracts and indexing services. From the creation of abstracts and the population of indices, end users are able to find not only publications from a specific source, but also publications from a specific area, by a specific author, etc.

During the early stages of Web content integration, when the Web was still young, developers were required to manually collect and hand code information into an HTML page. In information services, the service provider may need to put the collected data from various sources into a central place such as a database to do further data processing, such as data normalization, and to provide an indexing service. Under Web 2.0, O'Reilly (2005) views the Web as platform. Mashups use the Web itself as the programming and content delivery platform. Mashups access data or information directly from Web sites and programmatically create dynamic new Web sites or Web applications, presenting the data in a more integrated or useful way. Once the mashup process has been established, it will continue to automatically read, process, present, and update the content and data collected from different sources for the end user in the form of a Web site. Compared to the early stages of Web content integration, there is almost no manual intervention at any stage of the process. Similarly, in the information services field, there has traditionally never existed a central place to aggregate and normalize data from different sources.

To begin creating a mashup, there are three necessary components: content or data sources, a mashup algorithm or process, and a presentation platform.

Content and Data Sources

These are the foundation of any mashup: the raw objects the mashup will work with. Without content and data, a mashup has no definition. Content and data may be obtained via APIs, Web feeds, or screen scraping techniques.

Recently, many providers have taken steps to make their content and data more readily accessible. Some have developed application programming interfaces (APIs) to give developers access to their content and data via Web protocols such as REST (Representational State Transfer) and also through Web services. Others provide Web feeds (simple XML documents for content syndication) in popular formats such as RSS or Atom as a means of accessing their content and data. Through the use of APIs and Web feeds, developers are given access to content and data from the system backend and can gather and retrieve this data programmatically.

But not all data sources provide such means of programmatically accessing their content. To get content from these providers, a technique known as screen scraping must be deployed. Screen scraping is the process of retrieving a raw set of mixed data and extracting and formatting it to a data structure of the developer's liking to eventually be processed and mashed up. Comparatively, APIs and Web feeds provide a more reliable source of information, as they are managed directly by the data's originator. Screen scraping must adapt to the layout and content of its source Web site. Most modern Web sites tend to change frequently and employ complicated layout schemes using technologies such as Cascading Style Sheets (CSS), making screen scraping a process requiring occasional manual revision.

Mashup Algorithm or Process

This is where the mashup gets its name: during this design step, content and data from different sources are cohesively and seamlessly integrated. The mashup process may take place on the server or on the client side of a given transaction or may be a combination of the two.

On the server side, mashups can be deployed using server side scripting techniques such as CGI, PHP, ASP, etc. Here, data is retrieved and processed before being forwarded to the client. In this way, more complex retrievals and transformations of the data may be performed on one or many computers.

On the client side, mashups can be generated directly from an end user's Web browser through scripting technologies such as JavaScript and Ajax (Asynchronous JavaScript and XML). Some advantages of deploying a client side mashup include reduced communication overhead and more seamless user experience provided by running the mashup effectively on the user's Web browser as if it were an application as opposed to a Web page.

In practice, a careful combination of both techniques often yields the most efficient and user friendly solution by combining the power of server side content retrieval and processing with client side caching and manipulation of data.

Presentation Platform

This is the interface where end users will view and interact with mashed up content. In many cases, the presentation platform's job is to view only a single *slice* of mashup data and provide the necessary interface to transition between contiguous slices. An old-fashioned projector acts as an analogous presentation platform. It reduces the complexity of all of its slides by only displaying one at a time. If someone wishes to view all the slides, the projector provides a means of navigating between them in a predictable way. So too does a mashup's presentation platform.

MASHUPS ON THE WEB

With the rapid growth of mashups on the Internet, most can be classified under the following genres: map mashups, photo and video mashups, search mashups, and news mashups. They share many of the same access and display methods and we highlight the details of one of the most prominent ones (map mashups), below.

A large number of mashups present today are map mashups. This may be due in part to the readily available set of API tools and API access to online map service providers such as Google Maps, Yahoo Maps, Microsoft Virtual Earth, and AOL MapQuest. These tools make it possible for programmers, Web developers, and hobbyists to easily mash up data and content with online maps. Map mashup developers must first obtain geographic information, such as latitude and longitude, for their data set and then mash the data up into a customized online map. One example of a large-scale map mashup is HousingMaps.com which mashes up real estate listings from Craigslist with Google Maps. A second example, Chicagocrime.org, combines data from the Chicago Police Department's Citizen ICAM Web site with data from Google Maps.

When Google first launched its Map service, there existed no API to capture its data. Later, one was added, and other online services soon followed suit. In fact, there exist APIs for a variety of services. Some developers mash up photo APIs and video APIs with photo and video information. Others mash up search APIs or consumer market place APIs, news source Web feeds and more. Technologies such as RSS and Atom feeds for news stories make it possible to have personalized news content delivered directly to the end user.

In general, mashups can be classified into two distinct categories: visual mashups and non-visual mashups (Merrill, 2006). Visual mashups blend data and content from different sources and present it in a graphical interface, producing a tangible result for the end user. Non-visual mashups are used as a way of converting data from one type to another. Their data is, in turn, further refined for specific processes, data integration, and content integration.

From our mashup concept elaboration and the following mashup examples, we can identify connections between knowledge organization and mashups. Mashup can be used for knowledge organization either at personal knowledge level or at enterprise scale. Increasingly, individuals and companies are realizing the potential for use of mashups on a business intranet or within an enterprise environment. Indeed, although mashups can be creatively used in an amateur realm by developers and hobbyists, they have distinct benefits for businesses as well, especially in the areas of business process, data integration, and content integration. In this paper we will describe our experiment with a mashup for knowledge organization under an enterprise environment.

OUR EXPERIMENT

In our experiment, we combined HP Labs technical report information with HP's intranet People Finder, and created a mashup: the Technical Report Contextual Viewer. With this combination of data, we were able to put recently published technical reports under the lab and departmental organizational structure with a tag cloud section for each level of the organizational tree based on keyword frequency within the technical reports. By scanning the tag cloud, end users are provided with a sense of recent research and developments in labs and departments. These capabilities provide a novel way of organizing and displaying HP Labs technical reports within an enterprise environment.

Motivation

Initially, this project began out of the desire for easier, and more importantly faster, access to already-available data without the hassle of processing that data by hand. To us, this meant at the very least providing a larger view of the picture, but we extended this goal to include a mechanism which allowed our end users to narrow down their queries by sifting through an already optimized and established infrastructure: the organizational tree. Again, like in most mashups, the focus was on harvesting data which was already available for our use but was just not yet connected in a meaningful way.

Technical Reports and the Technical Report RSS Feed

HP Labs technical reports are research papers, reports, and articles published by HP Labs. They provide a means of letting researchers access various research developments, keep pace with the progress of research, and collaborate on projects internally. They are high-quality, scholarly research papers. Externally available technical reports are recognized and indexed by major information services and search engines such as Thomson Reuters, Elsevier, Google, etc. Technical reports are managed by the technical report publication department which also provides a technical report RSS feed for recent technical reports. The technical report RSS feed updates researchers with recently published technical reports and provides an alternative way for researchers to keep pace with the progress of their research and to collaborate on various projects internally.

The Enterprise Directory

The HP Enterprise Directory is a large internally stored and managed LDAP (Lightweight Data Access Protocol) database used to store basic employee information. This information can later be retrieved through simple calls to the database from a desktop application, a Web application, or manually through a browser. People Finder is the frontend interface to the Enterprise Directory. It allows employees to search for other employees' contact information when connected to the company intranet. People Finder is a Web application consisting of a simple text box used for inputting employee search terms that upon data entry dynamically changes to a list box containing possible hits from the Enterprise Directory.

Data within the Enterprise Directory is stored in LDIF (LDAP Data Interchange Format) which presents entries as a group of labeled attributes and separates entries with blank lines. To query the database, one needs only perform a simple

HTTP call to the address of the database, specifying which constraints are to be placed on the query results.

The HP Enterprise Directory is available for company-wide use and even has documentation and source code available for sample queries in various languages. These important resources are what made People Finder and our Technical Report Contextual Viewer possible.

Linking it All Together

In any mashup application, it is essential that all forms of data communicate correctly with one another; often this requires a translator of sorts to ensure all forms of data can interact and work together. This translator most often comes in the form of a programming language. The target programming language for a mashup is what takes the various mixed forms of data and translates them into structures which can be manipulated within the language.

In our application, we simply took data from the user describing the scope of data to a view based on their input from a Web page form; retrieved, extracted, and organized the corresponding RSS feed data; and queried the LDAP database, retrieving a dataset containing entries pertaining to the end user's scope. When all the data to be mashed up had been extracted, we joined the overlap between our two datasets using a common field: the names of authors. Our LDAP query returned a list of employee names under a particular branch of the organizational structure, and the HP Labs technical report RSS feed contained the relevant technical reports associated with those names. By selectively displaying only those technical reports from the RSS feed that corresponded to our LDAP queries, we were able to deliver the desired content to our end users.

Mashups by their very nature must be sensitive to their data. While it would be ideal to be able to design a mashup solely with a particular end result in mind, it is often necessary to meet halfway between what the data present provides (or what the content provider *chooses* to provide through their API) and what the designer has in mind to accomplish. In our own mashup, extra caution was required when dealing with variations of the names used as keys to match authors in the LDAP database to their corresponding technical reports in the RSS feed. Sometimes authors publish works under a different name from that which they use in the database. In our case, the Enterprise Directory LDAP database stored variations of employees' names, allowing us to have multiple names to match against, providing a high rate of success when locating their corresponding technical reports.

In the instance where an author publishes a technical report under a completely different name from the forms listed in the Enterprise Directory, the Technical Report Contextual Viewer *degrades gracefully*: notifies the end user of the problem and presents alternative options for tracking down the requested information. Disadvantages of using data sources without specific APIs include the possibility of on-the-fly format changes. Mashups which are tactful enough to anticipate these changes and degrade gracefully to help the user work through them (and give the developer time to fix them) instead of merely crashing are result of good programming practice.

Figure 1 is a flow chart illustrating a high-level mashup description.

In Figure 1, the mashup utility gathers data from two sources, extracts the meaningful entries, organizes them so they are easier to work with, and finally combines them in some fashion. Content is then generated for the end user with an optional process of allowing users to customize the data presented to them by querying a different data set and running the mashup on the new results.

Figure 1. Workflow for a generalized mashup

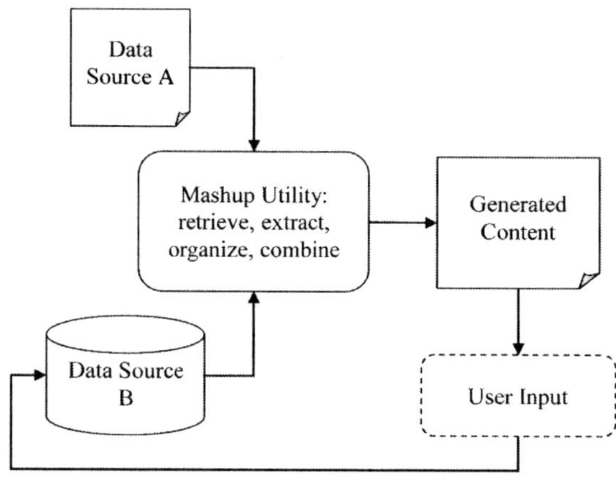

Our Mashup: The Technical Report Contextual Viewer

Upon navigating to the Technical Report Contextual Viewer frontend, the user is shown recent technical report information at a lab-wide scope—the largest view possible. At the top of the application are two *breadcrumb navigation* views showing a linked trail of where the user has traveled, both from a departmental standpoint as well as by the names of employees and their managers. Breadcrumb navigations show a user where they have been and how they got to a page by creating a trail of linked words denoting the sequential order of page accesses for a single session, and can be especially useful in hierarchically organized mashups.

Underneath the breadcrumb navigation is the name and a link to relevant contact information for the employee where the Technical Report Contextual Viewer's scope is rooted. If the employee manages other employees, their names are listed in a tabular format below for easy navigation and traversal; if any of these in turn manage employees, that fact is noted. It is important to understand that all information pertaining to the directory structure is inferred from the Enterprise Directory and is generated on the fly, making it robust against changes in the organizational structure.

Then the technical reports for the current scope are presented with links to their authors and the paper's abstracts (links to the papers themselves can be accessed from their respective abstracts). These are organized with the most recent technical reports appearing first (see Figures 2 and 3).

When a user navigates to more specific scopes, a tag cloud appears underneath the technical report listings, featuring in weighted font sized relevant keywords from the current abstracts. Clicking on one of the tags presents the user with a view of technical report abstracts containing the chosen keyword.

Keyword Tag Cloud

Tag clouds are a stereotypically classified Web 2.0 concept, although the notion they encapsulate has been around for a much longer time, stemming from roots in Information Services and Knowledge Management (Berry, et al). The idea of organizing data in such a manner that the most relevant portions are more visually accessible has always been a key design focus in many media. Tag clouds bring this concept to the digital realm, and do so in a dynamic fashion.

Several general paradigms may be presented when dealing with meaningful tag clouds:

Figure 2. A view of Technical Report Contextual Viewer

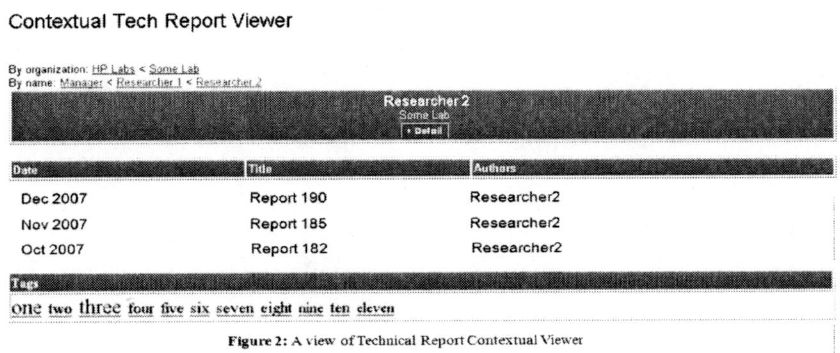

- *Capturing keywords (indexing).* Raw text must be read and processed in a meaningful way while keeping track of certain metrics. In our application, tag cloud keywords were captured by tallying the number of occurrences of each word present in all abstracts.
- *Filtering out noise (normalization).* Some results from indexing may be misleading or simply irrelevant and must be refines. In our mashup, once all possible keywords have been tallied, meaningless ones (such as articles and prepositions) must be sifted out.
- *Choosing candidates (reduction).* Too much data can be unpleasing to the eye and difficult to understand. After noisy data has been filtered out of our mashup, what remains is the keyword dataset, from which it is necessary to choose the *N* words with the highest hit counts.
- *Formatting the tags (organization).* In order to present the tag cloud information in a meaningful way, it is often helpful to scale the words relative to their frequency of appearance. This can often be performed by generating an absolute weight for each keyword based on how it ranks with every other keyword and then normalizing this number with respect to how it should appear within the presentation platform (in most cases, a Web browser).

The tag cloud provides a unique view of the data encapsulated within technical reports (see Figure 4). By glancing over the tag cloud, one can easily spot the most frequently cited abstract keywords. Comparing the font size of keywords

Figure 3. Sample breadcrumb navigation and gathered LDAP data. Note that all breadcrumb links and researcher data is generated at page access time through inference and user input

Figure 4. Keyword tag clouds provide both an easy-to-see glimpse of trends and links to related data

gives end users a sense of recent research and developments in labs and departments, especially key areas.

Tag clouds provide a useful kind of visual display for information and data. There are a few open-ended questions to consider when generating tag clouds. Some of them can also be applied for information and data visualization, a path for knowledge reasoning and knowledge relationship representation:

- Is the tag cloud a user-friendly feature? Does it help users find and access information? Does it provide additional information access points?
- Is it Web accessible? Is the tag cloud compliant with Web accessibility standards?
- How do you calculate the term frequency?
- How do you set the font size range for different term frequencies? As the frequency changes, the font size range may need to adjust or be set to accommodate the increase in frequency.

OUR FINDINGS

The mashup we created solved a specific business problem: quickly and easily finding recently published HP Labs technical reports under a lab and departmental organizational structure, providing a way to quickly scan the topics of technical reports as well. One of the primary reasons for creating enterprise mashups is to solve a specific business problem. Since there was already data from People Finder at the intranet level and data from the technical report publications system, there was no need to store data from these two sources in a third place. The Technical Report Contextual Viewer mashup was built to combine the data from these two sources *in-place*. Our mashup was created for data integration and content integration, two of the key areas of benefit for enterprise mashups. The Technical Report Contextual Viewer mashup is a lightweight integration—it relies on data from People Finder and the technical report RSS feed. There is an intrinsic serviced dependency. In addition, the Technical Report Contextual Viewer mashup exists only as an add-on to existing technical report data to provide a different view; the mashup will not replace the regular technical report process or delivery of data.

Our experiment indicates that creating an enterprise mashup will involve some form of the following process: gathering data from different sources, identifying the join point or the overlap area for mashing up, processing the data and generating mashed content, and presenting a formatted mashed content output.

We also identified some best practices for the process of creating a mashup, especially within an enterprise environment.

Gather Data from Different Sources

There is a huge amount of information on the Internet. There is a fair amount of information on an intranet as well. During the mashup preparation stage, one must analyze the sources available and find out which ones are mashable, that is, easy to extract data and content from, and which ones may need a lot of work to retrieve the relevant data (through methods such as screen scraping).

Remember to keep in mind the motivation for creating a mashup: to solve some business problem or issue. Narrow your scope of data sources to those within your enterprise purpose, making the process of identification of data and content more efficient and relevant, in turn allowing the mashup to succinctly serve the business process and purpose.

Once a set of sources has been identified, the owners of the sources may need to be contacted for permission. Even if a service is open for internal use through one interface, it might still be a good practice to notify its owner of its intended use. If the service were to change in any way in the future, its owner might take the initiative to notify the developer of the mashup. For an external service provider such as on the Internet, it is of course necessary to read any applicable license agreements for data access restrictions, API documentation, and End-User License Agreements (EULAs).

Identify the Join Point or the Overlap Piece for Mashing Up

Once the relevant sets of data have been identified, a common join point or overlap piece must be identified to tie them together. Sometimes, this match point might not be obvious or some massaging of the data might need to be done to enable one to blend and mix the data to create a more integrated and seamless mashup.

Process Data and Generate Mashed Content

As mentioned in the preceding stage, sometimes one may need to do further data processing and manipulation. It may be necessary to think about how to leverage the existing services and interfaces existing for the data. One may consider how to handle the retrieval and where to put the processing of data, on the client side or on the server side. It is also important to consider the scalability for future growth of the mashup.

Another consideration is keeping the mashup as a lightweight data accessor. You can lower the overhead of IT and business process by eliminating any unnecessary data processing and integration.

Finally, some internal data may be restricted or confidential. In that case you will need to consider how to blend and separate secured data. Governance and standards will come into play. There will be policies on who can classify data sources and how, who can access the data source and how, and who can build and view mashup products and how. From a technological point of view, some security architecture should be deployed and implemented for user access and resource crawling.

Present Generated Mashed Content

Once you have the mashed up content, you need to present the content in a user-friendly way. If there are existing organization and institutional standards for content deliver, these must be adhered to as well.

To present secure data in mashup, it may be necessary to have a mechanism to check a user's credentials.

FUTURE DEVELOPMENT

With the further development of mashups, individuals and companies are increasingly realizing the promise and potential use of this technology. Some companies are working on tools to make it easier to develop mashups, especially for non-programmers.

Following are some mashup tools developed by various companies:

- Yahoo Pipes (http://pipes.yahoo.com) – a visual composition tool to aggregate, manipulate and combine content on the Web. A pipe is a date processing pipeline with one or more data sources, such as RSS, Atom or XML feeds. It includes operators to filter and manipulate feeds. Via the visual interface, it makes it easier for non-programmers to weld and match data from different sources.

- Google Mashup Editor (http://code.google.com/gme/) -- provides a set of tools for developers to quickly create simple Web applications and mashups with Google services, such as using Google Maps.
- Microsoft Popfly (http://www.popfly.com/) – a visual tool to combine photos, RSS feeds and information to create mashups.
- Microsoft Sharepoint (http://www.microsoft.com/sharepoint/) – Sharepoint can be a mashup platform for enterprise usage. One can add Web parts, RSS feeds, enterprise search, plug-ins and connectors to business process and business data.
- Intel Mash Maker (http://mashmaker.intel.com) – a visualization engine lets you create mashup with data from various sources including annotated Web pages.
- QEDWiki (http://devzone.zend.com/node/view/id/678) – a wiki based mashup maker.

As mentioned before, enterprise mashups are primary intended to solve certain business problems. Because business users and domain experts understand their needs better than programmers, simple, yet powerful, tools help create mashups and instant applications to solve their business problems without much of a learning curve. We envision more and more mashup tools will be developed and deployed in the enterprise environment with a focus on making these tools easy to use and able to create instant mashup applications, avoiding a manual programming stage for data matching and mashing.

As for the *role* of mashups in the enterprise environment, we can foresee more innovative and creative uses of mashups to lower IT infrastructure and business process costs, and to solve business problems. A number of enterprise mashup use cases are suggested and presented here: a mashup that combines a knowledge system—such as publications, reports, and documents—with an expert system to create a personalized knowledge system or an expert-based knowledge system; a mashup that overlays publications, reports, and documents with organizational structure or project teams to create an organization portfolio or project portfolio; a mashup that blends sale data with sales staff information to provide further analysis of the sales force; a mashup that mixes sale data with geographic information and product information to provide a view of the market per product and per region, helping the company to form and improve its marketing strategy; a mashup that combines supply requests with business units and product lines to provide further analysis of produce process and production efficiency. The list can go on and on.

For enterprise mashups, there are two other important issues which need to be addressed when adopting mashups. First, security, authorization and compliance. One must make sure sensitive information and information with right permission will be handled and processed in the correct manner. Second, data readiness and trustworthiness. As the data may be scattered within the enterprise, there may be multiple, conflicting versions of the same information. This could cause issues when doing data matching and mashing.

All in all, the mashup is an old concept equipped with new technologies under the new Web 2.0 environment. More and more enterprise mashups will be developed to solve business problems and help business process. Using mashups to organize knowledge will help put knowledge in context, making knowledge more discoverable. Moreover, it will help the process to harvest knowledge, and share knowledge. Therefore, it will help reuse and leverage existing knowledge to create new sources of knowledge and stimulate innovation.

REFERENCES

Benslimane, D., Dustdar, S., & Sheth, A. (2008). Services mashups: the new generation of Web applications. *IEEE Internet Computing, 12*(5), 13–15. doi:10.1109/MIC.2008.110

Berners-Lee, T., & Lassila, O. (2001, May). The semantic web. *Scientific American Magazine, 284*, 34–43. doi:10.1038/scientificamerican0501-34

Berry, M. W., & Browne, M. (1999) *Understanding Search Engines: Mathematical Modeling and Text Retrieval*. Philadelphia, PA: Society for Industrial and Applied Mathematics.

Braga, D., Ceri, S., & Faniel, F. (2008). Mashing up search services. *IEEE Internet Computing, 12*(5), 16–23. doi:10.1109/MIC.2008.105

Daveport, T. H., & Prusak, L. (1998). *Working knowledge.* Boston, MA: Harvard Business School Press.

Fichter, D. (2006). Doing the monster mashup. *Online, 30*(4), 48–50.

Goodman, E., & Moed, A. (2006) Community in Mashups: The Case of Personal Geodata. Retrieved March 4, 2007, from http://mashworks.net/images/5/59/Goodman_Moed_2006.pdf

Gruman, G. (2006). Enterprise mashups. *InfoWorld, 28*(31). Retrieved March 4, 2007, from http://www.infoworld.com/article/06/07/28/31FEmashup_1.html

Hjerland, B (2003). Fundamentals of Knowledge organization. *Knowledge organization, 30*(2), 87-111.

Hodge, G. (2006). *Systems of knowledge organization for digital libraries: Beyond traditional authority files.* Washington, DC: The Digital Library Federation.

Hof, R. D. (2005, July 25). Mix, match, and mutate. *Business Week, 3942*, 72.

Huber, G. P., Davenport, T. H., & King, D. (1998). Some perspectives on organizational memory. In. F. Burstein, G. Huber, M., Mandviwalla, J. Morrison, & L. Olfman, (Eds.), *Task Force on Organizational Memory.* Presented at the 31st Annual Hawaii International Conference on System Sciences.

Jhingran, A. (2006). Enterprise information mashups: Integrating information, simply. *VLDB '06, 32,* 3-4.

Knowledge. (n.d.). Retrieved January 7, 2009, from http://en.wikipedia.org/wiki/Knowledge_organization

Knowledge organization. (n.d.). Retrieved January 7, 2009, from http://en.wikipedia.org/wiki/Knowledge

Koestler, A. (1964). *The act of creation.* London: Arkana, Penguin Group.

Linthicum, D. (2007). Enterprise mashups meet SOA. *InfoWorld, 29*(8). Retrieved March 4, 2007, from http://www.infoworld.com/article/07/02/19/08FEsaassoa_1.html

Macpherson, R. (2008). Critical management in knowledge organizations. *International Journal of Educational Management, 22*(7), 676–695. doi:. doi:10.1108/09513540810908584

Marks, P. (2006). Mashup websites are a dream come true for hackers. *New Scientist, 190*(2551), 28–30.

Merrill, D. (2006). *Mashups: The new breed of web app.* Retrieved March 2, 2007 from http://www-128.ibm.com/developerworks/xml/library/x-mashups.html

Mou, Y. Zhang. S., & Cao. J. (2004). Providing knowledge support in business process: a context based approach. *2004 IEEE International Conference on Systems, Man and Cybernetics, 3*(10-13), 2143-2149.

O'Brien, D., & Fitzgerald, B. (2006). Mashups, remixes and copyright law. *Internet Law Bulletin*, *9*(2), 17–19.

O'Reilly, T. (2005). *What Is Web 2.0*. Retrieved Feb 2, 2007 from http://www.oreillynet.com/pub/a/oreilly/tim/news/2005/09/30/what-is-web-20.html

Poll, R. (1996). Ontology for knowledge organization. In R. Green (Ed.), *Knowledge organization and change* (pp. 313-319). Indeks, Frankfurt.

Rau, L. F. (1987). Knowledge organization and access in a conceptual information system. *Information Processing & Management*, *23*(4), 269–281. doi:10.1016/0306-4573(87)90018-5

Sage. A. P. (2003). Knowledge management. In *Access Science*. Retrieved February 25, 2007, from http://dx.doi.org/10.1036/1097-8542.YB030820

Smiragila, R. P. (2002). The progress of theory in knowledge organization. *Library Trends*, *50*(3), 330.

Wilde, E. (2006). *Knowledge organization mashups*. Retrieved Feb 2, 2007 from http://dret.net/netdret/docs/wilde-tikrep245.pdf

Wilson, T. (2002). The nonsense of "knowledge management." *Information Research, 8*(1). Retrieved June, 20. 2007 from, http://informationr.net/ir/8-1/paper144.html

Wong, J., & Hong, J. I. (2007). Making mashups with Marmite: Towards end-user programming for the Web. *CHI 2007 Proceedings: Programming By & With End-Users* (pp. 1435-1444).

Yu, J., & Casati, F. (2008). Understanding mashup development. Mashing up search services. *IEEE Internet Computing*, *12*(5), 44–52. doi:10.1109/MIC.2008.114

Chapter 9
Knowledge Sharing Model of 24-Hour Knowledge Factory

Huosong Xia
Wuhan University of Science & Engineering, China

Amar Gupta
University of Arizona, USA

ABSTRACT

In order to improve the level of decision making and competitive advantage, organizations are actively trying to develop and incorporate new knowledge management techniques that are suited for the evolving global economy; the notion of globally distributed team environments represents one area of heavy focus. In implementing a globally distributed work environment, decision makers are faced with an increasingly daunting task of reconciling disparate distributed and heterogeneous data sources. Further, these data sources are growing every day as corporations dedicate more of their resources to a multinational scenario, rather than to a domestic or geographically-specific focus. In order to address this growing problem of knowledge sharing, the authors propose a knowledge sharing model that incorporates the notion of the 24-Hour Knowledge Factory, in conjunction with grid computing and case-based reasoning (CBR). This chapter begins with a description of the 24-Hour Knowledge Factory, the Enterprise Common Knowledge Shared (ECKS) methodology, and the evolving time-shift sharing model. Next, a CBR-adapted approach, based on grid computing, is presented for use in a 24-Hour Knowledge Factory environment. Finally, several types of enterprise knowledge transfer mechanisms are presented in this paper.

1. INTRODUCTION

In today's rapidly changing business environment, we have entered a new era of knowledge management; humans must now live and work in a knowledge-based society as knowledge workers (Drucker, 1993). Various streams of knowledge management (KM) research have emerged. Early research focused on understanding the differences among data, information, knowledge and classifications, such as tacit versus explicit knowledge (Polanyi, 1962; Nonaka, 1995), and individual

DOI: 10.4018/978-1-60566-954-0.ch009

versus collective knowledge (Spender, 1996). Other research has viewed knowledge as a source of competence and as a competitive resource (Hung et al., 2001). A goal of many KM initiatives is to develop a global knowledge community where knowledge is shared and utilized within the community. However, knowledge sharing is inherently a difficult process, and only partial knowledge fragments can be created and shared. Information technology (IT) has been long thought of as a way to facilitate sharing of knowledge; indeed, the use of IT to supplement knowledge sharing amongst communities of practice has been explored (Pan & Leidner, 2003), and the notion of 'virtual teams' has been proposed as a basic construct for this activity. Within virtual team environments, four key challenges exist: constraints on transaction memory; insufficient degree of mutual understanding; failure in sharing and retaining contextual knowledge; and inflexibility of organizational ties. Various knowledge management system approaches have been posited as potential solutions to meet these challenges (Alavi & Tiwana, 2002). Overall, the advent of knowledge management has transformed the way decisions are made and how companies manage common knowledge.

We are interested in knowledge management for decision support applications, especially as it pertains to enterprise knowledge shared in global, virtual teams. Decision makers are faced with a challenge: accurate and quick knowledge sharing is especially difficult when dealing with distributed, heterogeneous, and asynchronous knowledge assets that exist when dealing with geographically dispersed virtual teams. The skills and technologies utilized by virtual teams are a blend of both old and new concepts, each useful for a variety of different tasks and each with its own advantages and disadvantages (Gillam & Oppenheim, 2006). In order to address the problem of knowledge sharing in geographically dispersed environments, an integrated knowledge sharing framework is proposed; this incorporates concepts of the 24-Hour Knowledge Factory, grid computing, and case-based reasoning (CBR).

The 24-Hour Knowledge Factory (Gupta, 2009) is a paradigm that decision makers can employ for distributed, team-based work. For this paradigm to be employed in an effective manner, one needs to consider the following types of research questions:

(1) How can we build a common knowledge sharing model for decision support in the 24-Hour Knowledge Factory?
(2) How can CBR and grid computing concepts be utilized to enhance the capabilities of the 24-Hour Knowledge Factory, and what patterns and technologies must be used to facilitate this union?
(3) How can a time-shift model be developed for the 24-Hour Knowledge Factory using prior research that has largely disregarded the aspect of time-shifts within globally distributed sub-organizations?
(4) How does a distributed work sharing model address the KM issues brought up by the 24-Hour Knowledge Factory?

The chapter is organized as follows: Section 2 defines the 24-Hour Knowledge Factory; Section 3 adapts the CBR approach for the 24-Hour Knowledge Factory based on grid computing; Section 4 discusses the ECKS model for the 24-Hour Knowledge Factory based on decision evolution; Sections 5 and 6 present the ECKS modeling and service model based on grid computing; and, Section 7 provides the concluding remarks.

2. CHARACTERISTICS OF THE 24-HOUR KNOWLEDGE FACTORY

The term "24-Hour Knowledge Factory" is used to emphasize a global delivery model in which members of a globally distributed team work on separate parts of a project or a task around the clock; each member of the team working his or her normal workday hours in the unique time zone of his or her country, transferring completed work to the next geographical 'station' (Gupta, 2009). A globally distributed 24-hour call center is an example of a basic 24-Hour Knowledge Factory.

In a traditional software development environment, a code developer typically waits until a functional portion of the product is available before passing it on to the testing team, which is usually geographically collocated. However, by being able to send work to different time zones and receiving test results on overnight basis, a developer has a new, unprecedented opportunity to build portions of the product on an incremental and more daily basis (Gupta, 2008).

Software projects are well suited to the 24-Hour Knowledge Factory. Software development involves multiple sequential processes: a requirement drafting process, a systems analysis process, a system design process, a coding process, a testing process, and a customer application service process. The software product is made primarily through the transmission of knowledge between these sequential processes and the members of the development team. Since each distributed operation unit of a software development company is responsible for a separate sub-task, the overall efficiency of the project improves since each location perceives that progress is made "overnight". The technology and the system to support this type of factory are discussed in the following sections by different distributions of tasks depending on the appropriate needs for knowledge management. Obviously, effecting this sort of sweeping, fundamental organizational change is not easy: accurately transferring knowledge to offshore sites and having knowledge workers in other countries be able to start the cycle as soon as work is handed off is one of the primary issues in implementing this sort of work system.

3. USE OF CASE BASED REASONING APPROACH

Case Based Reasoning (CBR) is the process of using past cases to solve new problems. The theory of CBR appeared in 1982, and the first system in 1983 (Tsatsoulis & Williams, 2000). Memory organization packets were proposed; these constituted both generalized knowledge repositories and organizers of cases (Schank, 1982; Prentzas & Hatzilygeroudis, 2007).

The first commercially deployed CBR system was called Prism and was used for interbank financial telexes (Goodman, 1990). Founded on the psychological theory of human reasoning, CBR recognizes that humans often solve new problems by comparing them with similar ones that they resolved in the past (Chua et al., 2001). CBR has been successfully applied to different domains such as generating new product ideas (Wu, Lo & Hsu, 2006), financial forecasting (Chun and Park, 2006), and international market selection (Ozorhon, Dikmen & Birgonul, 2006).

CBR can be used as tool in the 24-Hour Knowledge Factory for supporting smooth knowledge transfer and problem resolution. The rationale is that the degree of reoccurrence of particular situations within the 24-Hour Knowledge Factory will be high enough to gain significant support from a CBR system implementation. Ostensibly what was done in one situation in a globally distributed workplace is likely to be applicable in other similar situations.

In general, a CBR system can be viewed as a composition of two modules: a case base and a problem solver (Malek & Amy, 1997). The case base, which contains historical problems and their corresponding solutions, acts as a source of knowledge. Given a new problem, the problem solver performs two actions: it retrieves similar cases from the case base using some measurement of similarity, and subsequently adapts the retrieved cases so that a solution to the new problem can be obtained.

Figure 1. Adapted CBR approach for 24-hour knowledge factory based on grid computing

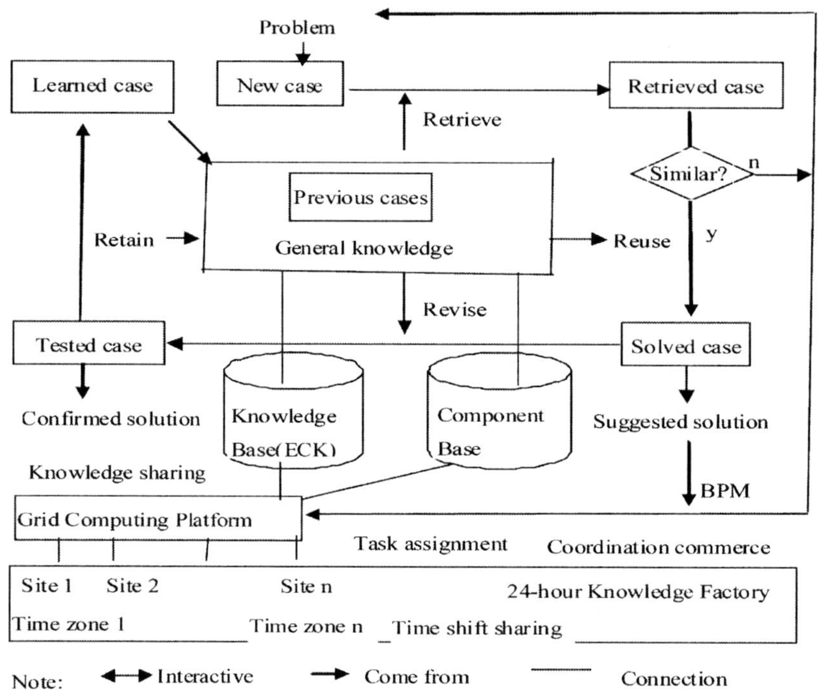

The main advantages of CBR are as follows: the ability to express specialized knowledge, modularity, easy knowledge acquisition, self-updatability, handling unexpected or missing inputs, and inference efficiency. At the same time, issues of CBR that may lead to problems are as follows: the inability to express general knowledge, knowledge acquisition difficulty, inference efficiency difficulty, and provision of explanations (Prentzas & Hatzilygeroudis, 2007).

Human experience is a special kind of knowledge, which captures previously experienced similar problem situations (cases) for human problem solving via different experience sharing and reused paths; items that can be logged and shared via all different mediums of communication. Since a knowledge worker interacting with minimal knowledge loss is pivotal to the success of the 24-Hour Knowledge Factory, we adopt CBR to support this paradigm using experience-sharing and reuse. This framework is depicted in Figure 1. The components of the framework are as follows:

- BPM: In the 24-Hour Knowledge Factory environment, we must understand how to accurately control the flow of work and knowledge as it relates to one particular business process at a time. This is difficult to achieve using traditional BPM methodologies.
- Grid computing platform: Grid computing embodies the use of an array of computers. The 24-Hour Knowledge Factory employs multiple computers too. However, the focus is different. In grid computing, the goal is primarily to achieve higher and more dependable computational power. In the 24-Hour Knowledge Factory, the primary goal is to complete a high-level task as fast as possible. Grid computing can serve as a platform for solving problems

within the 24-Hour Knowledge Factory that assigns task and coordinates work. Team members in different time zones can interact using the CBR approach for solving new problems, and grid computing for knowledge and information sharing. The growing success of grid technologies in different scientific communities is creating an increasing need for the development of tools and methodologies to support knowledge sharing and handling among people. Successful grid computing applications can be found in many domains, including workflow systems (Yu & Buyya, 2005) and medical support (Gurcan et al., 2007).

In the grid computing environment, the Intelligent Conversational Channel (ICC) (Mustapha, 2005) is envisaged as a community channel to facilitate knowledge sharing activities by utilizing multiple agents to create a virtual community. This concept can be extended for use in the 24-Hour Knowledge Factory environment. The CBR module will retain and reuse knowledge in the system while the parallelism of the grid computing network will help to learn and generalize the knowledge retained in the CBR.

Since the 24-Hour Knowledge Factory is based upon elements that can potentially prove to be hindrances in knowledge sharing; mainly because it is inherently global, distributed, heterogeneous, and asynchronous; a superior technology platform is needed to allow for a seamless transfer of knowledge. A grid computing platform can help to address this requirement. One of the first commonly known grid initiations is the SETI@home project, which is a distributed computing project that uses Internet-connected computers, hosted by the Space Sciences Laboratory at the University of California, Berkeley. The project was released to the public on May 17, 1999. The SETI@home project operates under the aegis of the Berkeley Open Infrastructure for Network Computing BOINC environment, which has enabled several millions of volunteers to download and analyze data (http://en.wikipedia.org/wiki/SETI@home; http://setiathome.berkeley.edu/).

Stanford University's Folding@home project, based on Playstation 3 gaming systems, is another good example of how grid computing platforms have evolved: on the second day of its release to the gaming community, the combined computing power of all gaming systems running Folding@home reached 367 Tera (trillion) Floating point Operations Per Second (TFLOPS), more than twice the amount of all of the other operating systems participating in the project combined (Huang, 2007).

Other relevant examples of grid computing include ones for parallel and distributed knowledge discovery (PDKD) (Cannataro, Talia & Trunfio, 2001) and for creating the infrastructure for semantic grids and knowledge grids (Cannataro & Talia, 2004).

The next-generation grid will include 4 layers in network technology perspective: Grid Fabric, Grid Services (data grid, computing grid, and information grid), Semantic Grid (meta data and ontologies), and Knowledge Grid (DM and knowledge discovery in database) (Cannataro & Talia, 2004). The configuration for the 24-Hour Knowledge Factory could include 3 layers: a knowledge-grid layer, a tool-grid layer, and a data grid layer, as described in Figure 2.

The data-grid layer will constitute the basic layer of resources for the 24-Hour Knowledge Factory. This layer will include documents in different time zones, records in database, standard rule sets in teams, cases in different places, and models of the 24-Hour Knowledge Factory. Within this layer, the directory and database access services will be key services, along with document management and Database Management Systems DBMS. In addition to these basic data processing resources, complex automated processing capabilities will be incorporated to give semantic meaning to each web resource. Hence the need for a tool-grid layer for communication, collaboration, and organiza-

Figure 2. Grid Computing Layer for 24-Hour Knowledge Factory

Knowledge-Grid Layer	Creation Knowledge Discovery & Innovation	Enterprise Common Knowledge General knowledge
Tool-Grid Layer	Tools Service Collaborative Technology	Communication (ICC), Sharing Tools Organizational Dynamic Design and Rules, Semantic Web
Data-Grid Layer	Directory Service Data Base, Document, Management	Recorder, Standard, Case, Model, Document

tion, as well as for addressing all data that the grid stores, maintains, and updates for users, applications, and operations. This is architecturally similar to the Globus Monitoring and Discovery Service environment that encompasses all the relevant data and metadata, grid services usage data, and application data sources and results. Grid middleware and grid applications currently maintain much of these data, so the key challenge for next-generation grids will be their seamless integration and use (Foster, 2006).

The tool-grid layer will provide the service tools and algorithms for collaboration and communication in the 24-Hour Knowledge Factory. This service will be responsible for searching, selecting, and downloading collaborative tools. While the metadata regarding the availability, location, and configuration will be stored in a database, documents will be managed by a directory service, while the data and tools will be stored in a local storage facility of each node. A node wishing to export data and documents to other users will need to publish them using the tools services (which store the metadata in the local portion of the node).

As advocated by Tim Berners-Lee, the next generation web will focus on semantics to allow effective communication between humans and machines, as well as to enable powerful collaboration between them to accomplish tasks (Berners-Lee, Hendler & Lassila, 2001). With the RDF (Resource Description Framework) and OWL (Web Ontology Language) the languages that power the semantic web becoming standards in their own right, and with new technologies reaching maturity for embedding semantics in existing web pages and querying RDF knowledge stores, exciting developments (Web 2.0, Web 3.0) are happening in this area (Lassila & Hendler, 2007). The semantic web is the collection of understanding tools at the heart of the knowledge grid. Although the semantic grid initiative is still developing, we think it will be a significant component of the next-generation grid. The use of semantics and ontology in grids can offer high-level support for managing grid resources and for designing complex applications that will benefit from the use of semantics.

The tool-grid layer includes the semantic platform in which autonomic computing principles are applied to ensure constant updates of the 24-Hour Knowledge Factory. As one of the most important grid computing tools, the Globus Toolkit (GT) can support the development of service-oriented, distributed virtual team's computing applications.

The knowledge grid layer is organized as a set of knowledge management operations. A software platform based on a knowledge grid model that organizes knowledge in three dimensional knowledge space (location, category, and level) has been implemented and used for knowledge sharing in research teams (Zhuge, 2002). A knowledge grid is an intelligent interconnection environment. It enables people or virtual teams (roles) to effectively capture, publish, share, and manage explicit knowledge resources. It also provides on-demand knowledge services to support people or services to conduct innovation, cooperative teamwork, problem solving, and decision making (Hai Zhuge, 2004). In order to facilitate knowledge discovery, the knowledge grid layer is organized in two hierarchic levels: the core K-grid layer and the high level K-grid layer (Cannataro, Talia & Trunfio, 2001).

Our knowledge-grid layer focuses on enterprise common knowledge (ECK) and general knowledge integration and knowledge diffusion, especially case reuse, innovation experience and case collection, and discovery in knowledge management (from a business decision making perspective). This is the key layer for the 24-Hour Knowledge Factory and provides the team with knowledge management capabilities of various types including: knowledge creation, common knowledge flow, team knowledge structure building, knowledge sharing modeling, and process engineering. Knowledge creation includes knowledge discovery and innovation; it is an idea driven by the team common knowledge. Common knowledge flow is a component of the content of knowledge flow, time, and direction. Team knowledge structure building and knowledge sharing modeling will be discussed in sections 5 and 6.

A knowledge grid allows the interaction of a team with distinct backgrounds, especially to address complex and multidisciplinary problems.

4. ECK SHARING MODEL BASED ON DECISION EVOLUTION

In the 24-Hour Knowledge Factory, we have to answer issues such as "what kind of knowledge can be shared in the team for decision evolution", "what is the business process", and "how can an enterprise make decisions"? To answer these questions, we should have a sharing model that can be utilized to build appropriate enterprise knowledge structures for the 24-Hour Knowledge Factory. Knowledge can be expressed in case-based format via enterprise knowledge structure.

Enterprise decision making is an interactive process characterized by information and knowledge sharing between various people. Factors that relate to enterprise decision making are varied and will change over time. The process of enterprise decision making relies on enterprise common knowledge sharing. Enterprise common knowledge sharing may speed up the process of making decisions because the sharing of knowledge throughout an organization can lead to shared knowledge, reducing the time that people need to learn and re-learn about projects. For this purpose, we propose an ECK sharing model for decision evolution as shown in Figure 3.

In the ECKS model for decision evolution, we analyze the details of components. Due to the complex environments inherent in knowledge diffusion, adaptive modeling is needed for effective decision making. Decision evolution is the process of decision making based on data, information, and knowledge. There are three main types of knowledge for decision evolution; static knowledge, which seldom changes; dynamic knowledge, which is often changing; and knowledge about business processing optimization. The 24-Hour Knowledge Factory has to cater to all of the above three categories of knowledge in order to ensure the best decision evolution.

Figure 3. ECK Sharing Model for Decision Evolution

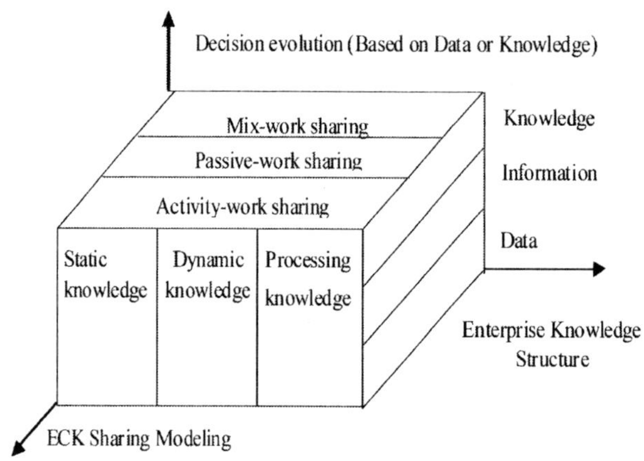

5. ENTERPRISE KNOWLEDGE STRUCTURE

Knowledge may be classified into various categories depending on the purpose of its use. For example, knowledge can be classified into explicit and tacit knowledge (Polanyi, 1962). As the most knowledgeable personnel in technically complex businesses approach retirement, there is a need to capture their knowledge. The temptation is for management to ignore the problem until it is too late.

A corporation's only enduring source of advantage is the knowledge housed within the minds of its employees and the knowledge built into its structures and systems. When discussing knowledge sharing, one must construct and analyze enterprise knowledge structures, such as the one shown in Figure 4, to understand what knowledge needs to be transferred in the 24-Hour Knowledge Factory environment.

Definition 1: given S=(P,W,D)representing the knowledge structure of enterprise:

- Where P is as a set of processing knowledge, $P=\{p_1,p_2,p_3\}$, p_1 representing decision processing knowledge, p_2 representing business processing knowledge, p_3 representing learning knowledge.
- Where W is as a set of static knowledge, $W=\{w_1,w_2\}$, w_1 representing knowledge work, w_2 representing knowledge description; D as a set of dynamic knowledge
- Where $D=\{d_1,d_2\}$, d_1 representing knowledge creation, d_2 representing knowledge acquisition.

Enterprise dynamic knowledge creation and knowledge acquisition require active interaction among decision processing; business processing; and learning from employees, teams, and business units. The knowledge acquisition process requires tools for data mining.

Enterprise static knowledge describes knowledge work and knowledge descriptions. Knowledge work is supported by explicit knowledge, rules, and enterprise forms. Knowledge descriptions for making knowledge easy to access are represented by the ontology in three layers: the rules, meaning, and usage layers. For example, knowledge can be described in terms of a specific business rule, the meaning of this rule in terms of the enterprise, and the specific use that this knowledge has within the enterprise.

Processing knowledge describes the knowledge creation and acquisition of enterprise in decision making process, business processing, and organization learning processing. Decision

Figure 4. Enterprise Knowledge Structure

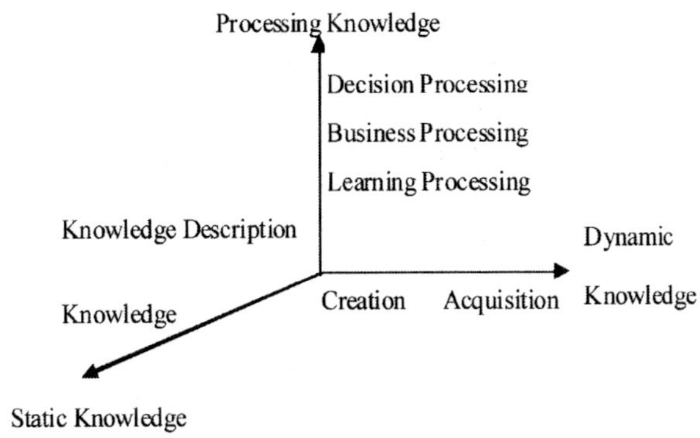

processing especially complex decision processing and emergency/real-time decision processing is the process of the creation of innovative within knowledge. Business processing also implies knowledge generation and knowledge transformation for different kinds of enterprise common knowledge. Learning processing helps in improving the integration of knowledge learning in communities from the experience of others.

6. ECK SHARING MODELING AND SERVICE MODEL BASED ON GRID COMPUTING

When discussing ECKS modeling, one confronts enterprise knowledge sharing in different perspectives: specifically, the three dimensional sharing model shown in Figure 5. To explain this concept more clearly, the following definition is provided:

Definition 2: given F(A,P,M) representing the ECK sharing modeling:

- Where A is as a set of activity-work sharing, $A=\{a_1,a_2\}$, a_1 representing enterprise knowledge base, a_2 representing enterprise knowledge ontology.
- Where P is as a set of passive-work sharing, $P=\{p_1,p_2\}$, p_1 representing knowledge sharing by team work, p_2 representing knowledge sharing by knowledge transfer.
- Where M is as a set of mix-work sharing, $M=\{m_1,m_2,m_3\}$, m_1 representing knowledge sharing by replying to requests for help, m_2 representing knowledge sharing by enterprise common knowledge grid, m_3 representing knowledge sharing by enterprise knowledge guide map. This is the ECKS modeling shown in Figure 5.

For this model to operate, teamwork is critical since the development of the enterprise common knowledge depends on social interaction and cooperation between team members to ensure sharing of knowledge by passive- work sharing.

Given $Dp=\{d_s,d_c\}$ which represents the processing of decisions for the 24-Hour Knowledge Factory:

- Where d_s represents the degree of simplicity in processing of a decision, which is structure decision processing
- And d_c represents the complexity of processing the decision, which is unstructured and complex processing of a decision.

Given $Bp=\{b_s,b_c\}$ which represents the processing of business for the 24-Hour Knowledge Factory:

Figure 5. ECK Sharing Modeling

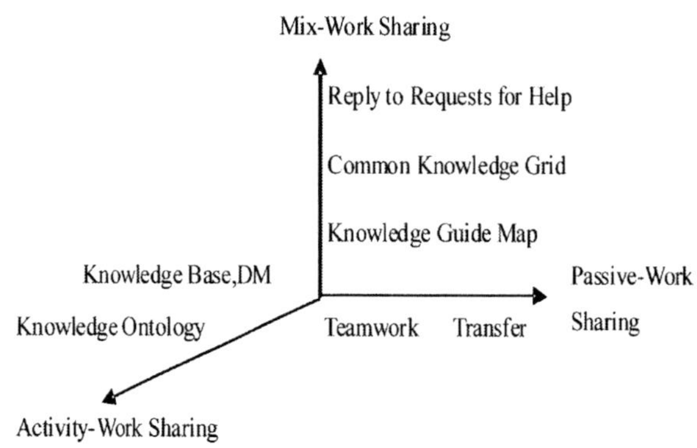

- Where b_s represents the simplicity of business processing, which is simple business processing (like standard simple processing).
- Also, b_c represents the complexity of business processing, which is difficult to standardize. For complex business processes, continuing optimality and reengineering are needed.

Given $Lp=\{l_s,l_c\}$ represents the processing of learning for the 24-Hour Knowledge Factory, where l_s represents the simplest degree of learning processing, which is learning from standard rules, cases, and simple components reuse, and l_c represents the most complex degree of the learning processing.

Most KM researchers consider knowledge transfer to be more a continuum. They focus on the cultural awareness and some other barriers between sender and receiver. For example, the concepts of Guanxi (personal connections) and mianzi (face) are fundamentally important in understanding cultural interactions in China. (Peter, Jeremy & Hui, 2006). In contrast, the aims of knowledge transfer in the 24-Hour Knowledge Factory are the processing of decisions, processing of business, and the processing of learning.

Then, ECK= {type (i),| i=1,2…8} represents the ways of enterprise common knowledge transfer in the 24-Hour Knowledge Factory.

We describe type (i) as follows: type $(i)=\{d_j,b_j,l_j,| j=s \text{ or } c\}$, type (i) as the type of enterprise common knowledge transfer.

The different types of knowledge transfer can be classified into categories by aims and dimensions. The types for knowledge transfer in this paper are based on three types of processing. Ways of enterprise common knowledge transfer include 8 types of combinatorial processing knowledge among one simple or complex decision processing, one simple or complex business processing and one simple or complex learning processing, as shown in table 1.

The enterprise common knowledge transfer described in type 1, is visible and expressible. These are easily shared and transferred formally and systematically; hence, we can build a system of the standard rules of knowledge transfer and collect the success cases and search in a case-base for solving similar problems based on sharing the case and adapting document management.

If the enterprise common knowledge transfer is of the type described in type 8, knowledge such as personal expertise, insights, and intuitions in this type are hard to see and express. These are inherently difficult to transfer, so in order to facilitate accurate transfer we can build a strong learning and innovation platform (and possibly apply a time-shift sharing model) in the 24-Hour Knowledge Factory. Because this paradigm is so elaborate and complex, we can help to facilitate

Table 1. Types of Enterprise Common Knowledge Transfer

	Type 1	Type 2	Type 3	Type 4	Type 5	Type 6	Type7	Type 8
Decision Processing	simple	Simple	Simple	Simple	Complex	complex	Complex	complex
Business Processing	Simple	simple	Complex	Complex	simple	simple	Complex	Complex
Learning Processing	Simple	complex	Simple	Complex	simple	complex	Simple	Complex

accurate knowledge transfer by doing such things as developing an intelligence based organization, adapting to collaboration based on grid computing, and adapting to a knowledge sharing environment via content services, communication services, and business transaction services.

If the way of enterprise common knowledge transfer is of the types described from type 2 to 7, the knowledge in this type is semi-easy and semi- hard to transfer. Thus, we can build different knowledge diffusion paths for knowledge transfer based on an activity knowledge warehouse.

In order to solve the problem of high complexity enterprise common knowledge transfer, we need to develop and setup a good sharing model. One of the most important things is to continue to develop activity-work sharing (as is described in Figure 5) through building knowledge base system and descriptions of enterprise common knowledge ontology.

Next we introduce a mix-work sharing model. In a mix-work sharing model, the ECK guide map may fulfill an important role in decision making. Knowledge is shared by a know-how database, a knowledge base, or some other type(s) of knowledge transfer. A common knowledge grid is a set of well-organized common knowledge that is accurately identified together with a set of KM operations. We can accurately store and retrieve common knowledge according to its coordinates, but it is complex and more expensive. Replies to requests for help may fulfill a task for peer to peer team knowledge sharing, or knowledge sharing in virtual communities, or face-to-face expert consulting.

In order to adapt the 24-Hour Knowledge Factory, a service model based on grid computing should be analyzed. Figure 6 is a simple model for service in the 24-Hour Knowledge Factory.

Currently, although the methods of global communication are extensive and varied, collaboration, email, ICC, and forums are the most important in the 24-Hour Knowledge Factory (although many complications with these mediums still remains).

Figure 6. Service Model Based on Grid Network

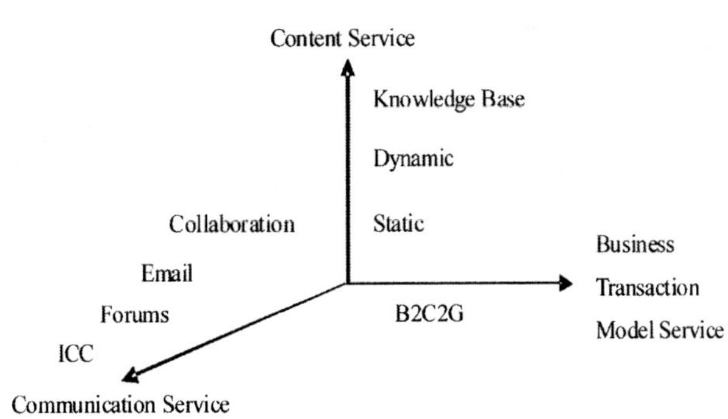

From a Web2.0 perspective, some of the matured Web-based applications, such as mashups, blogs, wikis, web feeds, tagging systems, user-created publications, and social networking applications can be used. From the knowledge content service perspective, the knowledge base, dynamic knowledge, and static knowledge (including case-reused knowledge) are the most important factors. A grid network is only a platform of technology. Content services need to be profoundly detailed for different tasks in the 24-Hour Knowledge Factory. From a business transaction perspective, the objects include governments, businesses, and customers. For a global operation service model of business transactions, building a mechanism of work flow and knowledge flow management in a common knowledge model from businesses, customers, and governments is also requisite.

7. CONCLUSION

Information transfer and knowledge sharing beyond one's organizational boundary in an extended enterprise model will be an inevitable trend forced by global scale competition. This study explores the relationship between decision making and knowledge sharing in an environment where the 24-Hour Knowledge Factory is embedded as grid computing and may be broken down physically, organizationally, and by area of technology.

A common knowledge sharing model such as the 24-Hour Knowledge Factory is complex, and we have only discussed some of the key issues. This paper has analyzed an enterprise common knowledge sharing model for decision evolution, as shown in the enterprise sharing structure in Figure 1. ECK modeling focuses on activity-work sharing, passive-work sharing, and mix-work sharing. For decision makers, this study is useful in demonstrating how an organization has developed the capability of making decisions to support the 24-Hour Knowledge Factory, based on enterprise common knowledge.

ACKNOWLEDGMENT

This research was supported by the National Philosophy and Social Science Fund (07BTQ010) of China, HuBei Province Fund of China (2007097, D200517003, 20040216), and the WUSE Fund (20063102). We deeply appreciate the suggestions from fellow members of the 24-Hour Knowledge Factory project team at the Eller College of Management, University of Arizona, USA. We thank Julie Ovadia, Tapasya Patki, and Hyo-mi Kim for their help in editing this paper. The authors thank the reviewers of this manuscript for their insightful comments.

REFERENCES

Alavi, M., & Tiwana, A. (2002). Knowledge integration in virtual teams: the potential of KMS. *Journal of the American Society for Information Science and Technology*, *53*(12), 1029–1037. doi:10.1002/asi.10107

Alexandre, F. (Ed.). *Connectionistsymbolic integration*. Hillsdale, NJ: Lawrence Erlbaum Associates.

Berners-Lee, T., Hendler, J., & Lassila, O. (2001). The semantic web. *Scientific American*, *5*(1).

Cannataro, M., & Talia, D. (2004). Semantics and knowledge grids: Building the next-generation grid. *IEEE Intelligent Systems*, (January/February): 56–63. doi:10.1109/MIS.2004.1265886

Cannataro, M., Talia, D., & Trunfio, P. (2001). Knowledge grid: High performance knowledge discovery services on the grid. In *Proc. of the 2nd International Workshop on Grid Computing (GRID 2001), Denver, USA* (LNCS 2242, pp. 38-50).

Chua, D.K.H., Li, D.Z., & Chan, W.T. (2001). Case-based reasoning approach in bid decision making. *Journal of Construction Engineering*, January/February, 35-45.

Chun, S., & Park, Y. (2006). A new hybrid data mining technique using a regression case based reasoning: Application to financial forecasting. *Expert Systems with Applications*, *31*, 329–336. doi:10.1016/j.eswa.2005.09.053

Drucker, P. (1993). *Post-capitalist society*. New York: Butterworth Heineman.

Foster, I. (2006). Globus toolkit version 4: Software for service-oriented systems. *J. Comput. Sci. & Technology*, *21*(4), 513–520. doi:10.1007/s11390-006-0513-y

Gillam, C., & Oppenheim, C. (2006). Review article: Reviewing the impact of virtual teams in the information age. *Journal of Information Science*, *32*(2), 160–175. doi:10.1177/0165551506062328

Goodman, M. (1990). Prism: A case-based telex classfier. In A. Rappaport & R. Smith (Eds.), Innovative applications of artificial intelligence (Vol. 2). Boston, MA: MIT Press.

Gupta, A. (2008). *Outsourcing and offshoring of professional services*. Hershey, PA: IGI Global.

Gupta, A. (2009). The 24-hour knowledge factory: Can it replace the graveyard shift? *IEEE Computer Magazine*, 66-77.

Gurcan, M., Pan, T., & Sharma, A. (2007). Gridimage: A novel use of grid computing to support interactive human and computer-assisted detection decision support. *Journal of Digital Imaging*, *20*(2), 160–171. doi:10.1007/s10278-007-9020-0

Huang, E. (2007). PS3 doubles folding@home's processing power. *Gamepro.com.*

Lassila, O., & Hendler, J. (2007). Embracing Web 3.0. *IEEE Internet Computing*, 90–93. doi:10.1109/MIC.2007.52

Malek, M., & Amy, B. (1997). A preprocessing model for integrating case-based reasoning and prototype-based neural network. In R. Sun & F. Alexandre (Eds.), Connectionist-Symbolic Integration: From Unified to Hybrid Approaches.

Mustapha, S. (2005). Extracting social knowledge in the intelligent conversational channel for agent communication. *19th International Conference on Advanced Information Networking and Applications, 2005 (AINA 2005)* (Vol. 2, pp. 733-738).

Nonaka, I., & Takeuchi, H. (1995). *The knowledge-creating company*. Oxford University Press.

Ozorhon, B., Dikmen, I., & Birgonul, M. (2006, September). Case-based reasoning model for international market selection. *Journal of Construction Engineering and Management*, 940–948. doi:10.1061/(ASCE)0733-9364(2006)132:9(940)

Pan, S., & Leidner, D. (2003). Bridging communities of practice with information technology in pursuit of global knowledge sharing. *The Journal of Strategic Information Systems*, *12*, 71–78. doi:10.1016/S0963-8687(02)00023-9

Peter, J. B., Jeremy, C., & Hui, T. (2006). Culture awareness in knowledge transfer to China-the role of guanxi and mianzi. *Journal of World Business*, *41*, 275–288. doi:10.1016/j.jwb.2006.01.008

Polanyi, M. (1962). *Personal knowledge: Towards a post-critical philosophy*. Chicago: University of Chicago Press.

Prentzas, J., & Hatzilygeroudis, L. (2007). Categorizing approaches combining rule-based and case-based reasoning. *Expert Systems: International Journal of Knowledge Engineering and Neural Networks*, *24*(2), 97–122. doi:10.1111/j.1468-0394.2007.00423.x

Schank, R. (1982). Dynamic memory: A theory of learning in computers and people, Cambridge: Cambridge University Press.

SETI@home. (n.d.). Retrieved Jan 29, 2009, from http://en.wikipedia.org/wiki/SETI@home

SETI@home. (n.d.). Retrieved Jan 29, 2009, from http://setiathome.berkeley.edu/

Spender, J.-C. (1996). Organizational knowledge, learning and memory: Three concepts in search of a theory. *Journal of Organizational Change Management*, *9*(1), 63–78. doi:10.1108/09534819610156813

Tsatsoulis, C., & Williams, A. (2000). Case-based reasoning. In T.C. Leondes (Ed.), *Knowledge-based systems: Techniques and applications*. CA: Academic Press.

Wu, M., Lo, Y., & Hsu, S. (2006). A case-based reasoning approach to generating new product ideas. *International Journal of Advanced Manufacturing Technology*, *30*, 166–173. doi:10.1007/s00170-005-0048-3

Yu, J., & Buyya, R. (2005). A taxonomy of scientific workflow systems for grid computing. *SIGMOD Record*, *34*(3), 44–49. doi:10.1145/1084805.1084814

Zhuge, H. (2002). A knowledge grid model and platform for global knowledge sharing. *Expert Systems with Applications*, *22*, 313–320. doi:10.1016/S0957-4174(02)00019-2

Zhuge, H. (2004). Semantics, resource and grid editorial. *Future Generation Computer Systems*, *20*, 1–5. doi:10.1016/S0167-739X(03)00159-6

Chapter 10
Challenges in Developing a Knowledge Management Strategy:
A Case Study of the Air Force Materiel Command[1]

Summer E. Bartczak
University of Central Arkansas, USA

Jason M. Turner
Air Force Institute of Technology, USA

Ellen C. England
ISN Software Corporation and Kaplan University, USA

ABSTRACT

It is widely acknowledged that knowledge management (KM) strategy is a desired precursor to developing specific KM initiatives. Strategy development is often difficult due a variety of influences and constraints. Using KM influences as a foundation, this case study describes issues involved in developing a KM strategy for the Air Force Materiel Command, including issues to be considered for future strategy development such as leadership support and understanding, conflicts with IT organizations, funding, technology usage and configuration, and outsourcing.

INTRODUCTION

Enablers, barriers, and influences of KM have been grouped into three broad categories: internal managerial influences, internal resource influences, and external environmental influences (Holsapple & Joshi, 2000, 2002). Managerial influences "emanate from the organizational participants responsible for administering the management of knowledge" (Holsapple & Joshi, 2000, p. 239); resource influences include human, financial, knowledge, and material resources that make KM a reality (p. 241); and environmental influences affect what "knowledge resources should or can be acquired in the course of KM, as well as what knowledge manipulation skills (e.g., human or technical) are available" (p. 242).

KM strategy is also generally regarded as essential to implementation and should be guided by organizational strategy (Zack, 1999). Earl (2001) provides a taxonomy of strategic starting points, seven "schools of knowledge management" and key attributes of each. Yet despite such insight, little is known about KM strategy within the military (Bower, 2001; Plant, 2000). Difficulties stem from the unique context in which KM must be implemented including culture, organization, and operating environment. Because of these unique attributes, an investigation of military KM may prove telling theoretically and practically.

CASE BACKGROUND

Headquartered in Dayton, Ohio, Air Force Material Command (AFMC) employs 85,000 military and civilian employees worldwide. AFMC has "cradle-to-grave" oversight for all aircraft, missiles, and munitions. The Directorate of Requirements (DR) is home to AFMC's Knowledge Management program.

In the early 1990s, AFMC/DR developed a repository of acquisitions regulations, process descriptions, and other miscellaneous information. The repository soon expanded into the Defense Acquisition Deskbook program and was managed by an interservice Joint Program Office. AFMC/DR continued updating Air Force (AF) documents within Deskbook; however, this did not require DR's entire budget. As a result, it was decided the excess funding was to be used for the development of an additional KM application that helped to document and disseminate overarching AF lessons learned.

AFMC/DR was also developing Web-based training for acquisitions personnel due to impending talent drains as more civilian personnel retired. To improve AFMC's preparedness, Deputy Director Robert Mulcahy became a KM champion. He consolidated deskbook, lessons learned, and web-based training into one KM system in order to provide better capture and dissemination of critical workforce knowledge.

Mulcahy assigned Randy Adkins to lead the consolidated AF knowledge management (AFKM) program. Initially, the AFKM program centered on the use of commercial KM processes and technologies for solving specific customer problems. Soon, however, the now-consolidated KM system grew beyond its original three components; by 2000, two new modules were added: the AFMC Help Center and Community of Practice (CoP) workspaces." The Help Center provided search capabilities for information across AFMC web sites; the CoP workspaces fostered information exchange, collaboration, and problem solving. The AFKM Hub/home page was a portal-like entrance into the entire system.

RESEARCH METHOD

AFMC was one of the first AF organizations to embrace KM; the AFKM team also faced significant challenges determining future directions for their efforts. It was therefore likely key issues impacting KM strategy development might be identified in this context. Additional case research was also needed to bridge the gap between KM theory and practical advice (Jennix, 2005, p. vii). Given these factors, an exploratory case study methodology was used.

Holsapple and Joshi's (2000, 2002) KM influences framework provided three foundational constructs for "analytic generalization" (Yin, 1994, p. 31); these factors—managerial, resource, and environmental—could be examined as potential barriers to KM strategy development. Considerations for design quality were made in accordance with Kidder and Judd (1986) and Yin (1994); however, internal validity was not addressed due to the study's exploratory nature.

Data included interviews, field notes, and physical traces. Open-ended interviews were taped and transcribed, then reviewed and approved by respondents. Twelve individuals were interviewed providing a cross-section of organizational leadership, the AFKM team, and AFKM customers. Transcripts were first searched and categorized according to a priori KM influence (and emergent) categories and themes. Resultant data was combined with field notes (capturing impressions about the interviews and observations of individual/organization dynamics) and physical traces (e.g., documents, Web sites, organizational charts, budget records, advertising media, etc.) to form a robust understanding of the case.

FINDINGS

The AFKM effort exhibited many of Holsapple and Joshi's (2000, 2002) influence factors; however, the military environment provided some unique constraints that further exacerbated the negative influences. On the whole, this study revealed a variety of latent and emergent issues that should be considered for any KM strategy development; key issues are discussed below.

Leadership Support and Understanding

Mulcahy had been a staunch supporter for KM efforts. David Franke replaced Mulcahy in 2000, and a new Director of Requirements was also appointed. Both were open to KM concepts and the AFKM program, but neither was as educated or enthused about KM as Mulcahy. Adkins indicated that Franke didn't see KM as needing emphasis above other AFMC programs, thereby increasing the difficulty of securing exposure and backing necessary to compete for scarce resources. Furthermore, few other individuals had much of an idea of what KM was about. Although it was easy to communicate the importance of individual applications (e.g., lessons learned, document repositories, corporate yellow pages), it was more difficult to explain comprehensive KM concepts. Adkins realized "learning about KM" took time, but the ignorance of those upon whom he relied for support threatened the program's survival before it had a chance to prove itself on a large scale.

Conflict with the IT Organization

Dealing with AFMC's information technology (IT) organization was a continual challenge because it perceived its role as providing technology solutions for the customer, as did AFMC/DR. Additionally, a conflict arose when the IT organization mandated LiveLink® as AFMC's only authorized collaboration tool. LiveLink® directly conflicted with CoP development and was generally more sophisticated than was needed by the average customer. While Adkins' team had a wealth of KM knowledge and system development expertise, the IT organization was the authorized policy maker, and continued conflicts risked AFKM being changed, dismantled, or absorbed.

Funding

A $600,00 budget cut loomed that would eliminate six personnel impacting AFKM systems development workload distribution. Furthermore, many AFKM customer-specific applications had been developed without charge. Without such assistance, some customers would never get their KM efforts off the ground and AFKM's support practices would have to be re-evaluated

System Usage Concerns

Despite rave customer reviews about AFKM systems, Adkins was disturbed by low usage rates. Access metrics showed usage generally rising, and yet it was a small portion of what it could be. Publicity capmpaigns did little overall; it was clear the AFKM system tools were still in their infancy and the low usage statistics didn't help the team adequately justify the benefits or budget.

Technological Challenges

The AFKM team became so efficient at developing technology solutions that they could develop a "CoP in a box" with a few minor customizations in only a few days. Instead of providing content (i.e., deskbook, lessons learned), the team now provided software frameworks, in which customers added information and knowledge. However, a new AF portal was decreed the de-facto access point for all AF information and knowledge. This raised the question of how to design future applications. Adkins' team was heavily involved in the technology of CoPs, but the community-based capabilities of the AF portal might change everything.

Outsourcing KM

With so many issues impacting AFKM; Adkins needed a strategic vision and implementation roadmap to guide future development. Adkins' foremost concern was the development of a strategic vision and plan. He needed documents that would provide starting points for decision-making and describe how to proceed to the envisioned business environment.

Unfortunately, AeroCorp's recommendations captured the complexities of AFMC's environment, and yet were so broad and involved it was difficult to determine a starting point. AeroCorp also had difficulty developing concise methodologies or "blueprints" that addressed the enormity of what AFMC needed to do to evolve into a true knowledge-sharing organization. In particular, AeroCorp applied integrated definition (IDEF) modeling to KM. IDEF modeling was developed for systems engineering and often depicts "as-is" enterprise processes and information requirements; it did not serve as a user-friendly methodology for fully explaining or depicting strategic KM needs.

After seeing the initial draft of the IDEF model, it was clear the process was "over-engineered." After a year of waiting, the promised roadmap was too unfamiliar and complicated for Adkins and others to practically implement. Faced with an impending budget cut, AeroCorp would likely not have an opportunity to make necessary changes. At this point, Adkins had no good answers.

LESSONS LEARNED

Adkins understood he needed a strategic vision to guide AFKM's direction and decision-making. When outsourcing KM strategy met with limited success, he rescoped and refocused the team on a few key areas under their immediate control. From 2002 forward, the AFKM team:

1. promoted CoPs as a key technique for KM across the AF,
2. provided enterprise Web search capabilities across AFMC and selected AF sites,

3. used a process approach for delivering CoP capability.

The team's strategy became one of building momentum by providing rapid KM services ("CoPs in a box") and following up with training and implementation support; leadership could observe successes at the grassroots level. Since the change in strategy, AFKM has enjoyed remarkable success. The AFKM Web site, now called AF Knowledge Now, continues to expand its capabilities and customer base. In 2004, Adkins secured key support from the AF Chief Information Officer; Adkins' team was dubbed the AF Center of Excellence for Knowledge Management, and AF Knowledge Now was integrated into the AF portal.

IMPLICATIONS AND CONCLUSION

This study highlighted some real-world examples of such barriers and several issues to be considered for strategy development: many of the same factors that act as barriers to implementation may also impede KM strategy development. This study highlighted some real-world examples, such as barriers and several issues to be considered for strategy development:

- KM is hard to define and communicate to others.
- KM initiatives must be championed and supported at the highest levels of any organization.
- KM strategy development is not easy, yet it is critical to the success of any KM initiative.
- Outsourcing KM can be very risky.
- Focusing on specific KM efforts is important for countering negative KM influences.

Despite rising awareness of KM and its benefits, we are reminded that such issues may well play out in any organization, military or otherwise, and should be accounted for preemptively during KM strategy development to improve the chances of improving long-term organizational performance.

REFERENCES

Bower, W. (2001). *Development of a decision framework for knowledge management projects.* Unpublished doctoral dissertation, Air Force Institute of Technology, Wright-Patterson AFB, Dayton, OH.

Earl, M. (2001). Knowledge management strategies: Toward a taxonomy. *Journal of Management Information Systems, 18*(1), 215-233.

Holsapple, C., & Joshi, K. D. (2000). An investigation of factors that influence the management of knowledge in organizations. *Journal of Strategic Information Systems, 9*, 235-261.

Holsapple, C., & Joshi, K. D. (2002). Knowledge management: A three-fold framework. *The Information Society, 18,* 47-64.

Jennix, E. (2005). *Case studies in knowledge management.* Hershey, PA: Idea Group Publishing.

Kidder, L., & Judd, C. M. (1986). *Research methods in social relations* (5th ed.). New York: Holt, Rhinehardt, and Winston.

Plant, T. (2000). *Introducing knowledge management into complex organizations* (unpublished manuscript). Australian Defense Force Academy, School of Computer Science, University College, University of New South Wales.

Yin, R. K. (1994). *Case study research: Design and methods* (2nd ed., Vol. 5). Thousand Oaks, CA: Sage Publications.

Zack, M. H. (1999). *Knowledge and strategy.* Boston: Butterworth-Heinemann.

ENDNOTE

[1] The views expressed in this case study are those of the authors and do not necessarily reflect the official policy or position of the Air Force, the Department of Defense, or the US Government.

This work was previously published in the International Journal of Knowledge Management, Vol. 4, Issue 1, edited by M. Jennex, pp. 46-50, copyright 2008 by IGI Publishing (an imprint of IGI Global).

Chapter 11
Impacts from Using Knowledge:
A Longitudinal Study from a Nuclear Power Plant

Murray E. Jennex
San Diego State University, USA

ABSTRACT

This is a longitudinal case study that explored the relationship between use of organizational memory and knowledge, knowledge management, and knowledge worker productivity within the engineering group at a nuclear power plant. Three data points were taken over 5 years. The group used a knowledge management system (KMS) and it was found that the system improved effectiveness/productivity of the organization. The organization had not identified measures for determining productivity improvements, so the key results of the case study are models showing the impact of knowledge use on productivity.

INTRODUCTION

This article explores the impact of using knowledge on the productivity in an engineering organization at a nuclear power plant. Intuitively, knowledge management (KM) researchers believe in the proposition that reusing knowledge will lead to improved organizational performance; however, while there is abundant anecdotal evidence to support this proposition, finding empirical evidence to support this proposition is difficult. Additionally, while the KM research community is generating KM success and effectiveness models, many of which include impacts on organizations and individuals, we are not doing a good job generating models to explain how this impact improves organizational or individual performance.

This article looks at an engineering organization over several years and presents results that answer this key research question: does reuse of knowledge lead to greater productivity, by showing that the reuse of knowledge results in improved individual and organizational productivity/performance. Additionally, models are presented to show how the reuse of knowledge improves individual and organizational performance.

BACKGROUND

Strassmann (1990) and Rubin (1994) propose that adding value to the organization or the organization's customers improves the productivity of the organization. Rubin (1994) defines "added value" as being the result of improved organizational performance. Kaplan and Norton's (1992) Balanced Business Scorecard measures the value of IS to the organization with one of the factors considered being the ability of the organization to sustain learning and improvement. Learning, and organizational learning, is the process by which experience is used to modify current and future actions. Huysman, Fischer, and Heng (1994), as well as Walsh and Ungson (1991) believe organizational learning has organizational memory (OM) as a component. Stein and Zwass (1995) and Walsh and Ungson (1991) define OM as the means by which knowledge from the past is brought to bear on present activities, thus resulting in higher or lower levels of organizational effectiveness. Improving effectiveness can result in improved organizational performance and adding value to the organization. Organizational learning uses OM as its knowledge base. Finally, Alavi and Leidner (2001) and Jennex and Olfman (2002) view organizational knowledge and OM as synonymous labels.

Davenport and Prusak (1998) view knowledge as an evolving mix of framed experience, values, contextual information, and expert insight that provides a framework for evaluating and incorporating new experiences and information. They found that in organizations, knowledge often becomes embedded in artifacts such as documents, video, audio, or repositories and in organizational routines, processes, practices, and norms. They also say that for knowledge to have value it must include the human additions of context, culture, experience, and interpretation. Nonaka (1994) expands this view by stating that knowledge is about meaning in the sense that it is context-specific. This implies that users of knowledge must understand and have experience with the context, or surrounding conditions and influences, in which the knowledge is generated and used for it to have meaning to them. This also implies that for a knowledge repository to be useful it must store the context in which the knowledge was generated. That knowledge is context specific argues against the idea that knowledge can be applied universally; however, it does not argue against the concept of organizational knowledge. Organizational knowledge is considered to be an integral component of what organizational members remember and use, meaning that knowledge is actionable. This longitudinal study focused on an engineering group in a single nuclear plant, as it was recognized that this organization had a shared context for understanding the knowledge that was being captured and reused.

Jennex (2005) utilized an expert panel, the editorial review board of the International Journal of Knowledge Management (IJKM), to generate a definition of KM as the practice of selectively applying knowledge from previous experiences of decision-making to current and future decision making activities with the express purpose of improving the organization's effectiveness. Another key definition of KM includes Holsapple and Joshi (2004) who consider KM as an entity's systematic and deliberate efforts to expand, cultivate, and apply available knowledge in ways that add value to the entity, in the sense of positive results in accomplishing its objectives or fulfilling its purpose. Finally, Alavi and Leidner (2001) concluded that KM involves distinct but interdependent processes of knowledge creation, knowledge storage and retrieval, knowledge transfer, and knowledge application. Taken in context, these definitions of KM focus on the key elements of KM: a focus on using knowledge for decision making and selective knowledge capture. This is important as the selective focus on knowledge capture separates KM from library science, which attempts to organize all knowledge and information, and the decision making focus emphasizes that KM is an action discipline focused on moving knowledge to where it can be applied. Ultimately, KM may best be described by the phrase "getting the right knowledge to the right people at the right time" and can be viewed as a knowledge cycle of acquisition, storing, evaluating, dissemination, and application.

KM is better understood when the concepts of Organizational Memory (OM), and Organizational Learning (OL) are incorporated. Jennex and Olfman (2002) found that the three areas are related and have an impact on organizational effectiveness. Organizational effectiveness is how well the organization does those activities critical to making the organization competitive. OL is the process the organization uses to learn how to do these activities better. OL results when users utilize knowledge. That OL may not always have a positive effect is examined by the monitoring of organizational effectiveness. Effectiveness can improve, get worse, or remain the same. How effectiveness changes influences the feedback provided to the organization using the knowledge. KM and OM are the processes used to identify and capture critical knowledge. Knowledge workers and their organizations "do" KM; they identify key knowledge artifacts for retention and establish processes for capturing it. OM is what IT support organizations "do"; they provide the infrastructure and support for storing, searching, and retrieving knowledge artifacts. Figure 1 illustrates these relationships and the following sections expand on these concepts.

Jennex (2005) views a KM system, KMS, as that system created to facilitate the capture, storage, retrieval, transfer, and reuse of knowledge. The perception of KM and KMS is that they holistically combine organizational and technical solutions to achieve the goals of knowledge retention and reuse to ultimately improve organizational and individual decision making. This is a Churchman (1979) view of KM that allows KMS to take whatever form necessary to accomplish these goals. Alavi and Leidner (2001, p. 114) defined a KMS as "IT (Information Technology)-based systems developed to support and enhance the organizational processes of knowledge creation, storage/retrieval, transfer, and application." They observed that not all KM initiatives will implement an IT solution, but they support IT

Figure 1. The KM/OM/OL Model (Jennex & Olfman, 2002)

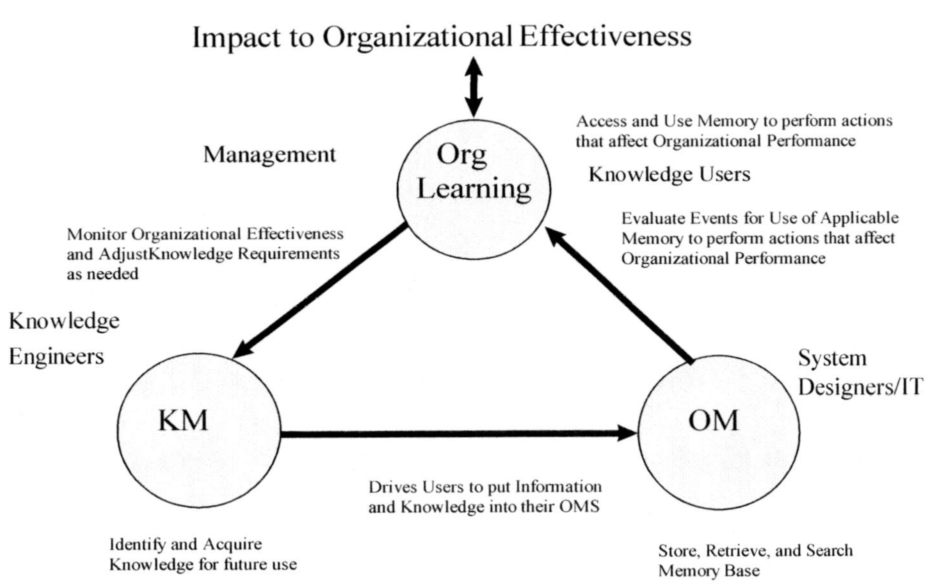

as an enabler of KM. Maier (2002) expanded on the IT concept for the KMS by calling it an ICT (information and communication technology) system that supported the functions of knowledge creation, construction, identification, capturing, acquisition, selection, valuation, organization, linking, structuring, formalization, visualization, distribution, retention, maintenance, refinement, evolution, accessing, search, and application.

An organization implements a KMS to improve its ability to capture, store, and reuse knowledge with the expectation that it will improve its learning and overall performance through improved decision making. Ultimately, organizations implement a KMS to help the organization learn and improve, with the expectation that organizational effectiveness/productivity will improve. This longitudinal case looks at an organization that manages and uses knowledge to determine if KM truly does improve productivity.

METHODOLOGY

The case study covers 5 years with data collected during three time periods. The first time period was in 1996 with the second time period being in 1998 and the third in 2001. The first data collection period utilized a survey and 40 interviews. The second data collection period occurred after the organization had completed a voluntary retirement program resulting in a 25% turnover in staff and utilized a survey and 10 interviews with new members to the organization. The third data collection period occurred while the organization was undergoing reorganization and reduction in force and utilized 22 interviews, 14 with interviewees from the first period, 6 with interviewees from the second period, and two with key managers leading the reorganization. All three data collection periods also included document review and direct observation for a period of several weeks during the data collection period.

ORGANIZATIONAL BACKGROUND

The subject engineering organization is part of a large, United States based, investor-owned utility. The utility is over 100 years old, has a service area of over 50,000 square miles, provides electricity to over 11 million people via 4.3 million residential and business accounts, and had operating revenues of approximately $8.7 billion in 2002. Utility net revenue has fluctuated wildly the last few years, with a $2.1 billion loss in 2000, $2.4 billion in earnings in 2001 (primarily due to one time benefits from restructuring and other initiatives), and decreasing to $1.2 billion in earnings in 2002. To service its customers, the utility operates a transmission and distribution system and several large electrical generation plants and is organized into 3 main line divisions, Transmission and Distribution, Power Generation, and Customer Service. Divisions such as Human Resources, Security, and Information Technology (IT) support the line divisions. The utility has approximately 12,500 employees.

The Power Generation division is organized into operating units dedicated to supporting specific power generation sites. Each operating unit has line organizations such as Operations, Maintenance, Engineering, and Chemistry/Health Physics. Power Generation operating units are supported by dedicated units from the corporate support divisions (Security, Human Resources, IT). The engineering organization used for this case study is part of the nuclear operating unit of the Power Generation division, and is located at the largest electrical generation site operated by the utility. IT support is provided to this operating unit by Nuclear Information Systems (NIS), which administratively is part of the corporate IT division and which operationally reports to both corporate IT and the nuclear unit of the Power Generation division. NIS supported engineering through its Engineering Support Systems group. This group consisted of a supervisor, two project manager/analysts, and two developers. This group was tasked with the maintenance of the 11 systems under NIS control. New systems or enhancements to existing systems were done at the instigation of engineering. Engineering through a charge back process paid costs associated with these projects and developers were hired as needed to support the work.

At the time of the study the engineering organization consisted of approximately 460 engineers disbursed among several different engineering groups reporting to the Station Technical, Nuclear Design Organization, Nuclear Oversight, and Procurement management structures. Industry restructuring was causing large drops in revenues that were driving the nuclear unit to reorganize engineering into a single organization consisting of 330 engineers under the management of the Nuclear Design Organization.

An engineering organization was selected for the case study as:

- Engineers are knowledge workers and make decisions as a part of their job function.
- Engineers use knowledge to make decisions.
- Engineer productivity is improved by increasing the speed or quality of the decisions they make.

This specific engineering organization was selected because it was accessible. Also, this organization resolves equipment and operational problems within a nuclear facility. They utilize performance and maintenance histories, lessons learned, and previous problem resolutions to arrive at new solutions or courses of action. How well they do this is reflected in how well the facility operates. The organization has approximately 100 engineers organized into groups that support specific facility systems or programs.

BASIC KM FINDINGS

The organization is driven to capture and use knowledge. Because it is a nuclear plant it falls under the guidance of the United States Nuclear Regulatory Commission (NRC). The NRC mandates that nuclear plants learn from events so that they are not repeated. Each nuclear site has an independent safety engineering group tasked with reviewing events from other sites for applicability to their site. Additionally, knowledge on event experience is promulgated to each site through official NRC documents. However, the result of this regulatory influence is that an inquiring and knowledge sharing culture is fostered throughout the nuclear industry. This site had an excellent knowledge sharing culture and interviews and surveys found that engineers were almost as likely to capture knowledge because they thought it a good idea as they were due to regulatory requirements. Table 1 shows the drivers that influence engineers to capture knowledge. These drivers are shown ranked by their importance. Additionally, their frequency of use is shown, as it shows that importance has little to do with how often the driver is used.

The organization did not have a formal KM strategy or KMS when the case began, although by the end of the case a formal KM organization had been formed. However, the organization did have KMS repositories and components, although they were not recognized as such. The organization's knowledge was found to reside in four major locations: documents, databases, your memory, and others' memories. Interviews and surveys found several repositories supporting these locations and it was determined that the de facto KMS was these components. Table 2 documents the de facto KMS and shows the type of repository, the system supporting the repository, and the types of knowledge found in the repository.

Table 1. Knowledge driver ratings

Driver or Reason Something is Captured in the KMS	n	Importance (Std Dev)	Frequency (Std Dev)
NRC requirement	19	1.05 (0.24)	3.26 (1.31)
You believe it is important to capture the knowledge	22	1.18 (0.41)	1.84 (1.30)
Procedure requirement	19	1.32 (0.47)	2.27 (1.03)
Near Miss Event	17	1.53 (0.64)	3.39 (0.96)
Management/Supervisor directive	20	1.55 (0.70)	2.29 (1.36)
Site Event	18	1.56 (0.62)	3.21 (1.22)
AR Assignment	20	1.60 (0.71)	2.19 (1.05)
Data/Trend Analysis	19	1.63 (0.49)	2.67 (0.90)
Lesson Learned	17	1.71 (0.59)	3.08 (0.76)
Other Regulatory requirement	14	1.71 (0.65)	2.93 (1.54)
Industry Event	20	1.75 (0.55)	3.44 (1.15)
Good Practice	19	1.79 (0.64)	2.67 (1.18)
INPO Recommendation	15	1.80 (0.56)	3.47 (1.25)
Group/Task Force recommendation	17	1.82 (0.35)	3.86 (1.03)
Coworker recommendation	18	1.83 (0.66)	2.56 (1.37)

n=# of respondents using the driver; Importance: 1=Very Important, 2=Important, 3=Not Very Important; Frequency: 1=Daily, 2=Weekly, 3=Monthly, 4=more than monthly, less than yearly, 5=Yearly

The above KMS components were found to be overlapping systems with each containing elements from the others. This was especially true for most IT components because process automation and reengineering led to the replacement of many documents and processes with IT substitutes. A few changes in the KMS were noted over the course of the case. The most significant was a decrease in the importance of e-mail. This was attributed to changing the e-mail system from CCMail to Lotus Notes. The change was performed without converting e-mail archives with the effect that knowledge was lost. This experience taught the organization not to rely on e-mail as a repository. Another important change was the reduction in the reliance on the "work done" sections of MOSAIC. Cost cutting process changes resulted in these sections being stored in the Corporate Document Management (CDM) system. This led to the addition of CDM to the KMS, which was the only component added during the course of the 5-year study.

An important observation on KMS use was that amount of use was not a good indicator of the impact of KMS use. Several long term organizational member during interviews echoed the sentiment that it was not how often engineers used the KMS but rather that it was the one time that they absolutely had to find knowledge or found unexpected knowledge that proved the worth of the KMS. An example of this was the use of the KMS to capture lessons learned and best practices associated with refueling activities. These activities occur on an approximate 18-month cycle that was sufficient time to forget what had been learned during the last cycle or to have new members with no experience taking over these activities.

This made evaluating the impact of the KMS on productivity difficult, as a common measure of impact is to multiple impact by the numbers of time

Table 2. KMS components

Repository	System	Contents
Document Based	CDM	Documents: memos, correspondence, drawings, procedures, vendor info, Records: completed procedures, tests, surveillances, Maintenance Orders, Reports
	Engineer Library	Drawings, Licensing Documents, Codes, Standards, NUREGS, Regulatory Guides, Design Basis Documents, System Descriptions, EPRI Documents, Reports, Old Nonconformance Reports, Correspondence, Vendor Info
	Training Master File	Qualification Guides, Answer Keys, Event evaluations, Lesson Plans, Task Analyses, Various Training Materials
Computer	MOSAIC	Equipment maintenance history, problem reports/resolutions, root cause and corrective actions, lessons learned.
	NCDB	Drawing Revision History, Base Engineering Info., Program History and Info., Document History, Calculations
	TOPIC	Hypertext files of Licensing Documents, ISEG Evaluations, Reports, Correspondence
	NDMS	Procedures, procedure history, and change basis documents
	Internet	Vendor/Utility/NRC Info.
Self	Your Files	E-mail archives, files, notebooks, in head memory, etc.
Other	Coworker	E-mail archives, files, notebooks, in head memory, etc.
	External various	Various external entity files, includes INPO and NPRDS, EPRI, NRC, Vendors, User's Groups, Trade Groups

CDM: Corporate Document Management, NUREGS: Nuclear Regulations, EPRI: Electric Power Research Institute, MOSAIC: Maintenance Order System, NCDB: Nuclear Consolidated Database, TOPIC: Text Management System, ISEG: Independent Safety Engineering Group, NDMS: Nuclear Document Management System, NRC: Nuclear Regulatory Commission, INPO: Institute of Nuclear Power Operation, NPRDS: Nuclear Plant Reliability Data System.

used. This measure would not have reflected the actual impact on productivity had it been the only way of assessing the KMS. This was especially true because engineers, supervisors, and managers were consistent in agreeing the KMS made them more productive and effective. It was decided that what was important was that engineers use the system when appropriate. To show this would be the case, an instrument from Thompson, Higgins, and Howell (1991) was adopted to measure engineer intent to use the KMS. The instrument, called the Perceived Benefit Model, was based on a study of workers' attitudes and behaviors with respect to optional computer usage. This work was based on Triandis' theory that the perception of future consequences predicts future actions. The implication was that the utilization of a PC in an optional use environment would be influenced by the individual's feelings, habits, and expected consequences of using PCs, and the social norms and environment governing PC use. They developed an instrument that was adapted to measure the relationships between social factors concerning KM use; perceived KMS complexity; perceived KM job fit; and perceived long-term consequences of KM use with respect to the utilization of KM. An additional factor, fear of job loss, was added to determine if that fear affected an engineer's willingness to contribute to the KM. Table 3 reflects measurements of the engineers with respect

Table 3. Perceptions affecting usage

Perceived Benefit Factor	Score	Result
Social factors	4.08	Organizational culture encourages use of the KMS
Complexity (inverse scored)	2.38	Not complex, supports use of the KMS
Job fit, near term consequences	4.56	Fit job well, supports use of the KMS
Job fit, long term consequences	3.36	Neutral
Fear of Job Loss	2.32	No support, no fear found

Note: Score is based on a 5-point scale where 5 is "strongly agree."

to their perceptions affecting future use of the KMS and show that the engineers will use the KMS when appropriate.

Finally, before it could be determined that the KMS had an impact on productivity, it had to be shown that the KMS was effective in performing its KM functions of capturing, storing, searching, and retrieving knowledge. This was done by using Stein and Zwass' (1995) adaptation of Quinn and Rhorbaugh's (1983) Competing Values Model to assess KMS effectiveness. Table 4 summarizes these findings. Data was collected via 20 interviews that were coded and analyzed using a 5-point Likert scale (1 is strongly agree). The scores lead to the conclusion that the KMS was considered to be effective.

Further qualitative analysis of effectiveness utilized structured interviews that asked for opinions and examples on the effectiveness of the KMS. A consensus was found that the KMS made the subject audience more effective. Nearly all agreed that most past decision information could be retrieved within a couple of hours and usually within minutes. However, nearly all agreed that the KMS could be better. Elements of these interviews were used in the stages 2 and 3 and found the same results. Examples of comments include:

It (the KMS) helps us to keep from reinventing the wheel. Every decision we make is not a new decision. Our systems help us to do this.

We have much more capability now than we did. As a Shift Technical Advisor (STA) we can do so much more than we could ten years ago. There is almost too much data.

The information is there but the tools are slow, systems crash, and the information and tools are unreliable.

The last comment demonstrates that while the KMS was considered effective, it was found wanting in the areas of hardware performance and overall integration. Users who had a PC with less than a Pentium processor (during the case study) or a lower level Pentium (during the latter two stages) found the systems slow and cumbersome. Lack of adequate RAM was a common issue (initially, 32 Mbytes were needed, expanding to 128 Mbytes for the final stage, and in each study over half the subjects had PCs with half (or less) of the necessary RAM). Also, users noted that there were many tools and sources but no observed intentional cohesion between them. It was noted that all the systems are on Windows so that data could be copied/cut and pasted, thus providing a basic level of integration. However, no master plan for developing or maintaining the KMS was developed during the period of the research and no evidence was found suggesting this would ever be done. This indicates that the KMS will continue to lack cohesion and will not improve in effectiveness. The two observed changes in the

Table 4. Results of effectiveness functions

Factor	Score	Result
Integration	2	Good time/spatial integration, support effective KMS
Adaptation	2	Boundary spanning done, outside information brought in, supports effective KMS
Goal Attainment	1	Goals/ performance tracked, support effective KMS
Pattern Maintenance	1.5	Procedures/revisions, individual skills tracked, supports effective KMS

Note: Score is based on a 5-point scale where 1 is "strongly agree."

KMS, noted above, actually reduced effectiveness by increasing access times. Also, reducing dependence on e-mail, while better for reliability, accuracy, and security, reduced individual effectiveness by removing an easy to use, readily accessible repository.

KEY KM FINDINGS

The key research question for this case was whether engineer use of the KMS results in improved productivity. Two areas of productivity were defined and examined. The first was individual engineer productivity, as it was assumed that for engineers to continue to use the KMS there must be a perceived benefit. The second was organizational productivity, as it was assumed that for organizations to continue to support a KMS there must be a benefit at the organizational level. This is consistent with the individual and organizational impact outcomes of DeLone and McLean's (1992) IS Success Model. The following paragraphs report the characterization of both forms of productivity.

Engineer Productivity

The standard measure for productivity is the ratio of resources used to products generated. This does not readily apply to most engineers. Instead, effectiveness was used as a measure of engineer productivity where effectiveness is a function of quantity and quality of engineering work accomplished. Engineering work in the context of the nuclear power facility was found to be related to decision support. Engineers performed evaluations and made recommendations to resolve plant issues, usually under time or resource pressure. Sometimes the work involved making and implementing the decision. In all cases, the engineer was measured on the timeliness, correctness, and quality of the decision support as determined by the supporting documentation and the satisfaction of the client. The case study explored engineering productivity and determined a model for it. Interviews were used to outline what measures the managers used to evaluate their engineers and to identify what measures the engineers' thought should be used. While no unique set of measures was identified, several factors together could be used for this measure: Figure 2 illustrates the personal productivity model derived for the subject organization.

The engineer productivity model has several quantitative, qualitative, and competency measures that are directly impacted by the use of the KMS. These measures are:

- Timeliness in completing assignments
- Number of assignments completed
- Identifying and completing high priority assignments

Figure 2. Engineer productivity model

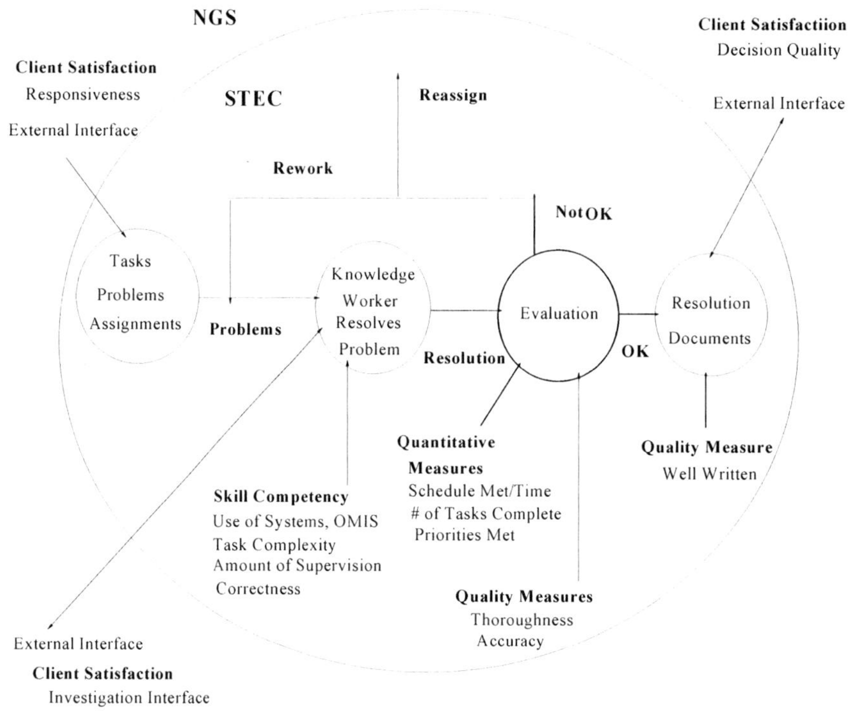

- Completeness of solutions (all the bases are covered)
- Quality of solutions (well written with complete documentation)
- Solving problems the first time
- Amount of work that has to be repeated
- Complexity of work that can be assigned to a worker
- Amount of backlog

Using this characterization of productivity, it was found that use of the KMS was considered a basic skill that each engineer was expected to possess. Use of the KMS was expected to improve the ability of the engineer to find and retrieve key information and knowledge that would aid the engineer in meeting deadlines and completing assigned work. As a result, it was expected that the work would include all available knowledge and be complete and accurate. Managers and supervisors rated the best engineers as those who used the KMS most effectively as manifested by timeliness and completeness of work and with sufficient quality such that little to no rework was required and the clients (i.e., those who had the problem the engineer was resolving) were satisfied with the recommendations or decisions. Engineers who met these expectations were rewarded with pay increases, promotions, and more interesting assignments, providing additional extrinsic motivation for the engineer to use the KMS.

Organizational Productivity

Identifying productivity measures for the organization was more difficult than identifying them for the engineers. Three approaches were used. The first looked at the performance assessments done by external organizations. These provide an effectiveness assessment of productivity. The second looked at performance relative to the goals in the business plan. The third looked at performance relative to preset key performance indicators. The second and third approaches are more traditional in their representation of productivity.

Approach #1

The first measure was based on the SALP, Systematic Assessment of Licensee Performance, Reports issued by the NRC. Review of scores issued since 1988 showed an increase from a rating of 2 to a rating of 1 in 1996, the time of the first stage of this research (see Table 5). Observed strengths in 1996 included the depth of component failure analysis; timely and thorough support for operations and maintenance activities; excellent diagnoses of equipment failures and investigation and resolution of emerging issues; operability determinations were well written and reflected conservative engineering judgment; and engineering self-assessments and resultant corrective actions were determined to be superior.

This rating dropped to a 2 in 1997 (time of the second stage) due to inconsistencies in management oversight and the quality in provision of engineering support to a few activities. However, it was noted that engineering had strong performance in resolving issues and determining corrective actions, self-assessment, and outage support (NRC News, 1997). The SALP program was suspended in 1998, as it was perceived that local government, insurance carriers, and others used ratings as objective measures of performance and not as self-assessment indicators. The SALP program was replaced by periodic plant performance reviews (NRC News, 1998). The plant performance review is a comprehensive review of plant processes with just the overall assessment released to the public; particular findings are given to the plant as guides for improvement, but are not made public. The subject site was given acceptable ratings for the remainder of the study period.

The other part of the external evaluation process is the site evaluation performed by the

Table 5. SALP ratings

Year	Engineering Rating	Overall Rating
1997	2	1.5
1996	1	1.5
1994	2	1.5
1993	2	1.43
1991	2	1.57
1990	2	1.43
1989	3	1.71
1988	2	1.82

Institute of Nuclear Power Operations (INPO). An evaluation was conducted during the spring of 1996, and resulted in a 1 rating. This rating was maintained throughout the 5 years of the study. A history of these ratings is not included, as the organization did not grant permission to publish it.

The external assessments identified several strengths directly related to engineer effectiveness. These include decision-making, root cause analysis, problem resolution, timeliness, and operability assessment documentation. This indicates a direct link between engineer productivity and organization productivity. Also, because internal engineering effectiveness assessments were positive and organization effectiveness is rated highly, it can be inferred that engineer effectiveness does directly impact organizational effectiveness.

Approach #2

The second measure was how well the organization's performance matched the expectations of its business plan. The first stage (case study) found only a few goals related to the subject organization and few performance indicators and goals that could be used to determine productivity. Two indicators were linked to knowledge use: unit capacity and unplanned automatic scrams. Unit

Table 6. Capacity factors, actual and cumulative (PRIS, 2003)

Year	U2 Capacity Factor %	U2 Cumulative%	U3 Capacity Factor%	U3 Cumulative%
1990	88.65	69.47	69.78	69.75
1991	61.55	68.48	91.89	72.91
1992	93.58	71.27	72.00	72.79
1993	81.67	72.31	75.34	73.08
1994	99.32	74.77	96.69	75.44
1995	69.3	74.31	79.29	75.79
1996	90.97	75.59	93.17	77.24
1997	71.01	75.27	72.33	76.86
1998	89.94	76.24	95.75	78.21
1999	87.95	76.98	88.96	78.93
2000	90.69	77.78	101.55	80.34
2001	101.27	79.09	60.03	79.15
2002	90.80	79.70	100.92	80.36

Note: A capacity factor greater than 100% is possible because capacity factor calculations are based on the original reactor rating of 1070 MW, but the reactors are approved for operation at 1105 MW.

capacity and unplanned scrams are influenced by how well the engineers evaluate and correct problems. Both factors improved over time. These two factors, plus unplanned outages and duration of outages, became the standard measure within the organization and throughout the industry during this study. Reporting and monitoring of these factors significantly improved during the course of the study. Originally, information on how the site was performing was distributed infrequently with little attention paid to it. During the last 2 years, as management became more aware of KM and the need for measuring their own effectiveness, the process was changed. Currently, performance information is available on the site's Intranet. Also, a quarterly report is produced that discusses how the site is performing and pays particular attention to lessons learned, what is working well, what is not working well, and where there are problems.

Originally, this approach was not considered valuable as a measure of effectiveness. However, it is now considered to be a very effective measure and has replaced the first SALP approach as the method of choice for assessing organizational effectiveness. Table 5 lists the capacity factors for the units of the site. The table also lists the cumulative capacity factor, because refueling outages cause lower capacity factors in the year they occur and the cumulative tends to show the overall impact of improvements in performance. Table 6 shows generally improving performance for both units during the period of the study (1996-2002). The dip in 1997 is due to special, first time cleaning activities that caused refueling outages to be extended, and is considered an anomaly in the generally improving trend. The dip for Unit 3 in 2001 is due to time needed to repair the turbine following an accident during startup following completion of the refueling outage. This accident was not due to activities performed by the subject-engineering group, and therefore was not considered a failure in KM.

Approach #3

The third productivity measure used performance indicators selected by the subject organization. These indicators are monitored monthly and graphs illustrating performance are printed and posted. This method provided less than useful results. It does tie in well with the organization's goals as defined in the second approach, but only addresses the quantifiable measures of the engineer productivity model. Because KM primarily affects the qualitative and competency skills of engineer productivity, this method does not provide any insight into whether or not KM improves productivity. However, as the organization progressed in its understanding of KM, this method was rolled into the second approach and is now used to report quantifiable results, as well as to report on qualitative measures such as lessons learned. Combining of the second and third approaches, first observed during the third stage, has provided an acceptable measure of organizational effectiveness. This approach consists of a digital dashboard of key performance indicators along with a summary of issues needing improvement and lessons learned that is available to all employees on the site Intranet. This measure indicated satisfactory performance during the data collection period with respect to quantifiable measures, such as capacity factor (the unit 3 turbine accident occurred after the data collection period) as indicated in Table 5. It also provided focus on what employees needed to focus on and improve to ensure continued acceptable capacity factor performance.

CHALLENGES FACING THE ORGANIZATION

Deregulation cost the organization dearly due to the ensuing energy crisis that caused many western utilities to suffer huge losses due to the difference between the cost of power and what they were allowed to charge for it. This utility was forced to reduce staff and cut significant budget. The result of this was that the subject organization developed an even finer appreciation for the impact of the KM on productivity, as well as the limitations of their KMS. The main challenge will be in improving the KMS while creating formal measures of KMS success and impacts on productivity and effectiveness. The organization has made a start in this direction by appointing a responsible manager for KM and by beginning to develop a formal KM strategy. This will be a challenge given the demand for resources from everyday operations.

CONCLUSION AND LESSONS LEARNED

Many organizations have reported difficulty in measuring the impact of KM on organizational productivity/effectiveness. This longitudinal case shows that an organization can find these measures if they look deep into the organization and comes to the ultimate conclusion that reuse of knowledge improves individual and organizational productivity/performance. The following reflect the lessons learned from this longitudinal case:

- Measures reflecting the impact of knowledge use can be found both for individuals and the organization, but will be organization specific. This research did not find measures that could be considered general and that could be used in all organizations and it may be that this type of generic measure may not exist for KM.
- Formal management of KM is needed to guide the development of KM and the KMS. Without this oversight the KMS tends to not be as integrated or usable as it could be. Additionally, the KMS may lack the capacity

or processing power needed to transfer and use knowledge.

- A KM strategy is needed to guide management in identifying and measuring the impacts of KM on the organization.
- Amount of use is not a good measure for KM or KMS success of effectiveness. However, intent to use is a good measure.

REFERENCES

Alavi, M., & Leidner, D. E. (2001). Review: Knowledge management and knowledge management systems: Conceptual foundations and research issues. *MIS Quarterly, 25(*1), 107-136.

Churchman, C. W. (1979). *The systems approach* (revised and updated). New York: Dell Publishing.

Davenport, T. H., & Prusak, L. (1998). *Working knowledge*. Boston: Harvard Business School Press.

DeLone, W. H., & McLean, E. R. (1992). Information systems success: The quest for the dependent variable. *Information Systems Research, 3*, 60-95.

DeLone, W. H., & McLean, E. R. (2003). The DeLone and McLean model of information systems success: A ten-year update. *Journal of Management Information Systems, 19*(4), 9-30.

Holsapple, C. W., & Joshi, K. (2004). A formal knowledge management ontology: Conduct, activities, resources, and influences. *Journal of the American Society for Information Science and Technology, 55*(7), 593-612.

Huber, G. P. (1991). Organizational learning: The contributing processes and the literatures. *Organization Science, 2*(1), 88-115.

Huysman, M. H., Fischer, S. J., & Heng, M. S. H. (1994). An organizational learning perspective on information systems planning. *Journal of Strategic Information Systems, (3)*3, 165-177.

Jennex, M. E. (2005). What is KM? *International Journal of Knowledge Management, 1*(4), i-iv.

Jennex, M. E., & Olfman, L. (2002). Organizational memory/knowledge effects on productivity, A longitudinal study. In *Proceedings of the 35th Hawaii International Conference on System Sciences, HICSS35*, IEEE Computer Society.

Kaplan, R. S., & Norton, D. P. (1992). The balanced scorecard, the measures that drive performance. *Harvard Business Review, 70*(1), 47-54.

Maier, R. (2002). *Knowledge management systems: Information and communication technologies for knowledge management*. Berlin: Springer-Verlag.

Nonaka, I. (1994). A dynamic theory of organizational knowledge creation. *Organization Science, 5*(1), 14-37.

Nuclear Regulatory Commission, NRC. (1998, October 2). *NRC Administrative Letter 98-07, Interim Suspension of the Systematic Assessment of Licensee Performance (SALP) Program.* United States Nuclear Regulatory Commission.

Nuclear Regulatory Commission News (NRC News). (1997, April 8). RIV-99-18, *NRC Finds Performance "Acceptable" at San Onofre in Latest Review.* United States Nuclear Regulatory Commission.

Nuclear Regulatory Commission News (NRC News). (1999, August 1). RIV-4497, NRC Rates *San Onofre Nuclear Plant "Good" and "Superior" in SALP Report.* United States Nuclear Regulatory Commission.

Power Reactor Information System (PRIS). (2003). *Power Reactor Details International Atomic Energy* Agency database. Retrieved August 12, 2007, from http://www.iaea.org/programmes/a2/

Quinn, R. E., & Rhorbaugh, J. (1983). A spatial model of effectiveness criteria: Towards a competing values approach to organizational analysis. *Management Science, 29*(3), 363-377.

Rubin, H. A. (1994). In search of the business value of information technology. *Application Development Trends, 1*(12), 23-27.

Stein, E. W., & Zwass, V. (1995). Actualizing organizational memory with information systems. *Information Systems Research, 6*(2), 85-117.

Strassmann, P. A. (1990). *The business value of computers*. New Canaan, CT: The Information Economics Press.

Thompson, R. L., Higgins, C. A., & Howell, J. M. (1991, March). Personal computing: Toward a conceptual model of utilization. *MIS Quarterly*, 125-143.

Walsh, J. P., & Ungson, G. R. (1991). Organizational memory. *Academy of Management Review, 16*(1), 57-91.

This work was previously published in the International Journal of Knowledge Management, Vol. 4, Issue 1, edited by M. Jennex, pp. 51-64, copyright 2008 by IGI Publishing (an imprint of IGI Global).

Chapter 12
Developing an Integrated Model for Understanding Knowledge Management Practices in an Arab Country:
Evidence from a Case Study

Minwir Al-Shammari
University of Bahrain, Kingdom of Bahrain

ABSTRACT

This chapter seeks to develop a model for understanding Knowledge Management (KM) practice in an Arab socio-economic context. To achieve the objectives of the study, a conceptual KM model was proposed and described; it was then illustrated using a case study. The chapter adopts a case study approach as a powerful source of understanding the KM specificities. Twelve interviews were conducted with executives of a telecommunications company, and then were systemically analyzed. Based on the findings of the study, a profile of KM in an Arab country is developed as well as a holistic and integrative KM model. The final model concludes with a proposed a three-layer KM model. The first layer includes KM drivers (market liberalization, technological advancements, and customers' preferences); the second includes KM processes (knowledge strategizing, sourcing, composing, sharing, and using), whereas the third layer includes KM enablers (KM buying behavior, convergence of business and technology, source-data quality, project championship, process-based structure, and sharing culture). However, the proposed model requires further testing through conducting more case studies to be able to capture the best practice of KM in this important region.

INTRODUCTION

Business organizations of the new economy operate in a highly competitive and turbulent business environment. Organizations are faced with fierce competitive pressures arising from technological advancements, globalization of markets, deregulation, liberalization, privatization, as well as rapid political and governmental changes that place huge demand on firms to remain flexible, responsive, and innovative (Drucker, 1995; Teece et al., 1997).

DOI: 10.4018/978-1-60566-954-0.ch012

The resource-based view of the firm recognizes the importance of organizational resources and capabilities as a principal source of creating and sustaining competitive advantage in market competition. According to this approach, resources are the main source of an organization's capabilities, whereas capabilities are the key source of its competitive advantage (Grant, 1991). As knowledge is one of the principal resources in service-oriented firms, effective usage and management of knowledge resources is a prerequisite of gaining distinctive advantage.

However, successful implementation of business concepts and practices in industrial Western economies may not necessarily replicate itself with success in emerging economies, e.g. the Arab region, if implementation was not carefully customized to fit the available organizational infrastructure and to the specific society and culture. The aim of the paper is to develop an understanding of Knowledge Management (KM) approach in a changing and fast growing Arab region, and to propose a model for a successful KM strategy in such a socio-cultural context.

THE IMPORTANCE OF KNOWLEDGE

The beauty of using knowledge as a base of sustainable competitive advantage is that it is a non-depleting resource. Unlike other business resources that diminish once shared, knowledge development follows the law of increasing returns - the more knowledge is used, the more value it creates. Furthermore, the more knowledge is shared, the more new knowledge is generated. Knowledge sharing, therefore, is becoming a successful way to increase the value of 'intellectual assets' in improving knowledge-intensive processes and adding value to customers and profitability to the business. There are several key attributes of knowledge, which must be factored into KM practices (Kluge, et al, 2001; and Davenport and Prusak, 2000):

- **Subjectivity:** context and individual background shape the interpretation of knowledge.
- **Transferability:** knowledge can be extracted and transferred to other contexts.
- **Embeddedness:** knowledge is often in static and buried form that makes it difficult to extract.
- **Self-reinforcement:** knowledge is the only unlimited resource, the one asset that its marginal utility increases and does not decrease once used or shared.
- **Perishability:** knowledge can become outdated.
- **Serendipity (spontaneity):** knowledge can develop unexpectedly in a spontaneous or incidental process (e.g., water cooler knowledge exchanges).
- **Velocity:** *speed* with which knowledge moves through an organization (e.g., computers and networks excel at enhancing the velocity of knowledge).
- **Viscosity:** *richness* or *stickiness* of detailed or subtle knowledge transferred (e.g., apprenticeship or mentoring relationship)

KM MODELS

Although KM is a young discipline for which no universally accepted model has been established, some authors were concerned with creating KM models. The role of KM models is to oversee, or provide guidance for, the discipline (Rubenstein-Montano et al., 2001a). KM strategy model is a high-level approach for outlining the processes, tools, as well as organizational and technological infrastructure needed to manage knowledge gaps or surpluses and to permit knowledge to flow effectively (Zack, 2002b). Some researchers argue that KM strategy may replace the firm's business strategy, or, a business strategy may evolve to become a KM strategy, or, the two strategies may complement one another (Civi, 2000; Vera,

2001; Krogh and Grant, 2002; and AlAmmari and Fung, 2008).

The KM strategy models, with their very general approach to KM, provide an excellent starting point for developing a business-specific KM process model. KM process models are approaches or methodologies that are more specific than models, detailing how to actually carry out KM in a manner consistent with a particular model.

There are a number of KM strategy models worthy of mention, including those that have incorporated models for the KM process, such as Wiig (1993), Holsapple and Joshi (1997), Wiig (1997), Beckman (1999), Probst et al. (1999), Davenport and Prusak (2000), Rubenstein-Montano et al. (2001a,b), Tiwana (2001) and Jashapara (2004), and Liebowitz (2004). In addition to these KM process models, there are a few KM successful implementation models presented by Lindsey (2002), Massey et al. (2002), and Jennex and Olfman (2003).

KNOWLEDGE ENVIRONMENT IN THE ARAB REGION

Many international and regional development agencies have put forward their contributions for the best utilization of knowledge for sustainable national development. The World Bank Institute (Aubert and Reiffers, 2003) offered its conceptual model for the creation of knowledge-based development strategies in different region of the world. The model is composed of the following five 'pillars':

- An economic and institutional model that provides incentives for the efficient creation, dissemination, and use of knowledge to promote growth and increase welfare;
- An educated and skilled population that can create and use knowledge;
- An innovation system of firms, research centers, universities, consultants, and other organizations that can tap into the growing stock of global knowledge, adapt it to local needs, and transform it into products valued by markets;
- A dynamic information infrastructure that can facilitate the effective communication, dissemination, and processing of information.
- An intangible component that makes a society function efficiently and move forward, such as the capacity to formulate a vision, the level of trust and self-confidence, and the appropriateness of guiding values.

United Nations Development Program (UNDP) published in 2002 the first Arab Human Development Report (AHDR, 2002) that addressed the most important development challenges facing human development in the Arab World at the beginning of the third millennium. The second report (AHDR, 2003) continues the process by examining in depth one of these challenges: the building of a knowledge society in Arab countries. Although it is a fact that Arab countries have greater resources than some developing countries that rank above them in various indices of human development, the need for sustainable human development in the Arab region is immense, as the region is "richer than it is developed" (AHDR, 2002). The second AHDR (2003) underlined the importance of knowledge to Arab countries as a powerful driver of economic growth through higher productivity. It also affirmed that knowledge could help the region to expand the scope of human freedoms, enhance the capacity to guarantee those freedoms through good governance.

The relevance of this study is based on the premise that leveraging of the firm's intellectual capital and core competencies is a mean to achieve efficiency and competitiveness in a region that is in immense need for sustainable development. Today's opportunity for the social and economic development of the Arab countries is to fuel banking and telecommunications industries as well as other relevant sectors with knowledge.

RESEARCH OBJECTIVES

The paper represents an exploratory study that follows the assumption that predictors of KM successful implementation and best practices in developed countries do not necessarily create value to other cultures, i.e. the Arab culture, when directly implemented. KM adoption needs to be customized to the organizational context and to the specific society and its national socio-cultural values.

This paper seeks to examine the implementation of KM in a telecommunications company in the Arab region, and to develop a model for KM strategy in such a cultural context. In particular, the paper sought to:

- Identify the business drivers for KM initiatives.
- Investigate the KM life cycle processes.
- Examine enabling factors that lead to a successful adoption of KM initiatives.
- Develop a profile of KM in an Arab country
- Develop a KM strategy model in an Arab context that integrates KM drivers, processes, and enablers.

THE RESEARCH MODEL

The review of KM models clearly showed that these models were predominantly similar in their main building blocks (acquire/create, codify/organize, share/distribute, and apply), almost any of the KM strategy models could serve as a reference preliminary theoretical base for KM studies. However, KM strategy models showed slight differences in some elements of process models, and some detailed KM models, e.g. Holsapple and Joshi (1997, 1998), Tiwana (2000), and Rubenstein-Montano et al. (2001a,b), have added some components (e.g. visions, strategic agendas, and objectives) prior to KM process or after it (e.g. infrastructure, culture, etc.).

The adopted KM research model integrates the main components of the aforementioned KM process and successful implementation models into a comprehensive one composed of three major layers (Figure 1):

- Layer One: KM environmental drivers' layer.
- Layer Three: KM enablers' layer.
- Layer Two: KM development processes' layer.

THE CASE METHODOLOGY

The present study is exploratory in nature that sought to understand the various issues concerning KM practices and to generate a model for a successful implementation of KM initiatives in the context of an Arab country. The exploratory nature of the study reflects an observation that the literature lacks an understanding of KM practices and success factors in Arab countries.

The exploratory nature of the study required a qualitative research methodology. The goal of a typical KM case study is to understand and explain technological, informational, and business phenomena with its socio-cultural and organizational context. A typical case study in KM adopts a qualitative research methodology based on interviews with experts.

A list of executives in the organization, who have direct relationship to KM, has been used as a primary source of data. There were 12 in-depth face-to-face interviews that have been conducted to solicit viewpoints of the concerned managers from different levels and functions. Interviews were conducted with general mangers, senior managers, managers, and other specialists from

Figure 1. The Conceptual Model

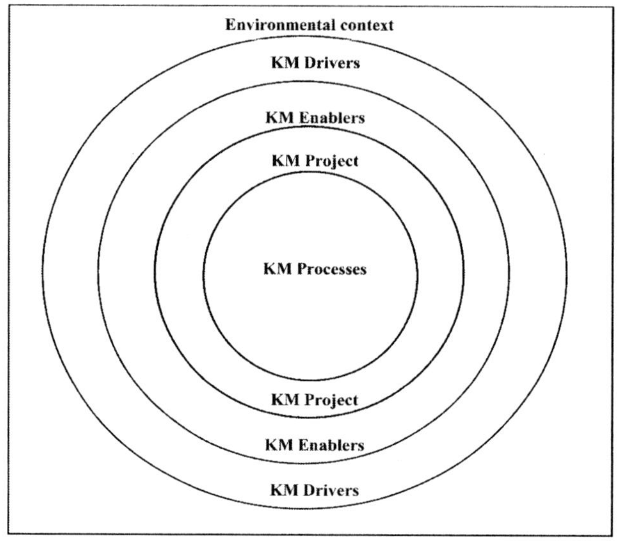

marketing, human resources, information and communication technology (ICT) applications and services, product development, customer support, and customer business development. Interviews at the company were voice recorded (except one un-recorded informal interview), enabling a later transcription of the text and afterwards a systematic analysis of the contents. Notes were also taken on some issues during the interviews. In addition, the company's newsletter and other appropriate organizational documents and reports were consulted and utilized as a source of secondary data in order to be able to achieve objectives of the study.

The researchers analyzed the contents, recognizing structures and patterned regularities in the text and makes replicable and valid inferences on the basis of these regularities. This process was assisted by a Qualitative Data Analysis (QDA) computer application called the NUD*IST (from QSR- Qualitative Solutions & Research International). NUD*IST stands for Non-numerical, Unstructured, Data: Indexing, Searching and Theorizing. Put simply, it works with textual documents, and facilitates the *indexing* of components of these documents; is able to *search* for words and phrases very quickly; and claims to support theorizing through enabling the retrieval of indexed text segments, related memos, and text and index searches.

Transcribed interviews were imported into the QSR NUD*IST package as text files. Subsequently every paragraph was thoroughly examined and categorized under one or more free nodes that represented the emerging issues. The process of assigning free codes to nodes is known as open coding in the grounded-theory methodology (Strauss et al., 1990). The grounded-theory is an inductive approach to create a detailed and integrative model at the end of the research project. Open coding is a process of reducing the data to a small set of themes that appear to describe the phenomenon under scrutiny.

CASE FINDINGS

While each one of the aforementioned KM issues was initially part of the cases study protocol, however, the results documented here cover only to the final list of categories of issues derived from the categorization of transcribed interviews using the NUD*IST software. New categories of themes emerged and others were regrouped as transcripts were analyzed.

KM DRIVERS

The undertaking of KM initiatives at the investigated company can be considered as an organizational response to several drivers in the business environment. The main drivers were market liberalization, ICT advancements, and customers' preferences.

Market Liberalization

In the company's under investigation, the government established the telecommunication regulatory commission (TRC) in 2001, and as a result, the local telecommunications market was officially declared deregulated in 2003. The market witnessed an entry of the first telecommunications competitor to the local market. Ever since the liberalization of the market, the company felt that it couldn't continue to run business the same traditional way using the same old technologies in the impending turbulent business environment. The main driver for a major KM initiative, i.e. Customer Relationship Management (CRM), was the impending competition due to deregulation of the local telecommunications market announced in 2001 and took effect in 2003.

ICTC Advancements

The CRM system intends to develop a better understanding of customer needs in order to better serve them, presents to employees' valuable information about different aspects of the business and the customers, and to equip them with knowledge to better perform their jobs and improve employee satisfaction. The CRM provides a single source of consolidated and integrated information through consolidated and integrated data and applications, which will improve productivity and information sharing processes. CRM also seeks to contribute to improving corporate image since the company will be seen as a company investing in enhancing its performance.

Customers' Preferences

In 1998/1999, the companies had some foresight that knowledge was critical to establishment of long-term relationships with customers and improvement of profitability in impending competitive environment. In 2001, it decided to initiate the development of a two-folded solution: CRM project to be able to manage their customer knowledge.

KM PROCESSES

The company's vision is to be the first choice communications partner for customers in the local market and in chosen markets across the region and to serve as a role model for other communications companies. The company's mission is to deliver a simple and complete customer experience -offering a full range of reliable, competitively priced communications services and solutions. The business strategic vision was cascaded down to the following specific corporate objectives:

- Enhancing customer satisfaction.
- Delivering impressive year-on-year profit growth.
- Increasing efficiencies across the company and its subsidiaries.
- Ensuring that we properly train, motivate, reward and retain its employees.
- Protecting and build upon its outstanding corporate image.

The KM development process included the following components:

- Sourcing Knowledge
- Composing Knowledge
- Sharing Knowledge
- Utilizing Knowledge

Sourcing Knowledge

Organizations interact with their environments (internal as well as external), absorb information, turn it into knowledge, and take action based on it (combined with their experience, values, and internal rules). Knowledge sources come from conscious and intentional techniques like acquisition (e.g. of Lotus by IBM, NCR by AT&T), rental (sponsorship of research in academic institutes, hiring a consultant), dedicated resources (research centers and universities like Xerox PARC, McDonald's universities), fusion (via brainstorming and retreats), adaptation (e.g. via learning sabbaticals), corporate universities, KM workshops, group dinners, and knowledge networking (Davenport and Prusak, 2000).

In order to maintain and enhance its competitive position, the company needs to continue to generate new ideas, products/services, or KM initiatives. The company's source of knowledge and KM awareness were found to come from the internal as well as external sources.

Internal Sources

The internal sources included examples such as professional training, on-job training and development, job rotation, and business meeting, committees, and task forces.

External Sources

The external sources included examples such as relationships with vendors (include selling ideas to top management through on-site presentations), partnership with a worldwide telecommunications company, and participation in knowledge fairs, workshops, seminars, or exhibitions, conferences, and professional meetings.

Composing Knowledge

The history of KM at the company started in 1995 with a cultural change towards a customer-centric organization, and since then, the company has been undertaking various KM activities. However, many of the KM initiatives were fragmented and didn't seem to be part of a formal corporate-wide action plan. Nevertheless, there was almost no disagreement among the senior managers and managers who participated in the study on the merit of the KM concept and its applications. In fact, they expressed their interest in the concept and acknowledged its importance and value to their business.

Organizational Transformation (OT)

During 1994-95, the company started thinking about introducing organizational change initiatives. In 1996, the company launched a major human-based organizational transformation program known as Organization Transformation (OT) project. The human resource management (HRM) department championed the project, which was mainly concerned with reengineering business processes and improving organizational performance. In 1996, the Organizational Transformation Phase 1 (OT1) initiative was completed, and followed by Phase 2 (OT2) and Phase 3 (OT3) in 1999, and 2001 respectively. Each initiative took almost a year of studying and two years of implementation.

In OT1, the company started questioning some of their old ways of doing things, i.e. bureaucratic procedures, and underwent a lot of organizational changes, which basically shifted the management system from a bureaucratic (control oriented, very top down management) to a democratic one. Some business procedures at the company were bureaucratic-type of operations that were there only to satisfy some people's quest for power and didn't add any value to the business; in fact, they wasted time, effort and money. In January 1996, and as part of the OT1 initiative, Communication and Audit Teams were formed. These teams met personally with every single employee of business groups in order to communicate to them the nature and objectives of the program, and to solicit their views and reactions as well.

In 1999, and after practicing OT1 for a few years, the company found some shortcomings that were not addressed, and as a result, launched Phase 2 (OT2). In the year 2000, the company decided that it was time to reengineer business processes by cutting out the non value-adding processes, and integrating information systems (IS) together. There were many fragmented or stand-alone systems that were doing many important things but they were not "talking" to each other.

Starting from 2001, and as part of OT3, the company foresaw the need for a transformation of the organization from an engineering-led (product-based) to customer-led business strategy. The end of the year 2002 witnessed the completion of the first stage called "Increased Business Value". In the year 2003, the second Phase ("Expansion and Growth") should have presumably started. In 2003, several work teams are looking at the various functions and processes for possible improvement and re-engineering. Phase 3 (OT3) was labeled "Get Ready", and was launched in mainly to help the company face the impending business competition by transforming the company from product-led to customer–led business Then, different organizational initiatives were carried out to promote that line of change. An outside consultant was called in to lead the organizational transformation process. However, the consultant faced some resistance when the issue of restructuring was tackled. Restructuring became part of the organizational politics and inertia emerged as a result.

One of the specific initiatives launched by the company under the newly emerged customer-led form was to increase the exchange and integration of knowledge across divisions, i.e. sales (customer-facing or front-end) and product development (marketing-oriented or back-end). These divisions never used to talk because they have a culture of "we got our own things to do; you got your own things to do".

At the beginning of 2003, the Sales and Product divisions were merged, and as a result of shared knowledge of these two units the company has launched its new Mobile Price Plan. That whole undertaking couldn't have done possible in the past with all of 'silos' or 'stovepipe' structure in place. A 'silo' or 'stovepipe' structure is a function-based form of organizations, supported with "islands" of data, which does not promote communication across departments or units.

Customer Relationship Management (CRM)

In 1998/1999, the company had some foresight that knowledge was crucial to establish long-term relationships with customers. In order to manage this knowledge they decided in early 2003 to implement the first formal KM initiative, viz. the CRM program. In 2000, the company tendered the CRM system and selected the supplier. In the first quarter of 2001, the initial stages of the project began. The operational side of the CRM system was up and running in 2005, but the analytical side is still under development.

The CRM is composed of Enterprise Data Warehouse (EDW), Operational CRM, and analytical CRM. The EDW initiative was announced in 2001 and it was up and running in early 2003. The EDW initiative was being used for KM purposes. The EDW is a repository of data coming from operational legacy systems, namely, customer care, billing system (including the three customer profiles: IT, GSM, and fixed line billing), finance system, accounts receivable and others. The system capitalizes all knowledge in terms of historical data and it can be used to improve decision making regarding product development, marketing plans, customer segmentation, product and services usage and others. The CRM system was thought to be a strategic system and major enabler for the company's continued success in the impending fierce competitive environment.

For the CRM project, the company formed different committees to oversee the EDW Phase of the project. These were the Business Intelligence Steering Committee (BISC) representing general managers (GMs) and Project Management Committee (PMC) consisting of the project manager of IT and the key business representatives from marketing, from sales, from back office, and customer care. There were also subcommittees looking into technical details of the system such as format of system reports and quality of data.

To be able to understand the whole business processes and objectives, the vendor of the CRM project redefined processes, identified key business deliverables and prioritized them into about 100 business cases, like customers, products, revenue, traffic, and sensitivity analysis. The vendor formulated some strategies, presented them to management, and came up with experiences and recommendations of how to best exploit knowledge in terms of processes and structure. At the same time the company formed a committee in order to align the system to business objectives in terms of who should be getting what access?, what sort of information should be going on it?, and how to structure the project phases?.

The vendor played a leading role in being the main source of knowledge for the company and in partnering with the business units to define their business requirements. So they could finalize the design and start to develop the CRM and extracting information from the source system into the CRM system.

Sharing Knowledge

Since 2002, and as a result of transformation of the company from bureaucratic to democratic management, and from a product-centered to a customer-centered business there has been more encouragement for internal sharing and absorption knowledge through committees. This may be due to the fact that the company will no longer be able to enjoy its monopoly of the market, and has to improve its competitive position through organizational transformation and leveraging of knowledge-based core competencies.

To transfer knowledge from experts to trainees in case of employees getting sick, having vacations or getting transferred, a twofold method is used. First, there is a direct transfer of knowledge through training and coaching, and second, there are knowledge gatherings that join together people undertaking similar activities. For example, watch keepers, who have two different shifts, overlap one hour for knowledge exchange.

Although the existing culture is remarkably different as knowledge is being shared through corporate manuals, guidelines, memos, meetings, and other relevant personal information related to employees themselves (e.g. through the HRM system) or related to employees' work are accessible electronically; nevertheless, there have been some down sides, due to the position/power differences among staff members. Some staff may be hesitant to ask a senior manager or a GM in particular.

Utilizing Knowledge

Since the company implemented CRM program and transformed its business, good financial performance results were achieved. Net profits climbed to about 25.2% during the first quarter of the year 2004 against the same period in 2003. This increase is attributed to a year-on-year rise in gross revenues, and a reduction in costs largely due to non-recurring exceptional items related to restructuring, which were successfully implemented in 2003.

KM Enablers

The company has worked hard to maintain its strong market position as competition is impending. Following the implementation of the CRM and OT initiatives, the company has achieved mixed results, i.e. remarkable performance at the financial side but almost complete failure at the level of operational excellence at the level of customer service and satisfaction. The significant financial performance gains may be attributed to the corporate downsizing that followed the transformation program. Yet technology-based KM initiatives, such as the CRM, has to mature into concrete corporate-wide change effort based on a clear plan and strategy still have a long way to go before being able to fully realize corporate-wide benefits.

In light of the case findings, the critical success factors (CSFs) of KM implementation were composed of six interrelated components that are in alignment 'equilibrium' with each other. Any change in one of the components would entail a need for a change in another component. These enablers were KM buying behavior, convergence of business and technology, source-data quality, project championship, process-based structure, and sharing culture.

KM Buying Behavior

It seems to be that due to lack of experience with KM projects in the region, the company's KM buying behavior looks like a 'solution buyer', which prefers all-in-one solutions, thinking that KM projects are same as ICT projects. The ICT-based KM initiatives at the company seemed to be created and used on the basis of 'vendor-push' rather than 'business-pull' buying behavior. The KM technology components were driving, instead of enabling the KM strategy. The focus of the vendor seemed to be limited to customization and implementation of ICT tools, but not ensuring that the process and organization elements are in place for effective management of the KCRM project. Effective vendor's role and involvement, as well as effective management of relationship with vendors are very essential to the CRM success.

Convergence of Business and Technology

In implementing KM projects, business should be the driver whereas ICT would be the enabler. Therefore, and in order to continue to keep KM projects 'business-driven' rather than 'technology-driven', and to secure a successful adoption of KM projects, it seems that it would be better to have business managers champion the KM project. Business managers and their staff are the power users of KM systems who are responsible for generating knowledge about different aspects of the business, the market, and the customers. Active involvement, support, and participation from senior-management levels and ICT managers are also essential for a successful implementation of KM projects.

Source-Data Quality

Data accuracy is very critical as KM systems, e.g. CRM, retrieve data from EDW and put them in the required format, but if the raw data were not completely filtered, then the validity of the project's information would be at risk. Poor data quality at the company resulted from accumulation of a lot of data inaccuracies over the years, and there is a need to conduct an urgent work on cleaning these data. Studies conducted by Jennex and Olfman (2006) and Finnegan and Sammon (2002) indicated that attention should be given to source-data quality for successful implementation of KM systems.

Project Championship

In the case of the CRM project, although there have been active involvement by senior management, ICT managers, business managers, and the vendor in its development process. The CRM project was not just a suite of software products but a business strategy to provide benefits to the business, e.g. improve levels of customer satisfaction, boost customer loyalty, and increase revenue from existing customers. However, an ICT manager rather than one of the knowledge users championed the CRM project at its beginning. It looks like that the technical mind-set of ICT people didn't fit the business nature of the ICT-driven KM projects. Soon the company understood that it had to be business driven and one of the general managers was appointed as the sponsor.

Process-Based Structure

The organizational structure is function-based that does not foster the concept of KM in a formal and cross-unit holistic approach through experimentation, documentation, sharing, and dissemination of knowledge across different departments. The change towards networked structure and business process-orientation will allow to improve performance of initiatives already in place and to promote new initiatives that might be needed, such as the establishment of an electronic library, 'yellow pages', 'knowledge maps', that can facilitate the buying and selling of specific knowledge created by workers in different departments within the company.

Sharing Culture

It was found from the case study that successful implementation of a KM strategy requires a major shift in organizational culture and commitment at all levels of an organization to initiate a focus on people and methods to enhance learning, improve communication, and encourage knowledge sharing instead of knowledge hoarding. In the company, some employees have misinterpreted the notion that 'knowledge is power', and therefore, tend not to cooperate in sharing their knowledge with other colleagues thinking that loss of power could mean loss of position. The situation has aggravated as the company undertook the OT3 initiative, wherein some positions have been cancelled. Such a finding was supported by Davenport et al. (1998), Jennex and Olfman (2000), Long and Fahey, (2000), and Alavi and Leidner (2001), and Hart and Warne (2006), and Usoro and Paisley (2006).

A PROFILE OF KM IN THE ARAB REGION

The work of Zhu (2004) questioned the claim that KM is a universal concept, and presented evidence that, despite growing overlaps, heterogeneity among KM styles is likely to continue due to differences in histories, cultures and institutional forces, which render a universal concept of KM unrealistic, counterproductive and undesirable. Zhu (2004) proposed KM in cross-cultural contexts that clearly reveal the unique associated problematics of different KM styles: the American, the Japanese, the European, and the Chinese. Based on the findings in this study, this paper adds a new KM profile for the Arab region (Table 1). The Arab KM profile is compared with other styles in line with the following dimensions set by Zhu (2004): motto, mentality, ideal-type, embodiment, mechanism, aim, focus, strategy, process, means, and metaphor.

A PROPOSED KM MODEL IN THE ARAB CONTEXT

Based on the findings of the study, a detailed integrative model for KM strategy was proposed (Figure 2). The model shows a three-layered cyclic diagram with multiple feedback loops. The first layer includes KM drivers; the second includes KM processes, whereas the third layer is KM enablers.

Table 1. A Profile of the Arab KM Style

Dimension	Arabic	Description
Motto	I codify, therefore, I am	The KM culture that prevails is 'data processing'-centric, wherein 'codification' is emphasized and 'personalization' is deemphasized.
Mentality	Functionalism/Incrementalism	Knowledge development is not looked at from a holistic process-perspective; rather, development of KM projects on a gradual and localized exploitation basis prevails. Silo knowledge mentality among employees in different departments is enhanced by functional structures. Silo mentality hinders knowledge sharing among employees.
Ideal-type	Knowledge as forgotten resource	Knowledge is rarely considered as a valuable resource to companies. Competition is traditionally product-centric, but is showing gradual concern with achievement of customer-centric competitive advantage. Personal knowledge is not usually shared.
Embodiment	Knowledge system	Emphasis on formal KM systems to capture/create structured knowledge, which in turn is stored, shared, and disseminated.
Mechanism	Knowledge outsourcing	Knowledge is created through internal and external sources. External sourcing dominates the knowledge scene and refers to out-of-the-house development or acquisition of ready-made KM systems. Sometimes, it follows a vendor-push mode where KM systems are pushed by vendors rather than pulled by companies.
Aim	Diffusion of environmental pressures	A critical response activity to environmental pressures such as competitors, liberalization of markets, advancement of ICT, and growing power of customers. Sometimes, KM projects end-up as vendor-push ICT projects introduced merely to follow the latest 'fashion' of the market? Vendors play a significant role in selling ideas of new ICT-based solutions that may end-up with no or little alignment with business strategies.
Focus	Explicit-structured knowledge	Explicit- structured knowledge is emphasized, whereas human and tacit-subjective knowledge is de-emphasized.
Strategy	Ad hoc	KM strategies are chaotic and still in their infancy. Lack of clear identification of business requirements, and more focus on computerized systems. A formal KM strategy hardly exists at a corporate level, although senior managers constantly stress the need to create, share and distribute knowledge.
Process	Buying	Vendors sell KM solutions formulate KM strategies; identify key business deliverables and present recommendations of process and structural changes to best exploit knowledge.
Means	ICTs People Vendors	ICTs People Vendors
Metaphor	Rich in data, yet poor in knowledge	Plenty of data exist, about customers for example, but rarely have these data been converted into knowledge and used to create sustainable competitive advantage.
Exemplar	Al-Shammari (2005). Implementing Knowledge-enabled CRM strategy in a large company	

DISCUSSION

Formal corporate-wide KM initiatives in the company were hardly been found in the investigated company. The KM initiatives were fragmented, same as the organization structure that was made up of many functional 'silos'. There also was an absence of an officially documented and declared

Figure 2. A Three-Layer KM Strategy Model (A: Drivers, B: Processes, and C: Enablers)

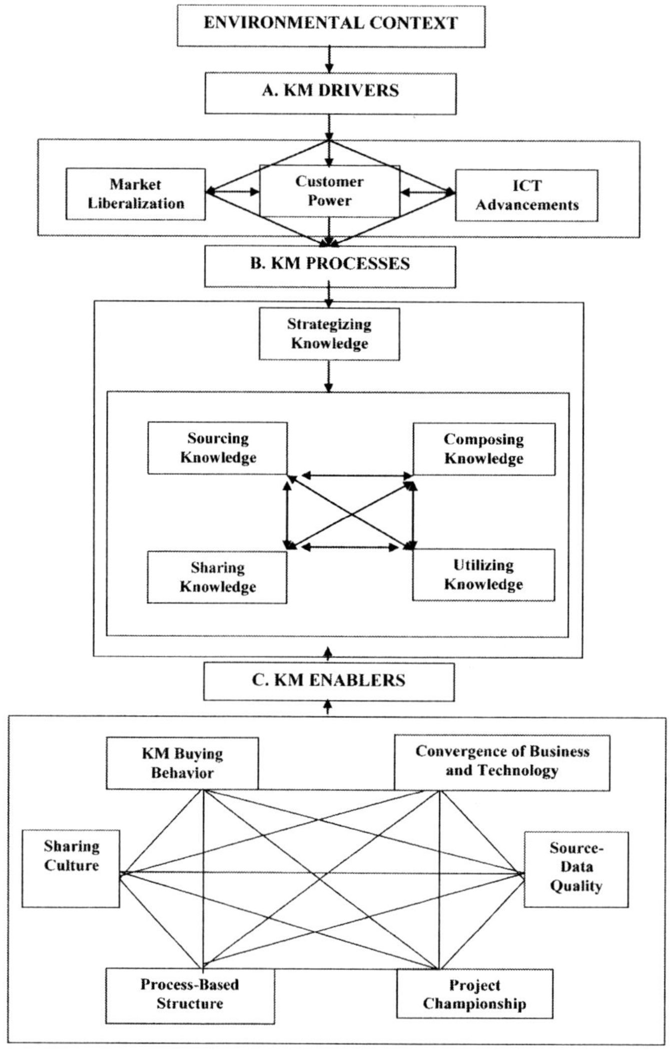

KM strategy embraced by the company, although senior managers stressed the need to create, share and distribute knowledge. According to Lessem and Neubauer (1993), the Anglo-Saxon orientation to knowledge creation can be categorized as pragmatic, the French-Nordic as rational, Japanese as holistic, Latin as humanistic. KM in the Arab region has not yet entered into the 'knowledge catch-up' stage prevalent in many emerging economies such as Korea (Kim, 2001). Therefore, KM effort in the Arab region creation can be categorized as 'chaotic' as it has not developed a structured and systematic approach or strategy. This finding is consistent with Jennex, et al. (2003) who investigated the need for having an organizational KM strategy to ensure that knowledge benefits gained from Y2K projects are captured for use in the organization. They found that benefits from projects were not being captured because the parent organizations did not have a KM strategy/process.

Davenport et al. (1998) observed that few firms employ the word 'knowledge' in strategy or planning documents. The very small numbers of firms that have a 'knowledge strategy' have not linked it to business strategy in any specific way. Despite theoretical linkages, KM is not yet tied to business strategy and performance in practice. Davenport et al. (1998) further noted that such concepts as 'communities of practice', 'knowledge sharing', 'and organizational learning' have been advanced by academics, consultants, and leading practitioners, but have yet to enter the realm of business strategy. As of the source of ideas for new KM projects, it was found that they come from internal as well as external sources. Internal sources come from human intellectual capital. In a study on KM in Kuwaiti organizations, Al-Athari and Zairi (2001) found that the most important sources of ideas come from existing knowledge of employees and organization. In another study on Egyptian software firms, Seleim et al. (2007) investigated three components of intellectual capital, human, structural, and customer-based relational capital, and found them associated with organizational performance and competitive advantage.

The KM initiatives taken by the company showed ICTs as the key enablers for KM. Major explicit KM initiatives, i.e. the CRM system, seemed to be created and used on the basis of 'push' by vendors of technology, not on the basis of 'pull' by real market need. The company has incorporated and maintained substantial technology-based knowledge distribution more than people-based knowledge sharing. The company has overemphasized explicit knowledge resources but deemphasized subtle ones, which means significant loss of the potential to utilize intellectual assets of human resources. The reason for such an overemphasis on explicit KM initiatives could be attributed to the prevailing 'data processing' culture in the company that is fetish of transactional processing of highly structured daily routines. The interviewees, at large, have many times mixed between KM and other business disciplines. Interviewees have on large perceived explicit KM initiatives, i.e. CRM, as synonymous to ICT, and implicit KM initiatives, such as organizational learning and knowledge sharing, as synonymous to human-based management fields, such as HRM, Organizational Behavior (OB), or Organizational Change and Development (OCD).

However, at the level of operational excellence (i.e., service time, lead time, quality of service, productivity), and satisfaction/loyalty of stakeholders (customers, employees, vendor, etc.), the results of technology-based KM solutions were not encouraging. The company faced and/or is still facing migration, workflow, and efficiency problems. Migration or testing problems lasted for couple of days; many data did not go through the operational CRM, as their data fields were not validated by the system. Workflow problems emerged as the people at network department for example could not trace the workflow of sales order processes, which in turn, adversely affected the ability to meet customer expectations. System's inefficiency was a result of the inability of the operational CRM to capture basic customer data; which would result in longer order fulfillment or service completion time, low productivity, customer dissatisfaction, and possible defect to competitors. The CRM system can be considered a good case of bad implementation.

As of the role of technology in KM, ICT-based approaches to KM particularly shine in the combination process, where explicit knowledge in documents, email and databases can be manipulated to create new kinds of knowledge. However, without the quality of connectivity and the simplicity and commonality offered by the software interface to application that is provided by an Intranet, for example, an organization's ability to create, share, capture and leverage knowledge is stuck in the 'stone age', just above the level of typewriters, faxes and snail mail (Rumizen, 2001).

Leading KM authors, e.g. Davenport and Prusak (2000), caution against a technology-push approach to KM, but argue that a technology ingredient is a necessary ingredient for successful KM projects. Senge (1990), the influential author in organizations, argued that organizations seeking to manage knowledge have placed too much emphasis on information technology and information management. Instead, he advocated organizational learning, which places too little emphasis on structured knowledge and use of technology to capture and leverage it. According to Senge (1999:3), learning organizations are 'organizations where people continually expand their capacity to create the results they truly desire, where new and expansive patterns of thinking are nurtured, where collective aspiration is set free, and where people are continually learning to see the whole together'. On a personal level, an individual in learning organizations work on developing 'personal mastery' of one's capacities, which refers to one's spiritual inner drive to learn and to be the best that one can be through developing one's vision, one's abilities, one's focus of energy (Senge, 1990). Siemens, one of the top KM-driven companies worldwide, has also affirmed its stand that the role of people is more important than technology in KM. Siemens KM program focused on a culture of sharing, synergy, and customer focus, especially in markets and fast-moving technology areas where the customer needs are more for total business solutions and sector intelligence than mere technology (Davenport and Probst, 2002).

The Arab region has greater resources than many developing countries (AHDR, 2003), but it has long suffered from 'digital divide' or 'knowledge gap', although it was known for presence of significant human capital, which under more promising conditions could offer a substantial base for an Arab knowledge renaissance in the business sector as well as in the society as a whole. Cultural impacts and differences in KM implementation have been recently the concern of many scholars, researchers, and conferences. In the Arab region, it seems that there is a widespread misconception that transferal or 'consumption' of technology alone is the key for bridging the 'knowledge/digital gap' with developed countries and achieving sustainable development. Arab countries' experiments with the transfer and adoption of technology have neither achieved the desired technological advancement nor yielded attractive returns on investment. Importing technology has not led to its adoption and internalization in the host country, let alone to its diffusion and production (AHDR, 2003).

One of the main features of this knowledge 'consumption' pattern prevailing in Arab countries, especially rich oil countries, is a high dependence on depleting resources, mainly oil, and reliance on external imports. This economic pattern attracts societies to import expertise and technology from outside because this is a quick and easy resort that ends up weakening local demand for knowledge and opportunities to produce it locally and employ it effectively in economic activity (AHDR, 2003). A large part of the Arab economic activity is not knowledge-intensive and is concentrated on primary commodities, as in agriculture, which remains largely traditional, and in industries specializing in the production of consumer goods, which depend heavily on franchising agreements with foreign companies. This definitely calls for a decisive move towards developing renewable resources through knowledge and technological capabilities and towards diversifying economic structures and markets to be more knowledge-based (AHDR, 2003).

The two biggest gaps that account for the failure in 'technology-based' knowledge development pattern in the Arab region have been the absence of effective innovation and knowledge production systems in Arab countries, and the lack of rational policies in the region that ingrain those essential values and institutional models that support knowledge development. The problems have been aggravated by the mistaken belief that knowledge can be built through the importation of scientific products without investing in the local production of knowledge through human creativity and innovation (AHDR, 2003).

The Arab educational system needs to equip successive generations with new approaches to knowledge acquisition, synthesis, sharing, and utilization through rigorous schooling. R&D, as a source and a way of applied knowledge, can assist Arab countries to identify gaps in strategically important and complex developmental issues. R&D should follow the concept of the KM lifecycle in generating and leveraging knowledge to offer competitive advantage. The hybridization of internal and external sources of knowledge is also critical in building synergy for innovation. Therefore, it is important to establish collaborative research support programs and/or strategic alliances, bilateral or multilateral cooperation between local and global universities, multinational companies, science and technology parks, research centers and international organizations. At the organizational level, there is a necessity for new forms of organizations to proactively undergo the process of "de-siloing" by transforming from the structure of rigid hierarchical silos to organic de-layered, knowledge-intensive organizations (Mirghani et al., 2008).

In an effort to revitalize knowledge, new strategies and action plans need to be explicated. The Arab world can revert from the status of "knowledge entropy" to the former "golden age" of Islam – if the principles of modern knowledge are effectively leveraged and cross-bred with traditions to result in a lucrative "knowmadism" (Mirghani et al., 2008). Specifically, epistemological pluralism is required for success in the realm of the "knowledge society". Hence, the relationship with the West should neither be contentious, nor submissive. A "coopetitive", or cooperative competition, relationship is good enough to build the "knowledge society". The Arab tribal system is more effective in sharing and synthesizing knowledge than is a systematic modern corporate system, which is demonstrated by cross-functional teams, communities of practice (CoPs), communities of interest and even flat organizational settings. CoPs can be considered the neoclassical version of tribal communication and relationships. The region has for centuries been equipped for knowledge nourishment. For instance, "Souk Oukaz" was the first known CoP in the region, and the very first command in the Holly Quran is strictly about knowledge. In some cases, ethnographic knowledge-sharing within the tribal system is more effective than some forms of corporate knowledge-sharing within CoPs or communities of interest. The Arab world needs to extend the same ideas to build the sense of a business system of "megatribe knowledge" that would blend all forms of business pluralism, such as strategic alliances, and "coopetition" considerations (Mirghani et al., 2008).

Arabic culture has been labeled as 'contact culture' in which stronger emphasis is placed on people and personal contact and much less on institutionally derived procedures and rules (Wagner et al. 2003; Zakaria et al., 2003), which in turn increases personalization in the design of business solutions (Scarborough, 1998). Zaharna (1995) points out that Arabic preference for oral communication connects with higher usage of metaphors, analogies, and story telling to establish the story telling of the message. These observations on Arabic cultural values should be able to help in paving the way for a 'personalized' KM approach that heavily relies on exchange of knowledge and experiences. Hansen et al's (1999) suggested that organizations need to select a single strategy to concentrate on, while using the other strategy in a support role yet also recognizes that this strategy will change as the organization's personnel become more experienced in the use of knowledge. As KM adoption in Arab companies is still in its early stage, it seems more appropriate to adopt a 'personalized' KM strategy before a 'codified' one, and use 'contact' KM tools before 'content' ones. KM contact tools encourage sharing and distribution of existing subtle knowledge among knowledge workers, whereas content tools are advanced enterprise KM systems, e.g. CRM, Data Mining, and Business Intelligence, which aim at discovery and creation of new knowledge.

To keep the momentum of the "knowledge" society in the Arab region, the new initiatives for knowledge organizations must expand and be sustained. Economic prosperity and growth in the Arab region is allegedly unsustainable due to its dependence on tangible resources. In the "knowledge economy", any solution that comes from a tangible commodity is considered local anesthesia and not an eternal panacea. The sustainability of this momentum needs uninterrupted diffusion and infusion of innovations and perpetually relevant knowledge, which may need restructuring at the organizational level. Senge (1990) argued that sustainable competitive advantage resulted from learning organizations where people learn faster than their competitors do; this is achieved when the resulting competitiveness of the whole organization is more than the sum of its parts. However, in the Arab world all Senge's principles are disrupted by non-economic parameters. For instance, the conflicts in the region caused periods of crises, ambiguity, turbulence, and acute, potentially irreversible, changes. The turbulent economy is highly affected by the conflicts in the region, which result in fluctuations of oil prices (Mirghani et al., 2008).

The work of Zhu (2004) presented evidence that, despite growing overlaps, heterogeneity among KM styles is likely to continue due to differences in histories, national cultures, and institutional forces. As a way out, the paper called for an interactionist, rather than a universal, strategy of constructing, connecting, and sharing knowledge across-cultural contexts, wherein cultural differences and diversity are important sources of competence rather than obstacles to overcome. The KAFRA model for KM (Okunoye and Bertaux, 2006) also called for an increased sensitivity to global diversity that could serve as a link between organizations and their environments in the creation of KM. The model ensures that KM is approached with consideration to the environment in which organizations operate. In the Tunis KM forum, papers have addressed the theory and practice of KM, with a distinctive focus on two complementary perspectives (francophone and Anglo-Saxon), but were able to integrate the discussion within the local environmental settings and needs of specific organizations (Passerini, et al., 2007).

This study came up with a set of enablers for successful implementation of KM initiatives, and, adds a socio-cultural perspective to practices and literature of KM strategy. The results of this study suggest that the link between KM strategy and business strategies need to be clearer in the Arab region, and calls for a formulation of organization-wide formal strategy for KM 'buying behavior' and for learning best practices and for the development for new projects. The results of the study also point out a major, not minor, role for human-based issues in KM. In the line of cross-cultural diversity in KM practices, the proposed KM model was thought to be useful to Arab companies in detecting areas of weakness in the existing situation and in helping them to concentrate their efforts on improving them. Knowledge gained from the model and embedded in the organization's core business processes and strategic decision-making processes may help Arab companies to create a profound impact on their organizational performance, productivity, and possibly competitive advantage but sometime in the future. However, the proposed model requires further testing through conducting more case studies to be able to capture the best practice of KM in this important region.

CONCLUSION

It should be noted, though, that at this stage any conclusions drawn from this research must remain to some extent provisional, and might not be generalized to other situations in other developing countries. The conclusions drawn from the case may not have implications beyond the specific context of the case that has been studied. This is especially true when only a single case is investigated; any generalizations made are tentative ones that must await further support from other studies- perhaps support from additional case studies or other kinds of qualitative studies. Thus, the type of study that future researchers might want to embark on would be to conduct more in-depth and multi-level analyses of multiple KM cases within the same Arab cultural context.

It seems that KM in the Arab region has not yet carved out its identity although there have been many KM initiatives that were undertaken but under different titles. This study clearly reflected the premise that KM in the Arab region is still in its infancy stage, and it is expected that projects that manage knowledge as an intellectual asset would offer very little to help Arab companies survive if not thrive. Due to these reasons as well as the inhomogeneous financial, educational, innovational, and technological infrastructures and constraints that prevail in the Arab region, it is suggested that Arab organizations need to develop a greater appreciation for their intangible human assets, captive in the minds and experiences of their knowledge workers. Management should encourage staff members to start thinking within their organizations of those of who could benefit from or in 'need' for their own knowledge, and determining which employees 'own' knowledge that, in turn, would be useful to them.

Arab companies may need to undertake KM projects that relate to the enhancement of the environment for knowledge sharing and collaboration, before projects that aim at creation of knowledge repositories, improving knowledge accessibility, and projects that manage knowledge as a strategic asset. Usage of simple KM sharing tools, rather than advanced KM enterprise solutions, might be the most suitable solution to start with in Arab socio-cultural context. Arab organizations need also to design performance appraisal and compensation systems in a way that incorporates knowledge sharing into employees' performance, and provide financial reward for those who share relevant and needed knowledge with others. When established procedures are not conducive to the sharing of knowledge, the company must be ready to restructure itself into an organization more amenable to knowledge sharing.

Knowledge gained from critical success factors once embedded in the organization's core business processes and strategic decision-making processes may help Arab companies to create a profound impact on organizational performance, productivity, and possibly competitive advantage. Moreover, the paper concludes that there is a need to redefine KM success. In designing a KM strategy, success shouldn't be confined to the success in technical implementation of ICT-based systems, but should be expanded to the adoption side relative to its local context. Successful implementation of a KM strategy relates to technical success in the development of a KM solution, whereas successful implementation of a KM strategy relates to the wider business-context success, from an internal perspective (e.g., operational efficiency) as well as an external perspective (e.g., customer satisfaction).

REFERENCES

AHDR. (2002). The first *Arab human development report: creating opportunities for future generations*. United Nations Development Programme. New York: UN Publications.

AHDR. (2003). The second *Arab human development report: building a knowledge society*. United Nations Development Programme. New York: UN Publications.

Al-Athari, A., & Zairi, M. (2001). Building benchmarking competence through knowledge management: an empirical study of the Kuwaiti context. *Benchmarking: an International Journal*, *8*(1), 70–80. doi:10.1108/14635770110383489

Al-Shammari, M. (2005). Implementing a Knowledge-enabled CRM strategy in a large company: a case study from a developing country. In M. E. Jennex (Ed.), *Case studies in knowledge management* (pp. 249-278). Hershey, PA: Idea Group Publishing.

AlAmmary, J., & Fung, C. C. (2008). Knowledge Management Strategic Alignment in the Gulf Cooperation Council Countries. [Retrieved from www.ejkm.com]. *Electronic Journal of Knowledge Management, 6*(2), 75–84.

Alavi, M., & Leidner, D. E. (2001). Review: knowledge management and knowledge management systems: Conceptual Foundations and Research Issues. *MIS Quarterly, 25*(1), 107–136. doi:10.2307/3250961

Aubert, J. E., & Reiffers, J. L. (2003). *Knowledge economies in the Middle East and North America: toward new development strategies*. World Bank Institute Series, Washington D.C.: The World Bank Press, Beckman, T. J. (1999). The current state of knowledge management. In J. Liebowitz (Ed.), *Knowledge management handbook* (pp. 1.1-1.22). Florida: CRC Press.

Blackler, F., & McDonald, S. (2000). Power, mastery and organizational learning. *Journal of Management Studies, 37*, 833–852. doi:10.1111/1467-6486.00206

Bontis, N. (2004). National intellectual capital index: a United Nations initiative for the Arab region. *Journal of Intellectual Capital, 5*(1), 13–39. doi:10.1108/14691930410512905

Civi, E. (2000). Knowledge management as a competitive asset: a review . *Marketing Intelligence & Planning, 18*(4), 166–174. doi:10.1108/02634500010333280

Davenport, T. H., Long, D. W., & Beers, M. C. (1998). Successful knowledge management projects. *Sloan Management Review, 39*(2), 43–57.

Davenport, T. H., & Probst, G. (2002). *Knowledge management book: Siemens best practices*. New York: John Wiley & Sons.

Davenport, T. H., & Prusak, L. (2000). *Working Knowledge: how organizations manage what they know*. Boston: MA: Harvard Business School Press.

Drucker, P. (1995). *Managing in a time of great change*. New York: Truman Tally.

Finnegan, P., & Sammon, D. (2002). Fundamentals of implementing data warehouseing in organizations. In S. Barnes (Ed.), *Knowledge Management Systems: Theory and Practice* (pp. 195-209). London: Thomson Learning.

Gamble, P., & Blackwell, J. (2001). *Knowledge management: a state of art guide*. London: Kogan Page Limited.

Grant, R. M. (1991). The resource-based theory of competitive advantage: implications for strategy formulation. *California Management Review, 33*, 113–135.

Grant, R. M. (2002). The Knowledge-based view of the firm. In N. Bontis & C. W. Choo (Eds.), *The Strategic Management of Intellectual Capital and Organizational Knowledge.* Oxford, U.K.: Oxford University Press.

Hansen, M. T., Nohria, N., & Tierney, T. (1999). What's your strategy for managing knowledge? *Harvard Business Review*, (March-April): 106–116.

Hart, D., & Warne, L. (2006). Comparing cultural and political perspectives of data, information, and knowledge sharing in organizations. *International Journal of Knowledge Management, 2*(2), 1–15.

Holsapple, C. W., & Joshi, K. D. (1997). Knowledge management: a three-fold framework. *Kentucky Initiative for Knowledge Management*. Paper No. (104).

Holsapple, C. W., & Joshi, K. D. (1998). In search of a descriptive framework for knowledge management: preliminary Delphi results. *Kentucky Initiative for Knowledge Management*. Paper No. (118).

Holsapple, C. W., & Joshi, K. D. (2000). An implementation of factors that influence the management of knowledge in organizations. *The Journal of Strategic Information Systems*, (9): 235–261. doi:10.1016/S0963-8687(00)00046-9

Jacobs, D. (1996). *The Knowledge Offensive: Compete Smartly in the Knowledge Society*. Netherlands: Alphen Aaan den.

Jashapara, A. (2004). *Knowledge management: an integrated approach*. Harlow, England: Prentice-Hall.

Jennex, M. E. (2000). Using an intranet to manage knowledge for a virtual Project team. In D. G. Schwartz, M. Diivitini, & T. Brasethvik (Eds.) *Internet-Based Organizational Memory and Knowledge Management* (pp. 241-259). Hershey, PA: Idea Group Publishing.

Jennex, M. E., & Olfman, L. (2006). A Model of Knowledge Management Success. *International Journal of Knowledge Management, 2*(3), 51–68.

Jennex, M. E., Olfman, L., & Addo, T. B. A. (2003). The Need for an Organizational Knowledge Management Strategy. *36th Hawaii International Conference on System Sciences, HICSS36*. IEEE Computer Society.

Kim, L. (2001). Absorptive capacity, co-opetition, and knowledge creation: Samsung's leapfrogging in semiconductors. In I. Nonaka and T. Nishiguchi (Eds), *Knowledge emergence: social, technical, and evolutionary dimensions of knowledge creation*. Oxford: Oxford University Press.

Kluge, J., Wolfram, S., & Licht, T. (2001). *Knowledge Unplugged: The McKinsey & Company global survey on knowledge management*. Palgrave Macmillan.

Krog, V. G., & Grand, S. (2002). From economic theory toward a knowledge-based theory of the firm: Conceptual building blocks. In N. Bontis & C. W.Choo (Eds.), *The Strategic Management of Intellectual Capital and Organizational Knowledge*. Oxford, U.K.: Oxford University Press.

Liebowitz, J. (2004). Conceptualizing and implementing knowledge management. In P. Love, P. Fong, & Z. Irani (Eds.), *Management of Knowledge in Project Environment* (pp. 1-18). Amsterdam: Elsevier Butterworth-Heinemann.

Lindsey, K. (2002). Measuring knowledge management effectiveness: a task-contingent organizational capabilities perspective. *Eight Americas Conference on Information Systems* (pp. 2085-2090).

Long, D. W., & Fahey, L. (2000). Diagnosing cultural barriers to knowledge management. *The Academy of Management Executive, 14*(4), 113–127.

Massey, A. P., Montoya-Weiss, M. M., & O'Driscoll, T. M. (2002). Knowledge management in pursuit of performance: insights from Nortel networks. *MIS Quarterly, 26*(3), 269–289. doi:10.2307/4132333

Mirghani, S. M., O'Sulivan, K. J., & Ribiere, V. (2008). A paradigm shift in the Arab region knowledge evolution . *Journal of Knowledge Management, 12*(5), 107–120. doi:10.1108/13673270810902975

Nonaka, I., & Takeuchi, H. (1995). *The Knowledge creating company*. Oxford: Oxford University Press.

Offsey, S. (1997). Knowledge management: linking people to knowledge for bottom line results. *Journal of Knowledge Management*, *1*(2), 113–122. doi:10.1108/EUM0000000004586

Okunoye, A., & Bertaux, N. (2006). KAFRA: A Context-aware framework of knowledge management in global diversity. *International Journal of Knowledge Management*, *2*(2), 26–45.

Passerini, K., Jennex, M. E., & Khaldoun, B. T. (2007). Perspectives from North Africa: the Tunis-2006 knowledge management forum. *International Journal of Knowledge Management*, *3*(1), 100–107.

Probst, G., Raub, S., & Romhardt, Kai. (1999). *Managing knowledge: Building blocks for success*. New York: John Wiley & Sons.

Rubenstein-Montano, B., Liebwowitz, J., Buchwalter, J., McCaw, D., Newman, B., & Rebeck, K. (2001a). A systems thinking framework for knowledge management. *Decision Support Systems*, *31*(1), 5–16. doi:10.1016/S0167-9236(00)00116-0

Rubenstein-Montano, B., Liebwowitz, J., Buchwalter, J., McCaw, D., Newman, B., & Rebeck, K. (2001b). SMARTvision: a knowledge-management methodology. *Journal of Knowledge Management*, *5*(4), 300–310. doi:10.1108/13673270110411724

Rumizen, M. C. (2001). *The complete idiot's guide to knowledge management*. New York: Penguin Putnam.

Scarborough, J. (1998). *The origins of cultural Differences and their Impact on Management*. Westport, Connecticut: Quorum Books.

Seleim, A. A. S., & Khalil, O. E. M. (2007). Intellectual Capital in Egyptian software firms. *The Learning Organization*, *11*(4/5), 332–346. doi:10.1108/09696470410538233

Senge, P. (1990). *The fifth discipline: the art and practice of learning organization*. New York: Doubleday/Currency.

Senge, P., Kleiner, A., Roberts, C., Ross, R., Roth, G., & Smith, B. (1999). *The dance of change: the challenges of sustaining momentum in learning organizations*. New York: Doubleday/Currency.

Strauss, A., & Corbin, J. (1990). *Basics of qualitative research: techniques and procedures for developing grounded theory* (2nd ed.). Thousand Oaks, CA: Sage Publications.

Teece, D., Pisano, G., & Shuen, A. (1997). Dynamic capabilities and strategic management. *Strategic Management Journal*, *18*(7), 509–533. doi:10.1002/(SICI)1097-0266(199708)18:7<509::AID-SMJ882>3.0.CO;2-Z

The Company. (2002, May 29)... *The Company's Newsletter*, *1*(1), 1.

Tiwana, A. (2001). *The essential guide to knowledge management: e-business and CRM applications*. Upper Saddle River, NJ: Prentice-Hall.

Turban, E., McLean, E., & Wetherbe, J. (2002). *Information technology for management: transforming Business in the Digital Economy* (3rd ed.). New York: John Wiley.

Usoro, A., & Kuofie, M. H. S. (2006). Conceptualization of cultural dimensions as a major influence on knowledge-sharing. *International Journal of Knowledge Management*, *2*(2), 16–25.

Vera, D. (2001). *CO-alignment between business strategy and knowledge strategy and impact on performance*. Paper presented at Academy of Management Conference, Washington, DC, USA.

Wagner, C., Cheung, K., Lee, F., & Ip, R. (2003). Enhancing e-governments in developing countries: managing knowledge through virtual communities. *The Electronic Journal on Information Systems in Developing Countries*, *14*(4), 1–20.

Wiig, K. (1993). *Knowledge management foundation*. Arlington, Texas: Schema Press.

Wiig, K. (1997). Knowledge management: where did it come from and where will it go*? Expert Systems with Applications*, *14*(Fall).

Zack, M. H. (1999). Managing codified knowledge . *Sloan Management Review*, *40*(4), 45–58.

Zaharna, R. S. (1995). Bridging cultural differences: American public relations practices and Arab communication patterns . *Public Relations Review*, (21): 241–255. doi:10.1016/0363-8111(95)90024-1

Zakaria, N., Stanton, J., & Sarkar-Barney, S. (2003). Designing and implementing culturally-sensitive IT applications: the interaction of culture values and privacy issues in the Middle East. *Information Technology & People*, *16*(1), 49–75. doi:10.1108/09593840310463023

Zhu, Z. (2001). What is to be managed: knowledge, knowing, or knower, and does it matter? In *Proceedings of the International Symposium on Knowledge and Systems Science* (pp. 29-45). Dalian University of Technology, Dalian, China.

Zhu, Z. (2004). Knowledge management: towards a universal concept or cross-cultural contexts? *Knowledge Management Research & Practice*, (2), 67-79.

Chapter 13
Applying Sense-Making Methodology to Design Knowledge Management Practices

Bonnie Wai-yi Cheuk
Environmental Resources Management (ERM), UK

Brenda Dervin
Ohio State University, USA

ABSTRACT

This chapter introduces readers to Dervin's Sense-Making Methodology (SMM) and demonstrates how it has been applied to design knowledge management projects for the public sector. The projects described in this chapter were implemented between November 2005 to June 2006 when the main author was the Head of Knowledge Management for the Improvement Service for the Scottish Government, a company limited by guarantee with a budget provided by the Scottish Executive, with the aim to improve the efficiency, quality and accountability of public services in Scotland through learning, sharing knowledge and delivering improvement solutions. Sense-Making Methodology is based on a set of assumptions which challenge some fundamental knowledge management thinking. The SMM assumptions imply the need for alternative procedures to be implemented to promote knowledge sharing. Three primary applications are discussed: (a) conducting user study to understand user needs; (b) designing web-based KM systems; and (c) facilitating dialogue to nurture communities of practice. This chapter aims at stimulating further thinking and debate in adopting theoretically informed approaches to implement knowledge management practices.

DOI: 10.4018/978-1-60566-954-0.ch013

INTRODUCTION

This chapter introduces Dervin's Sense-Making Methodology (SMM) a philosophically derived approach which allows knowledge management (KM) practitioners to more fully understand and listen to user's needs to inform the design of alternative KM practices. This chapter uses three examples to illustrate how SMM has been applied it to design knowledge management practices in the public sector in Scotland. The KM practices discussed were implemented between November 2005 to June 2006 as part of the public reform agenda with the aim to promote knowledge sharing across 32 Scottish local authorities to drive continuous improvement.

Sense-Making Methodology is a philosophically derived approach for studying communication as communication. SMM is built on a set of meta-theoretical assumptions about people, reality, information, power and context. SMM is user-oriented in that it is asking researchers and practitioners to more fully address what users "really" need. SMM assumes that to do this we need to enter into a dialogue with users as well as with system practitioners by attending to approaches to understanding communicating between users and systems and users and practitioners that are based on communicative principles, rather than transmission principles (Dervin, 2003, 2008).

Relating to the field of knowledge management, SMM redefines 'knowledge' and challenge the assumption that information or knowledge can bring out the realities (1998). Instead, 'realities' are considered always gappy and can only be understood from multiple perspectives in a given time-space moment and can be subjected to change over time. Therefore, knowledge cannot be treated as a commodity that can be captured, stored, retrieved and used. 'Knowledge' becomes 'sense-making' and 'sense-unmaking' or in this chapter refer to as a verb labeled 'knowledging'. Knowledge management becomes the designing of 'sense-making' and 'sense-unmaking' practices and systems to allow users to self-reflect as well as to gain multiple perspectives from listening to what others can offer and ultimately to address users' needs.

LITERATURE REVIEW: KM PHILOSOPHIES AND THE ASSOCIATED PRACTICES

A review of knowledge management (KM) literature shows a proliferation of publications in the last 10 years. The debate on what 'knowledge' is (and how to manage 'knowledge') has been intense and often contradictory. The confusion in this new, emergent field is created by a variety of ontological and epistemological assumptions. In this section, we will review KM literature which explicitly addresses philosophical assumptions and have informed KM practices.

In early 1990s, since Nonaka and Takeuchi (1995) introduce the concept of 'tacit' (i.e. knowledge in a person's head which has a personal quality and is hard to formalize and communicate) and 'explicit' knowledge (i.e. knowledge that is transmittable in formal, systematic language), scholar and practitioners have find ways to turn tacit knowledge into explicit. Knowledge is used interchangeably with 'information' and is managed as 'something which can be written down or codified' (Sutton, 2001). Knowledge is seen as objects which can be managed independent of the users or the recipients of the knowledge. The value of knowledge can be objectively assigned by experts according to a set of objective criteria.

This understanding of knowledge as objects has profound impact on the design of first generation KM practices which include:

1. Making 'tacit' knowledge explicit by investing in KM systems or global best practice databases which 'capture' the knowledge of experts. The 'capture' approach continued with an emphasis on capturing, storing,

retrieving knowledge in databases, manuals, books and reports, and then sharing it in a hard form (Hildreth and Kimble, 2002).
2. Measuring the benefits and bottom-line outcomes of knowledge capturing and transfer activities, assuming that 'codified' knowledge will have a linear impact on firms' operations. (Nonaka and Peltokorpi, 2006, p79; Dervin, 1998, p38)

At the other extreme, Wilson (2002) argues that everything outside the mind that can be manipulated in any way - such as journal articles, e-mail messages - is defined as 'data' or 'information'. Knowledge (i.e., what we know) can never be managed, except by the individual knower and, even then, only imperfectly.

This understanding of knowledge, shared by some academia and practitioners, led to the conclusion that:

1. KM is an umbrella term for a variety of organizational activities (such as management of information, staff and work practices), none of which are concerned with the management of knowledge.
2. KM is a 'nonsense' concept and a management fad
3. KM is difficult

In between these 2 views, there are scholars and practitioners who call for a more contextual and user-oriented approach in managing information, staff and work practices in order to facilitate knowledge flow between individuals, teams, departments, organizations and customers. They continue to explore KM by challenging and defining the dominant ontological and epistemological assumptions as well as giving new definitions to existing organisation activities.

What is in common amongst these scholars and practitioners is that they question the cost effectiveness of making tacit knowledge explicit through documentation and the building of global document repositories. They are not suggesting that we should abandon these 'first generation' KM practices, however, they call for recognising the limits of existing positivist philosophical assumptions (and the associated KM practices) and adopt alternative practices to bring advancement to KM as a multidisciplinary subject. While they all agree is that knowledge can sometimes be 'objective' and 'factual', at other times, it can be 'subjective' and 'emotional'. (Snowden & Stanbridge, 2004; Dervin, 1999; Brown and Duguid, 2000; Nonaka and Peltokorpi, 2006). Dervin (2003), in particular, posits sense-making and sense-unmaking as involving all of these simultaneously even though in a particular micro-moment of time there may be particular emphases.

These scholars challenge a number of fundamental assumptions about knowledge:

1. knowledge is not just a commodity that can be captured, stored, retrieved, used; and can be transferred from person to person and time-space to time-space. Knowledge transfer requires interrogation and interpretation and is seen from the recipients' perspectives (Dervin, 1999). It must include the cultivation of knowledge workers, for example, by allowing them to learn through self-descriptive awareness (Brown & Duguid, 2000, pp122)
2. Knowledge is not just about 'facts' which describe the 'complete reality'. Knowledge transfer is not just about providing people with facts, but also direction, ideas, support, confirmation and connection with other people etc. (Dervin, 1999; Wenger, 1998; Brown & Duguid, 2000)
3. Knowledge sits in a social context and is at least in part defined by power and in part defined by status. Knowledge transfer can be more or less effective depending how power is being used.

This renewed understanding of knowledge – through the eyes of the knowledge users – provides an alternative perspective and foundation to design KM practices. For example:

1. In the discourse of information management, Brown and Duguid (2000) propose that one must look at the social life of information, and highlight that it is important to look beyond information and understand the context in which people work and live to understand the real challenges in exploiting information and new information technologies.
2. In the discourse of learning and development, Wenger (1998) conducted research to understand how people learn in organizations, and have developed theories and practice to build and nurture communities of practice in which individuals develop the capacity to create and share knowledge.
3. In the discourse of management and decision support, Snowden puts narratives at the centre of knowledge transfer to support problem solving and decision making (Snowden, 2002). He argues that narratives sit between objective knowledge (which can be documented) and context (which is subjective, rich and difficult to capture). Narratives provide knowledge that is rich in context but requires less documentation. He introduces techniques to capture narrative from groups and individuals and then provides a broad range of analytical tools that help reveal organizational, behavioural, or thematic patterns both across and within organizations. The British Council has applied this technique to capture stories to understand how their staff have gone through a pilot new product development process and the stories revealed some major weaknesses and resulted in major improve of the final approach (Cheuk, 2007). World Bank has successfully introduced knowledge management to all staff by sharing a story about how an engineer in Pakistan managed to address a complicated highway structure engineering problem by getting immediate help from posting a request in the knowledge management system (Denning, 2000). Dervin (2008) has implicitly incorporate these assumptions and made their implementations explicit through a articulate approach to methodology for user studies, system design, and dialogue practice.

The move to understand knowledge through the eyes of the users can, nevertheless, cause potential problems. The more KM practitioner study their users' needs in-depth, the more the KM practitioners notice that different users have different needs at different times.

With the aim to better understand users' diverse needs, KM practitioners recognise that they need to study users' needs (and gather user requirements) by taking into account of the context that users are in. They tend to focus on contexts that are constant across time-space (such as age, gender, geography, work role, generation Y, department, function, service area, lifestyle etc), and tend to ask question such as 'what do users belonging to this context use/do to acquire knowledge using the given KM systems?'.

In doing this, they aim at arriving at generalisation as to what users want all the time or most of the time. The disappointing result is that:

- In statistical terms, the amount of difference between users grouped in these kind of context (that Dervin calls "noun boxes") tend to be small; users tend to report using similar approach to use KM systems
- the understanding of users' needs is limited because the experience that the users shared is very general and is too far from the micro-moments of their specific uses of KM systems.
- When digging deeper and focussing on actual work examples, KM practitioners learn

that the same user have different needs at different times.

The KM practitioners are challenged by this question: Is it possible to design KM systems to serve a wide range of users (and even the same user) across 24/7 time zones whose needs are extremely diverse?

There is a call to find pattern within diversity in order to bridge gaps between research and practice. The most disciplined and methodological approach to address gaps is found in the discourse community focussing on communication led by Dervin who since 1972 has systematically developed and continued to refine the Sense-Making Methodology as a methodology 'between the cracks'. Dervin argues that we need to study users needs and design KM practices by focusing on 'context' defined as person-in-situation-in-a-time-space-moment moving into the next time-space moment. The hope is to find systematic patterns out of diverse situations to understand human needs which may not surface if one only looks at users through static across-time-space attributes.

It should be noted that a variety of approaches focusing on sense-making (sometimes spelled as sensemaking) have emerged in recent literatures in numerous fields, primarily: knowledge management, human computer intersection, organizational communication, and communication. Dervin's approach is widely regarded as the most systematically developed. Recent papers provide comparisons (Dervin & Naumer, in press; Dervin & Reinhard, in press). Dervin's Sense-Making Methodology will be explored in detail in the next section.

AN OVERVIEW OF SENSE-MAKING METHODOLOGY

Devin's began to develop Sense-Making Methodology (SMM) in the late 1960s as an alternative approach to understand human communication. The approach has always been associated with a set of metatheorectical assumptions which inform the methodology chosen to study human needs. The best example to illustrate this point is the Sense-Making Micro-Moment Time-Line interviewing approach (Dervin, 2008). The approach was widely adopted by Library and Information Science researchers to study information seeking and using behaviour in the 1980s and became main stream in 1990s. Its applicability to design knowledge management practice is introduced by Dervin in 1998 and she calls for alternative KM practices (Dervin, 1998). She suggested that KM practitioners (and many other categories of system practitioners as well) are struggling with issues which she and colleagues have been zeroing in on since 1972 (Dervin and Foreman-Wernet, 2003).

Dervin's Sense-Making Methodology is defined as a set of meta-theoretic assumptions, a foundation for methodological guidance, specific research methods (both for data collection and for question framing and analysis), and a set of communication and design practices. All of these elements are generated from a philosophical perspective that regards information or knowledge as a human tool designed for making and unmaking sense of a reality that is simultaneously both chaotic and orderly (Dervin, 1992; Dervin, 2008)

Sense-Making makes no distinction between data, information, knowledge and wisdom. Knowledge is the sense made at a particular point in time-space by an individual. As Dervin says, sometimes it is shared and codified; sometimes a number of people agree upon it; sometimes it is entered into a formalized discourse and gets published; sometimes it gets tested in other times and spaces and takes on the status of facts; sometimes it is fleeting and unexpressed; sometimes it is hidden and suppressed; sometimes it gets imprimatured and becomes unjust law; sometimes it takes on the status of dogma.

In this chapter, the author uses the label 'knowledging' to refer to the gaining of new knowledge through the users' eyes in order to serve users' needs. This is informed by Dervin's (1998, 2003) call for understanding knowledge management as communication; and communication as communicatings, as verbings. Thus, knowledge management becomes the designing of 'sense-making' and 'sense-unmaking' (or 'knowledging') practices and systems to allow users to self-reflect as well as to gain multiple perspectives from listening to what others can offer, taking into account the power issues which can constraint what users are able to ask for, and ultimately to address their needs at specific moments in time-space.

In order to design KM practices and systems to understand the 'knowledging' process, Dervin argues that KM practitioners and researchers have to take into account changing 'contexts', i.e. one cannot assume context as constancy across time space (such as age, gender, geography, work role, generation Y, department, function, service area, task, lifestyle etc) . Nor can we assume that users will behave in the same way within the context all the time. Using a person carrying an umbrella as a metaphor, Dervin (2008) defines context as 'verb' which is constantly moving across time space together with the users. In practice, Dervin is asking KM researchers and practitioners to focus on studying and helping users-in-situations moving through time-space. These mandates inform user studies implements as well as system design and practice. In particular, they have led to a methodologically-based approach to interviewing users and analyzing study results. The approach has been applied to all kinds of interviewing, e.g. in person, phone, on-line; one-on-one, group. (Dervin, 2008; Dervin, 2007)

Also, Dervin has pointed out that by giving people access to use IT to access or contribute ideas, information, content or knowledge does not necessarily mean that the knowledge will get shared and be understood. For example, an intranet could potentially open up opportunity to allow all departments to build knowledge bases to publish their learning points. In the worse scenario, and it happens very frequently, information/knowledge residing in these KM systems are regarded as noise and are ignored by users. In face-to-face knowledge sharing events (such as training sessions, conferences, quality circles), while all participants are encouraged to share their learning points, it also happens too frequently, that participants leave with a lot of idiosyncratic personal experiences being shared but with little understanding of how these interconnect and are anchored in practice and material conditions. Dervin argues that these "spontaneous talking shop" events do not well serve the communicative design of systems and practices. The explicit design of communication procedures is critical to facilitate 'knowledging' and cannot be left to chance. Dervin argues that spontaneous communications practice reinforce current habits and reinforced current power structures. As a result, they miss the vital but hidden understandings that users have locked within them and do not readily share. She calls for a disciplined approach to the design and use of communications procedures to allow learning to be shared in a way that welcomes both majority and minority voices that allow users to connect internally within themselves across time-space as well as with each other. Ultimately, KM practices/systems should allow users to be able to move forward on what they need to make sense of at the time they need to do so.

Sense-Making Methodology is not about persuasion or dictating the outcomes on behalf of the users (e.g. deciding what users choose to do and think as a result of having access to knowledge residing in KM systems). Companies designing KM systems with the sole purpose of indoctrinating employees to adopt best practice policies, methodologies (as defined by experts) or to conform to senior managers' wish will not find SMM useful. Dervin, in fact, assumes that KM systems that make these assumptions may, under some circumstances, get obedience without understanding and, thus, impede long-term organizational growth. SMM focuses on communica-

Figure 1. Dervin's Sense-Making Metaphor (Dervin, 2008)

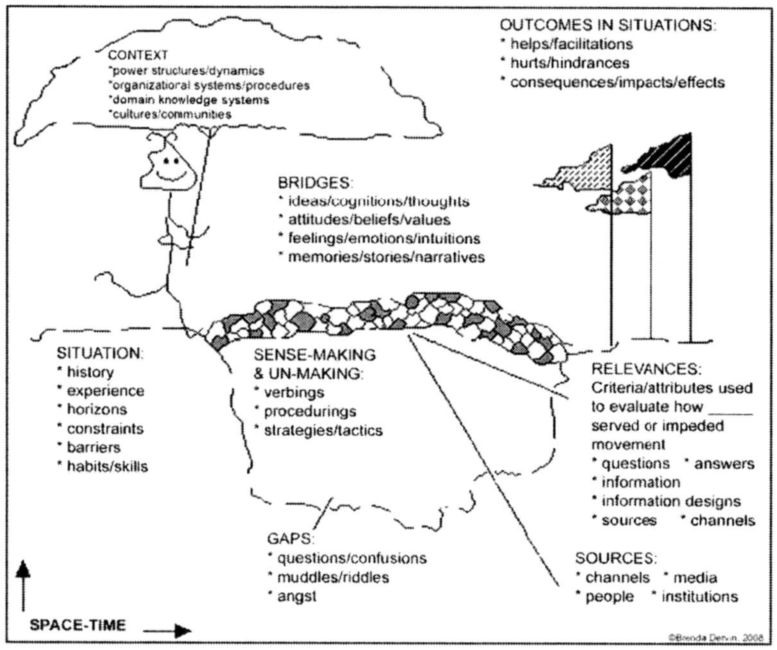

tion processes rather than outcomes. Accepting that SMM might be seen as utopian in its vision, Dervin believes that by introducing disciplined and dialogic communication practices, the methodology helps surface multiple perspectives, and open up dialogue and possibilities. Further, while applying SMM may increase uncertainty in some ways, it allows users to 'learn from within' and reflect deeply to understand and address their own needs as well as the needs of others and their organizations.

In introducing Sense-Making Methodology, Dervin has stated clearly that "the bottom-line goal of Sense-Making from its inception has been to find out what users – audiences, customers, patients, clients, patrons, employees – 'really' think, feel, want, dream" (Dervin, 1998, pp.39). Dervin always places the term "really" in quotes because she assumes that the best we can do is around that which we can not touch and cannot freeze and bend to our wills (see Figure 1).

She has elaborated that "Sense-Making uses a central metaphor – the metaphor of human beings traveling through time-space, coming out of situations with history and partial instructions, arriving at new situations, facing gaps, building bridges across those gaps, evaluating outcomes and moving on. Its central meta-theoretic concepts include: time, space, horizon, movement, gap and power. Its central operational concepts include: situation, history, gap, barrier, constraint, force, bridge, sense-making strategies, outcomes, helps and hurts.

"This metaphor provides guidance for thinking about people, talking to them, asking questions of them and designing systems to serve them. In capsule it says, look to the gap: this is where you will find the action in Sense-Making and sense-unmaking; in communicating; and, in the creating, seeking, using and rejecting of information and knowledge". This metaphor has been further refined in 2008 showing a person carrying an umbrella moving across time-space to better reflect how SMM defines context. It also shows gaps all over the picture to reflect the meta-theoretical assumption that 'gappiness' is a fundamental human experience which is at the core of SMM. (Dervin, 2008).

The SMM metaphor asks researchers to understand users' needs by looking at the Sense-Making triangle of 'situation', 'gaps' and 'help', and by asking these questions: (Dervin, 1992):

- What led you to this situation?
- Where did you want to get to?
- What gaps did you see?
- What got in the way?
- What help did you get along the way?
- What emotions / feelings did you experience?
- If you had a magic wand, what would you like to happen?

SMM applies this metaphor in difference ways depending on research purposes and to different ranges of time-space. For example, in some studies attentions are focused on entire situations. In others, on micro-moments of time-space within situations. Further, the depth of attentions to either situations or specific micro-moments in situations vary from purposively more shallow to purposively very intensive and deep. This choice depends on research purposes and the extent to which stereotyped understandings dominate the social context shielding from view how individual agents struggle to make sense of their relationships with themselves, with others, and with their organizational/social contexts.

In implementing methodologically this continual struggle of humans to navigate between their inner and outer worlds, their own senses of self and the demands of organizations and communities, Dervin is emphasizing that we must address issues relating to how power (internal and external) both can enable and/or constrain human sense-making and human knowledge sharing. Therefore, in designing KM practices and systems, she stresses that:

1. We must provide safe spaces for people to attend to power issues so that they are willing to tell us things that ordinary interviewing practices miss entirely. If this cannot be done in public arenas, then anonymity structures need to be added.
2. We should be cautious of one-way knowledge transfer from the experts to novices. We must be aware of power issues and consciously promote a discipline communications procedures to invite two-way sharing and negotiating of meanings (Dervin, 1989).
3. We should be careful not to design KM systems/processes from the experts' perspectives. Instead, we must look for differences in how people see their worlds (e.g. information that is presented to them), and also the differences in how they 'make their worlds' (i.e. construct a sense of their worlds in their subject domains and how things works). Years of SMM research has shown that if we conceptualise humans condition as a struggle through an incomplete reality, then the similar struggles of others become more informative to individual and collective sense-making.

WHY SENSE-MAKING METHODOLOGY?

Many KM projects are established with the aim to empower employees by giving them access to the content, systems, experts needed to get their work done. While most KM practitioners recognise the need to gather detailed user requirements through interviews, focus groups or surveys, many of these user-requirement studies fail to consider the real content needs of their end-users (Souto, Dervin & Savolainen, 2008). It is easy to assume that if we have asked users what they want then we can find ways to provide it. The reality is human beings are complex – their needs change over time, and in some cases, they may not know exactly what they want. Therefore, it is easy to conclude it impossible to design any KM systems/approach that can serve all employees' needs or to end up designing a compromised system hoping it will serve 80 per cent of customers but which, in practice, does not satisfy most employees.

SMM emphasizes that we can handle user diversity if we are willing to ask another set of questions and understand users' needs in a different and 'unconventional' way. SMM asks us to revisit the metatheorectical assumptions which define what knowledge is and what 'knowledging' is about, and then apply a methodological approach to studying these phenomena. By doing so, we can avoid drowning in the endless debate of what knowledge management really is and how one can manage knowledge effectively.

However, it has to be acknowledged that by doing so, some KM practitioners who adhere to the KM status quo, may see the alternative KM practices described in the next section as not meeting the current standards of 'knowledge management' practice.

In a more practical sense, the value of Dervin's Sense-Making Methodology above other traditional techniques have been demonstrated in a series of more than 150 studies conducted between 1976 and 2008 (Dervin & Foreman-Wernet, 2003; Cheuk & Dervin, 1999; Dervin's Sense-Making website. http://communication.sbs.ohio-state.edu/sense--making). The main author of this chapter has experienced the following benefits in her own KM projects:

1. Many users found it difficult to answer the survey question: 'What information do you need?', but felt more comfortable talking about their real-life experiences when they were asked: What situation you were in? What questions did you have? What struggles did you have?
2. Users were generally more able to share how they carry out their day-to-day work and accomplish tasks. They were also able to comment on whether they could get help at different stages of the business process;
3. Users could share their own views more freely which SMM interviewing expensive has shown is too often not when we seek to understand users through sets of predefined, closed-ended questions.
4. Users were able to free themselves from the constraints of what the current systems/process/structure can or cannot do and released their creativity to imagine new possibilities. For example, a number of respondents reported that if they had a magic wand, they would like to have a virtual collaborative space to allow them to meet virtually with other practitioners and work on projects.
5. Implementing SMM allowed the researchers to hear topics and answers which they had not considered and allowed them to discover 'what we didn't know we didn't know'.
6. Users were willing to give more time to the researcher to share their experience beyond the time they had allocated for interviews because they got value out of the self-reflection that is integral to the SMM interviewing process.

THE BUSINESS CONTEXT

In Scotland, the Improvement Service is devoted to improving the efficiency, quality and accountability of public services through learning, sharing knowledge and delivering improvement solutions. Formed in July 2005, it is a Company limited by guarantee with a budget provided by the Scottish Executive, the devolved government of Scotland responsible for most of the issues of day-to-day concern to the people of Scotland, including health, education, justice, rural affairs, and transport. It is a partnership between the Scottish Executive, the Convention of Scottish Local Authorities (COSLA) and the Society of Local Authority Chief Executives (SOLACE).

It aims to support continuous improvement by building on the expertise within local authorities and working in partnership with stakeholders in the public, private and voluntary sectors. It provides advice and support in the following areas: Best Value, Customer First, efficient government and performance management, elected members' development, knowledge management, management development, partnership and joint working, planning and development, as well as preparation for 2007 election.

The core objectives are to (a) promote a learning culture and support collaborative working across local authorities and partners; (b) build capacity within local government to improve the skills of officers and elected members; (c) promote good practice across Scottish local government; (d) promote the use of knowledge management within local authorities to support sharing and learning, e-governance and business re-design; (e) identify good practice and learning from outside Scotland and other areas of the public, private and voluntary sector to share with Scottish local government.

PUTTING SENSE-MAKING METHODOLOGY INTO PRACTICE

In this section, a number of KM projects will be discussed to demonstrate how Sense-Making Methodology has facilitated the process of 'knowledging'. The choice of a verb, is important here, because it reinforces that KM project is about giving users a journey of gaining knowledge as they move through time-space (Dervin, 2003). These projects were implemented between November 2005 to June 2006 when the main author was the Head of Knowledge Management for the Improvement Service for the Scottish Government. The projects were introduced to improve knowledge transfer across 32 Scottish local authorities.

CASE STUDY 1: CONDUCTING USER STUDY TO UNDERSTAND USERS' NEEDS

To prepare for the establishment of a KM strategy, the first KM project was to conduct a user study to find out what KM support colleagues need for improving local government services. A previous piece of work conducted by an external consultant highlighted the fact that when people were asked directly about 'KM support they need' out of context, they found it challenging to understand the phrase and also they interpret KM in different ways. As a result, not enough information was gathered to inform the development of a KM strategy.

To avoid this problem, SMM's Micro-Moment Time-Line interview approach was adopted to in-depth interview 39 councillors and senior officers based in different locations in Scotland. This interviewer invited each informant (i.e. interviewee) to share his/her real-life experience on a time-line. Respondents were then asked to divide up the time-line into mini time segments. The interviewer then zoomed into each mini time segment and asked each informant to share his/her experience using a set of SMM-guided questions which focused on 'situation', 'gaps' and 'helps'. The role of the interviewer was to help informants reflect on their own experiences, needs and dreams rather than looking for correct answers.

For this project, the respondents were asked these questions:

1. Reflect on the issues you are facing on a day-to-day basis, what do you see as a top priority area that you have to address to improve local government service?
2. Focus on this priority area, how would you describe the situation you are facing now to address priority the top area? How do you feel?
3. Where do you think you want to get to? What is the destination like?

4. What help do you need most to address the priority area and get to your destination?
5. Are you getting the help you need now? If yes, what is helping? What else?
6. If not, what are the barriers? What get in the way? What is missing?
7. What are the big questions you have and that you find difficult to get answers to?
8. If you have a magic wand, what would you like to happen?

In this exemplar study, SMM helped us get in-depth insight on the knowledge gaps which did not surface in the initial study carried out by the external consultant. and do not surface in typical interviewing approaches. The interviews proved to be very effective, because the councilors, chief executives and senior officers found it easy to talk about their work and the questions they had in specific context. The result of qualitative data analysis told us about:

1. Their main aspirations and what they saw as the top corporate policy priorities. When the main author and her colleagues compared their priorities against the Improvement Service business plan, they saw some gaps in terms of the support Improvement Services provided. Even though Improvement Service could not address all their needs, the findings helped Improvement Service, then a new company, to strategically position its role in supporting the 32 Scottish local authorities in area.
2. The situations councillors were facing in trying to meet these aspirations and policy priorities were pessimistic. When being asked publicly about their views on the outlook of local government, most councillors or elected members gave a positive picture. In this interview, 60% of the respondents reported they were feeling pessimistic or uncertain.
3. The help required to address priority issues were not obtained and they faced many barriers in reaching the desired goals. A number of informants wanted to remain anonymous and specifically pointed out to a power issue. One of the major barriers unearthed was the attitude of the Scottish Executive which was expressed by one informant as "a multiplicity of focuses and range of people were driving change; too many priorities. The Scottish Executive has been inconsistent; there were too many initiatives, inspections and audits."

Other findings which emerged from this project included a list of information needs of the respondents. For example, they want to know what innovative projects were being carried out by different local authorities; what external research reports/findings were available to support decision making; what toolkits and specific guidance were available to support partnership working etc.

The main author of this chapter then conducted a knowledge audit of all the information resources that were available to Scottish local authorities through desk research and additional interviews with colleagues working in the information centers in the local authorities. A range of internal and external information resources (including Communities of Practices) were identified. However, many of them were only available to employees working within a single local authority. There was not a one stop shop to share information resources across the 32 Scottish local authorities.

A comparison of the findings from these two studies -- the user study and the knowledge audit -- showed the information gaps. This project has informed the development of the IS website (www.improvementservice.org.uk) a platform for employees of the Scottish local authorities to collaborate and share knowledge, as well as triggered other projects in developing guidance and toolkits and connecting practitioners in topic areas where the local authorities need most help.

CASE STUDY 2: DESIGNING WEB-BASED KM SYSTEM

From a content management perspective, SMM asks KM practitioners not to solely focus on providing best practices to members. This is because "best practice" usually represent authoritative voices of the experts and freeze step-takings in time-space. Very often, what is considered 'politically correct' or 'best practices' at one time can be considered otherwise in another time. Further, SMM studies have shown that sense-makers learn more from understanding how others bridged gaps and anchoring these understandings in clear pictures of how others saw their gaps. Formulaic recipes for practices are far less helpful. Instead, we need to find ways to allow diverse practices to be captured and shared without pre-judgement. This is based on the assumption that a shared practice may be extremely relevant to some members at some point in time, but at other times, they can be totally irrelevant. Sense-Making trusts that each member can make the relevance judgement only when he/she is in a particular situation.

The author was conscious of the diverse approaches that users would like to take to look for information, and therefore of the need to complement all online content with opportunities for face-to-face networking. Informed by this thinking, the IS website does not have a 'best practice' area, rather it is implemented using such labels as 'communities' or 'toolkits', Initially when the site was launched, the KM principles were shared with our site users in order to emphasize that it is about supporting sharing amongst members (rather than Improvement Service telling members what they should do to achieve improvement targets).

A quote from the IS site on 13 Mar 2006 reads:

The site is built around a number of unconventional 'knowledge management' principles:

1. We do not assume that by putting up experts' opinion and best practices on the site, our users will adopt them without question and debate.

2. We do not assume that online interaction is always good. We understand that online resources and discussions may not always be the appropriate or preferred communications channels, and they cannot replace face-to-face meetings.

3. We do not assume there are 'right' answers out there. We believe there are difficult questions which we do not have answers to. Together with our users, we will facilitate and explore common understanding and solutions together.

4. We do not assume that the website alone will change people's behaviour and attitude. This website is an enabler (not a driver) of improvement initiatives. All our online resources and activities are supported by face-to-face events and capability building activities.

A positive outcome was the successful roll-out of the Improvement Service website which was commented by local government staff as engaging and inclusive. Many staff across the 32 local authorities registered as members in the first three months, and began to use 'community sites' to connect with others addressing similar issues at work. The website has allowed Improvement Service to demonstrate a quick win in achieving one of its goals to play a facilitator role rather than as the know-it-all 'expert' in promoting knowledge sharing across Scottish local authorities.

CASE STUDY 3: FACILITATING DIALOGUE TO NURTURE COMMUNITIES OF PRACTICE (COP)

Communities of Practice is an established KM practice to bring together like-minded practitioners to develop a shared vision to advance their practice area through sharing good and bad practices and testing emerging ideas. Very often, members of a COP meet face-to-face and are supported by a virtual collaborative space. In this example, the author was at the early stage of establishing establish a Communities of Practice to link up KM champions working in the Scottish local authorities to share ideas and learning to advance KM in their own area of work. She was in charge of facilitating this inaugural COP meeting which brought many KM champions who have never met into one single location.

Informed by SMM, the main author was conscious that knowledge sharing can be biased by power. For example, experts including the facilitators are generally allowed more time to voice their opinions and they tend to (perhaps unintentionally) dominate discussions, to the extent that other members do not have the chance to share their experiences, and do not feel they can contribute or are being valued. Eventually, the members become 'lurkers' or they 'drop out'.

In this kick off meeting of KM champions held in March 2006, all the participants were asked to prepare a 3 minute briefing to introduce their KM initiatives using a SMM informed template. The briefing note which was circulated to all participants reads:

Dear participants,

If you have some time this week (or even on your way to the event), I would like you to reflect on your (past or present) personal experience in promoting/facilitating knowledge sharing amongst your target users, and be prepared to share a three-minute story based on these questions.

1. What situation are/were you in? What am/were I trying to achieve?

2. What are/were the biggest 'gaps' or struggles? What gets/got in the way?

3. What is the one big lesson you have learnt so far?

4. What kind of tools seems to work well (or do not seem to work) to promote the sharing of ideas and experience?

5. If you have a magic wand, what help/support do you want?

To avoid the facilitator dominating the discussion, post-it notes were handed out to participants throughout the day, the participants were reminded that if they had any unanswered questions or comments, and if they did not have a chance to share it with the group, they were welcome to put them down on a post-in note and paste it on a flipchart board. These questions were then consolidated and typed up by the facilitator. They were then posted up on a open source collaboration wiki site to allow all participants to read as well as to provide additional comments for a period of 2 months after the event. The wiki also allowed other local government colleagues who could not attend the event to contribute to the discussion.

As each knowledge champion started to share their experience, a simple note-taking form was designed to allow participants to write down 'the help that I can give to this speaker', and they were encouraged to pass the notes to the speakers at the end of the sharing session. This has greatly increased the opportunity for meaningful dialogue, and allowed people to have discussion around topic areas which are of interests for a smaller number of participants.

The value of SMM, in this example, was that it offered a set of communications procedure to promote learning and listening. While KM events bring people together to learn from one another, SMM mandates avoiding the use of only spontaneous dialogue by introducing a set of structured communications procedures to ensure two-way dialogue which aims at maximizing learning, developing shared visions through self-reflection and connecting with others.

The positive outcome was the energy and commitment for all the participants to feel a part of this KM community and their willingness to further exchange ideas and practices online using the wiki site. This kick off meeting has resulted in many participants adopting lessons learnt from one another and kicked off a number of KM programs in the Scottish local authorities.

CONCLUSION

SMM challenges the traditional assumption that information or knowledge is seen as inherently beneficial, that it instructs members about their work, possible actions (best practices) and the potential consequences of these actions. Very often, it is too easy to assume the higher the input, the more benefits members are going to get.

Informed by SMM, Improvement Service recognized the limitation of measuring the return-on-investment (ROI) of KM projects by input (e.g. number of members, number of members participating in community events, number of best practices documents shared, number of discussion threads, number of hits to the intranet etc.) and weight these benefits against the cost of setting up, creating content and maintaining a community.

If knowledge is defined as the sense made at a particular point in time-space by an individual, we need to accept that sometimes no new discoveries are made, sometimes we create innovative ideas accidentally, and sometimes we identify new sales opportunities because of documents we have read or people we have spoken to. The value of KM projects is to provide that nurturing environment – or simply speaking, to deliberately design the dynamic water-cooler environment – for ideas exchange to take place even though the members are located in different geographical locations in Scotland and working for different local authorities. You can choose to leave these internal networking and learning opportunities to chances, but if you want it to happen, it has to be designed.

The return on investments (ROI) of a KM project is in effect the potential for innovations and creative ideas to happen, to avoid reinventing the wheel and to increase staff confidence and job satisfaction. The Improvement Service sees this as a an investment to drive cultural change and to transform the local government practice, to allow staff to see beyond what is possible currently, and to allow staff to learn on-the-job and to grow with the organization in times of change. We want colleagues to have the opportunity to inspire and challenge one another with their ideas, and provide help when possible, to bring their ideas into reality. Ultimately, the Improvement Service aims at consciously providing local government staff with the journey of 'becoming' someone different. KM investment is allocated as investment cost to support all the activities of Improvement Service, and requires no additional business case and ROI statement for the investment. It is what we need to do and one main reason for setting up the company.

In this chapter, Dervin's Sense-Making Methodology is introduced and practical examples are provided to demonstrate some alternative approaches to design KM projects for the public sector. The approaches and techniques used may appear to be obvious, but they are theoretically informed and backed by SMM research conducted since 1972. The literature review above highlighted that Knowledge Management as a discipline has developed out of multiple discourses, and carries with it conflicting definitions of knowledge. As a result 'KM' becomes something that is impossible to define and potentially mean little to too many. The design of knowledge management practices based on an explicit set of meta-theoretical assumptions is critical to develop common understanding, to allow for meaningful debates, and ultimately to advance the knowledge management discipline (Dervin, 2003).

There are, however, challenges in offering this kind of SMM journey to local government colleagues. It was in the application context described above a new way of doing things and definitely a new way of communicating with staff in the Scottish local government. We often heard employees say 'we do not have time to share knowledge with others' or 'we don't have the incentives to share knowledge with others'. Senior managers then asked 'what should we do to change our employees' thinking and make them more willing to share their knowledge and use others knowledge?'

Yet, by applying SMM as shown in the cases above, important and visible changes in these seemingly unmovable obstacles resulted. Thus, we saw that: the SMM's Micro-Moment Time-Line interview approach unearthed findings which did not come out from an initial study carried out by an external consultant. The design of the Improvement Service website informed by SMM has allowed Improvement Service to fully play its role as a knowledge sharing facilitator (which were much welcome by local authorities staff) rather than the know-it-all expert who give out recipes for local authorities to follow. The use of SMM to facilitate dialogue in the face-to-face meeting demonstrated the power of good conversation whereby every participant could fully take part and could connect ideas with oneself and with one another.

When applying SMM, every employee is conceptualized a theorist of his/her world, both subjective and objective, internal and external, interpretive and material. SMM assumes that, there must be a good reason for them to make the decision, to engage in knowledge sharing activities/events. Sense-Making Methodology asks KM practitioners to listen to the users on their own terms; and allow them to express their diverse perspectives (rather than trying to change them and make them listen to 'experts'). SMM does not provide recipes to implement KM projects. Rather, it provides a meta-theoretical framework and associated methodology to help KM practitioners design user studies, facilitate dialogue, and design systems and communications procedures which allow diverse needs to be heard in ways that are useful to both individual and collective sense-making. Perhaps, most important of all, it asks designers not to impose their own views on to their users.

For real cultural change to take place in the Scottish local authorities, SMM continually reminds us that KM is not just about asking staff working in the local authorities to change, instead it is asking the experts, the politicians in power, the senior managers and companies like Improvement Service to change – i.e. to lower their status and ego so that ordinary staff/users are empowered, are being listened to, are invited to be involved and have their say, and are given the nurturing environment for 'knowledging' and being a life long learners.

KM practices, informed by SMM, become genuinely communicative and dialogic, anchor in specific time-space moments of a living, breathing human being.

This chapter has aimed to stimulate interests and demonstrate potentials for designing KM practices that are informed by an explicit set of meta-theoretical assumptions. Dervin's Sense-Making Methodology has been considered by many to be the most methodologically developed approach. The authors of this chapter assume KM researchers and practitioners can reinvent the KM discipline by understanding users in different ways; and that KM practices can potentially take on very different shapes from what we see today,

REFERENCES

Brown, J. S., & Duguid, P. (2000). *The social life of information*. Boston, MA: Harvard Business School Press.

Cheuk, B. (2007). Applying Sense-Making and Narrative Techniques to capture lessons learnt. *Journal of Information & Knowledge Management, 6*(3), 1–7. doi:10.1142/S0219649207001494

Cheuk, B. & Dervin, B. (1999). A qualitative sense-making study of the information seeking situations faced by professionals in three workplace contexts. *The Electronic Journal of Communication, 9*(2-4).

Denning, S. (2000). *The Springboard: How Storytelling ignites action in knowledge-era organizations*. KMCI Press.

Dervin, B. (1989). Audience as listener and learner, teacher and confidante: The Sense-Making approach. In R. E. Rice & C. K. Atkin (Eds.), *Public communication campaigns* (2nd ed., pp. 67-86). Newbury Park, CA: Sage. Reprinted in: B. Dervin & L. Foreman-Wernet (with E. Lauterbach) (Eds.). (2003). *Sense-Making Methodology reader: Selected writings of Brenda Dervin* (pp. 215-232). Cresskill, NJ: Hampton Press.

Dervin, B. (1992). From the mind's eye of the user: The Sense-Making qualitative-quantitative methodology. In J. D. Glazier & R. R. Powell (Eds.), *Qualitative research in information management* (pp. 61-84). Englewood, CO: Libraries Unlimited.

Dervin, B. (1998, December). Sense-making theory and practice: an overview of user interests in knowledge seeking and use. *Journal of Knowledge Management, 2*(2), 36–46. doi:10.1108/13673279810249369

Dervin, B. (1999). Chaos, order and Sense-Making: A proposed theory for information design. In R. Jacobson (Ed.), *Information design*: 35-57. Cambridge, MA: MIT Press.

Dervin, B. (2003). Human studies and user studies: a call for methodological inter-disciplinarity. *Information Research, 9*(1). Retrieved from http://InformationR.net/ir/9-1/paper166.html

Dervin, B. (2003). Verbing communication: Mandate for disciplinary invention. In B. Dervin & L. Foreman-Wernet (with E. Lauterbach) (Eds.), *Sense-Making Methodology reader: Selected writings of Brenda Dervin* (pp. 101-110). Cresskill, NJ: Hampton Press.

Dervin, B. (2007). *Focus group for participatory research: design using systematic dialogic principles drawn from Sense-Making Methodology*. Paper presented at International Association of Media and Communication Research Meeting, Paris, France, UNESCO: July 23 – 25.

Dervin, B. (2008). *Interviewing as dialectical practice: Sense-Making Methodology as exemplar*. Paper presented at International Association of Media and Communication Research (IAMCR) Meeting, Stockholm, Sweden: July 20 – 25.

Dervin, B., & Foreman-Wernet, L. (2003) *Sense-Making Methodology Reader: selected writings of Brenda Dervin*. Cresskill, New Jersey: Hampton Press.

Dervin, B., & Naumer, C. (in press). Sense-Making. *Encyclopaedia of Library and Information Science*.

Dervin, B., & Reinhard, C. (in press). Communication and communication studies. *Encyclopaedia of Library and Information Science.*

Hildreth, P. M., & Kimble, C. (2002, October). The duality of knowledge. *Information Research, 8*(1). Retrieved from http://informationr.net/ir/8-1/paper142.html

Nonaka, I., & Peltokorpi, V. (2006). Objective and subjectivity in knowledge management: a review of 20 top articles. *Knowledge and Process Management, 13*(2), 73–82. doi:10.1002/kpm.251

Nonaka, I., & Takeuchi, H. (1995). *The knowledge-creating company*. New York: Oxford University Press.

Snowden, D. (2002). Complex acts of knowing: paradox and descriptive self-awareness. *Journal of Knowledge Management*, *66*(2), 100–111. doi:10.1108/13673270210424639

Snowden, D. & Stanbridge, P. (2004). "The landscape of management: creating the context for understanding social complexity. *E:CO Special double issue, 6*(1-2), 140-148.

Souto, P., Dervin, B., & Savolainen, R. (2008). *Designing for knowledge workers informings: an examplar applications of Sense-Making Methodology*. ASIS&T 2008 Annual Meeting (AM08 2008), Columbus, Ohio, October 24-29

Sutton, D. C. (2001). What is knowledge and can it be managed? *European Journal of Information Systems*, *10*(2), 80–88. doi:10.1057/palgrave.ejis.3000397

Wenger, E. (1998). *Communities of Practice: learning, meaning and identity*. New York: Cambridge University Press.

Wilson, T. (2002) The nonsense of 'knowledge management' *Information Research*, Vol. 8 No. 1, October 2002. http://informationr.net/ir/8-1/paper144.html#sch67 Retrieved on 8 July 2006.

Chapter 14
Using Soft Systems Methodology to Reveal Socio-Technical Barriers to Knowledge Sharing and Management:
A Case Study from the UK National Health Service

Alan C. Gillies
University of Central Lancashire, UK

Jeanette Galloway
North Mersey Health Informatics Service, UK

ABSTRACT

Nonaka (1998) argued that for companies to prosper they must move away from a view of organizations as information processing entities with a focus on formal and systematic knowledge to exploit tacit knowledge. Much of the subsequent literature relates to commercial companies, often in North America. Public services in the UK are undergoing rapid change to improve cost effectiveness, customer focus and improve outcomes. Reports such as Wanless (2002, 2004, 2007), Protti (2002) and Gray (2007) argue that this requires a more intelligent use of knowledge and information. However, authors such as Avison and Wood Harper, (1990) have long argued that systems to support such information-based innovations are context dependent and should be viewed as socio-technical systems rather than simply technological systems. This study uses Checkland's Soft systems Methodology (SSM) to consider the local factors operating within a case study from a local NHS health informatics service organization to assess the need to take account of local factors when applying knowledge management techniques in such cases, with a particular focus on managing the tacit knowledge components, highlighted by Nonaka.

DOI: 10.4018/978-1-60566-954-0.ch014

INTRODUCTION

Nonaka (1998) argued that for companies to prosper they must move away from a view of organizations as information processing entities with a focus on formal and systematic knowledge to exploit tacit knowledge. He argues that this view is deeply ingrained citing Taylor's principles of scientific management (1911) as the source. Taylor's premise that "the remedy for this inefficiency lies in systematic management, rather than searching for some unusual or extraordinary man" is still seen today in the emphasis on formal and systematic knowledge. For example, Keskin (2005) reports that organizations starting out in KM tend to initially concentrate on developing a strategy which is oriented towards explicit knowledge. On the other hand, writers such as Galliers and Newell (2003) define knowledge as something which is uniquely human. It labels the storage, generation and distribution activities of the computer as "information management", while reserving the "knowledge management" term for activities performed by humans, based upon the principle that information becomes knowledge only when it is processed by a human mind.

This study uses a case study focused upon IT help desks. These environments, perhaps because of the technical background of many of their staff and managers, tend to emphasize the role of technology in knowledge management and focus upon explicit knowledge that can be codified and structured in the Taylorian tradition.

Focusing on technology as the core of KM can lead to inadequate attention being paid to the human elements of KM including, culture, creativity, innovation, social networks etc. Reliance on a "technology push" (Damodaran and Olphert 2000) is not sufficient to achieve the organizational culture and context which will promote organizational learning. Cabrera, Collins and Salgado (2006) argue that technology alone cannot ensure that knowledge will be volunteered and shared and Kiluge et al (2001) suggested that those organizations most likely to fail at KM are those that implement technology-based solutions, and wait.

Holsapple (2005) argues that the exclusive and the identification perspective have "blind spots" (that obscure a clear vision of the relationship between technology and knowledge management. There is a more balanced, alternative "inclusive" perspective, which doesn't equate knowledge with information, or conversely, create a boundary between them. This perspective recognizes that modern KM has been enriched by advances in technology, for example, decision support technology, research support systems and communities of interest/practice. From this perspective a KM system is a socio-technical system which has as its objective the management and sharing of knowledge to support the achievement of organizational goals, recognizing the importance of human and cultural aspects of KM and the enabling role of technology.

This view is supported by Jennex et al (2008) Jennex and Olfman (2006) and Jennex and Olfman, (2005) who argue that "KM success is a multidimensional concept. It is defined by capturing the right knowledge, getting the right knowledge to the right user, and using this knowledge to improve organizational and/or individual performance. KM success is measured by means of the dimensions: impact on business processes, strategy, leadership, the efficiency and effectiveness of KM processes, the efficiency and effectiveness of the KM system, organizational culture, and knowledge content." and that "culture is a CSF but not an output of KM success."

This increasing emphasis upon culture as a critical success factor for KM, leads the authors to adopt a methodology designed to capture these aspects of culture, described in the next section. In particular, this study will seek to identify cultural barriers to effective knowledge sharing in support of the organizational goals, which might not be revealed using alternative approaches.

THE RESEARCH METHODOLOGY

The aim of the research is to investigate the importance of local and cultural factors in the successful deployment of knowledge management, particularly in the management of high value tacit knowledge. The specific findings from the case study are necessarily not generalizable, but their importance to the success of the local case can be used to demonstrate the validity of the principle that the KM system should be viewed is a socio-technical system rather than a technological innovation.

Avison et al (1998) argue that "Traditional approaches to information systems development can lead to an over-emphasis on the design and construction of computer-based artifacts such that insufficient attention is given to the social and contextual aspects of information systems development". Further, they argue that "any IS methodology that relies overmuch on technical rationality is, by itself, an insufficient foundation for IS development."

Therefore, this research seeks a more holistic approach, favored by Hirschheim et al. (1996) who argue that "sophisticated social theories are needed to understand and make sense of IS development activity". As a consequence, this research is based around an analysis of a case study using Checkland's soft systems methodology (Checkland, 1999; Checkland and Poulter, 2006).

Developed by Checkland and Scholes (1990), SSM has been described as "partly aiming to structure previously unstructured problems rather than to solve well structured problems" (Platt and Warwick 1995). It is an approach that has been widely used by public and private sector managers to deal effectively with problems associated with organizational change. We shall use it to seek to establish whether it can reveal critical local factors justifying the view of the knowledge management system as a socio-technical system.

SSM attempts to understand a given organization holistically by analyzing the structure of organizations as a whole and from many viewpoints. Checkland and Scholes (1990) have applied this methodology at the community level in the NHS, where they developed models of a system that could evaluate any health care project. They based this on the idea that health is a changing "norm" rather than an attainable goal.

SSM has been applied by a few authors in the Knowledge management area. For example, Fennessy (2002) used SSM in conjunction with SISTeM (Soft Information Systems and Technologies Methodology) to analyze KMS issues, human-computer interaction and the development of criteria for selecting a system. However, the study described herein uses SSM for a different purpose, to identify socio-technical factors which can influence the success of knowledge management across an organization.

Gao et al (2002) argue for the importance of taking multiple perspectives into account within knowledge management, and identify a range of soft systems approaches which may be used. (Ackoff, 1979; Beer, 1972; Churchman, 1970;

Flood and Jackson, 1991; Linstone, 1999; Mason, and Mitroff, 1981; Ulrich, W. 1983). SSM was chosen for this study because of its emphasis upon learning and its previous application within the UK public sector

The traditional SSM model is organized into seven distinct stages, which are summarized in Figure 1. The methodology contains real world activities which involve people in the problem domain (Stages 1-2, 5-7) and systems thinking activities (Stages 3 and 4) that may or may not involve those in the problem domain.

APPLYING SSM TO THE CASE STUDY PROBLEM

In stage one, the researcher seeks to data to define a view of the problem. The local case study was investigated using three complementary data collection techniques: an on-line questionnaire,

Figure 1. Stages of SSM, adapted from Macias-Chapula (1992)

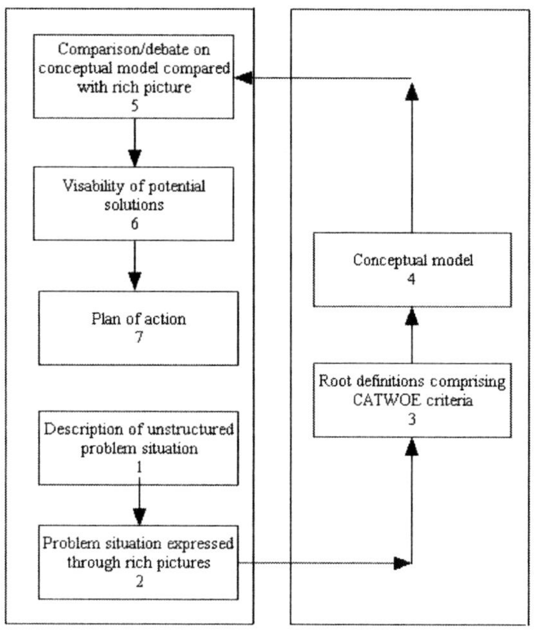

focus group and one hundred randomly selected incident descriptions.

A link to an online questionnaire was e-mailed to all thirty eight service desk agents employed by the HIS across its six service desks. An information sheet for participants was attached to the e-mail. The questionnaire is shown in Appendix 1.

Following this, all HIS service desk managers were invited to participate in a focus group. They were asked to consider two questions: "What barriers to knowledge sharing currently exist?" and "How can knowledge sharing be improved?"

They were asked to consider each question from three perspectives: within service desk teams, between HIS service desk teams and between service desk teams and local support teams, to enable a comparison to be made with the findings of the service desk agent survey.

The focus group was facilitated by one of the researchers. With the consent of participants, an audio recording was made of the session. This allowed the researcher to concentrate on listening and observing the session. It was also felt that a tape recording would provide a more reliable and comprehensive basis for analysis than field notes.

Finally, a download of one hundred randomly selected incident descriptions was obtained from one system. It was hoped that analysis of this data would help to achieve one of the key objectives of the knowledge audit, which was to identify the what proportion of incidents were resolved through the application of tacit knowledge and what proportion were resolved through the application of explicit knowledge.

At stage two of the SSM, the data gleaned from stage one is represented as a "rich picture", with all of the relevant relationships represented.

In stage three "root definitions" are constructed for the relevant Human Activity Systems (HAS) identified in stages one and two. The mnemonic CATWOE can be used as a checklist to ensure that the root definition is complete

(C)ustomer (people affected by the system)
(A)ctor (people participating in the system)
(T)ransformation (the transformation carried out by the system)
(W)eltanschauung (world view)
(O)wnership (person (s) authorized to decide on future of system)
(E)nvironment (the wider system)

In stage four a root definition is formed which provides the basis for a conceptual model containing all the elements of CATWOE.

In stages five and six the conceptual model is compared with the real world to highlight possible changes in the real world and these will result in recommendations.

In stage seven recommendations are implemented.

CASE STUDY: THE RESEARCH SETTING

North Mersey Health Informatics Service (HIS) provides information management and technology (IM&T) services to eight National Health Service (NHS) Trusts in North Merseyside in Liverpool, UK. There are currently six separate service desks.

According to the IT Infrastructure Library (ITIL 2007) the main goal of a service desk should be to provide a single point of contact for customers by receiving and recording calls from users, providing a initial asseSSMent of incidents, making a first attempt at incident resolution and monitoring and escalating incidents according to agreed service levels. This view reflects the Taylorian view of scientific management, where knowledge management is concerned with the systemization and codification of knowledge.

There is a paucity of published research concerning the implementation of KM systems within the IT service desk environment. However, research relating to the wider customer service industry must be considered to have some relevance.

Such research shows that many agents are reluctant to use KM tools (Downing 2004). Reasons cited include the lack of training in the use of the KM tools, using the tools takes too much time and are not personally fulfilling, and that the tool doesn't contain the required knowledge

The over-riding message from this research is that agents preferred to consult colleagues than to use the KM tool.

One service desk provides a service to three organizations. The other service desks are each dedicated to one organization. Each service desk has its own service desk system but the HIS has recently procured a new system which all desks will migrate to. The first service desk will migrate in August 2007.

The HIS has an organizational goal to increase the proportion of incidents resolved at first point of contact by its service desks. Limited performance data is available from existing service desk systems. However, a HIS customer satisfaction survey (HIS 2007) carried out in April 2007 indicated that, on average, across the six services desks, 42% of customers felt that their most recently reported incident had been resolved at first point of contact. There was a significant variation between the highest (71%) and the lowest (30%). These statistics suggest that there is scope to both improve the average performance and to achieve more consistent performance across the HIS.

Findings from SSM Stage 1: The Problem Situation Unstructured

Data collected from the survey of service desk agents, the focus group attended by service desk managers and the download of data from a HIS service desk system were used to provide an unstructured view of the problem situation, in our case study, the provision of help desk services . This elicited the following key findings:

Types of Knowledge Required by Service Desk Agents

Analysis of the data download resulted in the identification of 8 categories of incident, which are shown in Table 1, together with their relative frequency.

Further analysis of the data was undertaken in an attempt to determine the type of knowledge, explicit or tacit, that would have been required to resolve the incident. As the download included a description of the incident but not a description of the "fix" this proved to be difficult to achieve.

At a superficial level it could be observed that certain categories of incident were more likely to be "hard" than "soft" problems and therefore would probably have been resolved through the application of explicit rather than tacit knowledge. For example, 42% of incidents in the sample were concerned with national applications, and of these

Table 1. Categories of incident identified

Type	Examples	Frequency
National applications	requests for new smartcards, smartcard renewals and personal identification number resets, and some requests for PCs to be configured to enable access to national applications	42%
Hardware	eg requests to procure all types of hardware and reports of faults.	20%
Software	mainly reports of software applications running slowly or crashing	18%
Telecoms	requests for mobile phones, problems with mobile phones etc	5%
Security Incidents	requests for advice on possible breaches of security, for example e-mails containing patient identifiable information	3%
Administration	requests for changes to user profiles and e-mail accounts	2%
File Management	eg requests for the creation and moving of folders	2%
Network	reports of networks running slowly or problems with connectivity	2%

a substantial proportion were concerned with the issue and renewal of smartcards. In order to resolve these incidents service desk agents would need to access explicit knowledge in the form of registration authority policies and procedures

A significant proportion of the 20% of incidents that were concerned with hardware were requests for equipment. Again, in order to resolve these incidents service desk agents would need to access explicit knowledge in the form of local procurement policies and procedures

Use of Knowledge Sources

Findings from the survey showed that 79% of agents referred to colleagues for knowledge on a daily basis. Managers and "local experts" were also referred to on a daily basis by 44% of agents. The most commonly used "non-human" sources of knowledge were policies and procedures which were referred to on a daily basis by 42% of agents. Other sources, including known error bases, local knowledge bases and external vendor knowledge bases were used but on a less frequent basis.

The Role of the Service Desk Agent

Service desk agents were asked to assess the relative importance of various aspects of their role. The results show that respondents found it difficult to identify which particular aspect of their role was "most important". A majority (68%) of those who responded regarded incident resolution as the "most important" aspect of the role. However, most (52%) also thought that logging, assigning and escalating incidents was of equal importance. Only 44% felt that knowledge creation, for example recording details of fixes, fell into this category. Fewer still (40%) felt that sharing knowledge with colleagues was the most important aspect of the role

Sources of Knowledge

79% of respondents indicated that they consulted with service desk colleagues on a daily basis. A finding which seemed rather at odds with the fact that only 40% of service desk agents regarded information sharing as one of the most important aspects of the role.

Also referred to on a daily basis were, service desk managers (44%), "local experts" (44%).

This means that the three most commonly used internal sources of knowledge were "people" rather than "systems". This finding was rather surprising given that it had been observed from a high level analysis of incidents by category that the majority of incidents received by service desks were resolved through the application of explicit rather than tacit knowledge. This suggested that much of the knowledge being obtained from service desk colleagues, managers and local experts was knowledge that could be elicited, codified and made available via an internal knowledge base.

Policies and procedures were referred to on a daily basis by 42% of respondents and significant proportions of respondents indicated that, at least once or twice a week they accessed knowledge in known error databases (42%) and/or other local knowledge bases (53%). Real time system monitoring was used infrequently or never (32%), but this finding may reflect the fact that not all service desk teams have access to real time system monitoring. More surprising is the fact that 44% of respondents never access knowledge from service desk scripts.

External sources of knowledge were less used than internal sources. 47% of respondents used vendor knowledge bases at least once or twice a week. Only 26% indicated that they used online forums as a source of knowledge with the same frequency.

Recording and Sharing of Knowledge

According to the results of the survey, all respondents record new knowledge in some way. 45% of respondents indicated that they record new knowledge in a way that it can be accessed by other service desk agents in their own team. The fact that only 22% record new knowledge in the service desk system may reflect the fact that some of the existing service desk system in use across the HIS do not have a knowledge base. However, the key statistic to note is that a third of all new knowledge was recorded for personal use only.

Although all respondents felt that knowledge was shared within service desk teams, in the majority of cases (56%) this was on an ad hoc basis rather than in a systematic way (44%). 44% of respondents felt that knowledge was not shared between HIS service desk teams. Of those who felt that knowledge was shared, only 11% felt that this was done in a systematic way. The remaining 44% felt that knowledge sharing across HIS service desk teams took place on a purely ad hoc basis.

All respondents felt that some knowledge sharing did take place between the service desk team and other support teams, for example, server support teams and desktop support teams. However, again the majority (56%) felt that such sharing took place on an ad hoc basis rather than in any systematic way.

Almost a third of service desk agents (31%) felt that there were no barriers to knowledge sharing within service desk teams, eg "Everyone is very happy to help and share their knowledge." However, some technological and cultural barriers to knowledge sharing within teams were flagged:

Need for better knowledge base facilities within the service desk software.

People like to have power over things.

In the focus group, service desk managers described a situation which, in most respects, supported the data provided by service desk agents. That is, that knowledge was freely shared within service desk teams, but that knowledge sharing was ad hoc rather than systematic.

They also agreed that, as the survey findings had shown, colleagues and managers were the service desk agents' preferred source of knowledge. While the view was expressed that that this type of interaction within the team was a "good thing", there was also recognition that if certain individuals were being asked the same questions time and again, this could eventually lead to frustration.

Managers felt that the "knowledge is power" phenomenon was not usually encountered within service desk teams but they concurred with the service desk agents' view that lack of time to share knowledge in any systematic way was a key barrier.

Another barrier identified by managers, which had not been mentioned in survey results, related to working patterns. Some service desk agents work part-time and others, where service desks are open 24/7, work nights only. These individuals were seen as being disadvantaged in that they did not encounter the same diversity of problems as their full-time, nine- to- five colleagues, and therefore did not have to source the knowledge necessary to resolve such problems.

Analysis of service desk agents' responses again identified technological and cultural barriers.

Lack of centralized Knowledge Base.

A lot of people do not see the HIS as one big organization, a lot of people still have the mentality of 'them and us'.

However, a quarter of respondents pointed out that HIS service desks serve a range of organizations which currently use different systems. Therefore, service desk teams have differing knowledge requirements.

Different systems therefore, some fixes at one site would be inappropriate at another.

Service desk managers agreed with agents that it was the differences between the services that the various service desks currently support that was the main barrier to knowledge sharing, although it was acknowledged that there were some positive examples of knowledge sharing between those service desks which support national applications.

Managers did not feel that the absence of any significant sharing of knowledge between HIS service desks was as a result of resistance by staff, but rather that there was no pressing reason to do so at this point in time.

Some service desk managers felt quite strongly that there were significant barriers to knowledge sharing between their own service desk teams and other local support teams and that these barriers were mainly cultural rather than technological. One manager noted, "We don't have systems to do it, but that's the least of it!".

There was agreement that barriers to knowledge sharing between service desk agents and support teams were less significant on sites where teams were small. In small teams there was more need for flexibility of roles. In fact, in one small team, 1st, 2nd and 3rd line support staff worked on a rota basis. However, on sites where teams were larger, support staff seemed less willing to work flexibly. When 2nd and 3rd line support staff were occasionally required to provide cover on the service desk, they did so very unwillingly and the outcome was inevitably degradation in service to customers. Managers felt that this again pointed to a perception by support staff that the role of service desk agent has lower status than the role of a "technician".

Improving Knowledge Sharing

Almost half of the service desk agents' suggestions as to how knowledge sharing within service desk teams could be improved, were focused on better use of technology, for example,

A shared service desk software should have the facility to store a knowledge base, as this is where all service desk operators will spend most of their time, then they won't have to trawl through 1000s of folders on shared drives.

However, other suggestions were more concerned with cultural aspects of knowledge sharing, for example,

Time to be able to document and inform new starters.

Although managers had previously expressed the view that that there were no significant barriers to knowledge sharing within service desk teams, they did agree with service desk agents' view that a knowledge base could deliver benefits to the service.

They felt it was important that the knowledge base should be very easy to access and that adequate training should be provided to service desk agents, so that users weren't left on hold for long periods of time while service desk agents tried to find a solution to their problem.

More than half of service desk agents' thought that knowledge sharing between HIS service desk teams could be improved through improved use of technology. For example:

Instant messaging is a superb tool; I have used it on other help desks and it is fantastic as you can contact experts whilst on the phone to a client massively increasing first line fix rates.

Initially service desk managers had expressed the view that lack of commonality in the services supported by the various HIS service desks meant that there was no real driver to share knowledge. However, as the discussion progressed, a number of areas were identified where there was agreement that knowledge sharing could deliver benefits, and some suggestions were made as to how this could be achieved.

For example, some service desks which operate 24/7 provide an "out of hours" service to customers in other HIS partner organizations. There was agreement that the staff that provide this service could benefit from having access to "local" knowledge about the systems used in these other organizations.

Service desk managers felt that knowledge sharing between the service desk team and other local support teams was the area where there was most scope for improvement.

There was consensus that the quality of any knowledge base would be dependent upon the degree of "buy in" from support staff. If support staff were fully engaged with the knowledge base they would record and update knowledge about fixes as part of their daily routine. This would in turn improve the quality of knowledge available to service desk agents, and this in time would enable an increase in the proportion of incidents resolved at first point of contact.

However, it was clear to all that if this level of engagement was to be achieved, service desk teams and support teams would have to recognize that they share the same objectives for the service, and that these would only be achieved if knowledge is shared.

Although the responses to an earlier question (4.4.1) indicated that a third of all new knowledge was recorded by service desk agents for their own personal use only, surprisingly most service desk agents felt that little knowledge would be lost if they left the organization. However, further consideration of responses suggests that, for some service desk agents, the fact that their knowledge is stored on the shared drive leads them to believe that this knowledge would not be lost if they left the organization. This assumes that the knowledge is organized and recorded in such a way that it could be easily accessed by others.

I share all information and personal files are all on network drives.

SSM Stage 2: Graphical Representation of the Problem Situation

In stage 2 the key findings were represented as a "rich picture", reproduced in figure 2.

SSM Stage 3: Forming a Root Definition

In stage 3 a root definition was formed which expressed the purposeful activity of system described by the rich picture in a clear and explicit form.

Figure 2. Rich picture of support function

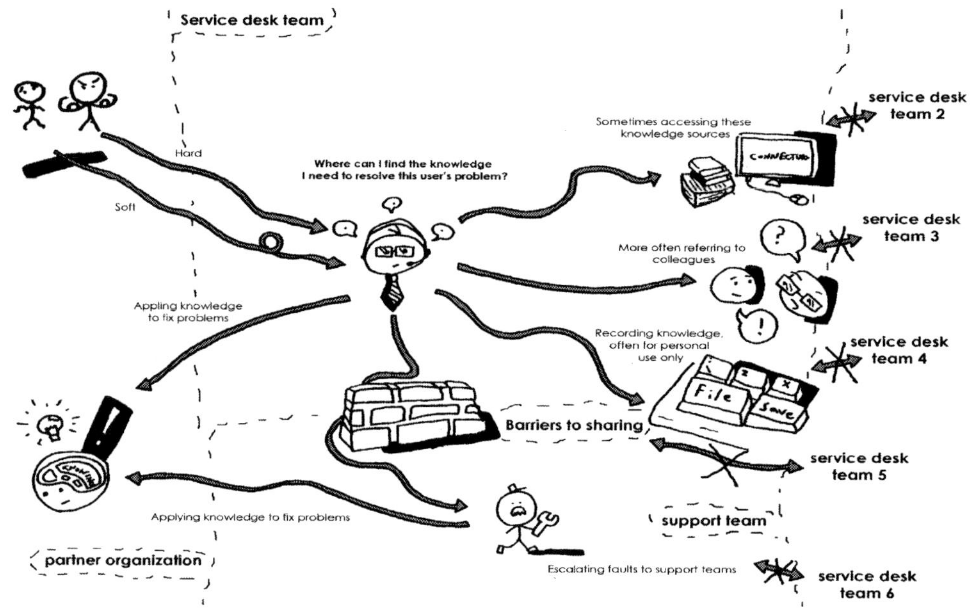

An effective system which supports the creation, storage, transfer and application of knowledge and enables service desk agents to improve the service they provide to IT users and helps to ensure that the North Mersey remains the preferred provider of IT support to its partner organizations.

The key elements of the definition, according to SSM CATWOE criteria were identified as in Table 2.

In stage 4 the root definition and the CATWOE criteria provided the basis for construction of a conceptual model. This model (see figure 3) illustrates the main activities necessary for the system and their logical dependencies.

In stage 5 the rich picture was compared with the conceptual model. The differences are noted in Table 3.

SSM Stage 6: Proposed Actions

Informed by the comparison of the rich picture with the conceptual model, in stage 6 a number of changes were recommended that would help to address the "problem" of knowledge sharing within and across HIS I.T. service desk teams.

Table 2. SSM CATWOE criteria

C	(Customers)	IT service users within North Mersey HIS partner organizations
A	(Actors)	Service Desk Agents
T	(Transformation)	The creation, storage, transfer and application of knowledge
W	(World view)	Working towards improved IT support services in the context of the concept of Trusts having a choice of IT Support Services providers
O	(Owner)	The IT Support Services Provider - The North Mersey HIS
E	(Environment)	There are barriers to knowledge sharing that need to be overcome

Figure 3. Conceptual model for IT Service Desk KM system

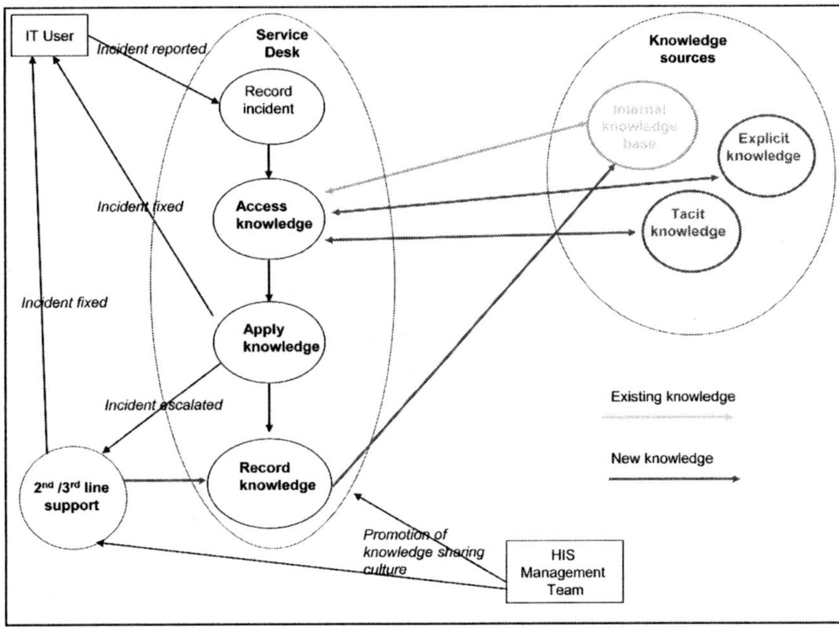

Table 3. Comparison of rich picture of current situation and conceptual model of desired state

Rich picture	Conceptual model
Most incidents reported to the service desk can be resolved through the application of explicit or "hard" knowledge	Explicit knowledge is codified and recorded in a single internal knowledge base.
Service desk agents prefer to ask colleagues and managers for knowledge, rather than refer to other sources	Service desk agents are fully trained in the use of the internal knowledge base and have confidence that they will find the knowledge they need there. The internal knowledge base is the first point of reference for explicit knowledge but service desk agents will continue to refer to colleagues and managers when a problem requires the application of tacit or "soft" knowledge, or when the internal knowledge base and other sources have failed to provide the necessary knowledge.
Some new knowledge is recorded by service desk agents, but often in a way that does not enable it to be shared with others	Service desk agents record new knowledge in the internal knowledge base. All explicit knowledge is codified and recorded.
Knowledge is shared within service desk teams, but on an ad hoc rather than systematic basis	The internal knowledge base enables systematic sharing of knowledge.
Most new knowledge is uncovered by support teams but is not shared with the service desk team	When an incident cannot be resolved by the service desk it is escalated to 2nd/3rd line support. Following resolution knowledge about the "fix" is recorded in the internal knowledge base.
Knowledge is not shared between HIS service desk teams	A single internal knowledge base is used by all HIS service desk teams.
There are both cultural and technological barriers to knowledge sharing	The internal knowledge base addresses many of the technological barriers to knowledge sharing. HIS Management team promotes a knowledge sharing culture across the organization.

1. Establish an internal HIS-wide knowledge base

The HIS has recently procured a new service desk system, the functionality of which includes a knowledge base. Implementation is scheduled to commence in August 2007. This will provide the technical capability needed to support an internal HIS wide knowledge base.

The more explicit knowledge is captured and recorded in the internal knowledge base, the more service desk agents will be enabled to resolve incidents without reference to colleagues and managers. A well populated knowledge base should enable even a "novice" to resolve the majority of straightforward incidents that are reported, and only complicated incidents, which are likely to be much fewer in number will need to be referred to an "expert".

2. Promote use of the knowledge base by service desk agents

Given service desk agents have expressed a preference for referring to colleagues for knowledge, it would be foolish to assume that they will immediately be enthusiastic users of the knowledge base. A strategy should be developed and implemented to address the following key issues which should help to encourage use of the knowledge base by service desk agents:

- the knowledge base must be easy to use
- agents must be trained to record and retrieve knowledge
- the knowledge base must be comprehensive, reliable and current

3. Promote the use of the knowledge base by support teams

The buy-in of support teams will be essential to the successful implementation of the knowledge base. This means that support team members must be committed to uploading and revising knowledge as part of their daily routine. It is clear from the findings of the research that this will require cultural change. An action plan should be developed and implemented to deliver the following:

Service desk teams and support teams should come together on a regular basis to develop shared service objectives, set targets and review progress.

Support staff should be encouraged to have shared ownership of the knowledge base with the service desk team

Support teams will need to receive training in the use of the knowledge base. Training should cover, what knowledge should be recorded, how it should be organized and recorded, when it should be revised.

4. Improve the management of tacit knowledge.

Tacit knowledge is more difficult to manage than explicit knowledge, but as evidence from the literature review has highlighted, it is extremely valuable to organizations and therefore should not be neglected in a knowledge management strategy.

Findings suggest that service desk agents and managers are in possession of tacit knowledge in the form of experiential and situational knowledge which would be difficult to elicit and codify. However, the findings of this research suggest that they are also in possession of "hard", factual knowledge that is not currently recorded, but could be. Steps should be taken to encourage managers and agents to proactively populate the internal knowledge base with this type of knowledge as this would help to achieve a more rapid population of the system and encourage use by service desk agents.

Although difficult to capture and make explicit, tacit knowledge can be shared in other ways. It is therefore essential that a knowledge strategy includes activities which will promote the sharing of tacit knowledge.

Stage 7 of the SSM methodology is concerned with the implementation of recommendations and is therefore yet to be completed.

CONCLUSION

The case study does not provide specific generalizable knowledge for the KM community, although with the current paucity of studies in UK public sector organizations, especially those that are knowledge intensive such as IT help desks, it may provide some useful insights.

However, it has much more significance to the wider community in demonstrating how a socio-technical approach can help gain a much greater understanding of the social and cultural factors acting as barriers and levers to knowledge management. Traditionally, there has been a view of a binary divide between explicit and tacit knowledge: tacit knowledge is often stated to be that which cannot be made explicit. This study reveals evidence of knowledge kept tacit for social or cultural reasons. This situation is schematically represented in Table 4.

The bottom right hand quadrant is key, because it represents knowledge that could be structured and codified, but generally is not.

The socio-technical analysis revealed a number of key features about this specific organization. Most incidents reported to a service desk can be resolved through the application of explicit rather than tacit knowledge. However, most new knowledge is uncovered by support teams and is not shared with the service desk team. Where new knowledge is recorded by service desk agents it is often done in a way that does not enable it to be shared with others. Similarly, knowledge is shared within service desk teams, but on an ad hoc rather than systematic basis

For more complex problems, service desk agents prefer to ask colleagues and managers for knowledge, rather than refer to other sources. There are both technical and cultural barriers to knowledge sharing. Within this organization, knowledge which could be systemized and made explicit is effectively kept within the tacit domain for cultural rather than technical reasons.

These characteristics may be specific to this organization. However, the authors assert that it is implausible to suggest that other similar barriers to knowledge management arising from the social rather than technical dimensions do not exist in other contexts.

This may be regarded as "tacit meta-knowledge" ie the tacit knowledge about the knowledge management function itself within an organization. Without tackling the management of this body of knowledge, the authors argue that the knowledge management function is likely to be sub-optimal.

The use of SSM to identify this tacit meta-knowledge has proved useful in this specific case,

Table 4.

	Explicit	Tacit
Technical view	Knowledge which can be structured and codified Should be codified to maximize access for staff and response times for customers	High value knowledge which cannot be readily structured and codified
Social and cultural view	Knowledge which can be structured and codified. Is codified because possession is not valued by staff	High value knowledge which is not structured and codified either because possession conveys prestige and value to staff, or because it is more convenient for the holder not to do so.

but it is offered as one useful approach rather than a unique solution.

REFERENCES

Ackoff, R. L. (1979). Resurrecting the future of operations research. *The Journal of the Operational Research Society, 30*(3), 189–199.

Avison, D. E., & Wood-Harper, A. T. (1990). *Multiview: An Exploration in Information Systems Development*. New York: McGraw-Hill.

Avison, D. E., Wood-Harper, A.-T., Vidgen, R. G., & Wood, J. R. G. (1998). A further exploration into information systems development: the evolution of Multiview2. *Information Technology & People, 11*(2), 124–139. doi:10.1108/09593849810218319

Beer, S. (1972). *Brain of the Firm*. London: Allen Lane.

Cabrera, A., Collins, W. C., & Salgado, J. F. (2006). Determinants of individual engagement in knowledge sharing. *International Journal of Human Resource Management, 17*, 245–264.

Checkland, P. (1999) *Systems thinking, systems practice*. Chichester: Wiley.

Checkland, P. B., & Poulter, J. (2006). *Learning for Action: A Short Definitive Account of Soft systems Methodology and its Use, for Practitioners, Teachers and Students*. Chichester: John Wiley and Sons Ltd.

Checkland, P. B., & Scholes, J. (1990). *Soft systems Methodology in Action*. Chichester: Wiley.

Churchman, C. W. (1970). Operations research as a profession. *Management Science, 17*(2), 37–53.

Damodaran, L., & Olphert, W. (2000). Barriers and facilitators to the use of knowledge management systems. *Behaviour & Information Technology, 19*, 405–413. doi:10.1080/014492900750052660

Fennessy, G. (2002). Understanding and selecting knowledge management systems for a health information provider. In *Proceedings of the 35th Annual Hawaii International Conference on System Science, 7-10 Jan. 2002* (pp.638-645).

Flood, R. L., & Jackson, M. C. (1991). *Creative Problem Solving: Total Systems Intervention*. Chichester: Wiley.

Galliers, R. D., & Newell, S. (2003). Back to the future: from knowledge management to the management of information and data. *Information Systems and E-Business Management, 1*, 5–13. doi:10.1007/BF02683507

Gao, F., Li, M., & Nakamori, Y. (2002). Systems thinking on knowledge and its management: systems methodology for knowledge management. *Journal of Knowledge Management, 6*(1), 6–14. doi:10.1108/13673270210417646

Gray, M. (2007, February 8). *Open access from the perspective of the NHS BioMed Central Colloquium*. The Royal College of Physicians, London, UK

Hirschheim, R., Klein, H. K., & Lyytinen, K. (1996). Exploring the intellectual structures of information systems development: a social action theoretical analysis. *Accounting . Management & Information Technology, 6*(1), 1–64. doi:10.1016/0959-8022(96)00004-5

IT Infrastructure Library. (2007). Retrieved from http://www.itil.co.uk/

Jennex, M. E., & Olfman, L. (2005). Assessing Knowledge management Success. *International Journal of Knowledge Management, 1*(2), 33–49.

Jennex, M. E., & Olfman, L. (2006). A Model of Knowledge management Success. *International Journal of Knowledge Management, 2*(3), 51–68.

Jennex, M. E., Smolnik, S., & Croasdell, D. (2008, January). *Towards Measuring Knowledge management Success*. Paper presented at the 41st Hawaii International Conference on System Sciences, HICSS41. IEEE Computer Society.

Keskin, H. (2005). The relationships between explicit and tacit oriented KM strategy, and firm performance. *The Journal of American Academy of Business*, *7*, 169–173.

Kiluge, J., Stein, W., & Licht, T. (2001). Knowledge Unplugged: the McKinsey global survey on Knowledge management.

KPMG. (2000). *Knowledge management research report 2000*. Retrieved from www.insite.cz/data/kpmg_km_report2000.pdf

Linstone, H. A. (1999). *Decision Making for Technology Executives: Using Multiple Perspectives to Improve Performance*. Boston, MA: Artech House.

Macias-Chapula, C. A., & Mason, R. O. (1995). Development of a soft systems model to identify information values, impact and barriers in a health care information system. *Journal of Information Science*, *21*(4), 283–288. doi:10.1177/016555159502100404

Mitroff, I. I. (1981). *Challenging Strategic Planning Assumptions*. New York: Wiley.

Nonaka, I. (1998). The Knowledge-creating company. In D. Neef, A. Siesfeld, & J. Cefola (Eds.), The Economic Impact of Knowledge (pp. 175-188). Butterworth-Heinemann.

North Mersey Health Informatics Service. (2007). *Customer Satisfaction Survey*. Internal document.

Platt, A., & Warwick, S. (1995). Review of soft systems methodology. *Industrial Management & Data Systems*, *95*, 19–21. doi:10.1108/02635579510086698

Protti, D. (2002). (submitted to). Implementing information for health: even more challenging than expected? [Department of Health Information Policy Unit, HMSO London.]. *Report*.

Taylor, F. W. (1911). *The Principles of Scientific Management* [trade edition]. New York: Harper and Brothers Publishers.

Ulrich, W. (1983). *Critical Heuristics of Social Planning*. New York: Wiley.

Wanless, D. (2002). *Securing Our Future Health: Taking a Long-Term View*. Final Report, HM Treasury,The Stationery Office, London.

Wanless, D. (2004). *Securing Good Health for the Whole Population*. Final Report, HM Treasury, The Stationery Office, London.

Wanless, D., Appleby, J., Harrison, A., & Patel, D. (2007, September) *Our Future Health Secured? A review of NHS funding and performance*.

APPENDIX 1: ONLINE QUESTIONNAIRE

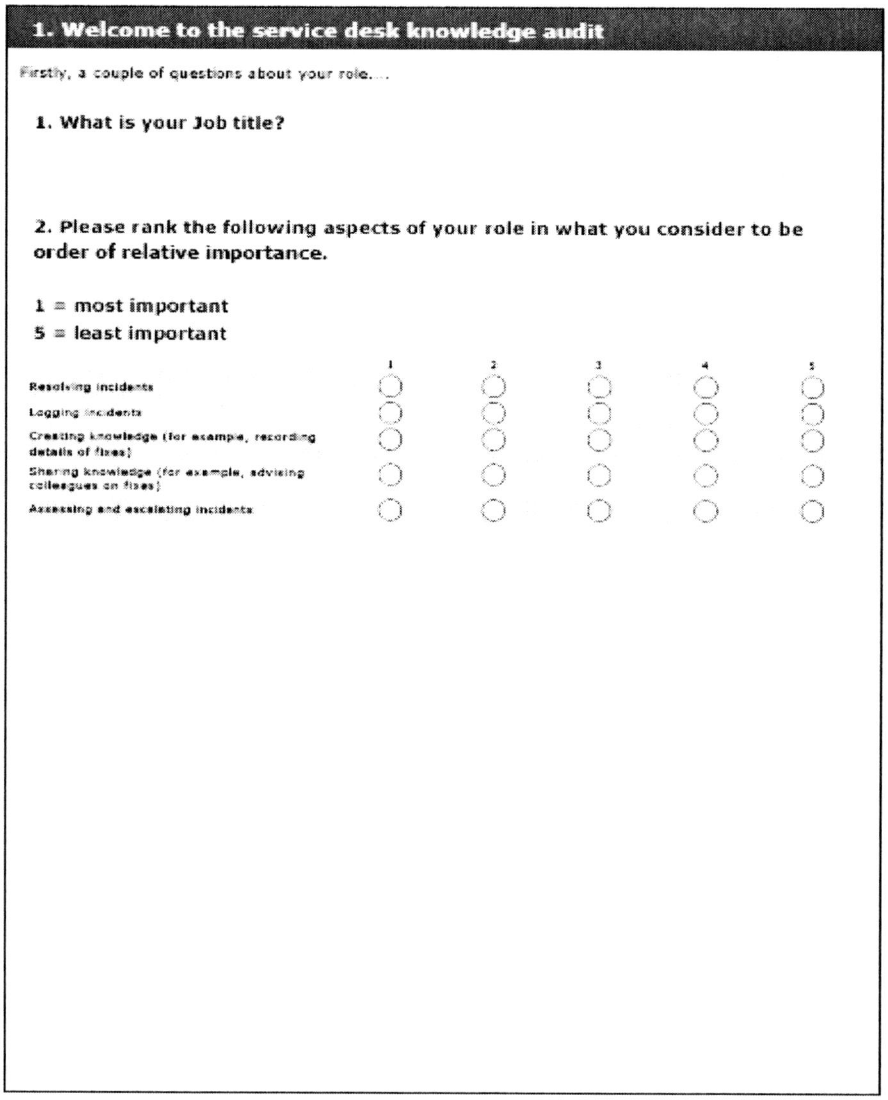

1. Welcome to the service desk knowledge audit

Firstly, a couple of questions about your role....

1. What is your Job title?

2. Please rank the following aspects of your role in what you consider to be order of relative importance.

1 = most important
5 = least important

	1	2	3	4	5
Resolving incidents	○	○	○	○	○
Logging incidents	○	○	○	○	○
Creating knowledge (for example, recording details of fixes)	○	○	○	○	○
Sharing knowledge (for example, advising colleagues on fixes)	○	○	○	○	○
Assessing and escalating incidents	○	○	○	○	○

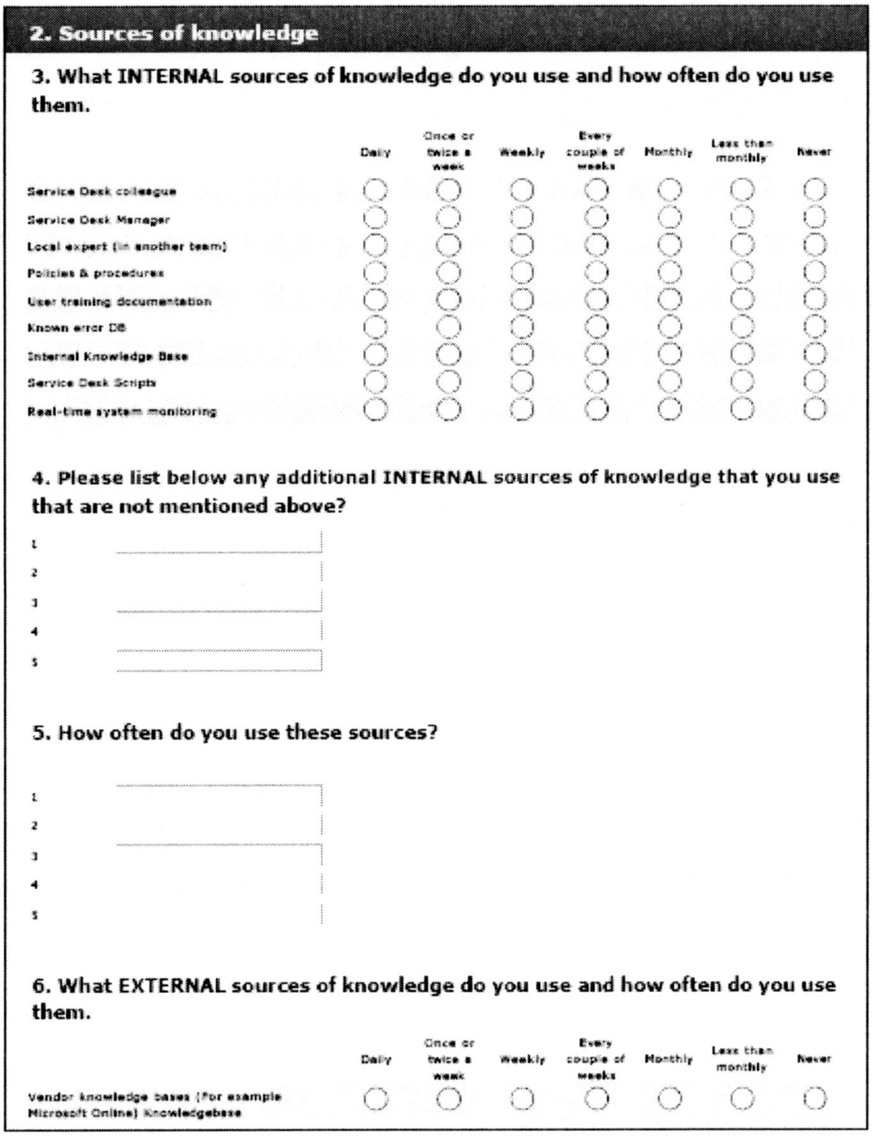

2. Sources of knowledge

3. What INTERNAL sources of knowledge do you use and how often do you use them.

	Daily	Once or twice a week	Weekly	Every couple of weeks	Monthly	Less than monthly	Never
Service Desk colleague	○	○	○	○	○	○	○
Service Desk Manager	○	○	○	○	○	○	○
Local expert (in another team)	○	○	○	○	○	○	○
Policies & procedures	○	○	○	○	○	○	○
User training documentation	○	○	○	○	○	○	○
Known error DB	○	○	○	○	○	○	○
Internal Knowledge Base	○	○	○	○	○	○	○
Service Desk Scripts	○	○	○	○	○	○	○
Real-time system monitoring	○	○	○	○	○	○	○

4. Please list below any additional INTERNAL sources of knowledge that you use that are not mentioned above?

1
2
3
4
5

5. How often do you use these sources?

1
2
3
4
5

6. What EXTERNAL sources of knowledge do you use and how often do you use them.

	Daily	Once or twice a week	Weekly	Every couple of weeks	Monthly	Less than monthly	Never
Vendor knowledge bases (For example Microsoft Online) Knowledgebase	○	○	○	○	○	○	○

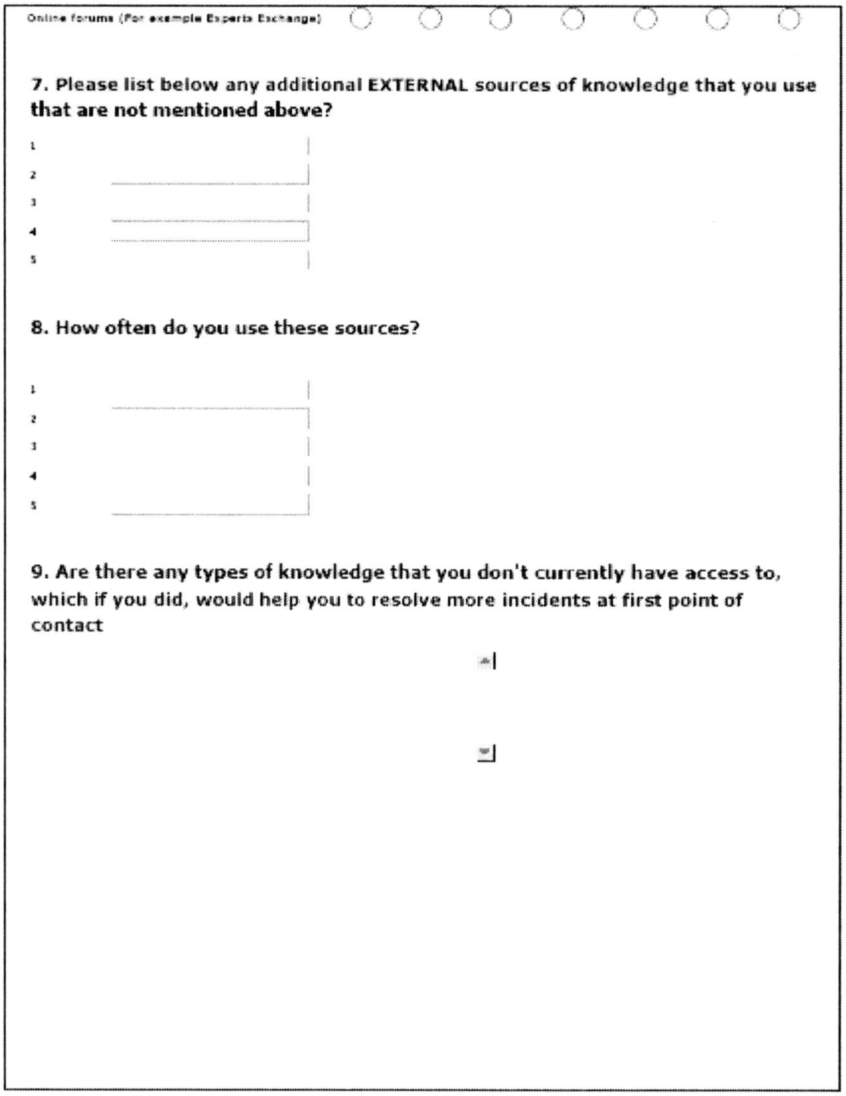

Online forums (For example Experts Exchange)

7. Please list below any additional EXTERNAL sources of knowledge that you use that are not mentioned above?

1
2
3
4
5

8. How often do you use these sources?

1
2
3
4
5

9. Are there any types of knowledge that you don't currently have access to, which if you did, would help you to resolve more incidents at first point of contact

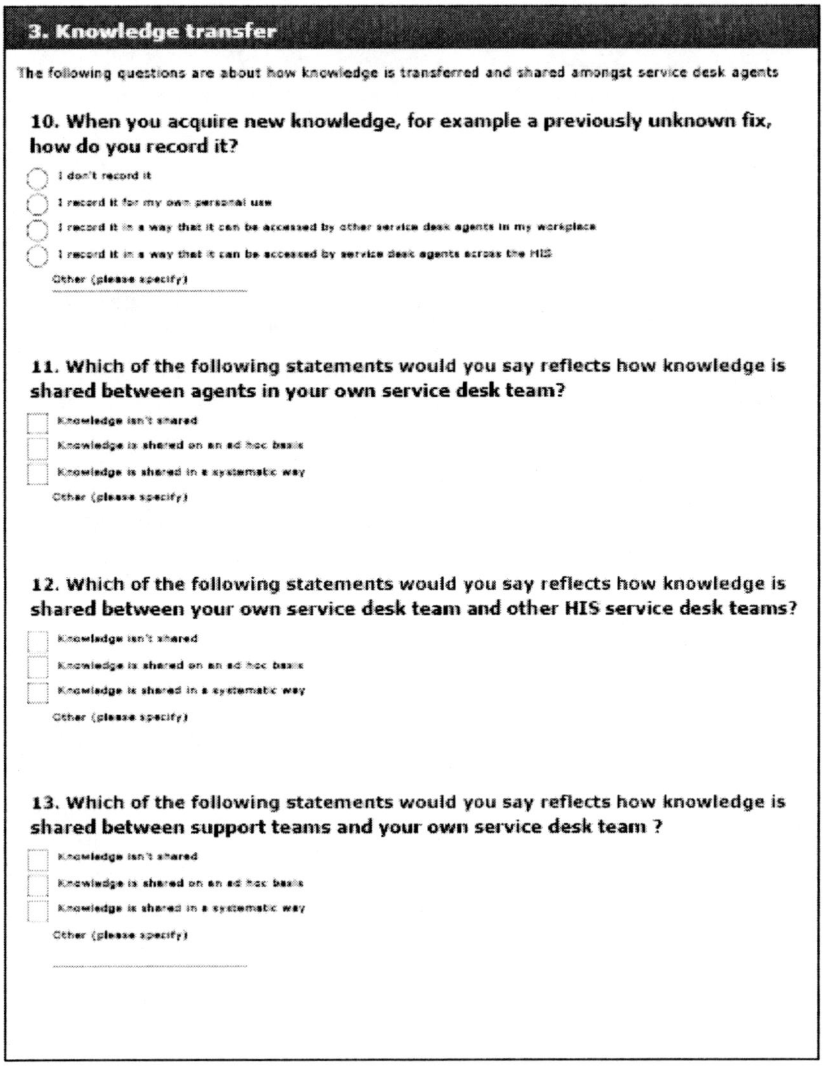

3. Knowledge transfer

The following questions are about how knowledge is transferred and shared amongst service desk agents

10. When you acquire new knowledge, for example a previously unknown fix, how do you record it?

- ○ I don't record it
- ○ I record it for my own personal use
- ○ I record it in a way that it can be accessed by other service desk agents in my workplace
- ○ I record it in a way that it can be accessed by service desk agents across the HIS

Other (please specify)

11. Which of the following statements would you say reflects how knowledge is shared between agents in your own service desk team?

- ☐ Knowledge isn't shared
- ☐ Knowledge is shared on an ad hoc basis
- ☐ Knowledge is shared in a systematic way

Other (please specify)

12. Which of the following statements would you say reflects how knowledge is shared between your own service desk team and other HIS service desk teams?

- ☐ Knowledge isn't shared
- ☐ Knowledge is shared on an ad hoc basis
- ☐ Knowledge is shared in a systematic way

Other (please specify)

13. Which of the following statements would you say reflects how knowledge is shared between support teams and your own service desk team ?

- ☐ Knowledge isn't shared
- ☐ Knowledge is shared on an ad hoc basis
- ☐ Knowledge is shared in a systematic way

Other (please specify)

4. Barriers to knowledge sharing

14. What do you think are the main barriers to knowledge sharing within your own service desk team, for example, technological, cultural?

15. What do you think are the main barriers to knowledge sharing between service desk teams across the HIS?

16. How do you think knowledge sharing could be improved in within your own service desk team?

17. How do you think knowledge sharing could be improved between service desks teams across the HIS?

5. and finally......................

18. When you joined the Service Desk Team, to what extent did your induction programme cover knowledge transfer, for example, introduction to internal and external sources, knowledge take-on from colleagues etc.

19. If you left the service desk team tomorrow, what knowledge would be lost and what would be the impact of this loss on the team ? For example, specialist knowledge, personal files etc

20. Please use this space to make any other comments that you think are relevant to this study.

Chapter 15
The Role of Situated Embodied Interaction in the Banking Customer Knowledge Creation Process

Sara Värlander
Stockholm University, Sweden

ABSTRACT

The increased reliance on Knowledge Management systems has made certain theorists to suggest that this will enable a surpassing of proximal knowledge creation, unequivocally leading up to more effective knowledge creation by easy codification and sharing of knowledge. However, in general, too much focus has been put on the potential of KM systems rather than its limits and the role of supporting social processes of knowledge creation has been largely ignored. The aim of the current research is to start to fill this gap in the KM literature by examining how social processes of knowledge creation are used in banking, taking the point of departure in an approach inspired from phenomenology. The paper illustrates how the increased use of KM systems has not decreased the need for relying on locally embedded service production, due to the invaluable knowledge creation processes that are generated through the embodiments of co-present interactions.

INTRODUCTION

Apocalyptic predictions have declared the advent of information technology to cause a gradual elimination of the reliance on physical place. As one example, Batty (1993, p. 615) meant that the Internet would entail 'a new kind of space, invisible to our direct senses, a space which might become more important than physical space itself.' Negroponte (1995, p. 2-3) suggested that the increased 'digitalization' would cause a move from 'the manipulation of atoms' to 'the management of bits,' insinuating a shift from whatever is tangible or physical to the intangible and virtual. Developing a similar argument Pitt, Berthon and Berthon (1999) suggested that the advent of the Internet would imply the death of distance, the homogenization of time and the irrelevance of location. In stark contrast to this view of a frictionless market unleashed from the impediments of time and space is the view that an increased reliance on information technology does not go hand in hand with a distanciation from physical place. Rather, some argue that it should instead be viewed as being closely intertwined with it (e.g., Graham, 1998; Shields, 2003; Woolgar, 2002; Yakhlef, 2005). Such claims draw to a certain extent on social embeddedness theory, which maintains that transactions embedded in social relationships are more efficient than placeless, arm's-length relationships (e.g., Granovetter, 1985, Uzzi, 1997; Uzzi & Gillespie, 2002), thereby claiming that such relationships will remain despite the advent of the Internet. This is because the social relationship instils trust and reciprocity that promote unique value creation, through the transfer of distinctive knowledge and resources (Uzzi & Gillespie, 2002) and 'fine-grained information,' which is embedded in social relationships (Uzzi, 1997). Similarly, Roberts (2000) emphasizes a continuing importance of human interaction in knowledge creation and argues for the importance of co-presence and co-location. Thus, drawing on this, it can be assumed that situated, embodied interaction remains important for the distinctive knowledge creation that it affords companies. In the knowledge management field, Handzic and Chaimungkalanont (2004) studied the role of socialization on organizational creativity. Their results show that informal socialization plays a significant role in enhancing organizational creativity and knowledge creation. However, enlightening as their results may be in showing the need for socialization in organizations, the limits of their study is that it does not show how various types of socialization leads to increased knowledge creation. The authors themselves underline this shortcoming, and calls for more explorative research on the links between socialization, creativity and knowledge creation.

Departing from an activity-theory, Ryu et al. (2005) made some contributions to the KM field by critically examining knowledge management systems, and how these need to be complemented by social interaction and learning from others. However, their study remains grounded in a discursive view on knowledge, in which social interaction is reduced to communication between individuals. Furthermore, their study is conceptual, which is a typical trait of much research in the knowledge management field.

The aim of the current research is to start to fill the gap in the KM literature by examining how social processes of knowledge creation are used in banking, taking the point of departure in an approach inspired from phenomenology. The banking context is fruitful for substantiating the aim, since it is an empirical context in which information technology is widely implemented and used to support customer knowledge creation. More specifically, the chapter draws on empirical data generated from 12 in-depth interviews with Swedish bank managers.

This chapter argues that understanding the knowledge creation process solely from a discursive, representative perspective, which has mainly been the case in studies on the role of IT in knowledge creation, is limiting and problematic. This is because it disregards the embodied, non-discursive dimension of knowledge creation (Küpers, 2005) taking place in proximal interaction. Thus, in this chapter, the human body is placed at the heart of knowledge management, rather than treating it as an 'absent presence.' In line with Hansen (2006) it is claimed that "discursive practices do constitute meaning making, [...but] discourse is often only a shadow of the phenomenological experience." Incorporating a phenomenological perspective to knowledge creation provides a lens through which the limits of IT in knowledge creation can be better understood, and will enable us to do away with assumptions of information technology rendering local embeddedness and social interaction obsolete.

Thus, for researchers, this chapter starts to lay the ground for a fresh perspective on knowledge management in relation to information technology, which help us to discover the discursive as well as the non-discursive practices of knowledge creation and to take situated embodiment seriously. For the practitioners within the knowledge management field, the chapter shows that situated embodiment generate knowledge about local markets derived from discursive as well as non-discursive experiences through four main sources, namely from embodying the context, from employees' local knowledge and networks, from face-to-face interactions with local community citizens and from face-to-face interactions with local customers. Thus, the main contribution is the chapter illustrating the interplay in the knowledge creation process between information technology and co-presence/co-location.

The main limitation of this chapter is the small empirical sample, which has enabled the author to tell only one story illustrating one specific case. This implies that the last word has not been said on this matter and more research is needed in order to provide additional stories, and to validate, complement or reject the findings presented here.

The chapter is outlined as follows. First, the conceptual framework is established. Second, the research methodology is discussed. Third, the findings are presented, and in section four these are discussed in the light of the conceptual framework, and the main conclusions are drawn. Finally, some limitations of the study and suggestions for further research are presented.

THEORETICAL FRAMEWORK

Social Embeddedness Theory

In order to shed light on the importance of social relationships in knowledge creation, and thus, the potential limits of relying too heavily on information technology, social embeddedness theory is a useful point of departure.

In large, social embeddedness theory is used for understanding how commercial transactions become embedded in webs of social attachments (Granovetter, 1985; Uzzi, 1997). It argues that the process of embedding commercial transactions in social attachments have a positive effect on the development and enforcement of contracts between actors. This is because the social relationship instills trust and reciprocity that promote unique value creation in the relationship through the transfer of distinctive knowledge and resources (Uzzi & Gillespie, 2002). Uzzi and Gillespie (2002) show that firms that maintain embedded ties and social networks gain increased financial performance.

Uzzi (1997) claims that what he refers to as 'fine-grained information' is embedded in such social relationships. This kind of information is more tacit than the information that is exchanged at arm's length interaction. Furthermore, this information is more detailed and has a holistic rather than a divisible structure that is difficult to communicate through more distant interaction and traditional market ties. The fine-grained information is more complex than data, but it is at the same time more fully understood because it is processed as 'chunks of information' rather than as pieces of dissimilar data (Uzzi, 1997). The social relationship between actors is the carrier of a meaning that is beyond what is actually uttered.'... The social relationship imbues information with veracity and meaning beyond its face value' (Uzzi, 1997, p. 46), which is the reason why valuable knowledge can be derived from such information.

Underlining the unique features of knowledge derived from lived experience Polanyi (1969, p. 189) states that 'the observed meaning of an experience structurally differs from one conveyed in a letter.' What is immediately experienced is different from that which is only present in thought (Polanyi, 1969). Hence, what is emphasized here is the role of physical proximity and relationships in customer knowledge creation. Nevertheless, social embeddedness theory does not go deeper into the phenomenological approach that implicitly underlies their claims. In the following I intend to develop this in an attempt to shed light on some of the fundamentals of social, proximal interaction in knowledge creation.

Knowledge Creation

There are a few dominant approaches to understanding knowledge creation. In the following, I will briefly go through these approaches, and argue for the reason why an approach to knowledge creation that is inspired from phenomenology is useful.

According to the cognitive approach to knowledge creation, knowledge is a storehouse of representations, which can be called upon for use in reasoning and which can be translated into language. This view has dominated the understanding of knowledge creation since the 1960s. According to this approach, human thinking is seen as "akin to a computer performing formal operations on symbols" (Bredo, 1994). Thus, thinking is viewed as a process of manipulating the representations, and the mind is considered as an information processor (Newell & Simon, 1972). Thus, thinking is conceived as something that goes on in the head without intimate physical interaction with the surroundings. This dominant position has however been increasingly challenged by proponents of the social approach, which acknowledges the role of human interaction.

Nonaka and Takeuchi (1995, p. 61) argue for a dynamic model of knowledge creation, in which tacit and explicit knowledge "interact with and interchange into each other in the creative activities of human beings." This reasoning rests on an assumption of knowledge being created through interaction between tacit and explicit knowledge, putting an emphasis on the social interaction between humans.

Von Krogh, Ichijo and Nonaka (2000) argue that the facilitation of conversations locally and increasingly among people in different locations is the key to enable knowledge creation. Thus, for them, knowledge management is about supporting conversations. Consequently, knowledge management does not simply involve increasing the quantity of information available, but rather of increasing the richness and quality of the available information sources.

Criticizing the cognitive approach underlying most research on (the potential of) information technology for knowledge creation, which in turn has driven the thesis of 'the death of geography,' Brown and Duguid (2002) claim that the high expectations on information technology have their roots in the understanding of humans as 'goal pursuing agents.' However, a technology-mediated interaction eliminates basic human social processes such as negotiation and discussion (Brown & Duguid, 2002). People negotiate all the time. The interesting point is that negotiation is so much more than matching supply and demand, it is an 'intricate process that tends to keep an eye on externalities such as the social fabric as well as on the immediate goal' (Brown & Duguid 2002, p. 50). Humans usually negotiate their behavior and continually accommodate themselves to one another. By contrast, the Internet can capture only the direct and explicit side of human negotiation, being 'blind to the complex social trade-offs between goals, rules and the social fabric' (Brown & Duguid 2002, p. 52).

In the social constructivist approach to knowledge creation, the focus is mainly on discursive and dialogic practices. Knowledge is considered as being created in processes of languaging (Maturana

& Varela, 1987). Nevertheless, what is missing in this approach is the role of the embodied, situated interaction with the world, a phenomenological approach that takes into account not only what is being discursively uttered (audio-oral features of the body), but also what we learn about the world based on our situated, immerged bodies, through perceptual cues, emotions, intuition, gazing, gesturing, and moving in specific ways. The embodied approach to knowledge creation departs from the phenomenological assumption of 'being-in-the-world' as constituting the basis for all our actions (Heidegger, 1962). Individuals are situated in visual, olfactory, tactile, and auditory settings, and relate to the world in terms of 'I experience' rather than 'I think,' where the former is contiguous to the body's enactments, using all senses (not just oral and auditory).

This implies that a focus is put not only on cognitive and social processes, but also on embodiment, that is, a body's engagement with its physical, perceptual, and spatial environment. Embodiments are for example ways of speaking, facial expressions, being friendly, showing signs of warmth, blushing, being angry, showing sadness, nodding one's head and waving good-bye, etc (Connerton, 1989). For instance, a 'smile, a handshake or words spoken in presence of someone we address, are all messages that a sender or senders impart by means of their own current bodily activity, the transmission occurring only during the time that their bodies are present to sustain that particular activity' (p. 72). These cannot be separated from their embodied medium, for they exist as such only when they are instantiated in a particular movement of the head or a particular kind of gesture. It is from this view on knowledge creation that this chapter takes its stance. The phenomenological approach to knowledge creation is useful since it questions the 'information-transfer' model of knowledge creation, which is based on an understanding of knowledge as being possible to codify and transfer without changing its content, to a view in which knowledge creation is to a large extent dependent upon social and bodily processes difficult to transfer to a technology-mediated context.

Locally Specific Information

The last pillar in the theoretical framework of this chapter is the incorporation of the notion of locally specific information, which relates to the contextual, experiential nature of knowledge creation. The tacit information that stems from experience has a further dimension, namely that of context (Polanyi, 1969). The importance of the local context has been addressed by various researchers. Clark and O'Connor (1997) argue that the local context provides a 'geography of information,' that is, locally specific information networks. To them, local markets are not only trading places, but also centers of information collection and formal and informal exchange of knowledge. Storper (1997) extends Clark and O'Connor's (1997) argument and claims that territorial, or local-specific soft assets, may involve information advantages, but also conventions of interaction and relation-specific skills, a sort of expertise that Storper (1997) refers to as noncodified traditions.

Yanow (2004) more specifically draws on a reasoning derived from phenomenology, defining local or contextual knowledge as the kind of knowledge that develops in interaction among people with the operations and objects that are specific to a local context. 'It develops out of the experience with the situation in question and much of it is tacitly known' (Yanow, 2004, p. 12). Such knowledge evolves from seeing and/or interacting with someone/some place/some thing over time. 'Local knowledge is the very mundane, yet expert understanding of and practical reasoning about local conditions derived from lived experience' (Yanow, 2004, p. 12). Local knowledge is situational and legitimates the experiential-contextual as a kind of specialization, in line with what Berger and Luckmann (1991) referred to as 'commonsense knowledge.'

The framework above sets the role of the local, co-present, embodied interaction at the forefront in knowledge creation by underlining its uniqueness in providing ingress to the social and discursive processes of knowledge creation, but also, and more importantly, to the embodied and the super-discursive practices, which are immediate, contextual and thus, impossible to codify and transfer. It is by understanding these latter practices that we are able to understand the limits of information technology in providing certain types of knowledge, and thus, to understand one of the reasons for why companies may need to remain locally embedded despite an increased reliance on information technology for knowledge creation.

METHOD

Data Generation Procedure

In this chapter, the empirical context is constituted out of the banking industry. The bank used in this chapter is the largest retail bank in Scandinavia. The author conducted semi-structured, face-to-face interviews with 10 senior branch managers representing a selection of the bank's branches, and in addition, interviews were conducted with the president and the vice president of the bank. The interviews were conducted between June and December 2005. The branches represented both rural and urban areas and were of varying size. The respondents were selected randomly from a list of the bank's branches, and all respondents agreed upon being interviewed. Semi-structured interviews were considered suitable due to their ability of providing rich insights in a complex area. The interview guide was designed by the author to probe topical areas evolving around the processes involved in knowledge creation. Typical questions posed in the interviews were: 'Could you tell me about how you create knowledge about your customers? 'What kind of information do you use?' 'What is the role of [the source of information] in the process?' To probe deeper into these issues I used follow-up questions such as: 'I am interested in those kinds of details, could you tell me more about that?' And 'Would you consider this typical or atypical?' The semi-structured interviews fostered a conversational style and elicited open, unstructured responses. Thus, rather than following the guide statically, the interview guide was used as a support to the conversation in order to focus it. Each interview lasted for around 1-1 1/2 hour.

The data generation was an iterative process, where each interview provided the author with new insights and new understandings, which could be further elaborated upon in the subsequent interview (Spiggle, 1994). The time span between the interviews was important, since it provided time to transcribe the recording of each interview, identify the main themes and eventual loose ends, and reflect upon the material (Ahrens & Dent, 1998).

Data Analysis

In accordance with the interpretive approach the analysis of data proceeded by means of an iterative, continuous part-to-whole and whole-to-part movement between each interview and the entire set of interviews (Spiggle, 1994; Patton, 2002).

The theorizing both emerged from and was intertwined with the empirical analysis, a procedure, which is sometimes referred to as a mix of inductive and deductive research, or abduction (Alvesson & Sköldberg, 1994). Thus, in a first step, each interview transcript was analyzed individually, bearing the theoretical framework in mind, but equally being 'open to the data' leaving room for new issues to emerge. In this step, chunks of data were classified and labeled (Spiggle, 1994). In a second step, the analysis was performed across interviewees in order to summarize the emerging, generic themes and abstract them into fewer, more general conceptual classes (Spiggle, 1994). The themes that are presented in the analysis section are the themes that were mentioned most frequently during the interviews.

In order to ensure that the interpretations of data mirrored the respondents' interpretations of their realities in a credible manner the interpretations were verified with three of the informants, who provided their comments on the text.

The presentation of the empirical material derived from the interviews is made in the form of quotations. Miles and Huberman (1994) describe these illustrations as 'vignettes,' which are focused descriptions typical to the empirical material, rather than evidence (Ahrens & Dent, 1998). Vignettes are like literary snapshots, which provide short, but rich, illustrations of common phenomena within the context of study.

FINDINGS

In the following, the most noteworthy themes emerging from the analysis of the interviews are presented. The themes illustrate the various complementary sources of knowledge, in addition to knowledge derived from various KM systems, that the bank is capitalizing on by being locally embedded. Before going on to discuss these various sources of complementary knowledge, a few voices of the role of the KM system used in the bank is in order.

The KM Systems and Its Role in Knowledge Creation

In the bank used as empirical illustration in this chapter, the use of credit scoring systems and CRM is standard. The credit scoring system is a sort of knowledge management system that is implemented and used to enhance the customer knowledge creation process when providing credits. Studying how the credit-scoring system is used in the customer knowledge generation process can enable us to better understand the potential limits of KM systems in knowledge creation, and how these may need to be complemented by embodied knowledge resources.

The credit-scoring system provides the bank tellers with ratings that are supposed to reflect the prospects of individuals and companies, as well as the overall economic outlook. The rating procedure is designed to ensure that the rating assigned to a company or a retail customer is unbiased and the bank tellers are instructed to follow the scorecards when providing credits. The credit score is a statistical calculation of the risk of loss, based on various kinds of information about the company's financial position, and provides a score between 1 (lowest risk) to 10 (highest risk). The bank managers explained that the aim with this system is to automate credit decisions and eliminate subjectivity and soft variables from face-to-face evaluations and replace it with measurable and objective knowledge. Thus, the aim with the KM system was to rule out proximal, 'subjective,' knowledge creation. The ultimate goal was to ensure a standard treatment of credits and to reduce risk. However, what is interesting for the purpose of this chapter is that the empirical data shows that in practice, the knowledge derived from the credit-scoring system is used as a 'first instance' in order to acquire a generic picture of the customer. The type of generic knowledge derived from the KM system helps the bank tellers to generate a rough picture of a customer. This was something that all branch managers agreed upon. One branch manager said:

We put in all the annual report numbers into the credit-scoring system and out from the machine comes a number. If it is a bad number we don't even need to meet the applicant or the customer. If the applicant doesn't pass this initial test you don't have to bother about soft variables. They are just gone. It is very simple. But for those who pass this first step, one needs to add more variables in a second step.

Paradoxically enough, it appears as if the attempt to eliminate soft variables creates new needs for soft variables. The soft variables are eliminated at one level, but are re-introduced at another. The credit-scoring system is apt to show stark contrasts, for example, it easily distinguishes the excellent customers and the poor ones. However, most of the time, it was argued that the credit-scoring system did not suffice to create a holistic picture of the customer, despite its processing of massive numerical information. It was even underlined that there was a risk for credit losses if the codified, system-based customer knowledge was not complemented by other sources. Seven of the branch managers clearly stated that it would be very risky to rely solely on the scoring system. The interview excerpt from an interview with another branch manager underlines this:

The competency of making evaluations based on more than the dry annual report numbers is extremely important. Because we need to have the crystal clear annual report analysis, but we also need to add softer variables in our evaluation... Because if you are strictly clinical in your analysis I think one will face credit losses.

Thus, since the system was perceived to be 'strictly clinical' and objective it was also considered to provide only a fraction of the knowledge needed about customers. In order to create a holistic knowledge of the customer, and of the local market in general, recourse to other, embodied information sources was considered necessary.

The CRM system is designed to store all the relevant data about each individual customer. First of all, the bank tellers can easily see the current financial situation of each customer, for example, house mortgages, pension savings, funds and shares. It was explained that when engaging with a customer, the CRM system is close to always verified in order to check whether the customer lacks some services that the bank teller considers could be suitable for the customer. Seven of the branch managers stated that they did. The other three, on the contrary, claimed that they relied to a very little extent on the CRM, but that they may glimpse at it during the interaction. Thus, in this way it was considered as a good support for cross-selling services. As one branch manager stated:

The CRM system is a good tool because you can put in important information about the customer that you may want to use in subsequent meetings. For example, if a customer tells me that they are expecting a baby I will note this in the CRM system, and for the next face-to-face meeting I will remember to ask whether they want a life insurance for their newly born.

However, even though most managers stated that they found the CRM system to be a good reminder tool, all of them claimed that they used it very little compared to what is intended and what was initially expected when investing in the system. According to the managers, this was due to many various reasons such as job stress (the bank tellers found that they did not have time to neither consult the system, nor to put in additional data in it), but the main reason was that customer knowledge was considered to be, to a large extent, situational and contextual rather than possible to store and retrieve. The knowledge about the customer is most and foremost generated in the situated, face-to-face interaction. As one branch manager explained:

Imagine if you have a customer with a wife, two children and a dog. I put in that information in the system. And then the customer calls me a few months later, and I automatically propose an insurance for his wife, drawing on the CRM system. Then he tells me that he has divorced. Then I propose an insurance for his dog, and he tells me that it was ran over by a truck some time ago. The question here is thus how effective it is to draw on data derived from the CRM system. I claim that it is better to draw on what emerges from the interaction with the customer. The best is to meet face-to-face, because you will acquire so much more knowledge about the customer, and you will be able to sell without making such mistakes.

Similar statements, underlining the role of the spontaneous interaction, were brought forward by all of the respondents.

Another branch manager claimed that even though the CRM system can contain much information, many of his employees claim they have most of their customer knowledge in their minds and their bodies. As one example, he explained that one of his employees has more than 400 customers, of which she claims that 370 she can perfectly remember.

When meeting the customer face-to-face, all of a sudden, I remember so many things about that customer that I would not have been able to tell if you asked me about the customer giving only the name of the person. In the interaction, the knowledge emerges, and is re-constituted. Actually, it is quite strange....

In the following, the various types of embodied knowledge creation are explored in more detail.

Embodying the Context

The first identified theme of knowledge complementing the knowledge management system was the importance of embodying the context in order to develop a local market feel. This was considered imperative in order to be able to adapt the business strategies to local conditions. All managers at the bank claim that they acknowledge the specificities of local contexts and attempt to learn and adapt continuously to local demands. The vice president explains this in the following quote:

We don't see Sweden as a totality. Rather it is about viewing the market according to the different parts in a way that acknowledges the uniqueness of every specific market. Because it is a huge difference in managing banking in Gavle [a city 200 km north from Stockholm] compared to Stockholm. So we have to adapt [...] It is about employees and specialization and things like that.

The possibilities to adapt the business to local contexts is dependent on the development of a local market feel, which in turn stems from employees being immerged in the local context. It was explained that this feel would be impossible to create without actively engaging with a market, 'being-there' in a phenomenological sense.

One manager vividly described how he acquired knowledge about the market and its customers based on embodied experiences of the context:

Closeness is important. We always want to visit a company before agreeing on a credit for example, because you want to see how it looks like - the machine park, the inventory - is it clean and proper or is the atmosphere chaotic? You can acquire so much information from being out on the field. You get a feeling for the company.

Thus, feeling and seeing the atmosphere, living it with the presence of your body, is the source to create a local market feel rather than relying on codified knowledge derived from the knowledge management systems.

Underlining the importance of creating knowledge from embodied experiences another manager stated:

The competency of making evaluations based on more than the dry annual report numbers is extremely important. [...] You need to have a good intuition and have the competency of feeling whether this is a credible customer or not.

Thus, also in this quote, we find that the role of being able to develop a feeling based on embodied experiences is underlined as a crucial source of knowledge in addition to knowledge derived from KM systems and documentation.

Employees' Local Knowledge and Networks

The second theme that emerged from the analysis was that an outcome from being locally embedded was an opportunity for the company to capitalize on employees' local networks. When analyzing the empirical data, it was found that nine of the branch managers explicitly stated that they always aimed to recruit their branch employees from the local area in which the branch was situated. This was due to the access that this provided to the employees' social networks, which enabled the bank to access important information and contacts. These networks were often informal, and consisted of for example employees' friends and former colleagues. The importance attributed to these networks was expressed by one branch manager:

It is an advantage if our employees are born in the local area, where the branch is situated, and if they know the area by heart. It has to do with their contact network. It makes work easier if they know which buttons to push, and whom to contact, and if you have grown up in the area you have a large network and you know which buttons to push much faster. Hence, you make fewer mistakes and business is much smoother.

Furthermore, recruiting employees from the local area enabled the bank to easier adapt to the 'noncodified traditions' (Storper, 1997) of the local market. The employees from the local area had an extensive incorporated, implicit knowledge about these traditions, which in turn enabled the bank to adapt to the local market in terms of interactional codes, for example social codes and the dialect. A quote from one branch manager vividly illustrates this:

I come from a small city situated in the northern parts of Sweden and I know that up there, in order to succeed, it takes a certain mentality, a certain way of being, a way of working, that is very different from here in Stockholm.

Such knowledge about local interactional codes cannot be acquired but through being immerged in the context. It is a kind of knowledge that is acquired through and manifested by your body, by the bodily postures, the dialect, and the way of interacting with people. Such knowledge cannot be codified and learned, but demands the active engagement with a context.

Face-to-Face Interaction with Local Community Citizens

The empirical data showed that the bank did not only reach employees' informal networks through a local recruitment strategy. It also had formalized interactions with various local community citizens in order to acquire a deeper knowledge about the local market.

First of all, the bank organizes 'local advisory boards,' which meet at the local bank branches every now and then, usually once a month. These boards consist of three representatives from the bank's business customers, who are experts in one business area each, for example, real estate, law, and auditing. Every branch has its own advisory board, and all but one branch manager mentioned these to be very important in order to gain knowledge about the local market. (The branch manager who did not find the board to be important claimed that this was due to a bad management from his side of how to use the board as an information source). A quote from one branch manager can illustrate this:

They [the advisory boards] provide us with information that you cannot gain by reading. It is information from someone you trust, information that can make you change your mind about something [...] you can see on them if they dislike a potential customer. Sometimes a gaze from one of the members, or someone nodding his head showing contentment, is enough to make us more cautious or more confident with a customer.

Thus, the embodied interaction with these advisory boards enabled the bank tellers to acquire not only discursive knowledge through the discussions, but also non-discursive knowledge through the body-languages, mimics, gazes, and so forth.

In addition to the advisory boards, the branch managers mentioned that they attend their local Rotary Club and similar 'social clubs' in order to meet the local people, to acquire information and to get to know the market. Even though this was not mentioned to be an explicit part of the bank's strategy, it was something that had developed to a sort of common practice. Mingling with the members of the clubs, and partaking in the chats of the latest rumors and trends was an important practice in the creation of a local market feel. Interestingly, this was often described using words connoting not only to the speaking/listening discourse, but also by using words such as 'feeling the atmosphere,' 'studying whom is talking to whom' etc, thus, once again underlining the role of embodiments.

In addition to the formalized advisory boards and the Rotary meetings, the quote from an interview with a branch manager illustrates how informal contacts in the local market, derived from being an active community citizen, can actually be an important source of knowledge:

You may acquire these soft variables from playing hockey with a police officer or having a beer with him and from talking to different persons as you do on a local market, and if you add these variables, taken together with some good sense, it is an important source of information and decision base.

Other examples of such informal types of interactions with community citizens were mentioned as important also by 6 other branch managers and the vice president. For example, some claimed that they used to have lunch with certain customers that also had positions within the local community, for example within the community council.

It was argued that the formal and informal networking conducted on the local markets was of importance for understanding the local customers and knowing how to adapt the service provisioning to the specific market. A quote from one branch manager illustrates this:

We are working on a market where we have some of the most demanding customers in Sweden, so we have to work in a way that suits these people. For example, in the area close to the water, if we would start telemarketing on those customers living there, they would be mad and never consider us as a potential bank. This is something that we have learnt from our networks, they told us, whatever you do, don't use telemarketing here. [...] This is why it is so important to be local, you must know your area so that you know how to work your market. If you don't, you will make plenty of mistakes.

The examples given show how the bank's embeddedness in a local market and the bank tellers' embodied interaction with various actors on that market help the company in acquiring invaluable knowledge difficult to obtain through codified knowledge management systems.

Face-to-Face Interactions with Local Customers

Finally, a theme, which was frequently mentioned to have a key role in local embeddedness was the importance of face-to-face meetings with customers in order to develop trustful relationships with them. This was perceived to be a source for acquiring valuable customer knowledge, since customers more easily and willingly reveal information about his or her needs and wants in these interactions. The bank has taken a proactive approach in order to ensure continuous face-to-face meetings. This is done by inviting customers to scheduled meetings with the bank clerks at least once a year, but by preference more often. This is explained by the president at the bank, who claims that the face-to-face meeting has even become more important since the increased use of information technology in customer knowledge creation:

10 years ago, the customer and the sales rep met on the demand of the customer. Today, it has become more anonymous, because the spontaneous meetings are fewer, so in order to ensure the relationship with the customer one has to plan meetings, one has to ask the customers if they would like to come visit us for an overview of their private financial situation, for example.

In similar lines, a branch manager said:

We must meet our customers face-to-face every now and then. This is in order to ensure that we keep in touch with their realities. What we hear from the customers when we meet them face-to-face we are unable to know in any other way. Between four eyes, with a bank man in whom they have trust, the customers reveal things about themselves and their situation.

This suggests that even though banks view their customers less often, the meetings have become qualitatively more important, something that all branch managers agreed upon. It appears as if today, the move is towards more interactional and qualitative face-to-face meetings.

The branch managers explained that the information about customers that they derived from meeting them face-to-face was invaluable and impossible to acquire elsewhere. This information was often to great help in determining customers' needs and wants, as explained in the following interview excerpt:

I could tell what customers want by the way they talk and behave, and also based on their looks. To a large extent it depends on gut feeling. If I sit down with a customer for 20 minutes half an hour and discuss and interact I am able to create a picture of the person that will stay in my mind. This could never be replaced by the information derived from a technological system. [...] By creating a personal experience you become a good banker.

Thus, based on perceptual cues, during a face-to-face interaction, it is possible to anticipate and 'guess' the specific needs of customers.

In similar lines another branch manager underlined the importance attributed to embodied experience through which knowledge about customers is created:

If I meet a person and he looks slack, or he does not look me in the eyes when he speaks, it says a lot about the person. On the contrary, a firm handshake, a constant eye contact, proper dressing, or shortly, charisma, often influence positively on my judgment about the company. It is just the way it works. What a person says does not become truthful if the rest does not match.

Thus, this quote illustrates the constant interaction between discursive and non-discursive knowledge creation, in which knowledge is created through one giving meaning to the other.

In addition to the face-to-face service encounters taking place at the branches, the bank organizes theme events, where customers are invited to a branch to attain various happenings, as illustrated in the following quote from a branch manager:

About once a month we organize some sort of theme evening. We have done wine tasting, Italian cooking and attended concerts together with our customers. It is free of charge and it has so far been very popular.

Interacting with customers in a relaxed manner was perceived to be important in order to acquire customer knowledge that was more in-depth that the knowledge that is possible to generate in more formal meetings. In the more relaxed atmosphere customers perceive the interaction with the bank to become more unpretentious. Thus, instead of conducting expensive market research, the organizing of theme events and ordinal customer meetings was considered to contribute to the customer knowledge creation. The creation of stronger ties with customers create opportunities for acquiring information, which is in line with Price and Arnould (1999), who stated that customers are more willing to divulge personal information in casual acquaintances.

DISCUSSION & CONCLUSION

The aim of this chapter was to start to fill the gap in the KM literature by examining how social processes of knowledge creation are used in banking, taking the point of departure in an approach inspired from phenomenology. The analysis shows that in addition to deriving knowledge from KM systems, the bank used as empirical illustration in this chapter perceive a need to complement the KM system with knowledge derived from non-discursive, embodied experiences. This is taking place through four main sources identified in the empirical material, categorized as 'embodying the context,' 'employees' local knowledge and networks,' 'face-to-face interactions with local community citizens,' and 'face-to-face interactions with local customers.' The findings illustrate how problematic the apocalyptic predictions about the 'death-of-distance' are (Batty, 1993; Negroponte, 1995; Pitt et al, 1999; Rayport and Sviokla, 1995) through the lens of knowledge creation. In contrast to this view, this chapter provides a contribution to extant KM literature by illustrating how the increased use of KM systems has not decreased the need for relying on physically embedded knowledge generation, due to the invaluable knowledge that is created in co-present interactions. This is in line with the propositions of Graham (1998), Woolgar (2002), Shields (2003) and Yakhlef (2005) who have argued for a view of a close intertwining between the virtual, technological systems and co-present interactions. Instead of being considered as substitutes they are considered as being closely interdependent. According to the approach taken in this chapter, this is because embodiments cannot be transferred to a technological context. 'Being-there,' in a phenomenological, embodied sense (Heidegger, 1962), contributes to a holistic knowledge about the local market and its customers, and such knowledge cannot be entirely codified into a system. In line with the phenomenological approach, this is because it is through our entire body that we generate knowledge – feelings, intuition, movements of the body, manner of speaking, dialect, and appearance all play in our knowledge creation processes (Connerton, 1989). The main contribution of this chapter is this illustration of how embodiments play a vital role in the knowledge creation process. Previous studies have underlined the importance of social interaction. However, these studies have treated the body as an 'absent presence' rather than an active part of the knowledge creation process and the body has tended to be reduced to the social. The findings in this chapter create the stepping stone for a fresh approach to studying knowledge management and knowledge management systems, shedding a light on the difficulties of reducing knowledge to solely being produced in discursive practices.

Thus, finding support also in social embeddedness theory (Granovetter, 1985; Uzzi, 1997), social interactions have an important influence on knowledge creation, and they promote unique value creation through the transfer of 'fine-grained information' and distinctive knowledge embedded in these relationships (Uzzi, 1997). However, this chapter draws this one step further, and argues that social relationships should not only be viewed as discursive interactions, but also as situated, embodied interactions.

Characteristic for the findings of this chapter is also the role attributed not only to co-presence but also to co-location. It is important to acknowledge that social relationships are necessarily local in their character, and that specific local markets may constitute a 'geography of information' (Clark & O'Connor, 1997) and have specific 'noncodified traditions' (Storper, 1997). In these noncodified traditions the body plays a significant role, because it is through the body that such traditions are learned and expressed. Such knowledge cannot be reduced into discursive practices and codified into a system. The bank is acknowledging this, and through its local embeddedness it becomes able to capture and capitalize on this knowledge by adapting the service provisioning to local contexts and customers.

LIMITATIONS AND FURTHER RESEARCH

The strength of the qualitative nature of this chapter is that it has allowed for the generation of rich insights. However, this can also be a shortcoming. The limitation of this piece of research is the small empirical sample, which has enabled me to tell only one story illustrating one specific case. Furthermore, qualitative and somewhat explorative research tends to generate ideas and hypotheses rather than to verify assumptions. This implies that the last word is not said on this matter and more research is needed in order to provide additional stories, and to validate, complement or reject the findings presented here. Studying other banks and service industries may provide a complementary picture of the processes of proximal knowledge creation and the role of embodiments.

REFERENCES

Ahrens, T., & Dent, J. F., (1998). Accounting and organizations: Realizing the richness of field research. *Journal of Management Accounting Research, 10,* 1-39

Alvesson, M., & Sköldberg, K. (1994). *Tolkning och reflektion. Vetenskapsfilosofi och Kvalitativ Metod (Interpretation and Reflection. The philosophy of Science and Qualitative method).* Lund: Studentlitteratur

Batty, M., (1993). The geography of cyberspace, Environment and planning B, *Planning and design, 20*(6), 615-16

Berger, P.L., & Luckmann, T. (1991). *The social construction of reality: a treatise in the sociology of knowledge.* London: Penguin

Bredo, E. (1994). *Cognitivism, situated cognition, and Deweyian pragmatism.* Philosophy of Education

Brown, J.S., & Duguid, P. 2002. *The social life of information.* Boston, MA: Harvard Business School Press.

Clark, G.L., & O'Connor, K. (1997). The informational content of financial products and the spatial structure of the global finance industry. In K.R. Cox (Ed), *Spaces of globalization. Reasserting the power of the local* (pp. 89-114). New York: The Guilford Press.

Connerton, P. (1989). *How societies remember.* Cambridge: Cambridge University Press.

Graham, S. (1998). The end of geography or the explosion of place? Conceptualizing space, place and information technology. *Progress in Human Geography, 22*(2), 165-185

Granovetter, M. (1985). Economic action and social structure: The problem of embeddedness. *American Journal of Sociology, 91*(3), 481-510

Handzic, M., & Chaimungkalanont, M. (2004). Enhancing organisational creativity through socialization. *The Electronic Journal of Knowledge Management, 2*(1), 57-64.

Hansen, H. (2006). The ethnonarrative approach. *Human Relations, 59*(8), 1049-1075.

Heidegger, M. (1962). *Being and time*. New York: Harper & Row

Küpers, W. (1998). Phenomenology of embodied productivity in services. *International Journal of Service Industry Management, 9*(4), 337–358

Maturana, H., & Varela, F. (1987). *The tree of knowledge: The biological roots of knowledge.* Boston, MA: Shambhala.

Miles, M.B., & Huberman, A.M. (1994). *Qualitative data analysis.* Thousand Oaks: CA Sage Publications.

Negroponte, N. (1995). *Being digital.* New York: Knopf.

Newell, A., & Simon, H.A. (1972). *Human problem solving.* Engelwood Cliff, NJ: Prentice-Hall

Nonaka, I., & Takeuchi, H. (1995). *The knowledge creating company: How Japanese companies create the dynamics of innovation.* Oxford: Oxford University Press.

Patton, M.Q. (2002). *Qualitative research & evaluation methods.* Thousand Oaks: Sage Publications.

Pitt, L., Berthon, P., & Berthon, J.P. (1999). Changing channels: The impact if the internet on distribution strategy. *Business Horizons, 42*(2), 19-28.

Polanyi, M. (1969). *Knowing and being.* London: Routledge and Kegan Paul.

Price, L.L., & Arnould, E.J. (1999). Commercial friendships: service provider-client relationships in context. *Journal of Marketing, 63*(4), 38-56.

Rayport, J.F., & Sviokla, J.J. (1995). Exploiting the virtual value chain. *Harvard Business Review, 73*(6), 75-85.

Roberts, J. (2000). From know-how to show-how? Questioning the role of information and communication technologies in knowledge transfer. *Technology analysis & Strategic management, 12*(4), 429-443.

Ryu, C., Kim, Y.J., Chaudhury, A., & Rao, H.R. (2005). Knowledge acquisition via three learning processes in enterprise information portals: learning-by-investment, learning-by-doing, and learning-from-others. *MIS Quarterly, 29*(2), 245-278.

Shields, R. (2003). *The virtual.* New York: Routledge

Spiggle, S. (1994). Analysis and interpretation of qualitative data in consumer research. *Journal of Consumer Research, 21*(December), 491-503.

Storper, M. (1997). Territories, flows, and hierarchies in the global economy. In K.R Cox (Ed), *Spaces of globalization. Reasserting the power of the local* (pp. 19-44). New York: The Guilford Press.

Uzzi, B., (1997). Social structure and competition in interfirm networks: The paradox of embeddedness. *Administrative Science Quarterly, 42*(1), 35-67.

Uzzi, B., & Gillespie, J.J. (2002). Knwoldege spillover in corporate financing networks: embeddedness and the firm's debt performance. *Strategic management Journal, 23*(7), 595-618.

Von Krogh, G., Ichijo, K., & Nonaka, I. (2000). *Enabling knowledge creation*. Oxford: Oxford University Press

Woolgar, S. (2002). *Virtual society? Technology, cyberbole, reality*. New York: Oxford University Press.

Yakhlef, A. (2005). Virtual organisation as spatial and temporal innovations. *Forthcoming in Space and Culture*.

Yanow, D., (2004). Translating local knowledge at organizational peripheries. *British Journal of Management, 15*(Special Issue 1), 9-25.

This work was previously published in the International Journal of Knowledge Management, Vol. 4, Issue 4, edited by M. Jennex, pp. 62-76, copyright 2008 by IGI Publishing (an imprint of IGI Global).

Chapter 16
Qualitative Pre-Processing for Semantic Search of Unstructured Knowledge

Shyamanta M. Hazarika
Tezpur University, India

ABSTRACT

This chapter describes semantic search of unstructured data through a qualitative pre-processor. Using the spatial representation language Region Connection Calculus, qualitative relationships inherent in the background knowledge is made explicit. The pre-processor obtained by exploiting such qualitative information can overcome some fundamental problems associated with information retrieval and is an efficient approach to retrieve relevant results.

INTRODUCTION

There has been a growing interest in treating *knowledge* as a significant organizational resource. Consistent with the interest in organizational knowledge, *knowledge management* has been constantly evolving over the last few years (Nonaka, 2005). Identification, acquisition, storage, dissemination, development and utilization of knowledge have been identified as the main tasks of knowledge management (Abecker and Decker, 1999). The advent of high throughput data acquisition technologies as well as digital storage technologies have made it possible to gather and store large amount of data in electronic form resulting in vast amount of information. Accurate and speedy access is required to such repositories, as knowledge is acquired by retrieving information (facts, text, document, images, audio, video etc.).

Knowledge Management Systems have to struggle to overcome the information overload. Finding particular piece of knowledge within large knowledge repositories can be very difficult. Two related problems to do with knowledge retrieval are - a. the issue of finding knowledge again, once it has been stored and b. the problem of retrieving the subset of content from the repository that is relevant to a particular problem. A large section of researchers within knowledge management is

DOI: 10.4018/978-1-60566-954-0.ch016

working on developing efficient tools for retrieving knowledge from such repositories.

Knowledge is seen as a mixture of various elements, which are sometimes codified and sometimes tacit. Knowledge is communicated through database entities, documents, workflows and e-mails etc (Dustdar, 2005). Such an item that allows knowledge to be communicated independently of its holder is a knowledge artifact. Knowledge artifacts may either be of structured, semi-structured, or unstructured nature (Hahn and Subramani, 2000). For subsequent discussion in this chapter, knowledge is interpreted as pieces of information (serving a specific need). The focus here is to retrieve these pieces of information.

Search and retrieval from unstructured information resources is usually by *best match*, i.e. to find documents which are *most relevant* to a given query (e.g. web searching, bibliographic database searches, digital libraries). Majority of unstructured information is either personal or developed through interaction between two or more individuals (Hicks et. al., 2002). Organizing and leveraging content from unstructured information has become a key concern today. There have been several attempts to bring 'structure' to this unstructured information. *Ontology* is used to capture implicit knowledge of the knowledge workers and to associate it with knowledge artifacts for classification, search, and browsing purposes (Decker et. al., 1999; Wang et. al., 2003). On the basis of ease and representational completeness, (Yang and Oh, 1993; Ounis and Pasca, 1998) argue in favor of general and intuitive knowledge representation formalisms such as *conceptual graphs*. Flexible and precise knowledge representation and retrieval can be achieved through *knowledge representation languages* that support logical inference. Many metadata languages (to support such inferences) are being developed to let people index Web information resources with knowledge representations (logical statements) and store them in Web documents (Martin and Eklund, 2000). However, these metadata languages are insufficient to satisfy several requirements necessary to allow precise, flexible, and scalable retrieval.

There has been work on design of knowledge management framework based on improved *information retrieval* (IR) systems (Yang et. al., 2002). An IR system helps to give answers to questions or find solutions by making relevant documents available via search queries. Each document contains search words (or descriptions) which can be used to describe the contents of the document. However, a user may want to retrieve on the basis of the conceptual content. The individual words provide unreliable evidence about the conceptual topic or meaning of a document. The two major problems of information retrieval systems are that of a. *synonymy* - literal terms in a user's query may not match those of a relevant document and b. *polysemy* - term in a user's query will literally match terms in documents that are of no interest to the user. To overcome such problems and provide relevant results for queries, a technique known as *latent semantic indexing* (LSI) (Deerwester et. al., 1990) have been developed. Improvements on LSI (Cegloski et. al., 2003; Dumais, 1990) have been reported in the literature.

Relevance has an important bearing and is crucial to information retrieval. Within an IR system, the retrieval strategy is to retrieve all the relevant documents, at the same time retrieving as few of the non-relevant as possible. Therefore, when characterisation of a document is worked out for subsequent use within an IR system, it should be such that it enables the document to be retrieved (when the document is relevant) in response to a query. One needs to construct a technique within which relevance decisions can be quantified. Research in IR for efficient and relevant retrieval frameworks seems to have been concerned with different aspects of such a technology (Deerwester et. al., 1990; Cegloski et. al., 2003; Dumais, 1990).

This chapter presents a method of searching unstructured knowledge artifacts. The technique presented is based on the *qualitative spatial knowledge representation* formalism - Region Connection Calculus (RCC) (Cohn et. al., 1997). The system is able to overcome few of the fundamental problems mentioned above and develop an approach to retrieve relevant results. This is based on a *qualitative pre-processor* for semantic search of unstructured data[1]. Using RCC the qualitative relationships inherent in the background knowledge is made explicit. Retrieval driven through meta-data obtained by exploiting such qualitative information can overcome some of the fundamental problems associated with information retrieval and is an efficient approach to retrieve relevant results.

In the rest of the chapter, first a review of *qualitative spatial reasoning,* particularly RCC – the qualitative spatial representation language is presented. Thereafter, the *qualitative pre-processor* is described. The results obtained for different sample document collections are evaluated. Finally, conclusions are drawn and pointers towards further work are presented.

QUALITATIVE SPATIAL REASONING

Knowledge Representation influence several issues in representation (Davis, 1993). A detailed discussion on *Knowledge Representation and Reasoning* (KR & R) here is neither feasible nor intended. In this section, elements of the knowledge representation formalism used are reviewed. A brief overview of qualitative spatial reasoning including RCC required for formulation of the qualitative pre-processor is presented.

Everyday spatial interactions are driven by qualitative abstractions. Research on mental models suggests that qualitative representations are an essential component of common-sense reasoning about the physical world (Davis, 1990). For computer systems to be intelligent, with many other facets of common-sense knowledge such as visual recognition, natural language processing and speech understanding, it would need more than ad hoc understanding of space and spatial interactions. Therefore there is increasing interest in the study of spatial concepts from a cognitive point of view. Qualitative Spatial Representation and Reasoning is concerned with providing calculi which allow a machine to represent and reason with spatial entities without resort to traditional quantitative techniques prevalent within for example, computer graphics or computer vision. Representation is concerned with different forms of spatial knowledge and how it can be formalized within a computational framework. Reasoning is concerned with methods and techniques for decision-making using spatial knowledge and developing efficient algorithms for doing so. The term Qualitative Spatial Reasoning (QSR) usually subsumes both the sub-fields of representation and reasoning. The main thrust of QSR is representation and reasoning about space in qualitative terms (Cohn and Hazarika, 2001).

The retrieval architecture described here exploits the area of QSR. Use of QSR for semantic search of unstructured data is motivated by the possibility to reason in terms of categories expressed as regions[2] in *conceptual space* (Gardenfors and Williams, 2001). This is bolstered by the fact that qualitative abstractions rather than complete quantitative knowledge a priori drive every day interaction (Escrig and Toledo, 2000). The pre-processing layer can exploit such qualitative relationships using RCC - the qualitative spatial representation language.

Region Connection Calculus

RCC is a qualitative spatial representation and reasoning formalism based on First Order Logic (Cohn et. al., 1997). The theory is a *region-based* theory of space i.e., basic entities of the theory are non-empty regions of space. The formal theory assumes a topological primitive: C(x, y) to mean that region ‘x’ is connected to region ‘y’. It is

Table 1. The five JEPD relations of RCC

Relation	Interpretation
DR(X,Y)	X is *disjoint* from Y
PO(X,Y)	X *partially overlaps* Y
EQ(X,Y)	X is *equal* to Y
PP(X,Y)	X is *proper part* of Y
PP^{-1} (X,Y)	Y is *proper part* of X

possible to define many relations and functions which capture interesting and useful topological distinctions through C. The relations employed here are limited to five *Jointly Exhaustive and Pair-wise Disjoint* (JEPD) binary predicates often referred to as RCC-5 (For a more detailed presentation of RCC including definitions the reader is referred to (Cohn et. al., 1997)). The language of RCC-5 consists of *region variables* X_0, X_1 … and the five JEPD binary relations (as tabulated in Table 1).

Figure 1 shows the JEPD set of RCC-5 relations[3].

The set of relations defined in terms of C can be embedded in a relational lattice with the top element as *tautology* and the bottom element as *contradiction*. The relational lattice is shown in Figure 2. The symbol T is interpreted as tautology and ⊥ as contradiction. In the lattice the most general relations are connected directly to the top and the most specific (strongest) relations to the bottom of the lattice. For example a PP is always a P and a P implies that it should always be a PP or EQ.

Given a fixed set of relations R, another important question is the relationship between the relations per se. Given two relations $R_1(x, y)$ and $R_2(x, y)$; what are the possible relations (from R) that can hold between x and y? A *composition table* (CT) enables one to answer such question (Cohn et. al., 1997).

The composition table for RCC-5 is given in Table 2. Multiple entries mean a disjunction of the relations is possible. The qualitative pre-processor uses the composition table in conjunction with the subsumption lattice.

Figure 1. Graphical representation of the JEPD set of RCC-5 relations

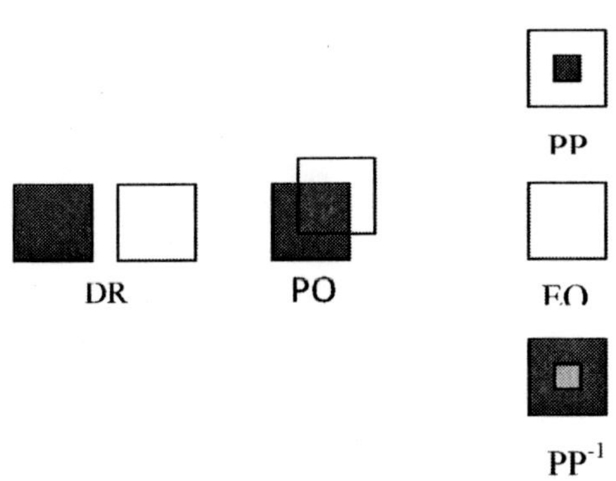

Figure 2. Subsumption lattice for RCC-5

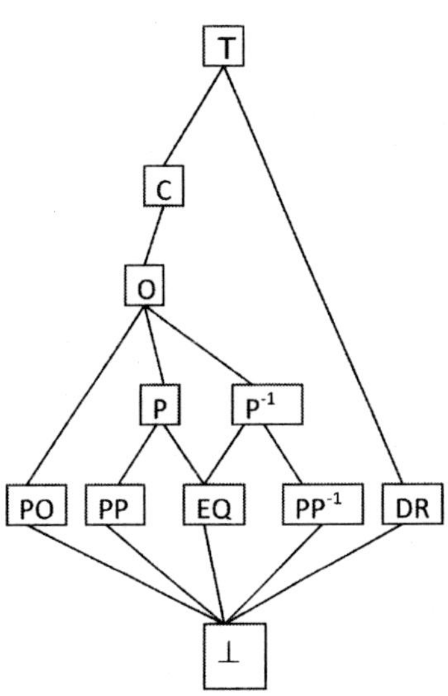

Table 2. Composition table for RCC-5

	DR	EQ	PP	PP^{-1}	PO
DR	PO, PP, PP^{-1}, EQ	DR	PP, DR, PO	DR	DR, PO
EQ	DR	EQ	PP	PP^{-1}	PO
PP	DR	PP	PP	EQ, DR, PP, PP^{-1}, PO	PO
PP^{-1}	PP^{-1}, DR, PO	PP^{-1}	EQ, PO PP^{-1}	PP^{-1}	PO, PP^{-1}
PO	DR, PO, PP^{-1}	PO	PO	PO, DR	PO, DR

PROPOSED ARCHITECTURE

The *Qualitative Pre-processor* (QP) exploits the qualitative relationships inherent in the background knowledge to maintain *meta-data*. This is similar to the use of RCC for reasoning about categories in conceptual space (Gardenfors and Williams, 2001). Unordered data is passed through a qualitative pre-processor where the data is categorised using RCC-5 base relations. The meta-data is fed to the search engine. The schematic diagram of the system is shown in Figure 3.

Qualitative Pre-Processor

Unordered data is categorised in terms of RCC-5 base relations. The schematic diagram of the QP is shown in Figure 4. The document is scanned to identify the *terms* or *content words*. Each of the term is regarded as a sub-category. RCC-5 relations between the terms are identified.

Figure 3. Proposed IR System using QP

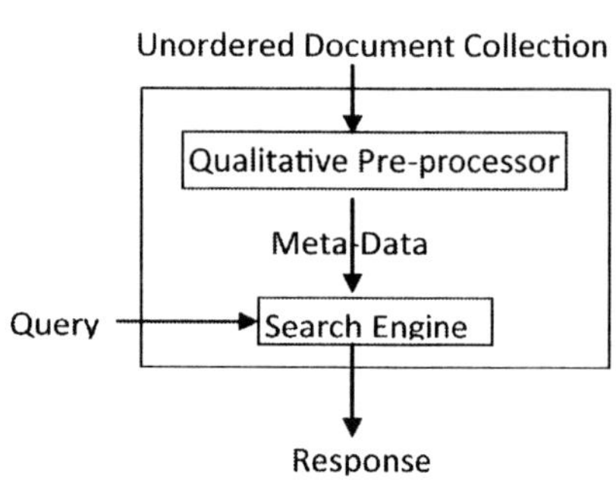

The design of the Qualitative Pre-processor is explained by taking a sample document. The terms in the documents are shown in *Italics*. The terms, also referred to as *content words* are extracted from the document collection following an 8-step process.

1. Make a complete list of all the words.
2. Discard articles, prepositions and conjunctions.
3. Discard common verbs.
4. Discard pronouns
5. Discard common adjectives.
6. Discard frilly words (therefore, thus, however, albeit, etc.)

Figure 4. Schematic diagram of the QP

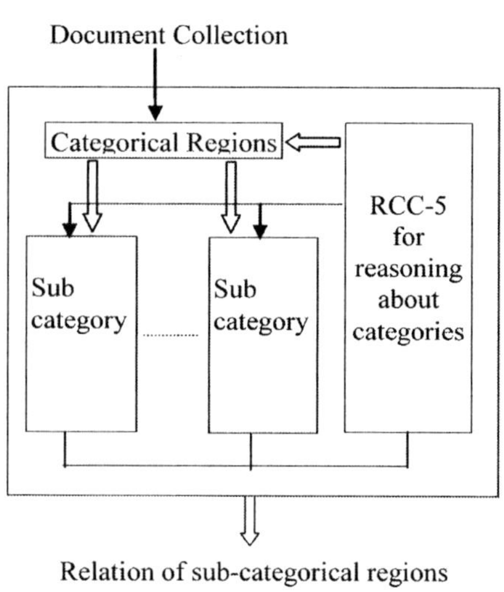

7. Discard any words that appear in every document.
8. Discard any words that appear in only one document.

Example 1 (Table 3)

The associated term list of the sample document collection - I is given in Table 4.

This process condenses the sample documents into sets of content words - words that are semantically significant and can be used to index the collection. Using background knowledge we express the qualitative relations amongst the above context words (in a *conceptual space*) in terms of RCC-5 base relations[4] (see Figure 5).

Search Architecture

The meta-data obtained from qualitative pre-processor has a semantic meaning. These terms are fed into the query processing system. The search architecture creates an index document. The index document uses *terms* as keys and the document that contain them as values. Retrieval of documents based on a given query is either *direct* or *enhanced.*

If any *term* in a query is already listed as a key in the index document, the documents linked to that key are retrieved. Such retrieval is direct. The CT is used for enhanced retrieval. CT enables one to identify terms that are linked to other term(s) in the original query. For example, given base relations PP(natural gas, energy) and PO(energy, price), the CT enables to identify relations that can hold between *natural gas* and *price*. The retrieval is enhanced accordingly.

EXPERIMENTAL RESULTS

For the sample document in Table 3, the following queries are given:

1. Economy of oil.
2. Price of oil in India.
3. Breakdown of nuclear energy.
4. Is ONGC related to oil?

Table 4. List of terms

Terms
Energy
Nuclear
ONGC
Gas
Natural gas
Price
India
Bombay
Oil

Table 3. Sample Document Collection- I

No	Document
1	The breakdown of *energy* supply sources including *oil, nuclear, coal,* and *natural gas*
2	Nation's largest independent *oil* and *gas* producer is Oil and Natural Gas Corporation (*ONGC*)
3	*India* is rich in *energy* sources including *oil* and *natural gas*
4	*Energy* consumption is a measure of the *economic*
5	Unit cuts crude *oil* posted *prices*
6	*ONGC* plans to drill more wells in the *Bombay*
7	confrontation after announcement of *oil* exploration plans, *economy* was hard hit by the rise in *price*

The experimental results obtained from the above queries are shown in Table 5. The QP increases the performance of the search.

For Query 1, it is seen that few but relevant documents are retrieved when QP is used. Response without QP also contains few irrelevant documents. The word *economy* is not present in the document collection; search result without QP gives documents that contain the term *oil*. Response with QP returns documents that contain both *oil* and *price* (synonym of *economy*). This is based on an attempt to solve synonymy by *parthood* - the relations EQ, PP and PP^{-1}.

For Query 1, the semantic representation of terms, expressed as RCC-5 base relations are PO(oil, natural gas) and PO(oil, ongc). PP^{-1}(economy, price) is added based on synonymy. There are two distinct vectors:

v1 (economy, oil)
v2 (price, natural gas, ongc)

With reference to Table 3, there is no document containing the term *economy*. Following terms would drive the direct retrieval (The corresponding documents are noted as well.):

oil 1, 3, 4, 5, 6, 7
economy None
price 4, 6. 7
natural gas 1, 7
ongc 7

Replacement by PP^{-1} would lead to enhancement of the number of documents retrieved based on *economy* as 4, 6 and 7. The final retrieval for Query 1 is based on vector v1(economy, oil) and

Figure 5. RCC-5 relations of terms in Table 4

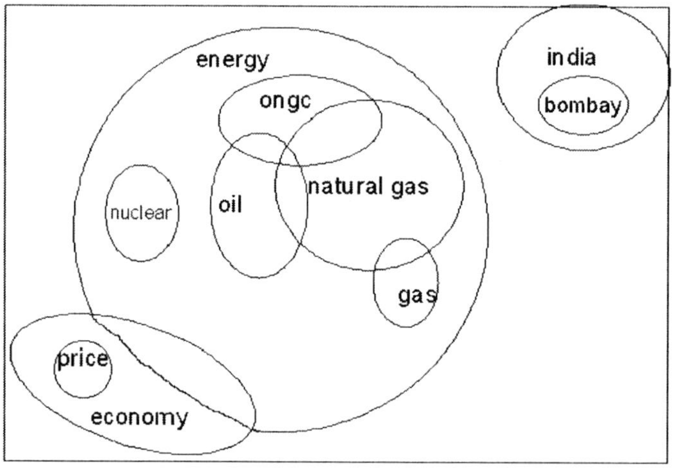

Table 5. Experimental Result of Sample - I

		Without Pre-processor	With Pre-processor
1	Economy of oil	1, 3, 4, 5, 6, 7	4, 6, 7
2	Price of oil in India	1, 3, 4, 5, 6, 7	7
3	Breakdown of nuclear energy	1, 4	1
4	Is ONGC related to oil	1, 3, 4, 5, 7	4, 7

Table 6. Sample Document Collection- II

No.	Document
1	*Glacial ice* often appears blue
2	*Glaciers* are made up of fallen *snow*
3	*Firn* is an intermediate state between *snow* and *glacial ice*
4	*Ice* shelves occur when *ice sheets* extend over the *sea*
5	*Glaciers* and *ice sheets* calve *icebergs* into the *sea*
6	*Firn* is half as dense as *sea water*
7	*Icebergs* are chunks of *glacial ice* under *water*

is the overlapped region of *economy* and *oil* i.e., documents 4, 6 and 7. Similarly for Query 2, retrieval based on *India* is enhanced by the term *Bombay*.

Further Illustrative Examples

In the following section, further examples are presented to illustrate the efficacy of the qualitative processor for efficient retrieval.

Example 2

Table 6 shows a standard sample document collection taken from (Cegloski et. al., 2003). The associated term list is in Table 7.

Figure 6 shows the collection of terms as a conceptual space with the relations between the terms expressed in RCC-5. Note that a given term is associated to another term through a RCC-5 relation from Table 1 with regards to the relationship between the *concept* and most general intended meaning of the terms.

Given the sample document in Table 6, the following queries are given:

1. Titanic hit iceberg in sea.
2. No ice is seen in river.
3. Formation of glacial ice is slow.
4. Firn is soft.

The experimental result based on above queries is shown in Table 8. Note that the retrieval with the QP has no irrelevant documents. Irrelevant documents are retrieved if retrieval is done without the qualitative pre-processor.

Example 3

Table 9 shows a standard sample document collection taken from (Deerwester et. al., 1990) with associated term list in Table 10.

Figure 7 shows the collection of terms as a conceptual space with the topological relations between the terms expressed in RCC-5.

Given the sample document in Table 9, the following queries are given:

Table 7. List of terms

Terms
Glacial ice
Ice
Glacier
Snow
Firn
Ice sheet
Sea
Water
Iceberg
Sheet

Figure 6. RCC-5 relations of terms in Table 7

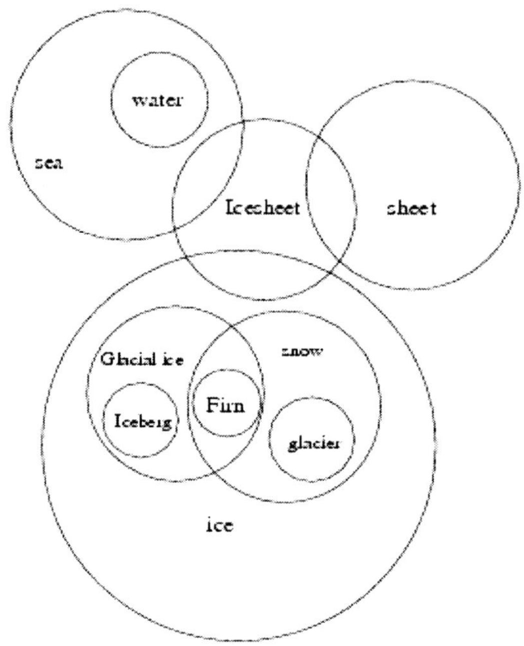

Table 8. Experimental Result of Sample – II

		Without Pre-processor	With Pre-processor
1	Titanic hit iceberg in sea	4, 5, 6, 7	5, 7
2	No ice is seen in river	1, 3, 4, 5, 7	4, 5, 7
3	Formation of glacial ice is slow	1, 3, 4, 5, 7	3
4	Firn is soft	3, 6	3, 6

Table 9. Sample Document Collection- III

No.	Document
1	*Human* machine *interface* for ABC *computer* applications
2	A *survey* of *user* opinion of *computer system response time*
3	The EPS *user interface* management system
4	The generation of random, binary, unordered *trees*
5	*System* and *human system* engineering testing of EPS
6	Relation of *user*-perceived *response time* to error measurement
7	The intersection *graph* of paths in *trees*
8	*Graph* minors: Width of *trees* and well-quasi-ordering
9	*Graph* minors: A *survey*

Table 10. List of terms

Terms
Human
Interface
Computer
User
System
Response
Time
Survey
Trees
Graph

1. Human computer interaction.
2. Interface of system.
3. Graph of response time.
4. Survey of Indian Education.

The experimental result based on above queries is shown in Table 11.

Above examples illustrates the efficiency of the QP for document retrieval. The QP retrieves only relevant documents.

Figure 7. RCC-5 relations of terms in Table 10

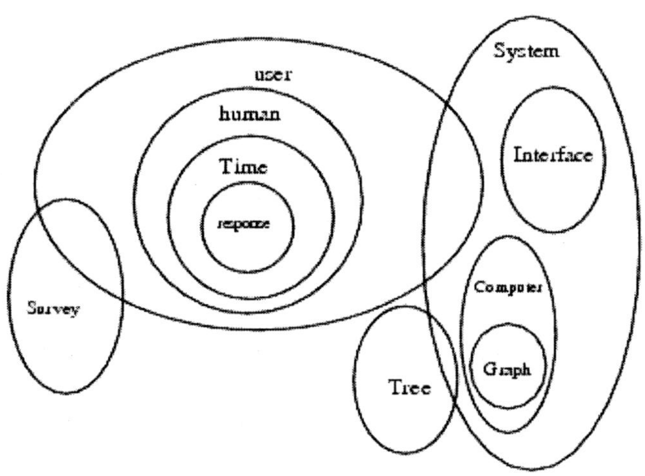

Table 11. Experimental Result of Sample - III

		Without Pre-processor	With Pre-processor
1	Human computer interaction	1, 2, 5	1, 2, 3
2	Interface of system	1, 2, 3, 5	1, 3
3	Graph of response time	2, 6, 7, 8, 9	No match
4	Survey of Indian Education	2, 9	No match

CONCLUSION

An approach to search relevant documents through use of a qualitative pre-processor is presented. The design of the QP is based on RCC-5 - the set of JEPD base relations of the spatial representation language Region Connection Calculus. The effectiveness of the QP is verified by comparing the results (of a given query) with the response obtained without the QP. No irrelevant documents are retrieved. The use of QP results in search space reduction based on identification of a sub set of the conceptual space where the related terms are found. A rudimentary approach to solve synonymy has been proposed.

The work reported here was to validate the proposed technique rather than put forward an efficient implementation of the proposal. Exploring efficient techniques of implementation of QP is part of on going research. While this study has limitations to its testing methodology, there is some real importance to KM researchers and practitioners once the described methodology is satisfactorily validated. The implications are not only better search engines, but more importantly perhaps a theoretical insight into how our cognitive processes work in making sense of acquired information. This remains to be explored further.

REFERENCES

Abecker, A., & Decker, S. (1999). Organizational Memory: Knowledge Acquisition, Integration, and Retrieval Issues. *Knowledge-Based Systems*, 113–124.

Cegloski, M., Coburn, A., & Cuadrado, J. (2003). Semantic Search of Unstructured Data using Contextual Network Graph. *National Institute for Technology and Liberal Education*, Middlebury, USA.

Cohn, A. G., Bennett, B., Gooday, J., & Gotts, N. M. (1997). Qualitative Spatial Representation and Reasoning with the Region Connection Calculus. *GeoInformatica*, *1*(3), 275–316. doi:10.1023/A:1009712514511

Cohn, A. G., & Hazarika, S. M. (2001). Qualitative Spatial Representation and Reasoning: An Overview. *Fundamenta Informaticae*, *46*(1-2), 1–29.

Davis, E. (1990). *Representations of Commonsense Knowledge*. CA: Morgan Kaufmann.

Davis, R., Shrobe, H., & Szobvits, P. (1993). What is Knowledge Representation? *AI Magazine*, *14*(1), 17–33.

Decker, S., Erdmann, M., Fensel, D., & Studer, R. (1999). Ontobroker: Ontology Based Access to Distributed and Semi-Structured Information. In R. Meersman et al. (Eds.), *Semantic Issues in Multimedia Systems*. Boston: Kluwer Academic Publisher.

Deerwester, S., Dumais, S., Furnas, G., Laundauer, T., & Harshman, R. (1990). Indexing by Latent Semantic analysis. *Journal of the American Society for Information Science American Society for Information Science*, *41*(6), 391–407. doi:10.1002/(SICI)1097-4571(199009)41:6<391::AID-ASI1>3.0.CO;2-9

Dumais, S. T. (1990). Enhancing Performance in Latent Semantic Indexing Retrieval (Tech Rep TM-ARH-017527). Bellcore.

Dustdar, S. (2005). Reconciling Knowledge Management and Workflow Management Systems: the Activity-based Knowledge Management Approach. *Journal of Universal Computer Science*, *11*(4), 589–604.

Escrig, M. & Toledo, F. (2000). Qualitative Spatial Reasoning: Theory and Practice - Application to Robot Navigation. *Frontiers in AI and Applications, 47.*

Gardenfors, P., & Williams, M.-A. (2001). Reasoning about categories in conceptual spaces. In . *Proceedings of, IJCAI-01*, 385–392.

Hahn, J., & Subramani, M. R. (2000). A Framework of Knowledge Management Systems: Issues and Challenges for Theory and Practice. In *Proceedings of 21st International Conference on Information Systems* (pp. 302–312).

Hicks, B. J., Culley, S. J., Allen, R. D., & Mullineux, G. (2002). A Framework for the Requirements of Capturing, Storing and Reusing Information and Knowledge in Engineering Design. *International Journal of Information Management, 22*, 263–280. doi:10.1016/S0268-4012(02)00012-9

Martin, P., & Eklund, P. W. (2000). Knowledge retrieval and the World Wide Web. *IEEE Intelligent Systems, 15*(3). doi:10.1109/5254.846281

Nonaka, I. (2005). *Knowledge Management: Critical Perspectives on Business and Management.* Taylor and Francis.

Ounis, I., & Pasca, M. (1998). Organizing Conceptual Graphs for Fast Knowledge Retrieval. In *Proceedings of 10th International Conference on Tools with Artificial Intelligence. IEEE Computer Society Press* (pp. 120-129).

Wang, Y., Yang, Z., Kong, P., & Gay, R. (2003). Ontology-based Web knowledge Management. *Information . Communications and Signal Processing, 3*, 1859–1863.

Yang, Z., Liu, Y., & Li, S. (2002). Applying Information Retrieval Technology to Incremental Knowledge Management. In *Proceedings of First International Conference on Engineering and Development of Cooperative Information Systems* (LNCS 2480, pp. 117-129).

Yang, Gi-Chul, & Oh, J. (1993). Knowledge acquisition and retrieval based on conceptual graphs. In *Proceedings of ACM/SIGAPP symposium on Applied Computing, Indianapolis* (pp. 476–481).

ENDNOTES

1 Unstructured data lacks definite structure. They are not organised in any way. They carry no meaning and therefore, no informational content.

2 Abstract regions constructed out of concepts.

3 Finer distinctions like *disconnected* (DC) and *externally connected* (EC) for DR, and *tangential* PP (TPP) and *non-tangential* PP (NTPP) for PP can be made. These relations, along with the inverses for the last two namely TPP^{-1} and $NTPP^{-1}$, constitute a JEPD set of base relations referred to as RCC-8 (Cohn et. al., 1997).

4 The qualitative relationships have been modelled manually, which does not in any way vitiate the idea of our proposed architecture of finding most relevant documents. Automated modelling using *Natural Language Processing* is a different issue and beyond the scope of this paper.

Chapter 17

Measuring the Dimensions of Tacit and Explicit Knowledge:
Enhancing Knowledge Management

Michael A. Chilton
Kansas State University, USA

James M. Bloodgood
Kansas State University, USA

ABSTRACT

Knowledge workers are often employed to extract knowledge from domain experts in order to codify knowledge held by these experts. The extent to which workers rely on tacit or explicit knowledge may produce inefficiencies and reduce productivity if the information is not shared among those who need it or if it encapsulates strategic goals and is inadvertently shared with those who might undermine the firm's competitive advantage. This chapter discusses the nature of tacit versus explicit knowledge in terms of the dimensions thought to contribute to its degree of tacitness. The authors present the results of an exploratory study in which they develop an instrument designed to elicit perceptions regarding the nature of knowledge used by workers and their degree of reliance on tacit knowledge. It is an indirect form of measurement that eliminates the need to render the knowledge entirely explicit prior to measurement. As an additional benefit, it allows the classification of knowledge along a continuum, ranging from entirely tacit to entirely explicit or somewhere in between. Use of this instrument by managers will help them identify pockets of tacit knowledge within the firm that could either be made explicit so that other workers can benefit from it or that could be prevented from becoming explicit should its strategic value require protection.

INTRODUCTION

Knowledge is created, stored, transferred, and used at all levels of an organization in an attempt to achieve the goals of the organization. The organization's performance is strongly influenced by the extent to which the appropriate knowledge is available and utilized by those who need it (Badaracco, 1991). The knowledge must also be aligned with an organization's innovation position and product/market position in order to establish an effective strategy (McDonough, Zack, Lin, & Berdrow,

DOI: 10.4018/978-1-60566-954-0.ch017

2008). Thus, organizations engage in a variety of methods of knowledge management in order to make available the knowledge that is needed. However, even when knowledge is available it is not always accessed by organization members (Nonaka & Takeuchi, 1995). Planning for the appropriate use of knowledge by organization members becomes very important (Flores, Catalanello, Rau, and Saxena, 2008). Some organization members may prefer or rely on certain types of knowledge rather than accessing all of the appropriate types of knowledge. This can result in suboptimal outcomes.

One knowledge characteristic that organization members may rely upon in differing amounts is its degree of tacitness. After Polanyi (1962, 1967) introduced the concept, the tacit character of knowledge has long been studied in the field of psychology and has begun to play a large role in other disciplines such as organizational behavior and management. Although success has been achieved in indirectly measuring tacit knowledge (cf. Scribner, 1986) research has not yet been conducted that aligns the degree to which individuals rely on tacit knowledge with tasks that are completed using varying degrees of tacit knowledge.

Increasing our understanding of what types of knowledge that organization members are most likely to utilize can help organizations improve their knowledge management practices. Primary reliance on either explicit or tacit knowledge, especially under varying degrees of complexity, can affect performance (van den Bos and Poletiek, 2008). For example, efforts by an organization to increase the amount of explicit knowledge that is created and made available to organization members for a particular project may be ineffective if organization members rely primarily on tacit knowledge. Instead the organization could consider increasing the amount of tacit knowledge available to the organization members or it could identify members who rely more on explicit knowledge and have them carry out the project. To do so implies that we can identify what tasks require a greater reliance on tacit knowledge to complete and which organizational members rely more on tacit and/or explicit knowledge in general.

An additional area of concern to managers is the degree to which tacit knowledge can affect competitiveness (Hall, 1992). Organizations can benefit competitively from attempts to conceal the adoption of certain practices (Terlaak and Gong, 2008), but when this proves inadequate innovative practices based on tacit knowledge can limit imitation by competitors. Even though absorptive capacity can influence the rate of interorganizational knowledge transfer (Todorova and Durisin, 2007), explicit knowledge is typically much easier for competitors to copy because it can be codified and transferred easily (Nonaka & Takeuchi, 1995). Therefore, if management can identify both the areas of their business that are more likely to use tacit knowledge and those in the organization who might be more inclined to rely on tacit knowledge, they can better match workers to tasks and thereby improve protection of knowledge which may have a strategic or other competitive value. Thus, a method to measure this type of knowledge would be useful to organizations to the extent that they would be better able to manage its use and protection.

From a researcher's perspective, the explicit/tacit character of knowledge is important to consider because studies that include knowledge as a variable of interest can have differing or erroneous outcomes if they do not measure the explicit/tacit character of the knowledge. For example, if organizations are being examined in regard to the amount of knowledge they possess and the resulting effect on organizational performance, the results may become muddled because firms may have a significant amount of explicit knowledge to help them create new products or processes, but those products and processes may be easily imitated by competitors and the organization's performance suffers as a result. Existing knowledge measurement approaches may show that the amount of knowledge in an organization may therefore not be positively associated with organizational performance. Moreover, researchers may find that a firm is very effective while appearing to possess limited knowledge when only explicit knowledge is measured and the amount of tacit knowledge is not also included in the measurement.

Grover and Davenport (2001) describe a framework for knowledge management research in which the process of knowledge begins with generation and ends in a realization or outcome. In the middle, knowledge can be codified and transferred and researchers are enjoined to discover impediments and enablers of this process and to look for ways in which firms can integrate these processes with its more familiar states and processes, such as its strategy, culture and behaviors (Grover & Davenport, 2001). While this is certainly necessary for knowledge not considered to have strategic value, another stream of research needs to investigate moving tacit knowledge directly into outcomes so that strategically important and competitive knowledge might be protected.

Kulkarni, Ravindran and Freeze (2006) formulated a knowledge management success model that focused exclusively on explicit knowledge, since successful knowledge management practices may not be uniform between the two types of knowledge. Another reason may have been the requirement to make tacit knowledge explicit in order to measure its quality, although this was not mentioned in their paper. Hansen, Nohria and Tierney (1999) found that successful consulting firms rely on a strategy of knowledge management that is primarily codified (explicit) or primarily personalized (tacit), depending upon the services offered. Consulting firms that offer solutions to repetitive problems rely primarily on a codification strategy, while those that offer highly customized solutions for unique problems rely primarily on a personalization strategy. Although there are many ways to capture tacit knowledge within organizations (Liebowitz, 2009),the personalization strategy attempts to make the reuse of tacit knowledge more efficient by changing it into explicit form before it can be managed.

We argue that not all tacit knowledge should be made explicit and that management of tacit knowledge is possible without having to make it explicit. In order to do so, however, the knowledge must first be identified and classified as tacit or explicit and its strategic importance must also be identified. To do so would require a reliable and valid metric to help knowledge managers resist the temptation to classify anything not well understood as "tacit." Although there are a variety of potential ways to measure tacit knowledge (Busch, 2008), we believe that tacit knowledge is identifiable based on its characteristics and that it need not be rendered explicit during this identification process.

The purpose of this paper is to present a description of the components of tacit and explicit knowledge and the results of the development of a survey instrument designed to tap these components. Tacit knowledge cannot be measured directly, but must first be made explicit (Osterloh & Frey, 2000). Such a transformation dilutes and skews the measurement and is analogous to the sort of destructive testing that occurs in manufacturing in the hopes that the measurement of a few products (which must be destroyed to complete the testing) is representative of those that remain. However, by allowing subjects to identify specific characteristics of the knowledge used in the completion of a task, we are able to classify the knowledge as being either tacit or explicit or somewhere in between. This eliminates the requirement to make tacit knowledge explicit and so can provide a more accurate estimate of its degree of tacitness. The following sections present the dimensions of tacit knowledge which have been drawn from previous research, discuss the nature of these dimensions and present an instrument aimed at measuring them. We then provide a discussion of how the scale might be used, the limitations of such a measurement, the implications to both theory and practice and some ideas for continued research in this area.

THE DIMENSIONS

Knowledge is considered to be *the* basis of competitive advantage for organizations (e.g. Conner & Prahalad, 1996; Ghemawat, 1986) and its management is key to the success of the firm (Becerra-Fernandez & Sabherwal, 2001). The knowledge-based view of the firm posits that organizations with better knowledge resources and the ability to utilize them will fare better than other organizations across the competitive landscape. The value of any particular knowledge resource is, of course, dependent on the situation to which it is being applied (Madsen, Riis, and Waehrens, 2008). However, characteristics of knowledge, such as its tacit and explicit character, can have a broader influence on the ability of a particular piece of knowledge to enhance an organization's performance. For example, good customer service is probably more valuable for high-end, women's clothing retailers than it is for self-service gas stations. However, if a high level of customer service at a women's clothing retailer is held tacitly by employees and later codified into easily teachable steps, this knowledge of how to serve customers well is more likely to leak to competitors. This leakage can prevent a competitive advantage from being sustainable, with competitive parity the result.

Tacit knowledge is knowledge that is difficult to describe and transmit to others, and in its pure form the user is unaware of its usage (Polyani, 1962). It typically is created through personal experience, but the experience has occurred in the past and to such a frequency or repetition that the possessor is no longer aware of the particulars of its existence (Hasher & Zacks, 1979). It becomes a habit or routine (Nelson & Winter, 1982). Explicit knowledge, on the other hand, is completely transmissible—users are consciously aware of its usage—and its creation and usage is either very recent or infrequent such that the user is aware of its particulars.

These characteristics are of vital importance to managers and researchers as the competitive playing field expands, because they influence the nature of the creation, storage, transfer and use of knowledge. As such, knowledge that is more explicit can be knowingly created, stored in an accessible manner, easily transferred, and used in a conscious and intentional manner.

The nature of explicit and tacit knowledge may cause one to initially believe that focusing on explicit knowledge seems to provide more benefits (Alavi & Leidner, 2001). This is particularly true when knowledge needs to be transferred to many organizational members. However, there are some disadvantages of explicit knowledge that enable tacit knowledge to be a preferred choice in a variety of situations (Bloodgood & Salisbury, 2001). For example, explicit knowledge is easily transferred to competitors, intentionally or otherwise. Additionally, when it is used intermittently, explicit knowledge can lead to a greater variance in outcomes. Thus, awareness and understanding of both types of knowledge within an organization is important for managers so that the creation, use, transfer and protection of the knowledge can be used to create and protect competitive advantage.

Our approach to measuring the degree to which knowledge is tacit is based on its characteristics. We can cite four characteristics within the literature: (1) the degree to which the holder of the knowledge is consciously aware of it, (2) the degree to which the knowledge is expressible in oral or written form, (3) the degree to which the knowledge is demonstrable to others, and 4) the degree to which the knowledge is applied in a formal or informal manner. Our reasoning is that if we can identify what a person relies on in each of these categories as they work through a task, then it follows that the knowledge used to complete the task can be identified as either tacit or explicit. We use a sliding scale to do this so that knowledge may be placed along a continuum that ranges from fully tacit to fully explicit. Such a method offers the advantage that the knowledge need not be made explicit to measure it and it allows for the dependent nature of the relationship between tacit and explicit knowledge—i.e., the two are not dichotomous, but reinforcing (Alavi & Leidner, 2001). We now discuss each of these characteristics since they represent the constructs in our model.

Conscious Awareness

Typically, when tacit knowledge is being used the user is not consciously aware of it. The tacit knowledge is built up over time and is stored in the individual in a manner that limits the individual's ability to explicate it. That is, although a knowledge base from previous experience is present, an individual may automatically (Nonaka & Takeuchi, 1995; Reber, 1993) utilize this knowledge base when needed but does not consciously think through the steps required to apply the knowledge. As an example, consider an experienced typist who does not consciously think about each key stroke but rather types words without being aware of exactly where each finger is on the keyboard at any given moment. Tacit knowledge is generally cued for use directly from the environment (Reber, 1993), thus bypassing the consciousness of the individual. This reduced conscious awareness, as shown in Reber's (1967, 1969) artificial grammar experiments, contributes to the inability of the individual to fully explain their behavior (Reber, 1969; Reber, 1989).

Conscious awareness is further described by cognitive load theory, which posits that the brain functions as a result of working memory and long term memory. Long term memory is formed by creating schemata from items found in working memory and that these schemata are automated as learning occurs (Paas, Renkl & Sweller, 2004). This automation in long term memory is what allows people to perform certain tasks without really thinking about it.

Expressibility

Tacit knowledge is difficult to express to others (Polyani, 1962; Polyani, 1967) in either written or oral form. The main issue is the extent to which the knowledge cannot be codified and directly communicated to another individual. Much of the extant research has focused on written expressibility, but oral explication is generally regarded as equivalent. Consider a real estate market as an example. The maxim, "location, location and location" tends to drive decision making regarding the placement of commercial enterprises. Although a myriad of quantitative data may support placement of a retail outlet in one place, an experienced realtor may possess intuition (based on market experience) that he is unable to clearly express to others as to why that particular location may not be optimal. If asked about his decision, he would likely be able to rank his ability to express his decision process along a continuum ranging from fully expressible to fully inexpressible. Doing so would reflect the nature of his knowledge without having to actually express it.

Demonstrability

Demonstrability is represented by a person's ability to perform the necessary tasks based only on seeing an activity performed or seeing the results of an activity. The greater this ability is, the greater the reliance on tacit knowledge and the better able is the person to complete all the steps within a task without as much detailed explicit instruction. This is especially true in complex situations that contain steps that are relatively observable. An individual with the appropriate tacit knowledge can more easily perform the functions necessary to complete the task (Godfrey & Hill, 1995). It is important to note that demonstrability may only have meaning if there is something that can be visualized as a final outcome or if steps are easily observable. Thus, working backwards may not always be appropriate, especially if it involves activities that have not yet been attempted (e.g. putting a man on the moon prior to 1969).

Formal or Informal Application

The dimensions cited thus far directly affect a person's ability to store and/or to transfer knowledge. We now introduce how knowledge is applied in a given situation as a measure of its degree of tacitness. When an individual undergoes training or experiences a task in a step by step fashion, the individual is initially cognizant of the steps he or she has learned. At these early stages of learning and practice, the individual is explicitly trying to remember and use the steps. Over time the steps become second nature, and the individual loses cognizance of their existence in their memory (Nelson & Winter, 1982). Reliance on the steps becomes automatic by nature. Individuals who use this knowledge at a later date are likely to appear to have jumped to a conclusion even though they have implicitly followed the steps without realizing it. In the case of an individual not realizing he or she has followed implicit steps learned long ago, it can appear that the individual is using a disorganized or informal approach to complete a task (Scribner, 1986) because specific steps are not consciously identified and explicitly followed. Thus the logic of the individual's actions appears to be missing when viewed by an outsider (similar to intuition, Reber, (1993). When the steps are not already learned, or at least not learned as well, the individual is more likely to knowingly follow the explicit steps in a formal manner. The degree to which a person can recall that the steps he or she used in performing a specific task is based on prior learning of the task is reflective of the degree of informality of his or her thought process. Thus, the higher the reliance on prior learning, relative to current learning, the greater the use of tacit knowledge by the individual. We distinguish prior learning from newer learning by the effect it has on how an individual uses it. While newer learning is characterized by adherence to specific rules that still require mindful application, prior learning is already committed to the subconscious through experience and is used without the individual being aware of the specific steps involved. The individual may realize he or she is relying on prior experiences but they are unable to accurately identify all of the steps that are followed. Thus, when knowledge is used from prior learning the mental process used to apply the prior learning appears more informal than when knowledge from current learning is used. When current learning is relied upon, the individual is more likely to be seen as using the specific, concrete steps associated with the current learning. This process takes on a more formal character as compared to when prior learning is used. These arguments follow from Scribner (1986), who suggests that the use of previously learned knowledge (working knowledge) is typified by an *ad hoc* approach and maintains a more informal character compared to currently learned knowledge that tends to be applied in a formal, step-wise fashion. We gain additional support from Wagner and Sternberg (1986) who reiterate this point when they speak of the perceived disorganized nature of tacit knowledge stemming from its prior learning. Therefore, our measurement of the use of formal or informal mental processes is indirectly captured using items relating to prior learning.

Our hypothesized model is depicted in figure 1.

THE METHOD AND MEASURE

It is apparent that the ability to measure knowledge would be very useful to organizations. Organizations could better determine the extent to which they can successfully complete future projects, improve existing processes, and, in general,

Figure 1. Hypothesized model

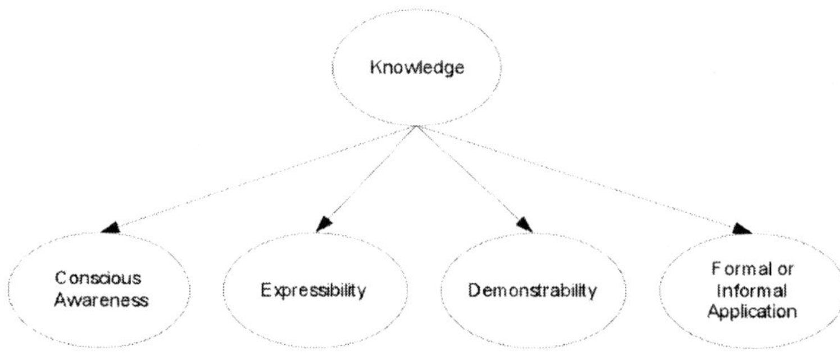

compete against other organizations so long as they know what is tacit and should be made explicit and what is tacit and should be protected (not made explicit). But measuring knowledge, and in particular tacit knowledge, has continued to be a thorn in the side of academic researchers and managers, because there are several aspects of knowledge that magnify its difficulty of measurement. There is the volume of knowledge, its form, its detail, and its value to name a few. The more of these aspects we simultaneously concern ourselves with, the more difficult measurement becomes. We suggest an initial step toward measurement would be to ascertain how much a particular type of knowledge is relied upon by an individual when working on a project. This approach would focus on the relative degree of a type of knowledge that is used.

Because the tacit nature of knowledge has received significant theoretical attention (cf. Alavi & Leidner, 2001), we have chosen it as the focus of this exploratory study. We have also selected information technology (IT) as the research domain because of the inherent nature, and therefore importance, of information and knowledge to this industry. IT organizations develop automated systems that help users process information into knowledge. In so doing, the IT worker must elicit both tacit and explicit knowledge from users. In addition, the IT workers themselves also possess both tacit and explicit knowledge that is used for developing these systems. These conditions make IT workers an excellent occupational group to use as the basis for the study.

Factor analytic techniques suggest that constructs and other manifest variables can be measured indirectly using indicators or observed variables that are reflective of the underlying constructs. The development of our instrument follows this technique by creating items thought to reflect conscious awareness (CA), expressibility (EX), demonstrability (D) and the degree of formal or informal application (F/I) of the knowledge with respect to a given task. As an example, we ask a subject to what extent he or she is consciously aware of the steps required to complete the task. Answers that indicate a greater awareness are reflective of explicit knowledge, while answers that indicate less awareness are reflective of tacit knowledge.

We created a 27 item pool, each of which was intended to capture one of the dimensions previously discussed so that we could identify a subject's perceived reliance on tacit and explicit knowledge and avoid the problems associated with attempting to identify the actual knowledge itself. We geared the items around a project task that would take about a week to complete. The items were worded in a manner that would identify the degree to which the subject relied upon either tacit or explicit knowledge to complete the project. By allowing the subject to rank each item from relied upon "completely" to relied upon "not at all" we are able incorporate the bipolar and continuous nature of the tacit/explicit knowledge construct and limit the subject's need to make the tacit knowledge explicit.

We next submitted these items to a number of knowledge management researchers who made suggestions for removing ambiguities in the wording of the items. They also categorized the items based on similarities into each of the four constructs we formulated according to our theory. We then compared the results of our experts and our original items and their groupings. As a result of these analyses, some adjustments were made to the wording of some of the items in order to remove ambiguities and to place each item clearly into one of the dimensions. The instrument uses a semantic differential presentation, which was converted into an electronic format that could be administered via the Internet. The instrument asks each subject to what extent each subject considered his or her actions taken during a specific assignment to be based on those things thought to reflect each dimension of tacit or explicit knowledge. The software then computes a score ranging from 1 to 5 depending upon where the subject places an electronic slider between the two anchors. Lower scores indicate a greater reliance on tacit knowledge; higher scores indicate a greater reliance on explicit knowledge. Some items are reverse scored since wording of those items elicited responses in the reverse direction.

The resulting instrument was then pilot tested using students in an advanced MIS course upon completion of a semester long project. Results were then tested for internal consistency and dimensionality using exploratory techniques. Further refinement of the precise wording of each item and the delivery protocol was made after analyzing these preliminary results. The resulting survey is presented in the appendix.

We next submitted the instrument to another class of advanced MIS students in computer networking fundamentals. These students were assigned a number of laboratory activities and wrote a report for each activity, which detailed their findings. The report included a synopsis of the work performed and a description of any variance from expected results. The activities chosen were ones for which the students had no prior experience, such as creating a web server, an e-mail server, imaging, setting up a Windows domain controller with DHCP and DNS services, public key encryption, packet sniffing and others; but for which each student was required to have a substantial knowledge base in order to complete. For example, in order to complete a lab on packet sniffing, the student must know what a packet is and what operations are performed on the packet when it is transmitted from one computer to another, including the structure and use of the TCP/IP protocol suite.

The sample consisted of 23 junior and senior level information systems students with varying degrees of prior experience. Although the laboratory activities were chosen so that the students had no prior experience, the group of students had been using computers in such activities as programming, system analysis and design and database design and querying. The students therefore brought with them approximately the same level of educational experience and had approximately similar knowledge bases. The average age was 21 and the group consisted of 20 men and 3 women.

A total of 10 lab experiments were performed by each subject and our survey instrument was administered after each experiment. Thus, a total of 201 observations were collected (accounting for some students who did not complete all the surveys). The results were analyzed both as a pooled group and as 10 sets of independent groups (accounting for each lab activity) for internal consistency and were factor analyzed. Factor analysis was performed to analyze the measurement model depicted in figure 1. Our premise is that if this model is supported by the data in terms of reliability and convergent and discriminant validity, then the resulting instrument can be used in subsequent tests in order to investigate the nature of the structural model. Our analysis therefore does not test any

Table 1. Reliability measurements

Factor	Alpha
All	0.83
CA	0.87
EX	0.81
F/I	0.65

hypotheses related to the underlying structural model, as would be performed in a confirmatory analysis (Anderson & Gerbing, 1988; Hatcher, 1994), but merely evaluates the "nature of the latent factors that are responsible for covariation in the data set…" (Hatcher, 1994, p. 69) This sort of restricted analysis, in which we have restricted some of the parametric values to zero based on the underlying theory allows us to respecify our model and re-estimate it in order to obtain an acceptable fit (Anderson and Gerbing, 1988). To do so, we eliminated those items that cross load or do not load on any one factor following accepted factor analytic techniques.

The results of our analysis are that a 16 item instrument demonstrates the best fit to our model. These items are marked with an asterisk in the appendix. Although one factor, demonstrability, had no significant loadings, it was stressed earlier that this dimension of tacit knowledge may not manifest itself in all cases. Because our subjects had no way of visualizing the final results of their projects, nor were the steps easily observed, we feel that the absence of this factor does not negate the theory. This dimension is very likely to appear in other situations where a clear picture of the final result is possible. In addition, the exploratory nature of this study and the unique problems which surface when using students involved in a learning situation compel us to include all 27 items of the instrument in the appendix. We discuss this further in the limitations section. Our analysis proceeds with our discussion of the statistical results from the 16 items we retained.

Figure 2. Data Supported Model

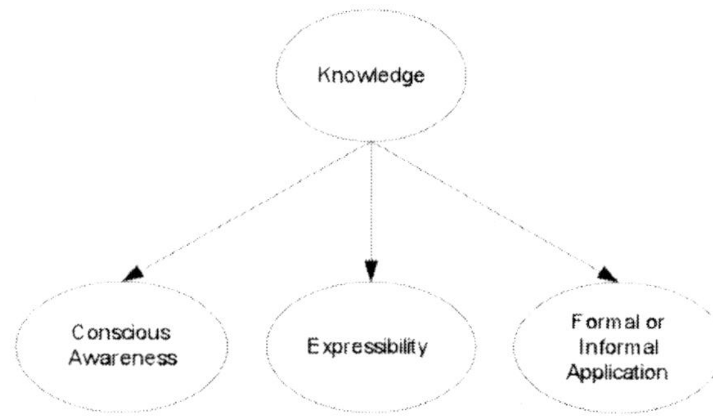

Coefficient alpha is used to estimate the internal consistency of the data and is reported in two different ways. In table 1, we provide the value of coefficient alpha for the entire data set and for the composite reliabilities of each factor. All values exceed generally accepted guidelines for minimum values (Hatcher, 1994).

Based on these values, we can say that the instrument appears to be measuring consistently and reliably.

Construct validity is demonstrated when the data collected fits the hypothesized model, and the results of the analysis show the items to load in such a way as to be interpreted according to the theory. The hypothesized model was shown earlier in figure 1, while the model supported by the data is now displayed in figure 2.

Exploratory factor analysis applied to the data set provides the following insight into the model. Three of the four factors which appear in the hypothesized model (figure 1), are supported by the data.

In order to assess convergent and discriminant validity, we attempt to determine whether the items converge to a particular factor (convergent validity) and only to a particular factor (discriminant validity). We use factor analysis to assess convergent validity and a chi-square test, a confidence interval test and a variance extracted test to assess discriminant validity (Anderson & Gerbing, 1988, Hatcher, 1994).

Table 2 displays the factor loadings, standard errors and t-values for each item. Good convergent validity is demonstrated when each t-value is significant (i.e., > 1.96 for a large sample at the 0.05 significance level) and should be at least twice the value of the standard error (Anderson & Gerbing, 1988). Data presented in table 2 support these requirements in every case, thus providing good support for convergent validity. The highest standard error (0.07) represents only 17.5% of the lowest factor loading (0.40, item 22, "Repetition"), and all t-values greatly exceed the 1.96 minimum.

To demonstrate discriminant validity, we perform a chi-square test, a confidence interval test and a variance extracted test on each of the factors (cf. Hatcher, 1994). Table 3 displays the results of the chi-square test, and it shows that the chi-square difference is significant to less than .1%. This indicates that the model with 3 factors provides a better fit than one with a single factor.

Table 4 shows that the confidence interval for the correlations of the three factors does not include the value, 1.0. This indicates that the factors are not perfectly correlated as would be indicated if the correlation coefficient equaled 1.0. In table 4, the name of each of the dimensions has been abbreviated (i.e., Conscious Awareness, CA, Expressibility, E, and Prior Learning, PL). Upper and lower limits are shown to the right of the inter-factor correlations, and the standard errors and p-values of each correlation are shown below.

A variance extraction test compares the results of the composite reliability for each factor (taken two at a time) with the squared correlation between them. This test is necessary because the size of the correlation between conscious awareness and prior learning as shown in table 4 is high enough that it is reasonable to question whether the items are measuring the same thing. Discriminant valid-

Table 2. Factor loadings, standard errors and t-values

		Conscious Awareness		
Item	**Description**	**Loading**	**Std. Err.**	**t-value**
I3	Outside Knowledge	0.56	-0.06	8.78
I16	Knowing	0.81	-0.06	13.01
I17	Instinctive	0.73	-0.06	12.53
I18	Familiar	0.96	-0.07	13.03
I21	Doing	0.74	-0.06	11.88
I26	Intuition	0.66	-0.06	11.04
		Expressibility		
I4	Written by self	0.55	-0.06	9.55
I5	Explaining	0.34	-0.06	5.47
I11	Written for others	0.62	-0.05	12.22
I12	Explained	0.68	-0.05	13.37
I14	Writing	0.53	-0.06	8.12
I22	Repetition	0.40	-0.07	5.89
I24	Clear about success	0.40	-0.06	7.03
I25	Success compared to others	0.45	-0.06	7.36
		Prior Learning		
I10	Reliance	0.72	-0.07	10.62
I20	Prior learning	0.72	-0.07	10.99

ity is demonstrated when the variance extracted estimate exceeds the correlation. This is shown in table 5 with the estimates of variance extracted on the diagonal.

Due to the nature of the research, our model fitting analysis seeks to specify an initial tentative model, which can be tested and modified in order to find a model that not only fits the data statistically, but also allows us to provide a meaningful interpretation of each parameter. Our process consisted first of screening the data for unreasonable values, outliers. We then performed an exploratory factor analysis to determine the number of factors to retain (discussed in an earlier section), and we evaluated the squared multiple correlations. We then examined the measures of overall fit.

We found no unreasonable values or anomalies, no outliers and the squared multiple correlations are reasonable. In addition, all fit indices indicate a good fit (e.g., adjusted goodness of fit, AGFI, = 0.86). The model fit seems to be more than adequate and is surprisingly good for an initial data collection set. The theorized relationships appear to hold, and the fitted model seems to accurately depict the hypothesized one.

DISCUSSION

Because of the usefulness of knowledge throughout an organization (Miller, Fern & Cardinal, 2007), a major goal of knowledge management in

Table 3. Chi-square statistics

Model	X^2	df
Uni-dimensional	862.84	104
Standard	186.94	101
Difference	675.9*	3

* p<0.001

Table 4. Inter-factor correlations, standard errors and confidence intervals

	CA	Lower Limit	Upper Limit	EX	Lower Limit	Upper Limit
EX	0.19	0.03	0.35			
	0.08					
	2.36					
PL	0.70	0.60	0.80	0.17	-0.01	0.35
	0.05			0.09		
	12.75			2.01		

Table 5. Variance extracted, squared interfactor correlations

	CA	EX	PL
CA	0.88		
EX	0.04	0.81	
PL	0.49	0.03	0.75

the organization is currently to codify knowledge so that more people in the firm have access to it (Klein, 1998). There are a number of valid reasons for this, and a number of ways employees can be motivated to do this (Osterloh & Frey, 2000), but when the knowledge held by workers is of such strategic importance that competitiveness may suffer if certain components are made public, then the current goal of codification may not always be appropriate. If managers are able to identify those portions of organizational projects that require tacit knowledge components, then a decision can be made to attempt to extract the knowledge and make it explicit for others in the organization or to protect it to help maintain competitiveness.

Without the means to measure the components of knowledge that determine its tacit or explicit character, managers will have difficulty optimizing the use of knowledge in their organizations. One of the primary goals of this study was to develop a measure for tacit and explicit knowledge. We are unaware of any scales that seek to classify activity components into either tacit or explicit, and so the development of our scale proceeded from scratch and was guided only by our knowledge of the theory. The resulting 16 item scale provides reliability and validity both from a statistical standpoint and from a theoretical one. Identification of tacit knowledge components is necessary to inform and train additional workers in these skills on the one hand and to protect competitiveness on the other.

As an example where the use of this scale might be appropriate within the IT field, consider a firm engaged in custom software development. A market leader in this field may enjoy a competitive position because it can expeditiously turn out products that are of the highest quality and of great use to end users. In short, the firm creates end user applications quickly that perform to the users' specifications. If the firm can identify the pockets of tacit knowledge among its senior developers, it might decide to make it explicit and allow less experienced developers to benefit from this knowledge. Such a decision, however, must be tempered with the realization that the newly codified knowledge may be easier for competing firms to exploit. In any event, the identification of those components of tacit knowledge is important and the scale presented herein is a first step towards achieving that goal.

LIMITATIONS, IMPLICATIONS AND FUTURE RESEARCH

This study has certain limitations that we now address. First, the study utilized subjects who were students engaged in a relatively explicit task. This could limit the generalizability of the findings. Although it is important to examine situations that range from highly tacit, mixed tacit/explicit, and highly explicit, this first study only examined a predominantly explicit task. Therefore, it may not generalize to tasks that are more tacit in nature. Certainly, future studies can focus on a variety of tacit and explicit situations in order to gain a more complete understanding of the usefulness of the instrument. One approach would be to utilize a field experiment design and obtain responses from practitioners with greater experience levels.

Another limitation with this study is the potential ambiguity surrounding the tacit end of the scale. There is some question as to whether tacit knowledge is being measured or the subjects' responses are simply demonstrating a lack of knowledge. To illustrate, consider a student who responds to item 17, which asks the subject to what extent his actions seemed instinctive versus reasoned or considered. If this student had not learned the material well, then his response might well be that it was instinctive (indicating a tacit component), since the student would be unable to explain it. Although the theory and research used to support the construction of the instrument provide extensive support for measuring the tacitness of knowledge, we felt that additional assurance that tacit knowledge was being measured (as opposed to a lack of knowledge) would be beneficial. Therefore, we decided to utilize a secondary examination of the data based on the Reber's (1993) theory from evolutionary psychology that states that the use of tacit knowledge results in relatively less variability in performance than does the use of explicit knowledge. In order to apply this theory and test our sample, we divided the sample into two parts—one part includes those whose score was below the theoretical mean ($n_1 = 37$) and the other includes scores above this mean ($n_2 = 140$)—and compared the standard deviation of performance scores between the groups. Performance scores for the group which relied more on tacit knowledge had a standard deviation of 2.3; while the standard deviation for the explicit group was 4.6. Although not conclusive, we believe that this computation provides additional support for the validity of the instrument itself.

Finally, a third limitation involves the inability to measure tacit knowledge directly. Based on the previous discussion about the nature of tacit knowledge and the problems associated with attempting to directly measure it, we felt that an indirect approach was the best way to examine it. By limiting the instrument to address a recall of behaviors that reflect the characteristics of the knowledge required to complete the task and not the actual knowledge used in the behavior, we feel that this problem is substantially reduced. At this point in time there is no perfect way to measure the exact amount of tacit and explicit knowledge possessed and used by an individual, however we believe that this study is an important first step toward that end.

The usefulness of the instrument will be established through its use and extension in future studies. If the instrument and/or future iterations of it are found to be useful in the identification of tacit and explicit knowledge, there are several areas within information systems that we see as potential users of information collected from the instrument. Here are but a few:

1) In the area of systems analysis, IT workers are charged with making sense of business processes and converting these processes into automated systems;
2) Knowledge workers who elicit tacit knowledge from domain experts can identify tacit and explicit components and focus their attention on those that need to be codified;
3) Data modeling and normalization of data structures is an enormously complex activity that contains largely tacit components. Identification of these components might make it easier to understand and model efficiently; and
4) Programmers are sometimes hired to be *ad hoc* systems analysts. For those companies who hire programmers who must figure out the business processes and convert them into systems, the use of tacit knowledge is pervasive and not easily passed along to new hires. For this group turning tacit knowledge into explicit knowledge might improve competitiveness by reducing development time (Madsen, et al., 2008).

Strategic value in information systems and therefore competitive advantage are obtained through such things as:

1) Knowledge appraisal systems that can accurately assess the value of individual and organizational knowledge (Rasmussen & Haggerty, 2008);
2) The time to implement a new system—the quicker one firm can do it, the more likely they are to acquire first mover advantages and increase market share;
3) Software quality: the higher the quality of the product, the higher the customer loyalty and the more business the firm is likely to receive;
4) Software capability: the more it is user friendly, the greater its ability to withstand adverse events (viruses, locking up or other

security issues), and the better its performance under load, the more likely the firm will obtain more business.

5) Worker-Task alignment: appropriate matching of workers with tasks may enable firms to increase utilization of tacit and explicit knowledge bases, thereby enhancing organizational performance (Chen & Edgington, 2005).
6) Paying attention to geographic career mobility of employees. Career mobility can influence knowledge transfer (Almeida & Kogut, 1999) so firms should identify the most strategically valuable human resources (those possessing important knowledge bases) and do more to increase their job satisfaction in order to increase employee retention where appropriate. If this proves too difficult or ineffective, firms can focus on knowledge extraction or codification before employees become disenchanted and leave the firm. The optimal course of action will depend on the explicitness or tacitness of the knowledge to be transferred.
7) Recognition of the trend toward self-forming, shared-access systems for engaging in knowledge work. Expert power is the principal force that provides leadership within these systems (Ehin, 2008), and organizations should recognize the consequential importance of tacit knowledge present in them.

Within these strategic areas, managers need to know what knowledge to protect and how to protect it from competitors. Competitors can hire away people with such knowledge or they can engage in less than honest methods of obtaining it, but in general the more tacit the knowledge is, the more difficult it is to extract and utilize.

These same characteristics hold true for internal transfer of knowledge. However, knowledge sharing can be amplified by paying attention to reputational enhancement of employees, experience levels, and network embeddedness (social capital) that employees possess (Wasko and Faraj, 2005). Thus, identifying when and where knowledge is more tacit and likely to result in protracted transfer procedures, organizations can introduce additional mechanisms to speed up transfer when and where it is deemed appropriate. For example, interdivisional knowledge has been shown to more strongly influence invention than either intra-divisional or inter-firm knowledge (Miller, Fern, & Cardinal, 2007). Moreover, not all existing knowledge about an organizational practice is useful in different parts of an organization (Madsen, Riis, and Waehrens, 2008). Thus, a focused knowledge transfer strategy would likely provide greater returns than would a more general policy for the organization. There are also additional benefits to this because a firm's future absorptive capacity can be positively influenced by accessing and transferring new knowledge (Todorova & Durisin, 2007). Therefore, a firm can increase its ability to manage knowledge it comes across in the future.

Finally, recent advances in research have identified social networks as informal, self-forming processes that are instrumental in the transfer of knowledge (Busch, 2009). These networks are capable of enhancing organizational learning and enabling organizations, and individuals within them, to act on knowledge with little or no formal involvement by managers. Thus, as time goes on, managers are likely to be less and less able to orchestrate the management of knowledge within their organizations (Ehin, 2008). Instead, they will be responsible for setting up the organizational structure that can influence network formation. In addition, managers may be able to assess the types of knowledge in use within these networks by using measurement devices, such as the one offered here, to identify various characteristics of the knowledge. Direct management of the knowledge may be less attainable, but some degree of awareness will still be possible and probably fruitful to achieve.

CONCLUSION

This study presents a theory of tacit and explicit knowledge in terms of the components that reflect the degree of tacitness of knowledge. We do so in order to present a scale that can be used to identify whether individuals rely more on tacit or explicit knowledge in the completion of a task and to identify what tasks might be more conducive to either tacit or explicit knowledge. That is, some work within organizations may require predominantly tacit or explicit knowledge by nature, and this nature may further be influenced by the individuals performing the work. To the extent that we can identify those areas in which people rely more on tacit knowledge, we can evaluate these areas in terms of competitiveness and decide whether to make this knowledge explicit or not. We may also be able to classify people as relying more on tacit or explicit knowledge in the performance of their duties and assign them accordingly. Such matching of individuals to type of knowledge work naturally would require additional research, and the instrument developed here may be helpful in that research.

REFERENCES

Alavi, M., & Leidner, D. E. (2001). Review: Knowledge management and knowledge management systems: Conceptual foundations and research issues. *MIS Quarterly*, *25*(1), 107–136. doi:10.2307/3250961

Almeida, P., & Kogut, B. (1999). Localization of knowledge and the mobility of engineers in regional networks. *Management Science*, *45*(7), 905–917. doi:10.1287/mnsc.45.7.905

Anderson, J. C., & Gerbing, D. W. (1988). Structural equation modeling in practice: A review and recommended two-step approach. *Psychological Bulletin*, *103*, 411–423. doi:10.1037/0033-2909.103.3.411

Badaracco, J. L. (1991). *The knowledge link.* Boston, MA: Harvard Business School Press.

Becerra-Fernandez, I., & Sabherwal, R. (2001). Organizational knowledge management: A contingency perspective. *Journal of Management Information Systems*, *18*(1), 23–55.

Bloodgood, J., & Salisbury, W. D. (2001). Understanding the influence of organizational change strategies on information technology and knowledge management strategies. *Decision Support Systems*, *31*, 55–69. doi:10.1016/S0167-9236(00)00119-6

Busch, P. (2008). *Tacit knowledge in organizational learning.* Hershey, PA: IGI Publishing.

Chen, A. N. K., & Edgington, T. M. (2005). Assessing value in organizational knowledge creation: Considerations for knowledge workers. *MIS Quarterly*, *29*(2), 279–309.

Conner, K. R., & Prahalad, C. K. (1996). A resource-based theory of the firm: Knowledge versus Opportunism. *Organization Science*, *7*(5), 477–501. doi:10.1287/orsc.7.5.477

Ehin, C. (2008). Un-managing knowledge workers. *Journal of Intellectual Capital*, *9*(3), 337–350. doi:10.1108/14691930810891965

Flores, L. G., Catalanello, R. F., Rau, D., & Saxena, N. (2008). Organizational learning as a moderator of the effect of strategic planning on company performance. *International Journal of Management*, *25*(3), 569–577.

Ghemawat, P. (1986). Sustainable advantage. *Harvard Business Review*, (September-October): 53–58.

Godfrey, P., & Hill, C. W. L. (1995). The problem of unobservables in strategic management research. *Strategic Management Journal*, *16*, 519–533. doi:10.1002/smj.4250160703

Grover, V., & Davenport, T. H. (2001). General perspectives on knowledge management: Fostering a research agenda. *Journal of Management Information Systems, 18*(1), 5–21.

Hall, R. (1992). The strategic analysis of intangible resources. *Strategic Management Journal, 13*, 135–144. doi:10.1002/smj.4250130205

Hansen, M. T., Nohria, N., & Tierney, T. (1999). What's your strategy for managing knowledge? *Harvard Business Review, 77*(2), 106–118.

Hasher, L., & Zacks, R. T. (1979). Automatic and effortful processes in memory. *Journal of Experimental Psychology. General, 108*(3), 356–388. doi:10.1037/0096-3445.108.3.356

Hatcher, L. (1994). *A step-by-step approach to using the SAS® system for factor analysis and structural equation modeling*. The SAS Institute, Cary, N.C.

Klein, G. (1998). *Sources of power*. Camridge, MA: The MIT Press.

Kulkarni, U. R., Ravindran, S., & Freeze, R. (2006). A knowledge management success model: Theoretical development and empirical validation. *Journal of Management Information Systems, 23*(3), 309–347. doi:10.2753/MIS0742-1222230311

Langer, E., Blank, A., & Chanowitz, B. (1978). The mindlessness of ostensibly thoughtful action: The role of "placebic" information in interpersonal interaction. *Journal of Personality and Social Psychology, 36*, 635–642. doi:10.1037/0022-3514.36.6.635

Liebowitz, J. (2009). *Knowledge retention.* New York: CRC Press.

Madsen, E. S., Riis, J. O., & Waehrens, B. V. (2008). The knowledge dimension of manufacturing transfers. *Strategic Outsourcing: An International Journal, 1*(3), 198–209. doi:10.1108/17538290810915272

McDonough, E. F., Zack, M. H., Lin, H., & Berdrow, I. (2008). Integrating innovation style and knowledge into strategy. *MIT Sloan Management Review, 50*(1), 52–58.

Miller, D. J., Fern, M. J., & Cardinal, L. B. (2007). The use of knowledge for technological innovation within diversified firms. *Academy of Management Journal, 50*(2), 308–326.

Nelson, R., & Winter, S. (1982). *An evolutionary theory of economic change*. Cambridge, MA: The Belknap Press of Harvard University Press.

Nonaka, I., & Takeuchi, H. (1995). *The knowledge-creating company*. New York: Oxford University Press.

Osterloh, M., & Frey, B. S. (2000). Motivation, knowledge, transfer, and organizational forms. *Organization Science, 11*(5), 538–550. doi:10.1287/orsc.11.5.538.15204

Paas, F., Renkl, A., & Sweller, J. (2004). Cognitive load theory: Instructional implications of the interaction between information structures and cognitive architecture. *Instructional Science, 32*, 1–8. doi:10.1023/B:TRUC.0000021806.17516.d0

Polanyi, M. (1962). *Personal knowledge*. Chicago: The University of Chicago Press.

Polanyi, M. (1967). *The tacit dimension*. London: Routledge & Kegan Paul.

Rasmussen, H. S., & Haggerty, N. (2008). Knowledge appraisal and knowledge management systems: Judging what we know. *Journal of Organizational and End User Computing, 20*(1), 17–34.

Reber, A. S. (1967). Implicit learning of artificial grammars. *Journal of Verbal Learning and Verbal Behavior, 6*, 855–863. doi:10.1016/S0022-5371(67)80149-X

Reber, A. S. (1969). Transfer of syntactic structure in synthetic languages. *Journal of Experimental Psychology, 81*(1), 115–119. doi:10.1037/h0027454

Reber, A. S. (1989). More thoughts on the unconscious: Reply to Brody and to Lewicki and Hall. *Journal of Experimental Psychology. General, 118*(3), 242–244. doi:10.1037/0096-3445.118.3.242

Reber, A. S. (1993). *Implicit learning and tacit knowledge*. New York: Oxford University Press.

Scribner, S. (1986). Thinking in action: Some characteristics of practical thought. In Sternberg & Wagner (Ed.), *Practical Intelligence*. Cambridge, UK: Cambridge University Press.

Terlaak, A., & Gong, Y. (2008). Vicarious learning and inferential accuracy in adoption processes. *Academy of Management Review, 33*(4), 846–868.

Todorova, G., & Durisin, B. (2007). Absorptive capacity: Valuing a reconceptualization. *Academy of Management Review, 32*(3), 774–786.

Van den Bos, E., & Poletiek, F. H. (2008). Effects of grammar complexity on artificial grammar learning. *Memory & Cognition, 36*(6), 1122–1131. doi:10.3758/MC.36.6.1122

Wagner, R. K., & Sternberg, R. J. (1986). Tacit knowledge and intelligence in the everyday world. In Sternberg & Wagner (Eds.), *Practical Intelligence*. Cambridge, UK: Cambridge University Press.

Wasko, M. M., & Faraj, S. (2005). Why should I share? Examining social capital and knowledge contribution in electronic networks of practice. *MIS Quarterly, 29*(1), 35–57.

APPENDIX

After completing a project, each subject was given a survey form on which he or she was asked to assess his or her agreement (from complete agreement to not at all) with 27 items. The phrase, "Now that you have completed your project, to what extent..." was placed at the top of the form, and the subject was asked to complete the phrase with each item and then indicate his or her level of agreement along a sliding scale, which ranged from completely to not at all. Scores were recorded electronically and converted to a 5-point Likert type score. Some items were reverse scored and items with an asterisk were included in the final 16.

1. Did you rely on written instructions?
2. Did you rely on material presented in class?
3.* Did you rely on knowledge gained from outside this class?
4.* Could the knowledge you used be written down?
5.* Would you have difficulty in explaining the steps?
6. Would viewing the finished product allow you to understand the steps involved?
7. Were you conscious of the steps required?
8. Did you utilize formal procedures?
9. Did you organize the steps you used?
10.* Did you rely on steps learned previously?
11.* Could the steps be written down so that any student could be successful?
12.* Could the steps be explained in class so that any student could be successful?
13. Did the solutions come to you step by step?
15. Would it be easier to show other students how to do this than tell them?
16.* Did you feel you knew how to do this without thinking about it?
17.* Did your actions seem instinctive instead of reasoned (or considered)?
18.* Were you already familiar with how to do this?
19. Did you spend more time planning the necessary steps or doing them?
20.* Did you rely on what you had learned previously?
21.* Were you able to do this without thinking about it?
22. Did you feel that you were repeating certain steps?
23.* Did you have to invent new steps?
24.* Are you clear about your success on your finished project?
25.* Could you explain why you did better or worse on this project than others?
26.* Did you rely on your intuition?
27. Did you change your typical approach to solving problems?

Chapter 18
Introducing Elasticity for Spatial Knowledge Management

David A. Gadish
California State University Los Angeles, USA

ABSTRACT

The internal validity of a spatial database can be discovered using the data contained within one or more databases. Spatial consistency includes topological consistency, or the conformance to topological rules. Discovery of inconsistencies in spatial data is an important step for improvement of spatial data quality as part of the knowledge management initiative. An approach for detecting topo-semantic inconsistencies in spatial data is presented. Inconsistencies between pairs of neighboring spatial objects are discovered by comparing relations between spatial objects to rules. A property of spatial objects, called elasticity, has been defined to measure the contribution of each of the objects to inconsistent behavior. Grouping of multiple objects, which are inconsistent with one another, based on their elasticity is proposed. The ability to discover groups of neighboring objects that are inconsistent with one another can serve as the basis of an effort to understand and increase the quality of spatial data sets. Elasticity should therefore be incorporated into knowledge management systems that handle spatial data.

INTRODUCTION

Geographic information systems (GIS) databases have gained popularity in different business sectors in recent years. GIS databases, which consist of vector based data elements including points, lines, and polygons (Aronoff, 1995). The elements in these databases are related to one another in terms of their location as well as in terms of their semantic interpretation (Clementini et al., 1993; Egenhoffer, 1991). Consistency is a measure of internal validity of these databases. Inconsistency is the opposite of consistency (Kainz, 1991). Inconsistency can be measured in terms of the number of objects that are in relations with one or multiple objects that do not satisfy one or more rules which describe the data (Cockcroft, 2004; Lutz et al., 2007; Xu, 2007). For example, it would be inconsistent to map a property boundary to the center of an adjacent road. Consistency is assessed using information contained within one or more databases. Spatial consistency includes topological consistency, or the conformance to topological rules (Kainz, 1995). An example of spatial inconsistency is illustrated in Figure 1 where two buildings slightly overlap their properties.

Detection of inconsistencies in spatial data is a key activity in an effort to manage the consistency of spatial data (Servigne et al., 2000). It is useful for evaluating, maintaining and enhancing spatial data quality. Since data in spatial databases is constantly evolving, there is an on-going need for detection and adjustment of inconsistencies. This need is amplified as two or more spatial databases are combined to discover and manage knowledge.

An approach for detecting inconsistencies in spatial data is presented. Inconsistencies between pairs of neighboring spatial objects (consisting of spatial geometry and non-spatial attributes) are detected by comparing relations between spatial objects to rules. A property of spatial objects (or simply objects), called elasticity, is defined to indicate the contribution of each of the objects to inconsistent behavior. Grouping of multiple objects, which are inconsistent with one another, based on their elasticity is proposed. These groupings become the basis for an effort to increase the quality of spatial data. This process is illustrated in Figure 2.

Elasticity and related concepts discussed in this paper could be incorporated into a Knowledge Management toolkits such as those covered by Balmisse et al. (2007). The ability to determine and enhance the quality of data will help quantify and strengthen the validity of discovered organizational knowledge.

More and more organizations in all business sectors are integrating spatial (location based) data with their existing non-spatial data sets. Spatial data integration and the resulting quality of this integration is therefore critical to integration of more and more non-spatial databases and to knowledge discovery in these combined data sets.

INCONSISTENCIES BETWEEN PAIRS OF NEIGHBORING OBJECTS

A particular object may be inconsistent with more than one of its neighbors. Detecting inconsistencies between pairs of neighboring objects in spatial databases is presented in this section.

First, objects that are neighbors with other objects are determined. The type of relations which exist between neighboring objects is essential. Rules that describe relations between

Figure 1. Example of inconsistencies in spatial data

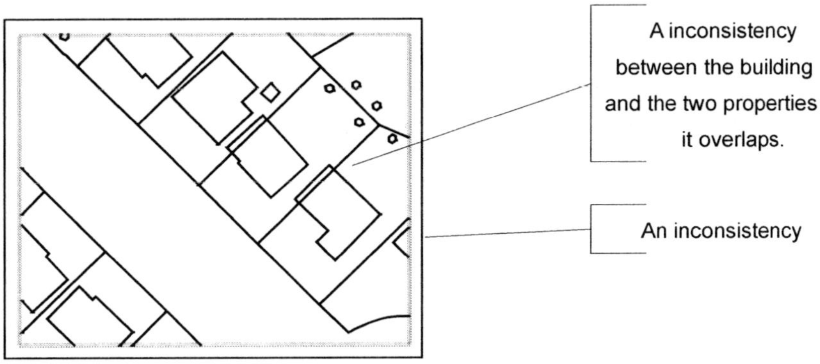

neighboring objects as well as rules that govern the relations of an object with its neighbors are identified. These rules are then used to compare each object's relations to other objects. The comparison produces a list of objects that do not satisfy rules applicable to relationships with their neighboring objects.

Detecting Neighboring Objects

Neighboring objects are determined for each object in the database.

A layer in a spatial database is a subset of objects with a common semantic interpretation. Consider object *i* on layer *L* and another object *j* on layer *M*. Layers *L* and *M* may originate from different data sets, from the same data set. These objects *i* and *j* may also belong to the same layer *L*.

A threshold distance *T* between all objects on layers *L* and *M* is used to determine whether two objects are at a close proximity or not. If the minimal Euclidean distance between two objects is less than or equals to *T*, the two objects O_i and O_j are said to be *Neighboring Objects*, otherwise they are not.

Each layer *L*, as well as each pair of layers *L* and *M* in a spatial database is assigned a corresponding threshold *T*. The threshold *T* may be set to the same or different value for each pair of layers.

Detecting the Type of Relation between Neighboring Objects

The relation between each pair of neighboring objects is determined. The criteria that must be satisfied for a pair of neighboring objects to be considered of a particular relation type are based on the nine-intersection model (Egenhofer et al., 1991) which classifies topological binary relations between shape objects. The classification is based on the intersection of the boundaries, interiors and exteriors of object pairs. These are represented as a 3x3 matrix:

$$\begin{bmatrix} \delta i \cap \delta j & \delta i \cap j^{o} & \delta i \cap j^{-1} \\ i^{o} \cap \delta j & i^{o} \cap j^{o} & i^{o} \cap j^{-1} \\ i^{-1} \cap \delta j & i^{-1} \cap j^{o} & i^{-1} \cap j^{-1} \end{bmatrix}$$

Each of these nine sets may be empty $\varnothing$ or non-empty $\neg\varnothing$. This results in a total of 9^2 possible

Figure 2. The process of creating elasticity-based groupings

combinations. Only eight of these combinations result in valid topological relations in R^2. The remaining combinations do not produce meaningful topological relations. The different relation types between pairs of shape objects are:

$$\begin{bmatrix} \varnothing & \varnothing & \neg\varnothing \\ \varnothing & \varnothing & \neg\varnothing \\ \neg\varnothing & \neg\varnothing & \neg\varnothing \end{bmatrix} \rightarrow i \quad Disjoint \quad j \tag{1}$$

$$\begin{bmatrix} \varnothing & \varnothing & \neg\varnothing \\ \neg\varnothing & \neg\varnothing & \neg\varnothing \\ \varnothing & \varnothing & \neg\varnothing \end{bmatrix} \rightarrow i \quad Contains \quad j \tag{2}$$

$$\begin{bmatrix} \varnothing & \neg\varnothing & \varnothing \\ \varnothing & \neg\varnothing & \varnothing \\ \neg\varnothing & \neg\varnothing & \neg\varnothing \end{bmatrix} \rightarrow i \quad Inside \quad j \tag{3}$$

$$\begin{bmatrix} \neg\varnothing & \varnothing & \neg\varnothing \\ \varnothing & \varnothing & \neg\varnothing \\ \neg\varnothing & \neg\varnothing & \neg\varnothing \end{bmatrix} \rightarrow i \quad Meet \quad j \tag{4}$$

$$\begin{bmatrix} \neg\varnothing & \varnothing & \varnothing \\ \varnothing & \neg\varnothing & \varnothing \\ \varnothing & \varnothing & \neg\varnothing \end{bmatrix} \rightarrow i \quad Equal \quad j \tag{5}$$

$$\begin{bmatrix} \neg\varnothing & \varnothing & \neg\varnothing \\ \neg\varnothing & \neg\varnothing & \neg\varnothing \\ \varnothing & \varnothing & \neg\varnothing \end{bmatrix} \rightarrow i \quad Covers \quad j \tag{6}$$

The relations *disjoint, contains, inside, meet, equal, covers, covered-by*, and *overlap* provide complete coverage for relations between pairs of shape objects, and are mutually exclusive, i.e. exactly one of these topological relations holds true between any two shape-objects in R^2. Therefore the *observed relation* between object i on layer L and j on layer M takes one of eight relation type values: *contains, inside, meet, equal, covers, covered-by*, and *overlap*.

The content of databases can now be analyzed to determine the relationship type of each pair of neighboring objects (which were identified in section 2.1).

Determining Rules that Govern Relations between Neighboring Objects

Rules, which consider topological relations alone, are based only on the shape of the object. This is not sufficient for detecting inconsistencies in spatial data, as this does not translate to a comprehensive description of real world situations. Semantic information is the meaning of real world entities described by the objects. This information is combined with topological relations to discover rules.

Considering the semantics of objects, it is possible to define which topological relations are consistent and which are not. For example, a building inside a residential property is a permitted relation, while a building inside a road is not. In either case, the topology of the scenario is described as a polygon inside another polygon. Therefore the semantics of each object is required to determine which relationship is allowed and which is not.

Rules governing relations between objects can be broadly classified based on the semantics of the real world entities that these objects represent. Since each layer's objects correspond to real world entities with a different semantic meaning, this discussion continues in terms of layers. Rules governing relations between objects are therefore determined based on the layers of corresponding objects.

Two types of rules are used in this chapter: (1) rules based on the analysis of the relation between each object and <u>each</u> of their neighbors and (2) rules based on the analysis of the relations between each object and <u>all</u> of its neighboring objects.

The first type of rule, describing the relationship between a pair of objects is called a P-Rule. The aim is to determine rules such as "A tree is inside a property" or "A road meets a property." Binary rules between pairs of objects on layers L and M that have relation type *Contains*.

The second type of rule, describing the relationship of an object with all its neighboring objects is called an M-Rule. The aim is to determine rules such as "a building is inside a property 1 time" or "A property meets a road between 0 and 2 times." These rules are defined in terms of two layers, a relation type, and upper and lower bounds for the number of objects on the second layer that can be in the specified relation type with the object on the first layer.

These P-Rules and M-Rules play important roles in detection and adjustment of inconsistencies.

Detecting Inconsistent Pair-Wise Relations (IPR)

An Inconsistent Pair-wise Relation, or IPR, is an observed relation between two objects *i* and *j* which does not satisfy any of the P-Rules or M-Rules that correspond to layers *L* and *M*. It is denoted as $IPR_{ij} = T$. If the rules that correspond to these layers are satisfied, an IPR does not exist; this is denoted as $IPR_{ij} = F$.

Each object's relation to its neighboring object is checked against P-Rules and M-Rules to determine if such an IPR exists.

Figure 3. An IPR due to a violation of a p-rule

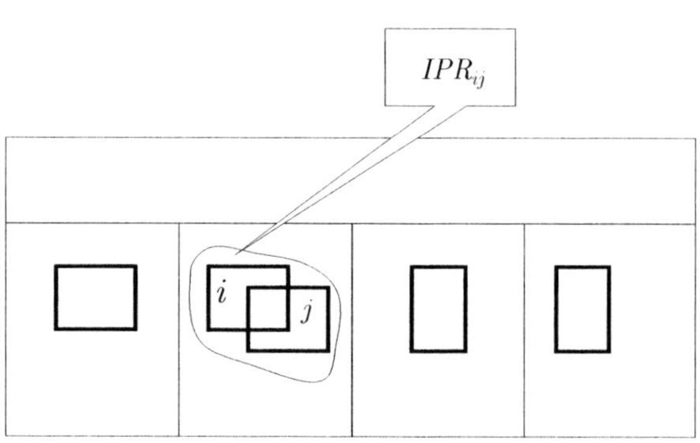

Examples of IPRs

Consider the following two examples to illustrate this process. Assume the following two rules exist: (1) "house disjoint house" (2) "fire hydrant inside property between 0 and 1 times." Then the objects in Figure 3 violate the first rule, as there are two houses which overlap one another.

The objects in Figure 4 violate the second rule, as there are two fire hydrants inside one property.

Graphical Representation of an IPR

An IPR is schematically represented in Figure 5 as two "object" nodes linked with a gray line indicating that an inconsistency exists between them.

Having proposed a process for identification of inconsistencies between pairs of objects, the next task is to formulate the identification of inconsistencies among multiple objects. Before this can be accomplished (Section 4), a property of objects is defined in the following section.

ELASTICITY ANALYSIS OF IPRs

The Elasticity Property of Objects

An inconsistency in a spatial database can involve two or more objects. A technique is proposed to characterize objects, which is then used to group all objects which form an inconsistency from multiple IPRs.

Consider an object that is inconsistent with one or more of its neighbors, that is, the object is involved in one or more IPRs. An example of such a situation is illustrated in Figure 6. In this case the inconsistency involves four objects, and three IPRs. They are: IPR_{ij}, IPR_{ik}, and IPR_{il}.

In such situations, a number of objects may be inconsistent with one another. This may be due to an inaccurate position of only one, or

Figure 4. An IPR due to a violation of an m-rule

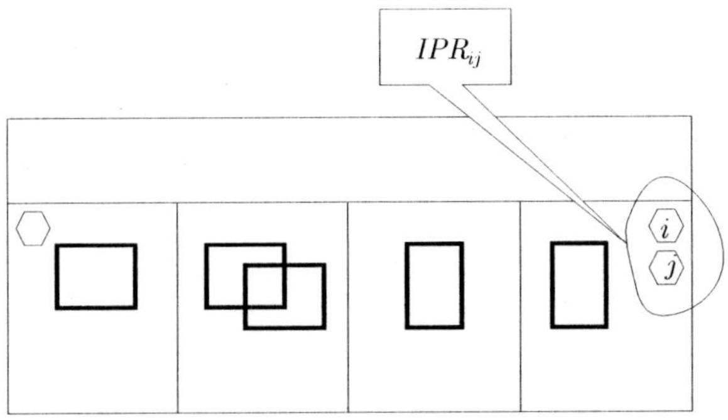

Figure 5. A schematic view of an IPR

Figure 6. An inconsistency involving four objects

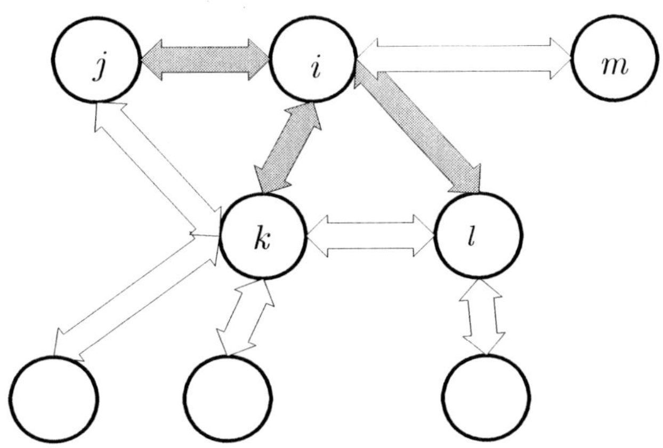

possibly more than one of these objects. That is, not all objects contribute to the existence of IPRs in this situation to the same extent. A weight is assigned to each object that is involved in one or more IPRs to reflect this disparity. This weight is the new elasticity property of an object, which is defined as follows:

Consider object *i*: Let I_i be the number of objects *j* that it is inconsistent with. Let N_i be the number of objects *j* that are neighbors with it. Then the elasticity property of object *i* is defined as:

$$ELS_i = \frac{I_i}{N_i}$$

Characteristics of Elasticity

The elasticity property of objects has a number of characteristics that are discussed in this section.

The elasticity has lower and upper bounds, that is $0 \leq ELS_i \leq 1$. The elasticity property of objects can be demonstrated with the following five scenarios:

Minimal Elasticity

Elasticity of a consistent object is zero. The elasticity of an object is zero if the object has no neighbors with which it is in an inconsistent binary relation. In this case, $ELS_i = 0$. This can only occur if

$$\frac{I_i}{N_i} = 0,$$

that is if $I_i = 0$. In other words i has no neighbor j such that IPR_{ij} exists.

Negative Elasticity

An object can not have negative elasticity. The elasticity of an object can not be less than zero. $ELS_i < 0$ would occur only if either I_i or N_i are negative values, which is not possible by their definition.

Maximal Elasticity

The elasticity of an object can not be greater than 1. $ELS_i > 1$ would occur only if $I_i > N_i$, that is i has more inconsistent neighbors than neighbors. This is not possible by definition of I_i and N_i.

Full Elasticity

The elasticity of an object may equal 1. $ELS_i = 1$ only when $I_i = N_i$, that is i is pair-wise inconsistent with all its neighbors.

Partial Elasticity

The elasticity of an object may be a value between 0 and 1. $0 < ELS_i < 1$ only when $I_i < N_i$, that is i is pair-wise inconsistent with at least one but not all of its neighbors.

Example of Elasticity

To understand the significance of the elasticity of an object, consider an example where two inconsistent pair-wise relations are detected between three objects $i, j,$ and k, which are neighbors with one another, such that $IPR_{ij} = T$ and $IPR_{ik} = T$. No IPR is detected between j, and k, and no additional IPRs are detected between $i, j,$ and k and any other of their neighbors. Suppose i has two neighbors (j, and k), and j and k each has 6 and 4 neighboring objects, respectively. Then

$$ELS_i = \frac{2}{2} = 1,$$

$$ELS_j = \frac{1}{6},$$

and

$$ELS_k = \frac{1}{4}.$$

Since object i is inconsistent with all objects it is neighbors with, it has a high elasticity value. This example is illustrated in Figure 7.

The higher the elasticity value, the more likely the object to contribute to the inconsistency. This is the case since an object that is inconsistent with all or many of its neighbors is likely to be the source of the inconsistency more so than an object that is inconsistent with relatively few of its neighbors.

FORMATION OF ELASTICITY-BASED IPR GROUPINGS (EIGS)

Real world inconsistencies are likely to occur between two or more objects. A technique to group the corresponding objects of a multi-object inconsistency in the spatial representation is required. This can be achieved by grouping objects using knowledge of the IPRs they are part of, as well as their elasticity.

Elasticity is used to group IPRs into multi-object structures that correspond to inconsistencies among multiple entities in the real world. The relative contribution of objects to these multi-object inconsistencies is established using elasticity.

Figure 7. Example of elasticity calculation for objects

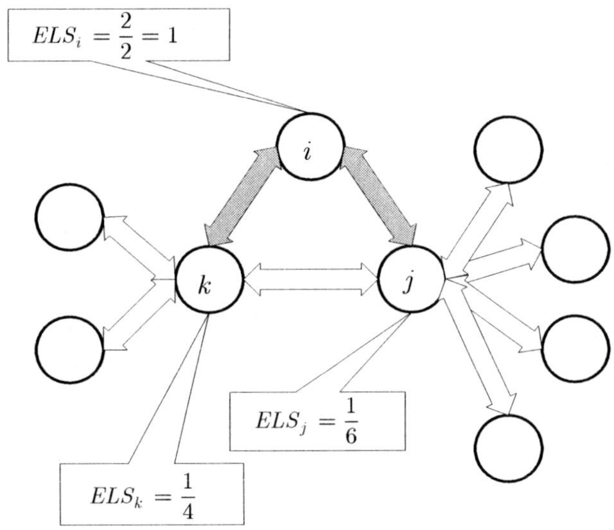

Interpretation of IPRs in Terms of Elasticity

A number of observations can be made about an IPR by looking at the elasticity of its member objects. The observations are later used for grouping IPRs into multi-object inconsistencies. Consider a pair of objects O_i and O_j such that $IPR_{ij} = T$. In determining the elasticity of each of the two objects, two types of IPRs are distinguished.

Unbalanced IPR

If $ELS_i > ELS_j$ then object *i* is referred to as the higher elasticity object and *j* as the lower elasticity object. This occurs if one of the following conditions is satisfied:

- The objects are inconsistent with one another and with no other objects. Object *i* has fewer neighbors than *j*. In this scenario we conclude that the object *i* that has fewer numbers of neighbors N is more likely to be used as the basis for grouping IPRs.
- Both objects have the same number of neighbors. Object *i* is inconsistent with more objects then *j*. In this scenario we conclude that the object, which is inconsistent with more of its neighbors, is more likely to be used as the basis for grouping IPRs.
- The rate of the number of objects *i* is inconsistent with, divided by the number of objects it is neighbors with, is greater than the rate of the number of objects *j* is inconsistent with divided by the number of objects it is neighbors with. In this scenario we conclude that the object with the higher rate is more likely to be used as the basis for grouping IPRs.

Balanced IPR

If $ELS_i = ELS_j$ then objects *i* and *j* have the same level of elasticity. This is referred to as a balanced IPR. It occurs if:

- The objects are inconsistent with one another and with no other objects. Object *i* has the same number of neighbors as does *j*. In this scenario, no further grouping is required.
- Both objects have the same number of neighbors. Object *i* is inconsistent with the

same number of objects as does j. In this scenario additional information is required to determine which object will be used as the basis for grouping IPRs.

- The number of objects i is inconsistent with, relative to the number of objects it is neighbors with, is the same as the number of objects j is inconsistent with, relative to the number of objects it is neighbors with. In this scenario the object that has a larger number of IPRs is more likely to be used as the basis for grouping IPRs.

Defining EIGs

An elasticity-based IPR grouping (EIG) is a set of one or more objects where the object of highest elasticity in the group forms an IPR with each of the remaining objects in the group.

Example of an EIG

To clarify this definition, consider the following situation: Consider three objects i, j, and k that are neighbors with one another, but with no other objects. Let i and j form an inconsistent pair-wise relation IPR_{ij} such that $ELS_i > ELS_j$. Let i and k form an inconsistent pair-wise relation IPR_{ik} such that $ELS_i > ELS_k$. Objects i, j, k are said to constitute an inconsistent set since object i has the highest elasticity value among the three objects and it forms an IPR with each of the other two objects. This is referred to as an elasticity-based IPR grouping (EIG) and denote it as ELS_{ijk}. This is illustrated in Figure 8.

Detecting EIGs

This is extended into a technique to analyze all IPRs in the database and group them into EIGs based on the elasticity of the objects which form the IPRs:

- *Determine all IPRs.*
- *Extract a list of all objects in all IPRs and determine their elasticity values.*
- *Sort the list of objects in descending order by elasticity.*
- *Sort objects that have the same elasticity values by the number of IPRs they are a part of, that is,* I_i *in descending order.*
- *Create the first empty EIG, to which objects will be assigned.*
- *For each object in the sorted list (whether it has or has not yet been assigned to constructed EIGs):*
    - o *Determine all IPRs in which this object participates.*
    - o *For each such IPR:*
        - ▪ *Identify the second object in the IPR.*
        - ▪ *Check the remaining objects in the sorted list (those objects with the same or smaller elasticity values) for occurrence of the second object regardless if they are already part of one or more EIGs.*
            - *If the second object is found:*
                - o *Assign the first object to the current EIG (if not assigned before to this EIG).*
                - o *Assign the second object to the current EIG.*
    - o *If there are still objects that have not yet been assigned to any EIGs, create the next empty EIG to which objects will be assigned.*

This results in a list of multi-object inconsistencies (EIGs). Each object's elasticity helps form these inconsistencies. In future work, we will explore how elasticity can be used to assist with object adjustment decisions that would eliminate or reduce the number and complexity of such multi-object inconsistencies.

Figure 8. A schematic view of an EIG

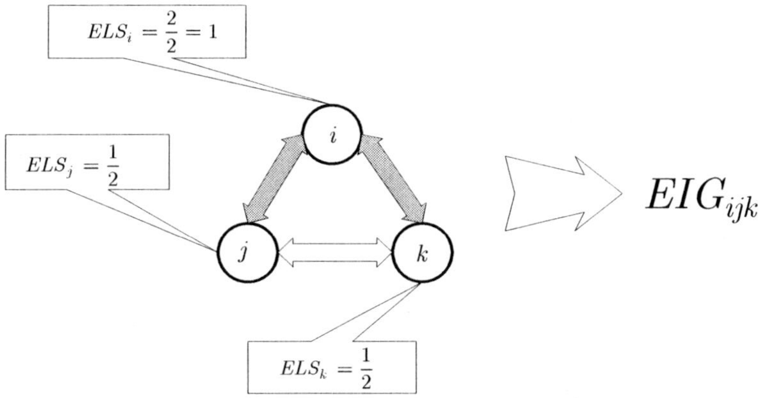

Table 1. Source data sets (SDS)

SDS ID	Geographic Coverage of Data Set	Data Source
SDS-1	Guelph	City of Guelph, Canada
SDS-2	Toronto (North York)	Teranet Inc., Canada
SDS-3	Toronto (North York)	North York Municipal Offices, Canada

Table 2. Experimental data set EDS-1

EDS ID	EDS-1		
Geographic Coverage	0.5 km by 0.6 km of Guelph.		
Number of Objects	749		
Layers			
Layer ID	Layer Description	Source SDS	Number of Objects
1	Residence.	SDS-1	202
2	Shed.	SDS-1	65
3	Property.	SDS-1	201
4	Tree.	SDS-1	281

EXAMPLE RESULTS

Experiments were conducted on GIS data from a number of public and private sector organizations. These geographic information systems consist of a cross section of utility infrastructure, commercial, land and taxation data.

A distinction is made between source data sets (SDS), which are the GIS databases analyzed in this research, and experimental data sets (EDS), which are subsets of one or more SDS on which the experiments were conducted. SDS is discussed in 5.1 and EDS are presented in Section 5.2.

Source Data Sets (SDS)

Each SDS examined in this research consists of numerous layers of raw spatial data built and maintained by highly-qualified and experienced people engaged in commercial applications. Three

Figure 9. EDS 1

Table 3. Experimental data set EDS-2

EDS ID		EDS-2	
Geographic Coverage		5100 ft by 5700 ft segment of North York.	
Number of Objects		9653	
Layers			
Layer ID	**Layer Description**	**Source SDS**	**Number of Objects**
1	Road.	SDS-2	112
2	Property.	SDS-2	3437
3	Building.	SDS-3	4991
4	Water Pipe Junction.	SDS-3	609
5	Sewer Manhole.	SDS-3	504

of these SDS are discussed in this section. They are listed in Table 1.

Experimental Data Sets (EDS)

Experimental data sets were created from the source data sets and used throughout this research. This section describes two such EDS that were constructed from the three SDS described in the previous section. The first EDS, denoted EDS-1, was created by selecting a number of layers of SDS-1 in a geographic region, while the second EDS, denoted EDS-2 was formed by combining selected layers from SDS-2 and SDS-3 in a geographic region.

The first experimental data set EDS-1 covers a portion of Guelph, Ontario, Canada and is discussed in Table 2.

The data in EDS-1 is shown graphically in Figure 9.

The second data set listed in Table 3 comprises of a portion of North York, which was created by combining data from two GIS databases, and adjusting them to common control points.

The data in EDS-2 is shown graphically in Figure 10.

The number of IPRs detected based on automatically observed relations that do not correspond to P-Rules or M-Rules are described in the first part of Table 4 and Table 5 for EDS-1 and EDS-2 respectively. Those automatically observed relations that correspond to M-Rules but have a frequency that is either smaller than the lower bound or larger than the upper bound of the M-Rules, are presented in the second part of these tables.

Figure. 10 EDS 2

Table 4. IPRs in EDS-1

EDS-1			
Observed Relation			**Number of IPRs based on Automatically Observed Relation**
Layer	**Layer**	**Relation**	
Residence	Property	Overlap	18
Shed	Property	Overlap	10
Tree	Residence	Overlap	4
Shed	Shed	Overlap	2
Tree	Tree	Overlap	6
Tree	Property	Overlap	1
M-Rule violated		**Nature of Violation**	**Number of IPRs based on Stationary M-Rules which were violated**
M-4		2 sheds in property	4
M-15		2 residences in property	2

The number of IPRs detected in each EDS is listed in Table 6.

The EIGs which were detected by grouping IPRs based on their semantic structure are listed in Table 7 and Table 8 for EDS-1 and EDS-2 respectively, along with the count of the number of such EIGs formed.

The types of objects with highest elasticity in the EIGs are summarized in Table 9 and Table 10 for EDS-1 and EDS-2 respectively.

The number of EIGs detected in each EDS is listed in Table 11.

The number of objects in EIGs, and the percent of objects that are in EIGs out of the total number of objects in each EDS are listed in Table 12.

DISCUSSION

The IPRs in EDS-1 listed in Table 4 indicate the existence of isolated incidents of IPRs of different

Table 5. IPRs in EDS-2

EDS-2			
Observed Relation			**Number of IPRs based on Automatically Observed Relation**
Layer	**Layer**	**Relation**	
Building	Building	Overlap	27
Building	Property	Overlap	142
Building	Road	Overlap	56
Sewer	Road	Overlap	11
Sewer	Property	Overlap	11
Sewer	Building	Overlap	10
Water	Road	Overlap	20
Water	Property	Overlap	20
Water	Building	Overlap	16
M-Rule violated		**Nature of Violation**	**Number of IPRs based on Stationary M-Rules which were violated**
M-12		Property contains 3 buildings.	24
M-12		Property contains 4 buildings.	4
M-12		Property contains 5 buildings.	5

Table 6. IPR summary

	Total IPRs	Number of Objects	IPR as Percent of Objects
EDS-1	47	749	6.27%
EDS-2	346	9653	3.58%

Table 7. Classification of EIGs in EDS-1

EDS-1		
Semantic Description of EIG	**Number of EIGs Automatically Detected**	**Number of EIGs Detected by Visual Inspection**
A Residence overlaps with one Property.	2	2
A Residence overlaps with more then one Property.	8	8
A Shed overlaps with more then one Property.	3	3
A Tree overlaps with a Residence.	4	4
A Shed inside one property overlaps with a second Shed. The second Shed overlaps two properties. (Show drawing here).	2	2
A Tree overlaps with more then one other Tree.	1	1
A Tree overlaps with one Tree.	3	3
A Tree overlaps with a Residence, and also with another Tree	1	1
A property contains two Sheds.	4	4
A property contains two Residences.	2	2

Table 8. Classification of EIGs in EDS-2

EDS-2		
Semantic Description of EIG	**Number of EIGs Automatically Detected**	**Number of EIGs Detected by Visual Inspection**
Two buildings inside one property overlap one another.	14	14
Two buildings overlap one another. One of the buildings is inside a property, the other building overlaps this same property as well as and adjoining property (drawing goes here).	9	9
A building overlaps two properties.	34	34
A building overlaps a property, a second building inside the same property as well as the adjoining road (drawing goes here).	4	4
A building overlaps a property as well as the adjoining road.	26	26
A Sewer overlaps a road and the adjoining property.	7	7
A Building overlaps a property and an adjoining road, as well as a Sewer that overlaps the same road and property.	4	4
A building that overlaps a property and adjoining road, and a sewer that is inside the property.	6	6
A Water Pipe Junction overlaps a road and the adjoining property.	13	13
A Building overlaps a property and an adjoining road, as well as a Water Pipe Junction that overlaps the same road and property.	7	7
A building that overlaps a property and adjoining road, and a Water Pipe Junction that is inside the property.	9	9
A property contains three buildings.	24	24
A property contains four buildings.	4	4
A property contains five buildings.	5	5

Table 9. EIG analysis for EDS-1

EDS-1		
Layer	**Number of EIGs whose Highest Elasticity Object is on the Layer**	**Percent of Total EIGs**
Residence	12	40%
Shed	9	30%
Property	0	0%
Tree	9	30%

Table 10. EIG analysis for EDS-2

EDS-2		
Layer	**Number of EIGs whose Highest Elasticity Object is on the Layer**	**Percent of Total EIGs**
Road	0	0%
Property	0	0%
Building	135	81.32%
Water	20	12.04%
Sewer	11	6.62%

Table 11. EIG Summary

	Total EIGs	**Number of Objects**	**EIG as Percent of Objects**
EDS-1	30	749	4.01%
EDS-2	166	9653	1.72%

Table 12. Percent of Objects in EIGs

	Number of Objects	**Number of Objects in EIGs**	**Percent of objects in EIGs**
EDS-1	749	68	9.07%
EDS-2	9653	467	4.83%

types in very small quantities. This same situation is seen when observing the types of EIGs detected in Table 7. The only exception to this is the number of residences which overlap with more then one property, indicating a possibility of some pattern of inconsistent behavior depending on their proximity. This pattern, if exists, would not be extensive, and therefore, there is no need for clustering EDS-1 or applying a regional strategy to this data set.

The IPRs in EDS-2 listed in Table 5 and the corresponding EIGs in Table 8 indicate an appreciable number of inconsistencies involving buildings, and to a lesser extent inconsistencies involving sewers and water pipe junctions. This situation is clearly demonstrated in Table 10 which shows that 135 buildings require adjustment, as do 20 water pipe junctions and 11 sewer manholes. This same table shows that over 81 percent of the inconsistencies are due to building objects, with 12 percent and 7 percent due to water pipe junctions and sewer manholes respectively. The building layer in EDS-2, which originates from aerial photography, is a likely cause of a significant number of the inconsistencies in EDS-2.

Both EDS-1 and EDS-2 were visually inspected for inconsistencies. All inconsistencies found during the visual inspection of the data sets were also automatically detected in terms of EIGs as seen in Table 7 and Table 8.

A measure of consistency of spatial data is proposed in terms of the number of EIGs, as shown in Table 11, and in terms of objects in EIGs as shown in Table 12. It is apparent from both tables that while EDS-2 has 5 times as many EIGs as EDS-1, EDS-1 is nearly twice as inconsistent as is EDS-2. It therefore seems that the merger of SDS-2 and SDS-3 to form EDS-2 produced consistency levels that are higher than that of EDS-1.

CONCLUSION

A method for detecting inconsistencies between pairs of objects, or IPRs, based on a comparison of observed relations against P-Rules and M-Rules was presented.

Elasticity, a property of objects was introduced to capture the relative contribution of objects to IPRs. Elasticity was then used to group IPRs into multi-object structures, called EIGs, correspond to inconsistencies among multiple neighboring entities in the real world. The relative contribution of objects in EIGs was established using elasticity, and will be applied to the EIG adjustment process in future publications.

Having systematically formulated inconsistent behavior in spatial databases, the regional aspects of some inconsistencies can be captured by clustering of EIGs. Future work is expected to discuss how elasticity and the clustering techniques are used in the process of finding local and global solutions to EIGs.

More and more organizations in all business sectors integrate spatial data with their existing non-spatial data sets. Spatial data integration and the resulting quality of this integration are becoming therefore critical to integration of more and more non-spatial databases. Integration of spatial databases in a way that minimizes inconsistencies in the combined data set leads to minimizing of inconsistencies when combining the non-spatial data sets that these spatial databases are linked to. Knowledge discovery in combined non-spatial databases is therefore likely to produce higher quality results.

REFERENCES

Abler, R. (1987). The national science foundation national center for geographic information and analysis. *International Journal of Geographic Information Systems, 1*(4), 303-326.

Aronoff, S. (1995). Geographic information systems: A management perspective. WDL Publications.

Balmisse, G., Meingan, D., & Passerini, K. (2007). Technology trends in knowledge management tools. *International Journal of Knowledge Management, 3*(2), 118–131.

Clementini, E., Felice, P.D., & Van Oosterom, P. (1993). A small set of formal topological relations suitable for end-user interaction, advances in spatial databases. In proceedings 3rd International Symposium, SSD'93, Singapore, Lecture Notes in Computer Science, Vol. 692 (Springer-Verlag, New York) (pp. 277-295).

Cockcroft, S. (2004). The design and implementation of a repository for the management of spatial data integrity constraints. Volume 8, Number 1 / March, Pages 49-69.

Davis, E. (1986). *Representing and acquiring geographic knowledge.* Los Altos, CA: Morgan Kaufmann Publishers, Inc.

Egenhofer, M.J. (1991). Reasoning about binary topological relations, Lecture notes

in computer science. *Advances in spatial databases, 2nd Symposium, SDD*'91, Zurich, Switzerland

Egenhofer, M.J., & Franzosa, R.D. (1995). On equivalence of topological relations. *International Journal of Geographical Information Systems, 9*(2), 133-152.

Egenhofer, M.J., & Franzosa, R.D. (1991). Point-set topological spatial relations. *International Journal of Geographic Information Systems, 5*(2), 161-174.

Egenhofer, M.J., & Herring, J.R. (1992). *Categorizing binary topological relations between regions, lines, and points in geographic databases.* Technical report, Department of Survey Engineering, University of Maine, Orono, ME.

Egenhofer, M.J., & Herring, J.R. (1991). *A mathematical framework for the definition of topological relations.* NCGIA technical paper 91-97

Egenhofer, M., & Herring, J. (1990). A Mathematical framework for the definition of Topological Relations. *Proceedings of 4th International Symposium on Spatial Data Handling,* (pp. 803-813). Zurich, Switzerland.

Hadzilacos, T., & Tryfona, N.. (1992). A Model for Expressing Topological Integrity Constraints in Geographic Databases. In A. Frank, I. Campari, & U. Formentini (Eds.), *Proceedings of the International Conference on Theories and Models of Spatio Temporal Reasoning in Geographic Space.* Pisa, Italy. Lecture notes in Computer Science, Vol. 639 (Springer Verlag, New York), (pp. 252-268).

Hayes-Roth, F., Waterman, D., & Lenat, D. (1983). *Building expert systems.* Reading, MA: Addison-Wesley Publishing Company.

Kainz, W. (1991). Logical consistency. In Guptil & Morison (Eds.), *Elements of spatial*

data quality (pp.109-137). Oxford.

Klien, A. (2007). A rule-based strategy for the semantic annotation of geodata. *Transactions in GIS, 11*(3), 437–452.

Lutz, M., & Kolas, D. (2007). Rule-based discovery in spatial data infrastructure. *Transactions in GIS, 11*(3), 317–336.

Mark, D., Frank, A., Egenhofer, M., Freundshuh, S., McGranghan, M., & White, R.M. (Eds.) (1989). *Languages of spatial relations: Report on the specialist meeting for NCGIA research initiative 2.* Technical Report 89-2, national Center for Geographic Information and Analysis.

Mark, D.M., & Egenhofer, M.J. (1992). An evaluation of the 9-intersection for region line relations. *In Proceedings of GIS/LIS '93*, San Jose, CA, (pp. 513-521).

Medeiros, C.B., & Cilia, M. (1995). Maintenance of binary topological constraints through active databases. *In Proceedings of 3rd ACM Workshop on GIS.*

Redman, T.C. (1992). *Data quality.* Bantam.

Servigne, S., Ubeda, T., Zuricelli, A., & Laurini, R. (2000). A methodology for spatial consistency improvement of geographic databases. *GeoInformatica, 4*(1), 7-34.

Smith, R., & Park, K.K. (1991). *An algebraic approach to spatial reasoning.* NCGIA technical paper 91-97.

Veregin, H. (1991). *Data quality measurement and assessment*. NCGIA Core Curriculum in Geographic Information Science.

Xu, J. (2007). Formalizing natural-language spatial relations between linear objects with topological and metric properties. *International Journal of Geographical Information Science, 21*(4), 377-395.

This work was previously published in the International Journal of Knowledge Management, Vol. 4, Issue 3, edited by M. Jennex, pp. 64-81, copyright 2008 by IGI Publishing (an imprint of IGI Global).

Chapter 19
A Specialized Evaluation and Comparison of Sample Data Mining Software

John Wang
Montclair State University, USA

Xiaohua Hu
Drexel University, USA

Kimberly Hollister
Montclair State University, USA

Dan Zhu
Iowa State University, USA

ABSTRACT

Finding the right software is often hindered by different criteria as well as by technology changes. The authors performed an AHP (Analytic Hierarchy Process) analysis using Expert Choice to determine which data mining package was most suitable. Deliberating a dozen alternatives and objectives led them to a series of pair-wise comparisons. When further synthesizing the results, Expert Choice helped provide a clear rationale for the decision. The issue is, data mining technology is changing very rapidly. This chapter focused only on the major suppliers typically available in the market place. The method and the process that was used can be easily applied to analyze and compare other data mining software or knowledge management initiatives.

INTRODUCTION

Based on the *Knowledge Life Cycle* model, four stages of knowledge creation, knowledge storage/retrieval, knowledge transfer, and knowledge application have been proposed by Alavi and Leidner (2001) and confirmed by Jennex (2006). "To be effective Knowledge Management Systems, KMS, must support the various knowledge management functions of knowledge capture, storage, search, retrieval, and use" (Jennex, 2006, p.3). Knowledge discovery is generally one of important stages or phases of KM. And while this incorporates identi-

DOI: 10.4018/978-1-60566-954-0.ch019

fying critical knowledge (this may also be what this stage is called), using data mining to aid in knowledge discovery is appropriate as being a useful KM tool.

Data mining is a promising tool that assists companies to uncover patterns hidden in their data. These patterns may be further used to forecast customer behavior, products and processes. It is important that managers who understand the business, the data, and the general nature of the analytical methods, are involved. Realistic expectation can yield rewarding results across a wide range of applications, from improving revenues to reducing costs (Davenport & Harris, 2007; Porter & Miller, 2001; Wang, 2008). It is crucial to properly collect and prepare the data, and to check the models against the real figures. The best model is often found after managers build models of several different types or by trying different technologies or algorithms. This alone demonstrates the active role managers play in the data mining or other knowledge management processes.

Selecting software is a practical yet very important problem for a company (James, Hakim, Chandras, King, & Variar, 2004). However, not enough attention is given to this critical task. Current literature is quite limited since selecting software is such a complex problem, due to many criteria and frequent technology changes (Elder IV & Abbott, 1998; Giraud-Carrier & Povel, 2003). Haughton, Deichmann, Eshghi, Sayek, Teebagy, & Topi (2003) generally reviewed several computer software packages for data mining including SPSS Clementine, XLMiner, Quadstone, GhostMiner, and SAS Enterprise Miner. Corral, Griffin, & Jennex (2005) examined the potential of knowledge management in data warehousing from an expert's perspective. Jennex (2006) introduced technologies in support of knowledge management systems.

Firstly, this article will take a brief look at data mining today, through describing some of the opportunities, applications and available technologies. We will then discuss and analyze several of the most powerful data mining software tools available on the market today. Ultimately we will also attempt to provide an analytical analysis and comparison among the brands we have selected. Our selection is based, in part, on our own experience using data mining software as well as writing data mining code, SQL code and our work as relational database administrators. For our analytical comparison we will be using *Expert Choice* (Version 11) advanced decision support software (Wang, Hu, Hollister, & Zhu, 2008).

DATA MINING SOFTWARE

Data mining software analyzes- based on open-ended user queries- relationships and patterns that are stored in transaction data. Available are several types of analytical software: statistical, machine learning and neural networks, decision trees, Naive-Bayes, K-Nearest Neighbor, rule induction, clustering, rules based, linear and logistical regression time sequence, etc. Along the lines of Mena (1998) and Martin (2005), the basic steps of data mining for knowledge discoveries are:

1. Define business problem
2. Build data mining data base
3. Explore data
4. Prepare data for modeling
5. Build model
6. Evaluate model
7. Deploy model
8. Results

Note: Each of these steps contains managerial issues which must be addressed.

The key to knowledge discovery is a true understanding of your data and your business. Without this understanding, no algorithm is going to provide you with a result in which you should confide. Moreover, without this background you will not be able to identify the problems you are trying to solve, prepare the data for mining, or correctly interpret the results. There are many tasks involved in the construction of a database: data collection, data description, selection, data quality assessment and data cleansing, consolidation and integration, metadata construction, and maintaining the database. In exploring the data, the manager must choose the appropriate hardware to accomplish this feat. The goal is to identify the most important fields in predicting an outcome, and determine which derived values may be useful. According to O Chan (2005), a good interface and fast computer response are very important in this phase because the very nature of your exploration is changed when you often have to wait up to 30 minutes for some graphs to be created.

Preparing data for modeling consists of four main parts: selecting variables, selecting rows, constructing new variables and transforming variables. The managerial decision in this case focuses on identifying key variables to examine, non-fully functional variables inclusive. The time it takes to build a model increases with the number of variables while blindly including extraneous columns can lead to incorrect models. The most important thing to remember about data model building is that it is an interactive process. Many alternative models may have to be examined to find one that is most appropriate in solving your business problem. A manager searching for a good model may go back and amend the data he/she is using or even modify his/her problem statement. In the evaluation and interpretation process, the accuracy rate found during testing applies only to the data on which the model was built. The accuracy may vary if the data to which the model is applied differ in important and unpredictable ways from the original data set.

Once a data mining model is built and validated, it can be used in two main ways. First, the manager may recommend actions based on simply viewing the model and its results. For example, the manager may look at the clusters the model has identified, the rules that define the model or the lift and ROI charts that depict the effect of the model. The second process involves applying the model to different datasets. The manager may use the model to flag records based on their classification or assign a score such as the probability of an action.

Data Mining Software Alternatives

As stated earlier in our introduction, there are numerous data mining software alternatives that vary in the number of modeling and visualization nodes as well as in price. We have elected the following eight software vendors for comparison due to a limitation of trial version of *Expert Choice* (Version 11):

- Clementine from SPSS
- DB2 Intelligent Miner from IBM
- Enterprise Miner from SAS
- GhostMiner by Fujitsu
- Insightful Miner V5.2 for Insightful
- Megaputer PolyAnalyst
- Microsoft SQL Server 2005 Enterprise Edition
- Oracle Data Miner

Although there are various other comparable programs available, we were limited in our selection. One of the limiting factors was the inadequacy of alternatives in our decision tools' evaluation copy.

Decision Tool

To aid in comparing our software choices, we used an evaluation copy of *Expert Choice* version 11, a leading software solution construed to analyze, categorize, prioritize, select, allocate and choose a selection based on relevant criteria (Expert Choice Inc, 2007). *Expert Choice* incorporates a process known as *Analytical Hierarchical Process* (AHP) into its software (Saaty & Vargas, 2006; Saaty, 1980; 1996; 2001; 2005). Research has demonstrated that AHP is a powerful decision-making tool that can help organizations avoid making costly mistakes caused by bad decisions (Hemaida & Schmits, 2006). AHP was developed by Saaty and Kearns and consists of four stages (Roper-Lowe, 1990). The first stage is to construct a hierarchy where the primary objective, or goal, is at the highest level. Criteria, which can also be sub-divided, follow in decreasing order. At the bottom of the hierarchy are the alternatives to be evaluated. The second stage calculates weights for the criteria using pair-wise comparisons. In the next stage, the alternatives are also compared to each other in respect to each criterion. Finally, all weighted scores are tallied to yield a final score. The alternative with the highest score is considered the best alternative.

SAMPLE PRODUCTS

In this section we will analyze the various features and benefits offered by each of our software alternatives that are to be considered, as well as researching product reviews and professional opinions. The information gathered from this analysis will serve as the basis for the pair-wise comparisons of the software alternatives with respect to each of our criteria In other words, we will investigate how important one choice is over the other alternative given a specific criterion, when comparing any two software alternatives,

CART by Salford Systems

CART is an easy to use decision tree tool that uses the CART algorithm and boosting. Its' main objective is to rifle through databases, identifying significant patterns and relationships, which are then used to generate predictive models. CART uses an exhaustive, recursive partitioning routine to generate binary splits by posing a series of yes-no questions. It searches for questions that split nodes into relatively homogenous child nodes. As the tree evolves, the nodes become more homogenous, identifying segments. CART supports more than 80 file formats, including SAP, SPSS databases such as Oracle and Informix, Excel spreadsheets, and Lotus 1-2-3 spreadsheets.

CART was formulated from the original CART code developed by Stanford University and University of California at Berkeley statisticians. The frequent addition of new features and capabilities continually enhances the procedure, strengthening the accuracy and reliability of the results. CART has a no-stopping rule, which makes it unique. This means that more data are read and compared, and it ensures that important data are not overlooked by stopping too soon. It produces an over-grown tree, and immediately prunes it back for the most optimal results. CART also uses a powerful binary split search approach. This means the trees are more sparing with data and detect more structure before too little data are left for learning. Next, CART uses automatic self-validation procedures, which are essential in avoiding the trap of finding patterns that apply only to the training data.

CART was designed for both technical and non-technical users. It can quickly identify important data relationships. It offers users some flexibility, with the choice of how to split criteria. It also offers different models for scalability. The results are easy to read and understand, with decision tree diagrams drawn out. Salford Systems understands that expert and timely technical support is a critical part of the business, which is why they offer many means of customer training and support. The company offers both public and private on-site instruction, user seminars, hand-on training courses, consultation services, and e-mail, NetMeeting, and phone support from offices worldwide.

SPSS: Clementine

Clementine data mining software by SPSS is useful for organizations using SPSS infrastructure as well as those with mixed platforms. This program supports both client and server platforms, including the Windows family of products and Sun Solaris, HP-UX11i, IBM AIX, and OS/400 server platforms.

With regard to reliability, Clementine by SPSS supports decision trees, neural networks, regression, self-organizing maps, clustering, and association rules (Lampe, 2004). However, the author states that Clementine implements "a broad set of statistical algorithms, but fewer than in the SAS and IBM packages" (Lampe, 2004 p. 18).

In the area of efficiency, Clementine works with SPSS, SAS and SQL and can export to C code and Predictive Model Markup Language (PPML) (Angus, 2006). It can also handle critical data preparation, rapid modeling, and model scoring tasks. These tasks are all performed using GUI graphical layouts, workflow diagrams, scatterplots, distribution, histogram, multiplot and web charts (which are unique to Clementine (Haughton et al., 2003)).

Training and support for Clementine are available from SPSS in the form of online tutorials, downloadable overview and demo of the program, along with online technical support and excellent help screens. The price of Clementine starts at $75,000 (Angus, 2006).

Enterprise Miner by SAS

Enterprise Miner was developed by SAS Corporation, which was originally called Statistical Analysis System. Enterprise Miner is an integrated software product that provides widespread business solutions for data mining based on SEMMA (Sample, Explore, Modify, Model, Assess) methodology. It has many different statistical tools including decision trees, clustering, linear and logistic regression and neural networks. Data preparation tools include outlier detection, variable transformations, random sampling, and the partitioning of data sets into training, test, and validation data sets. Its advanced GUI allows you to review large amounts of data in multidimensional histograms with ease as well as compare modeling results graphically.

Enterprise Miner includes several procedures that automate traditional analysis tasks, such as choosing the variables to include in a model and applying the appropriate transformations. The system also provides extensive visualization to help users explore the data to decide on additional manipulations that the system itself does not recommend. Enterprise Miners' graphical user interface and automated framework indicate that the user does not have to know how the tools work to use them. Release 8.2 provides cross-platform national language support that is especially important to international customers.

GhostMiner by Fujitsu

GhostMiner is a data mining software product from Fujitsu that not only supports common databases (or spreadsheets) and mature machine learning algorithms, but also assists with data preparation and selection, model validation, multi-models (like committees or k-classifiers), and visualization. GhostMiner provides large range of data preparation techniques; broad scope of selection of featured methods. Choice of data mining algorithms and visualization techniques are integrated.

GhostMiner offers several project features unique to their platform, which enables users to create simple interfaces for their specific needs. GhostMiner has a human machine interface (HMI) that is fairly user friendly and easy to start up right out of the box. The system is so easy to use that it actually has a feel of being too user friendly and may be missing some of the power of the larger server based data mining software tool such as Darwin IBM and Oracle. GhostMiner can be loaded directly onto a Windows based PC and is equally adept at data mining a system database as it is a series of spreadsheets, text or ASCII files.

GhostMiner contains both data pre-processing capabilities as well as data visualization capabilities. Data pre-processing includes data normalization, standardization and many preliminary statistical analysis functions, such as variance, standard deviation, mean and median across the entire database. GhostMiner does not have the inherent flexibility of some of the larger, more robust products, and also does not offer the same levels of support as the products offered by Oracle and IBM. GhostMiner is a product marketed to small to mid size users who are looking for a simple to use product at a lower price than some of its larger, well known counterparts.

Insightful: Insightful Miner

Insightful Miner is a cost effective data mining software program. The software has numerous model types, algorithms and visualizers, including decision trees, *Block Model Averaging*, linear and logistic regression, neural networks, Naïve Bayes, Cox proportional hazard models, K-means clustering and others. Insightful Miner offers highly scalable algorithms, which train models on very large data sets without the need for sampling or aggregation. Insightful also offers data pre-processing and data cleansing as well as exploratory data analysis and visualization. Insightful Miner's cost is typically $12,000.

According to a product review in *DM Review* (Lurie, 2004) the main strength of Insightful Miner is its ability to scale large data sets in an accessible manner. It provides the analytic tools required to transform fragmented raw data into "actionable knowledge" (Lurie, 2004, p. 88). Insightful Miner provides cutting edge analytics and reporting tools to identify patterns, trends and relationships in data. Insightfuls' simplicity allows users to quickly aggregate, clean and analyze data. Its powerful reporting and modeling capabilities allow users to deliver clear, usable analytics to designers and producers. Simple visual work maps make it easy for users to become productive relatively quickly. Insightful Miner provides excellent product support and its documentation is complete and easy to understand.

In another product review of Insightful Miner (Deal, 2004), the software was found to be a comprehensive data mining application that includes extensive data input, data manipulation, and analysis capabilities. Insightful Miner can efficiently process large amounts of data by using a chunking and processing algorithm that is intended to be scalable to the mass of data used for each analysis. Insightfuls' ability to integrate S-Plus strengthens and extends its functionality. Deal (2004) stated that Insightful Miner "is a very simple and intuitive process" (p. 46).

IBM: Intelligent Miner

IBM Intelligent Miner V7R1 is very user friendly software. It is an essential e-commerce tool, as it can aid in handling transactions as they come in. It has business intelligence applications, which allow it to make decisions that would be good for any business, large or small. The intelligence part of the software could cut costs and increase profits. The data screens help with decision making and improvement on processes that are out of date. It also makes maximizes the business to customer relationship, because of the personalization the software can provide for each client. This software package is also compatible with Windows, AIX, Solaris and Linux servers.

IBM Intelligent Miner V7R1 has IM Scoring, in which the user has an advantage, because scores and ranks are done in real time. This means that as a new transaction takes place, it would then reorganize the scores/ranks of the customers' information. For example, when a customer buys an item off the internet, the software would update for the payment due and when it should be posted. The same would apply for a dentist visit: after six months it would indicate that it is time for another check up for the particular patient. As the appointment would approach, the higher the person would be on the list, i.e. moving up the ranks. Another advantage with the IM Scoring is the high performance and scalability of mining functions, thus making sampling obsolete.

The best aspect of this product is its user friendliness. The whole staff would be content with it. It can also be updated easily, without any disruption to the business. IBM is currently promoting the DB2 Query Management Facility version 8.1, since in March 2006, IBM withdrew Intelligent Miner from all marketing and ended all its support for Intelligent Miner tools.

Megaputer: PolyAnalyst

Another data mining software package is PolyAnalyst (the newest version is 4.6) made by the Megaputer Company. This company is quite small, especially compared to some of the other companies we have profiled. Megaputer Intelligence Inc. is a leading developer and distributor of advanced software tools for data mining, text mining, and intelligent e-commerce personalization. The tools help reveal knowledge hidden in data. They add intelligence and insight to every step of the business decision-making process.

Since the Megaputer Company focuses primarily on data mining programs, they can offer a more comprehensive program than other companies who simply have a data mining component to existing products. They offer a vast array of algorithms from which a consumer can choose the ones they need specifically, making the product ready to be customized. The price for an older version of PolyAnalyst (the most recent pricing data found) is an affordable $2,300 for the base version and can go up to $14,900 with all the algorithms. Also, the developer kit for PolyAnalyst is available for $16,000.

PolyAnalyst can be run either on a stand-alone system or in a client/server configuration, where the server would handle the data processing. It only works with the Microsoft Windows O/S which shows that it is not as portable as some other products analyzed. Also, Megaputer offers possible users a free evaluation version to decide if this is the software right for them. The program offers a rich set of features. PolyAnalyst by Megaputer seems to be a feature rich data mining software package. The price and ala carte feature set seem more suited for a smaller company that cannot afford to use a more expensive data mining solution that would require the use of highly trained employees.

Oracle: Oracle Data Mining

Oracle Data Miner is the graphical user interface for Oracle Data Mining (Release 10.1 and above) that helps data analysts mine their Oracle data to find valuable hidden information, patterns, and new insights. Oracle Data Mining is a powerful data mining software embedded in the Oracle Database that enables you to discover new information hidden in your data and helps businesses target their best customers and find and prevent fraud.

Oracle provides unique portability across all major platforms including Windows, Solaris, HP-UX, IBM AIX, Compaq Tru64, and Linux and ensures that applications run without modification after changing platforms. There are two common ways to architect a database: client/server or multi-tier. Two basic memory structures are associated with Oracle software: the system global area and the program global area.

Oracle Data Miner facilitates interactive data preparation, data mining model creation, evaluation, refinement and model scoring. Oracle Data Mining provides the following supervised data mining algorithms: Naïve Bayes, Adaptive Bayes Network, decision trees, Support Vector Machines, attribute importance. Unsupervised algorithms are: clustering, association rules, feature selection, anomaly detection, text mining and unstructured data, life sciences algorithm. Mining Activity Guides provide structured templates for all users to explore and mine their data.

Oracle Data Mining (ODM) enables companies to extract information efficiently from the very largest databases, and build integrated business intelligence applications and support data mining problems such as: classification, prediction, regression, clustering, associations, attribute importance, feature extraction and sequence similarity searches and analysis. When the capabilities of Oracle Data Mining are combined with the ability of the RDBMS to access, pre-process, retrieve and analyze data, they create a very powerful platform for data analysis.

Oracle Data Mining can generate valuable new insights and reports that can help proactively manage your business, according to the Oracle Discoverer report. Oracle Data Miner models can be visualized graphically and can be display in tables, histograms, line graphs and pie graphs. Data may be in either Excel or the Database. Significant productivity enhancements are achieved by eliminating the extraction of data from the database to special-purpose data mining tools (Berger, 2005).

Data size is unlimited. The expert analyst can adjust some or all of the parameters manually, but the option to allow the algorithms to optimize the parameters intelligently, with no intervention, is available. There are free demos available: Oracle Data Mining, Integration with Oracle BI EE, Spreadsheet Add-in for Predictive Analytics, and Text Mining. The tutorial Oracle by Example series and online training provides valuable hands-on experience, step-by-step instructions on how to implement various technology solutions to business problems. Oracle Data Mining significantly reduces the cost of data mining. Savings are realized in the avoidance of additional hardware purchases for computing and storage environments, redundant copies and multiple versions of the data and duplication of personnel who perform similar functions. Database analytics includes: engine, basic statistics (free), data mining, text mining.

SQL Server 2005

SQL server 2005 is Microsoft's solution to database management and data mining. SQL Server database platform provides enterprise-class data management with integrated business intelligence (BI) tools. SQL Server 2005 combines analysis, reporting, integration, and notification. SQL server is closely integrated with Microsoft Visual Studio, the Microsoft Office System, and a suite of new development tools, including the Business Intelligence Development Studio (Bednarz, 2005).

Microsoft SQL Server series utilizes the Windows operating system and features four discrete algorithms. HMI features include a Windows' interface, as well as complete integration with the Microsoft Office suite. Reports that are served by the Report Server in Reporting Services can run in the context of Microsoft SharePoint Portal Server and Microsoft Office System applications such as Microsoft Word and Microsoft Excel (Fontana, 2005). SharePoint can be used to subscribe to reports, create new versions of reports, and distribute reports. SQL Server 2005 also supports rich, full-text search applications. Query performance and scalability have been improved dramatically, and new management tools will provide greater insight into the full-text implementation.

SQL Server also features an online restore function, database encryption and a fast recovery option. It also has a system with built-in scalability features such as parallel partition processing, creation of *remote relational online analytical processing* (ROLAP) or *hybrid online analytical processing* (HOLAP) partitions, distributed partitioned cubes, persisted calculations, and proactive caching.

COMPARISON

We use *Expert Choice* in the evaluation process and will attempt to analytically quantify the aspects of data mining software that best define overall product quality. Before we describe the decision making process, we would like to present several assumptions on which our decision will be based:

1) In addition to our experience, we will rely on manufacture specifications, descriptions and described attributes, along with third party reviews where available.
2) We will base our needs on fundamental business goals such as business-related decision making and business-driven information analysis. Although this definition may seem overly broad, we will attempt to further limit our scope by eliminating research and development, educational and political as well as most human resource applications.
3) Since we are using a trial version of *Expert Choice* advanced decision making software, there will be limits with respect to importing and exporting data as well as with printing and possibly some advanced analytical tools. Therefore, we will utilize screen captures embedded into this document, and will manually write any necessary data as opposed to systematic imports or exports.

Criteria Revisited

Our selection process will be centered on the below mentioned software quality criteria. We will attempt to compare all of our selections based on the specified criteria. Using *Expert Choice*, we will make objective ratings of each product, comparing in a pair-wise manner, attributes that define each element.

- Portability: the amount of platform independence; the number of support platforms and supported software architectures as well as any software requirements needed to run the software.
- Reliability: the degree of completeness, accuracy and consistency, any stated warranty and support provided by the vendor. The number of data models and algorithms available with the software as well as any templates or custom models available for creation of projects.
- Efficiency: the degree of efficiency and accessibility; the degree in which the product supports the general business goal assumptions and the number of tools available for data pre-processing.
- Human engineering: how well the software interfaces and communicates with the outside world, plus the quality of the human machine interface (HMI). Testability – how well the software is structured; how results are displayed and how results are re-introduced into the process if applicable.
- Understanding: degree of self-descriptiveness; the degree of simplicity of the machine interface, the use of graphical user interfaces, visual programming ability, summary reports, and data model visualization.
- Modifiability: the degree of augmentation ability and the ability to change over time and expand; the use of batch processing and any expert options as well as data size limitations.
- Price, training and support: price of product, availability of evaluation or demo versions, and the amount of post purchase support included in the package

Evaluation Model

Our evaluation criteria, as entered in the Expert Choice, are as follows:

- **Portability**, evaluated in terms of:
- Hardware platform (PC, Unix/Solaris workstation etc.)
- Software Architecture (standalone, client/server, thin client)
- Software requirements (DB2, SAS, Base, Java/JRE, Oracle, etc.

- **Reliability**, evaluated in terms of:
    - What model classes does the tool support?
    - How many algorithms does the tool use?
    - Does the tool allow custom model creation or simply uses templates?
    - What is the reputation of the vendor supplying the tool?
- **Efficiency**, evaluated in terms of:
    - How well does the product support our general business goal assumption?
    - Ability to perform data pre-processing.
- **Human Engineering**, evaluated in terms of:
    - Simplicity of HMI (human machine interface)
    - Graphical layout
    - Visual programming ability
- **Testability**, evaluated in terms of dissemination and deployment:
    - How well the results are re-introduced into the process "closing the loop"
    - How results are displayed
- **Understanding**, in terms of evaluation and interpretation of data:
    - Are summary reports available?
    - Can the model be visualized graphically?
- **Modifiability**, in terms of scalability and upgrades:
    - What is the data set size limit?
    - Are there expert options or batch processing?
- **Training and support**, evaluated in terms of:
    - Is a free demo available?
    - Is any free training or support available with the purchase?
- **Price** (where available) – if pricing is not available we will note our evaluation as price neutral.

PROCEDURE OF EXPERT CHOICE

Let's use five products to demonstrate the whole process of *Expert Choice* on a small scale. We commence with pair-wise comparisons for each of our criteria. Figure 1 is a screen capture of our initial results of priorities. As can be seen in Table 1, we placed a great deal of importance on Human Engineering (weight of .220), slightly less on Training and Support (w=. 193) and then on Understanding (w=. 190). Our main driver was that for the software to be successful, people had to know and understand it. Our next highest priority was Reliability, with a relative weight of .142, followed by Portability, which is platform and hardware independence, with a relative weight of .128.

Figure 1.

Ideal mode	PAIRWISE	PAIRWISE	PAIRWISE	PAIRWISE	PAIRWISE	PAIRWISE	PAIRWISE
Alternative	**Portability (L: .055)**	**Reliability (L: .145)**	**Efficiency (L: .130)**	**Human Engineering/ Testability (L: .201)**	**Understandability (L: .166)**	**Modifiability (L: .076)**	**Training and Support (L: .226)**
☑ Clementine	.793	.819	.806	.974	.988	.671	.861
☑ Enterprise Miner	.684	.725	1.000	.920	.944	.625	.677
☑ Oracle	1.000	1.000	.993	.984	.946	1.000	1.000
☑ Microsoft SQL	.236	.763	.862	.857	.951	.444	.968
☑ IBM DB2	.727	.806	.796	.714	.923	.389	.814
☑ Salford CART	.527	.738	.855	.783	1.000	.777	.767
☑ Megaputer	.360	.529	.268	1.000	.925	.826	.898
☑ Insightful Miner	.371	.607	.473	.858	.974	.923	.899

Next, we perform a pair-wise comparison of each software tool for each criterion; that is, we compare the components of each criterion on a case-by-case basis, assigning relative strengths and weaknesses to each product. Although this process is quite tedious, it provides an accurate measurement for each product. Table 2 shows an example of a pair-wise comparison for the contribution of hardware platform independence to overall platform independence, which is a contributor to overall portability within our quality structure.

Table 3 shows a graphical representation from the pair-wise comparison between all products for the hardware contribution, to overall portability. The screen capture shows a weight for each product with SQL Server as the best in class (with a weight of .269) and GhostMiner as last in class (with a weight of .109). These criteria are also weighted individually so as to roll up into the overall contribution towards portability.

Table 1. Weights Assigned to Criteria

Category	Priorities
Human Engineering	0.22
Training and Support	0.193
Understandability	0.19
Reliability	0.142
Portability	0.128
Modifiability	0.051
Efficiency	0.039
Testability	0.022
Price	0.016

Overall Results

Table 4 shows the overall results from *Expert Choice* advanced decision support software. From the first iteration of our selection process, the best solution for our chosen attributes and assigned priorities is the CART product, with an overall weight of .268, followed by SAS Enterprise with an overall weight of .223. We also performed several iterations, changing the weights of our criteria.

Table 5 shows the assigned weights of each category along with the overall score for all of the objects. This tool allows dynamic sensitivity analysis with respect to changing priorities. We used this tool to look at how much a change in one weight changes the overall goal. Using this tool is similar to the sensitivity analysis performed in

Table 3. Class Weightings for Overall Hardware Platform Independence

Vendor	Class Weighting
CART by Salford Systems	0.268
SAS Enterprise Miner	0.223
Oracle 8i	0.215
GhostMiner	0.141
SQP Server 2005	0.152
Overall inconsistency: 0.28	

Table 2. Pair-wise Comparison Grid WRT Hardware Platform

	CART by Salford Systems	SAS Enterprise Miner	Oracle 8i	GhostMiner	SQL Server 2005
CART by Salford Systems		3.0	3.0	3.0	7.0
SAS Enterprise Miner			2.0	3.0	4.0
Oracle 8i				3.0	3.0
GhostMiner					4.0
SQL Server 2005					
Inconsistency: 0.73					

Excel Solver; however, instead of listed ranges the Expert Choice tool allows for dynamic manipulation. From the chart we can see our weighted emphasis on Human Engineering (22%), Training and Support (19.3%) and Understandability. The window on the right shows which system best fits our stated criteria.

Table 4. Results from "Choosing a Data Mining Software Vendor"

Vendor	Overall Weight
CART by Salford Systems	0.191
SAS Enterprise Miner	0.215
Oracle 8i	0.222
GhostMiner	0.109
SQP Server 2005	0.263
Inconsistency: 0.73	

In Table 6 we change our requirements in order to verify the strength of our decision. We increase the importance of Price from 1.6% all the way up to 33.5%. We also change our Human Engineering requirement from 22% down to 5.8%, and also reduce Training and Technical Support, Portability, Reliability, Efficiency and Modifiability (flexibility) substantially and still came up with CART systems as our best overall choice (24% weight).

Table 5. Dynamic Sensitivity Analysis

Category	Category Weight	Vendor	Vendor Preference Weight
Portability	12.8%	CART by Salford Systems	26.8%
Reliability	14.2%	SAS Enterprise Miner	22.3%
Efficiency	3.9%	Oracle 8i	21.5%
Human Engineering	22.0%	GhostMiner	14.1%
Testability	2.2%	SQL Server 2005	15.2%
Understandability	19.0%		
Modifiability	5.1%		
Training and Support	19.3%		
Price	1.6%		

Table 6. Dynamic Sensitivity Analysis with Different Constraints

Category	Category Weight	Vendor	Vendor Preference Weight
Portability	0.1%	CART by Salford Systems	24.0%
Reliability	2.6%	SAS Enterprise Miner	18.5%
Efficiency	3.2%	Oracle 8i	17.1%
Human Engineering	5.8%	GhostMiner	20.8%
Testability	3.3%	SQL Server 2005	19.6%
Understandability	21.5%		
Modifiability	4.1%		
Training and Support	15.7%		
Price	33.5%		

SCENARIO ANALYSIS

We now start to compare eight leading data mining packages based on seven criteria. Determining the best software is a multiple objective decision-making process since different companies may have completely different needs. An array of software may each be the best choice because their design and performance are defined within a certain type of institution. Usually, one data mining software can not be the best for every scenario. This is because specific software can not meet the expectations of every type of institution; therefore the creation of scenarios is a very important tool in term of decision-making process.

In order to make this project more accurate and realistic, we have combined different scenarios. Factors, such as size, budget, type of business, and the type of data we have to manipulate, can affect the software we attempt to choose and the reasons why we choose it. Having simulated many scenarios, we found that size is a decisive factor. For instance, if we choose two companies with different sizes and follow a traditional reasoning, the tentative result may contradict with our intuition.

After researching all the alternatives, we used our decision tool, *Expert Choice*, to make pair-wise comparisons for each of them. A total of 392 pair-wise comparisons were required to compare each of the alternatives with respect to each of the criteria (196 comparisons for each scenario). This was in addition to the 42 pair-wise comparisons required to assign weights to each criterion with respect to the goal (21 comparisons for each scenario). After completing all of the pair-wise comparisons the software synthesized all of the weights of the alternatives with the weights of the criteria and selected the best alternative of each of the two scenarios. Tables 7 and 8 summarize the weights of the pair-wise comparisons for each of the alternatives with respect to each criterion. As with the weights of the criteria, there is also a direct relationship between the calculated weights in each column and the respective criterion. In other words, the higher a number is in a given column the more important that sized company views that particular software for that specific criterion.

Based on our research of all the alternatives and the weighted criteria calculated by our decision tool, the software has determined that for a small-sized company the top three alternatives are Insightful Miner, Megaputer PolyAnalyst, and SAS Enterprise Miner. These results were somewhat unexpected. We had anticipated that Insightful, Megaputer, and GhostMiner would be among the top three or four alternatives for a

Table 7. Weights assigned to each alternative for both a small and large-sized company.

Synthesized Weights - with respect to criteria	Efficiency		Human Engineering \ Understandability		Modifiability		Portability	
	Large	Small	Large	Small	Large	Small	Large	Small
Clementine	0.213	0.153	0.154	0.154	0.159	0.159	0.200	0.059
Enterprise Miner	0.176	0.174	0.155	0.155	0.151	0.151	0.221	0.059
GhostMiner	0.110	0.102	0.124	0.124	0.069	0.069	0.069	0.235
Insightful Miner	0.142	0.168	0.135	0.135	0.108	0.108	0.097	0.235
Intelligent Miner	0.106	0.130	0.112	0.112	0.155	0.155	0.097	0.059
Megaputer	0.086	0.091	0.090	0.090	0.060	0.060	0.067	0.235
Oracle Data Miner	0.102	0.103	0.104	0.104	0.151	0.151	0.148	0.059
SQL Server 2005	0.066	0.078	0.126	0.126	0.147	0.147	0.079	0.059

Table 8. Weights assigned to each alternative for both a small and large-sized company (cont.)

Synthesized Weights – continued	Reliability		Training and Support \ Price		Testability	
	Large	Small	Large	Small	Large	Small
Clementine	0.194	0.194	0.040	0.036	0.156	0.156
Enterprise Miner	0.206	0.206	0.027	0.025	0.149	0.149
GhostMiner	0.069	0.069	0.170	0.194	0.116	0.116
Insightful Miner	0.107	0.107	0.261	0.266	0.147	0.147
Intelligent Miner	0.110	0.110	0.029	0.024	0.099	0.099
Megaputer	0.147	0.147	0.261	0.349	0.151	0.151
Oracle Data Miner	0.101	0.101	0.108	0.051	0.096	0.096
SQL Server 2005	0.066	0.066	0.104	0.054	0.086	0.086

small-sized company, primarily because each of these vendors offer stand-alone versions of their software and are also the least expensive among all the alternatives. However, GhostMiner ranked lower than expected while SAS Enterprise Miner ranked higher. A closer analysis of the pair-wise comparisons shows that SAS was more efficient and had better human engineering than GhostMiner. Because of the weights given to these two criteria, SAS Enterprise Miner was able to beat all of the other alternatives despite its cost.

According to our decision tool, the top three alternatives for a large company are SPSS Clementine, followed by SAS Enterprise Miner and Insightful Miner. There was not one overwhelming choice for a large company. The differences in weight among the top three alternatives were relatively small (16.7%, 15.9%, and 13.5% respectively). These results were also a little unanticipated. All of the software reviews that we have read, rated SPSS and SAS among the top leading data mining software that are commercially available. We had not expected Insightful Miner to rank among the top three alternatives for a large company. We anticipated that Microsoft, IBM, or Oracle would round out the top three alternatives because these vendors offer enterprise class DBMS. Upon closer examination of the software analysis, Insightful Miner's visualization and modeling nodes were comparable to those of an enterprise class data mining software program such as Enterprise Miner and Clementine. In addition, a closer review of the pair-wise comparisons showed that Insightful Miner ranked higher than the other alternatives (with the exception of SAS and SPSS) in human engineering and efficiency. It also tied for top weight for Training and Support/Price. Table 9 summarizes the results of the Expert Choice software.

Certainly, different companies may have different priorities, preferences, and prerequisites. We have explored a few individual scenarios.

Special Case 1: This is a large international company, with thousands of employees, doing business between U.S., Mexico and other countries in Latin America. It is an import and export company. The main goal of using data mining software is to determine the best distribution methods in order to maximize profits. Keeping costs down so it can compete with other companies, is always a concern. The three main criteria this company is looking for in a software package are: Training and Support with multi-lingual support because of the language difference between the countries, Human Engineering to assure that employees in different countries with possibly different computer skill levels, will be able to adapt and use the software, and Portability because it is an established company with an IT department and different platforms that include Microsoft, IBM

Table 9. Summary of synthesized results for each sized company

Synthesized Weights - with respect to goal	Large Company	Small Company
Clementine	0.167	0.138
Enterprise Miner	0.159	0.140
GhostMiner	0.102	0.123
Insightful Miner	0.135	0.160
Intelligent Miner	0.112	0.104
Megaputer	0.106	0.146
Oracle Data Miner	0.115	0.098
SQL Server 2005	0.102	0.092
Overall inconsistency ratio	**0.010**	**0.020**

and Sun Microsystems, as well as a range of desktop operating systems that includes Windows 2000 and XP, Linux, and old legacy equipment. They must be certain that the software is compatible with all existing platforms. Because large amounts of data are processed, software must be robust and reliable as well (see Table 9).

- **Our goal is:** To find the best data mining software.
- **Our criteria are:** Listed seven factors (see Figure 1). The three most important criteria are Training and Support, Human engineering, and Portability.
- **Our alternatives are:** Clementine, Enterprise Miner, Oracle, Microsoft SQL, IBM DB2, Salford CART, Megaputer, and Insightful Miner (see Table 10).

Special Case 2: This is a large national corporation, between 500 and 1,000 employees, in the retail industry with many branches throughout the country. They already have an IT department and different types of platforms, including Unix Servers, Microsoft 2000 and 2003, as well as XP and 2000 Workstations. Portability is very important to make sure that the software is able to run with the platforms already in place. This company already has a well-established customer base, so the goal of choosing data mining software is to find the best way to maximize customer retention, while lowering costs. The three most important criteria that this company is looking for in a software package are: Portability, Efficiency to assure it supports the general business goal assumption, and Modifiability since it is a growing business-they want to be sure that they can go back and customize the software if necessary.

- **Our goal is:** To find the best data mining software.
- **Our criteria are:** Listed seven factors. The three most important criteria are portability, efficiency, and modifiability.
- **Our alternatives are:** Clementine, Enterprise Miner, Oracle, Microsoft SQL, IBM DB2, Salford CART, Megaputer, and Insightful Miner (see Table 11).

Special Case 3: This is a small start-up landscaping and construction company with less than 50 employees. The employees have limited knowledge of computers and software. The goal of using data mining software is to find the best way to attract new customers.

- **Our goal is:** To find the best data mining software.

Table 10.

Criteria	Weights	Software	Ranking
Portability	.215	Clementine	.136
Modifiability	.181	Enterprise Miner	.126
Training and Support	.147	Oracle	.162
Human Engineering / Testability	.130	Microsoft SQL	.109
Understandability	.119	IBM DB2	.117
Reliability	.109	Salford CART	.123
Efficiency	.100	Megaputer	.111
		Insightful Miner	.117

- **Our criteria are:** Listed seven factors. The three most important criteria we are looking for are Human engineering, Training and Support, and Understandability.
- **Our alternatives are:** Clementine, Enterprise Miner, Oracle, Microsoft SQL, IBM DB2, Salford CART, Megaputer, and Insightful Miner (see Table 12).

OTHER CASES

Online Company/E-Commerce

An online/e-commerce company in the recently growing industry. First of all, since an internet company has both actual and potential customers, it needs a tool that can hold and analyze large amount of data. Secondly, it might have engineers or a technical department, so it may not put weight on human engineering and training and support. Consequently, we put more weight on modifiability and less weight on engineering and support. As a result, Oracle would be the best tool for an online/e-commerce company because it scores the highest among 8 tools. If Oracle is not available, IBM would be the second choice.

Educational Institutions

Data mining software is used worldwide in the educational industry. One of Megaputer's data mining software called PolyAnalyst gets a majority

Table 11.

Criteria	Weights	Software	Ranking
Modifiability	.217	Clementine	.134
Portability	.171	Enterprise Miner	.127
Efficiency	.153	Oracle	.163
Reliability	.132	Microsoft SQL	.110
Training and Support	.126	IBM DB2	.115
Human Engineering / Testability	.123	Salford CART	.125
Understandability	.078	Megaputer	.108
		Insightful Miner	.117

Table 12.

Criteria	Weights	Software	Ranking
Training and Support	.226	Clementine	.132
Human Engineering / Testability	.201	Enterprise Miner	.124
Understandability	.166	Oracle	.150
Reliability	.145	Microsoft SQL	.124
Efficiency	.130	IBM DB2	.117
Modifiability	.076	Salford CART	.122
Portability	.055	Megaputer	.114
		Insightful Miner	.118

of its business from educational industry. Microsoft SQL came in first place with GhostMiner as the runner up.

Even though these scenarios can be used as references, they did not apply to every type of institution. Thus, it will be interesting to see what other choices are available in term of best data mining software. What would be the best data mining software for a medical institution?

CONCLUSION

With the use of *Expert Choice* we were able to analytically evaluate eight products within a complex yet controlled environment. The detailed analysis included prioritizing our constraints, evaluating the contributing criteria, entering comparative data and performing relevant sensitivity analysis. The software, *Expert Choice,* performed the analysis, based on our definition, priorities and data.

Data mining technology is changing very rapidly. Our paper focused only on the major suppliers typically available in the market place. There is no definite and explicit answer as to which tool is better suited to potential clients, mainly due to their unique priorities. As there are so many variables to quantify, the problem needs to be defined. Based on what approach the problem requires, then and only then can tools start being quantified. Certainly, the method and the process that we have used can be easily applied to analyze and compare other data mining software for each potential user. Although there is no pattern for pairing the correct software with the proper institution, with the use of this process, every institution should be able to determine which data mining software is the best for their operations.

ACKNOWLEDGMENT

We would like to thank Dr. Jennex, the *Edit-in-Chief of IJKM,* for his tremendous help and guidance during the period of revising our manuscript for more than one year. Dr. Jennex has suggested *Scenario Analysis*, a practical and wonderful idea, and offered many other specific suggestions.

REFERENCES

Alavi, M., & Leidner, D. E. (2001). Knowledge Management Systems: Emerging views and practices from the field. *32nd Hawaii International Conference on Systems Sciences, IEEE Computer Society.*

Angus, J. (2006). Clementine 8.1 melds BA with BI. *InfoWorld, 26*(19), 28–29.

Bednarz, A. (2005). Microsoft beefs up SQL Server database. *New World (New Orleans, La.)*, *22*(13), 12.

Berger, C., & Haberstroh, B. (2005). Oracle data mining 10g release 2: Know more, do more, spend less. Oracle White Papers. Retrieved January 9, 2009, from http://www.oracle.com/technology/products/bi/odm/pdf/bwp_db_odm_10gr2_0905.pdf

Chan, O, J. (2005). Enterprise information system strategy and planning. *Journal of American Business, Cambridge*, *6*(2), 148–154.

Corral, K., Griffin, J., & Jennex, M. E. (2005). Expert's perspective: The potential of knowledge management in Data Warehousing. *Business Intelligence Journal*, *10*(1), 36–40.

Davenport, T., & Harris, J. G. (2007). *Competing on analytics: The new science of winning*. Harvard Business School Press.

Deal, K. (2004). The quest for prediction. *Marketing Research*, *16*(4), 45–47.

Elder, J. F., IV, & Abbott, D. W. (1998). A comparison of leading data mining tools. *Fourth International Conference on Knowledge Discovery & Data Mining.* August 28, 1998. New York.

Expert Choice Inc. (2007). Expert Choice 11. Retrieved January 9, 2009, from http://www.expertchoice.com/software/

Fontana, J. (2005). Microsoft's future in BI market unclear. *New World (New Orleans, La.)*, *22*(43), 9–14.

Giraud-Carrier, C., & Povel, O. (2003). Characterizing data mining software. *Intelligent Data Analysis*, *7*(3), 181–192.

Haughton, D., Deichmann, J., Eshghi, A., Sayek, S., Teebagy, N., & Topi, A. (2003). A review of software packages for data mining. *The American Statistician*, *57*(4), 290–309. doi:10.1198/0003130032486

Hemaida, R., & Schmits, J. (2006). An analytical approach to vendor selection. *Industrial Management (Des Plaines)*, *48*(3), 18–24.

James, G., Hakim, J., Chandras, R., King, N., & Variar, G. (2004). Reviewers' choice: Only the best survive. *Intelligent Enterprise*, *7*(1), 34–38.

Jennex, M. E. (2006). Technologies in support of knowledge management systems, *6th International Forum on Knowledge Management* - Tunis, April, 2006.

Lampe, J. C., & Garcia, A. (2004). Data mining: An in-depth look. *Internal Auditing*, *19*(2), 4–20.

Lurie, I. (2004). Product Review: Insightful Miner. *DM Review*, *14*(6), 88.

Martin, W. E. (2005). *Managing Information Technology* (5th ed.). Saddle River: Prentice Hall.

Mena, J. (1998). Data mining FAQ's. *DM Review*.

Porter, M. E., & Miller, V. (2001). Strategy and the internet. *Harvard Business Review*, *72*(3), 62–68.

Roper-Lowe, G. C., & Sharp, J. A. (1990). The analytic hierarchy process and its application to an information technology decision. *The Journal of the Operational Research Society*, *41*(1), 49–59.

Saaty, T. L. 1980, *Multicriteria Decision Making: The Analytic Hierarchy Process*. Pittsburgh, PA: RWS Publications.

Saaty, T. L. (1996). *Decision Making with Dependence and Feedback: The Analytic Network Process.* Pittsburgh, PA: RWS Publications.

Saaty, T. L. (2001). *The Analytic Network Process* (2nd Version). Pittsburgh, PA: RWS Publications.

Saaty, T. L. (2005). *Theory and Applications of the Analytic Network Process*. Pittsburgh, PA: RWS Publications.

Saaty, T. L., & Vargas, L. G. (2006). *Decision making with the analytic network process: economic, political, social and technological applications with benefits, opportunities, costs and risks*. New York: Springer.

Wang, J. (Ed.). (2008). *Data Warehousing and Mining: Concepts, Methodologies, Tools, and Applications* (6 Volumes). Hershey, PA: IGI Global.

Wang, J., Hu, X. H., Hollister, K., & Zhu, D. (2008). A comparison and scenario analysis of leading data mining software. *International Journal of Knowledge Management*, *4*(2), 17–34.

Chapter 20
Operationalizing Knowledge Sharing for Informers[1]

Dianne P. Ford
Memorial University of Newfoundland, Canada

D. Sandy Staples
Queen's University, Canada

ABSTRACT

Knowledge sharing is a popular research topic; however, the construct has not been well defined theoretically or in terms of how to operationalize it, as there appears to be little consistency. This apparent lack of consistency is problematic for developing a cumulative understanding of the predictors and outcomes of this behavior. This study examines how other researchers have operationalized knowledge sharing, and conduct a qualitative study to further understand this construct. A knowledge sharing and hoarding classification system is developed, and six knowledge sharing behavioral categories are identified. Finally, recommendations are made for future research in knowledge management.

INTRODUCTION

Bill works in a highly competitive firm in the energy industry. When Denise, a junior associate in the firm, asks Bill for help, he is willing to share any bit of knowledge or expertise he can to help her learn and develop her skills. However, when his close colleague Jenna asks Bill for help, he calculates what knowledge she needs and what knowledge he's willing to give her and then shares accordingly. He refuses to share any knowledge that gives him his competitive edge over her for promotions; instead, he gives her more "basic knowledge" to assist her with the immediate problem at hand. When asked about sharing through intra-organizational broadcast media such as mass e-mail or the organization's intranet, Bill guffaws and remarks he hasn't the time.*

Darryl, a project manager in software development, considers himself to be exemplary when it comes to knowledge sharing. He believes very strongly that sharing his knowledge is a part of his job duties as a manager, but that it is also important to share knowledge to set an example for others. He shares not only with individuals directly, but also through

DOI: 10.4018/978-1-60566-954-0.ch020

the knowledge repository. There is very little that Darryl would consider withholding from a colleague, unless it was of a very confidential nature or on a need-to-know basis.

Allison is a programmer whose organization supports the use of a knowledge repository. Allison enjoys contributing to the repository and does so, on a regular basis. When asked why she enjoys using the repository she replies, "Well, that way I don't have to deal with all those annoying people asking annoying questions. I can just tell them where to go for the answers!"

** Names have been changed to protect anonymity.*

These above scenarios illustrate employees sharing their knowledge within their organizations. All three individuals believe their stories illustrate knowledge sharing, although none of them always fully disclose all of their knowledge. Knowledge sharing is thus a complex phenomenon that cannot be validly conceptualized as a simple binary yes/no behavior. The goal of this study is to examine the complexities of the knowledge sharing construct, from a theoretical and empirical perspective.

There are various ways to share one's knowledge, and a variety of behaviors can constitute knowledge sharing as illustrated in the opening vignettes. Previous approaches used by researchers to measure knowledge sharing include: media individuals use to communicate the knowledge (e.g., documents and manuals: Bock & Kim, 2002; Lin, 2008); types of knowledge intended to be shared or shared (e.g., Bock, Zmud & Kim, 2005; Kang, Kim & Chang, 2008; Szulanski, 2000); and a single, self-reported item that asks "Do you (intend to) share your knowledge?" (e.g., Fraser, Marcella & Middleton, 2000). Others assume knowledge sharing has occurred successfully or not successfully and investigate contextual variables and outcome variables to the knowledge sharing without actually measuring knowledge sharing (e.g., Buckman, 1998; Lahneman, 2004; Lemons, 2005; Pan & Scarbrough, 1998; Strickland, 2004). Therefore, not surprisingly, it has been noted that "no established and validated [knowledge sharing] measure exists" (Thompson & Heron, 2006, p. 37).

Multiple measures are problematic for the knowledge management field because different operationalizations of the same construct may influence relationships with other constructs and implies "Theory Shyness," (Kruglanski, 2001). Kruglanski defines theory shyness as the tendency for researchers to fall short of the goal of developing grand theory (theory that is generalizable across contexts and phenomena) and becoming more data-driven (e.g., Sutton & Staw, 1995). The negative consequences of theory shyness include inventing new names for similar concepts, fragmentation of the field, declining interest value of the field's articles, and isolation from general cultural dialogue (i.e., academic articles become disjointed from practitioner understanding and debate) (Kruglanski, 2001). Therefore, a comprehensive, theoretically-grounded operationalization of knowledge sharing, which is relevant to organizations, is needed. The purpose of this study is to operationalize knowledge sharing in a theoretical manner to enable future research to further develop a measure.

Whether we examine knowledge sharing from the perspective of the informer, the recipient, the knowledge itself, or the organization only compounds the difficulty of finding a cohesive theory. A multitude of terms have emanated to describe such differences of perspective. While *knowledge sharing* implies from the perspective of the informer, other terms describe other perspectives. *Knowledge sourcing* describes "a specific mechanism by which an individual accesses another's knowledge, including those recently proposed in the KM literature (e.g., knowledge repositories, virtual communities of practice) and well-established organizational practices (e.g., meetings, memos)" (Gray & Meister, 2004, p.

821). *Knowledge seeking* (Kankanhalli, Tan & Kwok-Kee, 2005; Reio & Wiswell, 2000; Saemundsson, 2004) and *knowledge transfer* (Ko, Kirsch & King, 2005; Sarker, Sarker, Nicholson & Joshi, 2005) are from the perspective of the recipient. *Knowledge stickiness* (Szulanski, 2000) and *transfer of best practices* (Elliott & O'Dell, 1999; O'Dell & Grayson, 2004) look at the ability to transfer a particular bit of knowledge. Finally, *knowledge flows* (Bih-Shiaw, Wang & Yen-Hao, 2006; Fey & Fury, 2008; Gupta & Govindarajan, 2000; Nissen, 2005; Singh, 2005; Suyeon, Hyunseok & Euiho, 2003) and *knowledge transfer* (Kane, Argote & Levine, 2005; Minbaeva & Michailova, 2004; Reagans & McEvily, 2003; Wang, Lin, Jiang & Klein, 2007) are terms used to describe knowledge sharing from an organizational perspective. *Knowledge transfer* is also used to describe inter-organizational or across divisions sharing (Argote, McEvily & Reagans, 2003; Inkpen & Tsang, 2005; Santoro & Saparito, 2006). The term *knowledge sharing* seems to be most consistently used to refer to intra-organizational sharing from an informer's perspective, although it has not been exclusively used in this manner. Thus, in keeping with the apparent trend on the use of the term *knowledge sharing*, we focused on the informer's perspective of sharing knowledge within the workplace.

We believe that there are two underlying causes to the variety of the operationalizations of knowledge sharing. The first is a lack of theoretical understanding of what constitutes knowledge sharing behaviors; the second is that knowledge sharing is a behavioral category (explained further below) and, as such, requires a behavioral index to properly measure it (e.g., Fishbein, 1979). To address these issues, we empirically examine "what is knowledge sharing?" to identify behaviors that constitute knowledge sharing. A qualitative study was used to explore the behaviors constituting knowledge sharing, and how knowledge sharing relates to knowledge hoarding and the usage of communication media channels. This study makes three contributions in the process of defining knowledge sharing. First, knowledge sharing as a behavior is analyzed. Second, the relationships between knowledge sharing and two related constructs, knowledge hoarding and the use of communication media channels, are examined. Third, future knowledge sharing research needs are identified.

OPERATIONALIZATIONS OF KNOWLEDGE SHARING

Before discussing the qualitative study, the proper measurement of behaviors that are categorical in nature (i.e., behavioral categories) like knowledge sharing will be described. Then past operationalizations of knowledge sharing will be briefly described and critiqued.

Knowledge Sharing and Behavioral Categories

Knowledge sharing is a behavior (i.e., an action or activity). The study of behaviors is not novel for the social or humanities fields, nor are the associated problems of operationalizing and obtaining valid measures of behavior (e.g., Sheppard, Hartwick & Warshaw, 1988). In psychology, Fishbein (1979) discusses the operationalization of behaviors within the context of the Theory of Reasoned Action (TRATRATRA: Fishbein & Ajzen, 1975). Fishbein contended that there are some fundamental caveats regarding the operationalization of behaviors that need to be met. Specifically, the behavior in question must be a behavior and not a behavioral category.

For example, exercising is a behavioral category consisting of many different behaviors (e.g., walking the dog, weight training, or training for a triathlon). Individuals, when asked whether they have exercised in the past week, will respond "Yes!" if one is training for a triathlon and the other is walking the dog; yet, these are hardly the same behavior. An injured tri-athlete may respond "Yes, I am exercising," when s/he is now 'just' walking the dog. A question regarding 'exercising' would not capture the change in behavior.

Knowledge sharing is also a behavioral category as illustrated by the opening vignettes (i.e., there are different ways and degrees to which one can share knowledge). As such, the relevant behaviors that constitute knowledge sharing need to be measured. Knowledge sharing should not be measured as a general construct, as it has been in past research as the review below shows. However, to date, we do not have a full understanding of what constitutes relevant knowledge sharing behaviors. This will be examined further in the review of the literature and the qualitative study.

Previously Used Approaches to Measuring Knowledge

The operationalizations of knowledge sharing have ranged from the intention or willingness to share knowledge (e.g., Constant, Kiesler & Sproull, 1994; Fraser et al., 2000; Huang, Davison & Gu, 2008), to what one should share (Connelly & Kelloway, 2003), to what one normally has shared (e.g., McLure Wasko & Faraj, 2000), to what one actually shares (e.g., Bock & Kim, 2002; Carraher, Sullivan & Crocitto, 2008; Ingram & Simons, 2002; Stoddart, 2001). Further discussion of the detail of each operationalization follows (see Table 1 for a summary).

Intention to Share Knowledge

Intentions are commonly used to operationalize knowledge sharing. However, it should be noted that intentions to share knowledge is not a behavior, but rather a *person's subjective probability that s/he will perform the knowledge sharing behavior in question* (Fishbeing & Ajzen, 1975). Intentions are easy to measure using Likert scale surveys and are potentially a sound predictor of actual behaviors, as illustrated by the Theory of Reasoned Action (Fishbein & Ajzen, 1974) and the Theory of Planned Behavior (Ajzen, 1991; Ajzen & Fishbein, 1980). However, we could not find research showing a strong predictive relationship between these two constructs for knowledge sharing (e.g., 1.4% of variance of actual KS explained by intentions, Bock & Kim, 2002; non-significant relationship between intentions and knowledge sharing, Kuo & Young, 2008).

Norms or Beliefs about Knowledge Sharing

The normative perspective, which examines what one should share, is another operationalization found in the literature (Connelly & Kelloway, 2003); however, the normative perspective is not a behavior either. It is an attitude towards knowledge sharing, not yet linked to actual knowledge sharing. The strengths of this operationalization are that it uses vignettes which help control for social desirability. However, the term "should" may actually increase social desirability as "should" statements do not necessarily reflect individuals' actual behaviors.

Actual Knowledge Sharing

The third operationalization of knowledge sharing is actual knowledge sharing which is a behavior and may be a more relevant measure for knowledge sharing research. Actual knowledge sharing has been measured in three ways: descriptive case studies, self-reported historical knowledge sharing, and observed actual knowledge sharing.

Descriptive case studies are a very rich and insightful methodology. Unfortunately the majority of the descriptive case studies found do not measure knowledge sharing explicitly. Rather, knowledge sharing either was assumed to have existed within the organization, or not to have existed in the case of failures of knowledge sharing (e.g., Buckman, 1998; Lahneman, 2004; Lemons, 2005; Pan & Scarbrough, 1998; Strickland, 2004).

With the failure to share knowledge, it is unclear as to what behavior is actually being addressed. What is "successful knowledge sharing" within these organizations? Without understanding the dependent variable, then it is difficult to create cumulative knowledge within the literature/field.

Two approaches are found in studies of self-reported measures of actual knowledge sharing. The first used Likert scale based measures to assess the individual's knowledge sharing behaviors (e.g., Bock & Kim, 2002; Carraher et al., 2008; Durham, Knight & Locke, 1997; Faraj & Sproull, 2000; Liao, Chang, Cheng & Kuo, 2004; Lin, 2008), although there is little consistency in the scales used. The operationalizations varied from sharing documents and manuals (explicit knowledge: Bock & Kim, 2002; Lin, 2008), sharing know-how (tacit knowledge: Bock & Kim, 2002; Lin, 2008), voluntary knowledge sharing like telling colleagues about a new lesson (knowledge donating: van den Hoof & de Leeuw van Weenen, 2004), requested knowledge sharing (knowledge collection: van den Hoof & de Leeuw van Weenen, 2004), frequency of contributing knowledge to electronic knowledge repositories (Kankanhalli, Tan & Wei, 2005), the extent that sharing knowledge voluntarily is the participant's pleasure (Liao et al., 2004), to whether or not sharing knowledge was a natural part of the organization's culture (McDermott & O'Dell, 2001). The second approach asked for verbal recollections of receiving and transferring knowledge (Ford & Chan, 2003).

Table 1. Summary of Knowledge Sharing Measures[3]

Construct	Operationalization
Intentions to Share Knowledge	**Descriptive** • "Preparedness of Knowledge Sharing" not measured but described the case of Australian academics (Jones, 2002). **Self-Reported** • Likert scale of Extremely Likely to Extremely Unlikely for items: "I will share my knowledge with more organizational members;" "I will always provide my knowledge at the request of other organizational members;" "I intend to share my knowledge with other organizational members more frequently in the future;" "I try to share my knowledge with other organizational members in an effective way;" "I will share my knowledge to anyone in the organization if it is helpful to the organization" (Bock & Kim, 2002). • Three-item Likert scale: "I will make an effort to share knowledge with my colleagues", "I intend to share knowledge with my colleagues when they ask", "I will share knowledge with my colleagues." (Huang, Davison & Gu, 2008) • Likert scale measure consisting of two dimensions: explicit knowledge sharing (two items based on sharing of documents, and sharing of manuals) and implicit knowledge sharing (three items based on sharing know-how "when asked", sharing know-how "more frequently", and sharing expertise from training/education "in a more effective way") (Bock et al., 2005, p.109; Chow & Chan, 2008). • Willingness to share knowledge is measured with a single question (Yes, No, Unsure) after a normative statement regarding knowledge is power is given in the questionnaire. An open-ended question follows asking the participant to explain the first answer (Fraser et al., 2000). • Willingness to share different types of knowledge is measured with 4 items: "I am willing to share my knowledge or know-how gained by my work", "I am willing to share my knowledge or know-how gained by training", "I am willing to share my insights and intuition gained by my work", "I am willing to share my data regularly with my co-workers." (Kang, Kim & Chang, 2008). • Scenario regarding of a typical day-to-day operation in which "Jones" found an error, and then the participants were asked what the likelihood that Jones would share his knowledge. They then followed up with an open-ended question for the reasons for their answer (Chow, Deng & Ho, 2000). • Two scenarios are given: one with self-interest highlighted and the other without self-interest. Then participants are asked if they would share the information in that situation (Wang, 2004). • A single vignette about a previously uncooperative colleague asking to have information (i.e., a computer program, which had been developed by the informer) was followed with Likert-scale items regarding willingness to share (Constant et al., 1994; Jarvenpaa & Staples, 2000; Wolfe & Loraas, 2008). **Observed** (None to date.)
Perceptions of Knowledge Sharing	**Self-Reported** • Vignettes were used describing different contexts with a Likert-scale question regarding should the character share the knowledge (Connelly & Kelloway, 2003). (No other operationalizations found.)

continued on the following page

Table 1. continued

Construct	Operationalization
Actual Knowledge Sharing	**Descriptive** • A description of various attributes of Buckman Labs was given. It was assumed that knowledge sharing occurred (Buckman, 1998; Pan & Scarbrough, 1998). • A description of the knowledge sharing practices in the U.S. intelligence community (Lahneman, 2004). • A description of knowledge sharing in a construction company (Styhre, 2008) • A description of knowledge management recommendations for U.S. governmental agencies. It was assumed that there was a failure in knowledge sharing practices within the U.S. governmental agencies leading to the 9/11 (Strickland, 2004). • A description of ways to ensure smooth knowledge sharing using Aerotek as an exemplar (Lemons, 2005). **Self-Reported** • Likert scale measure with five items: "How frequently do you share the following knowledge with your organizational members: reports, official documents; manuals, methodologies, models; know-where, know-whom; experience, know-how; expertise from education & training" (Bock & Kim, 2002; Lin, 2008). • Organizational knowledge-sharing was measured using a Likert scale with 12-items "I share my accumulated knowledge with members of my organization," "I share my organizational experiences and know-how with members my organization," and "I receive from others within the organization the information that I need to perform my job." (Carraher et al., 2008) • "Knowledge donating" and "Knowledge collecting" were two constructs for knowledge sharing. The items included both sides of the sharing behavior (i.e., receiving the knowledge and giving the knowledge) with various targets (van den Hoof & De Leeuw van Weenen, 2004). Knowledge donating consisted of 6 Likert-scale items that described voluntary knowledge sharing (e.g., "When I've learned something new, I tell my colleagues in my department about it"; "Knowledge sharing with my colleagues outside of my department is considered a normal thing": van den Hooff & de Leeuw van Weenen, 2004, p. 17). Knowledge collecting consisted of 8 Likert-scale items that describe requested knowledge sharing (e.g., "I share the information I have with colleagues within my department, when they ask me to;" "Colleagues outside my department tell me what their skills are, when I ask them about it": van den Hooff & de Leeuw van Weenen, 2004, p. 17). • Participants from a single firm (case study) respond to two Likert-scale items for knowledge sharing: "It is my pleasure to share my working experience and knowledge to my colleagues voluntarily;" "I will share my working experience and knowledge to my colleagues conditionally" (Liao et al., 2004, p.28). • A literature review identified 40 companies which were 'successful at knowledge management'. Questionnaires were sent to the companies to confirm whether or not "company representatives felt that sharing knowledge was a natural part of the culture" (McDermott & O'Dell, 2001). • Three self-report items: "What is your frequency of usage of EKRs [electronic knowledge repositories] to contribute knowledge?"; "I often use EKRs to contribute my knowledge in my work"; "I regularly use EKRs to contribute my knowledge in my work" (Kankanhalli et al., 2005, p.143). • Participants in a study by Thompson and Heron (2006) completed the 9 item Likert "advocacy participation" scale from organizational citizenship measure (van Dyne, Graham & Dienesch, 1994). • Participants in a study by Srivastava, Bristol and Locke (2006) completed 4-item Likert scale with questions like, "People in our team share their special knowledge and expertise with one another" (Faraj & Sproull, 2000) and 3-item Likert scale that ask questions like "…share information with…" (Durham et al., 1997). • In a case study, participants were interviewed and asked to identified work-related problems that they had to seek knowledge from others to solve, describe the knowledge and identify the informer. Participants were also asked to identify knowledge that they shared with others and who received that knowledge (Ford & Chan, 2003). • Two patterns of knowledge-sharing behaviors were rated by a 5-point Likert scale: (1) knowledge sharing in a large-group setting (3 items on the transmission of useful knowledge to a large number of people via internal and external education, training, and publications), and (2) knowledge sharing in a small-group setting (3 items on private sharing of useful knowledge with coworkers belonging to the same group. (Liu & Liu, 2008). **Observed** • Participants for the study were identified on the basis of having posted to one of three technical on-line communities (actual knowledge sharing was a selection criteria for the study: McLure Wasko & Faraj, 2000). • Participants for the study were identified on the basis of having posted to a national legal professional association in the United States. Knowledge contribution was measured two ways: volume of contributions (total number of contributions that were responses to a request for knowledge), and the helpfulness (content was coded by one of the authors and a domain expert) (McLure Wasko & Faraj, 2005). • Companies identified transfers of best practices (third party reporting the knowledge sharing behavior, confirmed by the parties involved: Szulanski & Cappetta, 2000). • Incidents of knowledge sharing were observed by the researchers in case studies (Berends et al., 2006; Ford & Chan, 2003). • Two quantifiable measures of knowledge sharing activities in F/OSS projects' mailing lists were created by analyzing substantial email exchanges between list participants: (1) the total number of posts externalized to the list (i.e., email messages potential knowledge seekers posted), (2) the total number of replies made by potential knowledge providers to questions posted to the lists. (Sowe, Stamelos & Angelis, 2008)

Finally, actual knowledge sharing was measured through observations. Observations were either made by the researcher after-the-fact (e.g., posting to on-line communities: McLure Wasko & Faraj, 2000, 2005; Sowe, Stamelos & Angelis, 2008), by the researcher in real-time (Berends, van der Bij, Debackere & Weggeman, 2006; Ford & Chan, 2003), or by others in the organization

(Szulanski & Cappetta, 2000). While observations mitigate social desirability (given the way knowledge sharing was measured in these studies), and are not susceptible to recall bias in the same way as self-reported behavior, observation does rely on others seeing and identifying the behavior as knowledge sharing. A third party might not consider something knowledge sharing, even if the informer and the recipient do. Also, as an observer within a natural setting, it is not possible to know if the informer is withholding some relevant knowledge while sharing some knowledge.

The constituent behaviors of a behavioral category such as knowledge sharing should be the different possible behaviors that constitute knowledge sharing, and these behaviors should be based on what the average person would do from the population in question (Fishbein, 1979). However, our review finds the typical operationalization of actual knowledge sharing behavior has not been specific behaviors, but generalized behaviors like "knowledge sharing" (e.g., Bock & Kim, 2002; Buckman, 1998; Srivastava, Bartol & Locke, 2006). The problem with this generalized operationalization is that it treats actual knowledge sharing as a categorical behavior like exercising (i.e., the previously described example). Although some specific behaviors with respect to actual knowledge sharing have been studied including verbal explanations (Palmer, 2001; Ford & Chan, 2003), personnel transfers (Gupta & Govindarajan, 2000), and use of intranets or knowledge repositories (Markus, 2001), the specific behaviors that comprise the behavioral category of knowledge sharing are not yet well defined. Therefore, to determine the behaviors that constitute knowledge sharing, an exploratory qualitative study was undertaken.

METHODS

Semi-structured telephone interviews were conducted with knowledge workers. Participants were first asked, "What does 'knowledge' mean to you?" This question served as a priming question for the topic, but also provided the researchers a conceptual framework for understanding what the individual was referring to when s/he discussed "knowledge." Finally, participants were asked, "How do you share your knowledge? Please list the types of behaviors that you would do to share your knowledge." They were prompted for more responses when their responses started to dwindle. The answers to this question and the subsequent unstructured discussion to clarify the behaviors listed and to identify as many as possible were the basis for identifying relevant behaviors for the construct of knowledge sharing. All but two of the interviews were recorded to ensure accuracy. In these two cases, transcripts of the handwritten notes from the interview were edited by the interviewees for accuracy. The interviews took approximately 25 to 45 minutes, depending on the amount of discussion from the participant.

Sample

To be accepted into the sample individuals had to satisfy the definition: *individuals who use information or knowledge as a primary input or output of their jobs*. Twenty employed knowledge workers working within North America formed the sample; nine male and eleven female participants whose age ranged from 24 to 55 years of age. The participants were from various industries (e.g., government, consultants, energy, information technology, and retail). The types of positions held were: lawyer, engineer, economic development officer, project manager in information systems, retail company marketing department employee, computer programmer, teacher assistant for special needs children. Geographically, they lived in several Canadian provinces and U.S. Central and Eastern states. Convergence was achieved as the last five interviews did not produce any new responses; thus further interviews were not sought.

Analysis

The analysis of the interviews followed an iterative process (Miles & Huberman, 1994). The transcripts were checked for accuracy; then the responses were examined to identify themes. To address the key research question, all possible behaviors identified by the participants were listed in a comprehensive list. The behaviors identified were then examined for redundancy. Finally, the list of behaviors was examined to identify dimensions or categories of behaviors.

RESULTS

Participants were asked to describe their behaviors when they share their knowledge after they had been asked to define "knowledge" in their own words. All the participants' definitions of knowledge contained at least two definitional components, implying that they perceived knowledge to be a complex construct subject to multiple different possible definitions. The common thread is that knowledge is related to information, that it is learned (either through experience, research, or education), and that it is applied.[2]

What is Knowledge Sharing?

Knowledge sharing behaviors identified by participants revolved around two themes. The first theme was based on the communication channels used. All of the participants identified various communication channels and communicated this theme as part of their initial response (20/20). One type of communication channel was in-person, for example: face-to-face (11/20), one-on-one discussions (7/20), meetings (9/20), cross-functional team meetings (2/20), group discussions (2/20), forums and conferences (3/20), walking over to people (2/20), talking in the hallway (1/20), and talking through the wall (1/20). Other communication channels were with the assistance of communication media, such as: e-mail (18/20), telephone (8/20), teleconferencing (2/20), videoconferencing (1/20), instant messaging (1/20), facsimile (1/20), intranet/websites (6/20), MS Share Point (1/20), MS PowerPoint presentations (2/20), and written documentation (10/20). Every participant listed at least three different means of sharing his/her knowledge with others at work as illustrated in the following quotes.

The best one is face-to-face. E-mail is good for covering tons of stuff. There's also walking over to people.

There's team meetings [sic], sending e-mail. I also use Lotus Notes database. There's one-on-one and one-on-few discussions, and face-to-face.

Walking to a cubicle and chit chat. Face-to-face, talk through the walls, round table at meetings, job shadowing, emails, group drive-publications, mass email, intranet. That's about it, that I can think of anyway.

Once participants listed the communication media, they were asked what they were doing when they were sharing their knowledge, which gave rise to the second theme. The second theme was based on the extent of sharing, such as sharing fully or hiding some knowledge. The responses for extent of sharing were: knowledge hinting or burying the knowledge (12/20), hiding some knowledge (10/20), sharing by demonstrating for better understanding (10/20), full disclosure (9/20), sharing as much as possible but withholding confidential knowledge (7/20), intentionally withholding some knowledge that is not confidential but still sharing some (7/20), referring the recipient to another person or database for the knowledge (7/20), following-up with the recipient at a later date to ensure understanding (6/20), mentoring the recipient (5/20), checking for understanding at the time of sharing the knowledge (2/20), and using case examples to illustrate points (1/20).

Again, all of the participants identified several behaviors. Interestingly, the following illustrate that the choice of level of sharing can be dependent upon various factors, such as the recipient (level of expertise, experience, their effort and past performance record), time constraints, and the risk inherent in the situation (business risk and personal career risk).

I fully share, especially in the work setting.... I won't hint at my knowledge if I'm under time constraints, but otherwise I would [hint at my knowledge] to play and learn or test the person for sharpness.... Hmmm... yeah I do that [hide knowledge] every day. This stuff I'll never share as it is my insurance against possible litigation.

I mentor once every month, demonstrate my knowledge (either voluntarily or by request) to increase people's efficiency. I role model efficient behaviors, and I follow-up all the time.... The level of detail I go into will depend on the person and the level of depth that they want or need. I consider confidentiality but I would rather err on the side of disclosing too much than too little.... I sometimes use hints when I'm doing project reviews [with subordinates]. I'm trying to help to increase the scope of their careers when I do that.... I will withhold some knowledge when it is a secret and I have to withhold it, but then I will inform the person that I am withholding something.

Full disclosure depends on what it is. If it is a "drive-by" conversation, then I just give them tidbits. If it is process oriented, then I will go into more detail and ensure that they understand it. I will refer people to others if necessary, and I contribute to the internet daily. I might also drop hints to make suggestions of how I might think to do it a better way. I will also hide knowledge if a peer might not have been doing all of their workload; I want equality, so effort is a key factor. I don't want them coming out smelling like a rose if I did all the work.

These two themes consist of several types of behaviors. For example, the communication channels theme includes behaviors such as: using e-mail, face-to-face discussions, talking on the phone, instant messaging, sharing knowledge in a meeting. Examples of behaviors that comprise the extent of knowledge sharing include: sharing the knowledge fully, mentoring, sharing knowledge and following-up to ensure understanding, sharing some knowledge but withholding other knowledge (for whatever reason), and withholding all aspects of the knowledge sought.

In previous work, it is assumed that knowledge sharing and knowledge hoarding are antitheses of each other (e.g., Hibbard & Carrillo, 1998; Husted & Michailova, 2002) which implies that knowledge sharing is a unidimensional construct that ranges from one extreme of knowledge hoarding to the other extreme of knowledge sharing. Since the two themes of knowledge sharing (communication channel and extent of sharing) were behaviors participants identified as "knowledge sharing," as part of our analysis, we attempted to map communication channels to the extent of sharing. However, we found the two themes could not be meaningfully mapped along the unidimensional knowledge sharing/knowledge hoarding continuum.

Specifically, communication channels do not map along the single continuum; more knowledge sharing and less hoarding do not occur necessarily with face-to-face as opposed to the telephone, for example. While it may be argued that nuances are better communicated through a richer face-to-face medium because of the existence of non-verbal communication and cues (e.g., Daft & Lengel, 1984; Daft & Lengel & Trevino, 1987; Zack, 1993, 1994) than the leaner phone medium, the verbal content can be exactly the same. One participant did identify that the extent to which knowledge sharing occurred was dependent on the media chosen: *I hope that people get the understanding; the amount of disclosure depends on the format. For example, in documents I am detailed, and instant*

Figure 1. Knowledge Sharing versus Knowledge Hoarding and Behavior Classifications

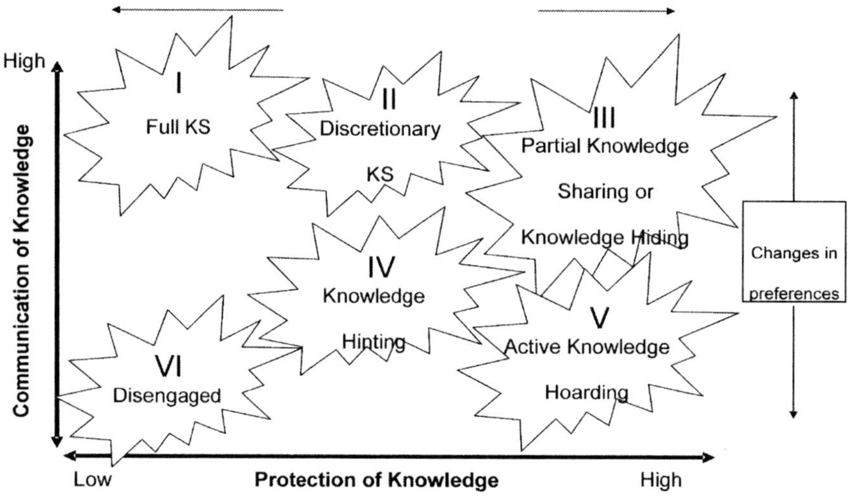

messaging is briefer and I hope that they get it. More pertinent, it is an erroneous assumption that more knowledge is always shared in face-to-face communication as opposed to other media, that an individual always hoards more knowledge using e-mail than by phone (a richer media). Thus, communication channels, in and of themselves, do not map meaningfully along this knowledge sharing/knowledge hoarding continuum.

The extent of sharing theme did map more meaningfully against knowledge sharing/knowledge hoarding, but the distances between the behaviors were not meaningful and the mapping was arbitrary at best. The fact that the responses of the participants did not fit well onto knowledge sharing/knowledge hoarding continuum led us to consider knowledge sharing and knowledge hoarding as two separate and distinct constructs (i.e., they are independent and can exist simultaneously). This led to a two-dimensional space with knowledge sharing on one axis and knowledge hoarding on the other axis instead of a single continuum (see Figure 1). However, to reduce confusion of multiple labels of "sharing" and "hoarding", we chose to label the "Knowledge Sharing" axis as "Communication of Knowledge," as one of the unifying themes of the existing definitions of knowledge sharing is that *something* (i.e., knowledge, expertise, understanding) is being *communicated* to a recipient somehow (e.g., Connelly & Kelloway, 2003; Lee, 2001). The "Knowledge Hoarding" axis is relabeled as "Protection of Knowledge" to reflect the most recent discussions on knowledge hoarding (Connelly, Zweig, & Webster, 2006; Webster et al., 2008).

Five of the six sets of behaviors vis-á-vis the knowledge sharing/hoarding space reflect responses from individuals in our study and one is implied.

Group I, Full Knowledge Sharing, is characterized by high or open communication of knowledge and low or no protection of knowledge. In this case, individuals would give everything they have (that is relevant); none of the relevant knowledge is withheld.

Group II, Discretionary Knowledge Sharing, is characterized by high/open communication of knowledge and moderate protection of knowledge. In this case, individuals share as much as possible subject to confidentiality or time constraints, etc. One participant commented that she would love to share everything, but there are times that she cannot, given confidentiality constraints. Interestingly, she also stated that in those instances, she would inform the recipient that she was withholding confidential information while trying to help them as much as possible.

Group III, Partial Knowledge Sharing, is characterized by high/open communication of knowledge and high protection of knowledge. In this case individuals actively share knowledge while simultaneously withholding relevant knowledge for reasons other than confidentiality or time constraints. These behaviors seem to be less altruistic and more self-serving in nature as illustrated by the opening vignette in which Bill only partially shares knowledge with his close colleague, Jenna, in order to preserve his competitive advantage. These motivational differences distinguish this category from Group II.

Group IV, Knowledge Hinting, is characterized by moderate communication of knowledge and moderate protection of knowledge. For example, in a meeting an individual may want to share knowledge with the group; however, doing so would make his/her superior lose face. Hinting or suggesting at the knowledge is intended to suggest to the superior to share that knowledge with the group. Alternatively, individuals may hint to junior colleagues to help them learn and arrive at the solution on their own. One participant hinted for less altruistic reasons as illustrated in this quote: *I won't hint at my knowledge if I'm under time constraints, but otherwise I would [hint at my knowledge] to play and learn or test the person for sharpness.* For her, hinting was like a cat and mouse game where she would have fun testing the recipient's mental acuity.

Group V, Knowledge Hoarding, is characterized by low communication of knowledge and high protection of knowledge. Active knowledge hoarding is likely the most self-serving of all the behaviors, as illustrated by one of the earlier quotes: *Yeah I do that [hide knowledge] every day. This stuff I'll never share as it is my insurance against possible litigation.*

Group VI, Disengaging, is implied theoretically from this two-dimensional space. Disengaging is characterized by low communication of knowledge and low protection of knowledge: the individual neither strives to share nor to hoard their knowledge. There were two examples in the data that might pertain to disengaging, both relating to reasons why the participants sometimes do not share knowledge at work. One participant explained that she does not share knowledge when experiencing premenstrual syndrome (PMS); another participant commented that when his back hurt, he did not put in the effort required to share knowledge. Neither of them was actively trying to hoard their knowledge, but they did not have the physical energy or perhaps mental focus or energy required to share their knowledge.

Recent research has examined the relationship between disengagement from knowledge sharing and disengagement as it relates to job performance as defined by Kahn (1990, 1992). In a qualitative study, Ford (2008) found that approximately 93% of the participants could describe a time when they were disengaged from knowledge sharing, and that 70% of all examples of "not sharing knowledge" constituted disengagement from sharing (17% were active knowledge hoarding and 13% were partial or discretionary knowledge sharing). Furthermore, she found that disengagement from knowledge sharing appeared to precede disengagement from other job tasks and possibly the organization, either temporarily or permanently. The most significant cause for disengagement from knowledge sharing was availability (emotional, physical and cognitive resources), more specifically, the lack thereof. Thus, even though this category was not well represented within the study presented here, subsequent research suggests this is a relevant behavioral category for organizations and individuals.

The results also suggested that communication channel behaviors can be mapped within this two-dimensional space. Participants used more communication channel behaviors (e.g., they chose to share via face-to-face, e-mail, meetings, sharing documents, teleconferencing, etc.) when they partook in one of the high/open communication of knowledge categories like full, discretionary or partial knowledge sharing. When there is moderate knowledge sharing (i.e., knowledge hinting), it appears as though individuals have fewer appropriate communication channels available from which to choose (e.g., they chose to share via face-to-face, meetings). In other words, none of the participants said that they would hint at or bury their knowledge within an e-mail or any other written communication channel, but that they might hint at their knowledge within a face-to-face setting. For example, one participant stated:

If a peer [makes me mad], then I might hint at the knowledge that they are asking for, but if it is a consistent problem, then I'm motivated to help them. If I like and respect the person, then NO I would not do that. Also I could not do that in email; it takes too long.

Knowledge hinting seems to require a communication channel with high to medium richness. Perhaps the non-verbal communication was needed for the informer to indicate to the recipient there was more s/he was trying to say than what s/he was saying verbally, like a facial expression, raised eyebrows or hand gestures. As explained by the Media Richness Theory, rich media has the ability to transmit these subtleties that leaner media (like e-mail and memos) do not (e.g., Daft & Lengel, 1984; Daft et al., 1987). Alternatively, as people share less knowledge, they might choose the verbal media over the written media as they may not want it on a "permanent" medium, such as paper or e-mails, to allow deniability if needed, or similarly, choose the written format if they share more to create accountability and increase the possibility for recognition.

When there is low or no communication of knowledge (i.e., disengaging or active knowledge hoarding), there appears to be few communication channel behaviors involved. Individuals wishing to actively hoard their knowledge might choose to avoid using communication channels altogether (e.g., not respond to e-mails or voice mail requests for knowledge, or avoid the knowledge seeker in the hallways) or use extremely lean media (e.g., respond with e-mail rather than a face-to-face or phone conversation) to conceal their hoarding behaviors. Lean media could conceal hoarding behaviors allowing them to appear to be sharing when they are sharing only information and not knowledge (e.g., Zack, 1993, 1994, 2007). Employees may be motivated to conceal hoarding since it may be seen as a work behavior that is counterproductive potentially resulting in disciplinary actions either formal (e.g., poor performance appraisals by supervisor) or informal (e.g., retribution and isolation by colleagues: Ford & Chan, 2003).

There is no differentiation among the choice or variety of communication channel behaviors along the protection of knowledge axis. We could not discriminate between full, discretionary, and partial knowledge sharing by the communication channel behaviors because the channels appeared to be the same (e.g., an individual may use e-mail to accomplish any of the three behaviors). Nor can one discriminate between disengaging and active knowledge hoarding by the communication channel behaviors. Communication channels capture the "How..." of knowledge sharing, but not the "What?" or "How much?"

DISCUSSION

We have seen in the review of the literature that there has been some general similarities in the previous operationalizations of "knowledge sharing" in that *something* is being *communicated* or *transferred* between the involved parties *(informer and recipient(s))*, and that *communication channels* are being used to accomplish this. The knowledge management literature has tended to operationalize knowledge sharing either through proxy variables (e.g., personnel transfers, use of communication media) or as a single categorical behavior (e.g., "Do you intend to share your knowledge?"). As discussed by Fishbein (1979), behavioral categories introduce noise and decrease predictive validity of intentions to actual behaviors. Thus, this research sought to identify what behaviors constitute knowledge sharing, so that future research could develop and use a more valid measure to move the knowledge sharing field ahead.

The results from this qualitative study suggest that knowledge sharing, while requiring the use of communication channels, is more than that; it is the extent to which the knowledge is communicated and shared. Furthermore, the commonly held assumption that knowledge sharing and knowledge hoarding are on a continuum may not be an accurate portrayal of these behaviors. Consequent to the proposal that knowledge sharing and knowledge hoarding are independent constructs that may co-occur, we extrapolate six possible behavioral categories: disengaging, knowledge hinting, partial knowledge sharing, discretionary knowledge sharing, full knowledge sharing, and active knowledge hoarding.

Why use six behavioral categories? For example, one can postulate only four: full knowledge sharing, partial knowledge sharing (which includes discretionary, hinting and self-serving partial withholding of knowledge), active knowledge hoarding, and disengaging. However, grouping all of the apparent "partial" sharing behaviors together loses richness as they appear to have different underlying motives (i.e., predictors). If two behaviors have different predictors they are different constructs and should be separated. However, empirical validation is necessary to determine whether these constructs are real or illusionary, to ensure we are not simply inventing more names for similar constructs and risking the "Theory Shyness" Kruglanski (2001) warns against.

The next step for future research is to develop and test specific measures for each of these six knowledge sharing behavioral categories. Behavioral categories may be measured in a number of different ways. However, the key issue is that the behavioral category should be broken into constituent behaviors. Occurrence or frequency of each of these behaviors would then be appropriate, as would behaviorally anchored rating scales (BARS: e.g., Fishbein, 1979; Schwab, Heneman III & DeCotiis, 1975; Smith & Kendall, 1963). For example, multiple-item scales could be developed for each category using the guidelines of Churchill (1979) or Straub, Gefen and Boudreau (2004). Operationalizations for each category and suggested items, drawn from our interviews, for measure development are provided in Table 2. These operationalizations could be a starting point for creating a behavioral index as suggested by Fishbein (1979). We also need to determine predictors for each of the six knowledge sharing behavioral categories outlined in Figure 1. To date, we do not fully understand what predicts full, partial, discretionary knowledge sharing, knowledge hinting, knowledge hoarding and disengaging behaviors and how these predictors may vary.

Another opportunity for future research is examining if relationships exist between these different behavioral categories. For example, do individuals prefer one behavioral category over the others (e.g., "Does Juan always try to fully share his knowledge; whereas, Joella is always disengaged?") or can a single individual display all six behavioral categories? Preliminary results from the interviewees suggest that while an individual may have a preference for one of the behavioral categories, they may also display all six behaviors given the right circumstances. For example, Darryl in the opening vignettes preferred full knowledge sharing; however, he would also use discretionary knowledge sharing if the knowledge was on a need-to-know basis. In person, Allison might appear to be disengaged; however, through the knowledge repository she exhibits full or partial knowledge sharing behaviors.

Table 2. Operationalizations and Suggested Items for Knowledge Sharing Behaviors

Full Knowledge Sharing: *"An individual describes or explains his/her understanding or expertise on the relevant subject fully without any withholding of the knowledge in question."*
I shared my understanding or expertise through mentorship.
I shared my understanding through job shadowing
I shared my understanding or expertise through demonstration
I described my knowledge in full detail and at a later date followed up with summary to ensure full understanding.
I described my knowledge in full detail and checked for understanding.
I described my expertise in full detail.
Discretionary Knowledge Sharing: *"An individual describes or explains his/her understanding or expertise on the relevant subject as much as s/he can, while simultaneously withholding some knowledge due to some external constraints (e.g., confidentiality)."*
I shared some of the knowledge, but withheld confidential aspects.
I shared as much knowledge as I could without infringing on privacy issues.
I described my understanding as much as I could, given the recipient's clearance level to this knowledge.
I could not share this knowledge fully because it's on a "need to know" basis and the recipient did not "need to know."
Partial Knowledge Sharing: *"An individual describes or explains his/her understanding or expertise on the relevant subject and withholds some relevant knowledge that could be shared."*
I shared some knowledge, but withheld other knowledge that was not confidential.
I described the knowledge that was to be shared in sufficient detail for basic understanding, but not in full detail.
Knowledge Hinting: *"An individual eludes to his/her understanding or expertise on the relevant subject without explicitly describing it."*
I shared knowledge by burying it in other knowledge or information.
I hinted at the knowledge with hopes the recipient would figure it out on their own.
I suggested at my understanding without explicitly stating it.
Active Knowledge Hoarding: *"An individual withholds all of the knowledge in question. They may state they are withholding the knowledge, or they may actively avoid sharing situations."*
I actively protect my knowledge.
I keep my knowledge to myself, even if I am asked to share it.
I refused to share my understanding when asked for help.
Disengaging: *"An individual does not actively share nor actively withholds their understanding and expertise. There is a withdrawal and a lack of engagement in these behaviors."*
I did not share any knowledge, as I was not asked to share any.
Did not share any knowledge, as doing so is not part of the job.
I couldn't be bothered to share any of my expertise.

For future studies on knowledge sharing from the informer's perspective, we recommend that observation or self-reports be used. Self-reports (although limited for various reasons) are the best alternative available for actual knowledge sharing, as suggested by this study due to the differentiation between full and partial knowledge sharing. Typically, only the informer could know if knowledge sharing occurred (the exception to this is the researcher may know what is not shared within an experimental setting). Recipients can report on the knowledge that is "shared" between them and the informed as they can judge what they learned; however, they do not know what knowledge was withheld from sharing. Additionally, knowledge sharing is a difficult behavior to observe from an external perspective due to the nature of knowledge in relation to information.

Therefore, the informer is the best judge as to whether or not knowledge was shared and self-reporting is a fair way to measure it.

We also recommend that future researchers be very clear on what they measure (such as intentions versus actual knowledge sharing, observations and third party assessments versus self-reports, process of sharing versus the outcomes of sharing like learning). The review of the previously used measures illustrates a lack of continuity within the knowledge sharing field, which hinders the development of a cumulative knowledge or understanding of the phenomenon.

Finally, we are left with the question, "Why were the communication channel behaviors the initial responses for all of the participants?" Possibly all of the participants responded with communication channel behaviors initially because the wording of the interview question, which was: "How do you share your knowledge? Please list the types of behaviors that you would do to share your knowledge." This may have created the response bias in which the participants assumed they were already *sharing something.* If they have already decided to share something, then they would be required to transmit this knowledge through some sort of communication channel.

This premise is supported by the Communication Theory (e.g., Gupta & Govindarajan, 2000), which argues that to communicate an idea or thought, the following process occurs. The communicator first thinks of the message which s/he would like to communicate and then, expresses the message, which must go through a medium (or communication channel) to reach the recipient. The recipient then senses/receives the transmission and subsequently interprets the message to arrive at his or her own understanding. In other words, once an individual decides what knowledge they want to share and the effort that they want to expend, then s/he must choose an appropriate communication channel to transmit the knowledge to the recipient.

Therefore, communication media captures only "How" knowledge is shared, not the underlying behaviors of sharing knowledge. Consequently, a measure based on use of communication media cannot capture the possible nuances of knowledge sharing because they fail to differentiate between the six behavioral categories and is therefore not the best choice for understanding why knowledge sharing occurs or what the outcomes are of knowledge sharing. Future research might want to examine if there is a relationship between the knowledge sharing behaviors and the choices of communication media.

Lastly, to note that "knowledge sharing is simply communication," results in an overly broad categorization of the behavior once again, as knowledge sharing also involves the "what is being communicated" and "to what extent," both of which have interpersonal, departmental and organizational implications. Being more specific about the behaviors involved allows for better refinement of measures and ultimately tighter predications and better understanding of the behaviors involved.

CONCLUSION

Given the importance of knowledge utilization for organizations and the key role sharing plays in generating value from knowledge, more research is needed to understand the contextual nuances of knowledge sharing in organizations. The results of this study provide a refined conceptualization of what constitutes knowledge sharing from the perspective of the provider and intra-organizational knowledge sharing. Knowledge sharing is clearly not a simple, single behavior that can be measured easily. Six types of knowledge sharing behavior classifications are identified: full knowledge sharing, partial knowledge sharing, discretionary knowledge sharing, knowledge hinting, active knowledge hoarding, and disengaged.

More research is required to validate these behavioral classes and create formal operationalizations and measures for each of these knowledge sharing behavioral classifications. We provide operationalizations and a list of possible items to include in the measures for each of the categories. Full knowledge sharing is operationalized as, *"An individual describes or explains his/her understanding or expertise on the relevant subject fully without any withholding of the knowledge in question."* Discretionary knowledge sharing is operationalized as, *"An individual describes or explains his/her understanding or expertise on the relevant subject as much as s/he can, while simultaneously withholding some knowledge due to some external constraints (e.g., confidentiality)."* Partial knowledge sharing is operationalized as, *"An individual describes or explains his/her understanding or expertise on the relevant subject and withholds some relevant knowledge that could be shared."* Knowledge hinting is operationalized as, *"An individual eludes to his/her understanding or expertise on the relevant subject without explicitly describing it."*

Active knowledge hoarding is operationalized as, *"An individual withholds all of the knowledge in question. They may state they are withholding the knowledge, or they may actively avoid sharing situations."* It will be a challenging construct for a self-reporting measure to capture due to potential social desirability issues that accompany this behavior. To that end, future research may need to include a social desirability measure for control, or word the items such that social desirability is minimized.

The last category, disengaging, is operationalized as, *"An individual does not actively share nor actively withholds their understanding and expertise. There is a withdrawal and a lack of engagement in these behaviors."* When developing a measure for this construct, the questions for this behavior should address the lack of sharing intentions but also the lack of hoarding intentions.

Future research needs to clearly define the context of the knowledge sharing behaviors within the research design and the measures used. This includes with whom the individuals are sharing (e.g., intra-organizationally to close colleagues or distant colleagues, or inter-organizationally with clients, partners, suppliers) and the timeframe of the sharing behaviours (e.g., today, yesterday, this past week, over the past month or year). Timeframe is relevant as some behaviors may occur very frequently within a day or week, but others may occur less frequently and require a longer timeframe to capture any activity (e.g., hinting might occur once a month as opposed to partial sharing which might occur daily) to avoid a ceiling or floor-effect.

Similarly, by including the context of the recipient, we may discover some behaviors may be more prevalent with subordinates or individuals from other departments (e.g., hinting or discretionary knowledge sharing) versus sharing with superiors (e.g., full knowledge sharing) versus sharing with close colleagues when promotions are competed for (e.g., partial knowledge sharing or active knowledge hoarding). Indeed, some behaviors may be benevolent and important with some types of recipients for the organization and should be encouraged by management, but be malevolent and harmful to the organization with other recipients and thus discouraged (e.g., discretionary sharing with members from other departments as opposed to members on the same project team).

This research examined knowledge sharing behaviors for intra-organizational sharing (and hoarding). Research is also required to examine if this conceptualization of knowledge sharing holds within different contexts (e.g., inter-organizational, within communities of practice, volunteer organizations, personal networks). We recommend that future researchers clearly identify which behavioral category of knowledge sharing they are assessing and how. Doing so will help to build cumulative knowledge on knowledge sharing.

REFERENCES

Ajzen, I. (1991). The theory of planned behavior. *Organizational Behavior and Human Decision Processes*, *50*(2), 179–211. doi:10.1016/0749-5978(91)90020-T

Ajzen, I., & Fishbein, M. (1980). Prediction of goal-directed behavior: Attitudes, intentions, and perceived behavioral control. *Journal of Experimental Social Psychology*, *22*(September), 453–474.

Argote, L., McEvily, B., & Reagans, R. (2003). Introduction to the Special Issue on Managing Knowledge in Organizations: Creating, Retaining, and Transferring Knowledge. *Management Science*, *49*(4), v–viii.

Berends, H., van der Bij, H., Debackere, K., & Weggeman, M. (2006). Knowledge sharing mechanisms in industrial research. *R & D Management*, *36*(1), 85–95. doi:10.1111/j.1467-9310.2005.00417.x

Bih-Shiaw, J., Yu Ping Wang, C., & Yen-Hao, C. (2006). Knowledge flows and performance of multinational subsidiaries: the perspective of human capital. *International Journal of Human Resource Management*, *17*(2), 225–244.

Bock, G. W., & Kim, Y. (2002). Breaking the myths of rewards: An exploratory study of attitudes about knowledge sharing. *Information Resources Management Journal*, *15*(2), 14–21.

Bock, G. W., Zmud, R. W., & Kim, Y. (2005). Behavioral intention formation in knowledge sharing: Examining the roles of extrinsic motivators, social-psychological forces, and organizational climate. *MIS Quarterly*, *29*(1), 87–111.

Buckman, R. H. (1998). Knowledge sharing at Buckman Labs. *The Journal of Business Strategy*, *19*(1), 11–15. doi:10.1108/eb039903

Carraher, S. M., Sullivan, S. E., & Crocitto, M. M. (2008). Mentoring across global boundaries: An empirical examination of home- and host-country mentors on expatriate career outcomes. *Journal of International Business Studies*, *39*(8), 1310. doi:10.1057/palgrave.jibs.8400407

Chow, C. W., Deng, F. J., & Ho, J. L. (2000). The openness of knowledge sharing within organizations: A comparative study of the United States and the People's Republic of China. *Journal of Management Accounting Research*, *12*, 65–95. doi:10.2308/jmar.2000.12.1.65

Chow, W. S., & Chan, L. S. (2008). Social network, social trust and shared goals in organizational knowledge sharing. *Information & Management*, *45*(7), 458. doi:10.1016/j.im.2008.06.007

Connelly, C. E., & Kelloway, K. (2003). Predictors of employees' perceptions of knowledge sharing cultures. *Leadership and Organization Development Journal*, *24*(5/6), 294–301. doi:10.1108/01437730310485815

Connelly, C. E., Zweig, D., & Webster, J. (2006, May 5th - 7th, 2006). *Knowledge hiding in organizations.* Paper presented at the Society for Industrial and Organizational Psychology 20th Annual Conference, Dallas, TX.

Constant, D., Kiesler, S., & Sproull, L. (1994). What's mine is ours, or is it? A study of attitudes about information sharing. *Information Systems Research*, *5*(4), 400–421. doi:10.1287/isre.5.4.400

Daft, R. L., & Lengel, R. H. (1984). Information richness: A new approach to managerial behavior and organizational design. In L. Cummings & B. M. Staw (Eds.), *Research in Organizational Behavior* (Vol. 6). Homewood, IL: JAI Press.

Daft, R. L., Lengel, R. H., & Trevino, L. K. (1987). Message equivocality, media selection, and manager performance: Implications for information systems. *MIS Quarterly*, *11*(3), 355–366. doi:10.2307/248682

Durham, C. C., Knight, D., & Locke, E. A. (1997). Effects of leader role, team-set goal difficulty, efficacy, and tactics on team effectiveness. *Organizational Behavior and Human Decision Processes*, *72*, 203–231. doi:10.1006/obhd.1997.2739

Elliott, S., & O'Dell, C. (1999). Sharing Knowledge & Best Practices: The Hows and Whys of Tapping Your Organization's Hidden. *Health Forum Journal*, *42*(3), 34.

Faraj, S., & Sproull, L. (2000). Coordinating expertise in software development teams. *Management Science*, *46*, 1554–1568. doi:10.1287/mnsc.46.12.1554.12072

Fey, C. F., & Furu, P. (2008). Top management incentive compensation and knowledge sharing in multinational corporations. *Strategic Management Journal*, *29*(12), 1301. doi:10.1002/smj.712

Fishbein, M. (1979). *A Theory of Reasoned Action: Some Applications and Implications*. Paper presented at the Nebraska Symposium on Motivation, Nebraska.

Fishbein, M., & Ajzen, I. (1975). *Belief, Attitude, Intention, and Behavior: An Introduction to Theory and Research*. Reading, MA: Addison-Wesley Publishing Co.

Ford, D. P. (2008). *Disengagement from Knowledge Sharing: The Alternative Explanation for Why People Are Not Sharing*. Paper presented at the Administrative Sciences Association of Canada.

Ford, D. P., & Chan, Y. E. (2003). Knowledge sharing in a multi-cultural setting: A case study. *Knowledge Management Research and Practice*, *1*(1), 11–27. doi:10.1057/palgrave.kmrp.8499999

Fraser, V., Marcella, R., & Middleton, I. (2000). Employee perceptions of knowledge sharing: Employment threat or synergy for the greater good? *Competitive Intelligence Review*, *11*(2), 39–52. doi:10.1002/(SICI)1520-6386(200032)11:2<39::AID-CIR7>3.0.CO;2-J

Gray, P. H., & Meister, D. B. (2004). Knowledge sourcing effectiveness. *Management Science*, *50*(6), 821–834. doi:10.1287/mnsc.1030.0192

Gupta, A. K., & Govindarajan, V. (2000). Knowledge flows within multinational corporations. *Strategic Management Journal*, *21*(4), 473. doi:10.1002/(SICI)1097-0266(200004)21:4<473::AID-SMJ84>3.0.CO;2-I

Gupta, A. K., & Govindarajan, V. (2000). Knowledge flows within multinational corporations. *Strategic Management Journal*, *21*, 473–496. doi:10.1002/(SICI)1097-0266(200004)21:4<473::AID-SMJ84>3.0.CO;2-I

Hibbard, J., & Carrillo, K. M. (1998). Knowledge revolution. *Informationweek*, *663*, 49–54.

Huang, Q., Davison, R. M., & Gu, J. (2008). Impact of personal and cultural factors on knowledge sharing in china. *Asia Pacific Journal of Management*, *25*(3), 451. doi:10.1007/s10490-008-9095-2

Husted, K., & Michailova, S. (2002). Diagnosing and fighting knowledge-sharing hostility. *Organizational Dynamics*, *31*(1), 60–73. doi:10.1016/S0090-2616(02)00072-4

Ingram, P., & Simons, T. (2002). The transfer of experience in groups of organizations: Implications for performance and competition. *Management Science*, *48*(12), 1517–1533. doi:10.1287/mnsc.48.12.1517.437

Inkpen, A. C., & Tsang, E. W. K. (2005). Social capital, networks, and knowledge transfer. *Academy of Management Review*, *30*(1), 146–165.

Jarvenpaa, S. L., & Staples, D. S. (2000). The Use of Collaborative Electronic Media for Information Sharing: An Exploratory Study of Determinants. *The Journal of Strategic Information Systems*, *9*(2-3), 129–154. doi:10.1016/S0963-8687(00)00042-1

Jones, S. (2002). Employee rights, employee responsibilities and knowledge sharing in intelligent organization. *Employee Responsibilities and Rights Journal, 14*(2-3), 69–78. doi:10.1023/A:1021119503782

Kahn, W. A. (1990). Psychological conditions of personal engagement and disengagement at work. *Academy of Management Journal, 33*, 692–724. doi:10.2307/256287

Kahn, W. A. (1992). To Be Fully There: Psychological Presence at Work. *Human Relations, 45*(4), 321. doi:10.1177/001872679204500402

Kane, A. A., Argote, L., & Levine, J. M. (2005). Knowledge transfer between groups via personnel rotation: Effects of social identity and knowledge quality. *Organizational Behavior and Human Decision Processes, 96*(1), 56–71. doi:10.1016/j.obhdp.2004.09.002

Kang, Y., Kim, S., & Chang, G. (2008). The impact of knowledge sharing on work performance: An empirical analysis of the public employees' perceptions in South Korea. *International Journal of Public Administration, 31*(14), 1548. doi:10.1080/01900690802243607

Kankanhalli, A., Tan, B. C. Y., & Kwok-Kee, W. (2005). Understanding seeking from electronic knowledge repositories: An empirical study. *Journal of the American Society for Information Science and Technology, 56*(11), 1156–1166. doi:10.1002/asi.20219

Kankanhalli, A., Tan, B. C. Y., & Wei, K.-K. (2005). Contributing knowledge to electronic knowledge repositories: An empirical investigation. *MIS Quarterly, 29*(1), 113–143.

Ko, D.-G., Kirsch, L. J., & King, W. R. (2005). Antecedents of knowledge transfer from consultants to clients in enterprise system implementations. *MIS Quarterly, 29*(1), 59–85.

Kruglanski, A. W. (2001). That "Vision Thing": The state of theory in social and personality psychology at the edge of the new millennium. *Journal of Personality and Social Psychology, 80*(6), 871–875. doi:10.1037/0022-3514.80.6.871

Kuo, F., & Young, M. (2008). A study of the intention-action gap in knowledge sharing practices. *Journal of the American Society for Information Science and Technology, 59*(8), 1224–1237. doi:10.1002/asi.20816

Lahneman, W. J. (2004). Knowledge-sharing in the intelligence community after 9/11. *International Journal of Intelligence and CounterIntelligence, 17*(4), 614–633. doi:10.1080/08850600490496425

Lee, J.-N. (2001). The impact of knowledge sharing, organizational capability and partnership quality on IS outsourcing success. *Information & Management, 38*, 323–335. doi:10.1016/S0378-7206(00)00074-4

Lemons, D. (2005). Ensuring smooth knowledge transfer through communities at Aerotek. *KM Review, 8*(1), 5.

Liao, S., Chang, J., Cheng, S., & Kuo, C. (2004). Employee relationship and knowledge sharing: A case study of a Taiwanese finance and securities firm. *Knowledge Management Research and Practice, 2*, 24–34. doi:10.1057/palgrave.kmrp.8500016

Lin, C. (2008). Clarifying the relationship between organizational citizenship behaviors, gender, and knowledge sharing in workplace organizations in Taiwan. *Journal of Business and Psychology, 22*(3), 241. doi:10.1007/s10869-008-9067-z

Liu, M., & Liu, N. (2008). Sources of knowledge acquisition and patterns of knowledge-sharing behaviors - an empirical study of Taiwanese high-tech firms. *International Journal of Information Management, 28*(5), 423. doi:10.1016/j.ijinfomgt.2008.01.005

Markus, M. L. (2001). Toward a theory of knowledge reuse: Types of knowledge reuse situations and factors in reuse success. *Journal of Management Information Systems, 18*(1), 57–93.

McDermott, R., & O'Dell, C. (2001). Overcoming cultural barriers to sharing knowledge. *Journal of Knowledge Management, 5*(1), 76–85. doi:10.1108/13673270110384428

McLure Wasko, M., & Faraj, S. (2000). "It is what one does": Why people participate and help others in electronic communities of practice. *The Journal of Strategic Information Systems, 9*, 155–173. doi:10.1016/S0963-8687(00)00045-7

McLure Wasko, M., & Faraj, S. (2005). Why should I share? Examining social capital and knowledge contribution in electronic networks of practice. *MIS Quarterly, 29*(1), 35–57.

Miles, M. B., & Huberman, A. M. (1994). *Qualitative Data Analysis: An Expanded Source Book* (2nd ed.). Thousand Oaks, CA: Sage Publications.

Minbaeva, D. B., & Michailova, S. (2004). Knowledge transfer and expatriation in multinational corporations: The role of disseminative capacity. *Employee Relations, 26*(6), 663–679. doi:10.1108/01425450410562236

Nissen, M. E. (2005). Dynamic Knowledge Patterns to Inform Design: A Field Study of Knowledge Stocks and Flows in an Extreme Organization. *Journal of Management Information Systems, 22*(3), 225–263. doi:10.2753/MIS0742-1222220308

O'Dell, C., & Grayson, C. J. (2004). Identifying and Transferring Internal Best Practices. *Handbook on Knowledge Management 1: Knowledge Matters*, 601-622.

Pan, S., & Scarbrough, H. (1998). A socio-technical view of knowledge-sharing at Buckman Laboratories. *Journal of Knowledge Management, 2*(1), 55–66. doi:10.1108/EUM0000000004607

Reagans, R., & McEvily, B. (2003). Network Structure and Knowledge Transfer: The Effects of Cohesion and Range. *Administrative Science Quarterly, 48*(2), 240–267. doi:10.2307/3556658

Reio, T. G. Jr, & Wiswell, A. (2000). Field Investigation of the Relationship Among Adult Curiosity, Workplace Learning, and Job Performance. *Human Resource Development Quarterly, 11*(1), 5–30. doi:10.1002/1532-1096(200021)11:1<5::AID-HRDQ2>3.0.CO;2-A

Saemundsson, R. G. J. (2004). Technical knowledge-seeking in a young and growing technology-based firm: Incentives and direction. *International Journal of Innovation Management, 8*(4), 399–429. doi:10.1142/S136391960400112X

Santoro, M. D., & Saparito, P. A. (2006). Self-Interest Assumption and Relational Trust in University-Industry Knowledge Transfers. *IEEE Transactions on Engineering Management, 53*(3), 335–347. doi:10.1109/TEM.2006.878103

Sarker, S., Sarker, S., Nicholson, D. B., & Joshi, K. D. (2005). Knowledge transfer in virtual systems development teams: An exploratory study of four key enablers. *IEEE Transactions on Professional Communication, 48*(2), 201–218. doi:10.1109/TPC.2005.849650

Schwab, D. P., Heneman, H. G. III, & DeCotiis, T. A. (1975). Behaviorally anchored rating scales: A review of the literature. *Personnel Psychology, 28*(4), 549–562. doi:10.1111/j.1744-6570.1975.tb01392.x

Sheppard, B. H., Hartwick, J., & Warshaw, P. R. (1988). The Theory of Reasoned Action: A meta-analysis of past research with recommendations for modifications and future research. *The Journal of Consumer Research, 15*, 325–343. doi:10.1086/209170

Singh, J. (2005). Collaborative Networks as Determinants of Knowledge Diffusion Patterns. *Management Science, 51*(5), 756–770. doi:10.1287/mnsc.1040.0349

Smith, P. C., & Kendall, L. M. (1963). Retranslation of expectations: An approach to the construction of unambiguous anchors for rating scales. *The Journal of Applied Psychology*, *47*, 149–155. doi:10.1037/h0047060

Sowe, S. K., Stamelos, I., & Angelis, L. (2008). Understanding knowledge sharing activities in tree/open source software projects: An empirical study. *Journal of Systems and Software*, *81*(3), 431. doi:10.1016/j.jss.2007.03.086

Srivastava, A., Bartol, K. M., & Locke, E. A. (2006). Empowering leadership in management teams: Effects on knowledge sharing, efficacy, and performance. *Academy of Management Journal*, *49*(6), 1239–1251.

Staples, D. S., & Webster, J. (2008). Exploring the effects of trust, task interdependence and virtualness on knowledge sharing in teams. *Information Systems Journal*, *18*(6), 617. doi:10.1111/j.1365-2575.2007.00244.x

Stoddart, L. (2001). Managing intranets to encourage knowledge sharing: Opportunities and constraints. *Online Information Review*, *25*(1), 19–28. doi:10.1108/14684520110366661

Strickland, L. S. (2004). The information shortcomings of 9/11. *Information Management Journal*, *38*(6), 34–41.

Styhre, A. (2008). The role of social capital in knowledge sharing: the case of a specialist rock construction company. *Construction Management and Economics*, *26*(9), 941–951. doi:10.1080/01446190802259035

Sutton, R. I., & Staw, B. M. (1995). What theory is *not*. *Administrative Science Quarterly*, *40*, 371–384. doi:10.2307/2393788

Suyeon, K., Hyunseok, H., & Euiho, S. (2003). A process-based approach to knowledge-flow analysis: a case study of a manufacturing firm. *Knowledge and Process Management*, *10*(4), 260–276. doi:10.1002/kpm.186

Szulanski, G. (2000). The process of knowledge transfer: A diachronic analysis of stickiness. *Organizational Behavior and Human Decision Processes*, *82*(1), 9–27. doi:10.1006/obhd.2000.2884

Szulanski, G., & Cappetta, R. (2000). *When credible sources share complex knowledge.* Unpublished manuscript, The Wharton School, University of Pennsylvania.

Thompson, M., & Heron, P. (2006). Relational quality and innovative performance in R&D based science and technology firms. *Human Resource Management Journal*, *16*(1), 28–47.

van den Hoof, B., & de Leeuw van Weenen, F. (2004). Committed to share: Commitment and CMC use as antecedents of knowledge sharing. *Knowledge and Process Management*, *11*(1), 13–24. doi:10.1002/kpm.187

Van Dyne, L., Graham, J. W., & Dienesch, R. M. (1994). Organizational citizenship behavior: Construct redefinition, measurement, and validation. *Academy of Management Journal*, *37*, 765–802. doi:10.2307/256600

Wang, C.-C. (2004). The influence of ethical and self-interest concerns on knowledge sharing intentions among managers: An empirical study. *International Journal of Management*, *21*(3), 370–381.

Wang, E. T. G., Chia-Lin Lin, C., Jiang, J. J., & Klein, G. (2007). Improving enterprise resource planning (ERP) fit to organizational process through knowledge transfer. *International Journal of Information Management*, *27*(3), 200–212. doi:10.1016/j.ijinfomgt.2007.02.002

Webster, J., Brown, G., Zweig, D., Connelly, C. E., Brodt, S. E., & Sitkin, S. B. (2008). Beyond knowledge sharing: Withholding knowledge at work. In J. J. Matocchio (Ed.), *Research in Personnel and Human Resources Management* (Vol. 27). Oxford, England: Elsevier.

Wolfe, C., & Loraas, T. (2008). Knowledge sharing: The effects of incentives, environment, and person. *Journal of Information Systems*, *22*(2), 53. doi:10.2308/jis.2008.22.2.53

Zack, M. H. (1993). Interactivity and communication mode choice in ongoing management groups. *Information Systems Research*, *4*(3), 207–239. doi:10.1287/isre.4.3.207

Zack, M. H. (1994). Electronic messaging and communication effectiveness in an ongoing work group. *Information & Management*, *26*(4), 231–241. doi:10.1016/0378-7206(94)90095-7

Zack, M. H. (2007). The role of decision support systems in an indeterminate world. *Decision Support Systems*, *43*(4), 1664–1674. doi:10.1016/j.dss.2006.09.003

ENDNOTES

1. This chapter is based on and extends "What is knowledge sharing from the informer's perspective?" by Ford, D.P. & Staples, D.S. which appeared in *International Journal of Knowledge Management, 4*(4), 1-20. © 2008 IGI Global. All tables and figures in this chapter are reproduced and extended with permission.
2. A more detailed description of the results from the knowledge definition question is available upon request to the principle author.
3. We would like to acknowledge that this summary of measures is not inclusive of all knowledge sharing research given its immense popularity.

Chapter 21
Sustainable Communities for Knowledge Management Systems in the New Technological Era

Elham Mousavidin
University of Houston, USA

Lakshmi Goel
University of North Florida, USA

ABSTRACT

The topic of knowledge management has received considerable attention in research as well as practice. However, the success of knowledge management systems remains elusive. This chapter provides a framework, which suggests that knowledge management success can be achieved by designing sustainable communities of practice. Communities of practice have proven to have significant economic and practical implications for organizations. A growing body of literature in knowledge management recognizes the importance of communities that foster collaborative learning in organizations and almost all knowledge management systems have a 'network' component that facilitates connecting people in communities of practice. Technological advancements in social systems such as weblogs, wikis, social networking sites, and virtual worlds enable new ways in which such communities can be supported. This study takes into account affordances of these technologies in facilitating knowledge management. This study draws on literature in knowledge management and communities of practice to arrive at properties of a community that make it sustainable. These properties can then be viewed as a blueprint of what a community needs to have to achieve its function of fostering collaboration and hence, generating knowledge. In sum, this research is intended to help practitioners arrive at how best to design communities in knowledge management systems.

DOI: 10.4018/978-1-60566-954-0.ch021

INTRODUCTION

The topic of knowledge management (KM) has received considerable attention in research as well as practice. However, the success of knowledge management systems (KMS) remains elusive (Akhavan et al. 2005; Hammer et al., 2004). There is a considerable body of literature that has studied factors for KMS success (Jennex and Olfman 2005). In this paper, our goal is to contribute to this line of research by identifying how these success factors may be achieved. Specifically, we restrict our scope of inquiry to a certain type of knowledge management systems; those that are designed to support communities of practice (CoPs).

Prior literature that has sought to identify important factors in KM success has adopted either the individual level of analysis (e.g. Bock et al., 2005; Kankanhalli et al., 2005), the organizational level of analysis (e.g. Brown and Duguid, 2000), or the technological level of analysis (e.g. Markus et al., 2002). We propose an approach that incorporates research on individuals, organizations, and the technology pertaining to knowledge management to suggest a set of design principles for sustainable communities of practice. Communities of practice have proven to have significant economic and practical implications on organizational practice (Brown and Duguid, 1999 and 20002000). A growing body of literature in knowledge management recognizes the importance of communities that foster collaborative learning in organizations and almost all knowledge management systems have a 'network' component that facilitates connecting people in communities of practice. Evidence has shown that community has been a key element in knowledge management systems of many companies including Xerox PARC, British Petroleum Co., Shell Oil Company, Halliburton, IBM, Proctor and Gamble, and Hewlett Packard (Brown and Gray, 1995; Cohen, 2006; Cross et al., 2006; McDermott, 1999a; McDermott, 1999b). Technological advancements in social systems such as weblogs, wikis, social networking sites, and virtual worlds enable new ways in which such communities can be supported. In this study we take into account properties of these technologies, which enable and constrain different uses of the technological environment (i.e. the technological affordances) (Gibson, 1977; Zammuto, 2007) in facilitating knowledge management.

Attributes of communities of practice, which we believe determine the success or failure of KM initiatives, have been thus far under-researched. KM can benefit from literature in virtual communities that looks at what properties of a community make it sustainable. These properties can then be viewed as a blueprint of what a community needs to have to achieve its function of fostering collaboration and hence, generating knowledge. In sum, this research is intended to help design communities in KMS, taking into account affordances of technologies, in order to achieve KM success.

KMS success models provide a strategic level process approach to achieving success. KMS success factors provide a means for evaluation of KMS success. Our goal is to suggest how these success factors could be achieved at an operational level. We draw on Jennex and Olfman's (2005b, 2006) work to arrive at a list of eight success factors that are applicable to our conceptualization of a KMS that supports CoPs. Table 1 provides a list of these factors.

This paper is structured as follows. In the next section we present a review of literature in knowledge management, KM success, and communities of practice. The literature helps provide the theoretical basis for our research. Our research methodology section follows the literature review. We elaborate on the process and method for arriving at our design recommendations, and discuss each recommendation in detail. We next provide a discussion, and conclude with our suggestions for future research.

Table 1. KMS success factors adopted from Jennex and Olfman (2005b and 2006)

Success Factor	Description
SF1	Identification of users, sources, knowledge, and links
SF2	Clear articulation of knowledge structure
SF3	Motivation and commitment of users
SF4	Senior management support
SF5	Measures for assessment of appropriate use
SF6	Clear goal and purpose
SF7	Support for easy knowledge use
SF8	Designing work processes to incorporate knowledge capture and use

LITERATURE REVIEW

The primary goal of this research is to contribute to literature in KM success. We provide a brief review of literature in knowledge management and knowledge management success to summarize the state of current research. We then focus on the literature in communities of practice, which we use to augment research on KM success.

Knowledge Management and Knowledge Management Systems

Managing knowledge is a focal task for organizations today. Appreciating the importance of knowledge as a core capability or resource (Grant, 1996; Alavi and Leidner, 2001) has underscored the need for managing it strategically. Though the effort to manage what a company 'knows' is not a recent phenomenon, new technologies and greater awareness fueled by a competitive business landscape have resulted in substantive attention paid to KM (Prusak, 2001).

Knowledge can be conceptualized in different ways. It can be seen as embedded in practices (Orlikowski, 2002) or processes (Epple and Argote, 1996), or as a separate entity or object (Schultze and Stabell, 2004). Another view of knowledge is that which is embedded in people's heads and is a "*fluid mix of framed experience, values, contextual information and expert insight that provide a framework for evaluation and incorporating new experiences and information*" (Davenport and Prusak, 1997, p. 5). This type of knowledge is referred to as tacit. While explicit knowledge is easily codified, stored, and transferred, by the use of technology (such as knowledge repositories, document control systems, or databases) tacit knowledge is 'stickier' (Hippel, 1994). Tacit knowledge, as conceptualized by Polanyi (1958) refers to knowing-how or embodied knowledge, and is the characteristic of an expert who can perform a task without deliberation of the principles or rules involved (Ryle, 1949/1984). This goes beyond a mere technical or physical know-how (Dretske, 1991) as it is highly contextual. Employees of a certain culture may have tacit knowledge about practices that employees of other cultures do not. Being able to deliberately leverage such tacit knowledge is hypothesized to generate value and be a key differentiator for an organization (Grant, 1996; Alavi and Leidner, 1999; Alavi and Leidner, 2001). It is tacit knowledge that resides in employees' heads, which is vital for problem solving and organizational learning (Davenport and Prusak, 1997). Due to the uneven distribution of expertise, the task of managing tacit knowledge is especially essential in today's dynamic and global business landscape. In the context of large, geographically distributed, multi-cultural firms where employees do not have the opportunity to interact face-to-face, communication and transfer of knowledge becomes even more challenging (Lapre and Van Wassenhove, 2003). Therefore, designing systems that facilitate tacit knowledge management is important. The focus of many design articles is on information or content management – which deals with explicit knowledge. In this paper, we focus on managing tacit knowledge.

We conceptualize knowledge management systems as systems designed specifically with the intent to manage organizational knowledge by connecting people. In this approach, KMS are primarily designed to support communities of practice. We elaborate on this further in the subsequent sections.

Knowledge Management Success

KMS success has been defined in many ways. Jennex and Olfman (2004, 2005b) provide an integrated framework of KM success factors identified by previous authors. We adopt a definition of KMS success as proposed by Jennex (2005a) as being able to reuse knowledge to improve organizational effectiveness by providing the required knowledge to those that need it when it is needed.

The attempt to manage knowledge is not always successful. IDC estimated an expenditure of USD 12.7 billion on KM in 2005. In 2007-2008 organizations were estimated to have spent USD 73 billion towards their knowledge management activities (Murphy and Hackbush, 2007). However, approximately 70% of KM initiatives are deemed unsuccessful (Akhavan et al., 2005; Hammer et al., 2004). Stories such as the struggle of General Motors (GM) and NUMMI (joint venture of GM and Toyota) in the initial stages of their initiatives for learning and knowledge transfer highlight the challenges (Inkpen, 2005). Though significant research in the field of information systems is directed toward how to successfully implement information technologies in general, KM presents unique challenges that are more complex than what models such as Technology Acceptance (TAM) (Davis, 1989) and Task Technology Fit (TTF) (Goodhue and Thompson, 1995) can explain. Issues such as employees' reluctance to share knowledge, coordination of knowledge management efforts, and adoption of the right model for knowledge creation, management, and transfer, present unique difficulties for KM system success (Jennex and Olfman, 2005a; Jennex et al., 2007).

Most research on factors of KM success can be seen to fall within one of three categories. First, using the individual as the unit of analysis, employee reluctance to share knowledge has been studied using frameworks such as identity theory (e.g. Constant et al., 1994), social-cognitive theory (e.g. Constant et al., 1994), social exchange theory (e.g. Kankanhalli et al., 2005), and the theory of reasoned behavior (e.g. Bock et al., 2005). Power has also been discussed as an important factor (Gordon and Grant, 2005; Porra and Goel, 2006). Findings indicate mixed results where employees want to share for reasons of 'showing-off' (Constant et al., 1994), altruism (Constant et al., 1994), or feeling of social obligation while employees are reluctant to share knowledge for reasons of fear of loss of hegemony (Shin, 2004), and costs (such as time and effort) (Butler, 2001) involved. Motivation (Ardichvili, 2003), and extrinsic reward structures (Shin, 2004, Yeu Wah et al., 2007) as predictors of knowledge sharing have also been studied.

Second, employing an organizational unit of analysis, management of KM activities has been examined. In particular, research in knowledge transfer (Argote and Ingram, 2000), organizational culture and norms (Constant et al., 1994; Hart and Warne, 2006; Usoro and Kuofie, 2006), and senior and middle management support (Brown and Duguid, 2000) have been studied. Here, KM success is related to favorable organizational factors for knowledge sharing.

Third, using the system as the unit of analysis, technical characteristics of KMS such as repository structure, directory capabilities, and collaboration tools have been investigated (Markus, 2001;

Markus et al., 2002; King, 2006). In this perspective, KM success is explained by theories such as Task-Technology Fit (TTF) (Goodhue and Thompson, 1995), which focus on choosing the right technology. Technological advancements offer new affordances that support aspects of tacit knowledge transfer in communities of practice. For example, social systems such as weblogs, wikis, and social networking sites (e.g. Facebook) afford informal communication and synergistic interactions that support communities of practice (Silva et al. 2006). The idea of social systems has been taken even further with the advent of three-dimensional (3D) virtual world technology (e.g. Second Life). These environments afford richer interactions where users can co-experience and co-create situations and virtual artifacts, as well self-express themselves through multiple cues (e.g. verbal as well as non-verbal) (Goel et al. 2008).

This paper investigates KMS from a perspective that incorporates the individual, organizational, and system units of analysis by using the lens of communities of practice (Lave and Wenger, 1991; Wenger, 1998; Brown and Duguid, 1999).

Communities of Practice

Communities of practice have been used by many to study KM practices (for example, see Cheuk, 2006; Koeglreiter et al., 2006); however, this perspective has not been applied to designing KMS per se (an exception is Stein, 2006 who proposes a descriptive model of the functions and structure of a successful CoP). Knowledge management systems are not particularly complex or technically different from other information systems (Alavi and Leidner, 1999). The difference between knowledge management systems and other systems such as group decision support systems (GDSS), electronic meeting systems (EMS), and expert systems lies not primarily in the technology, but in the purpose for their use. GDSS focus on connecting a particular group of employees for the goal of solving particular problems, or arriving at a decision. EMS focus on facilitating meetings and collaborative work among a certain group of people. Expert systems are typically rule-based, where the knowledge of an expert/s (where experts are identified by the organization) is captured in the system's knowledge base, and then queried by users. The goal of KMS, as we conceptualize them, is to connect all employees in an organization at all times. Unlike in expert systems, the roles of knowledge producers (experts) and consumers (users) are flexible. Groups are not dictated by organizational structures, but emerge ad-hoc as communities of employees with common interests and problems. Interaction within these communities may yield solutions to specific problems, but it is the interaction for the purpose of tacit knowledge exchange that is the goal of the system.

Since the central problem of KM is the creation and transfer of tacit knowledge, it is necessary to look at what facilitates these processes. Experiences and contextual insights have been traditionally transferred through methods such as story-telling (Brown and Duguid, 2000), sense-making (Brown and Duguid, 1999), or through conversations in informal social networks. Communities of practice are informal networks of like-minded individuals, where the process of learning and transfer of tacit knowledge is essentially social, involving a deepening process of participation (Lave and Wenger, 1991). Research shows that in the absence of decisive first-hand knowledge, an individual looks at successful decisions made by other like-minded, similarly-situated people (Nidumolu and Subramani, 2001) as filters or guides to identify potentially good choices (Hill et al., 1995). Prior case studies have shown that even for individuals armed with extensive know-what (explicit knowledge), collective know-how (tacit knowledge) can be highly significant (Brown and Duguid, 1999; Orr, 1989). KM practitioners and researchers recognize the importance of communities that foster collaborative learning in organizations (Pan and Leidner, 2003) and almost all knowledge management systems have a 'network' component that facilitates connecting people in communities of practice. The community perspective of knowledge management, which acknowledges the importance of informal networks and emphasizes collaboration, started in the late 1990s (Cross et al., 2006). Evidence has shown that communities have been a key element in knowledge management systems of many companies including Xerox PARC, IBM, and Proctor and Gamble (Brown and Gray, 1995; Cohen, 2006; Cross et al., 2006; McDermott, 1999a; McDermott, 1999b). Most of the companies that used IBM's first web-based knowledge management system organized their activities around communities, an element that IBM had not deliberately implemented in the system initially (McDermott, 1999b).

While studying design characteristics of communities, defining what is meant by a community and its sustainability is important. In attempting to do so, we refer to prior IS literature on virtual communities, since we consider communities in knowledge management systems as virtual. The term 'virtual' has been used here to distinguish these communities from real-life communities with face-to-face interaction. Borrowing from biology, virtual community sustainability has been regarded as the 'intrinsic longetivity' of the membership (e.g. Porra and Parks, 2005; Butler, 2001). Hence research has been devoted to studying how members can be encouraged to stay in a community. The concept of a 'community' has received much attention and there are different ideas as to what brings about a 'sense of community' (Blanchard and Markus, 2004). Reasons such as support (Blanchard and Markus, 2004), recognition (Blanchard and Markus, 2004), intimacy (Blanchard and Markus, 2004) and obligation (Wasko and Faraj, 2000), have all been studied as motivators of staying in a community. It has been acknowledged that in organizations tacit knowledge is shared in ad-hoc, informal settings (Brown and Duguid, 2000) that may not be replicable (such as brainstorming sessions, or when new hires approach veterans for specific advice). While the composition of members might change in a community, the community still serves the purpose as a platform for knowledge management. The existing literature does not reflect this functional aspect of communities. Therefore, we define a community as a platform for knowledge creation and exchange, and sustainability as how successful a community is in achieving its function of facilitating knowledge generation and exchange. This research attempts to draw on relevant literature and apply it to an organizational KM context in order to suggest how sustainable communities can be designed. Hence, the output of this paper is design recommendations or guidelines for communities of practice that are the central part of KMS.

One view of organizing CoPs is that the design structure should be emergent rather than imposed (Barab et al., 2003). However, it has been recognized that too little structure can also yield negative benefits, and a 'minimalist design' or a tentative platform for a community is needed (Wenger, 1998). Hence, while it is not recommended to have tightly controlled formal designs in place, informal structures and basic guidelines that allow flexibility, diversity, autonomy, creativity, and scalability are necessary (Wenger, 1998).

RESEARCH METHODOLOGY AND ANALYSIS

In this section we first elaborate on our method for arriving at design guidelines for sustainable communities in KMS. We next present our design recommendations each preceded by supporting literature. These are followed by examples in prior research, which evidence the recommendations.

Method

We conducted an extensive search in literature using engines such as Google Scholar and Social Sciences Index using key words such as knowledge, knowledge management, knowledge management system, knowledge management system success, communities, virtual communities, and communities of practice. Keeping in mind our research objective, we narrowed the results to papers that were relevant to the design of communities in the context of knowledge management. We support each proposed design guideline with results from prior studies, both qualitative and quantitative. The qualitative data includes quotes from case studies in knowledge management and virtual communities. Data from quantitative research mainly includes their supported hypotheses. The data immediately follows each design recommendation. The goal of using data from previous research was solely for clarification and better understanding, as well as demonstrating that the importance of these issues has been acknowledged explicitly by other researchers. Though the evidence was implicitly or explicitly observed in different papers, the related design guidelines were not the primary focus of these studies. One of our key contributions is thus the synthesis of the findings across the different studies and bringing to the forefront the importance of the design guidelines.

Design Recommendations

A community of practice is defined by the commonality of an interest shared by its members. Members of the community form communal bonds, construct collective identities through communicative action (Donath, 1999; Blanchard and Markus, 2004; Postmes et al., 2000), and reach common understanding (Habermas, 1984), thus generating collaborative knowledge. The concept of a community boundary is hence important and delineates what a community is about, and what it is not. In organizations, it is especially important to make sure a community is 'specialized' or focused on a particular topic in order to maximize the 'signal to noise' ratio and minimize the costs of obtaining relevant information. Thus,

Each community in a KMS should have a central focus which should be maintained throughout the life of the community by ensuring that all posts are relevant to the community's focus.

As will be discussed in the ensuing recommendations, a community manager, or a segmentation strategy, could play a key role in ensuring a topical focus. Jones and Rafaeli (2000) and Jones et al. (2004) conclude that in order for a virtual community to be sustainable, it has to have a topical focus because otherwise members might experience information overload, which is not tolerable by their cognition capacity. They add that,

It logically follows that beyond a particular communication processing-load, the behavioural stress zones encountered will make group communication unsustainable. (Jones and Rafaeli 2000, p. 219)

Overall, the empirical findings support the assertion that individual information-overload coping strategies have an observable impact on mass interaction discourse dynamics. Evidence was found [that] users are more likely to end active participation as the overloading of mass interaction increases. (Jones et al. 2004, p. 206)

Two complementary concepts discussed in literature are those of information overload (Rogers and Agarwala-Rogers, 1975) and critical mass (Licklider and Taylor, 1968; Markus, 1987). Critical mass refers to the required group size threshold for a sustainable community (Bieber et al., 2002). Information overload results from a higher number of messages, or messages that are not sufficiently organized in a sensible, linked structure, which makes it difficult for individuals to process. While critical mass indicates that a community that is too small will fail, information overload suggests that one that is too big will also fail. Hence, there is a maximum limit to the size of a community beyond which a low signal to noise ratio (Malhotra et al., 1997) and an upper bound on an individual's cognitive processing limits (Jones, 1997) will render it unsuccessful. This topic was the focus of studies conducted specifically on membership limits of communities (e.g. Jones and Rafaeli, 2000). While the limit is context dependent and varies with the nature of the community, a manager could determine an approximate threshold for when information overload or topical deviation occurs. When a community grows too large, a segmentation strategy can be employed to create an interrelated space (Jones and Rafaeli, 2000). Hence,

There should be a maximum limit set for the membership in the community in a KMS, beyond which the community should be split into interrelated sub-communities each with a central focus or topic.

Jones and Rafaeli (2000) provide examples of communities such as Amazon or Excite, in which a segmentation strategy has been used to keep the communities focused and prevent information overload.

'Segmentation strategy' refers here to any systematic method used to split discourse spaces with the aim of creating a system of interrelated virtual publics. As studies of usage show (e.g. Butler 1999), virtual publics are not 'scalable'. Therefore, a 'mega virtual public' cannot be sustained. Rather, virtual metropolises emerge from the creation of a series of related virtual publics, via the appropriate segmentation of discourse in different related cyberspaces. In turn, the resulting system of interconnected virtual publics encourages the expansion of user populations, while reducing the likelihood of overloaded virtual public discourse. (p. 221)

Moderation has been studied in virtual community literature (Markus, 2001). Human intervention is considered necessary for tasks such as maintaining community focus, preventing 'trolling' or 'flaming' (Malhotra et al., 1997), encouraging participation (Preece et al., 2003), and sanitizing data (Markus, 2001). Even though trolling and flaming are unlikely in organizational settings, moderation is required for the other reasons. Since moderators (often referred to as community or knowledge managers) are usually employees with regular duties, it is important that their work for the KM effort be recognized and that they are allowed to devote time to the community as part of their job (Davenport et al., 1998; Silva et al., 2006). Hence,

Each community should have at least one community manager with the authority and resources to manage and act for the benefit of the community.

The following remarks demonstrate the importance of the role of a community manager and the resources (e.g. people and time) that are available to him/her.

Knowledge managers have content leads that evaluate external knowledge resources and establish pointers to the new resources for specific domains. The searches are synthesized to allow higher level of reuse. Knowledge researchers strongly support sharing and reuse of knowledge probes: "The first thing I do is go check that database to make sure that no one hasn't already pulled that information before I go and start a whole new search. (Sherif and Xing 2006, p. 538)

One person per project is in charge of posting project deliverables onto the repository ... On a

weekly basis the knowledge manager goes in and makes sure it has been categorized correctly and the document has been zipped. He just makes sure it has been submitted according to all the standards and guidelines. (Sherif and Xing 2006, p. 536)

As seen in the following, lack of sufficient resources such as time can adversely affect the quality of community manager's job.

With the amount of time available to produce high quality and sanitized knowledge for dissemination ... It's not even just writing it ... I'm on the review committee and that's where a lot of time is as I've got to review every document ... The delay in implementing this second knowledge dissemination plan was due to ... the lack of resources to provide high quality, sanitized knowledge for consumption by customers. (Markus 2001, p. 80)

Research on information overload posits that information should be organized hierarchically in order to place new information in the correct context quickly. Also, costs of obtaining new knowledge are lower when messages are simple and contextually relevant (Jones et al., 2004). Blogs, wikis, and net forums use chronological and topical organizing successfully to map information. Site maps on websites provide a graphical view of how information is arranged – reducing the time and effort required to access it while also providing an overall picture of the website. More recent work on the semantic web enables tagging knowledge objects with keywords pertaining to the context and relevance of the topic (Daconta et al., 2003). Using descriptive tags enables searching and archiving information in a way that is most applicable to the topic. Semantic web technologies make a static hierarchical representation extraneous. Other new technologies such as virtual worlds allow the embedding of information in three-dimensional situational contexts. Here objects or virtual artifacts replace text-based representations of information (Lui et al., 2007). In other words information is tied to the virtual artifact, which is represented in a richer way than in traditional 2D textual virtual environment.

However, to make searches efficient, there needs to be standardization in the tags used to describe the same types of objects. The standards, while imposing a common structure, should also allow flexibility to reflect unique contextual information in the knowledge object (Geroimenko and Chen, 2003).

Site maps can be used to provide community-specific keywords that can be used to tag and search for community related topics. It should be noted that in 3D virtual worlds the notion of site maps could be dramatically different in that they are actual maps tied to virtual locations.

The importance of site maps in knowledge management systems has been suggested in prior research (e.g. Jennex and Olfman, 2000, 2005). This leads to the following design recommendations:

Each community in a KMS should have a site map showing how knowledge is arranged and accessible in the community.

All posts in the community should be categorizable according to the site map.

The importance of a well-designed site map (or an equivalent) can be seen below.

We've got to put tags on that content in a way that it's retrievable, in a way that makes sense as to how we do business. When you've done a particular type of project, creating [a] particular set of deliverables to a particular type of client, then you want to be able to hand this next person a path or a navigational metaphor or structure so that they can find what they are looking for and [if it]..is meaningful to them they can reuse it with a slight change. (Sherif and Xing 2006, p. 536)

You cannot just willy-nilly grab content and throw it into a big pot and then hope that it can be re-used. Obviously, you've got to put tags on that content in a way that it is retrievable. You have to be able to provide the knowledge contributor with the analog on the front end, so that they can categorize and catalog their knowledge in a way that makes it meaningful for the person who is now coming and going to repeat it all. (Sherif and Xing 2006, p. 536)

Costs in terms of effort and time can also be reduced by maintaining a community home page, which provides a quick overview of things such as the latest news related to the community topic, latest posts and replies. Virtual worlds have changed the representation of a home page from being text-based to one that is closer to the notion of a three-dimensional front.

An effective and efficient search function is important in order for members to be able to locate relevant information quickly, which also could reduce the amount of effort made (Markus, 2001). Hence,

The home page for the community should be fresh and dynamic, presenting all new relevant information for the community in a concise and easy-to-read manner.

The KMS should support an efficient and effective search function.

The following statements elaborate on these guidelines.

You go to this site that has the method and you click on the phases and read about the phases, you read about stages, and it shows what work products and what deliverables come out of those activities and stages. You can click on that and it will bring up the best examples of those deliverables and work products. (Sherif and Xing 2006, p. 537)

Say you have someone on the ExxonMobil team, and they need to keep up with what's going on with ExxonMobil, so we set up a search term for them and we tie it into our Dow Jones service that we use and everyday, Dow Jones uses that search term that we put in there and dumps these articles about ExxonMobil into a profiling container so the team member can use it. They don't have to go to Dow Jones, they don't have to look through 50 different articles, they go right here and they see right here, here's the 10 articles that came in today about ExxonMobil. (Sherif and Xing 2006, p. 537)

A core capability of the tool the team was provided was the ability to reference-link entries and apply multiple keywords, and then use powerful search capabilities to identify similar entries. (Markus 2001, p. 80)

Version control system for documents can be used to keep track of dates of multiple submissions of the same document. In addition to automatic checking, members can be encouraged by community managers to periodically review their submissions to the KMS and make sure that they are current and delete the obsolete, inconsistent entries (Kohlhase and Anghelache, 2004; Damodaran and Olphert, 2000).

Accuracy and currency of the information should be maintained by using tools such as version control systems, as well as by encouraging members to review their submissions.

The importance of the ability to revisit and revise posts and to keep the information accurate and up-to-date is seen below.

...the database author might know that the answer could be made more general in order to answer more questions. This might involve abstracting both the question and the answer. Occasionally, the author would feel it necessary to correct

incorrect, incomplete, or incoherent answers. (Markus 2001, p. 76)

The following shows how version control functionality benefits users of a web-based virtual learning environment for students.

Although this approach for providing group awareness is very simple, feedback from users of the BSCW system indicates that information such as 'A uploaded a new version of document X', or 'B has read document Y' is often very useful for group members in coordinating their work and gaining an overview of what has happened since they last logged in. (Appelt and Mambrey 1999, p. 1710)

Social network theory (Granovetter, 1973) and social identity theory (Tajfel and Turner, 1986) have been used to explain knowledge exchange and interactions in communities. According to social identity theory and theories of collective action, gaining self esteem and recognition for their expertise, and enhancing their reputation (Wasko and Faraj, 2005) motivate members to participate in communities (Postmes et al., 2000; Douglas and McGarty, 2001; Donath, 1999). 'Old-timers' in communities are frequently those whose advice is valued due to their track record in the community. Social network theory looks at relationships between members (Chae et al., 2005; Wellman, 1996; Wellman and Guila, 1997; Wasko and Faraj, 2004; Wellman et al., 1996; Garton and Haythornthwaite, 1997) and the normative structure of content and form in a group (Postmes et al., 2000; Wellman, 1996). While weak ties provide more opportunities for new knowledge (Hansen, 1999; Wellman, 1996), on-line strong ties provide more confidence in the information and reinforce real-life relationships (Wellman, 1996). With social network analysis (Wellman, 1996), a well connected member with a high social capital can be identified as a good information resource (Wasko and Faraj, 2005).

Technology should support multiple ways to connect people who need the information to those who have it (Garton and Haythornthwaite, 1997). Social technologies such as online networking sites (e.g. Facebook, MySpace) and virtual worlds (e.g. Second Life) can be used to support collaboration (Goel and Mousavidin, 2007). The affordance of virtual worlds of self-expression through actions, gestures, representation, and symbols allows for richer interaction and exchange of tacit knowledge (Goel et al., 2008). Expert directories are often an integral part of KMS and serve as transactive memory systems to identify 'who knows what' in the organization (Argote and Ingram, 2000).

If an employee knows exactly who to ask a particular question from, he/she should be able to contact the expert directly, and in the absence of the knowledge, the member can rely on the community to help arrive at an answer. Since members in a KMS can belong to multiple communities, these features apply to the entire system. This discussion leads to the following design recommendations:

The KMS should have the facility to maintain member profiles that indicate the number of posts, other member links, replies, and usage history of a member.

Members should be able to connect to other members directly through tools such as instant messaging as well as indirectly through forums and directories.

The user profile contains compulsory and optional information that a member provides upon registration. If a member of the community publishes a contribution or asks a question, the contributor's name is shown as a hyperlink. By clicking on this hyperlink, one obtains the user profile of the corresponding member. The extent of information other members see on the user profile depends on the level of anonymity the member has chosen. (Leimeister et al. 2005, p. 110)

In the remark below, Barab et al. (2003) discuss the importance of profiles in a community of practice called the "Inquiry Learning Forum" or ILF.

In fact, the ILF encourages its members to create and edit their member profiles so other ILF members can learn more about one another. This enables ILF members to control how they are perceived by others within the community, and ideally, these profiles help ILF members to decide who they want to communicate with and how they might interpret statements or attitudes of others. (Barab et al. 2003, p. 248)

In the context of virtual worlds, interaction can be non-textual and action-based as seen in Goel et al.'s (2008) findings in the quote below.

...a group of people interested in the design of a new structure can meet in Second Life and collectively work on a virtual version of the building by modifying it in real time to incorporate evolving ideas. Starwood Hotels, for instance, used Second Life as a platform to develop and design a new real-world site. A 3D blueprint of the new hotel was laid on a virtual floor with avatars of clients, architects, interior designers, and engineers were able to walk on the blueprint and to contribute ideas. Any avatar in Second Life was invited to make changes to the virtual hotel. Hence, the medium allowed people to pool their ideas and build a collective knowledge base. (p. 18)

Though social identity theory discourages anonymity, literature in MIS (especially in research on group decision support systems) has found anonymity to aid participation. However, an employee's trust in the content obtained from a KMS would be weaker if it were anonymous (Donath, 1999). Making authorship explicit adds legitimacy to the information. Literature in philosophy also discusses the importance of credentials in reliability on others for information (Hardwig, 1991). In addition, this makes the author responsible for making sure that the information he/she puts up is not erroneous. Investigating different levels of anonymity (such as using nicknames or real names) would be an interesting line of enquiry, as well. In virtual worlds, avatars can be designed to look like a person's real life self. For example, the avatar of CEO of IBM closely resembles his real life persona in meetings conducted in Second Life.

Submissions to a KMS should not be anonymous.

The statement below supports this guideline.

An interesting metric developed by the specialists to assess data quality was their use of incident authorship as an indicator of quality. Each incident that is entered is automatically assigned a unique number, which includes a code identifying the particular specialist who entered it ... You tend to evaluate information differently from different people. So if you see 40 items from a search you go to the incidents of those folks you've gotten good information from in the past ... I know that Arthur has a reputation for writing shorts novels as resolutions. I mean, he's a wonderful source of information ... So when I get an incident from him, I'm very comfortable with that information. Whereas, some of the other people in the department will put in one or two sentence resolutions. And it tends to make it a little vaguer and more difficult to be confident about. (Markus 2001, p. 68, 69)

Participation in a community needs to be encouraged (Cross et al., 2006; Davenport et al., 1998; Prandelli et al. 2006). Reluctance on behalf of employees to participate is a primary reason for the failure of KM efforts (Ardichvili, 2003; Alavi and Leidner, 1999). Specifically, perceived loss of power (Constant et al., 1994), fear of criticism and unintentionally misleading members (Ardichvili, 2003), and costs involved in terms of time and effort (Markus, 2001) are primary reasons why employees do not participate. While appropriate design of a system can help minimize the aforementioned costs (Bieber et al., 2002), the organization needs to make efforts to alleviate the other factors. Engendering an organizational culture which encourages pro-social behavior and knowledge sharing has been suggested in prior literature (Constant et al., 1994; Huber, 2001). At a community level, the moderator or community manager can play a vital role in increasing the level of participation. In particular, the community manager needs to ensure that knowledge is transferred from producers (experts) to consumers (users) (Markus, 2001; Cross et al. 2006) by ensuring that questions are answered and new knowledge is posted. These functions of a community manager maintain the value and usefulness of the community to its members (Preece et al., 2003). Hence,

A community manager should ensure that queries are answered.

Some of the responsibilities of community managers (Sysops, in this case) are shown in the statement below.

System operators (Sysops) were appointed to monitor the discussions in the forums, track requests and make sure they were answered. Sysops would try to get answers in 24 hours; if not they would contact people directly and ask them to respond. Additionally, they were to give positive feedback to those who did respond. Since there were likely to be cultural difference and sensitivities, Sysops were to monitor the content of messages ... Three translators were hired and Sysops would decide which messages were to be translated into English with technical replies to be translated back to the originator's own language. The goal for completion of translation was 48 hours. (Markus 2001, p. 85)

A community manager should encourage experts to contribute tacit knowledge (experiences, ideas, etc.) to the community.

Some techniques for encouraging participation were observed by Jones and Rafaeli.

Where sustained interactive discourse is a goal, various techniques can be used to gain critical mass. Administrators can seed discussions by systematically encouraging a group of key individuals to contribute. Economic incentives can be given and where a number of related virtual publics already exist, group segmentation can be used to gain instant critical mass for new virtual publics. (Jones and Rafaeli 2000, p. 221)

In addition to voluntarily accessing the system for information, a KMS can be made a central repository for electronically storable information such as required documents, templates, and forms. Since knowledge sharing cannot be forced and extrinsic rewards may not work (Kankanhalli et al., 2005; Huber, 2001), making the KMS an obligatory passage point (Callon, 1986) for explicit knowledge required for daily work would encourage employees who otherwise would not access the system, or make use of it. Most employees either do not think of using the KMS for posting such information, or may not want to spend the time and effort required to do so. More importantly, there should be a consistent format used for information posted. A community manager plays a key role in ensuring this consistency. Hence,

A community manager should encourage the posting of standardized documents, templates, forms, and other electronically storable information in a consistent manner.

The following shows some consequences of inconsistent postings.

We had to overhaul the [knowledge repository] after three years because nobody was following a consistent style [of classifying documents] ... [P] eople were building their case bases with different parameter settings, so it became like a soup of knowledge, and nobody could find anything. (Markus 2001, p. 81)

We summarize the design guidelines and highlight our contributions in the following section.

DISCUSSION AND FUTURE RESEARCH

The design recommendations derived from theory and past research are summarized in Table 2. In broad terms, the recommendations can be seen to fall into four categories – technological, membership, content, and organizational. To achieve our objective, we study KMS from a perspective that incorporates technical, individual, as well as organizational level literature. These are reflected in the technological, membership, and organizational categories. We tie our recommendations to prior research by suggesting how each of them could be used to achieve a particular success factor. In Table 2, each recommendation is followed by success factor(s) from Table 1 which we believe to be applicable.

Employing the lens of communities of practice allowed us to add a fourth level of analysis – that of a community. The guidelines regarding the content of KM communities address this level. In practice, most KMS incorporate communities as part of their architecture. By drawing on literature on virtual communities, we add to research in KMS by proposing design guidelines for the content and management of such communities. These categories are not mutually exclusive. For example, membership profiles need the corresponding technological features to support them. Also, the list is not intended to be exhaustive. Further research studying actual participatory behavior in KMS would help determine if there are other design characteristics that facilitate community participation.

It is important to note that the manner in which the design recommendations are implemented would differ based on specific technologies. While we give examples of how some may look in the context of technologies such as weblogs, wikis, social networking sites, and virtual worlds, it is hard to predict how the design features will be represented as these technologies evolve and new ones emerge. Hence the design recommendations have to be interpreted in the light of what new technologies afford.

Prior research in IS has not systematically studied design guidelines for knowledge management communities. While the design features discussed have been implemented in current KM practices, they have emerged more from a process of trial-and-error; not grounded in research. Organizations are spending considerable resources - both in terms of time and money - on knowledge management efforts, not all of which are successful. Results from this study could help managers concerned with KM increase their chances of success by designing sustainable communities.

Using a community of practice as a lens unifies the fragmented literature in knowledge management which, thus far, has studied the phenomenon separately at the individual, organizational, or system level. A shift of perspective of community sustainability from one that retains more members to one that serves as an effective and efficient platform for knowledge management also stimulates new lines of inquiry.

We looked at existing research on knowledge management and virtual communities, synthesized the literature, and applied it in the context of organizational KMS. Our goal was to conceptually identify guidelines for successful design of communities in KMS which can be used by practitioners who wish to implement KMS. Hence, these guidelines are intended as a blueprint to design KMS communities. Furthermore, they

Table 2. Summary of design recommendations for sustainable communities of practice in knowledge management systems

Design Guidelines		Success Factor
I. Technological features		
	1. Site Map	SF1, SF2, SF7
	2. Search features	SF7
	3. Document version control systems	SF1, SF2, SF7
II. Membership features		
	1. Non-anonymity	SF1
	2. Maintaining usage statistics and profiles	SF1, SF5
	3. Connectivity between members – Directories, Forums, IM capabilities	SF1
III. Content features		
	1. Making it an Obligatory Passage Point (OPP) for documents, templates, forms etc.	SF3, SF8
	2. Home page to represent community – fresh, dynamic	SF7
	3. Content on the home page for summary of new relevant topics, news, and highlights	SF2, SF7
	4. Moderation to ensure topical focus and relevance	SF2, SF3, SF5, SF6, SF7
	5. Moderation to ensure questions are answered	SF3, SF5
	6. Moderation to encourage 'experts' to contribute	SF3
	7. Moderation to ensure currency of documents	SF3, SF5, SF7
	8. Splitting into sub-communities, if size grows	SF3, SF5, SF6, SF7
IV. Organizational functions		
	1. Creating and supporting role of moderator/community manager	SF3, SF4

can also be used as an evaluative tool for existing KMS. Future research would add value by evaluating and testing these recommendations in a representative setting through possibly an action research. An exploratory case study of existing KMS that implement these features would also provide validity. Each recommendation could be the subject of a separate study. For example, the role of a knowledge manager or the design of the search features could constitute substantial research agendas.

This paper has the limitations associated with a conceptual study. It needs to be validated by empirical research. The suggestions presented for future research are intended to be a guide for a research program in this area. We draw on literature in virtual communities to inform us about the nature of communities in knowledge management systems. However, the design of these communities is contingent upon organizational factors such as organization culture, norms, practices, and structure. Hence, these guidelines may not be universally applicable but need to be tailored to the specific context and requirements. This research is intended to be a starting point for an inquiry on the topic.

REFERENCES

Akhavan, P., Jafari, M., & Fathian, M. (2005). Exploring Failure-Factors of Implementing Knowledge Management Systems In Organizations. *Journal of Knowledge Management Practice*.

Alavi, M. & Leidner, D. E. (1999). Knowledge Management Systems: Issues, Challenges, and Benefits. *Communications of the AIS, 1*(7).

Alavi, M., & Leidner, D. E. (2001). Review: Knowledge Management and Knowledge Management Systems: Conceptual Foundations and Research Issues. *MIS Quarterly, 25*(1), 107–136. doi:10.2307/3250961

Appelt, W., & Mambrey, P. (1999). Experiences with the BSCW Shared Workspace System as the Backbone of a Virtual Learning Environment for Students. In *Proceedings of ED Media '99, Charlottesville* (pp. 1710-1715).

Ardichvili, A. (2003). Motivation and barriers to participation in virtual knowledge-sharing communities of practice. *Journal of Knowledge Management, 7*(1), 64–77. doi:10.1108/13673270310463626

Argote, L., & Ingram, P. (2000). Knowledge Transfer: A basis for Competitive Advantage in Firms. *Organizational Behavior and Human Decision Processes, 82*(1), 150–169. doi:10.1006/obhd.2000.2893

Balasubramanian, S., & Mahajan, V. (2001). The Economic Leverage of the Virtual Community. *International Journal of Electronic Commerce, 5*(3), 103–138.

Barab, S. A., MaKinster, J. G. & Scheckler, R. (2003). Designing System Dualities: Characterizing a Web-Supported Professional Development Community. *The Information Society, 19*, 237–256. doi:10.1080/01972240309466

Bieber, M., Engelbart, D., Furuta, D., Hiltz, R., Noll, S. R., & Preece, J., J., Stohr, E. A., Turoff, M., & Van De Walle, B. (2002). Toward Virtual Community Knowledge Evolution. *Journal of Management Information Systems, 18*(4), 11–35.

Blanchard, A. L., & Markus, M. L. (2004). The Experienced 'Sense' of a Virtual Community: Characteristics and Processes. *The Data Base for Advances in Information Systems, 35*(1), 65–79.

Bock, G. W., Zmud, R. W., Kim, Y. G., & Lee, J. N. (2005). Behavioral Intention Formation in Knowledge Sharing: Examining the Roles of Extrinsic Motivators, Social-Psychological Forces, and Organizational Climate. *MIS Quarterly, 29*(1), 87–111.

Brown, J. S., & Duguid, P. (1999). Organizing Knowledge. *The Society for Organizational Learning, 1*(2), 28–44.

Brown, J. S., & Duguid, P. (2000). Balancing Act: How to Capture Knowledge Without Killing It. *Harvard Business Review*, 73–80.

Brown, J. S., & Gray, E. S. (1995). The People Are the Company. *FastCompany*. Retrieved from http://www.fastcompany.com/online/01/people.html

Butler, B. (1999). *The dynamics of electronic communities*. Unpublished Ph.D. dissertation, Graduate School of Industrial Administration, Carnegie Mellon University.

Butler, B. S. (2001). Membership Size, Communication Activity and Sustainability: A Resource-Based Model of Online Social Structures. *Information Systems Research, 12*(4), 346–362. doi:10.1287/isre.12.4.346.9703

Callon, M. (1986). Some Elements of A Sociology of Translation: Domestication of the Scallops and the Fishermen of St. Brieuc Bay. In J. Law (Ed.), *Power, Action and Belief* (pp. 196-233). London: Routledge & Kegan Paul.

Chae, B., Koch, H., Paradice, D., & Huy, V. (2005). Exploring Knowledge Management Using Network Theories: Questions, Paradoxes and Prospects. *Journal of Computer Information Systems*, *45*(4), 62–74.

Cheuk, B. W. (2006). Using Social Networking Analysis to Facilitate Knowledge Sharing in the British Council. *International Journal of Knowledge Management*, *2*(4), 67–76.

Cohen, D. (2006). What's Your Return on Knowledge? *Harvard Business Review*, *84*(12), 28–28.

Constant, D., Keisler, S., & Sproull, L. (1994). What's Mine is Ours, or Is It? A Study of Attitudes about Information Sharing. *Information Systems Research*, *5*(4), 400–421. doi:10.1287/isre.5.4.400

Cross, R., Laseter, T., Parker, A., & Velasquez, G. (2006). Using Social Network Analysis to Improve Communities of Practice. *California Management Review*, *49*(1), 32–60.

Daconta, M., Orbst, L., & Smith, K. (2003). *The Semantic Web*. Indianapolis: Wiley Publishing.

Damodaran, L., & Olphert, W. (2000). Barriers and Facilitators to the Use of Knowledge Management Systems. *Behaviour & Information Technology*, *19*(6), 405–413. doi:10.1080/014492900750052660

Davenport, T. H., De Long, D. W., & Beers, M. C. (1997). Building successful Knowledge Management Projects. *Center for Business Innovation Working Paper*, Ernst and Young.

Davenport, T. H., De Long, D. W., & Beers, M. C. (1998). Successful Knowledge Management Projects. *MIT Sloan Management Review*, *39*(2), 43–57.

Davenport, T. H., & Prusak, L. (1997). *Working Knowledge: How Organizations Manage What They Know*. Cambridge, MA: Harvard Business School Press.

Davis, F. D. (1989). Perceived Usefulness, Perceived Ease of Use, and User Acceptance of Information Technology. *MIS Quarterly*, *13*(3), 319–341. doi:10.2307/249008

Donath, J. S. (1999). Identity and deception in the virtual community. In M. A. Kollock (Ed.), *Communities in Cyberspace* (pp. 29-59). London: Routledge.

Douglas, K. M., & McGarty, C. (2001). Identifiability and self-presentation: Computer-mediated communication and intergroup interaction. *The British Journal of Social Psychology*, *40*, 399–416. doi:10.1348/014466601164894

Dretske, F. (1991). *Explaining Behavior: Reasons in a World of Causes*. Cambridge, MA: MIT Press.

Epple, D., & Argote, L. (1996). An Empirical Investigation of the Microstructure of Knowledge Acquisition and Transfer through Learning by doing. *Operations Research*, *44*(1), 77–86. doi:10.1287/opre.44.1.77

Garton, L., Haythornthwaite, C., & Wellman, B. (1997). Studying online social networks. *Journal of Computer-Mediated Communication*, *3*(1), 75–105.

Geroimenko, V., & Chen, C. (2003). *Visualizing the Semantic Web*. London: Springer.

Gibson, J. J. (1977). The Theory of Affordances. In R. Shaw & J. Bransford (Eds.), *Perceiving, Acting, and Knowing*. Hillsdale, NJ: Lawrence Erlbaum.

Goel, L., Junglas, I., & Ives, B. (2008). Virtual Worlds as Platforms for Communities of Practice. In King, W., (Ed.), *Annals of Information System series on Knowledge Management and Organizational Learning*. Springer.

Goel, L., & Mousavidin, E. (2007). vCRM: Virtual Customer Relationship Management. *The Data Base for Advances in Information Systems, 38*(4).

Goodhue, D. L., & Thompson, R. L. (1995). Task-Technology Fit and Individual Performance. *MIS Quarterly, 19*(2), 213–236. doi:10.2307/249689

Gordon, R., & Grant, D. (2005). Knowledge Management or Management of Knowledge? Why People Interested in Knowledge Management Need to Consider Foucault and the Construct of Power. *Journal of Critical Postmodern Organization Science, 3*(2), 27–38.

Granovetter, M. (1973). The strength of weak ties. *American Journal of Sociology, 78*, 1360–1380. doi:10.1086/225469

Grant, R. M. (1996). Toward a knowledge-based theory of the firm. *Strategic Management Journal, 17*(Winter Special Issue), 109-122.

Habermas, J. (1984). *The Theory of Communicative Action*. Boston: Beacon Press.

Hammer, M., Leonard, D., & Davenport, T. H. (2004). Why Don't We Know More About Knowledge? *MIT Sloan Management Review, 45*(4), 14–18.

Hansen, M. T. (1999). The Search-Transfer Problem: The Role of Weak Ties in Sharing Knowledge across Organizational Subunits. *ASQ, 44*, 82–111. doi:10.2307/2667032

Hardwig, J. (1991). The Role of Trust in Knowledge. *The Journal of Philosophy, 88*(12), 693–708. doi:10.2307/2027007

Hart, D., & Warne, L. (2006). Comparing Cultural and Political Perspectives of Data, Information, and Knowledge Sharing in Organisations. *International Journal of Knowledge Management, 2*(2), 1–15.

Hill, W., Stead, L., Rosenstein, M., & Furnas, G. (1995). Recommending and evaluating choices in a virtual community of use. *SIGCHI Conference on Human factors in computing systems*. Denver: Colorado.

Hippel, E. V. (1994). "Sticky Information" and the Locus of Problem Solving: Implications for Innovation. *Management Science, 40*(4), 429–440. doi:10.1287/mnsc.40.4.429

Huber, G. (2001). Transfer of knowledge in knowledge management systems: unexplored issues and suggested studies. *European Journal of Information Systems, 10*, 72–79. doi:10.1057/palgrave.ejis.3000399

Husted, K., & Michailova, S. (2002). Diagnosing and Fighting Knowledge-Sharing Hostility. *Organizational Dynamics, 31*(1), 60–73. doi:10.1016/S0090-2616(02)00072-4

Inkpen, A. C. (2005). Learning through Alliances: General Motors and NUMMI. *California Management Review, 47*(4), 114–136.

Jarvenpaa, S. L., & Staples, D. S. (2000). The Use of Collaborative Electronic Media for Information Sharing: An Exploratory Study of Determinants. *The Journal of Strategic Information Systems, 9*(2/3), 129–154. doi:10.1016/S0963-8687(00)00042-1

Jennex, M., & Olfman, L. (2000). Development recommendations for knowledge management/organizational memory systems. In *Proceedings of the Information Systems Development Conference*.

Jennex, M., & Olfman, L. (2004). Assessing Knowledge Management success/Effectiveness Models. In *Proceedings of the 37th Hawaii International Conference on System Sciences*.

Jennex, M. E. (2005a). What is Knowledge Management? *International Journal of Knowledge Management*, *1*(4), i–iv.

Jennex, M. E., & Olfman, L. (2005b). Assessing Knowledge Management success. *International Journal of Knowledge Management*, *1*(2), 33–49.

Jennex, M. E., & Olfman, L. (2006). A Model of Knowledge Management Success. *International Journal of Knowledge Management*, *2*(3), 51–68.

Jennex, M. E., Smolnik, S., & Croasdell, D. (2007). Knowledge Management Success. *International Journal of Knowledge Management*, *3*(2), i–vi.

Jones, Q. (1997). Virtual-Communities, virtual settlements and cyber archeology: A theoretical outline. *Journal of Computer-Mediated Communication*, *3*(3).

Jones, Q., & Rafaeli, S. (2000). Time to Split, Virtually: 'Discourse Architecture' and 'Community Building' Create Vibrant Virtual Publics. *Electronic Markets*, *10*(4), 214–223. doi:10.1080/101967800750050326

Jones, Q., Ravid, G., & Rafaeli, S. (2004). Information Overload and the Message Dynamics of Online Interaction Spaces: A Theoretical Model and Empirical Exploration. *Information Systems Research*, *15*(2), 194–210. doi:10.1287/isre.1040.0023

Kankanhalli, A., Tan, B. C. Y., & Kwok-Kei, W. (2005). Contributing Knowledge to Electronic Knowledge Repositories: An Empirical Investigation. *MIS Quarterly*, *29*(1), 113–143.

King, W. R. (2006). The Critical Role of Information Processing in Creating an Effective Knowledge Organization. *Journal of Database Management*, *17*(1), 1–15.

Koeglreiter, G., Smith, R., & Torlina, L. (2006). The Role of Informal Groups in Organisational Knowledge Work: Understanding an Emerging Community of Practice. *International Journal of Knowledge Management*, *2*(1), 6–23.

Kohlhase, M., & Anghelache, R. (2003). Towards Collaborative Content Management and Version Control for Structured Mathematical Knowledge. In *Proceedings of Second International Conference on Mathematical Knowledge Management (MKM)*.

Lapre, M. A., & Van Wassenhove, L. N. (2003). Managing Learning Curves in Factories by Creating and Transferring Knowledge. *California Management Review*, *46*(1), 53–71.

Lave, J., & Wenger, E. (1991). *Situated Learning: Legitimate peripheral participation*. Cambridge: Cambridge University Press.

Leimeister, J. M., Ebner, W., & Krcmar, H. (2005). Design, Implementation, and Evaluation of Trust-Supporting Components in Virtual Communities for Patients. *Journal of Management Information Systems*, *21*(4), 101–135.

Licklider, J. & Taylor, R. (1968). The computer as a communication device. *Science and Technology: For the Technical Men in Management*, 21-31.

Lippman, S. A., & Rumelt, R. P. (1982). Uncertain imitability: An analysis of interfirm differences in efficiency under competition. *The Bell Journal of Economics*, *13*, 418–438. doi:10.2307/3003464

Lui, T.-W., Picccoli, G., & Ives, B. (2007). Marketing Strategies in Virtual Worlds. *The Data Base for Advances in Information Systems*, *38*(4), 77–80.

Malhotra, A., Gosain, S., & Hars, A. (1997). Evolution of a Virtual Community: Understanding Design Issues Through a Longitudinal Study. In the *Proceedings of International Conference on Information Systems (ICIS)*.

Markus, L. M. (1987). Towards a "critical mass" theory of interactive media: Universal access, interdependence and diffusion. *Comm. Res.*, *14*, 491–511. doi:10.1177/009365087014005003

Markus, L. M. (2001). Towards a Theory of Knowledge Reuse: Types of Knowledge Reuse Situations and Factors in Reuse Success. *Journal of Management Information Systems*, *18*(1), 57–94.

Markus, L. M., Majchrzak, A., & Gasser, L. (2002). A Design Theory for Systems That Support Emergent Knowledge Processes. *MIS Quarterly*, *26*(3), 179–212.

McDermott, R. (1999a). How to get the most out of human networks: Nurturing Three-Dimensional Communities of Practice. *Knowledge Management Review*, *2*(5), 26–29.

McDermott, R. (1999b). Why Information Inspired But Cannot Deliver Knowledge Management. *California Management Review*, *41*(4), 103–117.

Murphy, J., & Hackbush, J. (2007). The Knowledge Management Spending Report, 2007–2008 The Market Hits $73B. *AMR Research Report*. Retrieved from http://www.amrresearch.com/Content/View.asp?pmillid=20744

Nidumolu, S. R., Subramani, M., & Aldrich, A. (2001). Situated Learning and the Situated Knowledge Web: Exploring the Ground Beneath Knowledge Management. *Journal of Management Information Systems*, *18*(1), 115–150.

Nonaka, I. (1994). A dynamic theory of organizational knowledge creation. *Organization Science*, *5*(1), 14–37. doi:10.1287/orsc.5.1.14

Orlikowski, W. J. (2002). Knowing in Practice: Enacting a Collective Capability in Distributed Organizing. *Organization Science*, *13*(3), 249–273. doi:10.1287/orsc.13.3.249.2776

Orr, J. E. (1989). Sharing Knowledge, Celebrating Identity: War Stories and Community Memory Among Service Technicians. In D. S. Middleton & D. Edwards (Eds.), *Collective Remembering: Memory in Society*. Newbury Park, CA: Sage Publications.

Pan, S. L., & Leidner, D. E. (2003). Bridging communities of practice with information technology in the pursuit of global knowledge sharing. *The Journal of Strategic Information Systems*, *12*, 71–88. doi:10.1016/S0963-8687(02)00023-9

Polanyi, M. (1958). *Personal Knowledge, Towards a Post-Critical Philosophy*. Chicago, IL: University of Chicago Press.

Porra, J., & Goel, L. (2006). Importance of Power in the Implementation Process of a Successful KMS: A Case Study. [Abstract] In 37th Annual Meeting of the Decision Sciences Institute, San Antonio, TX, November 18-21.

Porra, J. & Parks, M. S. (2006). Sustaining Virtual Communities: Suggestions from the Colonial Model. *Information Systems and e-Business Management, 4*(4), 309-341.

Postmes, T., Spears, R., & Lea, M. (2000). The formation of group norms in computer-mediated communication. *Human Communication Research*, *26*(3), 341–371. doi:10.1111/j.1468-2958.2000.tb00761.x

Prandelli, E., Verona, G., & Raccagni, D. (2006). Diffusion of Web-Based Product Innovation. *California Management Review*, *48*(4), 109–135.

Preece, J., Nonnecke, B., & Andrews, D. (2003). The top five reasons for lurking: improving community experiences for everyone. *Computers in Human Behavior*, *20*, 201–223. doi:10.1016/j.chb.2003.10.015

Prusak, L. (2001). Where did knowledge management come from? *IBM Systems Journal*, *40*(4), 1002–1007.

Rogers, E. M. & Agarwala-Rogers (1975). Organizational communication. In G. L. Hanneman, W. J. McEwen (Eds.), *Communication Behaviour* (pp. 218-236). Addision Wesley: Reading, MA.

Ryle, G. (1949/1984). *The Concept of Mind*. Chicago, IL: University of Chicago Press.

Schultze, U., & Leidner, D. (2002). Studying Knowledge Management in Information Systems Research: Discourses and Theoretical Assumptions. *MIS Quarterly*, *26*(3), 213–242. doi:10.2307/4132331

Schultze, U., & Stabell, C. (2004). Knowing What You Don't Know? Discourses and Contradictions in Knowledge Management Research. *Journal of Management Studies*, *41*(4), 549–573. doi:10.1111/j.1467-6486.2004.00444.x

Sherif, K., & Xing, B. (2006). Adaptive processes for knowledge creation in complex systems: the case of a global IT consulting firm. *Information & Management*, *43*(4), 530–540. doi:10.1016/j.im.2005.12.003

Shin, M. (2004). A framework for evaluating economics of knowledge management systems. *Information & Management*, *42*, 179–196.

Silva, L., Mousavidin, E., & Goel, L. (2006). Weblogging: Implementing Communities of Practice. In E. Trauth, D. Howcroft, T. Butler, B. Fitzgerald & J. DeGross (Eds.), *Social Inclusion: Societal and Organizational Implications for Information Systems* (pp. 295-317). New York: Springer-Verlag.

Stein, E. W. (2006). A Qualitative Study of the Characteristics of a Community of Practice for Knowledge Management and Its Success Factors. *International Journal of Knowledge Management*, *1*(4), 1–24.

Tajfel, H., & Turner, J. C. (1986). The social identity theory of intergroup behavior. In S. Worchel & W. G.Austin (Eds.), *Psychology of intergroup relations* (pp. 7-24), Chicago: Nelson-Hall.

Usoro, A., & Kuofie, M. H. S. (2006). Conceptualisation of Cultural Dimensions as a Major Influence on Knowledge Sharing. *International Journal of Knowledge Management*, *2*(2), 16–25.

Wasko, M. M., & Faraj, S. (2000). 'It is What One Does': Why People Participate and Help Others in Electronic Communities of Practice. *The Journal of Strategic Information Systems*, *9*(2/3), 155–173. doi:10.1016/S0963-8687(00)00045-7

Wasko, M. M., & Faraj, S. (2005). Why Should I Share? Examining Knowledge Contribution in Networks of Practice. *MIS Quarterly*, *29*(1), 35–57.

Wasko, M. M., Faraj, S., & Teigland, R. (2004). Collective Action and Knowledge Contribution in Electronic Networks of Practice. *Journal of the Association for Information Systems*, *5*(11-12), 493–513.

Wellman, B. (1996). For a Social Network Analysis of Computer Networks: A Sociological Perspective on Collaborative Work and Virtual Community. *SIGCPR/SIGMIS*, Denver, Colorado.

Wellman, B., & Gulia, M. (1997). Net Surfers Don't Ride Alone: Virtual Communities as Communities. *Communities and Cyberspace*, New York: Routledge.

Wellman, B., Salaff, J., Dimitrova, D., Garton, L., Gulia, M., & Haythornthwaite, C. (1996). Computer Networks as Social Networks: Collaborative Work, Telework, and Virtual Community. *Annual Review of Sociology*, *22*, 213–238. doi:10.1146/annurev.soc.22.1.213

Wenger, E. (1998). *Communities of Practice: Learning, Meaning, and Identity*. Cambridge University Press.

Yue Wah, C., Menkhoff, T., Loh, B., & Evers, H. D. (2007). Social Capital and Knowledge Sharing in Knowledge-Based Organizations: An Empirical Study. *International Journal of Knowledge Management*, *3*(1), 29–38.

Zammuto, R. F., Griffith, T. L., Majchrzak, A., Dougherty, D. J., & Faraj, S. (2007). Information technology and the changing fabric of organization. *Organization Science*, *18*(5), 749–762. doi:10.1287/orsc.1070.0307

Chapter 22
Risk Management:
Strengthening Knowledge Management

Suzanne Zyngier
La Trobe University, Australia

ABSTRACT

Deliberate exploitation of natural resources and excessive use of environmentally abhorrent materials have resulted in environmental disruptions threatening the life support systems. A human centric approach of development has already damaged nature to a large extent. This has attracted the attention of environmental specialists and policy makers. It has also led to discussions at various national and international conventions. The objective of protecting natural resources cannot be achieved without the involvement of professionals from multidisciplinary areas. This chapter recommends a model for the creation of knowledge-based systems for natural resources management. Further, it describes making use of unique capabilities of remote sensing satellites for conserving natural resources and managing natural disasters. It is exclusively for the people who are not familiar with the technology and who are given the task of framing policies.

INTRODUCTION

There are many approaches intended to aid the implementation of knowledge management (KM) strategies in an organization; there are also many frameworks that structure the rationale and management of organizational knowledge. In order for a KM practitioner to seriously reflect on practice and manage KM risks, he or she needs both a conceptual framework and tools. In this article, the capacity to manage risks to the effective implementation of strategy, and the capacity to review and to revise strategy according to need is presented as a tool for effective KM practice.

Risk management is the process of identifying, analyzing, evaluating, dealing with, and monitoring risk. Risks to knowledge management are both structural and cultural (Chua & Lam, 2005; DeLong & Fahey, 2000; Pfeffer & Sutton, 1999; Zyngier, 2002). The effective implementation of KM strategies demands that we manage risks to those strategies in order to realize the benefits of leveraging organizational knowledge to fulfill strategic aims and objectives.

This article is structured as follows: the following section discusses knowledge management strategies and observed risks to those strategies. KM governance is presented as a mechanism that includes risk management as an integral element in a suite of activities. It locates the responsibility for risk management and demonstrates how this is supported within the planning and implementation of strategy. Two case studies present find clear outcomes that support the role governance in ensuring risk management as a tool for strengthening practice in KM. Finally, it is concluded that risk management is part of a suite of activities that support the effective and sustainable implementation of an organizational KM strategy through KM governance.

KNOWLEDGE MANAGEMENT STRATEGIES

The effective practice of the management of knowledge acts to increase the effectiveness and profitability of an organization (Davenport, 1999; Davenport, De Long, & Beers, 1998; Davenport & Prusak, 2000; Nonaka & Takeuchi, 1995; O'Dell, Grayson, & Essaides, 1998). Managing knowledge ensures that the organization can leverage its key resource and has the right knowledge at the right time to fulfill its aims and objectives. Where systems are designed to support the capture, utilization, and re-utilization of knowledge using the experience of knowledge workers then innovation and creativity are enhanced throughout the value chain of organizational activity. This can improve revenue flows, staff quality, and staff and customer satisfaction. It can reduce the unit cost of the initial creation of knowledge and the overall of the service or product delivery process in an ongoing and continuous cycle (Nonaka & Takeuchi, 1995).

KM literature reflects multiple approaches to the understanding of what knowledge is important to an organization and how is can or should be leveraged to fulfill organizational aims and objectives. To this end many specific tools and techniques have been developed that can be parts of a strategy implemented to achieve KM objectives. These techniques are usually focused on a theoretical methodology that will provide the greatest leverage in implementation (Walsham, 2001). There are a broad variety of approaches to KM or combinations of approaches—each meeting a perceived need in the organization through a wide range of techniques to manage the transfer of organizational knowledge including those to leverage tacit and explicit resources.

Table 1 shows examples of the range of tools and techniques that have been developed by theoreticians and practitioners.

KM tools and techniques are selectively and variously employed according to the specific needs of an organization.

Acknowledging Risks: Obstacles to KM Strategy Implementation

A recurrent theme in KM research is the development of strategies to overcome obstacles to the successful implementation of a KM strategy. While many barriers are recounted as the responses of individuals, these people operate within and reflect the organizational environment. The KM strategy is implemented within that environment and therefore the responses of individuals are what can be measured to establish efficacy of organizational response. The unit of analysis in this research is KM strategy implementation within the organization. Within the literature cultural barriers seem to predominate.

Pfeffer and Sutton (1999) discuss fear and power relationships as a factor that can prevent organizations leveraging existing knowledge resources. Fear and distrust of management may affect to the ability of staff to act without being

Table 1. KM tools and techniques with author references

Individual strategies such as leveraging best practice	(O'Dell et al., 1998; O'Dell et al., 2000),
The capture of intellectual capital	(Sveiby, 1997, 2001);
The role and use of documents and databases for explicit knowledge resource storage and management	(Bawden, 1997; Kelleher & Courtney, 2003; Probst et al., 2000);
The role and use of KM portals and intranets	(McElroy, 2003).
The role and establishment of communities of practice	(O'Dell et al., 1998; Wenger et al., 2002; Wenger & Snyder, 2000);
The development of learning organizations	(Hong, 1999; Krogh et al., 2000; Lehaney et al., 2003; Senge, 1990a, 1990b); and
Exploring organizational cultural change management as it relates to the development of an environment in which knowledge sharing is a natural and desired part of organizational philosophy	(Davenport, 1999; Holsapple & Joshi, 2000; Kelleher et al., 2001; Swart & Kinnie, 2003).

punished either overtly or covertly. Fear for job security, self-esteem, and their future may influence employees against doing anything but what they have securely done in the past. It can be suggested that in order to understand the notion of a perceived cost of knowledge sharing we can take the notion of the cost of the transaction between people as borrowed from economics. Transactions include human capital investments: investment in training and learning by doing or mentoring are all costs that can be identified by the organization. The cost to the humans of participating in the transaction also requires recognition. Transaction cost economics is premised on the assumption that people are wholly rational and make decisions accordingly (Williamson, 1979). By contrast Foss and Mahnke (2003) use transaction cost economics to explain the financial, physical and emotional costs to employees of individual and of organizational economic exchange in the knowledge process and the management if associated risks.

Some researchers consider the role of executive management in developing an appropriate culture that fosters or hinders the management of knowledge as outlined by Nonaka and Takeuchi (1995), Davenport and Prusak (2000), Hackett (2000), Dixon (2000), Hauschild et al.(2001) and by Probst, Raub and Romhardt(2000).

Organizations limiting the application of new ideas may dull the knowledge creation process and stultify work practices. This in turn may lead to the diminution of product development and of service to clients. Organizational core rigidity can inhibit knowledge transfer when doing one thing well to the exclusion of anything else stifles creativity (Leonard, 1995). Further, 'best practice' solutions to a workplace problem may lead to the exclusion of a new innovative solution being ignored or never even exposed (O'Dell et al., 1998; O'Dell et al., 2000; Snowden, 2003)

Husted and Michailova (2002) suggest that obstacles to the effective management of knowledge are activity associated with three main classes of behavior. These are:

- Behaviors of the transmitter of knowledge;
- Behaviors of the receiver of knowledge and cultural; and
- Content related behaviors in the development of 'after action reviews' and the development of a 'learning organization' model so that knowledge acquisition is seen as normal and desirable.

Transmitter behavior where knowledge hoarding may be mild can be depicted as individual economic concern or alternatively strong hostility where it becomes apparent as an issue of survival in power games. Receiver behavior towards new knowledge can be mild resistance and would be characterized as professional pride. By contrast, strong resistance by receivers to acquiring new knowledge is described by Husted and Michailova (2002) as a strong push to maintain the status quo. A significant obstacle to knowledge sharing is the structure of an organization into divisions or departments that do not interact to share knowledge. These are referred to as organizational silos or cultural silos (Davenport & Prusak, 1997; De Long & Fahey, 2000; McDermott & O'Dell, 2000).

A complementary view of barriers to knowledge transfer is described by Szulanski as the 'internal stickiness' of knowledge (Szulanski, 1996, p. 27). Whether or not knowledge can be readily transferred depends on the intrinsic quality of knowledge and also on the people who are sharing it. Knowledge transfer is contingent on:

- The lack of the absorptive capacity of the recipient, their incapacity to understand or to (apply) utilize knowledge from a source that is outside their world view or experience.
- Causal ambiguity of the context—the person acquiring the knowledge cannot understand what the knowledge is for, how it relates to the task, the function of the task and the future purpose of the task or of the knowledge artefact; and
- An arduous, non-trusting or strained relationship between the source of the knowledge and the recipient—this applies regardless of the purpose, whether it is being transferred for the purposes of best practice or for innovation.

Transfer of knowledge and best practice are seen as two way or dual interpersonal exchange between a knowledge source and a knowledge recipient "in which the identity of the recipient matters" (Szulanski, 1996, p. 28). The transfer of knowledge is thus firmly seen as an exchange between individuals though it is not predicated on liking the other individual but rather on the notion of trust, mutual respect, mutual interests and mutual benefit (Seely-Brown & Duguid, 2000). This view is supported by Holsapple and Joshi, (2000) who propose that trust operates on two levels; interpersonal trust and trust in the organization. It is to be found in both the reciprocity between individuals and again separately between individuals and the organization.

As described above there are many barriers to implementation of KM strategies. What becomes apparent is a gap in the analysis of these obstacles. The gap reveals a problem in the implementation of authority, omission of specific risk management strategies, confusion of financial responsibility and little mention of review and revision of strategy and policy. These responsibilities are rarely explicitly mentioned in analysis or descriptions of strategies to manage organizational knowledge. There have been many frameworks used to support the implementation of KM strategies, to give structure and to assist practitioners (Del-Rey-Chamorro, Roy, Wegan, & Steele, 2003; European Committee for Standardization, 2004; Holsapple & Joshi, 2002; Jamieson & Handzic, 2003; Jennex & Olfman, 2005; Kemp, Pudlatz, Perez, & Ortega, 2002; Paulzen, 2002; Standards Australia, 2005; Tanudjojo & Braganza, 2005). The major weakness in these frameworks is that there is little mention of risk management, no defined role for the exercise of authority, decision-making, and the development of KM policy, and no mention of who has responsibility for financial management, of measurement and evaluation of the KM strategy or for review and revision of strategy and policy.

As will be shown in the following sections, governance can suggest a means to achieve effective risk management and, through authorized activity realize the benefits of KM strategy implementation.

RISK MANAGEMENT THROUGH KM GOVERNANCE

KM governance is a mechanism that authorizes KM activity, manages KM risks, maintains fiduciary duty over the financial investment in KM, and ensures the evaluation and review of KM strategy. These responsibilities focus on sustaining KM strategy through a realization of benefits from leveraging organizational knowledge resources. KM governance transparently aligns KM with the strategic aims of the organization through the development of policies. KM governance activities impact on and support the planning and development of the KM strategy and its successful implementation (Zyngier, 2005, 2006, 2007).

KM governance is a process through which organizations delegate responsibility and accountability for KM activities. It locates the source of authority in delivery of the outputs (Zyngier, 2005, 2006, 2007; Zyngier, Burstein, & McKay, 2004, 2005). The interpretation in this article of KM Governance goes beyond the interpretation of the EU framework that deals with the issue of control. (European Committee for Standardization, 2004). Governance of KM guides strategic thinking about policies and strategies implemented, both in the long term and in the medium term. KM strategies should not be regarded as static. Governance provides a mechanism for feedback, allowing the modification and development of existing processes and practices. Through development of policy KM governance determines how decisions are made and solutions developed for resolving obstacles, strategic alignment of strategy and corporate strategy, risk management, access to knowledge resources and under what conditions, and quality maintenance.

Emphasis on strategy, risk-management, delivering financial value and performance measurement indicates the ongoing management of best practice, reflects the stakeholder's needs and values, and drives the KM strategy. The importance of buy-in to the strategy is linked to managing the risk in uptake of new organizational strategies, and of KM in particular (Chua & Lam, 2005; Sohal & Fitzpatrick, 2002).

Risk management is a proactive means of analysis and anticipation of risks to the KM strategy before they arise. It becomes possible to develop plans for risk minimization by attempting to identify the possible risks in advance and for managing risks to the KM strategy as they occur during or after implementation. Management of the risks may require organizational change management, the provision of additional financial or infrastructural support, or a realignment of the original strategy in light of unforeseen or emergent activity within the organization (Standards Australia, 2004).

Risk is the likelihood of something happening to the planning, development and implementation of the KM strategy that will have an impact on its objectives. Risk is measured in terms of a combination of the consequences of an event and its likelihood and may have a negative impact on the strategy. Risk measurement also takes into account the notion of residual risk—that is risk that cannot be avoided even after a risk management strategy is in place (McKay & Marshall, 2004; Standards Australia, 2004). The Australian Standard on Risk Management (2004) specifies six steps in the risk management process: establishing the context, identifying the risks, analyzing the risks, assessing and prioritizing the risks, treating and finally monitoring and reviewing the risk management program.

The process of risk management also takes into account residual risk (Robson, 1994). Residual risk is when the organization is prepared to bear a small loss in order to avoid a greater cost. For example, an organization may be prepared to accept that an expert will not actively participate in a community of practice when forced participation may cause resignation. Another example could be that an organization may be prepared to bear the cost of a small level of duplication of knowledge capture in order to ensure that a single copy exists.

Risks to KM strategies are well researched and documented and can be specified together with the consequences that may flow from them. The need for risk management in KM was formally indicated in 2001 (Kelleher, Levene, & Price Waterhouse Coopers; Standards Australia) with the need to identify assets, the risks and controls associated with the planning, development and implementation of strategy. Obstacles to the effective management of organizational knowledge include a management culture in the organization that hinders KM or the philosophy of knowledge management is often poorly understood in an organization. Additionally there may be conflicts of organizational priorities as barriers to the development and initiation of a KM strategy (European Committee for Standardization, 2004). Another risk is that many organizations find the development of criterion for knowledge collection difficult (Chase, 1997; Zyngier, Burstein, & Rodriguez, 2003). This indicates the need for the establishment of policies to align KM with the firm's aims and objectives.

Governance involves identifying the risks of KM associated with the cultural issues, structural obstacles and other relevant concerns as they arise during the planning, development, implementation and ongoing operation and management of the KM strategy (British Standards Institution & Technical Committee BDD/3, 2002; IT Governance Institute & COBIT Steering Committee, 2000; Jamieson & Handzic, 2003). The management of these risks and assisting in their mitigation strengthens strategies to manage knowledge within the organization (Chua & Lam, 2005; Kelleher et al., 2001; Standards Australia, 2001). Risk management is an essential element of ensuring the successful implementation of a KM strategy. Governance locates the ultimate responsibility for ensuring risk management takes place.

RESEARCH DESIGN

A case study research method was selected to examine the phenomena within its particular context. It is a method that can use many sources of data in a single environment and in this instance; it included observation, semi-structured interviews and document analysis. The research from which this focus on KM risk management is drawn, collected data focused on understanding how governance processes in organizations utilize KM. Theories described in the literature provided the basis for focused observation and for the recording of the observations.

Research Methodology

This article compares and contrasts two cases from the collection of semi structured interview data, documents and observations of cases. Case study analysis took place over a period of several months collecting, examining and analyzing data in its original context - technique often used in an environment where theoretical constructs are unclear or not developed. The research established a purposive sample of the stakeholders in each entity being examined (Lincoln & Guba, 1985). The sample sought to include both users of the KM strategy and those who were implementing the strategy as stakeholders and collect data from them.

The interviews were transcribed and analyzed using QSR5 software as a tool for thematic analysis. In each case, the informants gave semi-structured; in-depth interviews each lasting approximately one hour. These questions canvassed:

- The organizational philosophy of KM;
- The history and implementation of the KM strategy;
- The process and allocation of responsibility for KM; and

- The organizational structures that support and govern the KM initiative.

RESEARCH FINDINGS: XYZ CONSULTING

XYZ consulting is a dispersed multinational enterprise selected purposively according to its large size and its distributed nature and as having a positive reputation as reflected in their Knowledge Group Global Director being invited as a participant in the Knowledge Group Global Director Summit (Oxbrow, 2003, 2004) and also as reflected in the business press as a knowledge intensive organization (Jennex & Zyngier, 2008).

XYZ consulting is a multinational management consulting firm ranked in the top six internationally. Its global headquarters is in Boston. It aims to work with leading organizations to improve their course and performance by stimulating innovative ideas. The company was started in the 1960s with a single consultant and now employs over 2,600 consultants worldwide through a network of offices. It has 60 offices in 37 countries. The company was established as and continues to operate as a Partnership. In 2003, the company recorded revenues of US$1.12 billion.

KM at XYZ Consulting

The current KM strategy was initiated when the partnership decided that they and their consultants needed to know "*how to know what we know and how to find the people who know*" (informant). When the informant was employed to develop the KM initiative as a global initiative for XYZ consulting, it was seen as being "*primarily to bring together what had been a completely uncoordinated set of researchers working in different places and in different ways.*" This was due to the informant's view that the company researchers and the KM initiative were separable. The thrust of this KM initiative was to create a global structure and set of processes to capture and manage explicit knowledge resources. Alternatively this could also be described as a global information management initiative.

A partner and the Knowledge Group Global Director are employed within the company corporate services division to lead KM:

- To satisfy the requirements of the development and implementation of a KM coordinated strategy;
- To manage knowledge as it is conforms to the aims and objectives of the organization;
- To develop a strategy that is specific to the needs of the organization;
- To resource the strategy to facilitate activity; and
- To authorize the implementation of KM activities.

The partner has a dual task. He has governance authority that is delegated through the legal structure of the Partnership agreement, over the strategy in general and takes responsibility for the technical aspects of the KM infrastructure. In this infrastructure role, he also collaborates with the Knowledge Group Global Director on KM strategy planning and strategy promotion. The Knowledge Group Global Director also takes responsibility for directing the staff who implement the strategy. Outcomes are reported back through company corporate services to the partnership. Collectively, the partners have no direct leadership role with respect to the KM strategy other than through the delegated KM role held by the one partner. Nor do the partners develop KM policy. They are both local and regional PA leaders and they "*have always been our champions and our chief customers*" (Informant). In this way the leadership of the strategy is demonstrably supported by the firm as a whole (De Tienne et al., 2004; O'Dell & Leavitt, 2004).

The informant is:

responsible for the strategy and platform for the knowledge group worldwide which comprises the practice area management, research analysts and the people who do the knowledge capture. But that's in a matrix ... except for our corporate that I manage directly. (Informant)

At the same time, funding for the strategy is derived from regional funding and from specific infrastructure allocations at the corporate level.

The team that captures knowledge is managed directly by the Knowledge Group Global Director. Additionally, there are two senior staff members reporting to the Knowledge Group Global Director for the Americas, although they are based in different offices and have local partners that sponsor the strategy locally. Budgeting and the review are done centrally but the KM team is managed in a team structure that is more culturally acceptable in their organizational context.

The strategy has been regionalized across the globe. The KM strategy allocates regional budgets but these are supervised by the central group. This is complete in Germany and the Americas, however it is yet to be achieved in the Asia Pacific and Europe.

Prior Systems: Cultural Risks

As previously described, the company had a practice of retaining PowerPoint presentation to clients together with the supporting documentation. These were kept in individual office locations on shared drives. One of the partners who sponsored the early KM initiative was a practice area leader who tried to encourage all the other practice area leaders to be systematic about the management of intellectual property. "*Specifically they had assistants who "kept the keys to the safe", you know and would dish out these decks that people would ask for by email or however*" (informant). This underlines the problems faced by the organization. There was little or no coordination or control over what was understood to be a highly valuable resource (Jennex & Zyngier, 2008).

Prior Systems: Structural Risks

The first specific problem was the risk of unauthorized access to material about client affairs and the preservation of client confidentiality. Responsibility for the management of these resources was handled by assistants, specifically the partner's secretary "*some of whom were very careful about it and others who weren't*" (informant).

The second problem was the risk to the management of these resources as "*there was not really good system of indexing or anything so the recovery or retrieval was a bit random and depended really on how much the secretary knew about the work*" (informant). Specifically the lack of a systematic, organization wide approach to search and retrieval of documents and related resources was a serious limitation on the availability of explicit knowledge resources.

Transfer of tacit knowledge was traditionally facilitated by pro-active staff education and training. The work structure in teams and by practice areas and practice interest groups creates a clustering of expertise within individual locations and regions. Working in specialist teams that were led where senior management played an active part resulted in mentoring of less experienced staff by those senior staff. There was little or no coordination or control over the transfer of tacit knowledge. The company grew from two consultants in one location in 1963, to 12 consultants in two countries in 1965 to its current size of 2600 consultants in 60 locations globally. The obvious consequence of this was the difficulties in personalization of knowledge to transfer knowledge between individuals locally and its transfer between locations globally (Hasen, Nohria, & Tierney, 1999; Nonaka, 1991).

Risk Management Outcomes from KM Governance Implementation: XYZ Consulting

Since the development of a KM governance mechanism, risks are identified and managed in a formal manner through review of the effectiveness of KM strategy implementation. Risks to the KM strategy are managed in a reactive rather than a proactive manner in that the organization waits until a problem occurs and then creates a solution through amending or changing strategy on a local or on a global scale.

The most substantive risk found was the rolling out a global KM strategy with a wide range of cultural approaches to motivating people to share.

For example in Germany early on ... they took the monetary approach and they gave incentives, cash incentives. We ended up negotiating with them to back off that because we were getting quantity rather than quality.(Informant)

As a cross-cultural management consulting practice the organization spans European, American and Asian cultures where sharing practices and motivations differ. Another area of risk management focus for the KM Team has and continues to be the management of risk for the continuity of the KM strategy "*and keep it get getting the resources that it needs.*"

Risk management attitudes expressed by the informant were couched in terms of ameliorating risks to the cultural and structural aspects of the KM strategy. In particular, at the global level KM team is responsible and report to the governance authority to:

1. Manage risk against "*the 'not invented here' syndrome*" (informant 1);
2. Manage cross-cultural difference to facilitate sharing of knowledge at a global level;
3. Mine databases to identify and leverage existing best practice;
4. Act on security issues for levels of access to electronic resources; and
5. Proactively report to and listen to partners and staff in order to ensure that the KM strategy continues to meet organizational needs.

Risk is jointly identified by the KM team together with the practice area leaders, who are partners and therefore the governing body, by reporting to them and *"listening to their ideas and their needs and meeting them"* (informant 1).

RESEARCH FINDINGS: ABC EXPLORATION AND DRILLING

ABC Exploration and Drilling is a publicly listed multinational oil and gas exploration and production company. Its global headquarters is in Western Australia. It has an international presence beyond its Australia ownership base. This enterprise was selected purposively according to its large size and its distributed nature and as having been a finalist in the 2004 Asian MAKE awards (Chase, 2004). Additionally it has been showcased and discussed at a number of Australian and European conferences as a knowledge intensive organization.

ABC Exploration and Drilling is Australia's leading company in its field. Established in 1954 the company has developed from being regarded as a junior player in the industry to being among Australia's largest independent listed oil and gas company with a market capitalization of approximately $10 billion. The company is the operator of multiple joint ventures with other companies and has substantial oil and gas production assets. During 2003, the company recorded revenues of AUD$2059.3 million.

KM at ABC Exploration and Drilling

The current KM strategy was developed according to the premise that: "*for knowledge to be sustainable we would need to embed* [KM] *into work practices. Into the day-to-day work practices and that actually is ...where we made a decision to look into the ways of working and building up communities of practice around business processes rather than [using] technology and portals*" (Informant). This meant a move away from the technological approach to KM. The new approach was defined as support for the transfer of tacit and explicit knowledge using techniques for personalizing knowledge, together with strategies to capture and store explicit knowledge supported by technology (Baily, 1995; Davenport, 1999; Debowski, 2006; Nonaka & Takeuchi, 1995; "Sarbanes Oxley Act," 2002).

The outcome was the creation of a small KM team of three people globally to manage knowledge across the company. The team started its activities with a pilot strategy in four business units. The growth of the strategy beyond those business units has been incremental and now functions across the company.

The informant was responsible for the knowledge strategy supported by a steering group that forms the KM governance structure. The strategy is described as being "*supported by a steering group*" comprising four of the directors:

One director from IT, another director from HR [Human Resources], one director from legal counsel ... and one director from the business. They are the steering group that review the strategy, review the work that I do and [review] the plans I have. (Informant)

There are two other members of the KM team. One works on KM and the other on the KM system. These roles are in reality "*a bit interchangeable*" (Informant). There is also company provision for staffing a third role on the communications and people side. Currently this role is being filled with the assistance of the HR staff to support the communications and people-focused elements of the strategy. This is common to other organizations but can cause conflicts of interest when the needs of a KM strategy are not in concert with the requirements of the HR department.

Prior Systems: Cultural Risks

Identified obstacles include that "*These people are too busy ... what's in it for me, or why should I change how I do things?*" (Informant). These change management risks are associated with process change and time management issues for the company. The other major obstacle relates to the introduction of collaborative tools: not everyone is willing to or able to contribute. "*Some are contributors, some are takers, and others just browse.*"

Prior Systems: Structural Risks

The initial KM strategy ABC Exploration and Drilling focused on explicit knowledge capture. This was achieved through purchase of collaboration tool and portal to manage explicit knowledge across the company. This was intended to structure, retain and support the range of work required by the firm and to the sharing of this work.

There had been no policies set in place to determine the alignment of the KM strategy with the aims and objectives of the company. There was no company wide KM strategy in place to establish priorities for explicit knowledge capture, nor for how it should be done. It was realized that while enabling all collaboration through a portal was an ideal, this was a limited approach to the understanding of how knowledge was transferred between people.

There were no specific strategies used to leverage tacit knowledge. Tacit knowledge transfer was ad hoc and took place incidentally to the structured activities of the firm.

Risk Management Outcomes from KM Governance Implementation: ABC Exploration and Drilling

Risk management as a tool of governance has resulted in strategies being developed to the specific identified obstacles to the implementation of this strategy. These can be seen as an outcome of the governance process in that while strategies are developed in accord with policy, they have been modified in order to overcome the obstacles (Jennex & Zyngier, 2008).

The Steering Group manages internal and external obstacles and risks to the KM strategy by requiring reviews of KM activities and by developing policies that take into account the regulatory, market and human resources issues that are identifiable by the stakeholders on the Steering Group.

Time availability and willingness to contribute have been recognized as being linked. The company sees that the recognition of the importance of knowledge as a key resource and the increased profile of the KM program of strategies has coincided with increased levels of participation. This is evidenced as a success in managing the cultural risk.

As a member of the group, the Team Leader Knowledge & Management Systems, also discusses these same issues with the Steering Group and with his implementation team. These issues are addressed by the Steering Committee with the assistance of the HR director and the business unit director. The strength of a stakeholder approach indicates that a broad input of advice aids the design of strategy and the implementation issues attached thereto (Korac-Kakabadse & Kakabadse, 2001; Peterson, 2000).

CONCLUSION AND FUTURE RESEARCH

The KM governance is a framework that is confirmed as useful to practitioners and theoreticians. It is a means of realizing the benefits and minimizing the risks to the successful development and implementation of organizational KM strategies.

As demonstrated through the experiences of XYZ Consulting and ABC Drilling, there is strong evidence to suggest that implementation of a KM governance mechanism improves the capacity of an organization to identify and manage KM risks. In the cases, the informants explicitly linked KM governance and management of KM risks. Risk management activities were not only identified but solutions to those risks were found through:

- Analysis of the KM risks
- Articulation of the KM requirements of the organizations;
- Strategic alignment of solutions; and
- Authorized activity to address the risks.

Informants presented risk management activity as a tangible benefit of governance and to the effective and ongoing continuation of their organizations' KM strategies.

As shown earlier, the extant KM literature documents many risks to the effective implementation of a KM strategy. Risk management supports action to resolve obstacles to existing problems Proactive approaches anticipate and manage risks by setting benchmarks and goals (Standards Australia, 2000, 2004). The main elements are communication and consultation, internal and external organizational context, identification, analysis, and evaluation. In the cases presented in these cases, risk management is an iterative and ongoing process. From the evidence, it can be suggested that successful risk management outcomes reported by informants can be attributed to support of such activity by the governing body.

What stands out in the research into these cases was that strategic benefits could be clearly identified and accounted for since the organizational implementation of risk management through each organization's KM governance framework. Strategic benefits were reported uniformly and enthusiastically from two perspectives. The first area of strategic benefit was in relation to the organization and its ability to realize benefits from the implementation of measures to manage and leverage organizational knowledge. The second area of strategic benefit was the support to the ongoing viability and continuity of KM strategy development and implementation. Strategic benefits from KM implementation were recounted by informants at each of the cases, both as perceptions and as measurable events. This confirmed that implementation of KM governance practices not only occurs but also contributes to the effective implementation of sustainable KM strategies in organizations.

This research has made a contribution to KM literature. It has identified bodies that are responsible for governance activities within this framework, their roles, and their tasks. It has made a new contribution to research literature through identification and analysis of processes that govern KM. This research facilitates effective implementation of KM strategies by providing a framework for organizations to use to ensure that authority, risk-management, financial control, and measurement are operationalized in order to realize benefits form KM strategy implementation. We strongly suggest that KM governance maximizes strategic benefits and manages the risks in successful implementation of KM strategies in specifically large, distributed organizations.

REFERENCES

Baily, A. (1995). *Tomorrow's company: The role of business in a changing world.* London: RSA.

British Standards Institution, & Technical Committee BDD/3. (2002). *BS 15000-1:2002 IT Service Management Part 1: Specification for service management.* London: British Standards Institution.

Chase, R. L. (1997). The knowledge-based organisation: An international survey. *Journal of Knowledge Management, 1*(1), 38-49.

Chase, R. L. (2004). *2004 Asian most admired knowledge enterprises—Executive summary.* Bedford, UK: Teleos – The KNOW Network.

Chua, A., & Lam, W. (2005). Why KM projects fail: a multi-case analysis. *Journal of Knowledge Management, 9*(3), 6-17.

Davenport, T. (1999). Knowledge management and the broader firm: Strategy, advantage and performance. In J. Leibowitz (Ed.), *Knowledge management handbook* (pp. 2-1 - 2-11). Boca Raton: CRC Press LLC.

Davenport, T., De Long, D. W., & Beers, M. C. (1998). Successful knowledge management projects. *Sloan Management Review, 39*(2), 43-58.

Davenport, T., & Prusak, L. (1997). *Information ecology: mastering the information and knowledge environment.* New York: Oxford University Press.

Davenport, T., & Prusak, L. (2000). *Working knowledge how organizations manage what they know.* Boston: Harvard Business School Press.

Debowski, S. (2006). *Knowledge management.* Milton, QLD: John Wiley & Sons.

Del-Rey-Chamorro, F. M., Roy, R., Wegan, B. V., & Steele, A. (2003). A framework to create key performance indicators for knowledge management solutions. *Journal of Knowledge Management, 7*(2), 46-62.

DeLong, D. W., & Fahey, L. (2000). Diagnosing cultural barriers to knowledge management. *The Academy of Management Executive; Ada, 14*(4), 113-127.

Dixon, N. M. (2000). *Common knowledge; How companies thrive by sharing what they know*. Boston: Harvard Business School Press.

European Committee for Standardization. (2004). *European guide to good practice in knowledge management - Part 1: Knowledge management framework CWA 14924-1:2004 (E)* (No. CWA 14924-1:2004 (E)). Brussels: European Committee for Standardization (Comite Europeen de Normalisation) CEN.

Foss, N. J., & Mahnke, V. (2003). Knowledge management: What can organizational economics contribute? In M. Easterby-Smith & M. A. Lyles (Eds.), *The blackwell handbook of organizational learning and knowledge management* (pp. xx, 676). Malden, MA: Blackwell Pub.

Hackett, B. (2000). *Beyond knowledge management: New ways to work and learn* (Research Report No. 1261-00-RR). New York: The Conference Board.

Hasen, M. T., Nohria, N., & Tierney, T. (1999). What's your strategy for managing knowledge. *Harvard Business Review, March-April*, 106-116.

Hauschild, S., Licht, T., & Stein, W. (2001). Creating a knowledge culture. *The McKinsey Quarterly*(1), 74-81.

Holsapple, C. W., & Joshi, K. D. (2000). An investigation of factors that influence the management of knowledge in organizations. *Strategic Information Systems, 9*, 235-261.

Holsapple, C. W., & Joshi, K. D. (2002). Knowledge management: A threefold framework. *The Information Society*(18), 47-64.

Husted, K., & Michailova, S. (2002). Diagnosing and Fighting Knowledge-Sharing Hostility. *Organizational Dynamics, 31*(1), 60-73.

IT Governance Institute, & COBIT Steering Committee. (2000). *COBIT Framework* (3rd ed.). Rolling Meadows, IL: IT Governance Institute.

Jamieson, R., & Handzic, M. (2003). A framework for security, control and assurance of knowledge management systems. In C. W. Holsapple (Ed.), *Handbook on knowledge management 1: Knowledge matters* (Vol. 1, pp. 477-505). Berlin: Springer-Verlag.

Jennex, M., & Olfman, L. (2005). Assessing knowledge management success *International Journal of Knowledge Management, 1*(2), 33-49.

Jennex, M., & Zyngier, S. (2008). Security as a contributor to knowledge management success. information systems frontiers. *A Journal of Research and Innovation, 9*(5), 493–504.

Kelleher, D., Levene, S., & PriceWaterhouse Coopers. (2001). *PAS 2001 Knowledge Management: A guide to good practice*. London: British Standards Institution

Kemp, J., Pudlatz, M., Perez, P., & Ortega, A. M. (2002). *KM framework; European KM Forum IST Project No 2000-26393*: The European KM Forum Consortium European Commission.

Korac-Kakabadse, N., & Kakabadse, A. (2001). IS/IT Governance: need for an integrated model. *Corporate Governance, 1*(4), 9-11.

Leonard, D. (1995). *The well springs of knowledge*. Boston: Harvard Business School Press.

Lincoln, Y. S., & Guba, E. G. (1985). *Naturalistic inquiry*. Beverly Hills, CA: Sage Publications.

McDermott, R., & O'Dell, C. (2000). Overcoming the 'Cultural Barriers' to sharing knowledge. *Journal of Knowledge Management, 5*(1), 76-85.

McKay, J., & Marshall, P. (2004). *Strategic management of e-business*. Milton, Qld.: John Wiley & Sons.

Nonaka, I. (1991). The knowledge-creating company. *Harvard Business Review(November-December)*, 96-104.

Nonaka, I., & Takeuchi, H. (1995). *The knowledge-creating company: How Japanese companies create the dynamics of innovation*. New York: Oxford University Press.

O'Dell, C., Grayson, C. J., & Essaides, N. (1998). *If Only We Knew What We Know; The Transfer of Internal Knowledge and Best Practice*. New York: The Free Press.

O'Dell, C., Hasanali, F., Hubert, C., Lopez, K., Odem, P., & Raybourn, C. (2000). Successful KM implementation: A study of best-practice organizations. In C. Holsapple (Ed.), *Handbook on knowledge management 2 knowledge directions, Vol. 2* (pp. 411-443). Berlin: Springer-Verlag.

Oxbrow, N. (2003). *Second CKO summit for the public sector*. London: TFPL.

Oxbrow, N. (2004). *'Sticky' knowledge strategies CKO summit 2004*. London: TFPL.

Paulzen, O. (2002). *A maturity model for quality improvement in knowledge management*. Chapter presented at the Enablling Organizations and Society Through Information Systems, Proceedings of the 13th. Australasian Conference on Information Systems (ACIS 2002), Melbourne.

Peterson, R. R. (2000). *Emerging capabilities of information technology governance: Exploring stakeholder perspectves in financial services*. Chapter presented at the 8th European Conference on Information Systems, Vienna.

Pfeffer, J., & Sutton, R. I. (1999). *The knowing-doing gap; how smart companies turn knowledge into action*. Boston MA: Harvard Business School Press.

Probst, G., Raub, S., & Romhardt, K. (2000). *Managing knowledge; Building blocks for success*. Chichester: John Wiley & Sons, Ltd.

Robson, W. (1994). *Strategic management and information systems; and integrated approach*. London: Pitman.

Sarbanes Oxley Act, HR 3763 (2002).

Seely-Brown, J., & Duguid, P. (2000). *The social life of information*. Boston: Harvard Business School Press.

Snowden, D. (2003). Managing for Serendipity or why we should lay off "best practice."KM. *Knowledge Management Journal*.

Sohal, A. S., & Fitzpatrick, P. (2002). IT Governance and management in large australian organisations. *International Journal of Production Economics, 75*, 97-112.

Standards Australia. (2000). *AS/NZS ISO 9000:2000 Quality management systems—Fundamentals and vocabulary* (3rd ed.). Sydney: Standards Australia, Standards New Zealand & International Organization for Standardization.

Standards Australia. (2001). *HB 275-2001 knowledge management: A framework for succeeding in the knowledge era*. Sydney: Standards Australia International Limited.

Standards Australia. (2004). *AS/NZS 4360:2004 Risk Management* (3rd ed.). Sydney: Standards Australia & Standards New Zealand.

Standards Australia. (2005). *AS 8015—2005 corporate governance of information and communication technology*. Sydney: Standards Australia.

Sveiby, K. E. (1997). *The new organizational wealth: managing and measuring knowledge-based assets*. San Fransisco: Berrett-Koehler Publishers, Inc.

Sveiby, K. E. (2001, July 2004). Methods for measuring intangible assets. Retrieved 3 August, 2004, from http://wwwsveiby.com/articles/IntangibleMethods.htm

Szulanski, G. (1996). Exploring internal stickiness: Impediments to the transfer of best practice within the firm. *Strategic Management Journal, 17*(Special Issue: Knowledge and the Firm - Winter).

Tanudjojo, S., & Braganza, A. (2005). *Overcoming barriers to knowledge flow: Evidence-based attributes enabling the creation, mobilization, and diffusion of knowledge.* Chapter presented at the 38th Hawaii International Conference on System Sciences (HICSS), Hawaii.

Walsham, G. (2001). Knowledge management: The benefits and limitations of computer systems. *European Management Journal, 19*, 599-608.

Williamson, O. E. (1979). Transaction-cost economics: The governance of contractual relations. *Journal of Law and Economics, 22*(2), 233-261.

Zyngier, S. (2005). Knowledge management governance. In D. Schwarz (Ed.), *The encyclopaedia of knowledge management.* Hershey, PA: Idea Group Publishing.

Zyngier, S. (2006). *The role of knowledge management governance in the implementation of strategy.* Chapter presented at the 39th. Hawaiian International Conference on System Sciences (HICSS39), Hawaii.

Zyngier, S. (2007). *Knowledge management governance: A framework for knowledge management benefits realization.* Chapter presented at the 8th International Research Conference on Quality, Innovation and Knowledge Management, New Delhi, India.

Zyngier, S., Burstein, F., & McKay, J. (2004). *Knowledge management governance: a multifaceted approach to organizational decision and innovation support.* Chapter presented at the Decision Support in an Uncertain World: Proceedings of the 2004 IFIP WG8.3 International Conference on Decision Support Systems (DSS2004), Prato, Italy.

Zyngier, S., Burstein, F., & McKay, J. (2005). Governance of strategies to manage organizational knowledge—a mechanism to oversee knowledge needs. In M. Jennex (Ed.), *Knowledge management case book.* Hershey, PA: Idea Group Books.

Zyngier, S., Burstein, F., & Rodriguez, M.-L. (2003). Knowledge management strategies in Australia. In H. Hasan & M. Handzic (Eds.), *Australian studies in knowledge management.* Woolongong: University of Wollongong Press.

This work was previously published in the International Journal of Knowledge Management, Vol. 4, Issue 3, edited by M. Jennex, pp. 19-32, copyright 2008 by IGI Publishing (an imprint of IGI Global).

Chapter 23
Managing Knowledge with Technology:
Current Trends in Local Government

Meliha Handzic
Sarajevo School of Science and Technology, Bosnia and Herzegovina

Amila Lagumdzija
Sarajevo School of Science and Technology, Bosnia and Herzegovina

Amer Celjo
Sarajevo School of Science and Technology, Bosnia and Herzegovina

ABSTRACT

This chapter reports on types and roles of information and communication technologies (ICT) implemented in knowledge management (KM) solutions in local governments. A sample of nine local councils were rated on usage of various generic and KM specific ICT in supporting knowledge exploitation or exploration, and codification or personalization strategies. The results indicate a marked preference for generic types of ICT, and support for knowledge exploitation and codification approaches. These findings and their implications are further interpreted in terms of three stages of KM development in organizations.

INTRODUCTION

Increased interaction, interdependency and volatility on a global scale are rapidly changing local governments' external environment, their community characteristics, as well as their organizational orientation. In circumstances of high uncertainty and ambiguity, the success of local governments depends to a greater extent on how well they utilize knowledge resources in adjusting to contextual changes. This requires special attention to knowledge management (KM). The major challenge for KM in local government is to foster the development of an enriched knowledge base that will enable local actors to better deal with adjustment and development issues of importance to their communities (Anttiroico, 2006). The purpose of this chapter is to address technical issues in organizational KM.

Referring to the theoretical work by Handzic (2004) the chapter considers the role of various information and communication technologies (ICT) in facilitating the processes in which knowledge is created, transferred and utilized in local governments. Findings reported in the chapter are part of an ongoing research project into the adoption of KM principles and practices in public sector organizations in Bosnia and Herzegovina (BiH). The role of ICT in local government KM solutions addressed in this chapter is only one of several aspects covered by the research project. Further project details can be obtained elsewhere (Handzic et al., 2008).

The current chapter is structured as follows. First, an overview of the literature on ICT and KM is presented in the next section. This is followed by a description of the methodology and the results of the empirical study related to ICT usage. The key findings are discussed next in the light of theoretical models relating technology use to different KM strategies and stages of KM development. Finally, conclusions and implications for practice and research are offered.

LITERATURE REVIEW ON ICT IN KM

The spectrum of views on the role of ICT in KM ranges from those that see knowledge as a uniquely human concept and consider that KM has little to do with technology, to those that see knowledge as an object and therefore KM as being mostly about technology (Snowden, 2003; Swan, 2003). The integrated approach advocated by Handzic (2004) bridges the artificial divide between two extreme perspectives by considering KM as a socio-technical phenomenon with both technology and people playing an important role.

Within the integrated framework, technology is placed among major influencing factors on knowledge processes. The functionalities of ICT are perceived as significant in shaping organizational efforts for knowledge creation, transfer and utilization, and thus for organizational learning, improvement and innovation. In order to better understand and appreciate the importance of technology in KM, this section surveys some ICT-based KM initiatives deployed in firms and their roles in supporting knowledge processes.

The KM literature offers a number of useful classifications of ICT tools for KM. Initially, Binney (2001) proposed a KM spectrum that consisted of six categories: transactional, analytical, asset management, process based, developmental and innovation/creation. Based on their functions and techniques, Tsui (2003) suggested a framework of commercial KM software tools including nine categories: search, meta/Web crawler, process modeling and mind mapping, case-based reasoning, data and text mining, taxonomy/ontological tools, groupware, measurement and reporting, and e-learning. More recently, Balmisse et al. (2007) grouped KM tools by functionalities into: explicit knowledge management, collaboration, knowledge discovery, expertise mapping tools and KM suites.

A typology of KM technologies developed by Handzic and Zhou (2005) is used to frame the discussion about the applications of ICT in KM in this chapter. This typology includes seven categories based on the distinction of basic KM processes they support. They include: knowledge storage, access, search/retrieval, sharing/delivery, discovery/visualization, utilization and platform technologies.

- Knowledge storage technologies cover databases, textbases, data warehouse, data marts and various multimedia systems used to capture and store organizational knowledge with the objective to enhance organizational memory and to provide broader access to knowledge resources (Alavi & Leidner, 2001). These technologies organize and make available knowledge in a variety of representational formats (e.g., data, text, images, audio and video), store current and retain historical and cross-functional aspects of knowledge.

- Knowledge access technologies such as knowledge maps, knowledge directories and yellow pages are tools used to improve access to knowledge stored in knowledge repositories and/or facilitate knowledge transfer among individuals. These systems act as navigation aids that help knowledge seekers to quickly locate important explicit and tacit knowledge sources (Wexler, 2001).
- Knowledge search/retrieval technologies including search engines and intelligent agents are tools used to locate internal knowledge on intranets or external knowledge on the Internet, with the objective of increasing the speed and accuracy of knowledge search. These software programs enable access to unstructured information and can carry out search tasks with some degree of independence and autonomy (Tsui, 2003).
- Knowledge sharing/delivery technologies represent various applications that use ICT to facilitate peer-to-peer communication and knowledge sharing (Hansen et al., 1999). E-mail systems, electronic bulletin boards, whiteboards, electronic forums, videoconferencing, voice mail, groupware are some examples of such tools used to provide the right knowledge to the right person at the right time. Specialized groupware applications also offer support for collaborative processes.
- Platform technologies comprise net-based tools such as internet, intranets, extranets and portals that are used to provide connectivity and support knowledge sharing inside and outside the organization. They are also commonly used by organizations to construct a single point of access to multiple sources of internal and external knowledge (Awad & Ghaziri, 2004). In general, they provide network platforms for knowledge collection, communication and analysis.
- Knowledge discovery/visualization technologies describe applications that look for hidden patterns in data in order to discover and make visible previously unknown patterns (Fayyad et al., 1996). Data mining, statistical tools, graphical representation and simulation technologies are technologies that use complex and sophisticated algorithms to extract and visualize new knowledge with a goal of supporting improvements and changes to the way knowledge is used, shared, and transferred.
- Knowledge utilization technologies such as knowledge-based systems, workflow systems, expert systems, rule induction, and decision trees are tools used to enable knowledge workers to apply the best decision-making expertise and improve performance (Becerra-Fernandez et al., 2004). These systems harness technology by imbedding knowledge into work processes, with the objective of facilitating knowledge integration and application. They can also enable people to learn more easily through experience.

The classes of technologies illustrated in Figure 1 can serve multiple purposes and can be combined in many ways to achieve synergic effects and tackle particular problems or support particular KM motives. According to Hansen et al. (1999), these technologies play a major role in supporting "codification" (i.e., strategy focusing on explicit knowledge forms) or "personalization" (i.e., strategy focusing on tacit knowledge forms). In addition, KM tools focus on facilitating "exploitation" (i.e., knowledge use and sharing of

Figure 1. Types and roles of ICT in KM

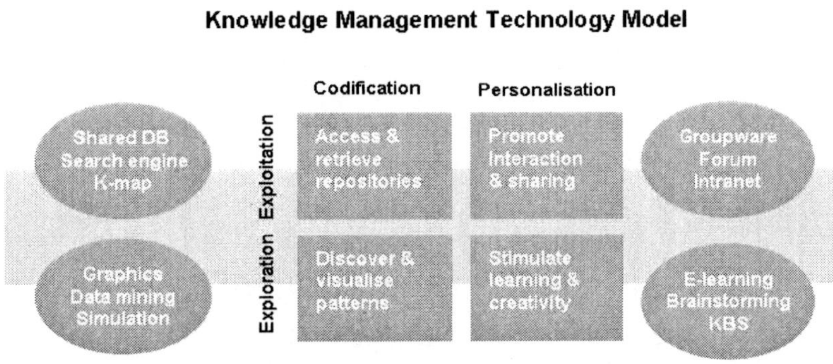

the existing knowledge) or improving "exploration" (i.e., people's ability to discover and create new knowledge).

Following this line of thinking Handzic (2004) specified the following four key functional requirements for KM systems: (i) building and making available knowledge repositories; (ii) promoting social interaction and networking; (iii) discovering and visualizing hidden patterns from data; and (iv) stimulating creativity and experiential learning. These priority areas where technology can help organizations to deliver KM are summarized in Figure 1. Practical implementations have been under way in both the private and public sectors. The emphasis of this article is on the latter.

Much prior empirical research in ICT-based KMS pursued in either local or federal government environments focused on specific initiatives. Some recent studies explored internal initiatives aimed principally at collaboration and knowledge sharing among employees (Cheuk, 2006). Others addressed the application of specialized KMS to achieving improvements in the speed and quality of government response actions (Murphy & Jennex, 2006). This study focused on the comprehensive set of technologies currently available to support KM initiatives with a goal of identifying their utilization trends in the local government environment. The typology and the model outlined earlier in this section served as a backbone of the research methodology applied for the investigation.

RESEARCH METHOD

Research Design and Instrument

Given that the intention in this study was to get a broad sense of the technological dimension of KM in the local government environment, a descriptive survey was selected as a preferred method for this research (Judd et al., 1991). The study also served as part of a pilot prior to undertaking a full-scale national survey of KM adoption in public administration in BiH.

This typology and model of KM technologies together with insights from prior related survey research (Anderson, 1998; Pillania, 2006; Zhou & Fink, 2003; Zyngier et al., 2003) informed the basis of the KM technology questionnaire used in this study. Modifications were made to the wording where necessary to reflect specifics of the organization being studied and to achieve consistency in framing among the questions. A list of the relevant questionnaire items is available in the appendix to this article. These items include: (i) organizational and individual demographics; (ii) availability and usage of different technology types; and (iii) comments and suggestions.

Table 1. Local councils participating in this study

Local council*	No. of participants	Brief description of each council
C1	11	inner city — commerce, consulting, finance etc.
C2	6	inner city — commerce, consulting, finance etc.
C3	11	inner city — commerce, consulting, finance etc.
C4	11	inner city — commerce, consulting, finance etc.
C5	8	outer city — predominantly rural
C6	13	outer city — predominantly rural
C7	8	outer city — predominantly industrial
C8	7	outer city — predominantly industrial
C9	4	outer city — predominantly rural

**Note: council names have been disguised for reasons of confidentiality*

The design of the survey took into account time requirements, emotional cost, trust and nature of the relationship between respondents and researchers. Thus, the survey form was compact, no personal information was required and the researchers' school logo was included in the cover letter as recommended by Zyngier et al. (2003). Short starting and ending instructions were added for clarity. Participants were also invited to indicate their interest in obtaining the results and in the follow-up interviews.

Subjects and Procedure

The case organization in our investigation was local government of the city of Sarajevo, capital of BiH. The target population comprised nine municipal councils with a total of 99 departments that provided government services across the capital territories. The normative goal of KM was to improve the efficiency of local government services. Target respondents were senior officials working in key council departments to enable focused observations (Vaus, 1995) and comparison with other surveys (Hauschild et al., 2001).

Questionnaires were distributed to the recipients personally by one of the researchers together with an explanatory cover letter. Follow-up telephone calls were made to maximize response rates as suggested by Dillman (2000). The distributed questionnaires were completed in the respondents' own time and without the researcher being present. Data collection ceased one month after the surveys were delivered. A total of 79 responses were received to 99 surveys distributed, achieving a response rate of 80 percent. Summary details of each participating council is provided in Table 1.

In responding to the survey, the participants were required to answer a series of questions and give optional comments and suggestions. Organizational demographics sought from the respondents included only their council and department names. Other information was known from the details provided on the government website. Personal demographics of the respondents were limited to the current position in the department for the purposes of verifying their senior status. In replying to the technology questions, the respondents were required to: (i) indicate the availability of each ICT category from the adopted typology; and (ii) rate the extent of its usage in KM relative to maximum and minimum endpoints of a seven-point Likert scale (7 being the maximum and 1 being the minimum).

Individual responses to items were collected, encoded and relevant descriptive statistics calculated for each council and technology type. Commonly used, but nevertheless arbitrary, cut offs of ">=5," "3-<5" and "1-<3," were used to indicate high (H), moderate (M) and low (L) values, while (N) referred to "=0" value assigned to unavailable technologies. Results are presented in the following section.

RESULTS

Types of ICT Used in KM

The results of the analysis presented in Table 2 indicate the extent of organizational usage of seven types of ICT in KM for nine local councils. The first four ICT types listed in the table are usually considered to have a more generic function, while the last three are seen as being more specific to knowledge management (Edwards & Shaw 2004).

With respect to results by technology types, the form of ICT most widely used for knowledge management was storage technology such as databases. This was identified as being in current extensive use (H) by all nine local councils. Second most common was sharing/delivery technology such as e-mail systems mentioned as currently in extensive use by six local councils. Platform technologies were the other type of ICT mentioned as being in considerable use (H or M) for knowledge management in six councils. The other type of ICT being used considerably was search/retrieval technology indicated by five councils. Three other classes of ICT were mentioned less frequently as being used significantly (H or M) for knowledge management. Access technologies received only four mentions and discovery/visualization and utilization technologies both received even fewer with three mentions. These technologies were little (L) or not in current use at all (N).

The analysis of results by councils reveals that, at one end of the scale are two councils (4, 9) who already make considerable use of all seven types of ICT in their knowledge management solutions. At the other end of the scale are three councils (5, 6, 8) where technology was seen as only of marginal relevance to knowledge management. In these councils only storage technologies were in significant use and all other technologies only marginally or not at all, as in council 8. In-between these two extreme groups are four councils (1, 2,

Table 2. Organisational usage of ICT for KM

Local council	Storage technology	Sharing technology	Platform technology	Retrieval technology	Access technology	Discovery technology	Utilization technology
C4	H	H	H	H	H	H	H
C9	H	H	H	H	H	H	H
C1	H	H	H	M	H	H	L
C7	H	H	H	H	H	L	L
C2	H	H	M	H	L	L	H
C3	H	H	H	L	L	L	L
C5	H	L	L	L	L	L	L
C6	H	L	L	L	L	L	L
C8	H	L	L	N	N	N	N

**Note: H (high), M (moderate), L (low), N (not in use)*

3, 7) who make very significant use of four generic ICT (sharing and platform, in addition to storage and retrieval), but make use of only some or none of three KM specific ICT (access, discovery and utilization). The only one exception is council 3, where several generic ICT systems were in use, but not search/retrieval. Overall, the results indicate that the majority of councils foster the use of technologies that are generic rather than specific to KM (72 percent versus 37 percent significant mentions).

Roles of ICT in KM

The results reported here focus on the roles played by ICT in supporting KM strategies of knowledge exploitation and/or exploration, codification and/or personalization. For analysis purposes, the empirical KM technology model presented in Figure 2 was built from local councils' ICT usage data.

Looking at the nature of ICT support for councils' KM strategies, there is a clear emphasis on facilitating exploitation of existing knowledge. All nine councils (1-9) demonstrate extensive use of technology to make available institutional knowledge repositories and to link organizational members to share personal knowledge. With respect to exploration, only two councils (4, 9) appear to use full technology potential to support creation of new knowledge, one council (1) makes some use of technology to support knowledge discovery and one (2) to facilitate experiential learning through knowledge application.

Further comparison of different ICT usage roles in local councils' KM as reflected in Figure 2 reveals a slightly greater emphasis placed on supporting codification than personalization KM strategies. All nine councils (1-9) show extensive use of generic storage ICT in creating and disseminating knowledge artefacts and documents. However, only six councils (1-4, 7, 9) show considerable use of generic sharing and platform technologies to link people for communication and collaboration purposes. KM specific technologies appear to play a much lesser role in supporting either KM strategy, with only four councils (1, 4, 7, 9) using technology to facilitate knowledge access, three (1, 4, 9) to support knowledge discovery from data, and three (2, 4, 9) for learning by doing through knowledge application to the task.

These results are consistent with our earlier reported findings (Handzic et al., 2008) showing that local government's overall approaches to KM

Figure 2. Empirical results for KM technology model

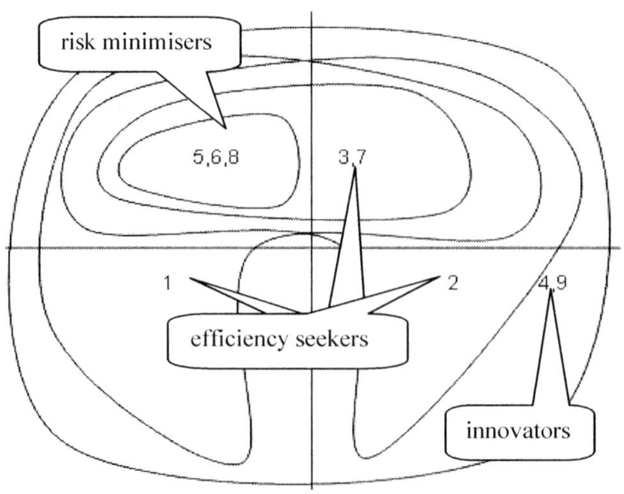

are divided between strategies that explore new knowledge sources and those that exploit existing explicit and tacit knowledge assets. Prior results reveal similar use of processes to acquire new needed knowledge and close the existing gaps in terms of gathering intelligence and looking for new ideas. With respect to existing knowledge, the results show that a greater emphasis is placed on transferring explicit knowledge (e.g., best practices, lessons learnt and documents) than on sharing tacit knowledge (e.g., people's ideas and experiences).

Stages of KM Development

Further analysis of findings presented in Figure 2 reveals that local councils examined are currently in different stages of KM development. Three councils (5, 6, 8) appear to be in the first stage, concentrating mainly on capture and storage of codified knowledge. Such KM approach is consistent with the goal of minimizing risk of losing valuable knowledge. Four councils (1, 2, 3, 7) appear to be in the second stage of KM development. They focus on sharing of the existing knowledge in people (not just in stores) through interaction. This approach is consistent with the goal of improving performance efficiency and effectiveness. The remaining two councils (4, 9) focus on creating knowledge environment conducive to innovation by balancing exploitation and exploration, and employing both codification and personalization strategies. This approach suggests that they are in the third and final stage of KM development.

In general, inner-city councils are at higher stages of KM development than outer-city councils. Three out of four inner-city councils are in stage 2 and one in stage 3. In comparison, three out of five outer-city councils are in stage 1, one in stage 2 and one in stage 3. These findings are largely consistent with their contextual circumstances. It is clear that the majority (7 out of 9) of local councils in this sample have some way to go in developing and implementing effective KM strategies. From the follow-up interviews with two innovative councils' officials, it is evident that both inner and outer city councils recognize new opportunities for local development and transform themselves to respond to new challenges. In particular, the inner-city council 4 sees its opportunity in creating an innovative media city and provision of information services to businesses, while the outer city rural council 9 sees its chance for advancement in wellness and eco tourism.

DISCUSSION

Main Findings

This study considered various types of ICT used in organizational KM initiatives in a sample of local councils in Bosnia and Herzegovina. The findings show clear emphasis on basic storage and sharing technologies that include files/databases and e-mail/net systems. These findings match earlier findings by Zhou and Fink (2003) and Edwards and Shaw (2004) reporting general preference for commonly known generic IT systems over those specifically labeled as being for KM. The findings also reinforce the most recent evidence by Handzic (2007) of greater benefits to decision makers from simple human-centered rather than from complex smart systems. Possible reasons for this focus on simple generic systems may be found in familiarity, convenience and obvious benefits of these systems. In contrast, sophisticated and complex intelligent systems are often rejected by people due to their "black-box" effect.

In terms of order of preference, storage technology was mentioned most often as being extensively used followed by sharing/delivery and platform technologies. This order is different from the Zhou and Fink (2003) Australian survey where e-mail, intranet and the Internet were rated as most effective ICT for KM. The fact that KM specific technologies often recommended elsewhere (Zyngier et al., 2003) were rarely mentioned in this study suggests that people might have been unaware of such technologies or lacking skills to implement them. Indeed, the frequent comment received by participants in this research project concerns obstacles to effective KM in terms of inadequate ICT literacy of public sector employees.

The study also considered how various ICT systems favoured by different local councils supported their organizational KM strategies. The findings indicate a clear emphasis on exploiting existing knowledge through shared repositories and personal interaction. Such strategic orientation is consistent with the currently stated business goal for BiH government administration of improving efficiency and effectiveness of its public services (Handzic et al., 2008). It is also consistent with empirical evidence from Australia showing its local government concerns with the loss of knowledge and the deployment of mechanisms for the sharing and reuse of knowledge (Martin, 2000).

Furthermore, the findings indicate that ICT played a relatively greater role in supporting codification than personalization KM strategy. This is not surprising, as codification approaches rely heavily on ICT to provide high-quality, reliable and fast systems to enable preservation and reuse of explicit knowledge (Hansen et al., 1999). In comparison, personalization approaches rely more on people and invest moderately in ICT to facilitate conversations and the exchange of their tacit knowledge. Despite this, Edwards and Shaw (2004) found Earl's (2001) process school of thought emphasizing personalization and sharing of knowledge as prominent in the UK organizations. In this sample, physical proximity may have contributed to the lesser need for computer mediated communication among employees.

Finally, the current state of ICT use in local councils is indicative of different stages in the evolutionary KM development. The majority of councils are in the early development stages, stressing reuse economics and explicit knowledge forms. These can ensure survival but not advancement as suggested by Von Krogh et al. (2000). In general, more developed and better resourced inner-city councils displayed greater sophistication and levels of KMT use than smaller and poorer outer-city ones. This indicates the importance of organizational factors in influencing KMS implementation and adoption (Vitari et al., 2007). In addition, it is important to note that ICT deployment cannot resolve all KM problems and warrant effective performance. There is also need for leadership support, learning culture and continued measurement and adjustment.

Implications for Practice and Research

The results of this study have a number of important implications for KM practice and research. Looking at the nature of ICT support for KM, it is obvious that technology was used more to facilitate exploitation of existing than exploration of new knowledge. This is one area for potential action by practice to move towards creation and innovation areas (Anttiroico, 2006). It is also true that technology was utilized more for supporting codification than personalisation. This calls for a remedial intervention aimed at facilitating and improving tacit knowledge sharing. For example, councils could create virtual communities of practice and/or design reward systems for contributions to develop more favorable attitudes towards sharing (Vitari et al., 2007)

In addition, the study found that local councils in this study fitted into the categories of risk minimisers, efficiency-seekers and innovators. This leaves a significant scope for further improvement in KM among the first two groups. In order to move towards innovation, Nonaka and Nishiguchi (2001) require from local government to take the strategic view of knowledge, formulate knowledge visions, tear down knowledge barriers, develop new institutional values and trust, catalyze and coordinate knowledge creation, develop a conversational culture, globalize local knowledge and localize global knowledge.

With respect to research, the current preference for simpler generic over sophisticated KM specific technologies reinforces earlier findings from UK and Australia. However, greater emphasis on information than on communication elements of ICT is contrary to UK and Australian studies. A possible explanation might lie in cultural differences. According to Hofstede (2001) values may differ considerably across national boundaries and certain features of KM technologies might be emphasized over others depending on the cultural context. This warrants further investigation into the factors influencing KMS acceptance (Vitari et al., 2007) and/or success (Jennex & Olfman, 2006). As a plausible future development, the follow-up quantitative study could test a set of external variables including cultural dimensions suggested by Hofstede.

The contingency view of KM implies that no one approach is best under all circumstances. From this study's findings, it can be seen that larger and better equipped inner-city councils dealt with their wider and more demanding customer base by high reliance on technology. In contrast, smaller and poorly resourced and financed outer-city councils operated successfully with a relatively minor support of technology, by using informal structures and cultures and by relying on people to complete many of the knowledge processes (Handzic et al., 2008). Generally, urban location, larger size and richer human and financial resources all had positive impacts on the level of KM technology implementation and adoption in the context of local administration. The output of future KM research should provide further answers for practice on what works and what does not and under what circumstances.

Finally, it is obvious that the findings of this study are limited by choice of BiH context, characteristics of the local government organizations, as well as by the participants' self-reporting their opinions. Therefore, further research is necessary to address current limitations and ensure that these findings have broad applicability.

CONCLUSION

This research was motivated by the need for better understanding of types and roles of ICT in managing knowledge in the local government environment. In order to gain insights into these issues we approached local government as a knowledge organization with an aim of identifying current trends in its KM technologies evolution.

As a result of our research, we are able to make two important contributions: (i) offer a theoretical KMT model that clusters major ICT types according to four key roles they play in supporting knowledge strategies; and (ii) show the usefulness of the model in practice for assessing the current stage of KMT development.

The research enabled us to determine preferred types of ICT in local government by studying local councils' usage patterns of different ICT types and positioning them along the exploration/exploitation and codification/personalization axes of the KMT model. We also acquired a valuable sense of where the local government under investigation is within the evolutionary development of KMT and were able to recommend directions for future: towards innovative government practice and contingency models research.

ACKNOWLEDGMENT

This study was supported by a research grant from the Ministry of Science and Education, Canton Sarajevo.

REFERENCES

Alavi, M., & Leidner, D.E. (2001). Knowledge management and knowledge management systems: Conceptual foundations and research issues. *MIS Quarterly, 25*(1), 107-136.

Andersen, A. (1998). *The knowledge management practices book*. Arthur Andersen.

Anttiroico, A. (2006). Strategic knowledge management in local government, In A. Anttiroiko and M. Malkia (Eds) *Encyclopedia of digital government* (pp. 268-298). Hershey, PA: IRM Press.

Awad, E.M., & Ghaziri, H.M. (2004). *Knowledge management*. Upper Saddle River, NJ: Pearson Education.

Balmisse, G., Meingain, D., & Passerini, K. (2007). Technology trends in knowledge management tools. *International Journal of Knowledge Management, 3*(2), 11 -131.

Becerra-Fernandez, I., Gonzales, A., & Sabherwal, R. (2004). *Knowledge management: Challenges, solutions, and technologies*. Upper Saddle River, NJ: Pearson Education, Inc.

Binney, D. (2001). The knowledge management spectrum: understanding the KM landscape. *Journal of Knowledge Management, 5*(1), 33–42.

Cheuk, B. W. (2006). Using social networking analysis to facilitate knowledge sharing in the british council. *International Journal of Knowledge Management, 2*(4), 67-76.

Dillman, D.A. (2000). *Mail and internet surveys: The tailored methods* (2nd ed.). New York: John Wiley & Sons.

Earl, M. (2001). Knowledge management strategies: Toward a taxonomy. *Journal of Management Information Systems, 18*(1), 215-233.

Edwards, J.S., & Shaw, D. (2004). Supporting knowledge management with IT. In Proceedings of the DSS 2004 conference, July, Prato, Italy.

Fayyad, U., Piatetsky-Shapiro, G., & Smyth, P. (1996). Knowledge discovery and data mining: Towards a unifying framework. In Proceedings of the Second International Conference on Knowledge Discovery and Data Mining, KDD-96, Oregon.

Handzic, M. (2004). *Knowledge management: Through the technology glass*. Singapore: World Scientific Publishing.

Handzic, M. (2007, July 3-6). Supporting decision makers with knowledge management systems. In Proceedings of the 11th Pacific Asia Conference on Information Systems (PACIS 2007) (pp. 46-54). Auckland, New Zealand.

Handzic, M., & Zhou, A.Z. (2005). *Knowledge management: An integrative approach*. Oxford, UK: Chandos Publishing.

Handzic, M., Lagumdzija, A., & Celjo, A. (2008). Auditing knowledge management practices in local government: Model and application. *Knowledge Management Research and Practice, 6*(1), 90-99.

Hansen, M.T., Nohria, N., & Tierney, T. (1999). What's your strategy for managing knowledge? *Harvard Business Review, 77*(2), 106-116.

Hauschild, S., Licht, T., & Stein, W. (2001). Creating a knowledge culture. *The McKinsey Quarterly, 1*, 74-81.

Hofstede, G. (2001). *Culture's consequences: Comparing values, behaviors, institutions, and organizations across nations*. Thousand Oaks, CA: Sage Publications.

Jennex, M.E., & Olfman, L. (2006). A model of knowledge management success. *International Journal of Knowledge Management, 2*(3), 51-68.

Judd, C.M., Smith, E.R., & Kidder, L.H. (1991). *Research methods in social relations* (6th ed.). Harcourt Brace Jovanovich College Publishers.

Martin, B. (2000). Knowledge based organisations: Emerging trends in local government in Australia, *Journal of Knowledge Management Practice*, October.

Murphy, T., & Jennex, M. E. (2006). Knowledge management and hurricane Katrina response. International *Journal of Knowledge Management, 2*(4), 52-66.

Nonaka, I., & Nishiguchi, T. (2001). *Knowledge emergence*. Oxford University Press, New York.

Pillania, R.K. (2006). State-of-art of knowledge storage and access in Indian industry. *Journal of Information and Knowledge Management, 5*(1), 55-61.

Snowden, D. (2003). Innovation as an objective of knowledge management. Part I: The landscape of management, *Knowledge Management Research & Practice, 1*(2), 113-119.

Swan, J. (2003). Knowledge Management in Action, in Holsapple. In C.W (ed) *Handbook on knowledge management 1: Knowledge matters* (pp. 271-296). Berlin: Springer.

Tsui, E. (2003). Tracking the role and evolution of commercial knowledge management software. In C. W. Holsapple (ed.), *Handbook on knowledge management 2: Knowledge directions* (pp. 5-27). Berlin: Springer.

Vaus DAD. (1995). *Surveys in social research* (4th ed). North Sydney: Allen and Unwin.

Vitari, C., Moro, J., Ravarini, A., & Bourdon, I. (2007). Improving KMS acceptance: The role of organizational and indivuduals' characteristics. *International Journal of Knowledge Management, 3*(2), 68-90.

Von Krogh, G., Ichijo, K., & Nonaka, I. (2000). *Enabling knowledge creation*. New York: Oxford University Press Inc.

Wexler, M.N. (2001). The who, what and why of knowledge mapping, *Journal of Knowledge Management, 5*(3), 249-263.

Zhou, A., & Fink, D. (2003). Knowledge management and intellectual capital: An empirical examination of current practice in australia. *Knowledge Management Research & Practice, 1*(2), 86-94.

Zyngier, S.M., Burstein, F., & Rodriguez, M.L. (2003). Knowledge management strategies in Australia: Analysis of uptake and understanding, In H. Hasan & M. Handzic (eds), *Australian Studies in Knowledge Management* (pp 487-451), Wollongong: UOW Press.

APPENDIX: KNOWLEDGE MANAGEMENT SURVEY (EXTRACT)

Survey Questionnaire

Instructions for completing the questionnaire

- Please answer all questions
- For the questions with a numeric scale, circle the number that best describes the factor being judged
- Circle only one number for each scale
- Read the specific instructions under each section where applicable

Demographics

Please give names of your council and department: ______________________________________

What is your position in the department: ____

Knowledge Management Technologies

Please indicate the extent of effective use of the following knowledge management technologies available in your organisation (or please indicate if not available):

Technology class	*Low*						*High*	*Not available*
a. Knowledge storage technologies (eg. databases, text-bases, data warehouses/marts)	1	2	3	4	5	6	7	
b. Knowledge guides/maps (eg. directories, yellow pages, expert locators etc)	1	2	3	4	5	6	7	
c. Knowledge search/retrieval technologies (eg. search engines, intelligent agents etc)	1	2	3	4	5	6	7	
d. Knowledge sharing/delivery technologies (eg. email, groupware, forums)	1	2	3	4	5	6	7	
e. Knowledge discovery and visualisation (eg. data mining, statistical tools, graphics, etc)	1	2	3	4	5	6	7	
f. Knowledge utilisation technologies (workflow system, expert systems, DSS etc.)	1	2	3	4	5	6	7	
g. Platform technologies (Internet, intranet, extranet, portals)	1	2	3	4	5	6	7	

Comments and Suggestions

Are there any other comments or suggestions you would like to make with respect to the adoption of knowledge management technology in your organisation?

Thank you for participating in this study

This work was previously published in the International Journal of Knowledge Management, Vol. 4, Issue 4, edited by M. Jennex, pp. 77-89, copyright 2008 by IGI Publishing (an imprint of IGI Global).

Chapter 24
Video Issues for Knowledge Management

Richard T. Herschel
Saint Joseph's University, USA

Ira Yermish
Saint Joseph's University, USA

ABSTRACT

This chapter reviews the plethora of user-generated video activity and the issues it creates for knowledge management activities. The ability for individuals to create and post videos online has become prolific and it has now become a source of potential liability for employees and the firm. Video can be used convey rich narratives that can facilitate sensemaking and knowledge sharing and transfer, but their needs to be standards and controls for content development and distribution. When video content is developed, structure and culture are important factors that must be considered in storytelling activities to increase the opportunity for effective sensemaking and message retention and to ensure the accuracy, relevance, and legitimacy of video content. Evidence and arguments are presented that should motivate organizations and academics to review video generation activities both internal and external to the organization. Issues concerning video content delivery, liability, spam, and search engine capabilities are discussed. Opportunities for new research inquiries are identified.

INTRODUCTION

Web users in the U.S. enjoy their video -- more than 11 billion clips were viewed online in July 2008 alone. That's up from nine billion videos in July 2007. On average, YouTube alone receives more than 60,000 uploads of copyrighted and uncopyrighted videos daily. YouTube, along with blogs and online networking sites MySpace and Facebook, have helped drive video sharing activity (Wall Street Journal, 2008).

The problem is that many of these videos frequently contain content that is protected by copyright. The use of copyrighted material without permission can lead to litigation – for the individual who posted it, the organization where they work, the site that hosted the material, or any combination of the above.

DOI: 10.4018/978-1-60566-954-0.ch024

Two years ago, illegal use of professionally created video was rampant on the Web, particularly on video sharing sites such as YouTube. Among those most visibly undercut was NBC Universal, which asked YouTube to take down the infamous "Lazy Sunday" video from Saturday Night Live, after 5 million unauthorized viewings, and Viacom, which filed a $1 billion suit against YouTube parent Google to stop illicit publishing of their content. Now, a year after YouTube introduced its Video Identification tool to stem misuse, automated systems are being used to identify and protect professionally produced content (Sandoval, 2008).

This paper examines the user-generated video phenomena and its implications for organizations and their knowledge management activities. It examines risk issues that user-generated video creates for organizations, especially video content liability. This issue is examined within the context of knowledgetransfer activities and storytelling. Organizational culture is shown to be an important factor in helping to shape what video content is developed and shared by firm employees. Video search engines and their potential role in protecting organizations from content liability issues are also examined. The objective of exploring user-generated video capabilities is to focus knowledge management's awareness on the rapid growth and proliferation of user-generated video so that effective approaches to managing user-generated video creation and sharing activities can be developed and deployed. In creating an organizational strategy, it is important that it be grounded in a clear understanding of how user-generated videos can be both a potential asset and a liability to the organization.

Video-related issues are now routinely in the press and many times matters relate to social networking and legal concerns. For example, MySpace plans to adopt a new video-identifying technology that will attempt to resolve copyright issues for some of the video clips users upload to its site. The technology, from a third-party company called Auditude, is in essence a form of fingerprinting technology that scans videos for professional –and often copyrighted -- content. Auditude's system indexes uploaded videos against more than one billion minutes of content from its library. Industry executives say such fingerprinting technology is key to resolving thorny copyright battles between media and technology companies over online video. Viacom's has employed its own similar technology and its use led to a $1 billion suit against Google Inc. Google's YouTube, accusing it of massive intentional copyright infringement and demanding that YouYube remove 100,000 infringing video clips. Viacom claimed that YouTube failed to prevent its users from posting pirated material to the site (Sandoval, 2008).

Video's generated by individuals is a social phenomenon that has not only affected social networking, but organizations as well. Melcrum (2007), a research firm, reports that while much of the interest in social media has centered on the adoption of blogging as a business tool for communicating with customers and staff, online video is, in fact, the number one application. They point out that corporations have taken note of the popularity of sites like MySpace, YouTube and Bebo and that they are beginning to integrate the same functionality and networking tools within their corporate intranets. Melcrum (2007) reports that the two most important applications for internal user-generated video are identified by organizations as improved employee engagement and improved internal collaboration.

Aniisu (2007) concurs that employee-generated videos are now becoming an integral part of internal organizational communication campaigns. He asserts that the medium is widely accepted due to its interactivity and its ability to treat content creatively.

That organizations are actively promoting and supporting user-generated video content can be illustrated. For example, at Southwest Airlines employees created and distributed videos to share their feelings about the September 11th World Trade Center Tragedy (Inside the Cubicle, 2006). Delta Airlines launched SiteSeer where employees are the stars of videos that provide travel tips for their customers (Webdriven, 2007). At Google, an employee posted videos for public access showing how the Google search engine works (Allen, 2006). And professionals and executives are now being observed using video-based social networking to consult with or commiserate with their peers online (Vascellaro, 2007).

RISK AND VIDEO CONTENT

Videos created by employees and customers are posted on web sites that discuss an organizations product, services, or processes. For example, some of the distributed user-generated videocontent on video sharing sites is commentary on the world's leading brands (Beasty, 2007), which can be either positive or negative. This activity is confirmed by a survey of corporate use of social networking applications conducted by Melcrum (2007). They found that while there is widespread enthusiasm for social media in the corporate world, 45% of respondents agreed that employees or customers discussing their organization or brands online posed a significant risk to its reputation.

An illustration of the potential liability issues that user-generated videos can create for organizations is further evidenced by a recent case in Great Britain where a supermarket employee posted a video on a social networking site of one worker hitting another worker. Because the clip revealed the internal activity of the supermarket, the employer decided to fire the employee. The employee then sued the supermarket's executives, won a claim for unfair dismissal, and was awarded compensatory damages (Popa, 2007).

On YouTube, one can find videos about corporations and their products, many of which are frankly unflattering. For example,

- A&P unceremoniously sacked two brothers for using the company facilities to film a faux-gangsta rap video (A&P is also suing them for one million dollars).
- A former AIG employee has posted a video on YouTube that "slams the company".
- There is a news report video posted on YouTube where McDonald's employees were frightened by a dwarf's appearance.
- A video was posted on YouTube of a worker celebrating his birthday by taking a bath in the kitchen sink of a Burger King. It got employees in trouble with the company, and the company in trouble with its customers and the local Health Commissioner.

Copyrightinfringement is one of the most immediate concerns for organizations. When an employee infringes copyrights, the employer may be held liable under two theories: contributory and vicarious infringement. Contributory infringement requires the employer have knowledge of the infringement and have made material contribution to the infringement. Actual knowledge, however, is not always necessary. Willful blindness is knowledge, in copyright law (where indeed it may be enough that the defendant *should* have known of the direct infringement). Thus, the fact that an employer is unaware of the illegal conduct of its employee does not fully preclude their liability. In addition, the second theory, vicarious infringement, contains no knowledge requirement, but only requires that the employer receive a direct financial benefit and have a right and ability to supervise the infringers. In the employment setting, the second element is virtually always found, leaving the question of financial benefit to control the inquiry.

Thus, unauthorized use of any copyrighted material may give rise to employer liability, especially when:

(i) the employer enjoys a benefit because of the employee's infringement,

(ii) the copyrighted material is shared using company time and equipment,
(iii) the employer has taken no steps to prevent such infringement and has turned a blind eye to the infringing activities.

When a third party brings charges for copyrightinfringement, which carries hefty fines of up to $150,000 per violation, the employer becomes a more profitable target than the employee because of the depth of employer pockets (Nyman, 2005).

Employer liability extends beyond copyright infringement into several other areas. Defamatory or libelous statements made by employees in e-mail communications or Internet video postings may give rise to employer liability. Employers may also be liable to their employees for claims of sexual harassment or employment discrimination when other employees create a hostile work environment by downloading and distributing inappropriate video content. Finally, even without the attribution of liability to other parties, employers should be concerned about employee Internet activity because it can contribute to a loss in employee productivity, significantly decreased bandwidth, and increased exposure to the viruses, worms, and spy-ware associated with downloading materials from untrusted and unknown Internet sources.

Liabilityfor the firm can come not only from employee actions, but from actions taken by others. For example, as part of Viacom's $1 billion copyright suit against Google's YouTube, a judge ordered the video-sharing site to disclose records, such as IP addresses and usernames. Google was also supposed to turn over records that included the viewing and uploading histories of YouTube employees, according to the sources.

There is little to no press concerning the sharing of copyrighted videocontent within organizations. Hence, there is little information available as to what firm's are doing to minimize their exposure to copyright infringement, despite the possibility that employees may be posting copyrighted video content on internal or external web sites that may potentially expose the firm to liability. One reason for this may be that most organizations are typically ill-equipped to monitor video posting activity as they do not possess the technology to adequately monitor video content. Moreover, Melcrum (2007) found that 70% of the organizations they surveyed admitted that they had no guidelines or policies relating to blogging or other social-media tools.

CONTENT LIABILITY

Video is a rich medium for sharing propaganda, misinformation, spam, and copyrighted material. The rise in video-related issues is seen to coincide with increased interest among video content providers in boosting the visibility of their of their video clips.

Content liability requires organizations to monitor and remove video content (especially user-generated content) that includes any material that violates legal (or ethical) standards, as defined by the organization standards of behavior, or by copyright or other laws. Firms need to monitor content to be certain that the videos posted and viewed do not include content that was not created by the poster and which may include clips of television shows, films, or professional training videos whose copyright belongs to other corporations. This issue is highlighted by the lawsuit that Viacom launched against YouTube and its owner Google over copyright infringing videos hosted by the site. This case focuses on the "safe harbor" protections for Internet service providers (ISPs) and it may influence other user-generated content sites, including enterprise sites (Wall Street Journal, 2007).

The legal action tests the limits the U.S. Digital Millennium Copyright Act (DCMA) of 1998. The Act creates a safe harbor for online service providers against copyright liability if they adhere to and qualify for certain prescribed safe harbor guidelines and promptly block access to allegedly infringing material (or remove such material from their systems) if they receive a notification claiming infringement from a copyright holder or the copyright holder's agent. Similar protections exist in European laws. Safe harbor was designed to protect companies from having to monitor the activity of every Internet user, something that was recognized as impractical. Companies do not have to prevent illegal use of their services proactively, but when properly notified they must "expeditiously" remove or disable access to infringing material.

VIDEO SEARCH TECHNOLOGY

Video files, including employee-generated videos, need to be cataloged and indexed so that employees can use enterprise and/or mobile search engines to ask for and secure video content meeting user-specified criteria. This means that sensemaking requires the provision of capabilities for retrieving a list of enterprise videos that match user search criteria and which are sorted with respect to some measure of relevance. Use of videosearch engines in this manner may provide a secondary benefit of promoting greater access to enterprise video content and increased viewing activity. For example, when YouTube was acquired by Google and then subsequently included on the Google Video Search Index, YouTube's site visits rose immediately by 18.5% (Tancer, 2007).

Because video clips are more ephemeral than Web pages, it is harder for search engines to assess any clip's relevance to a search query (Delaney, 2007). Image and video content upload systems typically rely on simple techniques like asking the user to file the image under a category, or to click a set of checkboxes of descriptive tags, or to type in a one-sentence description that can later be automatically parsed by the system to generate detailed metadata. The problem is that the requests for metadata are inefficient, oftentimes inaccurately reflecting the true video content and overburdening users by having them upload megabytes of images and video information that may or not be relevant to their informational needs.

As users capture and share more images the need for new and innovative search labeling services becomes essential. To that end, piXlogic has developed an enterprise search enginesfor images and videos. It is based on automatic indexing of the contents of the image without the need for any manually input textual metadata. piXlogic uses a concept called "notions" that are interpreted understandings about the context of the image and the objects in it and it has created a contextually rich and accurate search environment that exploits this. To catalog a repository of images or videos, the user points piXlogic's piXserve application software to that repository (or uses a Web crawler to collect images) and it automatically indexes the content of those files. Through a browser, users can then search using an image and/or point to one or more items in the image that are of interest to them. The software can also see and recognize any text that may appear anywhere in the field of view of the image (e.g., picking out names of recruitment candidates, knowledge videos and experts, and other online video resources). Where most image and video search enginetechnologies work by trying to match image signatures that are based on simple concepts such as textual labels, color histograms, texture, or edges, for example, piXserve literally "sees" the image as being composed of many objects, creates a representation describing the objects, and stores them in a database (Pepus, 2007). When concerns for video content liability arise, piXserve representations could be searched to determine whether there are images that may suggest content liability.

piXlogic provides an event alerting and notification feature that allows it to send out notices when it detects a particular object, text string, or notion within an image or video. This means that organizations can set up piXlogic servers to automatically search through incoming streams of images and video to find specific actions or objects and then respond to that information automatically. The response might be a simple e-mail notification or a more complex event processing activity, such as carrying out a database operation, or alerting the company of potential copying of copyrighted content from an external source (Pepus, 2007).

Another company, Altus (2007), also offers new video searching engine capabilities. Their product, Xtreme Knowledge Sharing 5.0, provides a word-by-word search capability of video and audio content via the software's generation of an automatic transcript of the source content. Users can search the video transcript and find the exact point of interest they need to be able to and jump to the exact slide or sentence in the video. The product incorporates the following capabilities:

- Socializes enterprise computing by capturing social networking features such as searchable video, podcasts, blogs, wikis and RSS, and brings them inside the enterprise to create an enterprise collaboration, knowledge sharing and on-demand information platform.
- Video synch and search allows workers to search video down to the spoken word to get just the right information instantly.
- Enables the creation of video learning portals to share the corporate knowledge captured from video training, meetings, conferences, PowerPoint presentations and more – making thousands of hours of expert knowledge searchable and accessible down to the spoken word.

A product with this capability could be used to search for videos potentially violating copyrights, but the process would probably be complex and time consuming.

Google recently released a search widget called Google Elections Video Search. Using speech recognition, videos uploaded to YouTube's Politicians Channels are transcribed and indexed. This lets users search for words that are spoken in a clip. Viewer can also automatically jump to the exact point in the video when a phrase is said. Again, while the ability to find words in videos is expedited, it is still difficult though feasible to find copied content that potentially compromises the firm.

Another possibility is that firms may eventually be able to subscribe to external search tools such as Google's Video Identification system, Auditude's video fingerprinting technology, or Viacom's video search engine to evaluate their internal video content. However, the potential for subscribing to these services is currently uncertain.

VIDEO AND KNOWLEDGE TRANSFER

Video search capabilities are important in knowledge management as they can help users find relevant and useful video content. If video content is unmanaged or difficult to find, it can exacerbate knowledge transfer problems in an organization. Knowledge transfer activities are already complicated by a number of other factors, including

- The inability to recognize and articulate "compiled" or highly intuitive competencies, e.g., tacit knowledge ideas (Nonaka & Takeuchi, 1995),
- geography or distance (Gailbraith, 1990)
- lack of a shared/superordinate social identity (Kane, Argote, & Levine, 2005),
- knowledge visualization issues (Burkhard, 2005), and
- faulty information (Kane, Argote, & Levine, 2005).

One important way of leveraging existing knowledge is through the transfer and reuse of existing firm-specific knowledge among different individuals or groups integral to the firms. These constituencies can include employees, business partners, value chain partners, customers, or solicited (or unsolicited) commentary from members of the public domain where the firm operates. Knowledge transfer is motivated by the desire to acquire, exploit, and maintain intellectual capital. It is a fundamental issue for firms. Knowledge transfer deals with the issue of moving knowledge from one part of the organization to other parts of the organization. It takes place whenever the discoveries or expertise of knowledgeable agents are disseminated more widely. Knowledge transfer is complex because (1) knowledge resides in organizational members, tools, tasks, and their subnetworks (Argote & Ingram, 2000) and (2) much knowledge in organizations is tacit or hard to articulate (Nonaka & Takeuchi, 1995).

Argote & Ingram (2000) define knowledge transfer as the process through which one unit (e.g., group, department, or division) is affected by the experience of another. They point out that the transfer of organizational knowledge (e.g., routine or best practices) can be observed through changes in the knowledge or performance of recipient units.

Argote (2005) contends that while there has been some theory on the issue of knowledge transfer (e.g., Argote & Ingram, 2000; Teece, Pisano, & Shuen, 1997), there has been little empirical analysis to support it. However, Watson and Hewett (2006) did conduct such research using a multi-theoretical model. They used social exchange theory to develop a set of hypotheses regarding the factors that influence the frequency with which individuals contribute their valuable knowledge to the knowledge management system. They also employed expectancy theory and the technology acceptance model to generate a new model of the factors that lead individuals to access and use knowledge from the knowledge management system, with particular emphasis on how companies can increase the extent to which individuals within the firm reuse knowledge (see Figure 1).

Social exchange theory (Tiwana & Bush, 2001, Bock & Young-Gul, 2002) has been used to examine the behavior of individuals in distributed web communities to discover factors that impede and facilitate knowledge sharing. Social factors are seen as important predictors of knowledge sharing behaviors. Social exchange theory provides a useful theoretical lens for examining knowledge sharing because it was developed to explain why individuals engage in cooperative behaviors that

Figure 1. Building an effective knowledge transfer system: a multi-theoretical approach (Watson and Hewett, 2006)

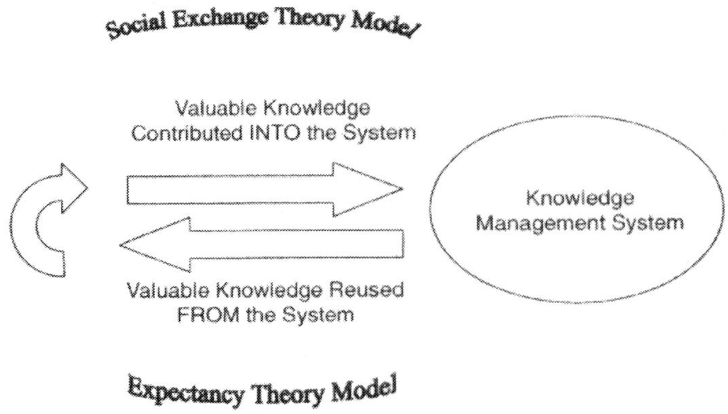

are not formally rewarded by the organization. Social exchange theory is used to understand why individuals would contribute their knowledge for the benefit of others.

Knowledge reuse is a way for an individual to obtain the knowledge necessary to work better or more efficiently. It becomes the motivational impetus that leads individuals to choose knowledge reuse over other methods of obtaining the necessary knowledge. Expectancy theory, a theory of motivation, can be used to explain this behavior and it can be linked to the issue of technology acceptance. Expectancy theory argues that an individual's motivations to use and share knowledge are influenced by the expected outcomes of using that knowledge (Bock & Young-Gul, 2002). The underlying motivations for the two different acts, knowledge contribution and knowledge reuse, are seen as quite different and Watson and Hewett (2006) argue that they are best explained by different theories. In their model, knowledge flows both *into* the system from individuals and *out of* the system to other individuals, as shown in Figure 1. The effectiveness of a firm's knowledge transfer system is dependent on the flow of knowledge in *both* directions.

By employing the simultaneous application of social exchange theory and expectancy theory to the knowledge transfer process, Watson and Hewett (2006) found that knowledge contribution depends upon frequency of knowledge reuse, organizational tenure, and advancement within the organization. They assert that knowledge access, training, and the perceived value of knowledge are all significant predictors of knowledge reuse.

What is not obvious in Watson and Hewett's assessment of factors affecting knowledge contribution and reuse is the impact of the use of content that may now expose the firm to liability or that proves to be otherwise unreliable or misinformed. In knowledge transfer, a prime opportunity for this danger to occur is when videos are used in storytelling activities.

VIDEO AND STORYTELLING

Stories are important for knowledge sharing because they illustrate patterns and help people to make visual connections between concepts and practice. Gill (2001) states that storytelling serves two purposes in knowledge management: it can (1) quickly disseminate information and (2) it can convey meaning at a high level of understanding. He asserts that the greatest benefit of using storytelling in knowledge management may come from its ability to capture tacit knowledge in an organization. Unlike explicit knowledge, which is written down in documents, manuals and other accessible sources, tacit knowledge is in the minds of people, many of whom don't know how much their experience has taught them. Storytelling allows for a stream of consciousness. Face-to-face and video-based storytelling help the viewer's imagination and cognition by providing concrete images and demonstrations of behaviors that help them understand the objective of the message and the meaning of the content.

Video is a viable alternative to face-to-face storytelling when the senses of smell taste, and touch are not essential to the story being told. As in face-to-face storytelling, effective structuring of the story is usually essential in video production to ensure logical flow and to facilitate the viewers understanding of the message.

Cynefin (Snowden, 2007) is a sensemaking framework that argues that use of structure in storytelling depends on the relationship between cause and effect. That is, the nature of cause and effect dictates how a narrative or story should be developed. *Cynefin* (Snowden, 2007) identifies five domains that describe the relationship between them cause and effect:

- Simple: the relationship between cause and effect is obvious.
- Complicated: the relationship between cause and effect requires analysis or some

other form of investigation and/or the application of expert knowledge.
- Complex: the relationship between cause and effect can only be perceived in retrospect.
- Chaotic: there is no relationship between cause and effect.
- Disorder: the state of not knowing what type of causality exists.

To enhance the potential for the understanding of complex cause and effect relationships the *Cynefin* framework (Snowden, 2007) requires more openness and less structure in the storytelling or narrative. It takes someone with vision to see the line that fits between observations and expectations. In these circumstances higher media richness may reduce the level of risk because more sensory information and greater opportunities for perceptions of patterns of relationships between narrative elements are made available.

Under any circumstance a storyteller's narrative must be validated because of the inherent limitations of human cognition. For example, it has been shown that the verbal areas of the brain have minimal interactions with the visual areas, making it difficult for humans to describe pictures with words. Moreover, the process of even attempting this seems to reduce the fidelity of the original image. This cognitive limitation provides a rationale for using rich media (e.g. video) to record the image. Also, when sharing, people sometimes adjust their own understanding to be more plausible to them. Hence, storytellers may change the way they remember an event or process to match what they described (Bogue, 2006). Increasing media richness may provide better opportunity to mitigate this bias.

Often times videos created by amateurs lack the considerations outlined above. Video effectiveness for knowledge sharing depends on the talent of the individual, how well the narrative describes the link between cause and effect, their ability to organize content, and the quality of the video presentation. Because amateurs oftentimes don't have the talent, the time, or the inclination to acquire these skills, they may find it simply easier to simply incorporate pre-existing content into their video with their own content added to it. This type of content is (or at least was) common on YouTube.

Organizational employees can use Apple's iMovie and Microsoft's Movie Maker 2 to create and edit video. Editing digital video on a computer, called non-linear editing, makes it easy to combine images, sounds, music and narration into a single finished production. This means that employees can easily create and distribute video's that combine their own content with materials that they have secured from other sources. In organizations, the extent to which such videos are made and the nature of their content oftentimes depends upon the culture of the organization.

VIDEO, CULTURE, AND SENSEMAKING

Culture plays a critical role in sensemaking activities (Hasanali 2004). It is evidenced through the artifacts and symbols used in the video-based stories that are created and shared in the firm. Culture contributes to knowledge and behavior by helping to construct what one knows, what one does, how one does it, what one verbalizes about what one knows, and what materials one selects and displays as evidence to support one's argument(s). It provides the underlying philosophical framework that identifies the tangible evidence needed to support the claim made. Culture is therefore expressed via the individual's espoused values and the assumptions that underlie his or her behavior – what is acceptable behavior and what isn't.

Video can be used as a vehicle to broadcast organizational cultural values and symbols that shape behavior, which means that the intent and use of video for tacit knowledge externalization can be either constructive or deconstructive in nature. For example, videos can be used to show someone how something is done or to show individuals or members of the firm how they should or should not behave. In other words, videos can be used to educate, to share information, and to shape employees values in a manner that is consistent with the cultural norms of the organization.

The value of video for sensemaking in organizational settings is that it again highlights the active requirement for managers and leaders to help employees to construct sensible accounts out of ambiguous, ambivalent, equivocal, and conflicting information that oftentimes exists. Knowledge management should help to define the purpose behind a video, the message to be conveyed, target what and whom to film, provide expertise as how to create and edit videos, and inform employees as to when and to whom to show the edited film to. In essence then, knowledge management should provide the rules of the road for videocreation and sharing.

Video provides a rich medium that leaders can also use to demonstrate their leadership and to shape employee's values. Video is an ideal form for sharing leadership form and content because it captures the essence of leadership thinking and behavior and any needed desired actions the leader wants to convey in the message. To be successful though, the leader must understand the nature and power of video if he or she intends to effectively influence employee behavior.

For example, managers should know that videos might be seen and interpreted in different ways by different people with varying cultural influences. If a video results in a change in an individual or group knowledge base, then that person or group has found some use and value for the information conveyed by the film. But the process of becoming knowledgeable cannot be managed from outside the individual. The only knowledge that can be expressed is that which can be accessed in consciousness and expressed in terms of words and/or behavior.

Managers should know that structured examination may be needed to determine whether the knowledge contained in a video can be absorbed and understood by viewers. The results of two studies conducted by Herschel, Nemati, and Steiger (2001, 2003) seem to indicate that people need help in articulating or demonstrating what they have learned from a video-based story. Their studies used video to convey rich narratives that varied by the amount of structure employed in both the presentation and the subsequent inquiry as to what was learned by the viewers from a video presentation. The results of both studies indicate that the use of structuring protocols or templates can substantially increase a video viewer's ability to articulate or demonstrate what they have learned from video-based information or storytelling.

The importance of this research is that one should not believe that simply sharing video content would result in the content being understood properly and absorbed by the recipient. Firms need a mechanism by which to monitor how video recipients interpret the content's meaning and whether the message is being effectively absorbed and comprehended.

Video sensemaking also depends upon the ability to find relevant and informed reference resources. These sources must be reliable, knowledgeable, and be able to convey their content effectively and their content must be examined to insure that there is nothing in it that exposes the firm to liability. In professionally developed videos, inclusion of any copyrighted content is typically done so only with prior written permission(s). However, in ad hoc user-generated videos, these permissions are oftentimes ignored. Whether intentional or not, use of copied materials puts the organization at risk.

User-generated storytelling activities, whether video-based or not, must always be scrutinized to insure adherence legal and ethical standards. With individuals now able to easily create, copy, and distribute video content, the need to insure information integrity and adherence to cultural, ethical and legal standards becomes critical. The now widespread and easy-to-generate video capabilities available to individuals requires greater levels of knowledge management diligence and scrutiny to insure that content adheres to the firm's cultural norms. This presents a daunting challenge to firms, as most of them have no idea as to the extent of video content being generated and shared by their employees. While organizations may be able to create stringent standards for video generation and sharing, these efforts may still prove to be insufficient. Firms will need to adopt and deploy video search technologies if they intend to have any hope of being able to enforce such standards. That is, organizations will need to develop or acquire substantial filtering and search tools to find and eliminate copyright or other types of infringing activities that can compromise the firm.

CONCLUSION: OPPORTUNITIES FOR RESEARCH

Daily usage of online video rose by 56% in 2007. In 2007, 14% of adults reported using online video every day, up from 9% in 2006. Weekly usage also rose 8% in 2007, with 52% of the Internet users viewing online video once a week or more, compared with 44% in 2006 (Luchter, 2007). Now the Federal Communications Commission has reserved a third of the airwaves next under auction for wireless networks, which could provide mobile users with the ability to receive more video services using whichever cell phone or wireless device they want.

Given the experiences of e-mail and web site development, there is every reason to expect that organizations and their employees' can and will eventually fully exploit video for internal and external knowledge sharing on a large scale. Hence, employers need to realize that employees may create and post more video information that is both relevant to and not relevant to workplace activities. This potential screams for the imposition of standards for the development and sharing of videos. External knowledge sharing videos created by individuals employed by the firm will warrant the firm making more proactive warnings to employees as to their potential ability to put the firm at risk by actions taken on their own time.

The arguments presented in this paper make clear that the rise in video creation and sharing warrant increased attention to the impact of video in knowledge management activities. Video provides an effective means for facilitating knowledge sharing, especially tacit knowledge because of the richness of the media. However, since videos can now be more easily generated and shared by various organizational stakeholders and because they pose such potential risk to organizations, knowledge transfer activities should be revisited.

It is still uncertain how user-generated video will affect knowledge contribution. Ease of video generation and sharing may help or hinder the frequency of knowledge reuse, mitigate the importance of organizational tenure, and/or be independent of advancement within the organization. It is also unclear how the plethora of user-generated videos will affect knowledge access, training, and the value of knowledge, especially if issues of content reliability and liability arise.

User-generated video has the potential to make content suspect and/or to provide so much of it that people won't be able to distinguish relevant information from spam when seeking sensory rich information. An expanded volume of videos may serve to compound the amount of equivocality and uncertainty in organizations and require the adoption of more advanced search and retrieval tools. So, in addition to concerns for liability, firms will need to devise schemes for assessing and monitoring what content is relevant and accurate in problem-solving activities and opportunity identification and what content isn't.

With employees able to generate videos easily and to share them widely across time and place, it is important that they understand organizational standards for video content generation. There is no reason to believe or assume that employees understand storytelling or that they are sensitive to copyright issues that can vary by culture. Organizations must be proactive in informing and educating employees in video development and production standards to foster effective use of the video medium. And while organizations should be exploring and using new video search engines to help their employees access content, they also need them to detect situations and content that could subject them to potential liability.

All of these issues provide new opportunities for research. Most of the academic inquiries into knowledge management and the propositions put forth to date were made at a time when technology limited the widespread creation, availability and distribution of video generated by individuals. This situation has now changed dramatically and will continue to do so, especially as wireless bandwidth expands, mobile video handsets are enhanced, and cell phone video sharing services become more widespread.

Extensive research, modeling, and simulation about how the human brain and its components actually work is helping improve computer systems, making them more intelligent and more contextually aware so that they can provide automatic context capabilities and derive meaning from digital content. These developments are creating new opportunities for knowledge management by providing intelligent systems that understand what we want and deliver what we need when we ask for it. However, the challenge for knowledge management researchers is to examine how these new systems and video-related knowledge transfer issues functionally affect organizational intellectual assets and their performance.

Case studies and survey research can be used to assess how frequently employees are creating and/or accessing internally or externally generated video and for what purposes. Organizations can also be queried to assess their efforts or plans for unifying communications, providing standards for user-generated video creation, viewing, and sharing, and for adopting more effective search mechanisms that will facilitate the anticipated or already existing increase in video content. And from a socio-technical research perspective, whether new video-oriented search engines will make a difference to the practice of knowledge management may depend to some degree on behavioral and cultural factors and legal precedents.

Use of user-generated video to improve employee engagement and improved internal collaboration depends upon how well organizations understand the factors that affect effective video usage and the strategies they use to manage it. Hence, both the need and the opportunity for research into user-generated video activity are compelling and immediate.

REFERENCES

Allen, P. (2006, November 21). *Google employee posts videos on how Google search engine really works*. Retrieved from http://www.paulallen.net/2006/11/21/google-employee-posts-videos-on-how-google-search-engine-really-works/

Altus. (2007, June 20). *First video-powered social networking application for the enterprise incorporated into Altus Xtreme Knowledge Sharing (XKS) Release 5.0*. Retrieved from http://www.altuslearning.com/news_other_detail.php?item=2007_0620

Aniisu. (2007, August 13). *Getting the best out of your employee videos*. Retrieved from http://intraskope.wordpress.com/2007/08/13/getting-the-best-out-of-your-employee-videos/

Argote, L. (2005). Reflections on Two Views of Managing Learning and Knowledge in Organizations. *Journal of Management Inquiry*, *14*, 43–48. doi:10.1177/1056492604273179

Argote, L., & Ingram, P. (2000). Knowledge transfer A Basis for Competitive Advantage in Firms. *Organizational Behavior and Human Decision Processes, 82*(1), 150–169. doi:10.1006/obhd.2000.2893

Beasty, C. (2007, July). Endless possibilities. *Customer Relationship Management, 11*(7), 41–44.

Bock, G. W., & Young-Gul, K. (2002). Breaking the myths of rewards: an exploratory study of attitudes about knowledge sharing. *Information Resources Management Journal, 15*, 14–21.

Bogue, R. L. (2006). Convert tacit knowledge into explicit knowledge to ensure better application development. Retrieved from http://downloads.techrepublic.com.com/download.aspx?docid=258623

Burkhard, R. (2005). Impulse: Using knowledge visualization in business oriented knowledge infrastructures. *Journal of Universal Knowledge Management, 0*(2), 170–188.

Delaney, K. (March 15, 2007). Spam hits video sites, misleading web viewers. *Wall Street Journal*. B1-2.

Gill, P. J. (2001). Once Upon an Enterprise: The ancient art of storytelling emerges as a tool for knowledge management. *Knowledge Management, 4*(5), 24-28. Retrieved from http://www.destinationcrm.com/km/dcrm_km_article.asp?id=823

Hasanali, F. (2004). Critical success factors of knowledge management. In E. Koenig & Srikantaiah (Eds.), *Knowledge management. Lessons learned* (pp. 55-69). Medford, NJ: ASIST Monograph Series.

Herschel, R., Nemati, H., & Steiger, D. (2001). Tacit to Explicit Knowledge Conversion: Knowledge Exchange Protocols. *Journal of Knowledge Management, 5*(1), 107–116. doi:10.1108/13673270110384455

Herschel, R., Nemati, H., & Steiger, D. (2003). Knowledge Exchange Protocols: A Second Study. *Journal of Information and Knowledge Management: Special issue of JIKM on " . Knowledge Management in Context and Context for Knowledge Management, 2*(2), 153–163.

Inside the Cubicle. (September, 2006). Southwest employers share a defining moment. Retrieved from http://insidethecubicle.blogs.com/blog/2006/09/southwest_emplo.html

Kane, A. A., Argote, L., & Levine, J. (2005). Knowledge transfer between groups via personnel rotation: Effects of social identity and knowledge quality. *Organizational Behavior and Human Decision Processes, 96*(1), 56–71. doi:10.1016/j.obhdp.2004.09.002

Luchter, L. (2007, June 19). Magid: 80% of 18-24 males watch online video weekly. *Online Media Daily*. Retrieved from http://publications.mediapost.com/index.cfm?fuseaction=Articles.showArticle&art_aid=62558

Melcrum. (2007, March 20). *New research shows social media is proving a big hit for global corporations inside and out, but risks remain*. Retrieved from http://www.melcrumblog.com/2007/03/social_media_is.html

Nonaka, I., & Takeuchi, H. (1995). *The Knowledge Creating Company*. New York: Oxford University Press.

Nyman, N. (2005). *Risky business: What must employers do to shield against liability for employee wrongdoings in the Internet age*. Retrieved from http://www.lctjournal.washington.edu/Vol1/a007Nyman.html

Pepus, G. (2007, June). Smart image and video search. *KMworld* (pp. 6-9).

Popa, B. (2007, September 4). *Supermarket employee won YouTube lawsuit*. Retrieved from http://news.softpedia.com/news/Supermarket-Employee-Won-YouTube-Lawsuit-64526.shtml

Sandoval, G. (2008, July 12). *Goofle, Vicom now clashing over YouTube employee records*. Retrieved from http://news.cnet.com/8301-1023_3-9989783-93.html

Snowden, D. (2007). *Cynefin*. Retrieved from http://en.wikipedia.org/wiki/Cynefin#The_Framework

Tancer, W. (2007, January 29). *YouTube and Google: Quantifying the Synergy*. Retrieved from http://weblogs.hitwise.com/bill-tancer/2007/01/youtube_and_google_quantifying.html

Teece, D., Pisano, G., Shuen, A., & Pisano, G. (1997). Dynamic capabilities and strategic management. *Strategic Management Journal, 18*(7), 509–533. doi:10.1002/(SICI)1097-0266(199708)18:7<509::AID-SMJ882>3.0.CO;2-Z

Tiwana, A., & Bush, A. (2001). A social exchange architecture for distributed Web communities. *Journal of Knowledge Management, 5*, 242–248. doi:10.1108/13673270110401220

Vascellaro, J. (2007, August 28). Social networking goes professional. *Wall Street Journal*. D1-D2.

Wall Street Journal. (2007, March 13). *Viacom sues Google and You Tube*. Retrieved from http://blogs.wsj.com/law/2007/03/13/viacom-sues-google-and-you-tube/trackback/

Wall Street Journal. (2008, October 30). *Beyond YouTube: New ways to find video on the web*. Retrieved from http://online.wsj.com/article/SB122532318320582165-search.html?KEYWORDS=online+video&COLLECTION=wsjie/6month

Watson, S., & Hewett, K. (2006). A multi-theoretical model of knowledge transfer in organizations: Determinants of knowledge contribution and knowledge reuse. *Journal of Management Studies, 43*(2), 141–173. doi:10.1111/j.1467-6486.2006.00586.x

Webdriven. (2007, August 15). *Delta Airlines employees make travel videos*. Retrieved from http://www.bewebdriven.com/blog/whats-hot/viral-travel-videos-delta-airlines.php

Compilation of References

Abbate, J. (1999). *Inventing the Internet*. Cambridge, MA: The MIT Press.

Abecker, A., & Decker, S. (1999). Organizational Memory: Knowledge Acquisition, Integration, and Retrieval Issues. *Knowledge-Based Systems*, 113–124.

Abler, R. (1987). The national science foundation national center for geographic information and analysis. *International Journal of Geographic Information Systems, 1*(4), 303-326.

Abou-Zeid, E. (2002). A Knowledge Management Reference Model. *Journal of Knowledge Management, 6*(5), 486–499. doi:10.1108/13673270210450432

Abou-Zeid, E. (2003). Developing Business Aligned Knowledge Management Strategy. In E. Coakes (Ed.), *Knowledge Management: Current Issues and Challenges* (pp. 156-172). IRM Press.

Ackerman, M., & Halverson, C. (2004). Organizational memory as objects, processes, and trajectories: An examination of organizational memory in use. *Computer Supported Cooperative Work (CSCW), 13*(2), 155-189.

Ackerman, M.S. (1996). Definitional and contextual issues in organizational and group memories. *Information Technology and People, 9*(1), 10-24.

Ackerman, M.S., & Halverson, C. (2000). Re-examining organizational memory. *Communication of the ACM, 43*(1), 58-64.

Ackermann, M., & Halverson, C. (1998). Considering an organization's memory. In Proceedings of CSCW'98 (pp. 39-48). Seattle, Washington.

Ackoff, R. L. (1979). Resurrecting the future of operations research. *The Journal of the Operational Research Society, 30*(3), 189–199.

Adams, D. A., Nelson, R. R., & Todd, P. A. (1992). Perceived usefulness, ease of use, and usage of information technology: A replication. *MIS Quarterly, 16*(2), 227-247.

Adams, G. L., & Lamont, B. T. (2003). Knowledge Management systems and developing sustainable competitive advantage. *Journal of Knowledge Management, 7*(2), 142–154. doi:10.1108/13673270310477342

AHDR. (2002). The first *Arab human development report: creating opportunities for future generations.* United Nations Development Programme. New York: UN Publications.

AHDR. (2003). The second *Arab human development report: building a knowledge society.* United Nations Development Programme. New York: UN Publications.

Ahrens, T., & Dent, J. F., (1998). Accounting and organizations: Realizing the richness of field research. *Journal of Management Accounting Research, 10*, 1-39

Ahuja, G. (2000). Collaboration networks, structural holes, and innovation: A longitudinal study. *Administrative Science Quarterly, 45*(3), 425-455.

Ahuja, M. J., & Galvin, J. E. (2003). Socialization in virtual groups. *Journal of Management, 29*, 161–185. doi:10.1177/014920630302900203

Ahuja, M. K., & Carley, K. M. (1999). Network structure in virtual organizations. *Organization Science, 10*, 741–757. doi:10.1287/orsc.10.6.741

Ahuja, M.K., & Carley, K.M. (1999). Network structure in virtual organizations. *Organization Science, 10*(6), 741-757.

Ajzen, I. (1985). From intentions to actions: A theory of planned behavior. In J. K. A. J. Beckman (Ed.), *Action control: From cognition to behavior* (pp. 11-39). New York: Springer-Verlag.

Ajzen, I. (1991). The theory of planned behavior. *Organizational Behavior and Human Decision Processes, 50*(2), 179–211. doi:10.1016/0749-5978(91)90020-T

Ajzen, I., & Fishbein, M. (1980). Prediction of goal-directed behavior: Attitudes, intentions, and perceived behavioral control. *Journal of Experimental Social Psychology, 22*(September), 453–474.

Akgun, A. E., Byrne, J. C. et al. (2006). Transactive memory system in new product development teams. *IEEE Transactions on Engineering Management, 53(1)*, 95-111.

Akhavan, P., Jafari, M., & Fathian, M. (2005). Exploring Failure-Factors of Implementing Knowledge Management Systems In Organizations. *Journal of Knowledge Management Practice*.

Al-Ammary, J., & Fung, C. C. (2008). Knowledge Management Strategic Alignment in the Gulf Cooperation Council Countries. [Retrieved from www.ejkm.com]. *Electronic Journal of Knowledge Management, 6*(2), 75–84.

Al-Athari, A., & Zairi, M. (2001). Building benchmarking competence through knowledge management: an empirical study of the Kuwaiti context. *Benchmarking: an International Journal, 8*(1), 70–80. doi:10.1108/14635770110383489

Alavi, M. & Leidner, D. E. (1999). Knowledge Management Systems: Issues, Challenges, and Benefits. *Communications of the AIS, 1*(7).

Alavi, M., & Leidner, D. (1999). Knowledge Management Systems: Issues, Challenges, and Benefits. *Communication of the AIS, 1*(7). Retrieved from http://cais.isworld.org/articles/1-7/

Alavi, M., & Leidner, D. E. (2001). Knowledge Management Systems: Emerging views and practices from the field. *32nd Hawaii International Conference on Systems Sciences, IEEE Computer Society.*

Alavi, M., & Leidner, D. E. (2001). Review: Knowledge management and knowledge management systems: Conceptual foundations and research issues. *MIS Quarterly, 25(*1), 107-136.

Alavi, M., & Tiwana, A. (2002). Knowledge integration in virtual teams: the potential of KMS. *Journal of the American Society for Information Science and Technology, 53*(12), 1029–1037. doi:10.1002/asi.10107

Alavi, M., Kayworth, T.R., & Leidner, D.E. (2006). An empirical examination of the influence of organizational culture on knowledge management practices. *Journal of Management Information Systems, 22*(3), 191-224.

Alexandre, F. (Ed.). *Connectionistsymbolic integration.* Hillsdale, NJ: Lawrence Erlbaum Associates.

Allen, P. (2006, November 21). *Google employee posts videos on how Google search engine really works.* Retrieved from http://www.paulallen.net/2006/11/21/google-employee-posts-videos-on-how-google-search-engine-really-works/

Almeida, P., & Kogut, B. (1999). Localization of knowledge and the mobility of engineers in regional networks. *Management Science, 45*(7), 905–917. doi:10.1287/mnsc.45.7.905

Al-Shammari, M. (2005). Implementing a Knowledge-enabled CRM strategy in a large company: a case study from a developing country. In M. E. Jennex (Ed.), *Case studies in knowledge management* (pp. 249-278). Hershey, PA: Idea Group Publishing.

Altus. (2007, June 20). *First video-powered social networking application for the enterprise incorporated into Altus Xtreme Knowledge Sharing (XKS) Release 5.0.* Retrieved from http://www.altuslearning.com/news_other_detail.php?item=2007_0620

Alvesson, M., & Kärreman, D. (2000). Taking the linguistic turn in organizational research: challenges, responses, consequences. *The Journal of Applied Behavioral Science, 36*, 136–158. doi:10.1177/0021886300362002

Alvesson, M., & Karreman, D. (2001). Odd couple: Making sense of the curious concept of knowledge management. *Journal of Management Studies, 38*(7), 995-1018.

Alvesson, M., & Sköldberg, K. (1994). *Tolkning och reflektion. Vetenskapsfilosofi och Kvalitativ Metod (Interpretation and Reflection. The philosophy of Science and Qualitative method)*. Lund: Studentlitteratur

Amin, A. (2002). Spatialities of globalisation. *Environment & Planning A, 34*, 385–399. doi:10.1068/a3439

Amit, R., & Shoemaker, P. J. H. (1993). Strategic Assets and Organizational Rents. *Strategic Management Journal, 14*(1), 33–46. doi:10.1002/smj.4250140105

Andersen, A. (1998). *The knowledge management practices book*. Arthur Andersen.

Anderson, J. C., & Gerbing, D. W. (1988). Structural equation modeling in practice: A review and recommended two-step approach. *Psychological Bulletin, 103*, 411–423. doi:10.1037/0033-2909.103.3.411

Anderson, J.R. (1983). *The architecture of cognition*. Cambridge, MA: Harvard University Press.

Andres, H., & Zmud, R. (2002). A contingency approach to software project coordination. *Journal of Management Information Systems, 18*(3), 41-70.

Angus, J. (2006). Clementine 8.1 melds BA with BI. *InfoWorld, 26*(19), 28–29.

Aniisu. (2007, August 13). *Getting the best out of your employee videos*. Retrieved from http://intraskope.wordpress.com/2007/08/13/getting-the-best-out-of-your-employee-videos/

Anttiroico, A. (2006). Strategic knowledge management in local government, In A. Anttiroiko and M. Malkia (Eds) *Encyclopedia of digital government* (pp. 268-298). Hershey, PA: IRM Press.

Appelt, W., & Mambrey, P. (1999). Experiences with the BSCW Shared Workspace System as the Backbone of a Virtual Learning Environment for Students. In *Proceedings of ED Media '99, Charlottesville* (pp. 1710-1715).

Ardichvili, A. (2003). Motivation and barriers to participation in virtual knowledge-sharing communities of practice. *Journal of Knowledge Management, 7*(1), 64–77. doi:10.1108/13673270310463626

Argote, L. (2005). Reflections on Two Views of Managing Learning and Knowledge in Organizations. *Journal of Management Inquiry, 14*, 43–48. doi:10.1177/1056492604273179

Argote, L., & Ingram, P. (2000). Knowledge Transfer: A basis for Competitive Advantage in Firms. *Organizational Behavior and Human Decision Processes, 82*(1), 150–169. doi:10.1006/obhd.2000.2893

Argote, L., McEvily, B., & Reagans, R. (2003). Introduction to the Special Issue on Managing Knowledge in Organizations: Creating, Retaining, and Transferring Knowledge. *Management Science, 49*(4), v–viii.

Argote, L., McEvily, B., & Reagans, R. (2003). Managing knowledge in organizations: An integrative framework and review of emerging themes. *Management Science, 49*(4), 571–582. doi:10.1287/mnsc.49.4.571.14424

Aronoff, S. (1995). Geographic information systems: A management perspective. WDL Publications.

Ashcraft, M.H. (1994). *Human memory and cognition (2nd ed.)*. New York, NY: HarperCollins College Publishers.

Asoh, D., Belardo, S., & Duchessi, P. (2003). Alignment: The missing link in knowledge management research. *Fourth European Conference on Knowledge Management* (pp. 39-47). Fergal McGrath University of Limerick.

Aubert, J. E., & Reiffers, J. L. (2003). *Knowledge economies in the Middle East and North America: toward new development strategies*. World Bank Institute Series, Washington D.C.: The World Bank Press, Beckman, T. J. (1999). The current state of knowledge management. In J. Liebowitz (Ed.), *Knowledge management handbook* (pp. 1.1-1.22). Florida: CRC Press.

Avison, D. E., & Wood-Harper, A. T. (1990). *Multiview: An Exploration in Information Systems Development*. New York: McGraw-Hill.

Avison, D. E., Wood-Harper, A.-T., Vidgen, R. G., & Wood, J. R. G. (1998). A further exploration into information systems development: the evolution of Multiview2. *Information Technology & People*, *11*(2), 124–139. doi:10.1108/09593849810218319

Awad, E.M., & Ghaziri, H.M. (2004). *Knowledge management*. Upper Saddle River, NJ: Pearson Education.

Bach, C., & Belardo, S. (2003). Scientific and Philosophical Aspects of Information and the Relationships Among Data, Information, and Knowledge. *Ninth Americas Conference on Information Systems*, Tampa Bay, Fl (pp. 2629-2639).

Badaracco, J. L. (1991). *The knowledge link*. Boston, MA: Harvard Business School Press.

Baily, A. (1995). *Tomorrow's company: The role of business in a changing world.* London: RSA.

Bakopoulos, J.Y. (1985). Toward a more precise concept of information technology. *In Proceedings of the 6th International Conference on Information Systems (ICIS)*, (pp. 17-24).

Balasubramanian, S., & Mahajan, V. (2001). The Economic Leverage of the Virtual Community. *International Journal of Electronic Commerce*, *5*(3), 103–138.

Balasubramanian, V. (1995). Organizational Learning and Information Systems, E-Papyrus, Inc. Retrieved January 17, 2008 from http://www.e-papyrus.com/personal/orglrn.html

Balmisse, G., Meingain, D., & Passerini, K. (2007). Technology trends in knowledge management tools. *International Journal of Knowledge Management, 3*(2), 11 -131.

Balmisse, G., Meingan, D., & Passerini, K. (2007). Technology trends in knowledge management tools. *International Journal of Knowledge Management, 3*(2), 118–131.

Bandura, A. (1977). Self-efficacy: Toward a unifying theory of behavioral change. *Psychological Review, 84*(2), 191-215.

Barab, S. A., MaKinster, J. G. & Scheckler, R. (2003). Designing System Dualities: Characterizing a Web-Supported Professional Development Community. *The Information Society, 19*, 237–256. doi:10.1080/01972240309466

Barney, J. (1991). Firm Resources and Sustained Competitive Advantage. *Journal of Management*, *17*(1), 99–120. doi:10.1177/014920639101700108

Barney, J. B. (1986). Organizational Culture: Can it be a Source of Sustained Competitive Advantage. *Academy of Management Review*, *11*(3), 656–665. doi:10.2307/258317

Bartczak, S. E., Turner, J. M., & England, E. C. (2007). Challenges in developing a knowledge management strategy: a case study of the Air Force Material Command. *International Journal of Knowledge Management*, *4*(1), 46–50.

Barthes, R. (1997). From work to text. In S. L. Feagin, & P. Maynard, P. (Eds.), *Aesthetics.* Oxford: Oxford University Press.

Batty, M., (1993). The geography of cyberspace, Environment and planning B, *Planning and design, 20*(6), 615-16

Beasty, C. (2007, July). Endless possibilities. *Customer Relationship Management*, *11*(7), 41–44.

Becerra-Fernandez, I., & Sabherwal, R. (2001). Organizational knowledge management: A contingency perspective. *Journal of Management Information Systems*, *18*(1), 23–55.

Becerra-Fernandez, I., Gonzales, A., & Sabherwal, R. (2004). *Knowledge management: Challenges, solutions, and technologies*. Upper Saddle River, NJ: Pearson Education, Inc.

Bednarz, A. (2005). Microsoft beefs up SQL Server database. *New World (New Orleans, La.)*, *22*(13), 12.

Beer, S. (1972). *Brain of the Firm*. London: Allen Lane.

Benslimane, D., Dustdar, S., & Sheth, A. (2008). Services mashups: the new generation of Web applications. *IEEE Internet Computing*, *12*(5), 13–15. doi:10.1109/MIC.2008.110

Berends, H., van der Bij, H., Debackere, K., & Weggeman, M. (2006). Knowledge sharing mechanisms in industrial research. *R & D Management*, *36*(1), 85–95. doi:10.1111/j.1467-9310.2005.00417.x

Berger, C., & Haberstroh, B. (2005). Oracle data mining 10g release 2: Know more, do more, spend less. Oracle White Papers. Retrieved January 9, 2009, from http://www.oracle.com/technology/products/bi/odm/pdf/bwp_db_odm_10gr2_0905.pdf

Berger, P.L., & Luckmann, T. (1991). *The social construction of reality: a treatise in the sociology of knowledge*. London: Penguin

Berman-Brown, R., & Woodland, M. J. (1999). Managing knowledge wisely: A case study in organisational behaviour. *Journal of Applied Management Studies*, *8*(2), 175-198.

Berners-Lee, T., & Lassila, O. (2001, May). The semantic web. *Scientific American Magazine*, *284*, 34–43. doi:10.1038/scientificamerican0501-34

Berners-Lee, T., Hendler, J., & Lassila, O. (2001). The semantic web. *Scientific American*, *5*(1).

Berry, M. W., & Browne, M. (1999) *Understanding Search Engines: Mathematical Modeling and Text Retrieval*. Philadelphia, PA: Society for Industrial and Applied Mathematics.

Bhattacharya, R., Devinney, T. M., & Pillutla, M. M. (1998). A formal model of trust based on outcomes. *Academy of Management Review*, *23*, 459–472. doi:10.2307/259289

Bieber, M., Engelbart, D., Furuta, D., Hiltz, R., Noll, S. R., & Preece, J., J., Stohr, E. A., Turoff, M., & Van De Walle, B. (2002). Toward Virtual Community Knowledge Evolution. *Journal of Management Information Systems*, *18*(4), 11–35.

Bierly, P., & Chakrabarti, A. (1996). Generic knowledge strategies in the U.S. pharmaceutical industry. *Strategic Management Journal*, *17*, 123-135.

Bih-Shiaw, J., Yu Ping Wang, C., & Yen-Hao, C. (2006). Knowledge flows and performance of multinational subsidiaries: the perspective of human capital. *International Journal of Human Resource Management*, *17*(2), 225–244.

Binney, D. (2001). The knowledge management spectrum: understanding the KM landscape. *Journal of Knowledge Management*, *5*(1), 33–42.

Birkinshaw, J., & Sheehan, T. (2002). Managing the knowledge life cycle. *MIT Sloan Management Review*, *44*(1), 75–83.

Blackler, F., & McDonald, S. (2000). Power, mastery and organizational learning. *Journal of Management Studies*, *37*, 833–852. doi:10.1111/1467-6486.00206

Blanchard, A. L., & Markus, M. L. (2004). The Experienced 'Sense' of a Virtual Community: Characteristics and Processes. *The Data Base for Advances in Information Systems*, *35*(1), 65–79.

Bloodgood, J., & Salisbury, W. D. (2001). Understanding the influence of organizational change strategies on information technology and knowledge management strategies. *Decision Support Systems*, *31*, 55–69. doi:10.1016/S0167-9236(00)00119-6

Bock, G. W., & Kim, Y. (2002). Breaking the myths of rewards: An exploratory study of attitudes about knowledge sharing. *Information Resources Management Journal*, *15*(2), 14–21.

Bock, G. W., Zmud, R. W., & Kim, Y. (2005). Behavioral intention formation in knowledge sharing: Examining the roles of extrinsic motivators, social-psychological forces, and organizational climate. *MIS Quarterly*, *29*(1), 87–111.

Bock, G.-W., Zmud, R. W., Kim, Y.-G., & Lee, J.-N. (2005). Behavioral intention formation in knowledge sharing: Examining the roles of extrinsic motivators, social-psychological forces, and organizational climate. *MIS Quarterly, 29*(1), 87-111.

Boettcher, S. (1998). The Netscape Intranet Solution: Deploying the Full-service Intranet. New York: John Wiley & Sons.

Bogue, R. L. (2006). Convert tacit knowledge into explicit knowledge to ensure better application development. Retrieved from http://downloads.techrepublic.com.com/download.aspx?docid=258623

Boland, R. J., & Tenkasi, R. V. (1995). Perspective making and perspective taking in communities of knowing. *Organization Science*, *6*, 350–372. doi:10.1287/orsc.6.4.350

Bollen, K. A. (1989). *Structural equations with latent variables*. New York: Wiley.

Bontis, N. (2004). National intellectual capital index: a United Nations initiative for the Arab region. *Journal of Intellectual Capital*, *5*(1), 13–39. doi:10.1108/14691930410512905

Booto Ekionea, J.-P., & Abou-Zeid, E.-S. (2005). Knowledge Management and Sustained Competitive Advantage: A Resource-Based Analysis. *IRMA (Information Resources Management Association International Conference), Proceedings*. San Diego (USA). May, 15-18.

Borghoff, U.M., & Pareschi, R. (1997). Information technology for knowledge management. *Journal of Universal Computer Science, 3*(8), 835-842.

Bower, W. (2001). *Development of a decision framework for knowledge management projects.* Unpublished doctoral dissertation, Air Force Institute of Technology, Wright-Patterson AFB, Dayton, OH.

Bowman, B. J. (2002). Building knowledge management systems. *Information Systems Management*, *19*, 32–40. doi:10.1201/1078/43201.19.3.20020601/37168.5

Braga, D., Ceri, S., & Faniel, F. (2008). Mashing up search services. *IEEE Internet Computing*, *12*(5), 16–23. doi:10.1109/MIC.2008.105

Breaugh, J.A. (1985). The work autonomy scales: Validity evidence. *Human Relations, 42*, 1033-1056.

Bredo, E. (1994). *Cognitivism, situated cognition, and Deweyian pragmatism*. Philosophy of Education

British Standards Institution, & Technical Committee BDD/3. (2002). *BS 15000-1:2002 IT Service Management Part 1: Specification for service management*. London: British Standards Institution.

Brockman, B. K., & Morgan, R. M. (2003). The role of existing knowledge in new product innovativeness and performance. *Decision Sciences, 34*(2), 385-419.

Brown, J. S., & Duguid, P. (1991). Organizational learning and communities-of-practice: toward a unified view of working, learning and innovation. *Organization Science*, *2*, 40–57. doi:10.1287/orsc.2.1.40

Brown, J. S., & Duguid, P. (1999). Organizing Knowledge. *The Society for Organizational Learning*, *1*(2), 28–44.

Brown, J. S., & Duguid, P. (2000). Balancing act: How to capture knowledge without killing it. *Harvard Business Review*, *78*(3), 73.

Brown, J. S., & Duguid, P. (2000). *The social life of information*. Boston, MA: Harvard Business School Press.

Brown, J. S., & Duguid, P. (2001). Knowledge and organization: a social-practice perspective. *Organization Science*, *12*, 198–213. doi:10.1287/orsc.12.2.198.10116

Brown, J. S., & Gray, E. S. (1995). The People Are the Company. *FastCompany.* Retrieved from http://www.fastcompany.com/online/01/people.html

Brown, J.S., & Duguid, P. 2002. *The social life of information*. Boston, MA: Harvard Business School Press.

Buckman, R. H. (1998). Knowledge sharing at Buckman Labs. *The Journal of Business Strategy*, *19*(1), 11–15. doi:10.1108/eb039903

Büchel, B., & Probst, G. (2000). From organizational learning to knowledge management. Retrieved January 5, 2008 from http://www.hec.unige.ch/recherches_publications/cahiers/2000/2000.11.pdf

Burkhard, R. (2005). Impulse: Using knowledge visualization in business oriented knowledge infrastructures. *Journal of Universal Knowledge Management*, *0*(2), 170–188.

Burt, R. S. (1997). The contingent value of social capital. *Administrative Science Quarterly, 42*, 339–365. doi:10.2307/2393923

Busch, P. (2008). *Tacit knowledge in organizational learning.* Hershey, PA: IGI Publishing.

Butler, B. (1999). *The dynamics of electronic communities.* Unpublished Ph.D. dissertation, Graduate School of Industrial Administration, Carnegie Mellon University.

Butler, B. S. (2001). Membership Size, Communication Activity and Sustainability: A Resource-Based Model of Online Social Structures. *Information Systems Research, 12*(4), 346–362. doi:10.1287/isre.12.4.346.9703

Byrne, B. M. (1998). *Structural equation modeling with LISREL, PRELIS, and SIMPLIS: Basic concepts, applications, and programming.* Mahwah, NJ: Lawrence Erlbaum Associates.

Cabrera, A., Collins, W. C., & Salgado, J. F. (2006). Determinants of individual engagement in knowledge sharing. *International Journal of Human Resource Management, 17*, 245–264.

CAIB. (2003). The Columbia accident investigation report. Retrieved August 12, 2007, from http://www.caib.us/news/report/pdf/vol1/full/caib_report_volume1.pdf

Callon, M. (1986). Some Elements of A Sociology of Translation: Domestication of the Scallops and the Fishermen of St. Brieuc Bay. In J. Law (Ed.), *Power, Action and Belief* (pp. 196-233). London: Routledge & Kegan Paul.

Campion, M, Medsker, G., & Higgs, C. (1993). Relations between work group characteristics and effectiveness: Implications for designing effective work groups. *Personnel Psychology, 46*, 823-850.

Cannataro, M., & Talia, D. (2004). Semantics and knowledge grids: Building the next-generation grid. *IEEE Intelligent Systems*, (January/February): 56–63. doi:10.1109/MIS.2004.1265886

Cannataro, M., Talia, D., & Trunfio, P. (2001). Knowledge grid: High performance knowledge discovery services on the grid. In *Proc. of the 2nd International Workshop on Grid Computing (GRID 2001), Denver, USA* (LNCS 2242, pp. 38-50).

Carlile, P. R., & Rebentisch, E. S. (2003). Into the black box: the knowledge transformation cycle. *Management Science, 1*(9).

Carlsson, S. A., Sawy, O. E., Eriksson, I., & Raven, A. (1996). Gaining Competitive Advantage Through Shared Knowledge Creation: In Search of a New Design Theory for Strategic Information Systems. In *Proceedings of the Fourth European Conference on Information Systems*, Lisbon, Portugal (pp. 1067-1076).

Carraher, S. M., Sullivan, S. E., & Crocitto, M. M. (2008). Mentoring across global boundaries: An empirical examination of home- and host-country mentors on expatriate career outcomes. *Journal of International Business Studies, 39*(8), 1310. doi:10.1057/palgrave.jibs.8400407

Cegloski, M., Coburn, A., & Cuadrado, J. (2003). Semantic Search of Unstructured Data using Contextual Network Graph. *National Institute for Technology and Liberal Education*, Middlebury, USA.

Chae, B., Koch, H., Paradice, D., & Huy, V. (2005). Exploring Knowledge Management Using Network Theories: Questions, Paradoxes and Prospects. *Journal of Computer Information Systems, 45*(4), 62–74.

Chan, O, J. (2005). Enterprise information system strategy and planning. *Journal of American Business, Cambridge, 6*(2), 148–154.

Chandler, A. D. (1990). *Scale and Scope - the Dynamics of Industrial Capitalism.* Cambridge, MA: Belknap Press.

Chang, S.-G., & Ahn, J.-H. (2005). Product and Process Knowledge in the Performance-oriented Knowledge Management Approach. *Journal of Knowledge Management, 9*(4), 8–18. doi:10.1108/13673270510610378

Chase, R. L. (1997). The knowledge-based organisation: An international survey. *Journal of Knowledge Management, 1*(1), 38-49.

Chase, R. L. (2004). *2004 Asian most admired knowledge enterprises—Executive summary*. Bedford, UK: Teleos – The KNOW Network.

Chase, W.G., & Simon, H. (1973). Perceptions in chess. *Cognitive Psychology, 4*(1), 55-81.

Chatman, J. A., & Jehn, K. A. (1994). Assessing the relationship between industry characteristics and organizational culture: How different can you be? *Academy of Management Journal, 37*(3), 522-553.

Checkland, P. (1999) *Systems thinking, systems practice*. Chichester: Wiley.

Checkland, P. B., & Poulter, J. (2006). *Learning for Action: A Short Definitive Account of Soft systems Methodology and its Use, for Practitioners, Teachers and Students*. Chichester: John Wiley and Sons Ltd.

Checkland, P. B., & Scholes, J. (1990). *Soft systems Methodology in Action*. Chichester: Wiley.

Chen, A. N. K., & Edgington, T. M. (2005). Assessing value in organizational knowledge creation: Considerations for knowledge workers. *MIS Quarterly, 29*(2), 279–309.

Chen, F. F., West, S. G., & Sousa, K. H. (2006). A Comparison of Bifactor and Second-Order Models of Quality of Life. *Multivariate Behavioral Research, 41*(2), 189–225. doi:10.1207/s15327906mbr4102_5

Cheuk, B. & Dervin, B. (1999). A qualitative sense-making study of the information seeking situations faced by professionals in three workplace contexts. *The Electronic Journal of Communication, 9*(2-4).

Cheuk, B. (2007). Applying Sense-Making and Narrative Techniques to capture lessons learnt. *Journal of Information & Knowledge Management, 6*(3), 1–7. doi:10.1142/S0219649207001494

Cheuk, B. W. (2007). Using social networking analysis to facilitate knowledge sharing in the British Council. *International Journal of Knowledge Management, 2*(4), 67–76.

Child, J. Faulkner, D. & Tallman, S. (2005). Cooperative Strategy: Managing Alliances, Networks, and Joint Ventures. Oxford: Oxford University Press.

Child, J., & Rodrigues, S. (2001). Social identity and organizational learning. In M. Easterby-Smith & M. A. Lyles (Eds.), *Handbook of organizational learning* (pp. 535-556). Oxford: Blackwell.

Chin, W.W. (1998). The partial least squares approach to structural equation modeling. In G.A. Marcoulides (Ed.), *Modern methods for business research* (pp. 295-336). Mahway, NJ: Erlbaum.

Chin, W.W. (2001). PLS-graph user's guide version 3.0 (User's manual that accompanies PLS-GRAPH version 3.00 build 1126 provided by Wynn Chin). Calgary, Canada: University of Calgary.

Choi, B., & Lee, H. (2003). An empirical investigation of km styles and their effect on corporate performance. *Information & Management, 40*, 403-417.

Chow, C. W., Deng, F. J., & Ho, J. L. (2000). The openness of knowledge sharing within organizations: A comparative study of the United States and the People's Republic of China. *Journal of Management Accounting Research, 12*, 65–95. doi:10.2308/jmar.2000.12.1.65

Chow, W. S., & Chan, L. S. (2008). Social network, social trust and shared goals in organizational knowledge sharing. *Information & Management, 45*(7), 458. doi:10.1016/j.im.2008.06.007

Choy, K. L., Lee, W. B. et al. (2005). A knowledge-based supplier intelligence retrieval system for outsource manufacturing. *Knowledge-Based Systems, 18*(1), 1-17.

Chua, A., & Lam, W. (2005). Why KM projects fail: a multi-case analysis. *Journal of Knowledge Management, 9*(3), 6-17.

Chua, D.K.H., Li, D.Z., & Chan, W.T. (2001). Case-based reasoning approach in bid decision making. *Journal of Construction Engineering*, January/February, 35-45.

Chun, S., & Park, Y. (2006). A new hybrid data mining technique using a regression case based reasoning: Application to financial forecasting. *Expert Systems with Ap-*

plications, *31*, 329–336. doi:10.1016/j.eswa.2005.09.053

Churchman, C. W. (1970). Operations research as a profession. *Management Science*, *17*(2), 37–53.

Churchman, C. W. (1979). *The systems approach* (revised and updated). New York: Dell Publishing.

Civi, E. (2000). Knowledge management as a competitive asset: a review. *Marketing Intelligence & Planning*, *18*(4), 166–174. doi:10.1108/02634500010333280

Clark, G.L., & O'Connor, K. (1997). The informational content of financial products and the spatial structure of the global finance industry. In K.R. Cox (Ed), *Spaces of globalization. Reasserting the power of the local* (pp. 89-114). New York: The Guilford Press.

Clementini, E., Felice, P.D., & Van Oosterom, P. (1993). A small set of formal topological relations suitable for end-user interaction, advances in spatial databases. In proceedings 3rd International Symposium, SSD'93, Singapore, Lecture Notes in Computer Science, Vol. 692 (Springer-Verlag, New York) (pp. 277-295).

Cockcroft, S. (2004). The design and implementation of a repository for the management of spatial data integrity constraints. Volume 8, Number 1 / March, Pages 49-69.

Cohen, D. (2006). What's Your Return on Knowledge? *Harvard Business Review*, *84*(12), 28–28.

Cohen, M.D. (1991). Individual learning and organizational routine: Emerging connections. *Organization Science, 2*(1), 135-139.

Cohen, M.D., & Bacdayan, P. (1994). Organizational routines are stored as procedural memory: Evidence from a laboratory study. *Organizational Science, 5*(4), 554-568.

Cohendet, P., & Llerena, P. (2003). Routines and incentives: the role of communities in the firm. *Industrial and Corporate Change*, *12*, 271–297. doi:10.1093/icc/12.2.271

Cohendet, P., Kern, F., Mehmanpazir, B., & Munier, F. (1999). Knowledge coordination, competence creation and integrated networks in globalised firms. *Cambridge Journal of Economics*, *23*, 225–241. doi:10.1093/cje/23.2.225

Cohn, A. G., & Hazarika, S. M. (2001). Qualitative Spatial Representation and Reasoning: An Overview. *Fundamenta Informaticae*, *46*(1-2), 1–29.

Cohn, A. G., Bennett, B., Gooday, J., & Gotts, N. M. (1997). Qualitative Spatial Representation and Reasoning with the Region Connection Calculus. *GeoInformatica*, *1*(3), 275–316. doi:10.1023/A:1009712514511

Coleman, R. (1990). *Foundations of Social Theory.* Cambridge, MA: Belknap Press.

Connelly, C. E., & Kelloway, K. (2003). Predictors of employees' perceptions of knowledge sharing cultures. *Leadership and Organization Development Journal*, *24*(5/6), 294–301. doi:10.1108/01437730310485815

Connelly, C. E., Zweig, D., & Webster, J. (2006, May 5th - 7th, 2006). *Knowledge hiding in organizations.* Paper presented at the Society for Industrial and Organizational Psychology 20th Annual Conference, Dallas, TX.

Conner, K. R. (1991). A Historical Comparison of Resource-Based Theory and Five Schools of Thought within IIndustrial Organization Economics: Do We Have a New Theory of the Firm? *Journal of Management*, *17*(1), 121–154. doi:10.1177/014920639101700109

Conner, K. R., & Prahalad, C. K. (1996). A resource-based theory of the firm: Knowledge versus Opportunism. *Organization Science*, *7*(5), 477–501. doi:10.1287/orsc.7.5.477

Connerton, P. (1989). *How societies remember.* Cambridge: Cambridge University Press.

Constant, D., Kiesler, S., & Sproull, L. (1994). What's mine is ours, or is it? A study of attitudes about information sharing. *Information Systems Research*, *5*(5), 400–421. doi:10.1287/isre.5.4.400

Constant, D., Sproull, L., & Kiesler, S. (1997). The kindness of strangers: on the usefulness of electronic weak ties for technical advice. In S. Kiesler (ed.), *Culture of the Internet.* Mahwah, NJ: Lawrence Erlbaum Associates.

Cooper, B. L., Watson, H. J., Wixon, B. H., & Goodhue, D. L. (2000). Data Warehousing Supports Corporate Strategy at First American Corporation. *MIS Quarterly*, *24*(4), 547–567. doi:10.2307/3250947

Cooper, R. (1994). The inertial impact of culture on IT implementation. *Information Management, 27*(1), 17-31.

Corral, K., Griffin, J., & Jennex, M. E. (2005). Expert's perspective: The potential of knowledge management in Data Warehousing. *Business Intelligence Journal*, *10*(1), 36–40.

Cowan, R., David, P. A., & Foray, D. (2000). The explicit economics of knowledge codification and tacitness. *Industrial and Corporate Change*, *9*, 211–253. doi:10.1093/icc/9.2.211

Cramton, C. D. (2001). The mutual knowledge problem and its consequences for dispersed collaboration. *Organization Science*, *12*, 347–371. doi:10.1287/orsc.12.3.346.10098

Creplet, F., Dupouet, O., Kern, F., Mehmanpazir, B., & Munier, F. (2001). Consultants and experts in management consulting firms. *Research Policy*, *30*, 1517–1535. doi:10.1016/S0048-7333(01)00165-2

Cronin, B. (2001). Knowledge management, organizational culture and Anglo-American higher education. *Journal of Information Science, 27*(3), 129-137.

Cross, R., & Baird, L. (2000). Technology is not enough: Improving performance by building or-ganizational memory. *Sloan Management Review, 41*(3), 69-78.

Cross, R., Laseter, T., Parker, A., & Velasquez, G. (2006). Using Social Network Analysis to Improve Communities of Practice. *California Management Review*, *49*(1), 32–60.

Cross, R., Parker, A., Prusak, L., & Borgatti, S.P. (2001). Knowing what we know: Supporting knowledge creation and sharing in social networks. *Organizational Dynamics, 30*(2), 100-120.

Cummings, J. L., & Teng, B. (2003). Transferring R&D knowledge: The key factors affecting knowledge transfer success. *Journal of Engineering and Technology Management*, *20*, 39–68. doi:10.1016/S0923-4748(03)00004-3

Cummings, J.N., & Cross, R. (2003). Structural properties of work groups and their consequences for performance. *Social Networks, 25*(3), 197-210.

Cummings, T.G. (1978). Self-regulating work groups: A socio-technical synthesis. *Academy of Management Review, 11*, 625-634.

Daconta, M., Orbst, L., & Smith, K. (2003). *The Semantic Web*. Indianapolis: Wiley Publishing.

Daft, R. L., & Lengel, R. H. (1984). Information richness: A new approach to managerial behavior and organizational design. In L. Cummings & B. M. Staw (Eds.), *Research in Organizational Behavior* (Vol. 6). Homewood, IL: JAI Press.

Daft, R. L., Lengel, R. H., & Trevino, L. K. (1987). Message equivocality, media selection, and manager performance: Implications for information systems. *MIS Quarterly*, *11*(3), 355–366. doi:10.2307/248682

Daft, R.L., & Lengel, R.H. (1986). Organizational information requirements, media richness and structural design. *Management Science, 32*(5), 554-571.

Daft, R.L., & MacIntosh, N.B. (1981). A tentative exploration into the amount and equivocality of information processing in organizational work units. *Administrative Science Quarterly, 26*, 207-224.

Daft, R.L., & Weick, K. (1984). Toward a model of organizations as interpretation systems. *Academy of Management Review, 9*, 284-295.

Damanpour, F. (1991). Organizational innovation: A meta-analysis of effects of determinants and moderators. *Academy of Management Journal, 34*, 555-590.

Damodaran, L., & Olphert, W. (2000). Barriers and Facilitators to the Use of Knowledge Management Systems. *Behaviour & Information Technology*, *19*(6), 405–413. doi:10.1080/014492900750052660

Damodaran, L., & Olphert, W. (2000). Barriers and facilitators to the use of knowledge management systems.

Behaviour & Information Technology, 19, 405–413. doi:10.1080/014492900750052660

Daniel, B., Schwier, R. A., & McCalla, G. (2003). Social capital in virtual learning communities and distributed communities of practice. *Canadian Journal of Learning and Technology, 29*, 113–139.

Davenport, T. (1999). Knowledge management and the broader firm: Strategy, advantage and performance. In J. Leibowitz (Ed.), *Knowledge management handbook* (pp. 2-1 - 2-11). Boca Raton: CRC Press LLC.

Davenport, T. H. (1998). Teltech: The Business of Knowledge Management Case Study. Retrieved from http://www.bus.utexas.edu/kman/telcase.htm.

Davenport, T. H., & Probst, G. (2002). *Knowledge management book: Siemens best practices*. New York: John Wiley & Sons.

Davenport, T. H., & Prusak, L. (2000). *Working knowledge: How organizations manage what they know*. Boston: MA: Harvard Business School Press.

Davenport, T. H., De Long, D. W., & Beers, M. C. (1997). Building successful Knowledge Management Projects. *Center for Business Innovation Working Paper*, Ernst and Young.

Davenport, T. H., Long, D. W., & Beers, M. C. (1998). Successful knowledge management projects. *Sloan Management Review, 39*(2), 43–57.

Davenport, T. H., Thomas, R. J., & Cantrell, S. (2002). The mysterious art and science of knowledge-worker performance. *Sloan Management Review, 44*(1), 23–30.

Davenport, T., & Harris, J. G. (2007). *Competing on analytics: The new science of winning*. Harvard Business School Press.

Davenport, T., & Prusak, L. (1997). *Information ecology: mastering the information and knowledge environment*. New York: Oxford University Press.

Davenport, T.H., & Klahr, P. (1998). Managing customer support knowledge. *California Management Review, 40*(3), 195-208.

Davis, E. (1986). *Representing and acquiring geographic knowledge*. Los Altos, CA: Morgan Kaufmann Publishers, Inc.

Davis, E. (1990). *Representations of Commonsense Knowledge*. CA: Morgan Kaufmann.

Davis, F. D. (1989). Perceived Usefulness, Perceived Ease of Use, and User Acceptance of Information Technology. *MIS Quarterly, 13*(3), 319–341. doi:10.2307/249008

Davis, F., Bagozzi, R., & Warshaw, P. (1989). User acceptance of computer technology: A comparison of two theoretical models. *Management Science, 35*(8), 982-1003.

Davis, R., Shrobe, H., & Szobvits, P. (1993). What is Knowledge Representation? *AI Magazine, 14*(1), 17–33.

Dawes, R. M. (1994). *House of Cards: Psychology and Psychotherapy Built on Myth*. New York: Free Press.

De Long, D. W., & Fahey, L. (2000). Diagnosing cultural barriers to knowledge management. *Academy of Management Executive, 14*(4), 113-127.

Deal, K. (2004). The quest for prediction. *Marketing Research, 16*(4), 45–47.

Debowski, S. (2006). *Knowledge management*. Milton, QLD: John Wiley & Sons.

Decker, S., Erdmann, M., Fensel, D., & Studer, R. (1999). Ontobroker: Ontology Based Access to Distributed and Semi-Structured Information. In R. Meersman et al. (Eds.), *Semantic Issues in Multimedia Systems*. Boston: Kluwer Academic Publisher.

Deerwester, S., Dumais, S., Furnas, G., Laundauer, T., & Harshman, R. (1990). Indexing by Latent Semantic analysis. *Journal of the American Society for Information Science American Society for Information Science, 41*(6), 391–407. doi:10.1002/(SICI)1097-4571(199009)41:6<391::AID-ASI1>3.0.CO;2-9

Deetz, S. A. (1992). *Democracy in an Age of Corporate Colonization: Developments in Communication and the Politics of Everyday Life*. Albany: State University of New York Press.

Delaney, K. (March 15, 2007). Spam hits video sites, misleading web viewers. *Wall Street Journal*. B1-2.

Delfabbro, P., & Winefield, A. (2000). Predictors of irrational thinking in regular slot machine gamblers. *The Journal of Psychology, 134*, 117-128.

DeLone, W. H., & McLean, E. R. (1992). Information systems success: The quest for the dependent variable. *Information Systems Research, 3*, 60-95.

DeLone, W. H., & McLean, E. R. (2003). The DeLone and McLean model of information systems success: A ten-year update. *Journal of Management Information Systems, 19*(4), 9-30.

DeLong, D.W., & Fahey, L. (2000). Diagnosing cultural barriers to knowledge management, *Academy of Management Executive, 14*(4), 113-128.

Del-Rey-Chamorro, F. M., Roy, R., Wegan, B. V., & Steele, A. (2003). A framework to create key performance indicators for knowledge management solutions. *Journal of Knowledge Management, 7*(2), 46-62.

Dembla, P., & Mao, E. (2002). A research framework for knowledge management. In D. White (Ed.), *Knowledge mapping and management* (pp. 297-310). Hershey, PA: Idea Group Publishing.

Denning, S. (2000). *The Springboard: How Storytelling ignites action in knowledge-era organizations*. KMCI Press.

Dervin, B. (1989). Audience as listener and learner, teacher and confidante: The Sense-Making approach. In R. E. Rice & C. K. Atkin (Eds.), *Public communication campaigns* (2nd ed., pp. 67-86). Newbury Park, CA: Sage. Reprinted in: B. Dervin & L. Foreman-Wernet (with E. Lauterbach) (Eds.). (2003). *Sense-Making Methodology reader: Selected writings of Brenda Dervin* (pp. 215-232). Cresskill, NJ: Hampton Press.

Dervin, B. (1992). From the mind's eye of the user: The Sense-Making qualitative-quantitative methodology. In J. D. Glazier & R. R. Powell (Eds.), *Qualitative research in information management* (pp. 61-84). Englewood, CO: Libraries Unlimited.

Dervin, B. (1998, December). Sense-making theory and practice: an overview of user interests in knowledge seeking and use. *Journal of Knowledge Management, 2*(2), 36–46. doi:10.1108/13673279810249369

Dervin, B. (1999). Chaos, order and Sense-Making: A proposed theory for information design. In R. Jacobson (Ed.), *Information design*: 35-57. Cambridge, MA: MIT Press.

Dervin, B. (2003). Human studies and user studies: a call for methodological inter-disciplinarity. *Information Research, 9*(1). Retrieved from http://InformationR.net/ir/9-1/paper166.html

Dervin, B. (2003). Verbing communication: Mandate for disciplinary invention. In B. Dervin & L. Foreman-Wernet (with E. Lauterbach) (Eds.), *Sense-Making Methodology reader: Selected writings of Brenda Dervin* (pp. 101-110). Cresskill, NJ: Hampton Press.

Dervin, B. (2007). *Focus group for participatory research: design using systematic dialogic principles drawn from Sense-Making Methodology*. Paper presented at International Association of Media and Communication Research Meeting, Paris, France, UNESCO: July 23 – 25.

Dervin, B. (2008). *Interviewing as dialectical practice: Sense-Making Methodology as exemplar*. Paper presented at International Association of Media and Communication Research (IAMCR) Meeting, Stockholm, Sweden: July 20 – 25.

Dervin, B., & Foreman-Wernet, L. (2003) *Sense-Making Methodology Reader: selected writings of Brenda Dervin*. Cresskill, New Jersey: Hampton Press.

Dervin, B., & Naumer, C. (in press). Sense-Making. *Encyclopaedia of Library and Information Science*.

Dervin, B., & Reinhard, C. (in press). Communication and communication studies. *Encyclopaedia of Library and Information Science*.

Dewett, T., & Jones, G. (2001). The role of information technology in the organization: A review, model, and assessment. *Journal of Management, 27*(3), 313-346.

Dieng, R., et al. (2000). *Méthodes et outils pour la gestion des connaissances*. Paris: Dunod.

Dierickx, I., & Cool, K. (1989). Asset Stock Accumulation and Sustainablity of Competitive Advantage. *Management Science*, *35*(12), 1504–1510. doi:10.1287/mnsc.35.12.1504

Dillman, D.A. (2000). *Mail and internet surveys: The tailored methods* (2nd ed.). New York: John Wiley & Sons.

Dirks, K. T., & Ferrin, D. L. (2001). The role of trust in organizational settings. *Organization Science*, *12*, 450–467. doi:10.1287/orsc.12.4.450.10640

Dixon, N. M. (2000). *Common knowledge; How companies thrive by sharing what they know*. Boston: Harvard Business School Press.

Dixon, W.J., & Massey, F.J. Jr. (1969). *Introduction to statistical analysis*. New York, NY: McGraw-Hill.

Dodgson, M. (1993). Organizational learning: A review of some literatures. *Organization Studies, 14*(3), 375-394.

Donath, J. S. (1999). Identity and deception in the virtual community. In M. A. Kollock (Ed.), *Communities in Cyberspace* (pp. 29-59). London: Routledge.

Dooley, K. J., Corman, S. R., & McPhee, R. D. (2002). A Knowledge Directory for Identifying Experts and Areas of Expertise. *Human Systems Management*, *21*, 217–228.

Douglas, K. M., & McGarty, C. (2001). Identifiability and self-presentation: Computer-mediated communication and intergroup interaction. *The British Journal of Social Psychology*, *40*, 399–416. doi:10.1348/014466601164894

Dretske, F. (1991). *Explaining Behavior: Reasons in a World of Causes*. Cambridge, MA: MIT Press.

Drucker, P. (1993). *Post-capitalist society*. New York: Butterworth Heineman.

Drucker, P. (1995). *Managing in a time of great change*. New York: Truman Tally.

Dumais, S. T. (1990). Enhancing Performance in Latent Semantic Indexing Retrieval (Tech Rep TM-ARH-017527). Bellcore.

Duncan, R., & Weiss, A. (1979). *Organizational learning: Implications for organizational design. Research in organizational behavior*. Greenwich, CT: JAI Press Inc.

Durham, C. C., Knight, D., & Locke, E. A. (1997). Effects of leader role, team-set goal difficulty, efficacy, and tactics on team effectiveness. *Organizational Behavior and Human Decision Processes*, *72*, 203–231. doi:10.1006/obhd.1997.2739

Dustdar, S. (2005). Reconciling Knowledge Management and Workflow Management Systems: the Activity-based Knowledge Management Approach. *Journal of Universal Computer Science*, *11*(4), 589–604.

Earl, M. (2001). Knowledge management strategies: Toward a taxonomy. *Journal of Management Information Systems, 18*(1), 215-233.

Earl, M. J. (1983). Emerging trends in managing new information technologies. Oxford Centre for Management Studies Research Paper 83/4. In Boland, R. J. & Hirschheim, R. A. (Eds.) (1987), *Critical Issues in Information Systems Research*. Chichester: Wiley.

Earl, M. J. (1990). *Proceedings of the International Conference on Information Systems*. Copenhagen, Denmark.

Earl, M. J. (2001). Knowledge management strategies: Toward a taxonomy. *Journal of Management Information Systems, 18*(1), 215-233.

Earl, M. J. (2003). Approaches to Information Systems Planning: Experiences in strategic information systems planning. In D. Leidner & R. Galliers (Eds.), *Strategic Information Management*. Oxford: Butterworth-Heinemann/Elsevier.

Edwards, J.S., & Shaw, D. (2004). Supporting knowledge management with IT. In Proceedings of the DSS 2004 conference, July, Prato, Italy.

Egenhofer, M., & Herring, J. (1990). A Mathematical framework for the definition of Topological Relations.

Proceedings of 4th International Symposium on Spatial Data Handling, (pp. 803-813). Zurich, Switzerland.

Egenhofer, M.J. (1991). Reasoning about binary topological relations, Lecture notes

Egenhofer, M.J., & Franzosa, R.D. (1991). Point-set topological spatial relations. *International Journal of Geographic Information Systems, 5*(2), 161-174.

Egenhofer, M.J., & Franzosa, R.D. (1995). On equivalence of topological relations. *International Journal of Geographical Information Systems, 9*(2), 133-152.

Egenhofer, M.J., & Herring, J.R. (1991). *A mathematical framework for the definition of topological relations.* NCGIA technical paper 91-97

Egenhofer, M.J., & Herring, J.R. (1992). *Categorizing binary topological relations between regions, lines, and points in geographic databases.* Technical report, Department of Survey Engineering, University of Maine, Orono, ME.

Ehin, C. (2008). Un-managing knowledge workers. *Journal of Intellectual Capital, 9*(3), 337–350. doi:10.1108/14691930810891965

El Louadi, M. (1996, June 13-14). *Interaction between Organizational Structure and IT on Infor-mation Needs and Provision in Small Businesses.* Proceedings of the 41st International Conference on Small Business (ICSB) (pp. 195-216). Stockholm (Sweden).

El Louadi, M. (1998). The relationship among organizational structure. Information technology and information processing in small Canadian firms. *Canadian Journal of Administrative Sciences, 15*(2), 180-199.

Elder, J. F., IV, & Abbott, D. W. (1998). A comparison of leading data mining tools. *Fourth International Conference on Knowledge Discovery & Data Mining.* August 28, 1998. New York.

Elliott, S. (1997). Case Corporation's Pilot Effort Proves Value of Knowledge Management. *Knowledge Management in Practice*, 10.

Elliott, S. (1998). Broderbund Builds Stong 'Case' for Internal, External Knowledge Sharing. Knowledge Management in Practice(14).

Elliott, S., & O'Dell, C. (1999). Sharing Knowledge & Best Practices: The Hows and Whys of Tapping Your Organization's Hidden. *Health Forum Journal, 42*(3), 34.

Ensign, P. C. (1998). Interrelationships and horizontal strategy to achieve synergy and competitive advantage in the diversified firm. *Management Decision, 36*, 657–668. doi:10.1108/00251749810245318

Epple, D., & Argote, L. (1996). An Empirical Investigation of the Microstructure of Knowledge Acquisition and Transfer through Learning by doing. *Operations Research, 44*(1), 77–86. doi:10.1287/opre.44.1.77

Escrig, M. & Toledo, F. (2000). Qualitative Spatial Reasoning: Theory and Practice - Application to Robot Navigation. *Frontiers in AI and Applications, 47.*

European Committee for Standardization. (2004). *European guide to good practice in knowledge management - Part 1: Knowledge management framework CWA 14924-1:2004 (E)* (No. CWA 14924-1:2004 (E)). Brussels: European Committee for Standardization (Comite Europeen de Normalisation) CEN.

Ewusi-Mensah, K. (1981). The external organization environment and its impacts on management information systems. *Accounting, Organizations and Society, 6*(4), 301-316.

Expert Choice Inc. (2007). Expert Choice 11. Retrieved January 9, 2009, from http://www.expertchoice.com/software/

Fahey, L., & Prusak, L. (1998). The eleven deadliest sins of knowledge management. *California Management Review, 40*(3), 265.

Falk, R., & Miller, N. B. (1992). *A primer for soft modeling.* Akron, OH: University of Akron Press.

Faraj, S., & Sproull, L. (2000). Coordinating expertise in software development teams. *Management Science, 46*, 1554–1568. doi:10.1287/mnsc.46.12.1554.12072

Fayyad, U., Piatetsky-Shapiro, G., & Smyth, P. (1996). Knowledge discovery and data mining: Towards a unifying framework. In Proceedings of the Second International Conference on Knowledge Discovery and Data Mining, KDD-96, Oregon.

Feldman, M.S., & March, J.G. (1981). Information in organizations as signal and symbols. *Administrative Science Quarterly, 26*(2), 171-186.

Fennessy, G. (2002). Understanding and selecting knowledge management systems for a health information provider. In *Proceedings of the 35th Annual Hawaii International Conference on System Science, 7-10 Jan. 2002* (pp.638-645).

Fey, C. F., & Furu, P. (2008). Top management incentive compensation and knowledge sharing in multinational corporations. *Strategic Management Journal, 29*(12), 1301. doi:10.1002/smj.712

Fichter, D. (2006). Doing the monster mashup. *Online, 30*(4), 48–50.

Figallo, C. (1998). *Hosting Web Communities: Building Relationships, Increasing Customer Loyalty, and Maintaining a Competitive Edge*. New York: John Wiley & Sons.

Finnegan, P., & Sammon, D. (2002). Fundamentals of implementing data warehouseing in organizations. In S. Barnes (Ed.), *Knowledge Management Systems: Theory and Practice* (pp. 195-209). London: Thomson Learning.

Fiol, C. M., & O'Connor, E. J. (2005). Identification in face-to-face, hybrid, and pure virtual teams: untangling the contradictions. *Organization Science, 16*, 19–32. doi:10.1287/orsc.1040.0101

Firestone, J. (1999). Enterprise Knowledge Management Modeling and Distributed Knowledge Management Systems. Retrieved from http://www.dkms.com/EKMDKMS.html.

Fishbein, M. (1979). *A Theory of Reasoned Action: Some Applications and Implications.* Paper presented at the Nebraska Symposium on Motivation, Nebraska.

Fishbein, M., & Ajzen, I. (1975). *Belief, attitude, intention and behavior: An introduction to theory and research.* Reading, MA: Addison-Wesley.

Flood, R. L., & Jackson, M. C. (1991). *Creative Problem Solving: Total Systems Intervention.* Chichester: Wiley.

Flores, L. G., Catalanello, R. F., Rau, D., & Saxena, N. (2008). Organizational learning as a moderator of the effect of strategic planning on company performance. *International Journal of Management, 25*(3), 569–577.

Fontana, J. (2005). Microsoft's future in BI market unclear. *New World (New Orleans, La.), 22*(43), 9–14.

Forbes. (2005). IT Competitiveness Network Readiness Index 2005. Retrieved April 9, 2005 from http://www.forbes.com/technology/2005/03/09/cx_0309wefranking.html, see also http://www.weforum.org/pdf/Gcr/GITR_2003_2004/Rankings.pdf

Ford, D. P. (2008). *Disengagement from Knowledge Sharing: The Alternative Explanation for Why People Are Not Sharing.* Paper presented at the Administrative Sciences Association of Canada.

Ford, D. P., & Chan, Y. E. (2003). Knowledge sharing in a multi-cultural setting: A case study. *Knowledge Management Research and Practice, 1*(1), 11–27. doi:10.1057/palgrave.kmrp.8499999

Fornell, C., & Larcker, D. (1981). Evaluating structural equation models with unobservable variables and measurement error. *Journal of Marketing, 18*(1), 39-50.

Foss, N. J., & Mahnke, V. (2003). Knowledge management: What can organizational economics contribute? In M. Easterby-Smith & M. A. Lyles (Eds.), *The blackwell handbook of organizational learning and knowledge management* (pp. xx, 676). Malden, MA: Blackwell Pub.

Foss, N. J., Knudsen, C., & Montgomery, C. A. (1997). An Exploration of Common Ground: Integrating Evolutionary and Strategic Theories of the Firm. In C.A. Montgomery (Ed.), *Resources-Based and Evolutionary of the firm.* Boston: Kluwer Academic Publishers.

Foster, I. (2006). Globus toolkit version 4: Software for service-oriented systems. *J. Comput. Sci. & Technology, 21*(4), 513–520. doi:10.1007/s11390-006-0513-y

Fowler, S. W., Lawrence, T. B., & Morse, E. A. (2004). Virtual embedded ties. *Journal of Management, 30*(5), 647–666. doi:10.1016/j.jm.2004.02.005

Franco, M., & Mariano, S. (2007). Information technology repositories and knowledge management processes: a qualitative analysis. *The Journal of Information and Knowledge Management Systems, 37*(4), 440–451.

Fraser, V., Marcella, R., & Middleton, I. (2000). Employee perceptions of knowledge sharing: Employment threat or synergy for the greater good? *Competitive Intelligence Review, 11*(2), 39–52. doi:10.1002/(SICI)1520-6386(200032)11:2<39::AID-CIR7>3.0.CO;2-J

Freeze, R. (2006). *Relating Knowledge Management Capability to Organizational Outcomes*. Dissertation, Completed August 10, 2006

Freeze, R., & Kulkarni, U. (2008). Validating Distinct Knowledge Assets: A Capability erspective. *International Journal of Knowledge Management, 4*(4).

Galbraith, J. (1977). *Organization design.* Reading, MA: Addison-Wesley.

Galbraith, J. R. (1973). *Designing complex organizations.* Reading, MA: Addison-Wesley.

Galletta, D.F., Durcikova, A., Everard, A., & Jones, B. (2005). Does spell-checking software need a warning label? *Communications of the ACM, 48*(7), 82-85.

Galliers, R. D. (1987). Information systems planning in the United Kingdom and Australia: a comparison of current practice. In P. I. Zorkorczy (Ed.), *Oxford Surveys in Information Technology, Vol. 4* (pp. 223-255). Oxford: Oxford University Press.

Galliers, R. D., & Newell, S. (2003). Back to the future: from knowledge management to the management of information and data. *Information Systems and E-Business Management, 1*, 5–13. doi:10.1007/BF02683507

Galunic, C., & Weeks, J. (1999). Managing knowledge at Booz-Allen & Hamilton: Knowledge On-line and Off, INSEAD, Fontainebleau, France. Retrieved August 23, 2007 from http://faculty.insead.edu/weeks/documents/Galunic-and-Weeks-Booz.pdf

Gamble, P., & Blackwell, J. (2001). *Knowledge management: a state of art guide*. London: Kogan Page Limited.

Gammelgaard, J., & Ritter, T. (2005). The knowledge retrieval matrix: Codification and personification as separate strategies, *Journal of Knowledge Management, 9*(4), 133-143.

Gao, F., Li, M., & Nakamori, Y. (2002). Systems thinking on knowledge and its management: systems methodology for knowledge management. *Journal of Knowledge Management, 6*(1), 6–14. doi:10.1108/13673270210417646

Gardenfors, P., & Williams, M.-A. (2001). Reasoning about categories in conceptual spaces. In. *Proceedings of, IJCAI-01*, 385–392.

Garton, L., Haythornthwaite, C., & Wellman, B. (1997). Studying online social networks. *Journal of Computer-Mediated Communication, 3*(1), 75–105.

Gefen, D., Karahanna, E., & Straub, D. (2003). Inexperience and experience with online stores: The importance of TAM and trust. *IEEE Transactions on Engineering Management, 50*(3), 307-321.

Geroimenko, V., & Chen, C. (2003). *Visualizing the Semantic Web*. London: Springer.

Gertler, M. S. (2003). Tacit knowledge and the economic geography of context or the undefinable tacitness of being (there). *Journal of Economic Geography, 3*, 75–99. doi:10.1093/jeg/3.1.75

Ghemawat, P. (1986). Sustainable advantage. *Harvard Business Review*, (September-October): 53–58.

Gibson, J. J. (1977). The Theory of Affordances. In R. Shaw & J. Bransford (Eds.), *Perceiving, Acting, and Knowing*. Hillsdale, NJ: Lawrence Erlbaum.

Gill, P. J. (2001). Once Upon an Enterprise: The ancient art of storytelling emerges as a tool for knowledge management. *Knowledge Management, 4*(5), 24-28. Retrieved from http://www.destinationcrm.com/km/dcrm_km_article.asp?id=823

Gillam, C., & Oppenheim, C. (2006). Review article: Reviewing the impact of virtual teams in the information age. *Journal of Information Science, 32*(2), 160–175. doi:10.1177/0165551506062328

Giraud-Carrier, C., & Povel, O. (2003). Characterizing data mining software. *Intelligent Data Analysis, 7*(3), 181–192.

Girod, M.S. (1995). La mémoire organisationnelle [Organizational Memory]. *Revue Française de Gestion, 105*, 30-42.

Girod, M.S. (1996). Pour une définition opérationnelle et une modélisation de la mémoire or-ganisationnelle [Towards an Operational and Modelization Definition of Organizational Memory]. *In Proceedings of the 5th Conference of the Association Internationale de Management Stratégique* (AIMS). Lille, May.

Gist, M., Rosen, B., & Schwoerer, C. (1988). The influence of training method and trainee age on the acquisition of computer skills. *Personnel Psychology, 41*(2), 255-265.

Godfrey, P., & Hill, C. W. L. (1995). The problem of unobservables in strategic management research. *Strategic Management Journal, 16*, 519–533. doi:10.1002/smj.4250160703

Goel, L., & Mousavidin, E. (2007). vCRM: Virtual Customer Relationship Management. *The Data Base for Advances in Information Systems, 38*(4).

Goel, L., Junglas, I., & Ives, B. (2008). Virtual Worlds as Platforms for Communities of Practice. In King, W., (Ed.), *Annals of Information System series on Knowledge Management and Organizational Learning*. Springer.

Goffee, R., & Jones, G. (1996). What holds the modern company together? *Harvard Business Review, 74*(6), 133-148.

Gold, A.H., Malhotra, A., & Segars, A.H. (2001). Knowledge management: An organizational capabilities perspective. *Journal of Management Information Systems, 18*(1), 185-214.

Goodhue, D. L., & Thompson, R. L. (1995). Task-Technology Fit and Individual Performance. *MIS Quarterly, 19*(2), 213–236. doi:10.2307/249689

Goodman, E., & Moed, A. (2006) Community in Mashups: The Case of Personal Geodata. Retrieved March 4, 2007, from http://mashworks.net/images/5/59/Goodman_Moed_2006.pdf

Goodman, M. (1990). Prism: A case-based telex classfier. In A. Rappaport & R. Smith (Eds.), Innovative applications of artificial intelligence (Vol. 2). Boston, MA: MIT Press.

Goodwill, J., & Hightower, R. (2004). *Professional Jakarta struts*. Hoboken, NJ: Wiley.

Gordon, R., & Grant, D. (2005). Knowledge Management or Management of Knowledge? Why People Interested in Knowledge Management Need to Consider Foucault and the Construct of Power. *Journal of Critical Postmodern Organization Science, 3*(2), 27–38.

Graham, S. (1998). The end of geography or the explosion of place? Conceptualizing space, place and information technology. *Progress in Human Geography, 22*(2), 165-185

Granovetter, M. (1973). The strength of weak ties. *American Journal of Sociology, 78*, 1360–1380. doi:10.1086/225469

Granovetter, M. (1985). Economic action and social structure: The problem of embeddedness. *American Journal of Sociology, 91*(3), 481-510

Grant, R. M. (1991). The resource-based theory of competitive advantage: Implications for strategy formulation. *California Management Review, 33*(3), 113–135.

Grant, R. M. (1996). Prospering in Dynamically-Competitive Environments: Organizational Capability as Knowledge Integration. *Organization Science, 4*(July-August), 375–387. doi:10.1287/orsc.7.4.375

Grant, R. M. (1996). Toward a knowledge-based theory of the firm. *Strategic Management Journal, 17*(Winter Special Issue), 109-122.

Grant, R. M. (2002). The Knowledge-based view of the firm. In N. Bontis & C. W. Choo (Eds.), *The Strategic Management of Intellectual Capital and Organizational Knowledge.* Oxford, U.K.: Oxford University Press.

Gray, M. (2007, February 8). *Open access from the perspective of the NHS BioMed Central Colloquium.* The Royal College of Physicians, London, UK

Gray, P. H., & Meister, D. B. (2004). Knowledge sourcing effectiveness. *Management Science, 50*(6), 821–834. doi:10.1287/mnsc.1030.0192

Gray, R. (2003). A Brief Historical Review of the Development of the Distinction Between Data and Information in the Information Systems Literature. *Ninth Americas Conference on Information Systems*, Tampa Bay, FL (pp. 2843-2849).

Grover, V., & Davenport, T. (2001). General perspectives on knowledge management: Fostering a research agenda. *Journal of Management Information Systems, 18*(1), 5.

Grover, V., & Davenport, T. H. (2001). General perspectives on knowledge management: Fostering a research agenda. *Journal of Management Information Systems, 18*(1), 5–21.

Gruman, G. (2006). Enterprise mashups. *InfoWorld, 28*(31). Retrieved March 4, 2007, from http://www.infoworld.com/article/06/07/28/31FEmashup_1.html

Gupta, A. (2008). *Outsourcing and offshoring of professional services.* Hershey, PA: IGI Global.

Gupta, A. (2009). The 24-hour knowledge factory: Can it replace the graveyard shift? *IEEE Computer Magazine*, 66-77.

Gupta, A. K., & Govindarajan, V. (2000). Knowledge flows within multinational corporations. *Strategic Management Journal, 21*(4), 473. doi:10.1002/(SICI)1097-0266(200004)21:4<473::AID-SMJ84>3.0.CO;2-I

Gupta, A. K., Govindarajan, V., & Malhorta, A. (1999). Feedback-seeking behavior within multinational corporations. *Strategic Management Journal, 20*, 205–222. doi:10.1002/(SICI)1097-0266(199903)20:3<205::AID-SMJ17>3.0.CO;2-H

Gupta, A.K., & Govindarajan, V. (2000). Knowledge flows within multinational corporations. *Strategic Management Journal, 21*(4), 473-496.

Gurcan, M., Pan, T., & Sharma, A. (2007). Gridimage: A novel use of grid computing to support interactive human and computer-assisted detection decision support. *Journal of Digital Imaging, 20*(2), 160–171. doi:10.1007/s10278-007-9020-0

Habermas, J. (1984). *The Theory of Communicative Action.* Boston: Beacon Press.

Hackett, B. (2000). *Beyond knowledge management: New ways to work and learn* (Research Report No. 1261-00-RR). New York: The Conference Board.

Hackman, J. R., & Oldham, G. R. (1980). *Work redesign.* Reading, MA: Addison-Wesley.

Hadzilacos, T., & Tryfona, N.. (1992). A Model for Expressing Topological Integrity Constraints in Geographic Databases. In A. Frank, I. Campari, & U. Formentini (Eds.), *Proceedings of the International Conference on Theories and Models of Spatio Temporal Reasoning in Geographic Space.* Pisa, Italy. Lecture notes in Computer Science, Vol. 639 (Springer Verlag, New York), (pp. 252-268).

Hahn, J., & Subramani, M. R. (2000). A Framework of Knowledge Management Systems: Issues and Challenges for Theory and Practice. In *Proceedings of 21st International Conference on Information Systems* (pp. 302–312).

Håkanson, L. (2007). Creating knowledge – the power and logic of articulation. *Industrial and Corporate Change, 16*(1), 51–88. doi:10.1093/icc/dtl033

Hall, R. (1992). The strategic analysis of intangible resources. *Strategic Management Journal, 13*, 135–144. doi:10.1002/smj.4250130205

Hammer, M., Leonard, D., & Davenport, T. H. (2004). Why Don't We Know More About Knowledge? *MIT Sloan Management Review*, *45*(4), 14–18.

Handley, K., Sturdy, A., Fincham, R., & Clark, T. (2006). Within and beyond communities of practice: making sense of learning through participation, identity, and practice. *Journal of Management Studies*, *43*(3), 641–653. doi:10.1111/j.1467-6486.2006.00605.x

Handzic, M. (2004). *Knowledge management: Through the technology glass*. Singapore: World Scientific Publishing.

Handzic, M. (2007, July 3-6). Supporting decision makers with knowledge management systems. In Proceedings of the 11th Pacific Asia Conference on Information Systems (PACIS 2007) (pp. 46-54). Auckland, New Zealand.

Handzic, M., & Chaimungkalanont, M. (2004). Enhancing organisational creativity through socialization. *The Electronic Journal of Knowledge Management, 2*(1), 57-64.

Handzic, M., & Zhou, A.Z. (2005). *Knowledge management: An integrative approach*. Oxford, UK: Chandos Publishing.

Handzic, M., Lagumdzija, A., & Celjo, A. (2008). Auditing knowledge management practices in local government: Model and application. *Knowledge Management Research and Practice, 6*(1), 90-99.

Hansen, H. (2006). The ethnonarrative approach. *Human Relations, 59*(8), 1049-1075.

Hansen, M. T. (1999). The search-transfer problem: the role of weak ties in sharing knowledge across organization subunits. *Administrative Science Quarterly*, *44*, 82–111. doi:10.2307/2667032

Hansen, M. T., Nohria, N., & Tierney, T. (1999). What's your strategy for managing knowledge? *Harvard Business Review*, *77*(2), 106–118.

Hansen, M.T. (1999). The search-transfer problem: The role of weak ties in sharing knowledge across organization subunits. *Administrative Science Quarterly, 44*(1), 82-111.

Hansen, M.T., & von Oetinger, B. (2001). Introducing T-shaped managers: Knowledge management's next generation. *Harvard Business Review, 3*, 107-116.

Hansen, M.T., Nohria, N., & Tierney, T. (1999). What's your strategy for managing knowledge? *Harvard Business Review, 77*(2), 106-116.

Hardwig, J. (1991). The Role of Trust in Knowledge. *The Journal of Philosophy*, *88*(12), 693–708. doi:10.2307/2027007

Harigopal, U., & Satyadas, A. (2001). Cognizant enterprise maturity model (CEMM). *IEEE Transactions on Systems, Man and Cybernetics. Part C, Applications and Reviews*, *31*(4), 449–459. doi:10.1109/5326.983928

Hart, D., & Warne, L. (2006). Comparing cultural and political perspectives of data, information, and knowledge sharing in organizations. *International Journal of Knowledge Management*, *2*(2), 1–15.

Hasanali, F. (2004). Critical success factors of knowledge management. In E. Koenig & Srikantaiah (Eds.), *Knowledge management. Lessons learned* (pp. 55-69). Medford, NJ: ASIST Monograph Series.

Haseman, W. D., Nazareth, D. L. et al. (2005). Implementation of a group decision support system utilizing collective memory. *Information and Management, 42*, 591-605.

Hasen, M. T., Nohria, N., & Tierney, T. (1999). What's your strategy for managing knowledge. *Harvard Business Review, March-April*, 106-116.

Hasher, L., & Zacks, R. T. (1979). Automatic and effortful processes in memory. *Journal of Experimental Psychology. General*, *108*(3), 356–388. doi:10.1037/0096-3445.108.3.356

Hatcher, L. (1994). *A step-by-step approach to using the SAS® system for factor analysis and structural equation modeling*. The SAS Institute, Cary, N.C.

Haughton, D., Deichmann, J., Eshghi, A., Sayek, S., Teebagy, N., & Topi, A. (2003). A review of software packages for data mining. *The American Statistician*, *57*(4), 290–309. doi:10.1198/0003130032486

Hauschild, S., Licht, T., & Stein, W. (2001). Creating a knowledge culture. *The McKinsey Quarterly, 1*, 74-81.

Hayes-Roth, F., Waterman, D., & Lenat, D. (1983). *Building expert systems.* Reading, MA: Addison-Wesley Publishing Company.

Hedberg, B. (1981). How organizations learn and unlearn. In P.C. Nystrom & W.H. Starbuck (Eds.), *Handbook of organizational design* (pp. 8-27). London.

Heidegger, M. (1962). *Being and time*. New York: Harper & Row

Hemaida, R., & Schmits, J. (2006). An analytical approach to vendor selection. *Industrial Management (Des Plaines)*, *48*(3), 18–24.

Henderson, J. C., & Venkatraman, N. (1993). Strategic Alignment: Leveraging Information Technology for Transforming Organizations. *IBM Systems Journal*, *32*(1).

Henderson, J.C., & Lee, S. (1992). Managing is design teams: A control theories perspective. *Management Science, 38*(6), 757-777.

Henry, C.M. (1998). Challenge of global capital markets to information-shy regimes: The case of Tunisia. Abu Dhabi. *The Emirates Center for Strategic Studies and Research, 53*(19).

Herschel, R., Nemati, H., & Steiger, D. (2001). Tacit to Explicit Knowledge Conversion: Knowledge Exchange Protocols. *Journal of Knowledge Management*, *5*(1), 107–116. doi:10.1108/13673270110384455

Herschel, R., Nemati, H., & Steiger, D. (2003). Knowledge Exchange Protocols: A Second Study. *Journal of Information and Knowledge Management: Special issue of JIKM on Knowledge Management in Context and Context for Knowledge Management*, *2*(2), 153–163.

Hibbard, J., & Carrillo, K. M. (1998). Knowledge revolution. *Informationweek*, *663*, 49–54.

Hicks, B. J., Culley, S. J., Allen, R. D., & Mullineux, G. (2002). A Framework for the Requirements of Capturing, Storing and Reusing Information and Knowledge in Engineering Design. *International Journal of Information Management*, *22*, 263–280. doi:10.1016/S0268-4012(02)00012-9

Hildreth, P. M., & Kimble, C. (2002, October). The duality of knowledge. *Information Research, 8*(1). Retrieved from http://informationr.net/ir/8-1/paper142.html

Hill, W., Stead, L., Rosenstein, M., & Furnas, G. (1995). Recommending and evaluating choices in a virtual community of use. *SIGCHI Conference on Human factors in computing systems.* Denver: Colorado.

Hippel, E. V. (1994). "Sticky Information" and the Locus of Problem Solving: Implications for Innovation. *Management Science*, *40*(4), 429–440. doi:10.1287/mnsc.40.4.429

Hirschheim, R., Klein, H. K., & Lyytinen, K. (1996). Exploring the intellectual structures of information systems development: a social action theoretical analysis. *Accounting. Management & Information Technology*, *6*(1), 1–64. doi:10.1016/0959-8022(96)00004-5

Hjerland, B (2003). Fundamentals of Knowledge organization. *Knowledge organization, 30*(2), 87-111.

Hodge, G. (2006). *Systems of knowledge organization for digital libraries: Beyond traditional authority files.* Washington, DC: The Digital Library Federation.

Hof, R. D. (2005, July 25). Mix, match, and mutate. *Business Week*, *3942*, 72.

Hofstede, G. (1980). *Culture's Consequences: International Differences in Work-related Values.* Beverly Hills CA: Sage.

Hofstede, G. (1991). *Cultures and organizations: Software of the mind.* New York: McGraw-Hill.

Hofstede, G. (2001). *Culture's consequences: Comparing values, behaviors, institutions, and organizations across nations.* Thousand Oaks, CA: Sage Publications.

Hofstede, G., Neuijen, B., Ohayv, D. D., & Sanders, G. (1990). Measuring organizational cultures: A qualilative and quantitative study across twenty cases. *Administrative Science Quarterly, 35*(2), 286-316.

Hollan, J., Hutchins, E. et al. (2000). Distributed cognition: Toward a new foundation for human-computer interaction research. *ACM Transactions on Computer-Human Interaction (TOCHI), 7(*2), 174-196.

Holsapple, C. W., & Joshi, K. (2004). A formal knowledge management ontology: Conduct, activities, resources, and influences. *Journal of the American Society for Information Science and Technology, 55*(7), 593-612.

Holsapple, C. W., & Joshi, K. D. (1998). In search of a descriptive framework for knowledge management: preliminary Delphi results. *Kentucky Initiative for Knowledge Management.* Paper No. (118).

Holsapple, C. W., & Joshi, K. D. (2002). Knowledge management: A threefold framework. *The Information Society*(18), 47-64.

Holsapple, C., & Joshi, K. (2000). An investigation of factors that influence the management of knowledge in organisations. *Journal of Strategic Information Systems, 9(*2-3), 235-261.

Holsapple, C., & Joshi, K. D. (2002). Knowledge management: A three-fold framework. *The Information Society, 18,* 47-64.

Holzner, B., & Marx, J. (1979). *The Knowledge Application: the Knowledge System in Society.* Boston: Allyn-Bacon.

Hornett, A., & Stein, E. W. (2007). Mapping the knowledge management domain of ideas: evidence from a practice group. *International Journal of Knowledge Management, 3*(3), 1–25.

Hoyle, R. H., & Panter, A. T. (1995). Writing about structural equation modeling. In R. H. Hoyle (Ed.), *Structural equation modeling: Concepts, issues, and applications* (pp. 158-176). Thousand Oaks, CA: Sage Publications.

Hu, L.-T., & Bentler, P. M. (1999). Cutoff criteria for fit indexes in covariance structure analysis: Conventional criteria versus new alternatives. *Structural Equation Modeling, 6*(1), 1-55.

Hu, P. J., Chau, P. Y. K., Sheng, O. R. L., & Tam, K. Y. (1999). Examining the technology acceptance model using physician acceptance of telemedicine technology. *Journal of Management Information Systems, 16(2),* 91-112.

Hu, W., Miller, W., & Nilakanta, S. (1998). PROMIS: A profiler of organizational memory and institutional systems. In *Proceedings of the International Conference of Information Resources Management Association,* Boston, MA, (pp. 399-405).

Huang, E. (2007). PS3 doubles folding@home's processing power. *Gamepro.com.*

Huang, Q., Davison, R. M., & Gu, J. (2008). Impact of personal and cultural factors on knowledge sharing in china. *Asia Pacific Journal of Management, 25*(3), 451. doi:10.1007/s10490-008-9095-2

Huber, G. (2001). Transfer of knowledge in knowledge management systems: unexplored issues and suggested studies. *European Journal of Information Systems, 10,* 72–79. doi:10.1057/palgrave.ejis.3000399

Huber, G. P. (1991). Organizational learning: The contributing process and the literatures. *Organization Science, 2,* 88–115. doi:10.1287/orsc.2.1.88

Huber, G. P., Davenport, T. H., & King, D. (1998). Some perspectives on organizational memory. In. F. Burstein, G. Huber, M., Mandviwalla, J. Morrison, & L. Olfman, (Eds.), *Task Force on Organizational Memory.* Presented at the 31st Annual Hawaii International Conference on System Sciences.

Huber, G.P. (1984). The nature and design of post-industrial organizations. *Management Science, 30*(8), 928-951.

Huber, G.P. (1990). A theory of the effects of advanced information technologies on organizational design, intelligence, and decision making. *Academy of Management Review, 15*(1), 47-71.

Hult, G.T.M. (2003). An integration of thoughts on knowledge management. *Decision Sciences, 34*(2), 189-195.

Husted, K., & Michailova, S. (2002). Diagnosing and fighting knowledge-sharing hostility. *Organizational Dynamics, 31*(1), 60–73. doi:10.1016/S0090-2616(02)00072-4

Huysman, M. H., Fischer, S. J., & Heng, M. S. H. (1994). An organizational learning perspective on information systems planning. *Journal of Strategic Information Systems, (3)*3, 165-177.

Huysman, M., Steinfield, C., Jang, C., & David, K., Huis In 'T Veld, M., Poot, J. & Mulder, I. (2003). Virtual Teams and the appropriation of communication technology: exploring the concept of media stickiness. *Computer Supported Cooperative Work, 12*, 411–436. doi:10.1023/A:1026145017609

Ibarra, H. (1999). Provisional selves: experimenting with image and identity in professional adaptation. *Administrative Science Quarterly, 44*, 764–791. doi:10.2307/2667055

Igbaria, M., Parasuraman, S., & Baroudi, J. J. (1996). A motivational model of microcomputer usage. *Journal of Management Information Systems, 13*(1), 127-143.

Ingram, P., & Simons, T. (2002). The transfer of experience in groups of organizations: Implications for performance and competition. *Management Science, 48*(12), 1517–1533. doi:10.1287/mnsc.48.12.1517.437

Inkpen, A. C. (2005). Learning through Alliances: General Motors and NUMMI. *California Management Review, 47*(4), 114–136.

Inkpen, A. C., & Tsang, E. W. K. (2005). Social capital, networks, and knowledge transfer. *Academy of Management Review, 30*(1), 146–165.

Inside the Cubicle. (September, 2006). Southwest employers share a defining moment. Retrieved from http://insidethecubicle.blogs.com/blog/2006/09/southwest_emplo.html

IT Governance Institute, & COBIT Steering Committee. (2000). *COBIT Framework* (3rd ed.). Rolling Meadows, IL: IT Governance Institute.

IT Infrastructure Library. (2007). Retrieved from http://www.itil.co.uk/

ITU. (2003, December 9). World Telecommunication Development Report – Access Indicators for the Information Society. *International Telecommunication Union.*

Jacobs, D. (1996). *The Knowledge Offensive: Compete Smartly in the Knowledge Society.* Netherlands: Alphen Aaan den.

James, G., Hakim, J., Chandras, R., King, N., & Variar, G. (2004). Reviewers' choice: Only the best survive. *Intelligent Enterprise, 7*(1), 34–38.

Jamieson, R., & Handzic, M. (2003). A framework for security, control and assurance of knowledge management systems. In C. W. Holsapple (Ed.), *Handbook on knowledge management 1: Knowledge matters* (Vol. 1, pp. 477-505). Berlin: Springer-Verlag.

Janz, B.D., & Prasarnphanich, P. (2003). Understanding the antecedents of effective knowledge management: The importance of a knowledge-centered culture. *Decision Sciences, 34*(2), 351-384.

Jarvenpaa, S. L., & Leidner, D. E. (1999). Communication and trust in global virtual teams. *Organization Science, 10*, 791–815. doi:10.1287/orsc.10.6.791

Jarvenpaa, S. L., & Staples, D. S. (2000). The Use of Collaborative Electronic Media for Information Sharing: An Exploratory Study of Determinants. *The Journal of Strategic Information Systems, 9*(2/3), 129–154. doi:10.1016/S0963-8687(00)00042-1

Jarvenpaa, S.L., & Staples, D.S. (2001). Exploring perceptions of organizational ownership of information and expertise. *Journal of Management Information Systems, 18(*1), 151-183.

Jashapara, A. (2004). *Knowledge management: an integrated approach.* Harlow, England: Prentice-Hall.

Jennex, M. E. (2000). Using an intranet to manage knowledge for a virtual Project team. In D. G. Schwartz, M. Diivitini, & T. Brasethvik (Eds.) *Internet-Based Organizational Memory and Knowledge Management* (pp. 241-259). Hershey, PA: Idea Group Publishing.

Jennex, M. E. (2005a). What is Knowledge Management? *International Journal of Knowledge Management, 1*(4), i–iv.

Jennex, M. E. (2006). Technologies in support of knowledge management systems, *6th International Forum on Knowledge Management* - Tunis, April, 2006.

Jennex, M. E., & Olfman, L. (2002). Organizational memory/knowledge effects on productivity, A longitudinal study. In *Proceedings of the 35th Hawaii International Conference on System Sciences, HICSS35*, IEEE Computer Society.

Jennex, M. E., & Olfman, L. (2005). Assessing Knowledge management Success. *International Journal of Knowledge Management, 1*(2), 33–49.

Jennex, M. E., & Olfman, L. (2006). A Model of Knowledge Management Success. *International Journal of Knowledge Management, 2*(3), 51–68.

Jennex, M. E., Olfman, L., & Addo, T. B. A. (2003). The Need for an Organizational Knowledge Management Strategy. *36th Hawaii International Conference on System Sciences, HICSS36*. IEEE Computer Society.

Jennex, M. E., Smolnik, S., & Croasdell, D. (2007). Knowledge Management Success. *International Journal of Knowledge Management, 3*(2), i–vi.

Jennex, M. E., Smolnik, S., & Croasdell, D. (2008, January). *Towards Measuring Knowledge management Success*. Paper presented at the 41st Hawaii International Conference on System Sciences, HICSS41. IEEE Computer Society.

Jennex, M., & Croasdell, D. (2004). Knowledge management, organizational memory & organ-izational learning cluster. In Proceedings of the 37th Hawaii International Conference on System Sciences, Hawaii, 1.

Jennex, M., & Olfman, L. (2000). Development recommendations for knowledge management/ organizational memory systems. In *Proceedings of the Information Systems Development Conference*.

Jennex, M., & Olfman, L. (2002). Organizational memory/knowledge effects on productivity, a longitudinal study. In *Proceedings of the 35th Annual Hawaii International Conference on System Sciences*.

Jennex, M., & Olfman, L. (2004). Assessing Knowledge Management success/Effectiveness Models. In *Proceedings of the 37th Hawaii International Conference on System Sciences*.

Jennex, M., & Olfman, L. (2005). Assessing knowledge management success. *International Journal of Knowledge Management, 1*(2), 33-49.

Jennex, M., & Zyngier, S. (2008). Security as a contributor to knowledge management success. information systems frontiers. *A Journal of Research and Innovation, 9*(5), 493–504.

Jennex, M.E., & Olfman, L. (2006). A model of knowledge management success. *International Journal of Knowledge Management, 2*(3), 51-68.

Jennix, E. (2005). *Case studies in knowledge management*. Hershey, PA: Idea Group Publishing.

Jhingran, A. (2006). Enterprise information mashups: Integrating information, simply. *VLDB'06, 32,* 3-4.

Ji, Y.G., & Salvendy, G. (2004). Interface methods for using intranet portal organizational memory information system. *Ergonomics, 47(*15), 1585-1597.

Jones, G. R., & George, J. M. (1998). The experience and evolution of trust: Implications for cooperation and teamwork. *Academy of Management Review, 23*, 531–546. doi:10.2307/259293

Jones, Q. (1997). Virtual-Communities, virtual settlements and cyber archeology: A theoretical outline. *Journal of Computer-Mediated Communication, 3*(3).

Jones, Q., & Rafaeli, S. (2000). Time to Split, Virtually: 'Discourse Architecture' and 'Community Building' Create Vibrant Virtual Publics. *Electronic Markets, 10*(4), 214–223. doi:10.1080/101967800750050326

Jones, Q., Ravid, G., & Rafaeli, S. (2004). Information Overload and the Message Dynamics of Online Interaction Spaces: A Theoretical Model and Empirical Exploration. *Information Systems Research, 15*(2), 194–210. doi:10.1287/isre.1040.0023

Jones, S. (2002). Employee rights, employee responsibilities and knowledge sharing in intelligent organization. *Employee Responsibilities and Rights Journal, 14*(2-3), 69–78. doi:10.1023/A:1021119503782

Judd, C.M., Smith, E.R., & Kidder, L.H. (1991). *Research methods in social relations* (6th ed.). Harcourt Brace Jovanovich College Publishers.

Kahn, W. A. (1990). Psychological conditions of personal engagement and disengagement at work. *Academy of Management Journal, 33*, 692–724. doi:10.2307/256287

Kahn, W. A. (1992). To Be Fully There: Psychological Presence at Work. *Human Relations, 45*(4), 321. doi:10.1177/001872679204500402

Kane, A. A., Argote, L., & Levine, J. (2005). Knowledge transfer between groups via personnel rotation: Effects of social identity and knowledge quality. *Organizational Behavior and Human Decision Processes, 96*(1), 56–71. doi:10.1016/j.obhdp.2004.09.002

Kane, A. A., Argote, L., & Levine, J. M. (2005). Knowledge transfer between groups via personnel rotation: Effects of social identity and knowledge quality. *Organizational Behavior and Human Decision Processes, 96*(1), 56–71. doi:10.1016/j.obhdp.2004.09.002

Kang, Y., Kim, S., & Chang, G. (2008). The impact of knowledge sharing on work performance: An empirical analysis of the public employees' perceptions in South Korea. *International Journal of Public Administration, 31*(14), 1548. doi:10.1080/01900690802243607

Kankanhalli, A., Tan, B. C. Y., & Kwok-Kee, W. (2005). Understanding seeking from electronic knowledge repositories: An empirical study. *Journal of the American Society for Information Science and Technology, 56*(11), 1156–1166. doi:10.1002/asi.20219

Kankanhalli, A., Tan, B. C. Y., & Wei, K.-K. (2005). Contributing knowledge to electronic knowledge repositories: An empirical investigation. *MIS Quarterly, 29*(1), 113–143.

Kankanhalli, A.M., Tanudidjaja, F., Sutanto, J., & Tan, B.C.Y. (2003). Role of information technology in successful knowledge management initiatives. Communications of the ACM, 46(9), 69-73.

Kaplan, R. S., & Norton, D. P. (1992). The balanced scorecard, the measures that drive performance. *Harvard Business Review, 70*(1), 47-54.

Kasper-Fuehrer, E. C., & Ashkanasy, N. (2001). Communicating trustworthiness and building trust in interorganizational virtual organizations. *Journal of Management, 27*, 235–254. doi:10.1016/S0149-2063(01)00090-3

Kelleher, D., Levene, S., & PriceWaterhouse Coopers. (2001). *PAS 2001 Knowledge Management: A guide to good practice*. London: British Standards Institution

Kelly, S., & Jones, M. (2001). Groupware and the social infrastructure of communication. *Communications of the ACM, 44*(12), 77-79.

Kemp, J., Pudlatz, M., Perez, P., & Ortega, A. M. (2002). *KM framework; European KM Forum IST Project No 2000-26393*: The European KM Forum Consortium European Commission.

Keskin, H. (2005). The relationships between explicit and tacit oriented KM strategy, and firm performance. *The Journal of American Academy of Business, 7*, 169–173.

Kidder, L., & Judd, C. M. (1986). *Research methods in social relations* (5th ed.). New York: Holt, Rhinehardt, and Winston.

Kiluge, J., Stein, W., & Licht, T. (2001). Knowledge Unplugged: the McKinsey global survey on Knowledge management.

Kim, L. (2001). Absorptive capacity, co-opetition, and knowledge creation: Samsung's leapfrogging in semiconductors. In I. Nonaka and T. Nishiguchi (Eds), *Knowledge emergence: social, technical, and evolutionary dimensions of knowledge creation*. Oxford: Oxford University Press.

King, W. R. (2006). The Critical Role of Information Processing in Creating an Effective Knowledge Organization. *Journal of Database Management, 17*(1), 1–15.

King, W. R., Marks, P. V., & McCoy, S. (2002). The most important issues in knowledge management. *Communications of the ACM, 45*(9), 93–97. doi:10.1145/567498.567505

Klein, G. (1998). *Sources of power*. Camridge, MA: The MIT Press.

Klein, K. J., & Sorra, J. S. (1996). The challenge of innovation implementation. *Academy of Management Review, 21*(4), 1055-1080.

Klien, A. (2007). A rule-based strategy for the semantic annotation of geodata. *Transactions in GIS, 11*(3), 437–452.

Kluge, J., Wolfram, S., & Licht, T. (2001). *Knowledge Unplugged: The McKinsey & Company global survey on knowledge management*. Palgrave Macmillan.

Knowledge organization. (n.d.). Retrieved January 7, 2009, from http://en.wikipedia.org/wiki/Knowledge

Knowledge. (n.d.). Retrieved January 7, 2009, from http://en.wikipedia.org/wiki/Knowledge_organization

Ko, D.-G., Kirsch, L. J., & King, W. R. (2005). Antecedents of knowledge transfer from consultants to clients in enterprise system implementations. *MIS Quarterly, 29*(1), 59–85.

Koeglreiter, G., Smith, R., & Torlina, L. (2006). The Role of Informal Groups in Organisational Knowledge Work: Understanding an Emerging Community of Practice. *International Journal of Knowledge Management, 2*(1), 6–23.

Koestler, A. (1964). *The act of creation*. London: Arkana, Penguin Group.

Kogut, B., & Zander, U. (1992). Knowledge of the firm: combinative capabilities, and the replication of technology. *Organization Science, 3*, 383–397. doi:10.1287/orsc.3.3.383

Koh, J., & Kim, Y.-G. (2004). Knowledge sharing in virtual communities: an e-business perspective. *Expert Systems with Applications, 26*, 155–166. doi:10.1016/S0957-4174(03)00116-7

Kohlhase, M., & Anghelache, R. (2003). Towards Collaborative Content Management and Version Control for Structured Mathematical Knowledge. In *Proceedings of Second International Conference on Mathematical Knowledge Management (MKM).*

Korac-Kakabadse, N., & Kakabadse, A. (2001). IS/IT Governance: need for an integrated model. *Corporate Governance, 1*(4), 9-11.

Korthaus, A., Henke, S., Aleksy, M., & Schader, M. (2006). A distributed topic map architecture for enterprise knowledge management. In *Proceedings of the 5th IEEE/ACIS International Conference on Computer and Information Science, ICIS-COMSAR 2006*, (pp. 96-102).

Koskinen, K. U. (2003). Evaluation of tacit knowledge utilization in work units. *Journal of Knowledge Management, 7*(5), 67–81. doi:10.1108/13673270310505395

KPMG. (2000). *Knowledge management research report 2000*. Retrieved from www.insite.cz/data/kpmg_km_report2000.pdf

Kransdorff, A. (1998). *Corporate amnesia: Keeping know-how in the company*. New York, NY: Butterworth-Heinemann.

Kraut, R., Patterson, M., Lundmark, V., Kiesler, S., Mukopadhyay, T., & Scherlis, W. (1998). Internet paradox. *The American Psychologist, 53*, 1017–1031. doi:10.1037/0003-066X.53.9.1017

Krippendorff, K. (1975). Some principles of information storage and retrieval in society. *General Systems, 20*, 15–35.

Krog, V. G., & Grand, S. (2002). From economic theory toward a knowledge-based theory of the firm: Conceptual building blocks. In N. Bontis & C. W.Choo (Eds.), *The Strategic Management of Intellectual Capital and Organizational Knowledge*. Oxford, U.K.: Oxford University Press.

Kruglanski, A. W. (2001). That "Vision Thing": The state of theory in social and personality psychology at the edge of the new millennium. *Journal of Personality and Social Psychology, 80*(6), 871–875. doi:10.1037/0022-3514.80.6.871

Küpers, W. (1998). Phenomenology of embodied productivity in services. *International Journal of Service Industry Management, 9*(4), 337–358

Kuhn, T. S. (1962). *The Structure of Scientific Revolutions*. Chicago: The University of Chicago Press.

Kulkarni, U. R., Ravindran, S., & Freeze, R. (2006). A knowledge management success model: Theoretical development and empirical validation. *Journal of Management Information Systems*, *23*(3), 309–347. doi:10.2753/MIS0742-1222230311

Kuo, F., & Young, M. (2008). A study of the intention-action gap in knowledge sharing practices. *Journal of the American Society for Information Science and Technology*, *59*(8), 1224–1237. doi:10.1002/asi.20816

Kwan, M. M., & Balasubramanian, P. (2003). KnowledgeScope: Managing knowledge in context. *Decision Support Systems*, *35*(4), 467-486.

Lahneman, W. J. (2004). Knowledge-sharing in the intelligence community after 9/11. *International Journal of Intelligence and CounterIntelligence*, *17*(4), 614–633. doi:10.1080/08850600490496425

Lam, A. (2000). Tacit knowledge, organizational learning and societal institutions: An integrated framework. *Organization Studies*, *21*(3), 487-513.

Lampe, J. C., & Garcia, A. (2004). Data mining: An in-depth look. *Internal Auditing*, *19*(2), 4–20.

Lane, C. (1998). Introduction. In C. Lane, & R. Bachmann (eds.), *Trust Within and Between Organizations*. New York: Oxford University Press.

Lane, P. J., & Lubatkin, M. (1998). Relative absorptive capacity and interorganizational learning. *Strategic Management Journal*, *19*, 461–477. doi:10.1002/(SICI)1097-0266(199805)19:5<461::AID-SMJ953>3.0.CO;2-L

Langer, E., Blank, A., & Chanowitz, B. (1978). The mindlessness of ostensibly thoughtful action: The role of "placebic" information in interpersonal interaction. *Journal of Personality and Social Psychology*, *36*, 635–642. doi:10.1037/0022-3514.36.6.635

Lansdale, M. (1988). The psychology of personal information management. *Applied Ergonomics*, *19*(1), 55-66.

Lapre, M. A., & Van Wassenhove, L. N. (2003). Managing Learning Curves in Factories by Creating and Transferring Knowledge. *California Management Review*, *46*(1), 53–71.

Lassila, O., & Hendler, J. (2007). Embracing Web 3.0. *IEEE Internet Computing*, 90–93. doi:10.1109/MIC.2007.52

Lave, J., & Wenger, E. (1991). *Situated Learning: Legitimate peripheral participation*. Cambridge: Cambridge University Press.

Lave, J., & Wenger, E. (1991). *Situated Learning: Legitimate Peripheral Participation*. New York: Cambridge University Press.

Lawrence, P. R., & Lorsch, J. W. (1967). *Organization and Environment*. Boston, MA: Harvard University Press.

Lea, M., & Spears, R. (1991). Computer-mediated communication, deindividuation and group decision-making. *International Journal of Man-Machine Studies*, *34*, 283–301. doi:10.1016/0020-7373(91)90045-9

Lee, G. K., & Cole, R. E. (2003). From a firm-based to a community-based model of knowledge creation: the case of the Linux kernel development. *Organization Science*, *14*, 633–649. doi:10.1287/orsc.14.6.633.24866

Lee, H., & Choi, B. (2003). Knowledge management enablers, processes, and organizational performance: An integrative view and empirical examination. *Journal of Management Information Systems*, *20*(1), 179-229.

Lee, J.-N. (2001). The impact of knowledge sharing, organizational capability and partnership quality on IS outsourcing success. *Information & Management*, *38*, 323–335. doi:10.1016/S0378-7206(00)00074-4

Lee, T., Chams, M. et al. (1999). Information integration with attribution support for corporate profiles. In *Proceedings of the Eighth International Conference on Information and Knowledge Management*, Kansas City, MO, United States: ACM Press.

Lehner, F., Maier, R., & Klosa, O. (1998). Organisational memory systems - application of advanced database & network technologies. Research Paper No. 19, University of Regensburg, Department of Business Informatics.

Leidner, D., & Galliers, R. (Eds.). (2003). *Strategic Information Management*. Oxford: Butterworth-Heinemann/ Elsevier.

Leidner, D., Alavi, M., & Kayworth, T. (2006). The role of culture in knowledge management: A case study of two global firms. *The International Journal of Electronic Collaboration, 2(1),* 17-40.

Leidner, D.E., & Elam, J.J. (1995). The impact of executive information systems on organizational design, intelligence, and decision making. *Organization Science, 6*(6), 645-665.

Leimeister, J. M., Ebner, W., & Krcmar, H. (2005). Design, Implementation, and Evaluation of Trust-Supporting Components in Virtual Communities for Patients. *Journal of Management Information Systems, 21*(4), 101–135.

Lemons, D. (2005). Ensuring smooth knowledge transfer through communities at Aerotek. *KM Review, 8*(1), 5.

Leonard, D. (1995). *The well springs of knowledge*. Boston: Harvard Business School Press.

Lesser, E. L., & Storck, J. (2001). Communities of practice and organizational performance. *IBM Systems Journal, 40*(4), 831-841.

Lesser, E., & Everest, K. (2001). Using communities of practice to managing intellectual capital. *Ivey Business Journal, 65*, 37–41.

Levitt, B., & March, J.G. (1988). Organizational learning. *Annual Review of Sociology, 14*(3), 319-340.

Li, M., & Gao, F. (2003). Why Nonaka highlights tacit knowledge: a critical review. *Journal of Knowledge Management, 7*(4), 6–14. doi:10.1108/13673270310492903

Li, W., Ardichivili, A., Maurer, M., Wentling, T., & Studemann, R. (2007). Impact of Chinese culture values of knowledge sharing through online communities of practice. *International Journal of Knowledge Management, 3*, 46–59.

Liao, S., Chang, J., Cheng, S., & Kuo, C. (2004). Employee relationship and knowledge sharing: A case study of a Taiwanese finance and securities firm. *Knowledge Management Research and Practice, 2*, 24–34. doi:10.1057/palgrave.kmrp.8500016

Licklider, J. & Taylor, R. (1968). The computer as a communication device. *Science and Technology: For the Technical Men in Management*, 21-31.

Liebowitz, J. (2004). Conceptualizing and implementing knowledge management. In P. Love, P. Fong, & Z. Irani (Eds.), *Management of Knowledge in Project Environment* (pp. 1-18). Amsterdam: Elsevier Butterworth-Heinemann.

Liebowitz, J. (2009). *Knowledge retention.* New York: CRC Press.

Lin, C. (2008). Clarifying the relationship between organizational citizenship behaviors, gender, and knowledge sharing in workplace organizations in Taiwan. *Journal of Business and Psychology, 22*(3), 241. doi:10.1007/s10869-008-9067-z

Lincoln, Y. S., & Guba, E. G. (1985). *Naturalistic inquiry*. Beverly Hills, CA: Sage Publications.

Lindsey, K. (2002). Measuring knowledge management effectiveness: a task-contingent organizational capabilities perspective. *Eight Americas Conference on Information Systems* (pp. 2085-2090).

Linstone, H. A. (1999). *Decision Making for Technology Executives: Using Multiple Perspectives to Improve Performance*. Boston, MA: Artech House.

Linthicum, D. (2007). Enterprise mashups meet SOA. *InfoWorld, 29*(8). Retrieved March 4, 2007, from http://www.infoworld.com/article/07/02/19/08FEsaassoa_1.html

Lippman, S. A., & Rumelt, R. P. (1982). Uncertain imitability: An analysis of interfirm differences in efficiency under competition. *The Bell Journal of Economics, 13*, 418–438. doi:10.2307/3003464

Liu, M., & Liu, N. (2008). Sources of knowledge acquisition and patterns of knowledge-sharing behaviors - an empirical study of Taiwanese high-tech firms. *International Journal of Information Management, 28*(5), 423. doi:10.1016/j.ijinfomgt.2008.01.005

Long, D. W., & Fahey, L. (2000). Diagnosing cultural barriers to knowledge management. *The Academy of Management Executive*, *14*(4), 113–127.

Luchter, L. (2007, June 19). Magid: 80% of 18-24 males watch online video weekly. *Online Media Daily*. Retrieved from http://publications.mediapost.com/index.cfm?fuseaction=Articles.showArticle&art_aid=62558

Luftman, J. N., et al. (2004). *Managing the IT Resource: Leadership in the Information Age*. Pearson, Prentice Hall.

Lui, T.-W., Picccoli, G., & Ives, B. (2007). Marketing Strategies in Virtual Worlds. *The Data Base for Advances in Information Systems*, *38*(4), 77–80.

Lurie, I. (2004). Product Review: Insightful Miner. *DM Review*, *14*(6), 88.

Lutz, M., & Kolas, D. (2007). Rule-based discovery in spatial data infrastructure. *Transactions in GIS*, *11*(3), 317–336.

Macias-Chapula, C. A., & Mason, R. O. (1995). Development of a soft systems model to identify information values, impact and barriers in a health care information system. *Journal of Information Science*, *21*(4), 283–288. doi:10.1177/016555159502100404

Macpherson, R. (2008). Critical management in knowledge organizations. *International Journal of Educational Management*, *22*(7), 676–695. doi:. doi:10.1108/09513540810908584

Madsen, E. S., Riis, J. O., & Waehrens, B. V. (2008). The knowledge dimension of manufacturing transfers. *Strategic Outsourcing: An International Journal*, *1*(3), 198–209. doi:10.1108/17538290810915272

Magnus, S., & Niclas, O. (2003). Behavioral intentions in satisfaction research revisited. *Journal of Consumer Satisfaction, Dissatisfaction and Complaining Behavior*, *16*, 53-66.

Maier, R. (2001). Towards a Framework for Knowledge Management Strategies: Process Orientation as Strategic Starting Point. In *Proceedings of the 34th Hawaii International Conference on System Sciences*. IEEE Computer Society.

Maier, R. (2002). *Knowledge management systems: Information and communication technologies for knowledge management*. Berlin: Springer-Verlag.

Majchrzak, A., Malhotra, A., & John, R. (2005). Perceived individual collaboration know-how development through information technology-enabled contextualization: Evidence from distributed teams. *Information Systems Research*, *16*(1), 9-27.

Makadok, R. (2001). Toward a synthesis of the resource-based and dynamic-capability views of rent creation. *Strategic Management Journal*, *22*(5), 387–401. doi:10.1002/smj.158

Malek, M., & Amy, B. (1997). A preprocessing model for integrating case-based reasoning and prototype-based neural network. In R. Sun & F. Alexandre (Eds.), Connectionist-Symbolic Integration: From Unified to Hybrid Approaches.

Malhotra, A., Gosain, S., & Hars, A. (1997). Evolution of a Virtual Community: Understanding Design Issues Through a Longitudinal Study. In the *Proceedings of International Conference on Information Systems (ICIS)*.

Malhotra, Y. (1997). Profile of the Ideal Knowledge Manager/Architect. http://www.brint.com/wwwboard/messages/273.html.

Mark, D., Frank, A., Egenhofer, M., Freundshuh, S., McGranghan, M., & White, R.M. (Eds.) (1989). *Languages of spatial relations: Report on the specialist meeting for NCGIA research initiative 2*. Technical Report 89-2, national Center for Geographic Information and Analysis.

Mark, D.M., & Egenhofer, M.J. (1992). An evaluation of the 9-intersection for region line relations. *In Proceedings of GIS/LIS '93*, San Jose, CA, (pp. 513-521).

Marks, P. (2006). Mashup websites are a dream come true for hackers. *New Scientist*, *190*(2551), 28–30.

Markus, L. M. (1987). Towards a "critical mass" theory of interactive media: Universal access, interdependence and diffusion. *Comm. Res.*, *14*, 491–511. doi:10.1177/009365087014005003

Markus, M. L. (2001). Toward a theory of knowledge reuse: Types of knowledge reuse situations and factors in reuse success. *Journal of Management Information Systems*, *18*(1), 57–93.

Markus, M. L., Majchrzak, A., & Gasser, L. (2002). A design theory for systems that support emergent knowledge processes. *MIS Quarterly, 26*(3), 179-212.

Martin, B. (2000). Knowledge based organisations: Emerging trends in local government in Australia, *Journal of Knowledge Management Practice*, October.

Martin, P., & Eklund, P. W. (2000). Knowledge retrieval and the World Wide Web. *IEEE Intelligent Systems*, *15*(3). doi:10.1109/5254.846281

Martin, W. E. (2005). *Managing Information Technology* (5th ed.). Saddle River: Prentice Hall.

Massey, A. P., Montoya-Weiss, M. M., & O'Driscoll, T. M. (2002). Knowledge management in pursuit of performance: insights from Nortel networks. *MIS Quarterly*, *26*(3), 269–289. doi:10.2307/4132333

Maturana, H., & Varela, F. (1987). *The tree of knowledge: The biological roots of knowledge*. Boston, MA: Shambhala.

Mayer, R. C., Davis, J. H., & Schoorman, F. D. (1995). An integrative model of organizational trust. *Academy of Management Review*, *20*, 709–734. doi:10.2307/258792

McDermott, R. (1999). Why information technology inspired but cannot deliver: Knowledge management. *California Management Review, 41*(4), 103-117.

McDermott, R. (1999a). How to get the most out of human networks: Nurturing Three-Dimensional Communities of Practice. *Knowledge Management Review*, *2*(5), 26–29.

McDermott, R., & O'Dell, C. (2001). Overcoming cultural barriers to sharing knowledge. *Journal of Knowledge Management*, *5*(1), 76–85. doi:10.1108/13673270110384428

McDonough, E. F., Zack, M. H., Lin, H., & Berdrow, I. (2008). Integrating innovation style and knowledge into strategy. *MIT Sloan Management Review*, *50*(1), 52–58.

McElroy, M. (2002). Social innovation capital. *Journal of Intellectual Capital*, *3*, 30–39. doi:10.1108/14691930210412827

McKay, J., & Marshall, P. (2004). *Strategic management of e-business*. Milton, Qld.: John Wiley & Sons.

McKnight, B., & Bontis, N. (2002). E-improvisation: collaborative groupware technology expands the reach and effectiveness of organizational improvisation. *Knowledge and Process Management*, *9*, 219–227. doi:10.1002/kpm.154

McKnight, D. H., Cummings, L. L., & Chervany, N. L. (1998). Initial trust formation in new organizational relationships. *Academy of Management Review*, *23*, 473–490. doi:10.2307/259290

McLure Wasko, M., & Faraj, S. (2000). "It is what one does": Why people participate and help others in electronic communities of practice. *The Journal of Strategic Information Systems*, *9*, 155–173. doi:10.1016/S0963-8687(00)00045-7

McLure Wasko, M., & Faraj, S. (2005). Why should I share? Examining social capital and knowledge contribution in electronic networks of practice. *MIS Quarterly*, *29*(1), 35–57.

Medeiros, C.B., & Cilia, M. (1995). Maintenance of binary topological constraints through active databases. *In Proceedings of 3rd ACM Workshop on GIS.*

Medsker, G. J., Williams, L. J., & Holahan, P. J. (1994). A review of current practices for evaluating causal models in organizational behavior and human resources management research. *Journal of Management Information Systems, 20*(2), 439-464.

Melcrum. (2007, March 20). *New research shows social media is proving a big hit for global corporations inside and out, but risks remain.* Retrieved from http://www.melcrumblog.com/2007/03/social_media_is.html

Mena, J. (1998). Data mining FAQ's. *DM Review*.

Merrill, D. (2006). *Mashups: The new breed of web app.* Retrieved March 2, 2007 from http://www-128.ibm.com/developerworks/xml/library/x-mashups.html

Meyerson, D., Weick, K. E., & Kramer, R. M. (1996). Swift trust in temporary groups. In R. M. Kramer, & T. R. Tyler (eds.), *Trust in Organizations: Frontiers of Theory and Research.* Thousand Oaks: Sage Publications.

Michalisin, M. D., Smith, R. D., & Kline, D. M. (1997). In Search of Strategic Assets. *The International Journal of Organizational Analysis*, (4): 360–387. doi:10.1108/eb028874

Miles, M. B., & Huberman, A. M. (1994). *Qualitative Data Analysis: An Expanded Source Book* (2nd ed.). Thousand Oaks, CA: Sage Publications.

Miles, R. E., & Snow, C. C. (1978). *Organizational Strategy, Structure and Process.* New York: McGraw-Hill.

Miller, D. J., Fern, M. J., & Cardinal, L. B. (2007). The use of knowledge for technological innovation within diversified firms. *Academy of Management Journal*, *50*(2), 308–326.

Miller, D., & Friesen, P. H. (1982). Innovation in conservative and entrepreneurial firms: Two modes of strategic momentum. *Strategic Management Journal, 3*, 1-25.

Miller, L. L., Honavar, V., Wong, J., & Nilakanta, S. (1998). Object-oriented data warehouse for information fusion from heterogeneous distributed data and knowledge sources. In *Proceedings of the IEEE Information Technology Conference*, (pp. 27-31).

Miller, L. L., Lu, Y., Zhou, Y., & Hurson, A. R. (2000). A data warehouse based on materializing object-oriented views. In *Proceedings of the International Conference on Computers and Their Applications.* New Orleans, LA, (pp. 68-71).

Minbaeva, D. B., & Michailova, S. (2004). Knowledge transfer and expatriation in multinational corporations: The role of disseminative capacity. *Employee Relations*, *26*(6), 663–679. doi:10.1108/01425450410562236

Miner, A.S. (1990). Structural evolution through idiosyncratic jobs: The potential for unplanned learning. *Organization Science, 1*(2), 195-210.

Miranda, S. M., & Saunders, C. S. (2003). The social construction of meaning: An alternative perspective on information sharing. *Information Systems Research, 14*(1), 87-106.

Mirghani, S. M., O'Sulivan, K. J., & Ribiere, V. (2008). A paradigm shift in the Arab region knowledge evolution. *Journal of Knowledge Management*, *12*(5), 107–120. doi:10.1108/13673270810902975

Mitroff, I. I. (1981). *Challenging Strategic Planning Assumptions.* New York: Wiley.

Money, W., & Turner, A. (2005). Assessing knowledge management system user acceptance with the technology acceptance model. *International Journal of Knowledge Management, 1*(1), 8-26.

Moore, G. C., & Benbasat, I. (1991). Development of an instrument to measure the perceptions of adopting an information technology innovation. *Information Systems Research, 2*(3), 192-222.

Moorman, C., & Miner, A.S. (1998). Organization improvisation and organizational memory. *Academy of Management Review, 23*(4), 698-723.

Moran, T.P., & Carroll, J.M. (1996). *Design rationale: Concepts, techniques, and use*. Mahwah, NJ: Lawrence Erlbaum.

Mou, Y. Zhang. S., & Cao. J. (2004). Providing knowledge support in business process: a context based approach. *2004 IEEE International Conference on Systems, Man and Cybernetics, 3*(10-13), 2143-2149.

Murphy, J., & Hackbush, J. (2007). The Knowledge Management Spending Report, 2007–2008 The Market Hits $73B. *AMR Research Report*. Retrieved from http://www.amrresearch.com/Content/View.asp?pmillid=20744

Murphy, T., & Jennex, M. E. (2006). Knowledge management and hurricane Katrina response. International *Journal of Knowledge Management, 2*(4), 52-66.

Mustapha, S. (2005). Extracting social knowledge in the intelligent conversational channel for agent communication. *19th International Conference on Advanced Information Networking and Applications, 2005 (AINA 2005)* (Vol. 2, pp. 733-738).

Nahapiet, J., & Ghoshal, S. (1998). Social capital, intellectual capital, and the organizational advantage. *Academy of Management Review*, *23*, 242–266. doi:10.2307/259373

Naughton, J. (1999). *A Brief History of the Future: The Origins of the Internet*. London: Weidenfield & Nicholson.

Negroponte, N. (1995). *Being digital*. New York: Knopf.

Nelson, R. R., & Winter, S. G. (1982). *An evolutionary theory of economic change*. Cambridge, MA: Belknap Press of Harvard University Press.

Nemati, H. R., Steiger, D. M. et al. (2002). Knowledge warehouse: An architectural integration of knowledge management, decision support, artificial intelligence and data warehousing. *Decision Support Systems 33*(2), 143.

Nevo, D., & Wand, Y. (2005). Organizational memory information systems: A transactive memory approach. *Decision Support Systems, 39*, 549-562.

Newell, A., & Simon, H.A. (1972). *Human problem solving*. Engelwood Cliff, NJ: Prentice-Hall

Nickols, F. W. (2000). The Knowledge in Knowledge Management. In J.W. Cortada & J.A. Woods (Eds), *The knowledge management yearbook 2000-2001* (pp. 12-21). Boston, MA: Butterworth-Heinemann.

Nidumolu, S. R., Subramani, M., & Aldrich, A. (2001). Situated Learning and the Situated Knowledge Web: Exploring the Ground Beneath Knowledge Management. *Journal of Management Information Systems*, *18*(1), 115–150.

Nilakanta, S., Miller, L. L. et al. (2006). Organizational memory management technological and research issues. *Journal of Database Management, 17*(1), 85-94.

Nissen, M. E. (2005). Dynamic Knowledge Patterns to Inform Design: A Field Study of Knowledge Stocks and Flows in an Extreme Organization. *Journal of Management Information Systems*, *22*(3), 225–263. doi:10.2753/MIS0742-1222220308

Nissen, M., Kamel, M., & Sengupta, K. (2000). Integrated Analysis and Design of Knowledge Systems and Processes. In Y. Malhotra (Ed.), *Knowledge Management and Virtual Organizations* (pp. 214-244). Idea Group Publishing.

Nolan, R. (1979). Managing the crises in data processing. *Harvard Business Review*, *57*(2).

Nonaka, I. (1991). The knowledge-creating company. *Harvard Business Review (November-December)*, 96-104.

Nonaka, I. (1994). A dynamic theory of organizational knowledge creation. *Organization Science*, *5*(1), 14–37. doi:10.1287/orsc.5.1.14

Nonaka, I. (2005). *Knowledge Management: Critical Perspectives on Business and Management*. Taylor and Francis.

Nonaka, I., & Konno, N. (1998). The concept of "Ba": Building a foundation for knowledge creation. *California Management Review, 40*(3), 40-54.

Nonaka, I., & Nishiguchi, T. (2001). *Knowledge emergence*. Oxford University Press, New York.

Nonaka, I., & Peltokorpi, V. (2006). Objective and subjectivity in knowledge management: a review of 20 top articles. *Knowledge and Process Management*, *13*(2), 73–82. doi:10.1002/kpm.251

Nonaka, I., & Takeuchi, H. (1995). *The knowledge creating company: How Japanese companies create the dynamics of innovation*. Oxford: Oxford University Press.

Nonaka, I., Toyama, R., & Konno, N. (2001). SECI, Ba and leadership: a unified model of dynamic knowledge creation. In I. Nonaka, & D. J. Teece (eds.), *Managing Industrial Knowledge: Creation, Transfer and Utilization*. London: Sage Publications.

North Mersey Health Informatics Service. (2007). *Customer Satisfaction Survey.* Internal document.

Nuclear Regulatory Commission News (NRC News). (1997, April 8). RIV-99-18, *NRC Finds Performance "Acceptable" at San Onofre in Latest Review.* United States Nuclear Regulatory Commission.

Nuclear Regulatory Commission News (NRC News). (1999, August 1). RIV-4497, NRC Rates *San Onofre Nuclear Plant "Good" and "Superior" in SALP Report.* United States Nuclear Regulatory Commission.

Nuclear Regulatory Commission, NRC. (1998, October 2). *NRC Administrative Letter 98-07, Interim Suspension of the Systematic Assessment of Licensee Performance (SALP) Program.* United States Nuclear Regulatory Commission.

Nunnally, J. C. (1967). *Psychometric theory.* New York: McGraw-Hill.

Nyman, N. (2005). *Risky business: What must employers do to shield against liability for employee wrongdoings in the Internet age.* Retrieved from http://www.lctjournal.washington.edu/Vol1/a007Nyman.html

O'Brien, D., & Fitzgerald, B. (2006). Mashups, remixes and copyright law. *Internet Law Bulletin, 9*(2), 17–19.

O'Dell, C., & Grayson, C. J. (1998). If only we knew what we know: Identification and transfer of internal best practices. *California Management Review, 40*(3), 154–174.

O'Dell, C., & Grayson, C. J. (2004). Identifying and Transferring Internal Best Practices. *Handbook on Knowledge Management 1: Knowledge Matters*, 601-622.

O'Dell, C., Hasanali, F., Hubert, C., Lopez, K., Odem, P., & Raybourn, C. (2000). Successful KM implementation: A study of best-practice organizations. In C. Holsapple (Ed.), *Handbook on knowledge management 2 knowledge directions, Vol. 2* (pp. 411-443). Berlin: Springer-Verlag.

O'Reilly, C. A., Chatman, J. A., & Caldwell, D. F. (1991). People and organizational culture: A profile comparison approach to assessing person-organization fit. *Academy of Management Journal, 14*(1), 487-516.

O'Reilly, T. (2005). *What Is Web 2.0.* Retrieved Feb 2, 2007 from http://www.oreillynet.com/pub/a/oreilly/tim/news/2005/09/30/what-is-web-20.html

Offsey, S. (1997). Knowledge management: linking people to knowledge for bottom line results. *Journal of Knowledge Management, 1*(2), 113–122. doi:10.1108/EUM0000000004586

Okunoye, A., & Bertaux, N. (2006). KAFRA: A Context-aware framework of knowledge management in global diversity. *International Journal of Knowledge Management, 2*(2), 26–45.

Olson, E.M., Slater, S.F., & Hult, G.T.M. (2005). The performance implications of fit among business strategy, marketing organization structure, and strategic behavior. *Journal of Marketing, 69*(3), 49-65.

Orlikowski, W. J. (2002). Knowing in Practice: Enacting a Collective Capability in Distributed Organizing. *Organization Science, 13*(3), 249–273. doi:10.1287/orsc.13.3.249.2776

Orr, J. E. (1989). Sharing Knowledge, Celebrating Identity: War Stories and Community Memory Among Service Technicians. In D. S. Middleton & D. Edwards (Eds.), *Collective Remembering: Memory in Society.* Newbury Park, CA: Sage Publications.

Ortenblad, A. (2001). On differences between organizational learning and learning organization. *The Learning Organization, 8*(3/4), 125-133.

Osterloh, M., & Frey, B. S. (2000). Motivation, knowledge, transfer, and organizational forms. *Organization Science, 11*(5), 538–550. doi:10.1287/orsc.11.5.538.15204

Ounis, I., & Pasca, M. (1998). Organizing Conceptual Graphs for Fast Knowledge Retrieval. In *Proceedings of 10th International Conference on Tools with Artificial Intelligence. IEEE Computer Society Press* (pp. 120-129).

Oxbrow, N. (2003). *Second CKO summit for the public sector.* London: TFPL.

Oxbrow, N. (2004). *'Sticky' knowledge strategies CKO summit 2004*. London: TFPL.

Ozorhon, B., Dikmen, I., & Birgonul, M. (2006, September). Case-based reasoning model for international market selection. *Journal of Construction Engineering and Management*, 940–948. doi:10.1061/(ASCE)0733-9364(2006)132:9(940)

Paas, F., Renkl, A., & Sweller, J. (2004). Cognitive load theory: Instructional implications of the interaction between information structures and cognitive architecture. *Instructional Science*, *32*, 1–8. doi:10.1023/B:TRUC.0000021806.17516.d0

Paepcke, A. (1996). Digital Libraries: Searching is not enough. *D-Lib Magazine*, (May): 1996.

Palmer, R. (1993). *Write in Style – A Guide to Good English*. London: E & FN Spon.

Pan, S. L., & Leidner, D. E. (2003). Bridging communities of practice with information technology in the pursuit of global knowledge sharing. *The Journal of Strategic Information Systems*, *12*, 71–88. doi:10.1016/S0963-8687(02)00023-9

Pan, S., & Scarbrough, H. (1998). A socio-technical view of knowledge-sharing at Buckman Laboratories. *Journal of Knowledge Management*, *2*(1), 55–66. doi:10.1108/EUM0000000004607

Passerini, K., Jennex, M. E., & Khaldoun, B. T. (2007). Perspectives from North Africa: the Tunis-2006 knowledge management forum. *International Journal of Knowledge Management*, *3*(1), 100–107.

Patton, M.Q. (2002). *Qualitative research & evaluation methods*. Thousand Oaks: Sage Publications.

Paulzen, O. (2002). *A maturity model for quality improvement in knowledge management*. Chapter presented at the Enablling Organizations and Society Through Information Systems, Proceedings of the 13th. Australasian Conference on Information Systems (ACIS 2002), Melbourne.

Peffers, K., Tuunanen, T. et al. (2006). The design science research process: A model for producing and presenting information systems research. In *Proceedings of the International Conference on Design Science Research in Information Systems and Technology*, Claremont, CA.

Penrose, E. (1959). *The Theory of the Growth of the Firm*. New York: Wiley.

Pentland, B. T. (1995). Information systems and organizational learning: the social epistemology of organizational knowledge systems. *Accounting. Management and Information Technologies*, *5*, 1–21. doi:10.1016/0959-8022(95)90011-X

Peppart, J., & Ward, J. (2004). Beyond Strategic Information Systems: towards an IS capability. *The Journal of Strategic Information Systems*, *13*, 167–194. doi:10.1016/j.jsis.2004.02.002

Pepus, G. (2007, June). Smart image and video search. *KMworld* (pp. 6-9).

Perrow, C. (1967). A framework for the comparative analysis of organizations. *American Sociological Review*, *32*, 194-208.

Peter, J. B., Jeremy, C., & Hui, T. (2006). Culture awareness in knowledge transfer to China-the role of guanxi and mianzi. *Journal of World Business*, *41*, 275–288. doi:10.1016/j.jwb.2006.01.008

Peterson, R. R. (2000). *Emerging capabilities of information technology governance: Exploring stakeholder perspectves in financial services*. Chapter presented at the 8th European Conference on Information Systems, Vienna.

Pfeffer, J., & Sutton, R. I. (1999). *The knowing-doing gap; how smart companies turn knowledge into action*. Boston MA: Harvard Business School Press.

Pickering, J. M., & King, J. L. (1995). Hardwiring weak ties: interorganizational computer-mediated communication, occupational communities, and organizational change. *Organization Science*, *6*, 479–486. doi:10.1287/orsc.6.4.479

Pillania, R.K. (2006). State-of-art of knowledge storage and access in Indian industry. *Journal of Information and Knowledge Management*, *5*(1), 55-61.

Pitt, L., Berthon, P., & Berthon, J.P. (1999). Changing channels: The impact if the internet on distribution strategy. *Business Horizons, 42*(2), 19-28.

Plant, T. (2000). *Introducing knowledge management into complex organizations* (unpublished manuscript). Australian Defense Force Academy, School of Computer Science, University College, University of New South Wales.

Platt, A., & Warwick, S. (1995). Review of soft systems methodology. *Industrial Management & Data Systems, 95*, 19–21. doi:10.1108/02635579510086698

Podsakoff, S., MacKenzie, B., Lee, J.Y., & Podsakoff, N.P. (2003). Common method biases in behavioral research: A critical review of the literature and recommended remedies. *Journal of Applied Psychology, 88*(5), 879-903.

Polanyi, M. (1962). *Personal knowledge: Towards a post-critical philosophy.* Chicago: University of Chicago Press.

Polanyi, M. (1967). *The tacit dimension.* London: Routledge & Kegan Paul.

Polanyi, M. (1969). *Knowing and being.* London: Routledge and Kegan Paul.

Polanyi, M. (1975). *Personal Knowledge*. Chicago: University of Chicago Press.

Poll, R. (1996). Ontology for knowledge organization. In R. Green (Ed.), *Knowledge organization and change* (pp. 313-319). Indeks, Frankfurt.

Popa, B. (2007, September 4). *Supermarket employee won YouTube lawsuit.* Retrieved from http://news.softpedia.com/news/Supermarket-Employee-Won-YouTube-Lawsuit-64526.shtml

Porra, J. & Parks, M. S. (2006). Sustaining Virtual Communities: Suggestions from the Colonial Model. *Information Systems and e-Business Management, 4*(4), 309-341.

Porra, J., & Goel, L. (2006). Importance of Power in the Implementation Process of a Successful KMS: A Case Study. [Abstract] In 37th Annual Meeting of the Decision Sciences Institute, San Antonio, TX, November 18-21.

Porter, M. E., & Miller, V. (2001). Strategy and the internet. *Harvard Business Review, 72*(3), 62–68.

Postmes, T., Spears, R., & Lea, M. (2000). The formation of group norms in computer-mediated communication. *Human Communication Research, 26*(3), 341–371. doi:10.1111/j.1468-2958.2000.tb00761.x

Power Reactor Information System (PRIS). (2003). *Power Reactor Details International Atomic Energy* Agency database. Retrieved August 12, 2007, from http://www.iaea.org/programmes/a2/

Prandelli, E., Verona, G., & Raccagni, D. (2006). Diffusion of Web-Based Product Innovation. *California Management Review, 48*(4), 109–135.

Preece, J. (2000). *Online Communities: Designing Usability, Supporting Sociability.* Chichester: John Viley & Sons.

Preece, J., Nonnecke, B., & Andrews, D. (2003). The top five reasons for lurking: improving community experiences for everyone. *Computers in Human Behavior, 20*, 201–223. doi:10.1016/j.chb.2003.10.015

Premkumar, G., Ramamurthy, K., & Saunders, C.S. (2005). Information processing view of organizations: An exploratory examination of fit in the context of interorganizational relationships. *Journal of Management Information Systems, 22*(1), 257-298.

Prencipe, A., & Tell, F. (2001). Inter-project learning: Processes and outcomes of knowledge codification in project-based firms. *Research Policy, 30*(9), 597-621.

Prentzas, J., & Hatzilygeroudis, L. (2007). Categorizing approaches combining rule-based and case-based reasoning. *Expert Systems: International Journal of Knowledge Engineering and Neural Networks, 24*(2), 97–122. doi:10.1111/j.1468-0394.2007.00423.x

Price, L.L., & Arnould, E.J. (1999). Commercial friendships: service provider-client relationships in context. *Journal of Marketing, 63*(4), 38-56.

Probst, G., Raub, S., & Romhardt, K. (2000). *Managing knowledge; Building blocks for success*. Chichester: John Wiley & Sons, Ltd.

Protti, D. (2002). (submitted to). Implementing information for health: even more challenging than expected? [Department of Health Information Policy Unit, HMSO London.]. *Report*.

Prusak, L. (2001). Where did knowledge management come from? *IBM Systems Journal*, *40*(4), 1002–1007.

Purvis, R. L., Sambamurthy, V., & Zmud, R. W. (2001). The assimilation of knowledge platforms in organizations: an empirical investigation. *Organization Science*, *12*, 117–135. doi:10.1287/orsc.12.2.117.10115

Quinn, R. E., & Rhorbaugh, J. (1983). A spatial model of effectiveness criteria: Towards a competing values approach to organizational analysis. *Management Science, 29*(3), 363-377.

Randall, D., Hughes, J., O'Brien, J., Rouncefield, M., & Tolmie, P. (2001). 'Memories are made of this:' Explicating organisational knowledge and memory. *European Journal of Information Systems, 10*(2), 113-121.

Rasmussen, H. S., & Haggerty, N. (2008). Knowledge appraisal and knowledge management systems: Judging what we know. *Journal of Organizational and End User Computing*, *20*(1), 17–34.

Rau, L. F. (1987). Knowledge organization and access in a conceptual information system. *Information Processing & Management*, *23*(4), 269–281. doi:10.1016/0306-4573(87)90018-5

Rayport, J.F., & Sviokla, J.J. (1995). Exploiting the virtual value chain. *Harvard Business Review, 73*(6), 75-85.

Reagans, R., & McEvily, B. (2003). Network Structure and Knowledge Transfer: The Effects of Cohesion and Range. *Administrative Science Quarterly*, *48*(2), 240–267. doi:10.2307/3556658

Reber, A. S. (1967). Implicit learning of artificial grammars. *Journal of Verbal Learning and Verbal Behavior*, *6*, 855–863. doi:10.1016/S0022-5371(67)80149-X

Reber, A. S. (1969). Transfer of syntactic structure in synthetic languages. *Journal of Experimental Psychology*, *81*(1), 115–119. doi:10.1037/h0027454

Reber, A. S. (1989). Implicit Learning and Tacit Knowledge. *Journal of Experimental Psychology. General*, *118*(3), 219–235. doi:10.1037/0096-3445.118.3.219

Reber, A. S. (1989). More thoughts on the unconscious: Reply to Brody and to Lewicki and Hall. *Journal of Experimental Psychology. General*, *118*(3), 242–244. doi:10.1037/0096-3445.118.3.242

Reber, A. S. (1993). *Implicit learning and tacit knowledge*. New York: Oxford University Press.

Reddy, M. L. (1979). The conduit metaphor: a case of frame conflict in our language about language. In A. Ortony (Ed.), *Metaphor and thought*. Cambridge: Cambridge University Press.

Redman, T.C. (1992). *Data quality*. Bantam.

Reed, A., & DeFillippi, R. J. (1990). Causal Ambiguity, Barriers to Imitation, and Sustainable Competitive Advantage. *Academy of Management Review*, *15*(1), 88–102. doi:10.2307/258107

Reio, T. G. Jr, & Wiswell, A. (2000). Field Investigation of the Relationship Among Adult Curiosity, Workplace Learning, and Job Performance. *Human Resource Development Quarterly*, *11*(1), 5–30. doi:10.1002/1532-1096(200021)11:1<5::AID-HRDQ2>3.0.CO;2-A

Rice, R.E. (1992). Task analyzability, use of new media, and effectiveness: A multi-site exploration of media richness. *Organization Science, 3*(4), 475-500.

Roberts, J. (2000). From know-how to show-how: the role of information and communication technologies in the transfer of knowledge. *Technology Analysis and Strategic Management*, *12*(4), 429–443. doi:10.1080/713698499

Roberts, J. (2003). Limits to communities of practice. *Journal of Management Studies*, *43*(3), 623–639. doi:10.1111/j.1467-6486.2006.00618.x

Robey, D., Wishart, N. A., & Rodriguez-Diaz, A. G. (1995). Merging the metaphors for organizational improvement: Business process reengineering as a component of organizational learning. *Accounting, Management and Information Technologies, 5*(1), 23-39.

Robson, W. (1994). *Strategic management and information systems; and integrated approach.* London: Pitman.

Rogers, E. M. & Agarwala-Rogers (1975). Organizational communication. In G. L. Hanneman, W. J. McEwen (Eds.), *Communication Behaviour* (pp. 218-236). Addision Wesley: Reading, MA.

Rogers, E. M. (2003). *Diffusion of innovations* (5th ed.). New York: Free Press.

Roper-Lowe, G. C., & Sharp, J. A. (1990). The analytic hierarchy process and its application to an information technology decision. *The Journal of the Operational Research Society, 41*(1), 49–59.

Roth, J. (2003). Enabling knowledge creation: learning from an R&D organization. *Journal of Knowledge Management, 7*(1), 32–48. doi:10.1108/13673270310463608

Royston, J.P. (1982). An extension of shapiro and wilk's W test for normality to large samples. *Applied Statistics, 31*(2), 115-124.

Rubenstein-Montano, B., Liebwowitz, J., Buchwalter, J., McCaw, D., Newman, B., & Rebeck, K. (2001). A systems thinking framework for knowledge management. *Decision Support Systems, 31*(1), 5–16. doi:10.1016/S0167-9236(00)00116-0

Rubenstein-Montano, B., Liebwowitz, J., Buchwalter, J., McCaw, D., Newman, B., & Rebeck, K. (2001). SMARTvision: a knowledge-management methodology. *Journal of Knowledge Management, 5*(4), 300–310. doi:10.1108/13673270110411724

Rubin, H. A. (1994). In search of the business value of information technology. *Application Development Trends, 1*(12), 23-27.

Ruggles, R. (1998). The state of the notion: Knowledge management in practice. *California Management Review, 40*(3), 80-89.

Rumelt, R. P. (1984). Towards a Strategic Theory of the Firm. In A. B. Lamb (Ed.), *Competitive Strategic Management* (pp. 566-570). Englewood Cliffs, NJ: Prentice Hall.

Rumizen, M. C. (2001). *The complete idiot's guide to knowledge management.* New York: Penguin Putnam.

Ruppel, C. P., & Harrington, S. J. (2001). Sharing knowledge through intranets: A study of organizational culture and intranet implementation. *IEEE Transactions on Professional Communication, 44*(1), 37-52.

Russo, M. V., & Fouts, P. A. (1997). A Resource-based Perspective on Corporate Environmental Performance and Profitability. *Academy of Management Journal, 40*(3), 534–559. doi:10.2307/257052

Ryle, G. (1949/1984). *The Concept of Mind.* Chicago, IL: University of Chicago Press.

Ryssen, S. V., & Godar, S. H. (2000). Going international without going international: multinational virtual teams. *Journal of International Management, 6*, 49–60. doi:10.1016/S1075-4253(00)00019-3

Ryu, C., Kim, Y.J., Chaudhury, A., & Rao, H.R. (2005). Knowledge acquisition via three learning processes in enterprise information portals: learning-by-investment, learning-by-doing, and learning-from-others. *MIS Quarterly, 29*(2), 245-278.

Saaty, T. L. (1996). *Decision Making with Dependence and Feedback: The Analytic Network Process.* Pittsburgh, PA: RWS Publications.

Saaty, T. L. (2001). *The Analytic Network Process* (2nd Version). Pittsburgh, PA: RWS Publications.

Saaty, T. L. (2005). *Theory and Applications of the Analytic Network Process.* Pittsburgh, PA: RWS Publications.

Saaty, T. L. 1980, *Multicriteria Decision Making: The Analytic Hierarchy Process.* Pittsburgh, PA: RWS Publications.

Saaty, T. L., & Vargas, L. G. (2006). *Decision making with the analytic network process: economic, political, social and technological applications with benefits, opportunities, costs and risks*. New York: Springer.

Sabharwal, R., & Chan, Y. (2001). Alignment between business and IS strategies: A configurational approach. *Information Systems Research, 12*(1), 11–33. doi:10.1287/isre.12.1.11.9714

Sabherwal, R., & Becerra-Fernandez, I. (2003). An empirical study of the effect of knowledge management processes at individual, group, and organizational levels. *Decision Sciences, 34*(2), 225-260.

Saemundsson, R. G. J. (2004). Technical knowledge-seeking in a young and growing technology-based firm: Incentives and direction. *International Journal of Innovation Management, 8*(4), 399–429. doi:10.1142/S136391960400112X

Sage. A. P. (2003). Knowledge management. In *Access Science*. Retrieved February 25, 2007, from http://dx.doi.org/10.1036/1097-8542.YB030820

Sandoval, G. (2008, July 12). *Goofle, Vicom now clashing over YouTube employee records*. Retrieved from http://news.cnet.com/8301-1023_3-9989783-93.html

Santoro, M. D., & Saparito, P. A. (2006). Self-Interest Assumption and Relational Trust in University-Industry Knowledge Transfers. *IEEE Transactions on Engineering Management, 53*(3), 335–347. doi:10.1109/TEM.2006.878103

Sarbanes Oxley Act, HR 3763 (2002).

Sarbaugh-Thompson, M., & Feldman, M.S. (1998). Electronic mail and organizational communication: Does saying "hi" really matter? *Organizational Science, 9*(6), 685-698.

Sarker, S., Sarker, S., Nicholson, D. B., & Joshi, K. D. (2005). Knowledge transfer in virtual systems development teams: An exploratory study of four key enablers. *IEEE Transactions on Professional Communication, 48*(2), 201–218. doi:10.1109/TPC.2005.849650

Sarvary, M. (1999). Knowledge management and competition in the consulting industry. *California Management Review, 41*(2), 95-107.

Satyadas, A., Harigopal, U., & Cassaigne, N. P. (2001). Knowledge management tutorial: An editorial overview. *IEEE Transactions on Systems, Man and Cybernetics. Part C, Applications and Reviews, 31*(4), 429–437. doi:10.1109/5326.983926

Scarborough, J. (1998). *The origins of cultural Differences and their Impact on Management*. Westport, Connecticut: Quorum Books.

Schank, R. (1982). Dynamic memory: A theory of learning in computers and people, Cambridge: Cambridge University Press.

Scheepers R., Venkitachalam K., & Gibbs, M.R. (2004). Knowledge strategy in organizations: Refining the model of Hansen, Nohria and Tierney. *Journal of Strategic Information Systems, 13*(3), 201-222.

Schendel, D. (1994). Introduction to Competitive Organizational Behavior: Toward an Organizationally Based Theory of Competitive Advantage. *Strategic Management Journal, 15*, 1–4. doi:10.1002/smj.4250150901

Schenkel, A., & Teigland, R. (2008). Improved organizational performance through communities of practice. *Journal of Knowledge Management, 12*(1), 106–118. doi:10.1108/13673270810852421

Schultz, M. (2003). Pathways of relevance: Exploring inflows of knowledge into subunits of multinational corporations. *Organization Science, 14*, 440–459. doi:10.1287/orsc.14.4.440.17483

Schultze, U., & Leidner, D. (2002). Studying Knowledge Management in Information Systems Research: Discourses and Theoretical Assumptions. *MIS Quarterly, 26*(3), 213–242. doi:10.2307/4132331

Schultze, U., & Stabell, C. (2004). Knowing What You Don't Know? Discourses and Contradictions in Knowledge Management Research. *Journal of Management Studies, 41*(4), 549–573. doi:10.1111/j.1467-6486.2004.00444.x

Schulz, M. (2001). The uncertain relevance of newness: Organizational learning and knowledge flows. *Academy of Management Journal, 44*(4), 661-681.

Schulz, M., & Jobe, L.A. (2001). Codification and tacitness as knowledge management strategies: An empirical exploration. *Journal of High Technology Management Research, 12,* 139-165.

Schwab, D. P., Heneman, H. G. III, & DeCotiis, T. A. (1975). Behaviorally anchored rating scales: A review of the literature. *Personnel Psychology, 28*(4), 549–562. doi:10.1111/j.1744-6570.1975.tb01392.x

Scott, J.E. (1998). Organizational knowledge and the Internet. *Decision Support Systems, 23,* 3-17.

Scott, S.G., & Bruce, R.A. (1994). Determinants of innovative behavior: A path model of individual innovation in the workplace. *Academy of Management Journal, 37*(3), 580-607.

Scribner, S. (1986). Thinking in action: Some characteristics of practical thought. In Sternberg & Wagner (Ed.), *Practical Intelligence.* Cambridge, UK: Cambridge University Press.

Seely-Brown, J., & Duguid, P. (2000). *The social life of information.* Boston: Harvard Business School Press.

Segars, A. H. (1997). Assessing the unidimensionality of measurement: A paradigm and illustration within the context of information systems research. *Omega, 25*(1), 107-121.

Seleim, A. A. S., & Khalil, O. E. M. (2007). Intellectual Capital in Egyptian software firms. *The Learning Organization, 11*(4/5), 332–346. doi:10.1108/09696470410538233

Senge, P. (1990). *The fifth discipline: the art and practice of learning organization.* New York: Doubleday/Currency.

Senge, P., Kleiner, A., Roberts, C., Ross, R., Roth, G., & Smith, B. (1999). *The dance of change: the challenges of sustaining momentum in learning organizations.* New York: Doubleday/Currency.

Servigne, S., Ubeda, T., Zuricelli, A., & Laurini, R. (2000). A methodology for spatial consistency improvement of geographic databases. *GeoInformatica, 4*(1), 7-34.

SETI@home. (n.d.). Retrieved Jan 29, 2009, from http://setiathome.berkeley.edu/

Shapiro, S.S., & Wilk, M.B. (1965). An analysis of variance test for normality (Complete Samples). *Biometrika, 52*(3, 4), 591-611.

Sharkie, R. (2003). Knowledge creation and its place in the development of sustainable competitive advantage. *Journal of Knowledge Management, 7*(1), 20–31. doi:10.1108/13673270310463590

Sharma, R., & Yetton, P. (2003). The contingent effects of management support and task interdependence on successful information systems implementation. *MIS Quarterly, 27*(4), 533-555.

Shaw, M.E. (1964). Communication networks. In L. Berkowitz (Ed.), *Advances in experimental social psychology* (Vol. 1, pp. 111-147). New York: Academic Press.

Sheppard, B. H., Hartwick, J., & Warshaw, P. R. (1988). The Theory of Reasoned Action: A meta-analysis of past research with recommendations for modifications and future research. *The Journal of Consumer Research, 15,* 325–343. doi:10.1086/209170

Sheridan, T.B., Vamos, T., & Aida, S. (1983). Adapting automation to man, culture and society. *Automatica, 19*(6), 605-612.

Sherif, K., & Xing, B. (2006). Adaptive processes for knowledge creation in complex systems: the case of a global IT consulting firm. *Information & Management, 43*(4), 530–540. doi:10.1016/j.im.2005.12.003

Shields, R. (2003). *The virtual.* New York: Routledge

Shin, M. (2004). A framework for evaluating economics of knowledge management systems. *Information & Management, 42,* 179–196.

Shotter, J. (1993). *Conversational Realities: Constructing Life through Language.* London: Sage Publications.

Silva, L., Mousavidin, E., & Goel, L. (2006). Weblogging: Implementing Communities of Practice. In E. Trauth, D. Howcroft, T. Butler, B. Fitzgerald & J. DeGross (Eds.),

Social Inclusion: Societal and Organizational Implications for Information Systems (pp. 295-317). New York: Springer-Verlag.

Simon, H.A. (1982). *Designing organizations for an information-rich world, models for bounded rationality.* Cambridge, MA: MIT Press.

Singh, J. (2005). Collaborative Networks as Determinants of Knowledge Diffusion Patterns. *Management Science, 51*(5), 756–770. doi:10.1287/mnsc.1040.0349

Singley, M.K., & Anderson, J.R. (1989). *The transfer of cognitive skill.* Cambridge, MA: Harvard University Press..

Smiragila, R. P. (2002). The progress of theory in knowledge organization. *Library Trends, 50*(3), 330.

Smith, P. C., & Kendall, L. M. (1963). Retranslation of expectations: An approach to the construction of unambiguous anchors for rating scales. *The Journal of Applied Psychology, 47,* 149–155. doi:10.1037/h0047060

Smith, R., & Park, K.K. (1991). *An algebraic approach to spatial reasoning.* NCGIA technical paper 91-97.

Smolnik, S., & Erdmann, I. (2003). Visual navigation of distributed knowledge structures in groupware-based organizational memories. *Business Process Management Journal, 9*(3), 261.

Snowden, D. & Stanbridge, P. (2004). The landscape of management: creating the context for understanding social complexity. *E:CO Special double issue, 6*(1-2), 140-148.

Snowden, D. (2002). Complex acts of knowing: Paradox and descriptive self-awareness. *Journal of Knowledge Management, 66*(2), 100–111. doi:10.1108/13673270210424639

Snowden, D. (2003). Innovation as an objective of knowledge management. Part I: The landscape of management, *Knowledge Management Research & Practice, 1*(2), 113-119.

Snowden, D. (2003). Managing for Serendipity or why we should lay off "best practice."KM. *Knowledge Management Journal.*

Snowden, D. (2007). *Cynefin.* Retrieved from http://en.wikipedia.org/wiki/Cynefin#The_Framework

Sohal, A. S., & Fitzpatrick, P. (2002). IT Governance and management in large australian organisations. *International Journal of Production Economics, 75,* 97-112.

Song, S., & Teng, J.T.C. (2006). Effective work unit knowledge management (KM): An exploratory investigation of the roles of network, task environment, and KM strategies. In *Proceedings of the 27th International Conference on Information Systems*, Milwaukee, WI.

Soo, C., Devinney, T., Midgley, D., & Deering, A. (2002). Knowledge management: philosophy, processes and pitfalls. *California Management Review, 44,* 129–150.

Souren, P., Haseman, W.D., & Ramamurthy, K. (2004). Collective memory support and cognitive-conflict group decision-making: An experimental investigation. *Decision Support Systems, 36*(3), 261-281.

Souto, P., Dervin, B., & Savolainen, R. (2008). *Designing for knowledge workers informings: an examplar applications of Sense-Making Methodology.* ASIS&T 2008 Annual Meeting (AM08 2008), Columbus, Ohio, October 24-29

Sowe, S. K., Stamelos, I., & Angelis, L. (2008). Understanding knowledge sharing activities in tree/open source software projects: An empirical study. *Journal of Systems and Software, 81*(3), 431. doi:10.1016/j.jss.2007.03.086

Spender, J.-C. (1994). Organizational Knowledge, Collective Practice and Penrose Rents. *International Business Review, 3*(4), 353–367. doi:10.1016/0969-5931(94)90028-0

Spender, J.-C. (1996). Organizational knowledge, learning and memory: Three concepts in search of a theory. *Journal of Organizational Change Management, 9*(1), 63–78. doi:10.1108/09534819610156813

Sperber, D., & Wilson, D. (1995). *Relevance: Communication and Cognition.* Oxford UK: Blackwell.

Spiegler, I. (2000). Knowledge Management: A New Idea or a Recycled Concept? *Communications of AIS (June), 3*(14).

Spiggle, S. (1994). Analysis and interpretation of qualitative data in consumer research. *Journal of Consumer Research, 21*(December), 491-503.

Srivastava, A., Bartol, K. M., & Locke, E. A. (2006). Empowering leadership in management teams: Effects on knowledge sharing, efficacy, and performance. *Academy of Management Journal, 49*(6), 1239–1251.

Standards Australia. (2000). *AS/NZS ISO 9000:2000 Quality management systems—Fundamentals and vocabulary* (3rd ed.). Sydney: Standards Australia, Standards New Zealand & International Organization for Standardization.

Standards Australia. (2001). *HB 275-2001 knowledge management: A framework for succeeding in the knowledge era*. Sydney: Standards Australia International Limited.

Standards Australia. (2004). *AS/NZS 4360:2004 Risk Management* (3rd ed.). Sydney: Standards Australia & Standards New Zealand.

Standards Australia. (2005). *AS 8015—2005 corporate governance of information and communication technology*. Sydney: Standards Australia.

Staples, D. S., & Webster, J. (2008). Exploring the effects of trust, task interdependence and virtualness on knowledge sharing in teams. *Information Systems Journal, 18*(6), 617. doi:10.1111/j.1365-2575.2007.00244.x

Stein, E. W. (2006). A Qualitative Study of the Characteristics of a Community of Practice for Knowledge Management and Its Success Factors. *International Journal of Knowledge Management, 1*(4), 1–24.

Stein, E. W., & Zwass, V. (1995). Actualizing organizational memory with information systems. *Information Systems Research, 6*(2), 85–117. doi:10.1287/isre.6.2.85

Steiner, K., Essmayr, W., & Wagner, R. (2001). Topic maps - an enabling technology for knowledge management. In *Proceedings of the 12th International Workshop on Database and Expert Systems Applications*, (pp. 472-476).

Stenmark, D. (2000). Leveraging tacit organization knowledge. *Journal of Management Information Systems, 17*(3), 9-24.

Stewart, G.L., & Barrick, M.R. (2000). Team structure and performance: Assessing the mediating role of intra-team process and the moderating role of task type. *Academy of Management Journal, 43*(2), 135-148.

Stoddart, L. (2001). Managing intranets to encourage knowledge sharing: Opportunities and constraints. *Online Information Review, 25*(1), 19–28. doi:10.1108/14684520110366661

Storck, J., & Hill, P. A. (2000). Knowledge diffusion through "strategic communities". *Sloan Management Review, 41*, 63–74.

Storper, M. (1997). Territories, flows, and hierarchies in the global economy. In K.R Cox (Ed), *Spaces of globalization. Reasserting the power of the local* (pp. 19-44). New York: The Guilford Press.

Strassmann, P. A. (1990). *The business value of computers*. New Canaan, CT: The Information Economics Press.

Stratte-McClure, J. (2000). Taking the information highway to efficiency. International Herald Tribune, March 20.

Strauss, A., & Corbin, J. (1990). *Basics of qualitative research: techniques and procedures for developing grounded theory* (2nd ed.). Thousand Oaks, CA: Sage Publications.

Strickland, L. S. (2004). The information shortcomings of 9/11. *Information Management Journal, 38*(6), 34–41.

Styhre, A. (2008). The role of social capital in knowledge sharing: the case of a specialist rock construction company. *Construction Management and Economics, 26*(9), 941–951. doi:10.1080/01446190802259035

Sutton, D. C. (2001). What is knowledge and can it be managed? *European Journal of Information Systems, 10*(2), 80–88. doi:10.1057/palgrave.ejis.3000397

Sutton, R. I., & Staw, B. M. (1995). What theory is not. *Administrative Science Quarterly, 40*, 371–384. doi:10.2307/2393788

Suyeon, K., Hyunseok, H., & Euiho, S. (2003). A process-based approach to knowledge-flow analysis: a case study of a manufacturing firm. *Knowledge and Process Management, 10*(4), 260–276. doi:10.1002/kpm.186

Sveiby, K. E. (1997). *The new organizational wealth: managing and measuring knowledge-based assets*. San Fransisco: Berrett-Koehler Publishers, Inc.

Sveiby, K. E. (2001, July 2004). Methods for measuring intangible assets. Retrieved 3 August, 2004, from http://wwwsveiby.com/articles/IntangibleMethods.htm

Swain, D. & Ekionea, J.-P. B. (2008). A Framework for Developing and Aligning a Knowledge Management Strategy. *Journal of Information and Knowledge Management (June), 7*(2).

Swan, J. (2003). Knowledge Management in Action, in Holsapple. In C.W (ed) *Handbook on knowledge management 1: Knowledge matters* (pp. 271-296). Berlin: Springer.

Swan, J., Scarbrough, H., & Robertson, M. (2002). The construction of "communities of practice" in the management of innovation. *Management Learning, 33*, 477–496. doi:10.1177/1350507602334005

Szulanski, G. (1996). Exploring internal stickiness: Impediments to the transfer of best practice within the firm. *Strategic Management Journal, 17*(Special Issue: Knowledge and the Firm - Winter).

Szulanski, G. (2000). The process of knowledge transfer: A diachronic analysis of stickiness. *Organizational Behavior and Human Decision Processes, 82*(1), 9–27. doi:10.1006/obhd.2000.2884

Szulanski, G., & Cappetta, R. (2000). *When credible sources share complex knowledge.* Unpublished manuscript, The Wharton School, University of Pennsylvania.

Tabachnick, B.G., & Fidell, L.S. (1989). *Using multivariate statistics, (2nd ed.)*. New York, NY: Harper Collins Publishers, Inc.

Tajfel, H., & Turner, J. C. (1986). The social identity theory of intergroup behavior. In S. Worchel & W. G.Austin (Eds.), *Psychology of intergroup relations* (pp. 7-24), Chicago: Nelson-Hall.

Tancer, W. (2007, January 29). *YouTube and Google: Quantifying the Synergy*. Retrieved from http://weblogs.hitwise.com/bill-tancer/2007/01/youtube_and_google_quantifying.html

Tanriverdi, H. (2005). Information technology relatedness, knowledge management capability, and performance of multibusiness firms. *MIS Quarterly, 29*(2), 311-334.

Tanudjojo, S., & Braganza, A. (2005). *Overcoming barriers to knowledge flow: Evidence-based attributes enabling the creation, mobilization, and diffusion of knowledge.* Chapter presented at the 38th Hawaii International Conference on System Sciences (HICSS), Hawaii.

Taylor, F. W. (1911). *The Principles of Scientific Management* [trade edition]. New York: Harper and Brothers Publishers.

Te'eni, D. (2001). A cognitive-affective model of organizational communication for designing IT. *MIS Quarterly, 25*(2), 251-312.

Teece, D. J. (1998). Capturing value from knowledge assets: The new economy, markets for know-how, and intangible assets. *California Management Review, 40*(3), 55.

Teece, D. J. (1998). Research directions for knowledge management. *California Management Review, 40*(3), 289–292.

Teece, D. J. (2001). Strategies for managing knowledge assets: the role of firm structure and industrial context. In I. Nonaka, I. & D. J. Teece (eds.), *Managing Industrial Knowledge: Creation, Transfer and Utilization*. London: Sage Publications.

Teece, D. J., Pisano, G., & Shuen, A. (1997). Dynamic capabilities and strategic management. *Strategic Management Journal, 18*(7), 509–533. doi:10.1002/(SICI)1097-0266(199708)18:7<509::AID-SMJ882>3.0.CO;2-Z

Teece, D.J. (2000). *Managing intellectual capital: Organizational, strategic, and policy dimensions.* Oxford University Press.

Terlaak, A., & Gong, Y. (2008). Vicarious learning and inferential accuracy in adoption processes. *Academy of Management Review, 33*(4), 846–868.

The Company. (2002, May 29). *The Company's Newsletter, 1*(1), 1.

Thompson, J.D. (1967). *Organizations in action.* New York: McGraw-Hill.

Thompson, M. (2005). Structural and epistemic parameters in communities of practice. *Organization Science, 16*(2), 151–164. doi:10.1287/orsc.1050.0120

Thompson, M., & Heron, P. (2006). Relational quality and innovative performance in R&D based science and technology firms. *Human Resource Management Journal, 16*(1), 28–47.

Thompson, R. L., Higgins, C. A., & Howell, J. (1991). Personal computing: Toward a conceptual model of utilization. *MIS Quarterly, 15*(1), 124-143.

Thompson, R. L., Higgins, C. A., & Howell, J. M. (1991, March). Personal computing: Toward a conceptual model of utilization. *MIS Quarterly,* 125-143.

Tiwana, A. (2000). *The Knowledge Management Toolkit.* Prentice Hall: Upper Saddle River, NJ.

Tiwana, A. (2001). *The essential guide to knowledge management: e-business and CRM applications.* Upper Saddle River, NJ: Prentice-Hall.

Tiwana, A., & Bush, A. (2001). A social exchange architecture for distributed Web communities. *Journal of Knowledge Management, 5,* 242–248. doi:10.1108/13673270110401220

Tiwana, A., & Mclean, E. R. (2005). Expertise integration and creativity in information systems development. *Journal of Management Information Systems, 22*(1), 13–43.

Todorova, G., & Durisin, B. (2007). Absorptive capacity: Valuing a reconceptualization. *Academy of Management Review, 32*(3), 774–786.

Tornatzky, L. G., & Klein, K. J. (1982). Innovation characteristics and innovation adoption-implementation: A meta-analysis of findings. *IEEE Transactions on Engineering Management, 29*(1), 28-45.

Tsatsoulis, C., & Williams, A. (2000). Case-based reasoning. In T.C. Leondes (Ed.), *Knowledge-based systems: Techniques and applications.* CA: Academic Press.

Tsui, E. (2003). Tracking the role and evolution of commercial knowledge management software. In C. W. Holsapple (ed.), *Handbook on knowledge management 2: Knowledge directions* (pp. 5-27). Berlin: Springer.

Tunney, R. J. (2003). Implicit and explicit knowledge decay at different rates: A dissociation between priming and recognition in artificial grammar learning. *Experimental Psychology, 50*(2), 124–130. doi:10.1026//1618-3169.50.2.124

Tuomi, I. (2000). Data is more than knowledge: Implications of the reversed knowledge hierarchy for knowledge management and organizational memory. *Journal of MIS, 16*(3), 103-117.

Turban, E., McLean, E., & Wetherbe, J. (2002). *Information technology for management: transforming Business in the Digital Economy* (3rd ed.). New York: John Wiley.

Tushman, M.L., & Anderson, P. (1986). Technological discontinuities and organizational environments. *Administrative Science Quarterly, 31*(3), 439-465.

Ulrich, W. (1983). *Critical Heuristics of Social Planning.* New York: Wiley.

Usoro, A., & Kuofie, M. H. S. (2006). Conceptualisation of Cultural Dimensions as a Major Influence on Knowledge Sharing. *International Journal of Knowledge Management, 2*(2), 16–25.

Uzzi, B. (1997). Social structure and competition in interfirm networks: The paradox of embeddedness. *Administrative Science Quarterly, 42,* 35–67. doi:10.2307/2393808

Uzzi, B., & Gillespie, J.J. (2002). Knowledge spillover in corporate financing networks: embeddedness and the firm's debt performance. *Strategic management Journal, 23*(7), 595-618.

Van Bruggen, G.H., Lilien, G.L., & Kacker, M. (2002). Informants in organizational marketing research: Why use multiple informants and how to aggregate responses. *Journal of Marketing Research, 39*(4), 469-478.

Van de Ven, A., Delbecq, A., & Koenig, R. (1976). Determinants of coordination modes within organizations. *American Sociological Review, 41*, 322-338.

Van den Bos, E., & Poletiek, F. H. (2008). Effects of grammar complexity on artificial grammar learning. *Memory & Cognition, 36*(6), 1122–1131. doi:10.3758/MC.36.6.1122

van den Hoof, B., & de Leeuw van Weenen, F. (2004). Committed to share: Commitment and CMC use as antecedents of knowledge sharing. *Knowledge and Process Management, 11*(1), 13–24. doi:10.1002/kpm.187

Van der Vegt, G., Van de Vliert, E., & Oosterhof, A. (2003). Informational dissimilarity and organizational citizenship behavior: The role of intra-team interdependence and team identification. *Academy of Management Journal, 46*, 715-727.

Van der Vegt, G.S., Emans, B.J.M., & Van de Vliert, E. (2001). Patterns of interdependence in work teams: A two-level investigation of the relations with job and team satisfaction. *Personnel Psychology, 54*(1), 51-72.

Van Dyne, L., Graham, J. W., & Dienesch, R. M. (1994). Organizational citizenship behavior: Construct redefinition, measurement, and validation. *Academy of Management Journal, 37*, 765–802. doi:10.2307/256600

Vascellaro, J. (2007, August 28). Social networking goes professional. *Wall Street Journal*. D1-D2.

Vaus DAD. (1995). *Surveys in social research* (4th ed). North Sydney: Allen and Unwin.

Venkatesh, V., & Morris, M. (2000). Why don't men ever stop to ask for directions? Gender, social influence, and their role in technology acceptance and usage behavior. *MIS Quarterly, 24*(1), 115-139.

Venkatesh, V., Morris, M. G., Davis, G. B., & Davis, F. D. (2003). User acceptance of information t technology: Toward a unified view. *MIS Quarterly, 27*(3), 425-478.

Vera, D. (2001). *CO-alignment between business strategy and knowledge strategy and impact on performance*. Paper presented at Academy of Management Conference, Washington, DC, USA.

Veregin, H. (1991). *Data quality measurement and assessment*. NCGIA Core Curriculum in Geographic Information Science.

Vitari, C., Moro, J., Ravarini, A., & Bourdon, I. (2007). Improving KMS acceptance: The role of organizational and indivuduals' characteristics. *International Journal of Knowledge Management, 3*(2), 68-90.

Vizcaino, A., Soto, J. P., Portillo-Rodríguez, J., & Piattini, M. (2007). Developing knowledge management systems form a knowledge-based and multi-agent approach. *International Journal of Knowledge Management, 3*(4), 67–83.

von Krogh, G. (2002). The communal resource and information systems. *Journal of Strategic Information Systems, 11*, 85-107.

Von Krogh, G., Ichijo, K., & Nonaka, I. (2000). *Enabling knowledge creation*. Oxford: Oxford University Press

Wageman, R. (1995). Interdependence and group effectiveness. *Administrative Science Quarterly, 40*, 145-180.

Wagner, C., Cheung, K., Lee, F., & Ip, R. (2003). Enhancing e-governments in developing countries: managing knowledge through virtual communities. *The Electronic Journal on Information Systems in Developing Countries, 14*(4), 1–20.

Wagner, R. K., & Sternberg, R. J. (1986). Tacit knowledge and intelligence in the everyday world. In Sternberg & Wagner (Eds.), *Practical Intelligence*. Cambridge, UK: Cambridge University Press.

Wall Street Journal. (2007, March 13). *Viacom sues Google and You Tube*. Retrieved from http://blogs.wsj.com/law/2007/03/13/viacom-sues-google-and-you-tube/trackback/

Wall Street Journal. (2008, October 30). *Beyond YouTube: New ways to find video on the web.* Retrieved from http://online.wsj.com/article/SB122532318320582165-search.html?KEYWORDS=online+video&COLLECTION=wsjie/6month

Walls, J. G., Widmeyer, G. R., & Sawy, O. A. (1992). Building an information system design theory for vigilant EIS. *Information Systems Research*, *3*(1), 36-59.

Walsh, J. P., & Ungson, G. R. (1991). Organizational memory. *Academy of Management Review*, *16*(1), 57-91.

Walsh, J.P. (1995). Managerial and organizational cognition: Notes from a trip down memory lane. *Organization Science*, *6*(3), 280-321.

Walsham, G. (2001). Knowledge management: The benefits and limitations of computer systems. *European Management Journal*, *19*(6), 599-608.

Walsham, G., & Barrett, M. (2005). *ICTs and changing processes of knowing in a global development agency. Judge Institute of Management Working Papers*, No.02/2005, University of Cambridge. Retrieved April 20, 2005 from www.jbs.cam.ac.uk/research/working_papers/2005/wp0502.pdf

Walther, J. B. (1995). Relational aspects of computer-mediated communication: experimental observations over time. *Organization Science*, *6*, 186–203. doi:10.1287/orsc.6.2.186

Wang, C.-C. (2004). The influence of ethical and self-interest concerns on knowledge sharing intentions among managers: An empirical study. *International Journal of Management*, *21*(3), 370–381.

Wang, E. T. G., Chia-Lin Lin, C., Jiang, J. J., & Klein, G. (2007). Improving enterprise resource planning (ERP) fit to organizational process through knowledge transfer. *International Journal of Information Management*, *27*(3), 200–212. doi:10.1016/j.ijinfomgt.2007.02.002

Wang, J. (Ed.). (2008). *Data Warehousing and Mining: Concepts, Methodologies, Tools, and Applications* (6 Volumes). Hershey, PA: IGI Global.

Wang, J., Hu, X. H., Hollister, K., & Zhu, D. (2008). A comparison and scenario analysis of leading data mining software. *International Journal of Knowledge Management*, *4*(2), 17–34.

Wang, Y., Yang, Z., Kong, P., & Gay, R. (2003). Ontology-based Web knowledge Management. *Information. Communications and Signal Processing*, *3*, 1859–1863.

Wanless, D. (2002). *Securing Our Future Health: Taking a Long-Term View.* Final Report, HM Treasury,The Stationery Office, London.

Wanless, D. (2004). *Securing Good Health for the Whole Population.* Final Report, HM Treasury, The Stationery Office, London.

Wanless, D., Appleby, J., Harrison, A., & Patel, D. (2007, September) *Our Future Health Secured? A review of NHS funding and performance.*

Wasko, M. M., & Faraj, S. (2000). 'It is What One Does': Why People Participate and Help Others in Electronic Communities of Practice. *The Journal of Strategic Information Systems*, *9*(2/3), 155–173. doi:10.1016/S0963-8687(00)00045-7

Wasko, M. M., & Faraj, S. (2005). Why should I share? Examining social capital and knowledge contribution in electronic networks of practice. *MIS Quarterly*, *29*(1), 35-57.

Wasko, M. M., Faraj, S., & Teigland, R. (2004). Collective Action and Knowledge Contribution in Electronic Networks of Practice. *Journal of the Association for Information Systems*, *5*(11-12), 493–513.

Watson, R. T. (1999). *Data Management: Databases and Organizations* (2nd ed.). New York.

Watson, S., & Hewett, K. (2006). A multi-theoretical model of knowledge transfer in organizations: Determinants of knowledge contribution and knowledge reuse. *Journal of Management Studies*, *43*(2), 141–173. doi:10.1111/j.1467-6486.2006.00586.x

Webdriven. (2007, August 15). *Delta Airlines employees make travel videos.* Retrieved from http://www.bewebdriven.com/blog/whats-hot/viral-travel-videos-delta-airlines.php

Webster, J., Brown, G., Zweig, D., Connelly, C. E., Brodt, S. E., & Sitkin, S. B. (2008). Beyond knowledge sharing: Withholding knowledge at work. In J. J. Matocchio (Ed.), *Research in Personnel and Human Resources Management* (Vol. 27). Oxford, England: Elsevier.

Welch, D., Welch, L., & Piekkari, R. (2005). Speaking in tongues: The importance of language in international management processes. *International Studies of Management and Organization, 1*, 10–27.

Wellman, B. (1996). For a Social Network Analysis of Computer Networks: A Sociological Perspective on Collaborative Work and Virtual Community. *SIGCPR/SIGMIS*, Denver, Colorado.

Wellman, B., & Gulia, M. (1997). Net Surfers Don't Ride Alone: Virtual Communities as Communities. *Communities and Cyberspace*, New York: Routledge.

Wellman, B., & Gulia, M. (1999). Virtual communities as communities: net surfers don't ride alone. In M. A. Smith, & P. Kollock, (eds.), *Communities in Cyberspace*. London: Routledge.

Wellman, B., Salaff, J., Dimitrova, D., Garton, L., Gulia, M., & Haythornthwaite, C. (1996). Computer Networks as Social Networks: Collaborative Work, Telework, and Virtual Community. *Annual Review of Sociology, 22*, 213–238. doi:10.1146/annurev.soc.22.1.213

Wenger, E. (1998). Communities of practice: Learning as a social system. *The Systems Thinker, 9*(5).

Wenger, E. (1998). *Communities of Practice: learning, meaning and identity*. New York: Cambridge University Press.

Wenger, E. C., & Snyder, W. M. (2000). Communities of Practice: The Organizational Frontier. *Harvard Business Review, 78*, 139–145.

Wenger, E., McDermott, R., & Snyder, W. M. (2002). *Cultivating Communities of Practice: A Guide to Managing Knowledge*. Boston, MA: Harvard Business School Press.

Wernerfelt, B. (1984). A resource-based view of the firm. *Strategic Management Journal, 5*(2), 171–180. doi:10.1002/smj.4250050207

West, S. G., Finch, J. F., & Curran, P. J. (1995). Structural equation models with nonnormal variables. In R. H. Hoyle (Ed.), *Structural equation modeling: Concepts, issues, and applications* (pp. 56-75). Thousand Oaks, CA: Sage Publications.

Wexler, M.N. (2001). The who, what and why of knowledge mapping, *Journal of Knowledge Management, 5*(3), 249-263.

Wiesenfeld, B. M., Raghuram, S., & Garud, R. (1999). Communication patterns as determinants of organizational identification in a virtual organization. *Organization Science, 10*, 777–790. doi:10.1287/orsc.10.6.777

Wiig, K. (1993). *Knowledge management foundation*. Arlington, Texas: Schema Press.

Wiig, K. (1997). Knowledge management: where did it come from and where will it go? *Expert Systems with Applications, 14*(Fall).

Wijnhoven, F. (1999). Development scenarios for organizational memory information systems. *Journal of MIS, 16*(1), 121-146.

Wilde, E. (2006). *Knowledge organization mashups*. Retrieved Feb 2, 2007 from http://dret.net/netdret/docs/wilde-tikrep245.pdf

Williamson, O. E. (1979). Transaction-cost economics: The governance of contractual relations. *Journal of Law and Economics, 22*(2), 233-261.

Wilson, T. (2002). The nonsense of 'knowledge management' *Information Research*, Vol. 8 No. 1, October 2002. http://informationr.net/ir/8-1/paper144.html#sch67 Retrieved on 8 July 2006

Wilson, T. (2002). The nonsense of "knowledge management." *Information Research, 8*(1). Retrieved June, 20. 2007 from, http://informationr.net/ir/8-1/paper144.html

Winter, S. G. (1987). Knowledge and Competence as Strategic Assets. In D. J. Teece (Ed.), *The Competitive Challenge: Strategies for Industrial Innovation and Renewal* (pp. 159-184). Cambridge, MA: Ballinger Publishing Company.

Witzel, M. (2003). The world's first virtual business organization. *European Business Forum,* Issue 13, 72-74.

Wolfe, C., & Loraas, T. (2008). Knowledge sharing: The effects of incentives, environment, and person. *Journal of Information Systems, 22*(2), 53. doi:10.2308/jis.2008.22.2.53

Wong, J., & Hong, J. I. (2007). Making mashups with Marmite: Towards end-user programming for the Web. *CHI 2007 Proceedings: Programming By & With End-Users* (pp. 1435-1444).

Woolgar, S. (2002). *Virtual society? Technology, cyberbole, reality.* New York: Oxford University Press.

Wu, M., Lo, Y., & Hsu, S. (2006). A case-based reasoning approach to generating new product ideas. *International Journal of Advanced Manufacturing Technology, 30,* 166–173. doi:10.1007/s00170-005-0048-3

Xu, J. (2007). Formalizing natural-language spatial relations between linear objects with topological and metric properties. *International Journal of Geographical Information Science, 21*(4), 377-395.

Yakhlef, A. (2005). Virtual organisation as spatial and temporal innovations. *Forthcoming in Space and Culture.*

Yang, Gi-Chul, & Oh, J. (1993). Knowledge acquisition and retrieval based on conceptual graphs. In *Proceedings of ACM/SIGAPP symposium on Applied Computing, Indianapolis* (pp. 476–481).

Yang, Z., Liu, Y., & Li, S. (2002). Applying Information Retrieval Technology to Incremental Knowledge Management. In *Proceedings of First International Conference on Engineering and Development of Cooperative Information Systems* (LNCS 2480, pp. 117-129).

Yanow, D., (2004). Translating local knowledge at organizational peripheries. *British Journal of Management, 15*(Special Issue 1), 9-25.

Yates, J., Orlikowski, W., & Okamura, K. (1999). Explicit and Implicit Structuring of Genres in Electronic Communication: Reinforcement and Change of Social Interaction. *Organization Science, 10*(1), 83–103. doi:10.1287/orsc.10.1.83

Yen, C. H., & Miller, L. L. (1995). An extensible view system for multidatabase integration and interoperation. *Integrated Computer-Aided Engineering, 2*(2), 97-123.

Yin, R. K. (1994). *Case study research: Design and methods* (2nd ed., Vol. 5). Thousand Oaks, CA: Sage Publications.

Yu, J., & Buyya, R. (2005). A taxonomy of scientific workflow systems for grid computing. *SIGMOD Record, 34*(3), 44–49. doi:10.1145/1084805.1084814

Yu, J., & Casati, F. (2008). Understanding mashup development. Mashing up search services. *IEEE Internet Computing, 12*(5), 44–52. doi:10.1109/MIC.2008.114

Yu, S.-H., Kim, Y.-G., & Kim, M.-Y. (2004). *Linking Organizational Knowledge Management Drivers to Knowledge Management Performance: An Exploratory Study.* Paper presented at the 37th Hawaii International Conference on System Sciences. HICSS36, IEEE Computer Society.

Yue Wah, C., Menkhoff, T., Loh, B., & Evers, H. D. (2007). Social Capital and Knowledge Sharing in Knowledge-Based Organizations: An Empirical Study. *International Journal of Knowledge Management, 3*(1), 29–38.

Zack, M. H. (1993). Interactivity and communication mode choice in ongoing management groups. *Information Systems Research, 4*(3), 207–239. doi:10.1287/isre.4.3.207

Zack, M. H. (1994). Electronic messaging and communication effectiveness in an ongoing work group. *Information & Management, 26*(4), 231–241. doi:10.1016/0378-7206(94)90095-7

Zack, M. H. (1999). *Knowledge and strategy.* Boston: Butterworth-Heinemann.

Zack, M. H. (1999). Managing codified knowledge. *Sloan Management Review, 40*(4), 45–58.

Zack, M. H. (1999). Developing a knowledge strategy. *California Management Review, 41*(3), 125–145.

Zack, M. H. (2007). The role of decision support systems in an indeterminate world. *Decision Support Systems, 43*(4), 1664–1674. doi:10.1016/j.dss.2006.09.003

Zaharna, R. S. (1995). Bridging cultural differences: American public relations practices and Arab communication patterns. *Public Relations Review*, (21): 241–255. doi:10.1016/0363-8111(95)90024-1

Zakaria, N., Stanton, J., & Sarkar-Barney, S. (2003). Designing and implementing culturally-sensitive IT applications: the interaction of culture values and privacy issues in the Middle East. *Information Technology & People*, *16*(1), 49–75. doi:10.1108/09593840310463023

Zammuto, R. F., Griffith, T. L., Majchrzak, A., Dougherty, D. J., & Faraj, S. (2007). Information technology and the changing fabric of organization. *Organization Science*, *18*(5), 749–762. doi:10.1287/orsc.1070.0307

Zand, D. E. (1972). Trust and managerial problem solving. *Administrative Science Quarterly*, *17*, 229–239. doi:10.2307/2393957

Zhang, W., & Watts, S. (2008). Online communities as communities of practice: a case study. *Journal of Knowledge Management*, *12*(4), 55–71. doi:10.1108/13673270810884255

Zhou, A., & Fink, D. (2003). Knowledge management and intellectual capital: An empirical examination of current practice in australia. *Knowledge Management Research & Practice*, *1*(2), 86-94.

Zhu, Z. (2001). What is to be managed: knowledge, knowing, or knower, and does it matter? In *Proceedings of the International Symposium on Knowledge and Systems Science* (pp. 29-45). Dalian University of Technology, Dalian, China.

Zhu, Z. (2004). Knowledge management: towards a universal concept or cross-cultural contexts? *Knowledge Management Research & Practice*, (2), 67-79.

Zhuge, H. (2002). A knowledge grid model and platform for global knowledge sharing. *Expert Systems with Applications*, *22*, 313–320. doi:10.1016/S0957-4174(02)00019-2

Zhuge, H. (2004). Semantics, resource and grid editorial. *Future Generation Computer Systems*, *20*, 1–5. doi:10.1016/S0167-739X(03)00159-6

Zollo, M., & Winter, S.G. (2002). Deliberate learning and the evolution of dynamic capabilities. *Organization Science*, *13*(3), 339-351.

Zucchermaglio, C., & Talamo, A. (2003). The development of a virtual community of practice using electronic mail and communicative genres. *Journal of Business and Technical Communication*, *17*, 259–284. doi:10.1177/1050651903017003001

Zyngier, S. (2005). Knowledge management governance. In D. Schwarz (Ed.), *The encyclopaedia of knowledge management*. Hershey, PA: Idea Group Publishing.

Zyngier, S. (2006). *The role of knowledge management governance in the implementation of strategy.* Chapter presented at the 39th. Hawaiian International Conference on System Sciences (HICSS39), Hawaii.

Zyngier, S. (2007). *Knowledge management governance: A framework for knowledge management benefits realization.* Chapter presented at the 8th International Research Conference on Quality, Innovation and Knowledge Management, New Delhi, India.

Zyngier, S., Burstein, F., & McKay, J. (2004). *Knowledge management governance: a multifaceted approach to organizational decision and innovation support.* Chapter presented at the Decision Support in an Uncertain World: Proceedings of the 2004 IFIP WG8.3 International Conference on Decision Support Systems (DSS2004), Prato, Italy.

Zyngier, S., Burstein, F., & McKay, J. (2005). Governance of strategies to manage organizational knowledge—a mechanism to oversee knowledge needs. In M. Jennex (Ed.), *Knowledge management case book*. Hershey, PA: Idea Group Books.

Zyngier, S., Burstein, F., & Rodriguez, M.-L. (2003). Knowledge management strategies in Australia. In H. Hasan & M. Handzic (Eds.), *Australian studies in knowledge management*. Woolongong: University of Wollongong Press.

Zyngier, S.M., Burstein, F., & Rodriguez, M.L. (2003). Knowledge management strategies in Australia: Analysis of uptake and understanding, In H. Hasan & M. Handzic (eds), *Australian Studies in Knowledge Management* (pp 487-451), Wollongong: UOW Press.

About the Contributors

Murray E. Jennex is an associate professor at San Diego State University, editor in chief of the International Journal of Knowledge Management, editor in chief of Idea Group Publishing's Knowledge Management book series, co-editor in chief of the International Journal of Information Systems for Crisis Response and Management, and president of the Foundation for Knowledge Management (LLC). Dr. Jennex specializes in knowledge management, system analysis and design, IS security, e-commerce, and organizational effectiveness. Dr. Jennex serves as the Knowledge Management Systems Track co-chair at the Hawaii International Conference on System Sciences. He is the author of over 100 journal articles, book chapters, and conference proceedings on knowledge management, end user computing, international information systems, organizational memory systems, ecommerce, security, and software outsourcing. He holds a B.A. in chemistry and physics from William Jewell College, an M.B.A. and an M.S. in software engineering from National University, an M.S. in telecommunications management and a Ph.D. in information systems from the Claremont Graduate University. Dr. Jennex is also a registered professional mechanical engineer in the state of California and a Certified Information Systems Security Professional (CISSP) and a Certified Secure Software Lifecycle Professional (CSSLP).

* * *

Minwir Al-Shammari is Professor Operations Management & Technology at the University of Bahrain's College of Business Administration. He holds a Ph.D in Industrial Management from University of Glasgow, UK (1990) and M.S in industrial management from University of Central Missouri, USA (1986). He has been involved for about 20 years in teaching, research, training, and/or consultancy in the areas of operations management, knowledge management, supply chain management, management information systems, business process re-engineering, project management, spreadsheet modeling, management science, and research methodology. Prof. Al-Shammari served as a member of a number of national, regional, and international professional associations. He has received a number of local, regional, and international research awards, grants, and scholarships. He served as a consultant to the UN on a Knowledge Management project in the ESCWA region. He served on the editorial boards of such refereed international publications as Journal of Systems and Management Sciences, International Journal of Applied Decision Science, International Journal of Management Innovation Systems, and Cross-Cultural Management: An International Journal. He has authored/co-authored over 30 research papers, and served as a reviewer for several regional and international research journals such as Logistics Information Management, International Journal of Production Economics, Journal of Information Systems Education, and International Journal of Production & Operations Management. Al-Shammari's publications have appeared in such refereed international journals as International Journal of Knowledge Management, Logistics Information Management, International Journal of Information Management, European Journal of Operational Research, Expert Systems with Applications, Journal of Computer Information Systems, International Journal of Operations and Production Management, Production and Inventory Management Journal, International Journal of Commerce and Management, International Journal of Computer Applications in Technology, Cross-Cultural Management, International Journal of Management, Leadership and Organization Development Journal, and Creativity and Innovation Management.

Summer Bartczak is an adjunct assistant professor of management information systems at the University of Central Arkansas. She also serves as a knowledge analyst and strategy consultant with Sawdey Solution Services, Inc. in support of the Department of Defense. She worked for 21 years in the communications, computer, and information management field as an officer in the US Air Force. She holds a PhD in management information systems (Auburn University), MS in information resource management (Air Force Institute of Technology), a MA in military operational art (Air University), and a BS(US Air Force Academy). Her research interests include knowledge management strategy and implementation.

James M. Bloodgood is an associate professor of management at Kansas State University. He received his Ph.D. in strategic management from the University of South Carolina. His research interests include knowledge management, organizational change, international entrepreneurship, and business ethics. He has published in a variety of journals including Academy of Management Review, Decision Support Systems, Journal of Management, and Journal of Management Studies.

Amer Celjo is a lecturer at Sarajevo School of Science and Technology and Application Manager at MIMS Group. He completed his bachelor of EET at Oklahoma State University, USA and MBA at Schiller International University, Germany. Amer's interest is in information technology. His work focuses on researching technical factors contributing to effective organisational learning and knowledge management.

Bonnie Cheuk has over 10 years of experience facilitating knowledge sharing and managing information in both private and public organisations. Since 2006, she has worked for Environmental Resources Management (ERM), the world's largest environmental consultancy, and heads a global program which aims at promoting cross-boundary collaboration and knowledge sharing both internally and with clients. Prior to joining ERM, she headed up a knowledge management consultancy unit promoting knowledge sharing across the 32 Scottish local authorities and their partners. She was with the British Council (2002 to 2005) and with Arthur Andersen business consulting (1999 to 2002) where she helped clients to establish and implement knowledge strategy in Asia Pacific region and in the United States. Bonnie received her Ph.D. 1999 and since then has been applying Dervin's Sense-Making Methodology and Snowden's complexity theory to help companies design and implement user-oriented knowledge management projects and systems. Her KM projects have won awards such as Top 10 Best Intranet Awards 2009 for ERM; Information Management Award IM2004 and IM2005 for British Council. Bonnie is recognized internationally for promoting information literacy in the workplace context. She can be contacted at bonnie.cheuk@gmail.com.

Michael A. Chilton is an associate professor of management information systems at Kansas State University. He received his Ph.D. from the University of Arkansas. His research interests include knowledge management, IT performance metrics, and IT pedagogy. He has published in a variety of journals including the Journal of Management Information Systems, the Database for Advances in Information Systems and the Journal of Information Systems Education.

Andrew P. Ciganek is an assistant professor of computer information systems at Jacksonville State University. He earned his PhD from the University of Wisconsin – Milwaukee in 2006. His research interests include examining the managerial and strategic issues associated with the decision-making process of innovative technologies. He has had several refereed conference publications and has also published book chapters examining topics related to mobile computing devices and enterprise application integration.

Brenda Dervin is Full Professor of Communication and Joan N. Huber Fellow in Social and Behaviorial Sciences, Ohio State University. She has worked on the development of Sense-Making Methodology for 33 years. She and colleagues have applied the approach in multiple contexts focusing in particular on user and audience studies intended to implement the design of communication/information systems and the improvement of system interfaces with users. She got her PhD in communication from Michigan State University and holds an honorary doctorate in the social sciences from the University of Helsinki. A prolific author, she has received top researcher awards from both the American Society for Information Science and Technology and the International Communication Association. She is former president and a fellow in the latter organization and for more than a decade served as an elected member of the council of the International Association of Media and Communication Research. She can be contacted at dervin.1@osu.edu.

Jean-Pierre Booto Ekionea is a PhD candidate in information systems, an independent senior consultant in IS/IT/KM, and a lecturer in the Management and Technology Department at the University of Quebec in Montreal (UQAM), Canada since 2001. He received his master's degree in computer science from UQAM and bachelor's degree in computer science from ISIPA-Computer Institute in Kinshasa (DR Congo). His research interests are business performance and the sustainability of competitive advantage as defined by IT/IS and KM strategies. Additional areas of study for Booto include the acquisition, development, deployment and use policies. He is currently focusing on the relationship of KM with software management and on the maturity model for KM capabilities. Booto has professional and academic experiences in IS analysis and design, user needs analysis and modeling, software management, IT/IS project management, knowledge management engineering, strategic aspects of IT/IS/KM. He is currently working for Celtel DR Congo as an independent consultant.

Mohamed El Louadi is an associate professor of management information systems at the University of Tunis, Higher Institute of Management (ISG). He has published in several IS and management journals and participated in numerous international conferences covering topics related to the adoption of information and communication technologies (ICT) and MIS. He is also the author of three books on ICT and MIS. He has held research and teaching positions at the University of Pittsburgh (U.S.), the Université du Québec à Trois-Rivières (Canada), Concordia University (Canada), the Higher Colleges of Technology (Dubai), and the American University of Beirut (Lebanon).

Ellen England is currently an industrial hygiene and safety consultant for ISN Software Corporation and adjunct professor with Kaplan University. She worked for 21 years in the environmental engineering, occupational health, and academic fields as an officer in the US Air Force. She holds a PhD in environmental engineering (University of Missouri-Rolla), MS environmental health(University of Minnesota), MS general administration (Central Michigan)and BS Industrial Engineering (University of Iowa).

Dianne P. Ford, Ph.D., is an Assistant Professor in the Faculty of Business Administration at Memorial University of Newfoundland, St.John's, Canada. Her research interests focus at areas that utilize her double major in MIS/OB and include: knowledge management, perceived value of knowledge, cross-cultural implications for MIS and knowledge flows, trust, and disengagement. Dianne has published articles in IEEE: Transactions in Engineering Management, and various knowledge management journals and has presented papers at Academy of Management Annual Meeting, Hawaii International Conference for Systems Sciences, and Administrative Sciences Association of Canada.

Ronald Freeze is an assistant professor of information systems in the accounting and information systems department at Emporia State University in Kansas. He received his PhD from Arizona State University. His current research interests include knowledge management, capability assessment and SEM modeling. Ron's emphasis in his research is the measurement and validated contribution of knowledge to organizational performance. Freeze teaches object oriented programming, micro-computing applications, software analysis & design and business computing at the undergraduate level. His publications have appeared in the Journal of Management Information Systems and Journal of Knowledge Management. Freeze has also presented and had proceedings published from the ACIS, ECIS, AMCIS, ICIS and HICSS international conferences.

David Gadish is a faculty member at the Information Systems Department at the College of Business and Economics, California State University Los Angeles. His research interests include GIS, spatial data, information technology for real estate and financial sector organizations. Prof. Gadish has worked and consulted for government and industry since 1991 in GIS, information technology, and business process management.

Jeanette Galloway is communications and software development manager of the North Mersey Health Informatics Service in Liverpool, England. The North Mersey HIS provides information technology and management services to the National Health Service in the city. It is a shared service meeting the needs of hospitals, primary care, and community services. Jeanette graduated from the University of Central Lancashire's MSc programme in health informatics with distinction in 2007. The case study at the heart of this paper informed the development of a knowledge management strategy for the North Mersey HIS.

Jens Gammelgaard is associate professor of international business at the Department of International Economics and Management at the Copenhagen Business School. He joint the Copenhagen Business School in April 1998. His main research interest is knowledge management practices of multinational corporations, international mergers and acquisitions, and subsidiary development. His work has been widely published in journals like Management International Review, Journal of International Management, Journal of Knowledge Management, International Journal of Knowledge Management and edited volumes. Jens Gammelgaard has taught various courses on bachelor, MSc, and MBA, and is currently Program Director of the Bachelor of International Business program at Copenhagen Business School.

Alan Gillies has been professor of information management at UCLAN in Preston, England since 1994. He graduated from The Queen's College, Oxford in 1984 in chemistry. His PhD, probably the first to be awarded by UCLAN in 1992, was in problem solving methodology using KBS. He has also held a part time position in medical education at the University of Oxford, and in 2001 was awarded Doctor Honoris Causa by the University of Medicine and Pharmacy in Cluj Napoca, Romania. He is a member of the European Association of Health Information and Librarianship, a Chartered IT professional, and a Fellow of the British Computing Society. He has written over 100 publications including over 30 peer reviewed articles, and 18 books.

Lakshmi Goel is an Assistant Professor in Management at the Coggin College of Business, University of North Florida. She received her Ph.D. from the C.T. Bauer College of Business, University of Houston. Her research interests include knowledge sharing, organizational learning, and strategic management using social technologies such as weblogs, wikis, and three-dimensional virtual worlds. Lakshmi can be reached at: l.goel@unf.edu.

Amar Gupta is Thomas R. Brown Endowed Professor of Management and Technology; Professor of Entrepreneurship, Management and Organizations, and MIS; Senior Director for Research and Business Development; Eller College of Management (as well as Professor of Computer Science, College of Science), at the University of Arizona, USA. Earlier, he was at MIT from 1979 to 2004 and served as the founding Co-Director of the Productivity from Information Technology (PROFIT) Initiative. His current areas of interests include: Knowledge Acquisition; Knowledge Discovery and Data Mining; Knowledge Management; and Knowledge Dissemination. He is an Associate Editor of ACM Transactions of Information Technology (TOIT) He is one of the co-inventors of a new approach for reading handwritten numbers, and has advocated the use of electronic techniques for nationwide paper-less check processing. He serves as an advisor to a number of corporations and international organizations. He introduced a new course on outsourcing of professional activities at MIT in 2004 and is currently leading several initiatives that involve the use of geographically distributed teams of workers in diverse professions.

Meliha Handzic is an associate professor at Sarajevo School of Science and Technology, a partner of the University of Buckingham, UK. She earned her PhD in information systems from the University of New South Wales, Australia. Handzic's research interests include knowledge management, decision support systems, e-learning and more recently e-government. She has published on these topics widely in books, journals, and conference proceedings. Her latest monograph, Socio-Technical Knowledge Management: Studies and Initiatives, provides a valuable insight into the potential and limitations of various social and technical approaches to managing knowledge.

Shyamanta M. Hazarika is an Associate Professor of Computer Science & Engineering at School of Engineering, Tezpur University, India. He received his PhD from University of Leeds, England. Prior to that, he had completed M.Tech from Indian Institute of Technology, Kanpur, India and Bachelor's in

Engineering from Assam Engineering College, Guwahati, India. His research interests include Knowledge Representation and Reasoning, Cognitive Robotics and Intelligent Assistive Systems.

Richard Herschel is Chair of the Decision & System Sciences Department in the Haub School of Business at Saint Joseph's University in Philadelphia. His research has appeared in the International Journal of Knowledge Management, Knowledge Management Review, the Journal of Knowledge Management, Decision Support Systems, the International Journal of Information Knowledge, Culture, and Change, Information Strategy: the Executive's Journal, Small Group Research, the Journal of End User Computing, the Journal of Data Warehousing, the Journal of Information and Management Sciences, Technology Studies, and Sex Roles: A Journal of Research. Richard has taught courses in knowledge management both in the United States and China, and he teaches courses on the subject to both MBA and Executive MBA students. Dr. Herschel received his Ph.D. from Indiana University in Management Information Systems. Prior to academia, he worked as a systems analyst at Johnson & Johnson, Columbia Pictures, Schering-Plough Corporation, and Maryland National Bank.

Xiaohua (Tony) Hu is currently an associate professor and the founding director of the data mining and bioinformatics lab at the College of Information Science and Technology, Drexel University. He is the now also serving as the IEEE Computer Society Bioinformatics and Biomedicine Steering Committee Chair and the IEEE Computational Intelligence Society Granular Computing Technical Committee Chair (2007-2009). Tony's current research interests are in biomedical literature data mining, bioinformatics, text mining, semantic web mining and reasoning, rough set theory and application, information extraction and information retrieval. He has published more than 160 peer-reviewed research papers in various journals, conferences and books such as various IEEE/ACM Transactions (IEEE/ACM TCBB, IEEE TFS, IEEE TDKE, IEEE TITB, IEEE Computer), JIS, KAIS, CI, DKE, IJBRA, SIG KDD, IEEE ICDM, IEEE ICDE, SIGIR, ACM CIKM, IEEE BIBE, IEEE CICBC etc, co-edited 9 books/proceedings. He has received a few prestigious awards including the 2005 National Science Foundation (NSF) Career award,(the most prestigious award from NSF to young faculty in USA), the best paper award at the 2007 International Conference on Artificial Intelligence, the best paper award at the 2004 IEEE Symposium on Computational Intelligence in Bioinformatics and Computational Biology, the 2007 IEEE Bioinformatics and Bioengineering Outstanding Contribution Award, the 2006 IEEE Granular Computing Outstanding Service Award, and the 2001 IEEE Data Mining Outstanding Service Award. He has also served as a program co-chair/conference co-chair of 14 international conferences/workshops and a program committee member in more than 50 international conferences in the above areas. He is the founding editor-in-chief of the International Journal of Data Mining and Bioinformatics, an associate editor/editorial board member of four international journals (KAIS, IJDWM, IJSOI and JCIB). His research projects are funded by the National Science Foundation (NSF), US Dept. of Education, and the PA Dept. of Health and he has obtained more than US$3.8 millions research grants in the past 4 years as PI or Co-PI.

Ming Hua is a PhD student in the department of computer science at the Iowa State University.

Xia Huosong is a professor at the Department of Information Management and Information Systems of the Wuhan University of Science and Engineering. He was the visiting scholar in MIS, at Eller College of Management, at the University of Arizona. He received a Ph.D. degree in management science and engineering, and an M.S. degree in MIS from Management School at Huazhong University of Science and Technology. He received a B.S. degree in mathematics from Huazhong Normal University. His main research interests are: data mining and knowledge management, MIS, DSS, e-Commerce, and Logistics Information Systems.

Kimberly Killmer-Hollister, Ph.D. is an Associate Professor in the Department of Management & Information Systems at Montclair State University, Upper Montclair, New Jersey. Dr. Hollister's research falls into two main categories: Applied Operations Management and Educational Program Assessment of Management Information Systems and Operations Management curriculums. Dr. Hollister's research has been published in many peer-reviewed journals including: European Journal of Operational Research, Journal of Informatics and Education Research, Journal of Accountancy, Journal of Business & Economic Studies. Dr. Hollister is actively engaged in sharing her work with the greater academic community at regional, national, and international conferences.

Uday Kulkarni is an associate professor of information systems at the W. P. Carey School of Business at Arizona State University. He got his PhD from the University of Wisconsin-Milwaukee. Kulkarni teaches graduate courses in business intelligence and business IT strategy and has received several teaching awards. His research interests lie in the area of knowledge management–metrics development and assessment, decision-making support using data and knowledge based systems, and application of knowledge based/AI techniques to business processes. His research has appeared in journals such as IEEE Transactions on Knowledge and Data Engineering, IEEE Transactions on Software Engineering, Decision Support Systems, Decision Sciences, European Journal of Operations Research, and Journal of Management Information Systems.

Amila Lagumdzija is a lecturer at Sarajevo School of Science and Technology. She completed her bachelor of information systems at DePaul University, USA and MBA at Schiller International University, Germany. Amila teaches a wide range of subjects in Information Systems. Her research work is primarily focused on the social and organisational aspects of knowledge management. She has published and presented internationally in the field.

En Mao is an assistant professor of information systems and Agnes Candies Endowed professor at Nicholls State University. She joined Nicholls State University's College of Business Administration in 2006. She earned her PhD from the University of Memphis. Her current research interests include information technology diffusion and acceptance, end-user behavior, knowledge management, global IT, and cross-cultural issues. She has published in the Journal of Global Information Technology Management, Information & Management, Data Base, and Communications of the AIS. Her research has also appeared as book chapters in Knowledge Mapping and Management and Global Information Technology Management. Currently, she is serving as an associate editor on the editorial board of the Journal of Information Privacy and Security. She is also a member of the editorial review board of the Journal of Global Information Technology Management.

Justin Meza is an undergraduate student at the University of California at Los Angeles, majoring in Computer Science, as well as a researcher in the Exascale Computing Lab at Hewlett-Packard Laboratories. As a freelance web developer, he focuses on compliance with web standards without compromising the delivery of engaging, dynamic, and scalable content to a variety of audiences and actively seeks out ways in his research to leverage new and upcoming technologies to help distribute information to those seeking it more efficiently and effectively. His research in the area of information management at the enterprise business level continues to aid those in search of answers through its manifestation in several pervasive business applications. He can be contacted via email: justin.meza@hp.com.

Leslie Miller received a BA (1967) and an MA (1974) in mathematics at University of South Dakota, and a PhD (1980) in computer science from Southern Methodist University. At Iowa State University, he was an assistant professor (1984-1987), an associate professor (1987-1991), and a professor (1991-on-going) in computer science. He served as department chairman of computer science from 1998-2001. His major research interests are in: object oriented databases, organizational decision support systems, data warehouses, database semantics, organizational memory, parallel searching methods, multi-agent systems, database design, data-mining and computational biology. Dr. Miller is currently looking at the developing infrastructure for providing geospatial data to field survey and exploration applications. Other work on geospatial data focuses on developing accuracy models. Current activity in the organizational decision support systems area centers around the use of object based database systems to support the decision process. Work on organizational memory is focused on the capture of organizational semantics and the integration of corporate documents into the meeting process.

Elham Mousavidin is a Ph.D. candidate in the Decision and Information Sciences department at the C.T. Bauer College of Business, University of Houston. She received her MBA from C. T. Bauer College of Business. Her research interest lies in the area of information systems development (ISD). Currently she is studying Social Construction of Technology (SCOT) in the process of ISD. She has also been involved in research on web-enabled communities (e.g. weblogs) and three-dimensional virtual worlds, and their potential applications in organizations. Elham can be reached at: emousavi@mail.uh.edu.

Sree Nilakanta is an associate professor of management information systems at Iowa State University. He received his MBA and PhD in information systems from University of Houston. Dr. Nilakanta also holds a BS in mechanical engineering from Madras University. His research straddles both behavioral and technical domains of information systems with emphasis on technology innovation, database management, and organizational memory. His research has appeared in Management Science, Journal of Management Information Systems, Decision Support Systems, Information & Management, Journal Software and Information Technology, Journal of Strategic Information Systems, Omega, and others.

Seokwoo Song, PhD, is an associate professor of information systems & technology at Weber State University. He holds a MBA from Syracuse University and a PhD in information systems from the University of Wisconsin at Milwaukee. His current research interests are in the areas of knowledge management, social network, information retrieval and filtering, and IT implementation. His research publications have appeared in several journals including Communications of the ACM and DATA BASE for Advances in Information Systems.

Yunan Song graduated with an MS in computer science from Iowa State University in 2006. She currently works for SAP America.

Mark Srite is an associate professor of MIS at the University of Wisconsin – Milwaukee. He received his PhD from Florida State University in 2000. His research interests include the acceptance, adoption, and use of information technologies, cross-cultural IT issues, and group decision-making. His work has been published, or been accepted for publication, in Management Information Systems Quarterly, the Journal of MIS, Decision Support Systems, Information & Management, the Journal of Global Information Management, the Journal of Global Information Technology Management, the Journal of Computer Information Systems, and elsewhere. He is on the editorial review board of the Journal of Global Information Technology Management.

Sandy Staples, Ph.D., is a Professor and Distinguished Faculty Research Fellow of Management Information Systems in the School of Business at Queen's University, Kingston, Canada. His research interests include: knowledge management, distributed working practices at both the team and individual levels, and assessing the effectiveness of information systems and IS practices. Sandy has published articles in various journals, books and magazines including Organization Science, Information Systems Research, Small Group Research, Knowledge Management Research & Practice, Information & Management, Journal of Strategic Information Systems, Journal of Management Information Systems, International Journal of Management Reviews, Information Systems Journal, Research in Personnel and Human Resources Management and KM Review. He has served as an Associate Editor for MIS Quarterly and on the editorial boards of other journals.

Deborah E. Swain, PhD, is an assistant professor in the School of Library and Information Sciences at NC Central University in Durham, NC. She has over 20 years experience for corporations such as IBM, AT&T, and Lucent Technologies/Bell Labs. In 1999, she completed her doctorate in Information Science at the University of North Carolina at Chapel Hill. She also has an MA from UNC-CH in English and a BA from Duke University. Dr. Swain has taught at UNC-Chapel Hill, NC State University, and Campbell University. As a project manager and systems engineer, she applied research in knowledge management to the writing of requirements and specifications. Her areas of research are collaboration, knowledge management, health informatics, and digital libraries. She is currently involved in studies to define knowledge management for healthcare facilities and nursing education organizations. She has presented papers and workshops for the ICKM, ASIST, STC, and IEEE.

Imen Tounsi teaches at the University of Sousse, Institute of Higher Business Studies (IHEC) in Tunisia. She is finishing her dissertation at the University of Tunis, Higher Institute of Management (ISG). Her research interests include the study of collective memory at the group, team, organization, and community levels. She is presently working on transactive memory, its characteristics and the implication of group composition.

Jason Turner is presently serving as director of the Air Force Institute of Technology's Information Resource Management Program and assistant professor of Information Resource Management. He has worked for 15 years as an officer in the US Air Force in a variety of leadership, management, and policy-making capacities focused on providing in-garrison and deployed information, computer, and communication systems and services at various levels of command both stateside and overseas. He holds a PhD in information science (University of Texas at Austin), a MS in information resource management (Air Force Institute of Technology), and a BS in psychology (University of Wisconsin at

Madison). His research interests include social and organizational uses of information and information technology and their impacts on organizational and interpersonal behavior, cognition, decision-making, and work processes.

Sara Värlander. PhD, is an assistant professor at the Stockholm University School of Business, Sweden. Her research interests include the interplay between the physical and the virtual and the emergent practices from the use of information technology in organizations. Another area of interest is the role of the situated interaction in knowledge creation.

John Wang is a full professor at Montclair State University. Having received a scholarship award, he came to the USA and completed his PhD in operations research from Temple University. He has published over 100 refereed papers and six books. He has also developed several computer software programs based on his research findings. He is the Editor-in-Chief of Int. J. of Data Mining, Modelling and Management, Int. J. of Operations Research and Information Systems, Int. J. of Information Systems and Supply Chain Management, and Int. J. of Information Systems in the Service Sector. He has served as a guest editor and referee for many other highly prestigious journals. He has served as track chair and/or session chairman numerous times on the most prestigious international and national conferences. His long-term research goal is on the synergy of data mining, operations research and cybernetics.

Ira Yermish is an Assistant Professor of Decision and System Sciences in the Haub School of Business. He has been at Saint Joseph's University since 1984. His teaching and research areas include systems analysis and design, data base management, data communications, information resource management, and business intelligence and has been active in executive education. Dr. Yermish was awarded a certificate for Excellence in Teaching in 1988. In addition to his current academic activities, he is an active management and information systems consultant. Dr. Yermish earned degrees from Case Western Reserve University, Stanford University the University of Pennsylvania. His early professional experience included positions with Univac, Control Data, RCA Corporation, the Institute for Scientific Information, and was founder of MagnaSystems, Inc.Dr. Yermish is an accomplished singer and photographer, avid cyclist, runner, and triathlete, having completed marathons and Ironman events all over the world.

Dan Zhu is an associate professor of Information Systems and Computer Science at the Iowa State University. She received her Ph.D. in Information Systems from Carnegie Mellon University. She also has M.S. and B.E. degrees in Computer Science. Prior to joining Iowa State, she was an assistant professor of Management Sciences in the College of Business at the University of Iowa in Iowa City, IA. Her general research centers on developing and applying intelligent and learning technologies to business and management. Dr. Zhu's research has appeared in the Proceedings of National Academy of Sciences, Information System Research, Decision Sciences, Naval Research Logistics, Annals of Statistics, Annals of Operations Research, Journal of Database, Journal of Electronic Commerce Research, Journal of Information System and Security, Journal of Scheduling, International Journal on Business Intelligence and Data Mining, Journal of Information and Software Technology, Journal of Knowledge Management, Omega, etc.

Lei Zhu graduated with an MBA and MS in information systems from Iowa State University in 2006. She is a business system analyst at Capital One.

Qin Zhu is the information developer and systems analyst at HP Labs Research Library. She holds the degree, Master of Library and Information Science. Prior to HP Labs Research Library, she was an information consultant at Ajilon Consulting. At HP Labs Research Library, she works in the digital library areas, such as integrating digital resources, maintaining and establishing resource reference and linking in digital environment. She focuses on emerging technologies in digital library and information management and organization areas. She also keeps pace with developments on information standards from national and international standard organizations. She has multiple papers published in leading publications for information professionals and academic peer review journals. Her research areas include information organization; information management; information retrieval; search engine and search engine optimization; data analysis, data mapping, and data modeling. She can be contacted via email: qin.zhu@hp.com.

Suzanne Zyngier is currently a research fellow in the School of Business at La Trobe University, Melbourne. Her research centres on the governance of knowledge management strategies and the development of a framework for the effective, sustainable implementation of those strategies. The knowledge management governance framework structures and describes the roles and tasks involved at each point of governance: authorization, planning and development, and the implementation of such programs. Zyngier has worked at Monash and Swinburne Universities and has written journal articles, technical reports, book chapters. She regularly presents papers at international conferences and to industry. Zyngier has conducted her own business as a consultant to the professional, corporate and not-for profit as a knowledge management and information services analyst.

Index

D

E

F

G

H

I

J

K

L

M

N

O